Taxing Wages 2016

OECD
BETTER POLICIES FOR BETTER LIVES

Please cite this publication as:
OECD (2016), *Taxing Wages 2016*, OECD Publishing, Paris.
http://dx.doi.org/10.1787/tax_wages-2016-en

ISBN 978-92-64-25187-8 (print)
ISBN 978-92-64-25249-3 (PDF)

Annual
ISSN 1995-3844 (print)
ISSN 2072-5124 (online)

Foreword

This annual publication provides details of taxes paid on wages in all 34 member countries of the OECD. The information contained in the Report covers the personal income tax and social security contributions paid by employees, the social security contributions and payroll taxes paid by their employers and cash benefits received by families. The objective of the Report is to illustrate how personal income taxes, social security contributions and payroll taxes are calculated and to examine how these levies and cash family benefits impact on net household incomes. The results also allow quantitative cross-country comparisons of labour cost levels and of the overall tax and benefit position of single persons and families.*

The Report shows the amounts of taxes, social security contributions, payroll taxes and cash benefits for eight family-types, which differ by income level and household composition. It also presents the resulting average and marginal tax rates. Average tax rates show that part of gross wage earnings or total labour costs which are taken in personal income taxes (before and after cash benefits), social security contributions and payroll taxes. Marginal tax rates show the part of an increase of gross earnings or total labour costs that is paid in these levies.

The focus of the Report is the presentation of new data on the tax/benefit position of employees in 2015. In addition, the new data is compared with corresponding data for the year 2014. It is important to note that, the average worker is designated as a full-time employee (including manual and non-manual) in either industry Sectors B-N inclusive with reference to the International Standard Industrial Classification of All Economic Activities, Revision 4 (ISIC Rev. 4) or industry Sectors C-K inclusive with reference to the International Standard Industrial Classification of All Economic Activities, Revision 3 (ISIC Rev. 3).

The Report is structured as follows:

- *Chapter 1 contains an overview of the main results for 2015.*
- *Chapter 2 examines the tax burdens on second earners.*
- *Part I (International Comparisons) reviews the main results for 2014 and 2015 and is divided into 3 chapters (Nos. 3 to 5). Chapter 3 reviews the main results for 2015, which are summarised in comparative tables and figures included at the end of that section. Chapter 4 presents a graphical exposition of the estimated tax burden on labour income in 2015 for gross wage earnings between 50% and 250% of the average wage. Then Chapter 5 reviews the main results for 2014, which are summarised in the comparative tables at the end of the chapter and compares them with the 2015 figures.*
- *Part II (Chapter 6) focuses on the historical trends in the tax burden for the period 2000-15.*
- *Part III contains individual country tables specifying the wage levels considered and the associated tax burdens for eight separate family types, together with descriptions of each tax/benefit system.*

* *Previous editions were published under the title* The Tax/Benefit Position of Employees *(1996-98 editions) and* The Tax/Benefit Position of Production Workers *(editions published before 1996).*

- *The Annex describes the methodology and its limitations.*

The Report has been prepared under the auspices of the Working Party on Tax Policy Analysis and Tax Statistics of the Committee on Fiscal Affairs. This document has been produced with the financial assistance of the European Union. The Views expressed herein can in no way be taken to reflect the official opinion of the European Union.

Table of contents

Part III

Country details, 2015

Tables

Figures

Executive summary

After increasing each year since 2011, the tax burden on the average worker remained at 35.9% in OECD countries for a second consecutive year in 2015. The tax burden or tax wedge is measured by taking the total taxes and social security contributions (SSCs) paid by employees and employers, minus family benefits received as a proportion of the total labour costs for employers. This measure provides an analysis of how these levies and cash benefits combine together to impact on net household income.

Although the OECD average remained stable, 24 OECD countries have experienced a higher labour tax burden compared with 2014, however, this was offset by reductions in the tax burden in 8 countries. Among these, the countries with the largest decreases were Estonia, Greece and Spain, all with decreases of at least one percentage point.

In those countries where there was a higher tax burden on the average worker, the main factor contributing to the increase were changes to personal income taxes (PIT), even though only 2 countries raised statutory PIT rates at the average wage level (Denmark and the Netherlands). Most of the PIT increases were driven by a higher proportion of earnings becoming subject to tax as the value of tax free allowances and tax credits fell relative to earnings. In most countries where there was a fall in the tax burden, reductions in PIT were the key factor, however, lower SSCs also played a significant role in the case of Estonia, Greece and the Netherlands.

Over the past five years, the labour tax burden has increased in 24 OECD countries and fallen in 9 others. At the same time, PIT burdens have risen in 25 out of 34 countries. In 2015, only 7 countries had higher statutory PIT rates for workers on average earnings than in 2010, although 2 others had higher surtaxes. In 8 countries, the PIT rates were lower compared with 2010. This report looks at how these changes affect various types of household, such as single earners, families with or without children, or single parents. In all OECD countries, the tax wedge for families with children is either lower or, in a small minority of cases, the same as single earners without children.

The report also contains a Special Feature examining how the tax and in-work benefit systems, including provisions targeted at children, have impact on the incentives for second earners to enter the workforce. The size of the second earners' average tax burden, and therefore the incentives to enter the labour market, not only depend on the underlying PIT and SSCs levied on the second earner's income, but are also influenced by a number of design aspects of PIT systems, including the withdrawal of dependent spouse tax provisions and family-based taxation.

There are two main reasons for this. First, the second earner average tax burden may be higher because a dependent spouse tax allowance or tax credit – which lowers the tax burden on the income of a primary earner who has a dependent (i.e. non-working) spouse –

is fully or partially lost when the second earner moves into employment. Second, the tax wedge can be higher for second earners due to the adoption of family-based rather than individual-based taxation. Family-based taxation has been adopted by a number of countries for equity purposes as it ensures that families with the same total income pay the same total income tax – irrespective of who has earned the income. However, under family-based taxation, the second earner effectively pays tax at a higher part of the income tax rate schedule than they would under individual-based taxation because the primary earner is already gaining the full benefit from the lower part of the tax rate schedule. This effect increases with the level of the primary earner's income.

Key findings

The average tax burden in the OECD remained unchanged in 2015

- Across OECD countries, the average tax and social security burden on employment incomes remained at 35.9% for a second consecutive year in 2015. This followed a rise totalling 0.9 percentage points between 2010 and 2014. This reversed the decline from 36.0% to 35.0% between 2007 and 2010.
- The highest average tax burdens for childless single workers earning the average national wage were in Belgium (55.3%), Austria (49.5%), Germany (49.4%) and Hungary (49.0%). The lowest were in Chile (7%), New Zealand (17.6%) and Mexico (19.7%).
- In 2015, the tax wedge increased in 24 of 34 countries, fell in 8 and remained unchanged in Chile and Hungary.
- There was an increase of more than 0.4 percentage points in the overall tax burden in 5 countries – Australia, Luxembourg, Israel, Italy and Portugal. All of these countries had significant PIT increases and two also had significant SSC increases.
- A decline of one percentage point or more was experienced in 3 countries – Greece (-1.3 percentage points), Spain (-1.2 percentage points) and Estonia (-1.0 percentage point). Another 2 countries – Ireland and the Netherlands – had decreases of more than -0.4 percentage points. Of these 5 countries, 3 had significant SSC decreases and 3 had significant PIT decreases.
- Changes to the PIT were the main contributor to an increasing total tax wedge in 20 of the 24 countries. The largest increase was in the Netherlands (+1.23 percentage points) although the overall tax wedge decreased by 0.59 percentage points as there was a shift away from SSCs towards PIT.
- Changes to PIT were also the primary contributing factor in most countries where the tax burden fell in 2015. The exceptions were the Netherlands, where the employee SSCs fell by 1.71 percentage points, and Greece, where the employer SSCs declined by 0.92 percentage points.

Tax burdens in families with children

- The highest tax wedges for one-earner families with two children at the average wage were in France (40.5%) and Belgium (40.4%). Austria, Finland and Italy had tax wedges of between 39% and 40%. New Zealand had the smallest tax wedge for these families (4.9%), followed by Chile (7%), Ireland (9.5%) and Switzerland (9.8%). The average for OECD countries was 26.7%.

- The largest increases in the tax burden for one earner families with children were in Iceland (1.5 percentage points) and New Zealand (1.2 percentage points) and the largest fall in Estonia (-4.4 percentage points) mainly due to increased cash benefits.
- The tax wedge for families with children is lower than that for single individuals without children in all OECD countries except in Chile and Mexico, where both family types have the same level of tax burden. The differences are more than 15% of labour costs in the Czech Republic, Germany, Ireland, Luxembourg and Slovenia.

Chapter 1

Overview

This chapter presents the main results of the analysis of the taxation of labour income across OECD member countries in 2015. Most emphasis is given to the tax wedge – a measure of the difference between labour costs to the employer and the corresponding net take-home pay of the employee – which is calculated by expressing the sum of personal income tax, employee plus employer social security contributions together with any payroll tax, minus benefits as a percentage of labour costs. The calculations also focus on the net personal average tax rate. This is the term used when the personal income tax and employee social security contributions net of cash benefits are expressed as a percentage of gross wage earnings. The analysis focuses in the single worker with no children on average earnings and makes a comparison with the single earner married couple with two children.

This Report provides unique information for each of the thirty four OECD countries on the income taxes paid by workers, their social security contributions, the family benefits they receive in the form of cash transfers as well as the social security contributions and payroll taxes paid by their employers. Results reported include the marginal and average tax burden for one- and two-earner households, and the implied total labour costs for employers. These data are widely used in academic research and in the formulation and evaluation of social and economic policies. The taxpayer specific detail in this Report enables it to complement the information provided annually in the *Revenue Statistics*, a publication providing internationally comparative data on tax levels and tax structures in OECD countries. The methodology followed in this Report is described briefly in the introduction section below and in more detail in the Annex.

The tables and charts present estimates of tax burdens and of the tax "wedge" between labour costs and net take-home pay for eight illustrative family types on comparable levels of income. The key results for 2015 are summarised in second section below. Part I of the Report presents more detailed results for 2015, together with comparable results for 2014 and discusses the changes between the two years. Part II of the Report reviews historical changes in tax burdens between 2000 and 2015.

Introduction

This section briefly introduces the methodology employed for this Report, which focuses on full-time employees. It is assumed that their annual income from employment is equal to a given percentage of the average full-time adult gross wage earnings for each OECD economy, also referred to as the *average wage* (AW). This covers both manual and non-manual workers for either industry Sectors C-K inclusive with reference to the International Standard Industrial Classification of All Economic Activities, Revision 3 (ISIC Rev. 3) or industry Sectors B-N inclusive with reference to the International Standard Industrial Classification of All Economic Activities, Revision 4 (ISIC Rev. 4).[1] Further details are provided in Table 1.6 as well as in the Annex of this Report. Additional assumptions are made about the personal circumstances of these wage earners in order to determine their tax/benefit position. The taxes included in the present Report are confined to personal income tax, social security contributions and payroll taxes (which are aggregated with employer social contributions in the calculation of tax rates) payable on gross wage earnings. Consequently, any income tax that might be due on non-wage income and other kinds of taxes – e.g. corporate income tax, net wealth tax and consumption taxes – is not taken into account. The benefits included are those paid by general government as cash transfers, usually in respect of dependent children.

For most OECD countries, the tax year is equivalent to the calendar year, the exceptions being Australia, New Zealand and the United Kingdom. In the case of New Zealand and the United Kingdom, where the tax year starts in April, the calculations apply a "forward looking" approach. This implies that, for example, the tax rates reported for 2015 are those for the fiscal year 2015-16. However, in Australia, where the tax year starts in July, it has been decided to take a "backward looking" approach in order to present more reliable results. So, for example, the year 2015 in respect of Australia has been defined to mean its fiscal year 2014-15.

The Report presents several measures of taxation on labour. Most emphasis is given to the tax wedge – a measure of the difference between labour costs to the employer and the corresponding net take-home pay of the employee – which is calculated by expressing the sum of personal income tax, employee plus employer social security contributions together with any payroll tax, minus benefits as a percentage of labour costs. Employer social security contributions and – in some countries – payroll taxes are added to gross wage earnings of employees in order to determine a measure of total labour costs. However, it should be recognised that this measure may be less than the true labour costs faced by employers because, for example, employers may also have to make non-tax compulsory payments. The average tax wedge measures identify that part of total labour costs which is taken in tax and social security contributions net of cash benefits. In contrast, the marginal tax wedge measures identify that part of an increase of total labour costs that is paid in these levies.

The calculations also focus on the net personal average tax rate. This is the term used when the personal income tax and employee social security contributions net of cash benefits are expressed as a percentage of gross wage earnings. The net personal marginal tax rate shows that part of an increase of gross wage earnings that is paid in personal income tax and employee social security contributions net of cash benefits.

Review of results for 2015

Tax wedge

Table 1.1 shows that the tax wedge between total labour costs to the employer and the corresponding net take-home pay for single workers without children, at average earnings levels, varied widely across OECD countries in 2015 (see column 1). While in Austria, Belgium, France, Germany, Hungary and Italy, the tax wedge is around 50% or higher, it is under 20% in Chile, Mexico and New Zealand. The highest tax wedge is observed in Belgium (55.3%) and the lowest in Chile (7.0%).

The changes in tax wedge between 2014 and 2015 for the average worker without children are described in column 2 of Table 1.1. The tax wedges increased in twenty four countries and fell in eight. The increases were of less than one percentage point, Portugal being the highest at 0.86 percentage points. In contrast, decreases of one percentage point or more were observed in Greece (-1.27 percentage points), Spain (-1.16 percentage points) and Estonia (-1.00 percentage point). There was no change in the tax wedge for Chile and Hungary.

In general, the rises in tax wedge rates are driven by higher income taxes (see column 3). This was the major factor in twenty of the countries showing an overall increase. The largest increase in income taxes as a percentage of labour costs was in the Netherlands (1.23 percentage points), although the overall tax wedge decreased by 0.59 percentage points as a result of lowered social security contributions. The employee social security contributions notably declined by more than one percentage point (-1.71 percentage points).

By contrast, higher social security contributions account for virtually all of the increased tax wedge in Finland and Japan, and over half of it in Luxembourg. Increasing employee social security contributions have the largest part in the rise in tax wedges in Luxembourg (0.45 percentage points) and Finland (0.19 percentage points).

Table 1.1. **Comparison of total tax wedge**

As % of labour costs

Country[1]	Total Tax wedge 2015	Annual change 2015/14 (in percentage points)[2]			
		Tax wedge	Income tax	Employee SSC	Employer SSC[3]
	(1)	(2)	(3)	(4)	(5)
Belgium	55.3	-0.28	-0.22	0.00	-0.07
Austria	49.5	0.09	0.19	0.02	-0.12
Germany	49.4	0.18	0.11	0.03	0.04
Hungary	49.0	0.00	0.00	0.00	0.00
Italy	49.0	0.76	0.76	0.00	0.00
France	48.5	0.05	0.13	0.14	-0.23
Finland	43.9	0.20	0.00	0.19	0.00
Czech Republic	42.8	0.17	0.17	0.00	0.00
Sweden	42.7	0.24	0.25	0.00	0.00
Slovenia	42.6	0.08	0.08	0.00	0.00
Portugal	42.1	0.86	0.86	0.00	0.00
Slovak Republic	41.3	0.10	0.10	0.00	0.00
Spain	39.6	-1.16	-1.16	0.00	0.00
Greece	39.3	-1.27	-0.09	-0.25	-0.92
Estonia	39.0	-1.00	-0.59	-0.30	-0.11
Turkey	38.3	0.22	0.22	0.00	0.00
Luxembourg	38.3	0.64	0.19	0.45	0.00
Norway	36.6	-0.25	-0.25	0.00	0.00
Denmark	36.4	0.21	0.25	0.00	-0.13
Netherlands	36.2	-0.59	1.23	-1.71	-0.10
Poland	34.7	0.08	0.08	0.00	0.00
Iceland	34.0	0.37	0.49	-0.04	-0.09
Japan	32.2	0.26	-0.01	0.13	0.13
United States	31.7	0.02	0.04	0.00	-0.02
Canada	31.6	0.05	0.03	-0.02	0.04
United Kingdom	30.8	-0.15	-0.18	0.02	0.01
Australia	28.4	0.69	0.68	0.00	0.01
Ireland	27.5	-0.47	-0.47	0.00	0.00
Switzerland	22.2	0.05	0.05	0.00	0.00
Korea	21.9	0.19	0.12	0.04	0.04
Israel	21.6	0.49	0.25	0.00	0.24
Mexico	19.7	0.20	0.15	0.00	0.05
New Zealand	17.6	0.31	0.31	0.00	0.00
Chile	7.0	0.00	0.00	0.00	0.00

Note: Single individual without children at the income level of the average worker.

1. Countries ranked by decreasing total tax wedge.
2. Due to rounding, the changes in tax wedge in column (2) may differ by one tenth of percentage point from the sum of columns (3)-(5). For Denmark, the Green Check (cash benefit) contributes to the difference as it is not included in columns (3)-(5).
3. Includes payroll taxes where applicable.

Source: Country submissions, *OECD Economic Outlook Volume 2015* (No. 98).

StatLink http://dx.doi.org/10.1787/888933341170

Table 1.2 and Figure 1.1 show the constituent components of the tax wedge in 2015, i.e. income tax, employee and employer social security contributions (including payroll taxes where applicable), as a percentage of labour costs for the average worker without children. The labour costs in Table 1.2 are expressed in terms of dollars with equivalent purchasing power. Figure 1.1 shows that the average tax wedge in OECD countries was 35.9% in 2015.

Table 1.2. **Income tax plus employee and employer social security contributions**

As % of labour costs, 2015

Country[1]	Total tax wedge[2]	Income tax	Social security contributions		Labour costs[4]
			Employee	Employer[3]	
	(1)	(2)	(3)	(4)	(5)
Switzerland	22.2	10.5	5.9	5.9	74 255
Belgium	55.3	21.6	10.8	22.9	74 137
Germany	49.4	16.1	17.2	16.2	71 579
Austria	49.5	13.1	14.0	22.4	69 060
Luxembourg	38.3	16.0	11.4	10.9	68 267
Norway	36.6	17.9	7.3	11.5	68 030
Netherlands	36.2	15.2	12.1	8.9	66 838
France	48.5	10.7	10.3	27.5	63 562
Sweden	42.7	13.5	5.3	23.9	61 345
Australia	28.4	22.7	0.0	5.6	59 258
Finland	43.9	18.4	6.7	18.7	58 458
United Kingdom	30.8	12.8	8.4	9.7	56 929
United States	31.7	16.5	7.0	8.1	55 457
Iceland	34.0	26.7	0.3	7.0	55 015
Italy	49.0	17.5	7.2	24.3	54 484
Denmark	36.4	35.8	0.0	0.8	54 473
Japan	32.2	6.7	12.4	13.1	54 308
Korea	21.9	4.9	7.6	9.4	52 173
Spain	39.6	11.6	4.9	23.0	51 348
Canada	31.6	14.1	6.8	10.8	46 759
Ireland	27.5	14.2	3.6	9.7	45 467
Greece	39.3	7.1	12.4	19.7	42 681
New Zealand	17.6	17.6	0.0	0.0	39 493
Portugal	42.1	14.0	8.9	19.2	36 744
Israel	21.6	8.9	7.5	5.1	36 094
Slovenia	42.6	9.7	19.0	13.9	35 596
Czech Republic	42.8	9.2	8.2	25.4	32 805
Estonia	39.0	12.6	1.2	25.3	32 125
Hungary	49.0	12.5	14.4	22.2	31 236
Turkey	38.3	10.6	12.8	14.9	30 463
Poland	34.7	5.0	15.3	14.4	29 939
Slovak Republic	41.3	7.4	10.2	23.8	28 555
Chile	7.0	0.0	7.0	0.0	19 338
Mexico	19.7	8.0	1.2	10.5	14 375

Note: Single individual without children at the income level of the average worker.

1. Countries ranked by decreasing labour costs.
2. Due to rounding, the total in column (1) may differ by one or more percentage points from the sum of columns (2)-(4). For Denmark, the Green Check (cash benefit) contributes to the difference as it is not included in columns (2)-(4).
3. Includes payroll taxes where applicable.
4. Dollars with equal purchasing power.

Source: Country submissions, *OECD Economic Outlook Volume 2015* (No. 98).

StatLink http://dx.doi.org/10.1787/888933341188

The percentage of labour costs paid in income tax varies considerably within OECD countries. The lowest figures are in Chile (zero) and Korea (4.9%). The highest values are in Denmark (35.8%), with Australia, Belgium and Iceland all over 20%. The percentage of labour costs paid in employee social security contributions also varies widely ranging from zero in Australia, Denmark and New Zealand to 17.2 % in Germany and 19.0% in Slovenia. Employers in France pay 27.5% of total labour costs in social security contributions, the highest amongst OECD countries. The corresponding figures are also more than 20% in

Figure 1.1. **Income tax plus employee and employer social security contributions, 2015**

As a % of labour costs

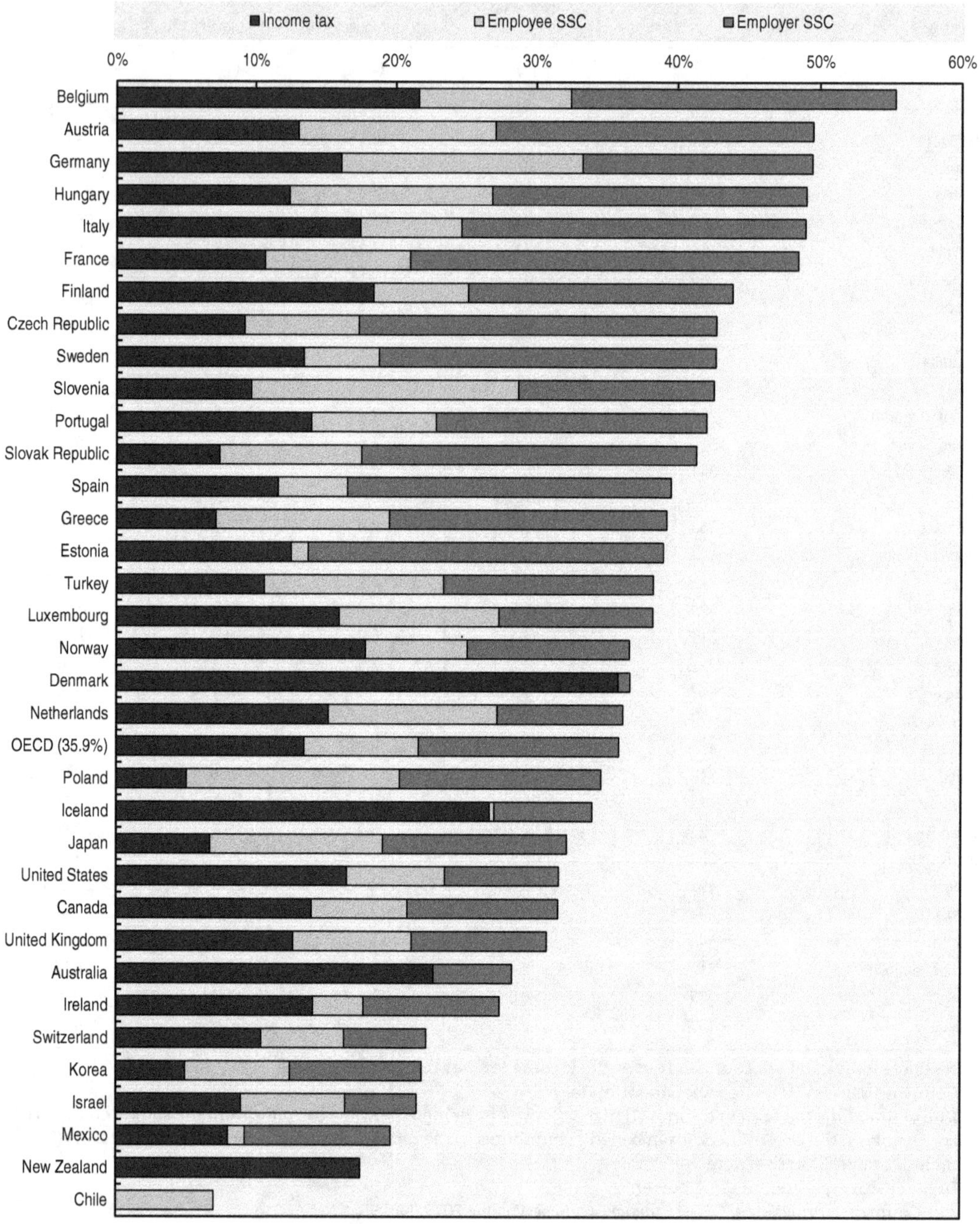

Notes:

Single individual without children at the income level of the average worker.

Includes payroll taxes where applicable.

StatLink http://dx.doi.org/10.1787/888933340355

nine other countries – Austria, Belgium, the Czech Republic, Estonia, Hungary, Italy, the Slovak Republic, Spain and Sweden.

As a percentage of labour costs, the total of employee and employer social security contributions exceeds 20% in more than half of the OECD countries. It also represents one-third of total labour costs or more in eight OECD countries: Austria, Belgium, the Czech Republic, France, Germany, Hungary, the Slovak Republic and Slovenia.

Personal average tax rates

The personal average tax rate is defined as income tax plus employee social security contributions as a percentage of gross wage earnings.[2] Table 1.3 and Figure 1.2 show the personal average tax rates in 2015 for a single worker without children at the average

Table 1.3. **Income tax plus employee social security contributions, 2015**

As % of gross wage earnings

Country[1]	Total payment[2]	Income tax	Empoyee social security contributions	Gross wage earnings[3]
	(1)	(2)	(3)	(4)
Switzerland	17.4	11.1	6.3	69 887
Netherlands	29.9	16.7	13.3	60 867
Luxembourg	30.7	17.9	12.8	60 812
Norway	28.4	20.2	8.2	60 203
Germany	39.7	19.2	20.5	59 987
Belgium	42.0	28.1	14.0	57 166
Australia	24.1	24.1	0.0	55 921
Denmark	36.1	36.1	0.0	54 013
Austria	34.9	16.8	18.1	53 565
United Kingdom	23.4	14.1	9.3	51 431
Iceland	29.1	28.7	0.4	51 181
United States	25.6	18.0	7.7	50 964
Finland	30.9	22.7	8.3	47 503
Korea	13.8	5.4	8.4	47 286
Japan	22.0	7.7	14.3	47 205
Sweden	24.7	17.7	7.0	46 678
France	28.9	14.7	14.2	46 103
Canada	23.4	15.8	7.6	41 719
Italy	32.6	23.1	9.5	41 250
Ireland	19.7	15.7	4.0	41 054
Spain	21.5	15.1	6.4	39 529
New Zealand	17.6	17.6	0.0	39 493
Greece	24.3	8.8	15.5	34 266
Israel	17.3	9.4	7.9	34 241
Slovenia	33.3	11.2	22.1	30 660
Portugal	28.3	17.3	11.0	29 692
Turkey	27.5	12.5	15.0	25 926
Poland	23.7	5.9	17.8	25 637
Czech Republic	23.3	12.3	11.0	24 482
Hungary	34.5	16.0	18.5	24 308
Estonia	18.4	16.8	1.6	24 010
Slovak Republic	23.0	9.6	13.4	21 764
Chile	7.0	0.0	7.0	19 338
Mexico	10.3	8.9	1.4	12 865

Note: Single individual without children at the income level of the average worker.
1. Countries ranked by decreasing gross wage earnings.
2. Due to rounding total may differ one percentage point from aggregate of columns for income tax and social security contributions
3. Dollars with equal purchasing power.

Source: Country submissions, *OECD Economic Outlook Volume 2015* (No. 98).

StatLink http://dx.doi.org/10.1787/888933341192

Figure 1.2. **Percentage of gross wage earnings paid in income tax and employee social security contributions, 2015**

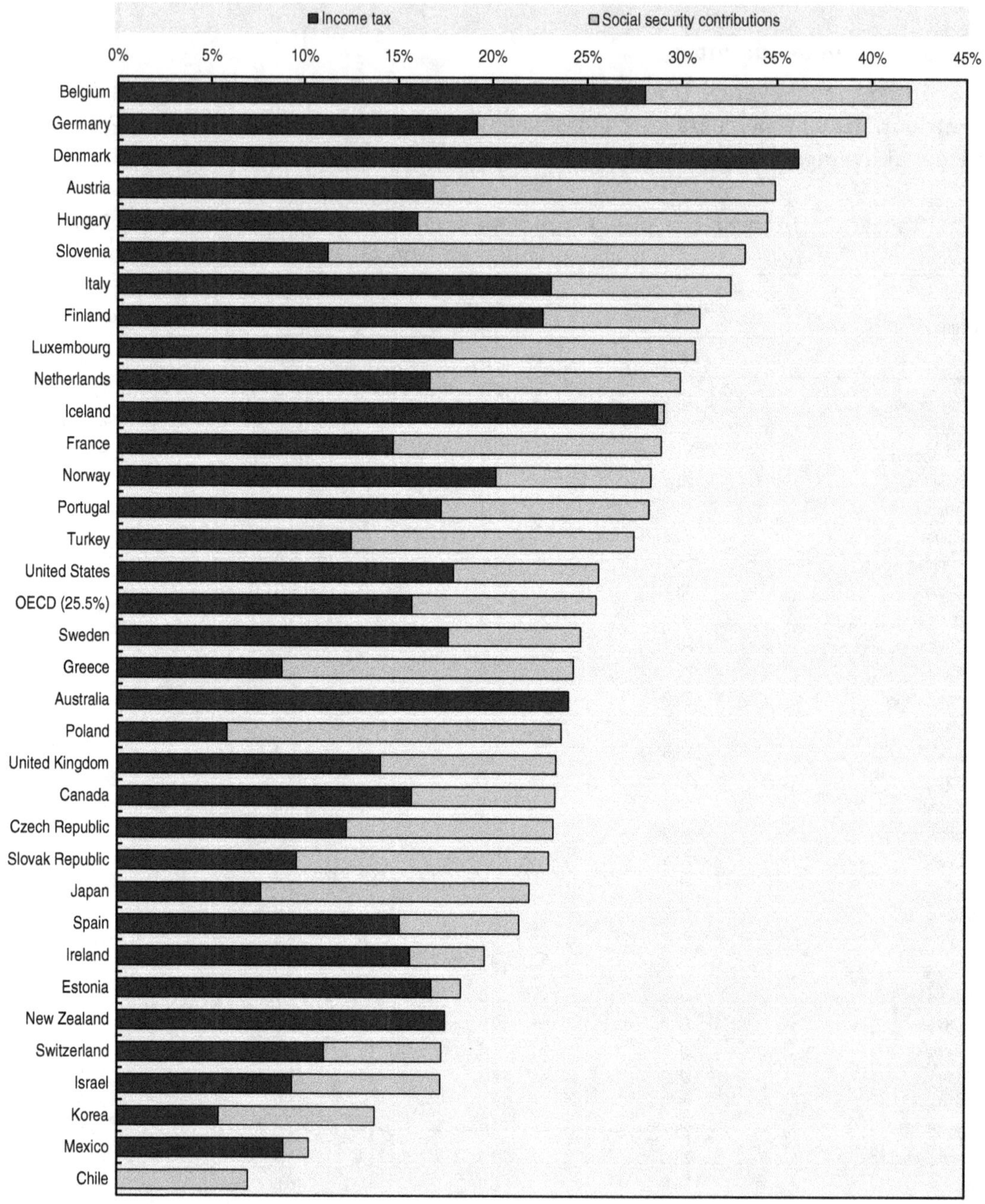

Notes:
Countries ranked by decreasing tax burden.
Single workers at the income level of the average worker.

StatLink http://dx.doi.org/10.1787/888933340366

earnings level. The gross wage earnings figures in Table 1.3 are expressed in terms of dollars with equivalent purchasing power. Figure 1.2 provides a graphical representation of the personal average tax rate decomposed between income tax and employee social security contributions.

Figure 1.2 shows that on average, the personal average tax rate in OECD countries is 25.5%. Belgium at 42.0% of gross earnings has the highest rate with Denmark and Germany being the only other countries with rates of more than 35%. Chile and Mexico have the lowest personal average tax rates with 7.0 and 10.3% of gross average earnings respectively. Korea is the only other country with a rate of less than 15%.

The impact of taxes and benefits on a worker's take-home pay varies greatly among OECD countries. Such wide variations in the size and make-up of tax wedges reflect in part differences in:

- the overall ratio of aggregate tax revenues to Gross Domestic Product; and,
- the share of personal income tax and social security contributions in national tax mixes.

The mix of taxes paid out of gross wage earnings also varies greatly between countries as illustrated in Figure 1.2.

In 2015, the share of income tax within the personal average tax rate is more important than the share of the employee social security contributions for 23 of 34 OECD member countries. No employee social security contributions are levied in Australia, Denmark and New Zealand and the rates are 4% or less of gross earnings in Estonia, Iceland, Ireland and Mexico. In contrast, the single worker at the average wage level paid substantially more (i.e., over 6 percentage points) in employee social security contributions than in personal income tax in five countries – Greece, Japan, Poland, Slovenia and Chile, where the average worker did not pay personal income tax in 2015. In eight countries – Austria, the Czech Republic, France, Germany, Hungary, Israel, Korea and Turkey – the shares of personal income tax and employee social security contributions as percentages of gross earnings are very close (i.e., differences of 3 percentage points or less).

Family tax rates

Table 1.4 compares the tax wedges for a one-earner married couple with two children and a single individual without children, at average earnings levels. These tax wedges varied widely across OECD countries in 2015 (see columns 1 and 2). The size of the tax wedge for the family is generally lower than the one observed for the individual without children, since many OECD countries provide a fiscal benefit to families with children through advantageous tax treatment and/or cash transfers.

The savings realised by a one-earner married couple compared to a single worker are greater than 20% of labour costs in Luxembourg, and greater than 15% of labour costs in four other countries – the Czech Republic, Germany, Ireland and Slovenia. The tax burdens are the same in Chile and Mexico and different by less than three percentage points in Greece, Israel, Korea and Turkey (see columns 1 and 2).

In 28 of 34 OECD countries, there is only a small change (not exceeding plus or minus one percentage point) in the tax wedge of an average one-earner married couple with two children between 2014 and 2015 (see column 3). There is no change in Chile. There are increases of greater than 1 percentage point in two countries: Iceland (1.50) and New Zealand (1.17). In 2015, the tax wedge for families fell by 4.35 percentage points in Estonia mainly due to increased cash benefits. It also decreased by more than one percentage point in Greece (-1.29), in Poland (-1.25) and in Spain (-1.12). It decreased by less than one percentage point in seven other countries: Belgium, Canada, France, Ireland, the Netherlands, Norway and the United Kingdom. By comparison, the change in the tax

Table 1.4. **Comparison of total tax wedge by family type**

As % of labour costs

Country[1]	Family[2] total tax wedge 2015	Single[3] total tax wedge 2015	Annual change 2015/14 (in percentage points)		
			Family tax wedge	Single tax wedge	Difference between single and family (4)-(3)
	(1)	(2)	(3)	(4)	(5)
France	40.5	48.5	-0.04	0.05	0.09
Belgium	40.4	55.3	-0.22	-0.28	-0.06
Italy	39.9	49.0	0.93	0.76	-0.17
Finland	39.3	43.9	0.54	0.20	-0.34
Austria	39.0	49.5	0.12	0.09	-0.03
Greece	38.1	39.3	-1.29	-1.27	0.02
Sweden	37.8	42.7	0.40	0.24	-0.16
Turkey	36.9	38.3	0.28	0.22	-0.06
Hungary	35.3	49.0	0.53	0.00	-0.53
Germany	34.0	49.4	0.24	0.18	-0.06
Spain	33.8	39.6	-1.12	-1.16	-0.04
Norway	31.9	36.6	-0.14	-0.25	-0.10
Portugal	30.7	42.1	0.88	0.86	-0.03
Netherlands	30.6	36.2	-0.42	-0.59	-0.17
Estonia	28.5	39.0	-4.35	-1.00	3.34
Slovak Republic	28.4	41.3	0.34	0.10	-0.24
Poland	28.4	34.7	-1.25	0.08	1.33
Japan	26.8	32.2	0.30	0.26	-0.04
Czech Republic	26.6	42.8	0.08	0.17	0.10
United Kingdom	26.3	30.8	-0.10	-0.15	-0.05
Denmark	26.0	36.4	0.40	0.21	-0.19
Slovenia	23.7	42.6	0.18	0.08	-0.10
Iceland	22.4	34.0	1.50	0.37	-1.13
United States	20.7	31.7	0.09	0.02	-0.07
Mexico	19.7	19.7	0.20	0.20	0.00
Korea	19.6	21.9	0.23	0.19	-0.04
Israel	18.9	21.6	0.23	0.49	0.26
Canada	18.8	31.6	-0.48	0.05	0.53
Australia	17.8	28.4	0.46	0.69	0.23
Luxembourg	15.9	38.3	0.71	0.64	-0.08
Switzerland	9.8	22.2	0.07	0.05	-0.02
Ireland	9.5	27.5	-0.22	-0.47	-0.25
Chile	7.0	7.0	0.00	0.00	0.00
New Zealand	4.9	17.6	1.17	0.31	-0.85

1. Countries ranked by decreasing tax wedge of the family.
2. One earner married couple with two children and earnings at the average wage level.
3. Single individual without children and earnings at the average wage level.

Source: Country submissions, *OECD Economic Outlook Volume 2015* (No. 98).

StatLink http://dx.doi.org/10.1787/888933341208

wedge of a single taxpayer without children at the average wage level was greater than one percentage point in two OECD countries (Greece and Spain, both of which experienced a decrease). Detailed explanations on the latter are given in section on the tax wedge above.

A comparison of the changes in tax wedges between 2014 and 2015 for the one-earner married couples with two children and single persons without children, at the average wage level, is shown in column 5 of Table 1.4. The fiscal preference for families increased in eight OECD member countries: Australia, Canada, the Czech Republic, Estonia, France, Greece, Israel and Poland. Additionally, the effects of changes in the tax system on the tax

Figure 1.3. **Income tax plus employee contributions less cash benefits, 2015**

As % of gross wage earnings, by family-type

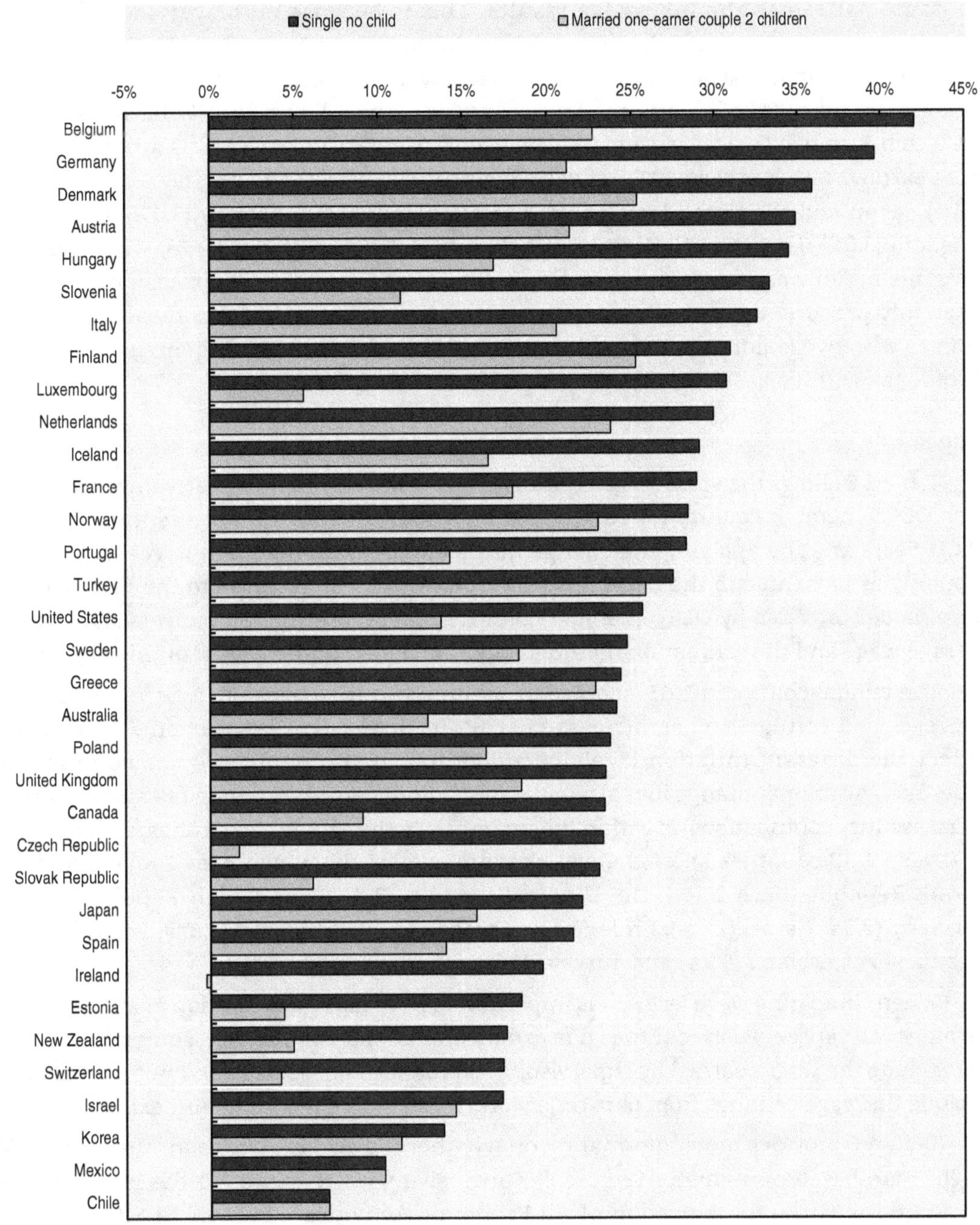

Notes:

Countries ranked by decreasing rates for single taxpayer without children.

Family types: A single individual without children and earnings at the average wage level and a one earner married couple with two children and earnings at the average wage level.

StatLink http://dx.doi.org/10.1787/888933340375

wedge were independent of the family type in Mexico. In seven other countries; Austria, Japan, Korea, Portugal, Spain, Switzerland and the United Kingdom, the differences in the changes in the tax wedge for the two family types were 0.05 percentage points or less. There were no changes at all in Chile.

Figure 1.3 compares the net personal average tax rate for the average worker between single individuals and a one-earner married couple with two children. These results show the same pattern as the tax wedge results. This is because employer social security contributions which are not taken into account in the former but included in the latter are independent of family type. The savings realised by a one-earner married couple are close to or greater than 20% of earnings in four countries – Luxembourg (25.1%), Slovenia (22.0%) the Czech Republic (21.6%) and Ireland (19.9%). In contrast, the savings as a percentage of gross earnings are less than 10% in twelve countries – Spain (7.5%), Poland (7.3%), Sweden (6.4%), Japan and the Netherlands (both 6.2%), Finland (5.7%), Norway (5.4%), the United Kingdom (5.0%), Israel (2.8%), Korea (2.5%), Turkey (1.7%) and Greece (1.5%). The burden is the same in Chile and in Mexico. It is also interesting to note that when cash benefits are taken into account, the net personal average tax rate for the average one-earner married couples with two children in Ireland becomes negative (-0.3%) as cash benefits exceed the income tax and social security payments.

Wages

Table 1.5 shows the gross wage earnings in national currency of the average worker in each OECD member country for 2014 and 2015. The figures for 2015 are estimated by the OECD Secretariat by applying the change in the compensation per employee in the total economy as presented in the *OECD Economic Outlook* (No. 98) database to the final average wage values provided by OECD member countries. More information on the values of the average wage and the estimation methodology is included in the Annex of this Report.

The annual change in 2015 – shown in column 3 – varied between a decrease of -0.8% in Greece and Portugal and an increase of 16.6% in Turkey. To a large extent, the changes reflect the different inflation levels of individual OECD countries – see column 4 of Table 1.5. The annual change in real wage levels (before personal income tax and employee social security contributions) is within the range of -2% to +2% for 21 countries; see column 5 of Table 1.5. 13 countries show changes that are outside this range: New Zealand and the Slovak Republic (both 2.1%), the United Kingdom (2.2%), the Czech Republic (2.6%), Germany (2.8%), Israel (2.9%), Chile (3.1%), Sweden (3.2%), Hungary (3.8%), Poland (4.1%), Estonia (4.7%), Iceland (4.9%) and Turkey (8.6%).

When comparing wage levels, it is important to note that the definition of average wage earnings can vary between countries due to data limitations. For instance, some countries do not include the wages earned by supervisory and managerial workers and not all countries exclude the wage earnings from part-time workers (see Table A.4 in the Annex).

Table 1.6 provides more information on whether the average wages for the years 2000 to 2015 are based on industry Sectors C-K inclusive with reference to the International Standard Industrial Classification of All Economic Activities, Revision 3 (ISIC Rev. 3) or industry sectors B-N inclusive with reference to the International Standard Industrial Classification of All Economic Activities, Revision 4 (ISIC Rev. 4).

Most OECD countries have calculated average wage earnings on the basis of sectors B-N in the ISIC Rev. 4 Industry Classification at least since 2008. The exceptions are Chile and Mexico. Some countries have revised the average wage values for prior years as well. Average wage values based on the ISIC Rev. 4 Classification or any variant are available for all years for Australia, Canada, the Czech Republic, Estonia, Finland, Greece, Hungary, Iceland, Italy, Japan, the Slovak Republic, Slovenia, Spain, Sweden and Switzerland.

Table 1.5. **Comparison of wage levels**

Country	Gross wage in national currency		Annual change 2015/14 (in percentage)			
	2014	2015	Gross wage	Inflation[1]	Real wage before tax	Change in personal average tax rate[2]
	(1)	(2)	(3)	(4)	(5)	(6)
Australia	79 409	80 774	1.7	1.6	0.1	0.7
Austria	42 814	43 484	1.6	0.9	0.7	0.2
Belgium	46 451	46 693	0.5	0.6	-0.1	-0.3
Canada	49 821	50 877	2.1	1.2	1.0	0.0
Chile	7 019 299	7 556 043	7.6	4.4	3.1	0.0
Czech Republic	308 688	317 924	3.0	0.4	2.6	0.2
Denmark	397 600	405 876	2.1	0.5	1.6	0.3
Estonia	12 338	12 926	4.8	0.1	4.7	-1.2
Finland	43 035	43 536	1.2	-0.2	1.3	0.2
France	37 307	37 792	1.3	0.1	1.2	0.3
Germany	45 700	47 042	2.9	0.1	2.8	0.2
Greece	20 450	20 296	-0.8	-0.9	0.2	-0.7
Hungary	3 054 276	3 172 122	3.9	0.1	3.8	0.0
Iceland	6 960 000	7 440 480	6.9	1.9	4.9	0.5
Ireland	34 178	34 847	2.0	0.1	1.8	-0.5
Israel	134 748	137 958	2.4	-0.5	2.9	0.3
Italy	30 400	30 710	1.0	0.2	0.9	1.0
Japan	4 972 455	5 005 807	0.7	0.8	-0.2	0.2
Korea	41 428 224	42 162 723	1.8	0.7	1.0	0.2
Luxembourg	54 920	55 553	1.2	0.1	1.1	0.7
Mexico	103 246	105 924	2.6	2.9	-0.3	0.2
Netherlands	49 155	49 235	0.2	0.3	-0.1	-0.6
New Zealand	54 733	56 110	2.5	0.4	2.1	0.3
Norway	537 195	552 012	2.8	2.1	0.6	-0.3
Poland	44 083	45 521	3.3	-0.8	4.1	0.1
Portugal	17 411	17 280	-0.8	0.5	-1.3	1.1
Slovak Republic	10 422	10 616	1.9	-0.2	2.1	0.1
Slovenia	17 948	18 109	0.9	-0.6	1.6	0.1
Spain	26 191	26 259	0.3	-0.6	0.8	-1.5
Sweden	408 188	421 364	3.2	0.1	3.2	0.3
Switzerland	89 779	90 286	0.6	-1.2	1.7	0.1
Turkey	27 487	32 048	16.6	7.4	8.6	0.3
United Kingdom	35 182	36 017	2.4	0.1	2.2	-0.2
United States	50 099	50 964	1.7	0.0	1.7	0.0

1. Estimated percentage change in the total consumer price index.
2. Difference in the personal average tax rate of the average worker (single without children) between 2015 and 2014.
Source: Country submissions, *OECD Economic Outlook Volume* 2015 (No. 98).

StatLink http://dx.doi.org/10.1787/888933341212

Australia (for all years) and New Zealand (years 2004 to 2015) have provided values based on the 2006 ANZSIC industry classification, divisions B to N, which substantially overlaps the ISIC Rev. 4, Sectors B to N. For New Zealand, the years prior 2004 continue to be based on sectors C-K in ANZSIC. Turkey has provided values based on the NACE Rev. 2 classification sectors B-N for years 2007 to 2015. Values for the years prior to 2007 are based on the average production worker wage (ISIC rev. 3.1, sector D).

In general, the change in the industry classification from ISIC Rev. 3 to ISIC Rev. 4 has had only a small impact on the level of the average wage earnings but the results reported in this Report for the years before 2015 may slightly deviate from the values reported in last year's edition on this account.

Table 1.6. **Average Wage Industry Classification**

	years for which ISIC Rev. 3.1 or any variant (Sectors C-K) has been used to calculate the AW	years for which ISIC Rev. 4 or any variant (Sectors B-N) has been used to calculate the AW
Australia[1]		2000-15
Austria[2]	2004-07	2008-15
Belgium	2000-07	2008-15
Canada		2000-15
Chile[3]	2000-15	
Czech Republic		2000-15
Denmark	2000-07	2008-15
Estonia		2000-15
Finland		2000-15
France	2000-07	2008-15
Germany	2000-05	2006-15
Greece[4]		2000-15
Hungary		2000-15
Iceland[5]		2000-15
Ireland[6]	2000-07	2008-15
Israel[7]	2000-12	2013-15
Italy		2000-15
Japan		2000-15
Korea[8]	2000-07	2008-15
Luxembourg	2000-04	2005-15
Mexico[9]		
Netherlands	2000-07	2008-15
New Zealand[10]	2000-03	2004-15
Norway	2000-08	2009-15
Poland	2000-06	2007-15
Portugal	2000-05	2006-15
Slovak Republic[11]		2000-15
Slovenia		2000-15
Spain		2000-15
Sweden		2000-15
Switzerland		2000-15
Turkey[12]		2007-15
United Kingdom	2000-07	2008-15
United States	2000-06	2007-15

Notes:

1. Australia: Based on ANZSIC06 such that the categories substantially overlap with ISIC 4, sectors B-N.
2. Austria: 2000-03 average wage values are not based on the NACE (ISIC) classification.
3. Chile: The AW values are based on sectors C to O from years 2006 to 2015. From 2010 onwards sectors L (7522) and L (7523) are excluded.
4. Greece: The average annual earnings refer to full time employees for the Sectors B to N of NACE Rev 2, including Division 95 and excluding Divisions 37, 39 and 75 for 2008 onwards.
5. Iceland: Using national classification system that corresponds with the NACE rev. 2 classification system.
6. Ireland: Values from 2000 to 2007 are based on sectors C-E (NACE). From 2008 onwards, they are based on sectors B-E (NACE rev.2).
7. Israel: The statistical data for Israel are supplied by and under the responsibility of the relevant Israeli authorities. The use of such data by the OECD is without prejudice to the status of the Golan Heights, East Jerusalem and Israeli settlements in the West Bank under the terms of international law.
8. Korea: Average wage values are based on 6th Korean Standard Industrial Classification (KSIC) C-K for 2000-2001, 8th KISC C-M for 2002 to 2007 and 9th KISC B-N except E for 2008 onwards.
9. Mexico: 2000-14 AW values are based on the Mexican Classification of Economic Activities (Clasificación Mexicana de Actividades Económicas [CMAE]) which is based on one of the first versions of ISIC.
10. New Zealand: See the note for Australia which applies from 2004.
11. Slovak Republic: Average wage values based on ISIC Rev. 4 classification (B to N) and still include the self-employment data.
12. Turkey: The average wage is based on the average production worker wage ISIC rev. 3.1 sector D for years 2000 to 2006.

StatLink http://dx.doi.org/10.1787/888933341229

Notes

1. Not all national statistical agencies use ISIC Rev. 3 or Rev. 4 to classify industries. However, the Statistical Classification of Economic Activities in the European Community (NACE Rev. 1 or Rev. 2), the North American Industry Classification System (US NAICS 2002). the Australian and New Zealand Standard Industrial Classification (ANZSIC 2006) and the Korean Standard Industrial Classification (6th to 9th KISC) include a classification which broadly conforms either with industries C-K in ISIC Rev. 3 or industries B-N in ISIC Rev. 4.
2. In the Netherlands, the division made between personal income taxes and employee social security contributions is slightly different to the methodology generally applied in this Report.

Chapter 2

Special feature: Measuring the tax wedge on second earners

This special feature examines how the tax and in-work benefit systems, including tax and benefit provisions targeted at children, in OECD countries impact on the incentives for second earners to enter (or re-enter) the workforce. While all income taxes discourage work, the specific design of an income tax system can affect the exact incentives workers face. This is particularly the case for second earners where a number of policy choices significantly affect the incentives for workers to enter the workforce (as well as incentives once in the workforce).

Introduction

This special feature examines how the tax and in-work benefit systems, including tax and benefit provisions targeted at children, in OECD countries impact on the incentives for second earners to enter (or re-enter) the workforce. While all income taxes discourage work, the specific design of an income tax system can affect the exact incentives workers face. This is particularly the case for second earners where a number of policy choices significantly affect the incentives for workers to enter the workforce (as well as incentives once in the workforce).

The choice between individual- and family-based taxation is a prime example. Family-based taxation has been adopted by a number of countries for equity purposes as it ensures that families with the same total income pay the same total income tax – irrespective of who has earned the income.[1] However, in such a system a second earner is effectively taxed at higher marginal tax rates than a single individual would be. Similarly, the withdrawal of tax allowances and credits on the basis of family income and the presence of dependant spouse allowances (which are both also strongly justifiable on equity grounds) can act to reduce second earner participation incentives.

While this special feature focuses solely on the tax and in-work benefit systems, it is important to bear in mind that there are a variety of broader factors that also influence the incentives for individuals to enter the workforce. These include: income received when out of work (unemployment insurance and assistance; social assistance); the availability and cost of child care; paid leave provisions (e.g. maternity, parental and sickness leave) and the existence of other unearned income (e.g. investment income, spouse's income). The calculation of "participation tax rates" can be useful in examining the impact of both tax and out-of-work benefits (though not broader factors) on second earner participation incentives (see, e.g. OECD, 2015), but such analysis is beyond the scope of this special feature.

The analysis in this special feature is based on the *Taxing Wages* models and builds on work contained in OECD Tax Policy Study No. 21 – *Taxation and Employment* (published in 2011). It identifies the impact of tax and in-work benefit systems on the incentives for second earners to enter the workforce by calculating the average tax wedges and rates faced by second earners when they move into employment.[2] More specifically, it presents:

- Average tax wedges of second earners with and without children moving into employment earning 67% of the average wage (AW) in 2014. In each case the primary earner is assumed to earn the AW.
- Net personal average tax rates of second earners with and without children moving into employment earning 67% of the AW for 2014. Again, the primary earner is assumed to earn the AW.
- A comparison of average tax wedges on second earners in 2010 with those in 2014.
- A comparison of net personal average tax rates on second earners in 2010 with those in 2014.

In this analysis, the assumptions underlying the second earner average tax wedge (and rate) calculations are that the decision for the second earner to enter the workforce is made: 1) subsequent to the primary earner's decision to participate; and 2) at the **family level** rather than the individual level.[3] As such, the second earner average tax wedge measures how much extra personal income tax (PIT) plus employee and employer social security contributions (SSCs) the family will have to pay as a result of the second earner entering employment, as a proportion of the second earner's gross earnings plus the employer SSCs due on the second earner's income. It therefore takes into account any additional tax liability on the principal earner that results from the second earner entering the workforce. As emphasised by Jaumotte (2003), this is the appropriate tax rate to measure the disincentive facing a second earner to participate in employment. The average tax wedge (ATW) and net personal average tax rate (ATR) can be expressed, respectively, as follows:

$$ATW = \frac{\text{Increase in income tax, employer and employee SSCs(net of inwork benefits) paid by the family as a result of the second earner entering the workforce}}{\text{Increase in family gross income and employer SSCs as a result of the second earner entering the workforce}}$$

$$ATR = \frac{\text{Increase in income tax and employee SSCs(net of inwork benefits) paid by the family as a result of the second earner entering the workforce}}{\text{Increase in family gross income as a result of the second earner entering the workforce}}$$

Note that the second earner average tax wedges and net personal average tax rates calculated in this paper do not necessarily conform with the legal ones in all countries, for example Germany (see further Box 1).

Box 1. **Assumptions underlying the second earner tax wedge calculations**

As noted in the introduction, that the underlying assumptions in the second earner tax wedge calculations are that the decision for the second earner to enter the workforce is made: 1) subsequent to the primary earner's decision to participate; and 2) at the family level rather than the individual level. Consequently, the second earner average tax wedge calculation measures the additional tax burden borne by the family relative to the increase in income of the family (including employer SSCs) when the second earner enters employment. As this is a family-based calculation, it does not draw any conclusions as to how the tax burden is allocated between the primary and second earner.

If different assumptions are made then this may affect the calculations made. For example, if the second earner's participation decision is assumed to be made contemporaneously with the primary earner, then the average tax wedge faced by the entire family may be the preferable measure of the tax burden on both partners entering employment.

Alternatively, if the second earner's participation decision is assumed to be made at the individual rather than family level (and where the second earner disregards any change in the primary earner's tax burden), then it may be appropriate to only take into account the tax burden legally imposed on the second earner as opposed to the increase in tax on the whole family. With an individual based tax system, the resulting average tax wedge calculation would remain relatively simple – the legal tax burden (including SSCs) imposed on the second earner would be divided by the second earner's income (plus employer SSCs). This means that any loss by the primary earner of, for example, a dependent spouse allowance/tax credit or a transferable allowance/tax credit would not be considered in the calculation of the second earner average tax wedge. As a result, the second earner average tax wedge would tend to be lower than that calculated under the paper's current methodology for countries with such provisions. Consistent with this approach, the primary earner's average tax wedge would increase when the second earner enters employment.

Box 1. **Assumptions underlying the second earner tax wedge calculations** *(cont.)*

Under family-based taxation, the calculation of the second earner average tax wedge would become more complicated due to the fact that the increase in tax burden would be legally attributable to the family rather than either partner. Then the way to calculate a second earner average tax wedge would be to consider the sharing of the whole household income within the family prescribed by law and use the second earner's allocated income in the calculations. That just results in applying the average income tax rate of the entire family to the second earner.

Following this latter approach, the second earner average tax wedge would be lower than in the calculations in this report. Consider, for example, Germany which treats the family as the taxable unit via an income splitting system. As per Figure 2.1a, a second earner faces an average tax wedge of 54.7% on entering employment under the assumption and calculations used in this paper, and hence the total additional tax burden on the family is included in the average tax wedge calculation. Under the legal splitting method attributing the tax wedge of the entire family to the second earner would result in a tax wedge of 47.4%. As per Figure 2.1b in the case of a family with two children, using this paper's approach, a second earner also faces an average tax wedge of 54.7%. Instead the application of the legal splitting method would result in a tax wedge of 42.1%.

Beyond such methodological issues, it is also important to bear in mind that – as was noted in the introduction – the average tax wedge indicator only takes account of the influence of tax on the participation decision, not of broader factors. For example, consider female labour force participation in Germany. Although German family-based taxation has not changed, the female employment rate* has increased significantly by 10 percentage points between 2005 and 2014. Since 2010 it has increased by more than 3 percentage points to almost 70% in 2014. This is well above the OECD average of 57.9%. It seems that, in the case of Germany, factors other than the tax system are more important for the work incentives of second earners. These might be, among others, the overall labour market situation, out-of-work benefits or the availability of child care facilities.

* OECD Short-Term Labour Market Statistics, Employment rate, Aged 15-64, Females.

Average tax wedges and rates for second earners

Tax wedges on second earners in 2014

Figure 2.1a presents the average tax wedge for second earners without children earning 67% of the AW in 2014. The primary earner is assumed to earn the average wage. Second earner average tax wedges range from 60.2% in Belgium to 7.0% in Chile.

The size of these average tax wedges is driven not just by the underlying PIT and SSC rates, but also by a number of design aspects of PIT systems. In many countries, the second earner average tax wedge is increased because a dependent spouse allowance/tax credit – which lowers the tax burden on the income of a primary earner who has a dependent (i.e. non-working) spouse – is (fully or partially) lost when the second earner moves into employment. For example, in Slovenia the primary earner loses the *dependent family member allowance* when the second earner enters the workforce, while in Canada the primary earner loses the *spouse tax credit*.

In a number of other countries, the tax wedge is increased for second earners due to the adoption of family-based rather than individual-based taxation.[4] Under family-based taxation, the second earner effectively pays tax at a higher part of the income tax rate schedule than they would under individual-based taxation because the primary earner is already gaining the full benefit from the lower part of the tax rate schedule. This effect is exacerbated the greater the level of the primary earner's income. Even when the income

Figure 2.1. **Average tax wedges on second earners, 2014**

a. Second earner at 67% of the AW (primary earner at the AW level), no children

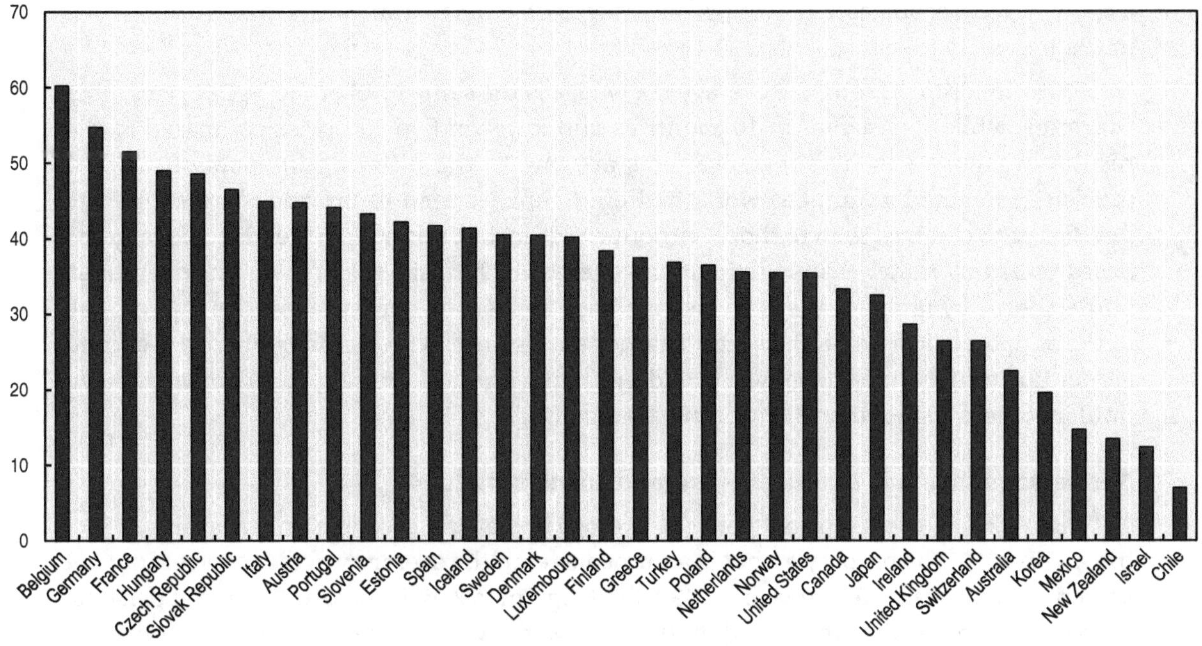

b. Second earner at 67% of the AW (primary earner at the AW level), 2 children

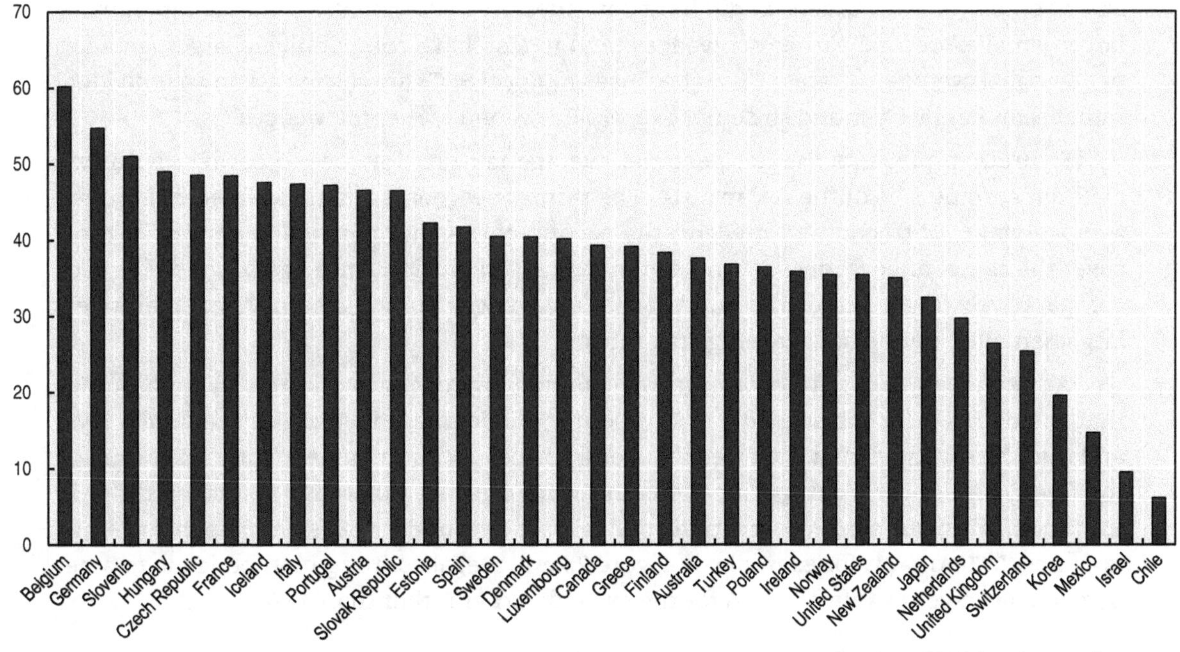

StatLink http://dx.doi.org/10.1787/888933340387

tax thresholds for a family are higher than for an individual, this still generally results in the second earner facing higher marginal income tax rates than they would under individual-based taxation. For example, in Switzerland, the primary earner's income of approximately CHE 90 000 (the average wage) means that the first franc that the second earner receives (once their basic allowance is exhausted) is taxed at a personal income tax rate of 18.33% rather than the zero rate.

Figure 2.1b presents the average tax wedge for second earners with two children earning 67% of the AW in 2014. The primary earner is once again assumed to earn the average wage. Second earner average tax wedges now range from 60.2% in Belgium to 6.1% in Chile.

With children present, the average tax wedge is the same in 19 of the 34 OECD member countries, while it is higher in 10 countries and lower in five countries compared to the results in Figure 2.1a. The mixed effects are due to the differing impacts of support provisions targeted at families with children. Countries tend to provide more support to families with children than to those without children, but this support tends to be targeted based on family rather than individual income. As such, while they reduce the overall tax burden borne by families, they can also increase the second earner tax wedge if part or all of the support is lost when the second earner enters employment. Meanwhile, the second earner tax wedge can be lower with children than without if the support is not withdrawn until income is higher than 167% of the average wage.

Net personal average tax rates on second earners in 2014

Figure 2.2a presents the net personal average tax rate for second earners earning 67% of the AW in 2014. The primary earner is assumed to earn the average wage. Second earner net personal average tax rates range from 49.1% in Belgium to 2.9% in Mexico. These net personal average tax rate results are lower than the average tax wedge results due to the absence of employer SSCs in the calculations. Rankings also change to some degree due to the differing size of employer SSC burdens in different countries. However countries with comparatively larger (smaller) second earner tax wedges tend to also have comparatively larger (smaller) net personal average tax rates. This is because employer SSCs are calculated on an individual rather than family basis and so do not exacerbate second earner tax wedges.

Figure 2.2b presents the net personal average tax rate for second earners with two children earning 67% of the AW in 2014. The primary earner is again assumed to earn the average wage. With children present, the second earner net personal average tax rates cover the same range from 49.1% in Belgium to 2.9% in Mexico. Once again, countries with comparatively larger (smaller) second earner tax wedges tend to also have comparatively larger (smaller) net personal average tax rates.

As explained in detail in Box 1, the calculation approach used in this paper assumes that the decision for the second earner to enter employment is made at the family level and that the second earner's tax wedge takes into account the change in total taxes paid by the family. Under the legal specifications the second earner tax wedge result can differ in some countries. The same observation applies for the second earner's net personal average tax rates. In Germany, for example, in Figure 2.2a the legal splitting method leads to a net personal average tax rate of 37.2% for the second earner rather than 46.0%.

Comparison of average tax wedges and rates for second earners between 2010 and 2014

Changes in tax wedges for second earners between 2010 and 2014

This section examines how second earner average tax wedges have changed between 2010 and 2014.

Figure 2.3a shows that the average tax wedge for second earners without children increased in 18 countries between 2010 and 2014. The largest increases in percentage point

Figure 2.2. **Net personal average tax rates on second earners, 2014**

a. Second earner at 67% of the AW (primary earner at the AW level), no children

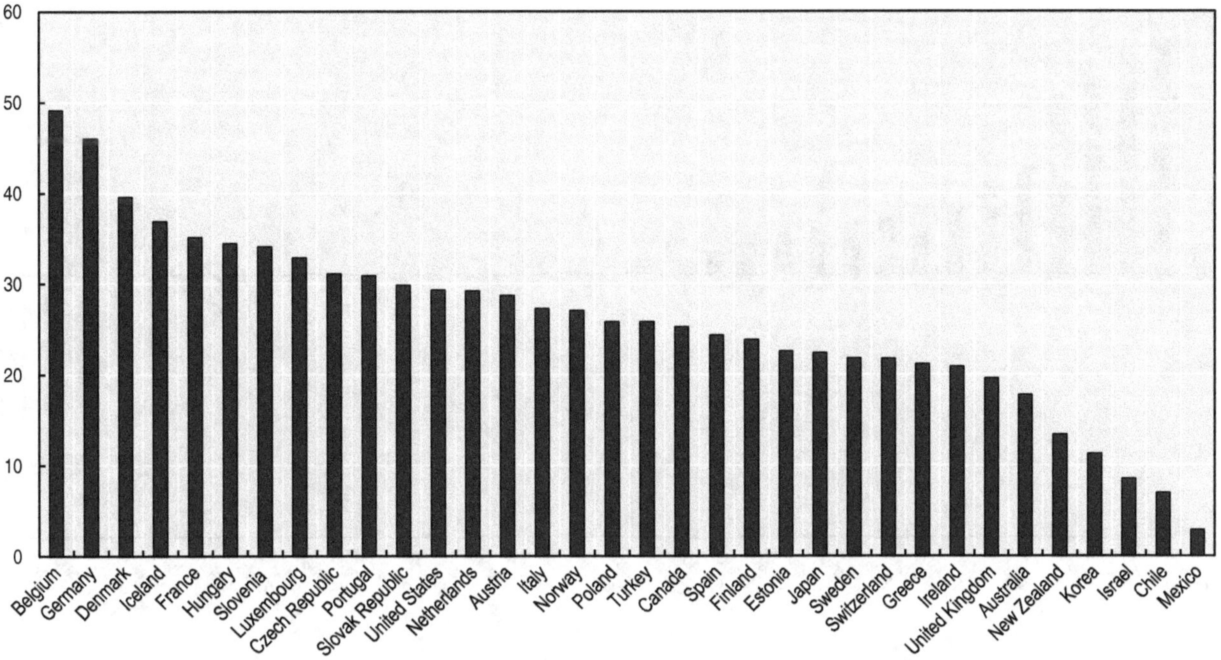

b. Second earner at 67% of the AW (primary earner at the AW level), 2 children

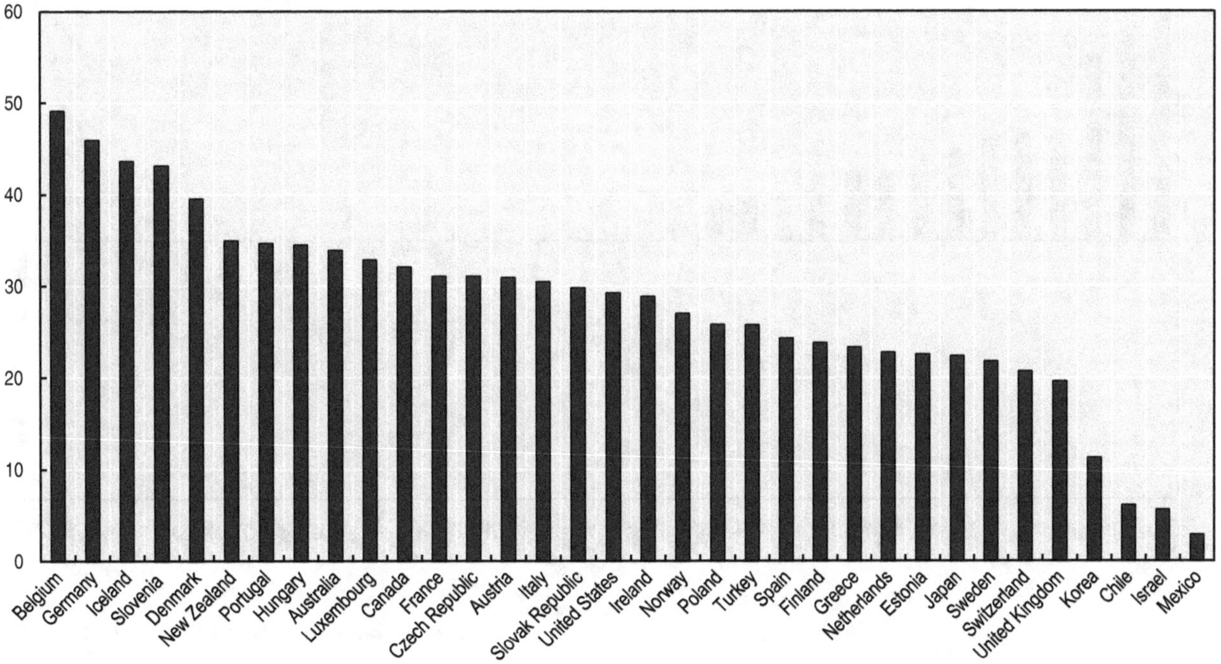

StatLink http://dx.doi.org/10.1787/888933340398

terms were in Portugal (5.4), Hungary (5.2), Luxembourg (4.3) and Ireland (4.1). The increase in Portugal is due to both an increase in marginal personal income tax rates and a reduction in the basic tax credit. In Hungary, the increase is due to the removal of the general Employee Tax Credit (in 2012) which was replaced by more targeted tax reliefs focused on certain categories of second earners (such as mothers returning from child-care

Figure 2.3. **Changes in average tax wedges between 2010 and 2014**

a. Second earner at 67% of the AW, 0 children, in percentage points

b. Second earner at 67% of the AW, 2 children, in percentage points

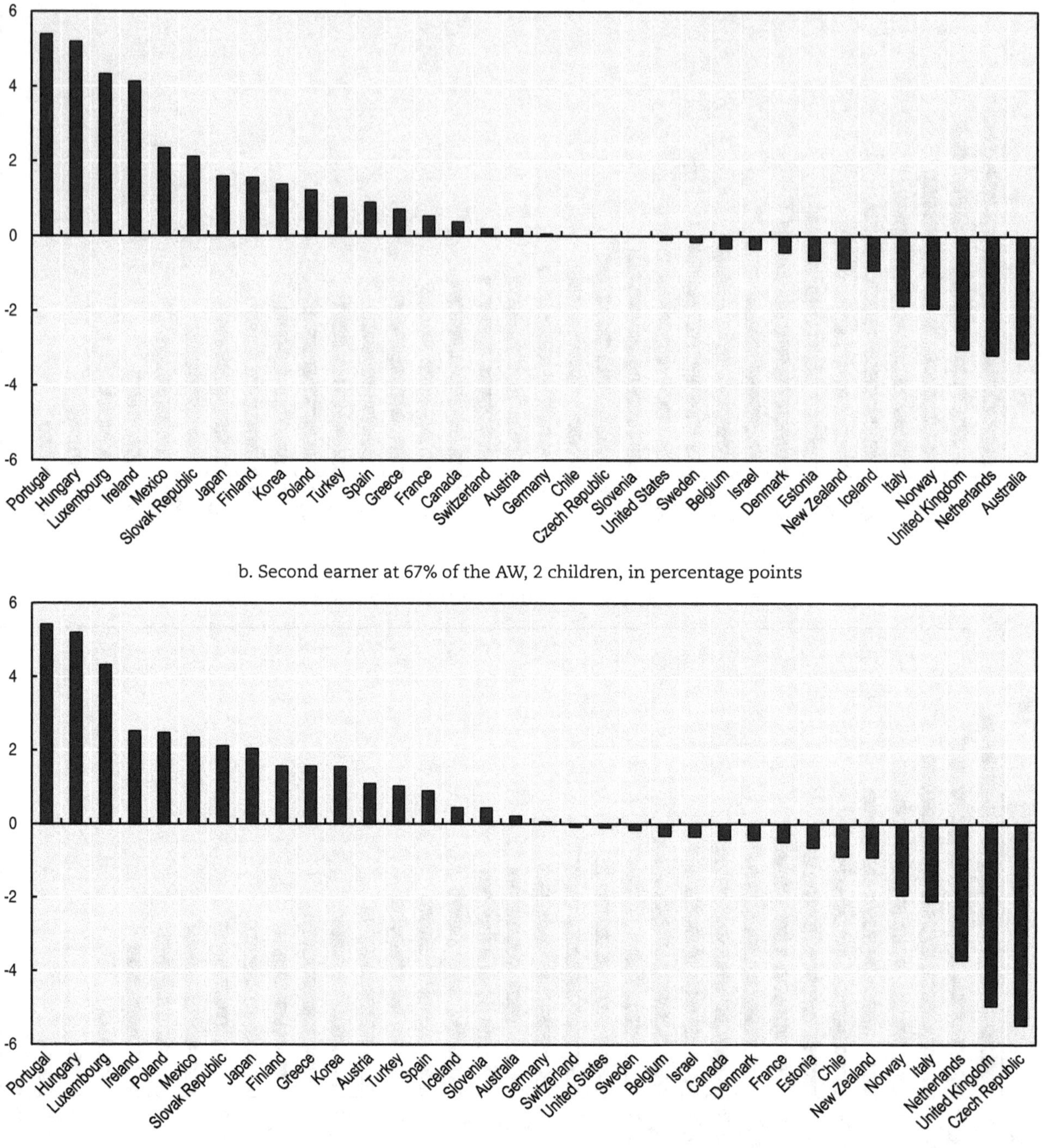

StatLink http://dx.doi.org/10.1787/888933340407

leave) that are not reflected in the general indicator. In Luxembourg, the basic tax allowance and credits have been frozen, while the marginal tax rates remained unchanged at the observed family's income range and the lump sum deduction for travel expenses has been abolished (in 2013). In Ireland, the Universal Social Charge replaced the Income and Health levies in 2011 and applies higher rates for the observed family's income range. In addition, in 2013, exemptions that reduced the employee SSCs were abolished. The average tax wedge increased by one percentage point or more in seven other countries: Finland, Japan, Korea, Mexico, Poland, the Slovak Republic and Turkey.

In contrast, the average tax wedge for second earners without children decreased in 13 countries between 2010 and 2014. The largest decreases in percentage point terms were observed in Australia (-3.3), the Netherlands (-3.2) and the United Kingdom (-3.0). The decrease in Australia is due to restrictions in eligibility for the *Dependant Spouse Tax Offset*.[5] In the Netherlands, reformed tax credits reduced the tax burden within the households when the spouse moved from non-employment to employment between 2010 and 2014. In the United Kingdom, the reduction is due to an increase in the basic personal allowance. The average tax wedge also decreased by more than one percentage point in Norway (-1.9) and Italy (-1.8). There were no changes in the tax burden during that period of time in Chile, the Czech Republic and Slovenia.

Figure 2.3b shows that the average tax wedge for second earners with two children also increased in 18 countries between 2010 and 2014. The largest increases in percentage point terms were once again in Portugal (5.4), Hungary (5.2) and Luxembourg (4.3) for the reasons noted above. The tax wedge increased by one percentage point or more in ten other countries: Austria, Finland, Greece, Ireland, Japan, Korea, Mexico, Poland, the Slovak Republic and Turkey.

In contrast, the average tax wedge for the second earner with two children decreased in 16 countries. It decreased the most in percentage point terms in the Czech Republic (-5.5), the United Kingdom (-4.9) and the Netherlands (-3.7). It also decreased by more than one percentage point in Italy (-2.1) and Norway (-1.9). The reduction in the Czech Republic is due to the removal of a *social allowance* (that was withdrawn when the non-employed spouse took up an employment).

Changes in net personal tax rates for second earners between 2010 and 2014

This section examines how the net personal average tax rates for second earners have changed between 2010 and 2014. While the magnitudes of changes vary to an extent, the same overall pattern in the changes can be observed as for the average tax wedges.

Figure 2.4a shows that the net personal average tax rate for second earners without children increased in 17 countries between 2010 and 2014. Similar to the changes observed for the average tax wedge, the largest increases in percentage points were in Hungary and Portugal (both by 6.7), Ireland (4.6) and Luxembourg (4.4). The increases for those countries are mainly due to the changes in the income tax systems noted in the previous section. Net average personal tax rates increased by more than one percentage point in seven other countries: Finland, France, Greece, Japan, Korea, Mexico and Spain.

In contrast, the net personal average tax rate for second earners without children decreased in 13 countries between 2010 and 2014. The largest decreases in percentage point terms were observed in the Netherlands (-3.6), Australia (-3.3) and the United Kingdom (-3.0). Once again, the decreases for those countries are mainly due to the changes in the income tax systems noted in the previous section. The net personal average tax rates also decreased by more than one percentage point in Italy (-2.4) and Norway (-2.3). There were no changes in the tax burden during that period of time in Chile, the Czech Republic, the Slovak Republic and Slovenia.

Figure 2.4b shows that the net personal average tax rate for second earners with two children also increased in 18 countries between 2010 and 2014. The largest increases in

Figure 2.4. **Changes in net personal average tax rates between 2010 and 2014**

a. Second earner at 67% of the AW, 0 children, in percentage points

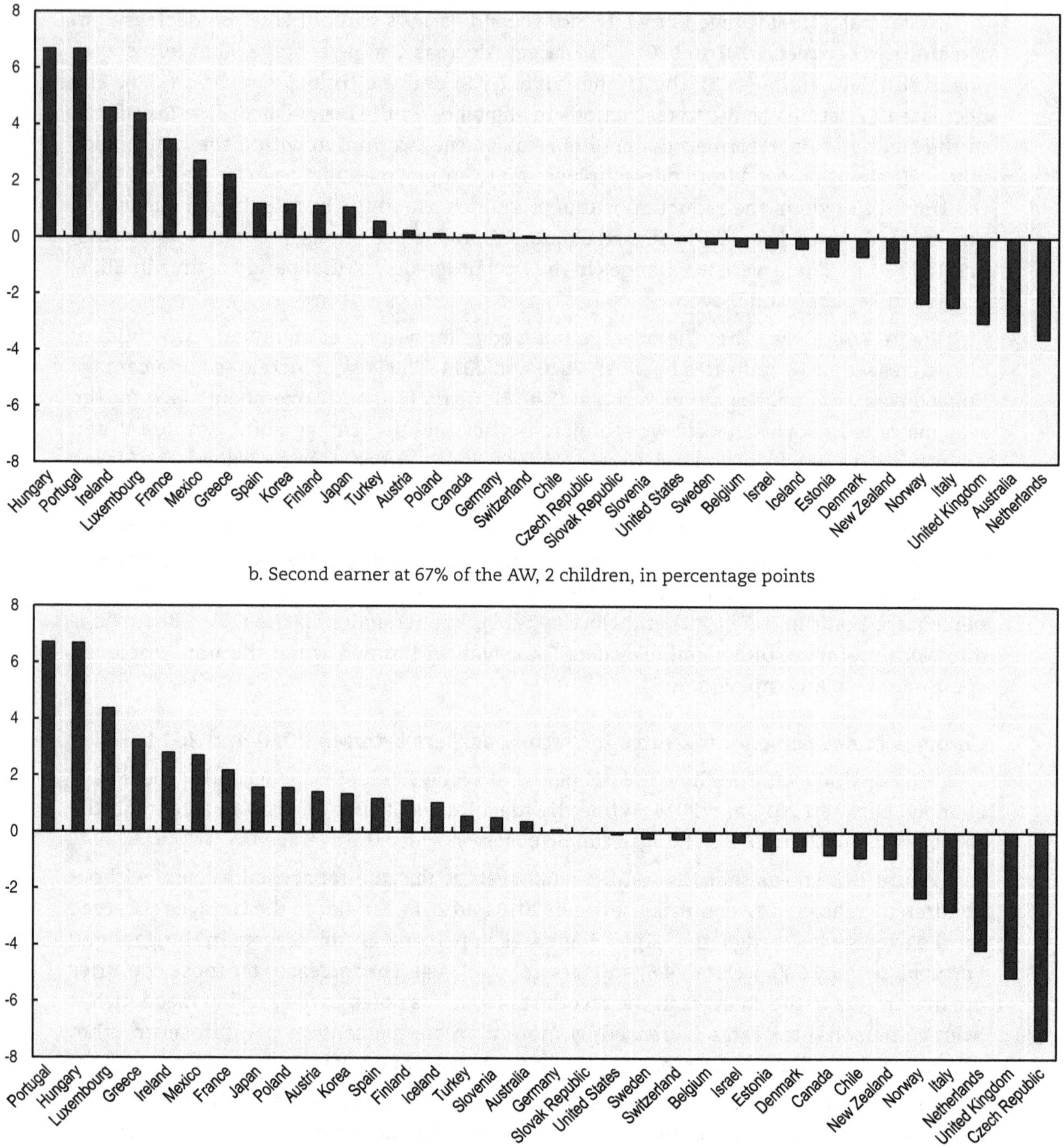

StatLink http://dx.doi.org/10.1787/888933340417

percentage points were in Hungary and Portugal (both 6.7) and Luxembourg (4.4). Those countries also experienced the largest increases in the average tax wedge for the second earner with children. The net personal average tax rates increased by one percentage point or more in 11 other countries; Austria, Finland, France, Greece, Iceland, Ireland, Japan, Korea, Mexico, Poland and Spain.

In contrast, the net personal tax rate for second earners with two children decreased in 15 countries. It decreased the most in percentage point terms in the Czech Republic (-7.3), the United Kingdom (-5.1) and the Netherlands (-4.2). It also decreased by more than one percentage point in Italy (-2.8) and Norway (-2.3). There were no changes in the net personal tax rate for the second earner in the Slovak Republic.

In the Slovak Republic, the net personal average tax rate did not change for second earners with and without children between 2010 and 2014, whereas the average tax wedge for the second earner with and without children increased by 2.1 percentage points. The changes were driven by increased employer SSCs between 2010 and 2014. In the Slovak Republic, the retirement insurance rate of 14% is divided between the government (5%) and a privately managed fund (9%). Since 2012, the government contribution rate has been increased from 5% to 10% (and the privately managed fund rate reduced from 9% to 4%). Only the payments to government are considered to be taxes and hence included in the *Taxing Wages* calculations.

Notes

1. Note though that there are also equity arguments for individual taxation. For example, it is arguable that a one-earner family is actually better off than a two-earner family with the same total income because the one-earner family has additional time available for leisure or for non-market work (such as child care) that the two-earner family would have to pay for. Individual taxation ensures that the one-earner family pays more tax than the two-earner family in this situation.
2. In this report, a "second earner" is defined as a married person who may or may not be working, but whose spouse – the "primary earner" – is working. If the second earner is working, they are assumed to earn less than the primary earner.
3. Under this assumption the decision as to whether the second earner enters employment is made based on what is best for the whole family, rather than what is best just for the second earner.
4. With respect to family based taxation, the personal income tax is calculated on the combined spouses' earnings in several countries, notably: Estonia, France, Germany, Ireland, Luxembourg, Poland, Portugal, and Switzerland. In Germany, Norway, Spain and the United States, married couples have the option of either an individual- or a family-based assessment. In Norway and Spain the *Taxing Wages* model allows for the most advantageous of these options to be chosen. In the United States, the modelling is based on family-based taxation only. In Germany, Luxembourg, Poland and Portugal, joint taxation is based on a splitting method between spouses. In Germany, this results in identical average and marginal legal tax rates for both the principal and second earner (see further Box 1). The income-splitting system in France also allocates a weighting to each child.
5. During the fiscal year 2013-14, the eligibility conditions for the *Dependant Spouse Tax Offset* were restricted (requiring the spouse to have been born before 1 July 1952), and consequently the tax credit is not included in the 2014 *Taxing Wages* calculations. The offset was entirely abolished as of the 2014-15 fiscal year.

References

Jaumotte, F. (2003) "Female labour force participation: Past trends and main determinants in OECD countries", *OECD Economics Department Working Papers*, No. 376. *www.oecd.org/officialdocuments/publicdisplaydocumentpdf/?doclanguage=en&cote=eco/wkp%282003%2930*.

OECD (2015) "Benefits and Wages Database", *www.oecd.org/social/benefits-and-wages.htm*.

OECD (2011) "Taxation and Employment", *OECD Tax Policy Studies*, No. 21, OECD, Paris, *http://dx.doi.org/10.1787/9789264120808-en*.

PART I

International comparisons

This section provides unique information for each of the OECD countries on the income taxes paid by workers, their social security contributions, the family benefits they receive in the form of cash transfers as well as the social security contributions and payroll taxes paid by their employers. It provides results for 2015 and 2014 and discusses the changes between the two years. Results reported cover the marginal and average tax burden for eight different family types.

PART I

Chapter 3

2015 tax burdens

The 2015 tax burden results based on the eight model family types are presented in Tables 3.1 to 3.11 and Figures 3.1 to 3.6. The model family types vary by marital status, number of children and economic status: single taxpayers without children earning 67%, 100% and 167% of the average wage (AW); a single parent with two children earning 67% of the AW; a single earner couple at the AW level with two children; two-earner couples at 133% and 167% of the AW with two children; and a two-earner couple without children at 133% of the AW.

The chapter presents different measures for the average tax burdens (tax wedge, personal tax rate, net personal tax rate, personal income tax rate and employee social security contribution rate) and marginal rates (tax wedge and net personal tax rate). The results for two measures of tax progressivity are also considered: tax elasticity on gross earnings and labour costs.

Average tax burdens

Table 3.1 and Figure 3.1 show the average tax wedge (combined burden of income tax, employee and employer social security contributions) taking into account the amount of cash benefits each specific family-type is entitled to. Total levies due minus transfers received are expressed as a percentage of total labour costs, defined as gross wage *plus* employers' social security contributions (including payroll taxes). In the case of a single person at the average wage level the wedge ranges from 7.0% (Chile) and 17.6% (New Zealand) to 49.5% (Austria) and 55.3% (Belgium). For a one-earner married couple with two children at the same wage level the wedge is lowest in New Zealand (4.9%) and Chile (7.0%) and highest in France (40.5%) and Belgium (40.4%). As stated in Chapter 1, the wedge tends to be lower for a married couple with two-children at this wage level than for a single individual without children due to both receipt of cash benefits and/or more advantageous tax treatment. It is also interesting to note that the wedge for a single parent with two children earning 67% of the average wage level is negative in Australia (-1.4%), Canada (-5.9%), New Zealand (-14.4%) and Ireland (-18.6%). This is due to the amount of cash benefits received by these families plus any applicable non-wastable tax credits that exceed the sum of the total tax and social security contributions that are due.

Table 3.2 and Figure 3.2 present the combined burden of the personal income tax and employee social security contributions, expressed as a percentage of gross wage earnings (the corresponding measures for income tax and employee contributions separately are shown in Tables 3.4 and 3.5). A single person at the average wage level without children is liable to an average tax plus contributions burden of more than 40% only in Belgium (42.0%). The lowest average rates were in Chile (7.0%), Mexico (10.3%), Korea (13.8%), Israel (17.3%), Switzerland (17.4%), New Zealand (17.6%), Estonia (18.4%) and Ireland (19.7%).

Table 3.3 shows the combined burden of income tax and employee social security contributions with the levies due being reduced by the entitlement to cash benefits for each family-type. Figure 3.3 illustrates this burden for single individuals without children and one-earner married couples with two children at average earnings, respectively. Comparing Tables 3.2 and 3.3, the average tax rates for families with children (columns 4 -7) are lower in Table 3.3 because most OECD countries support families with children through cash benefits.

A lower burden is also observed for a single individual *without* children at 67% of the average wage in Canada because of a cash transfer paid to mitigate the burden imposed by the federal consumption tax (further details can be found in the country chapter contained in Part III of this Report). The same is true in Denmark for single taxpayers at 67% and 100% of the average wage and two-earner married couples without children at 133% of the average wage who receive a green check to compensate for increased environmental taxes.

For single parents with two children earning 67% of the average wage level, 27 countries provide cash benefits. In Ireland these represent 38.7% of income and they are at least 25% of income in 5 other countries: Canada (30.0%), New Zealand (29.3%), Slovenia (26.5%), Australia

(25.9%) and Denmark (25.8%). 26 countries provide benefits for a one-earner married couple with two children earning the average wage level, although these are less generous relative to income, ranging up to 13.6% (Slovenia) and 13.5% (Luxembourg). The lower level of importance of cash benefits for the married couple can be attributed to three reasons: single parents may be eligible for more generous treatment; the benefits themselves may be fixed in absolute amount; or the benefits may be subject to income testing.

Table 3.4 shows personal income tax due as a percentage of gross wage earnings. For single persons without children at the average wage (column 2) – the income tax burden varies between 0% (Chile) and 36.1% (Denmark). In most OECD member countries, at the average wage level, the income tax burden for one-earner married couples with two children is substantially lower than that faced by single persons (compare columns 2 and 5). These differences are clearly illustrated in Figure 3.4. In nine OECD countries, the income tax burden faced by a one-earner married couple with two children is less than half that faced by a single individual (the Czech Republic, Germany, Luxembourg, Poland, Portugal, the Slovak Republic, Slovenia, Switzerland and the United States). In contrast, there is no difference in seven countries – Australia, Chile, Israel, Mexico, New Zealand, Sweden and the United Kingdom.

There are only three OECD member countries where a married average worker with 2 children has a negative personal income tax burden. This is due to the presence of non-wastable tax credits, whereby credits are paid in excess of the taxes otherwise due. This results in tax burdens of -4.7% in the Czech Republic, -2.0% in the Slovak Republic and -1.5% in Poland. Similarly, in seven countries – the Czech Republic, Germany, Poland, the Slovak Republic, Spain, the United Kingdom and the United States – single parents with two children earning 67% of the average wage show a negative tax burden. In four other countries – Chile, Israel, Korea and Slovenia – this family-type pays no income tax.

A comparison of columns 5 and 6 in Table 3.4 demonstrates that if the previously non-employed spouse finds a job which pays 33% of the average wage level, the income tax burden of the family (now expressed as 133% of the average wage level) is slightly higher in seventeen countries, the largest differences being in the Czech Republic (7.0 percentage points) with Germany (5.7 percentage points) and the Slovak Republic (5.6 percentage points). At the same time, the income tax burden is lower in fifteen countries, the largest differences being in Finland (-4.6 percentage points), Australia and Mexico (both -4.4 percentage points). There is no impact on the tax burden in Chile and France.

An important consideration in the design of an income tax is the level of progressivity – the rate at which the income tax burden increases with income. A comparison of columns 1 to 3 in Table 3.4 provides an insight into the levels of progressivity in the income tax systems of OECD countries. Comparing the income tax burden of single individuals at the average wage level with their counterparts at 167% of the average (columns 2 and 3), the lower paid worker faces a lower tax burden in all countries except in Hungary. There, a flat tax rate is applied on labour income and all households without children pay the same percentage of income tax. The same is true for single individuals at 67% of the average wage level compared with the average with an additional exception in Chile where these workers do not pay income tax. Finally the burden faced by single individuals at 67% of the average wage level represents one-quarter or less of the burden faced by their counterparts at 167% in only five OECD countries: Chile (0%), Mexico (15%), Greece (17%), Korea (18%) and the Netherlands (25%).

The addition of social security contributions to the average tax rate reduces this progressivity as well as the proportional fiscal savings enjoyed by families (compare Table 3.2 and Table 3.4). The OECD personal average tax burden of single individuals at 67% of the average wage level is only 32% lower than their counterparts at 167% compared to the OECD average savings of 50% for personal income taxes alone. The average fiscal savings observed for one-earner married couples with two children at the average wage level relative to single individuals falls from 37% to 20%. These lower figures reflect that there is little variation between social security contribution rates across family types, as shown in Table 3.5.

Table 3.5 shows employee social security contributions as a percentage of gross wage earnings. For a single worker without children at the average wage level (column 2) the contribution rate varies between zero (Australia, Denmark and New Zealand) and 22.1% (Slovenia). Australia, Denmark and New Zealand do not levy any employee social security contributions paid to general government and there are four other countries with very low rates – Iceland (0.4%), Mexico (1.4%) and Estonia (1.6%). Social security contributions are usually levied at a flat rate on all earnings, i.e. without any exempt threshold. In a number of OECD member countries a ceiling applies. However, this "capping" provision usually applies to wage levels higher than 167% of the average wage. These rate structures reflect a roughly constant average burden of employee social security contributions for most countries between 33% and 167% of average wage earnings. Some examples of a constant proportional burden for employee social security contributions for over the eight model family types, are (in decreasing order) Slovenia (22.1%), Hungary (18.5%), Poland (17.8%), Greece (15.5%), Turkey (15.0%), the Czech Republic and Portugal (11.0%), Norway (8.2%), the United States (7.7%), Chile (7.0%) and Estonia (1.6%).

In addition, at the average wage level only Germany and the Netherlands impose different burden of social security contributions on employees; according to their family status (see Figure 3.5).

Marginal tax burdens

Table 3.6 and Figure 3.6 show the percentage of the rise in labour costs that is deducted through the personal income tax and both employee and employer (including payroll taxes) social security contributions for a marginal increase in labour costs. This is the marginal wedge. In most cases, the marginal tax wedge absorbs 25%-55% of a rise in labour costs for single individuals without children at the average wage level. However, in eight OECD countries these individuals face higher marginal wedges – Belgium (66.3%), Austria (60.5%), Germany (60.2%), France (59.3%), Italy (56.0%), Ireland (55.8%), Finland and Luxembourg (both 55.5%). Mexico (25.2%) and Chile (7.0%) have the lowest marginal tax rates.

In twenty two OECD member countries, the marginal tax wedge for one-earner married couples at average earnings with 2 children is either the same or within 5 percentage points as that for single persons at average wage earnings with no children. The marginal wedge is more than 5 percentage points lower for the one-earner married couples in eight countries: Ireland (18.1 percentage points), Luxembourg (16.1 percentage points), France (15.8 percentage points), Portugal (14.1 percentage points), Switzerland (9.7 percentage points), the United States (9.3 percentage points), Germany (7.9 percentage points) and Slovenia (7.4 percentage points). In contrast, in New Zealand (21.2 percentage points), Canada (20.9 percentage points), Australia (18.9 percentage points) and Iceland (8.9 percentage points), the marginal rate for one-earner married couples with two children is more than 5 percentage points higher than it is for single workers with no children.

Table 3.7 and Figure 3.7 show the incremental change to personal income tax and employee social security contributions less cash benefits when gross wage earnings rise marginally. As in the case of the tax wedge, in most cases personal income tax and employee social security contributions absorb 25% - 55% of a worker's pay rise for single individuals without children at the average wage level. The marginal tax rate is lower than 25% only in Chile (7.0%), Mexico (19.5%), Estonia (21.3%) and Korea (21.9%).

In twenty one OECD member countries, the net marginal personal tax rate for one-earner married couples with two children at the average wage level is either the same or within five percentage points as that for single persons with no children. The marginal rate is more than 5 percentage points lower for the one-earner married couples in nine countries: France (21.8 percentage points), Ireland (20.0 percentage points), Luxembourg (18.1 percentage points), Portugal (17.5 percentage points), Switzerland (10.4 percentage points), the United States (10.0 percentage points), Germany (9.4 percentage points), Slovenia (8.5 percentage points) and Spain (5.6 percentage points). In contrast, in Canada (22.9 percentage points), New Zealand (21.2 percentage points), Australia (20.0 percentage points) and Iceland (9.6 percentage points), the marginal rate for one-earner married couples with two children is more than 5 percentage points higher than it is for single persons with no children. These higher marginal rates arise because of the phase out of income-tested tax reliefs and/or cash transfers. When an income-tested measure is being phased out, the reduction in the relief or benefit compounds the increase in the tax otherwise payable. These programmes are set out in greater detail in the relevant country chapters, in Part III of the Report.

Table 3.8 shows the percentage increase in net income when gross wage earnings increase by 1 currency unit, i.e. the elasticity of after-tax income.[1] Under a proportional tax system, net income would increase by the same percentage as the increase in gross earnings, in which case the elasticity is equal to 1. The elasticity is measured as 0.8 when an increase of gross wage by 1 currency unit leads to a corresponding rise of net take-home pay of only 0.8 of a unit. The more progressive the system is – at the income level considered – the lower this elasticity will be. In the case, for example, of the one-earner married households with two children at the average wage level, column 5 of Table 3.8 shows that of all OECD member countries Canada (0.46), Australia (0.47), New Zealand (0.51) and Belgium (0.58) have, on this measure, the most progressive systems of income tax plus employee social security contributions taking into account tax provisions and cash transfers for children at this income level. In contrast, Chile (1.00), France (0.95), Turkey (0.91) and Mexico (0.90) either implement or are close to a proportional system of income tax plus employee social security contributions – at least for this family type.

It is interesting to note that the elasticity exceeds one for a single individual at 167% of the average earnings in Austria (1.03), indicating that the income tax system at this point in the income scale is regressive. In other words, a percentage increase in gross pay leads to an increase in net income in excess of the percentage increase in gross wage earnings.

Table 3.9 provides a different elasticity measure: the percentage increase in net income when labour costs (i.e. gross wage earnings plus employer social security contributions and payroll taxes) rise by 1 currency unit.[2] In this case taxes and social security contributions paid by employers are also part of the analysis. In most OECD member countries the value of this elasticity lies between 0.5 and 0.97 for the eight selected family-types. This elasticity is below 0.5 for single parents earning 67% of the average wage level in Australia (0.41), Canada (0.37), Ireland (0.27) and the United Kingdom (0.25), for one-earner married households at the average wage level with two children in Australia and Canada (both 0.47) and for two-earner married households where one spouse earns the average wage and the other 33% of it with two children in Australia (0.38). In contrast, the elasticity is between 0.97 and 1.0 for some family types in Chile, Estonia, Hungary, Japan, Korea, Mexico and Poland. It is interesting to mention that under this elasticity measure the income tax system is regressive for a single individual at 167% of average earnings in Spain (1.11), Germany (1.14) and Austria (1.21).

Table 3.10 sets out figures for gross wage earnings and net income for the eight family-types after all amounts have been converted into U.S. dollars with the same purchasing power. Single workers with the average wage take home (see Table 3.10, column 4) over USD 37 000 in eight countries: Switzerland (USD 57 756), Norway (USD 43 104), the Netherlands (USD 42 650), Australia (USD 42 456), Luxembourg (USD 42 134), Korea (USD 40 748), the United Kingdom (USD 39 381) and the United States (USD 37 899). The corresponding lowest levels were in Mexico (USD 11 539), Hungary (USD 15 922) and the Slovak Republic (USD 16 748). In the case of a one-earner married couple with two children at the average earnings level, families take home over USD 50 000 in Luxembourg and Switzerland; with the lowest level again being in Mexico. It is interesting to observe that with the exceptions of Chile and Mexico, the one-earner married couple takes home more than the single individual at the average wage due to the favourable tax treatment of this family and/or the cash transfers to which they are entitled.

Table 3.11 shows the corresponding figures to Table 3.10 for labour costs and net income. So the 'net' columns in Tables 3.10 and 3.11 are identical. Usually, labour costs are found to be much higher than gross wages, because any employer social security contributions (including payroll taxes) are now taken into account. If measured in US dollars with equal purchasing power, labour costs for single workers earning the average wage level are the highest in Switzerland (USD 74 255) and Belgium (USD 74 137), and the lowest in Mexico (USD 14 375) and Chile (USD 19 338). It is interesting to note that the annual labour costs are equal to the annual gross wage in Chile and New Zealand. In those countries neither compulsory employer social security contributions nor payroll taxes are levied on wages. However, employers in Chile are subject to non-tax compulsory payments related notably to pension schemes.

Notes

1. The reported elasticities in Table 3.8 are calculated as (100-METR)/(100-AETR), where METR is the marginal rate of income tax plus employee social security contributions less cash benefits reported in Table 3.7 and AETR is the average rate plus employee social security contributions less cash benefits reported in Table 3.3.
2. The reported elasticities in Table 3.9 are calculated as (100-METR)/(100-AETR), where METR is the marginal rate of income tax plus employee and employer social security contributions less cash benefits reported in Table 3.6 and AETR is the average rate plus employee and employer social security contributions less cash benefits reported in Table 3.1.

Table 3.1. **Income tax plus employee and employer contributions less cash benefits, 2015**

As % of labour costs, by family-type and wage level

	Single no ch 67 (% AW)	Single no ch 100 (% AW)	Single no ch 167 (% AW)	Single 2 ch 67 (% AW)	Married 2 ch 100-0 (% AW)	Married 2 ch 100-33 (% AW)[2]	Married 2 ch 100-67 (% AW)[2]	Married no ch 100-33 (% AW)[2]
Australia	23.1	28.4	34.0	-1.4	17.8	22.7	26.3	24.2
Austria	45.0	49.5	52.2	29.3	39.0	38.4	42.1	45.4
Belgium	49.5	55.3	60.7	35.8	40.4	41.4	48.1	47.7
Canada	26.6	31.6	33.4	-5.9	18.8	23.7	26.9	28.5
Chile	7.0	7.0	7.9	6.1	7.0	4.7	6.6	7.0
Czech Republic	39.9	42.8	45.1	24.5	26.6	32.7	35.4	40.5
Denmark	34.3	36.4	42.4	7.6	26.0	29.8	31.8	34.5
Estonia	38.0	39.0	39.9	21.5	28.5	31.7	33.6	38.0
Finland	38.3	43.9	49.7	28.3	39.3	36.5	38.9	39.9
France	43.5	48.5	54.3	35.9	40.5	37.9	43.1	43.7
Germany	45.3	49.4	51.3	30.8	34.0	38.7	42.3	45.2
Greece	34.7	39.3	46.8	30.9	38.1	37.5	38.0	38.3
Hungary	49.0	49.0	49.0	27.2	35.3	38.7	40.8	49.0
Iceland	29.9	34.0	38.3	19.5	22.4	28.6	32.3	30.1
Ireland	21.6	27.5	38.8	-18.6	9.5	14.0	19.8	20.3
Israel[1]	14.6	21.6	30.6	2.7	18.9	15.9	15.3	17.9
Italy	42.0	49.0	54.6	26.5	39.9	39.5	42.7	43.8
Japan	30.8	32.2	34.9	24.6	26.8	28.3	29.2	31.4
Korea	18.6	21.9	24.0	17.0	19.6	19.3	19.5	20.7
Luxembourg	31.1	38.3	45.2	7.1	15.9	20.3	26.0	29.4
Mexico	15.0	19.7	22.8	15.0	19.7	17.6	17.8	17.6
Netherlands	31.0	36.2	41.5	8.8	30.6	27.6	29.7	32.2
New Zealand	13.5	17.6	23.3	-14.4	4.9	12.0	16.5	16.2
Norway	33.6	36.6	42.4	22.1	31.9	31.1	33.2	33.9
Poland	33.4	34.7	35.7	24.0	28.4	30.2	31.7	33.4
Portugal	36.2	42.1	48.0	25.2	30.7	31.1	35.6	36.1
Slovak Republic	38.8	41.3	43.4	27.2	28.4	31.7	35.7	37.6
Slovenia	38.6	42.6	46.5	10.1	23.7	30.8	34.6	40.2
Spain	36.0	39.6	44.2	24.1	33.8	35.6	36.4	36.7
Sweden	40.7	42.7	51.0	33.4	37.8	37.3	39.0	41.0
Switzerland	19.4	22.2	26.8	4.7	9.8	12.9	16.0	20.0
Turkey	36.1	38.3	41.9	34.8	36.9	35.7	36.9	36.4
United Kingdom	26.0	30.8	37.3	5.4	26.3	22.4	26.2	25.9
United States	29.5	31.7	36.4	12.1	20.7	24.7	26.6	29.5
Unweighted average								
OECD-Average	**32.1**	**35.9**	**40.4**	**17.2**	**26.7**	**28.3**	**31.0**	**32.7**
OECD-EU 21	**37.7**	**41.8**	**46.5**	**21.2**	**31.1**	**32.6**	**35.8**	**38.0**

Note: ch = children

Disclaimer: *http://oe.cd/disclaimer*

1. Information on data for Israel: *http://oe.cd/israel-disclaimer*.
2. Two-earner family.

StatLink http://dx.doi.org/10.1787/888933341274

Figure 3.1. **Income tax plus employee and employer contributions less cash benefits, 2015**

As a % of labour costs, by family-type

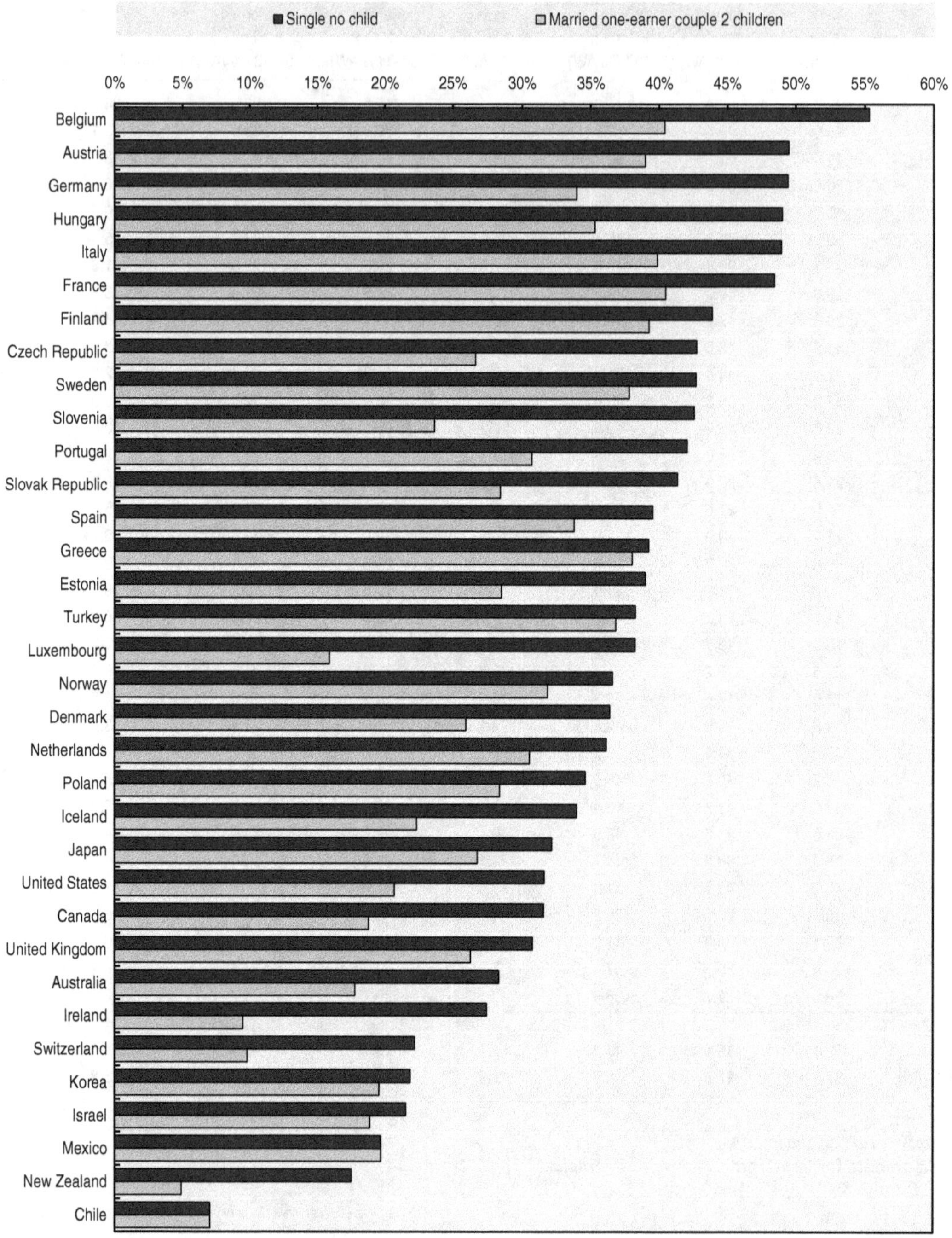

Note: The family type "single no child" corresponds to a wage level of 100% of average wage. The family type "married one earner couple 2 children" corresponds to a combined wage level of 100%-0% of average wage.

Source: OECD calculations based on country submissions and *OECD Economic Outlook, Volume 2015* (No. 98).

StatLink http://dx.doi.org/10.1787/888933340421

Table 3.2. **Income tax plus employee contributions, 2015**

As % of gross wage earnings, by family-type and wage level

	Single no ch 67 (% AW)	Single no ch 100 (% AW)	Single no ch 167 (% AW)	Single 2 ch 67 (% AW)	Married 2 ch 100-0 (% AW)	Married 2 ch 100-33 (% AW)[2]	Married 2 ch 100-67 (% AW)[2]	Married no ch 100-33 (% AW)[2]
Australia	18.5	24.1	30.1	18.5	24.1	19.7	21.9	19.7
Austria	29.0	34.9	39.4	26.2	32.9	29.3	32.3	29.6
Belgium	35.4	42.0	49.1	30.0	30.8	32.2	37.9	34.1
Canada	19.0	23.4	27.1	11.4	18.7	19.9	21.5	20.0
Chile	7.0	7.0	7.9	7.0	7.0	7.0	7.0	7.0
Czech Republic	19.4	23.3	26.4	5.7	6.3	13.3	16.2	20.2
Denmark	33.8	36.1	42.1	32.2	32.2	34.0	35.2	34.0
Estonia	17.0	18.4	19.6	12.7	12.7	14.8	16.1	17.0
Finland	24.1	30.9	38.1	24.1	30.8	26.0	28.1	26.1
France	25.9	28.9	34.4	22.1	22.1	22.1	25.5	26.6
Germany	34.7	39.7	43.8	17.5	21.2	26.9	31.2	34.6
Greece	18.6	24.3	33.7	18.6	25.7	23.2	23.7	23.2
Hungary	34.5	34.5	34.5	23.2	26.9	28.8	30.0	34.5
Iceland	24.6	29.1	33.7	24.6	20.9	24.9	27.3	24.9
Ireland	13.2	19.7	32.2	7.3	12.0	12.2	16.7	12.2
Israel[1]	10.8	17.3	26.3	5.9	17.3	13.9	12.7	13.9
Italy	23.4	32.6	40.0	15.7	25.7	22.3	26.0	25.8
Japan	20.4	22.0	25.8	20.4	20.6	21.1	21.4	21.1
Korea	10.2	13.8	17.2	8.4	11.3	11.0	11.1	12.5
Luxembourg	22.6	30.7	38.5	15.9	19.1	20.7	25.1	20.7
Mexico	3.2	10.3	15.0	3.2	10.3	5.9	7.5	5.9
Netherlands	24.4	29.9	37.6	18.0	27.5	23.5	25.1	25.7
New Zealand	13.5	17.6	23.3	14.9	17.6	16.2	16.5	16.2
Norway	25.0	28.4	34.9	21.5	27.2	25.4	27.0	25.4
Poland	22.2	23.7	24.9	11.3	16.4	18.5	20.2	22.2
Portugal	21.1	28.3	35.6	14.7	18.3	17.5	20.3	20.9
Slovak Republic	19.7	23.0	25.8	12.5	11.4	16.0	18.8	19.7
Slovenia	28.7	33.3	37.9	22.1	25.0	25.9	27.8	30.5
Spain	16.8	21.5	27.7	1.4	14.0	16.3	17.3	17.7
Sweden	22.1	24.7	35.6	22.1	24.7	22.4	23.7	22.4
Switzerland	14.4	17.4	22.2	8.6	10.8	12.4	14.8	15.0
Turkey	24.9	27.5	31.8	23.4	25.8	24.5	25.9	25.2
United Kingdom	19.2	23.4	29.8	4.1	23.4	19.1	21.7	19.1
United States	22.9	25.6	31.1	3.9	13.7	17.6	20.0	22.8
Unweighted average								
OECD-Average	**21.2**	**25.5**	**31.0**	**15.6**	**20.1**	**20.1**	**22.2**	**22.0**
OECD-EU 21	**24.1**	**28.8**	**34.6**	**17.0**	**21.9**	**22.1**	**24.7**	**24.6**

Note: ch = children

Disclaimer: *http://oe.cd/disclaimer*

1. Information on data for Israel: *http://oe.cd/israel-disclaimer.*
2. Two-earner family.

StatLink http://dx.doi.org/10.1787/888933341281

Figure 3.2. **Income tax plus employee contributions, 2015**

As % of gross wage earnings, by family-type and wage level

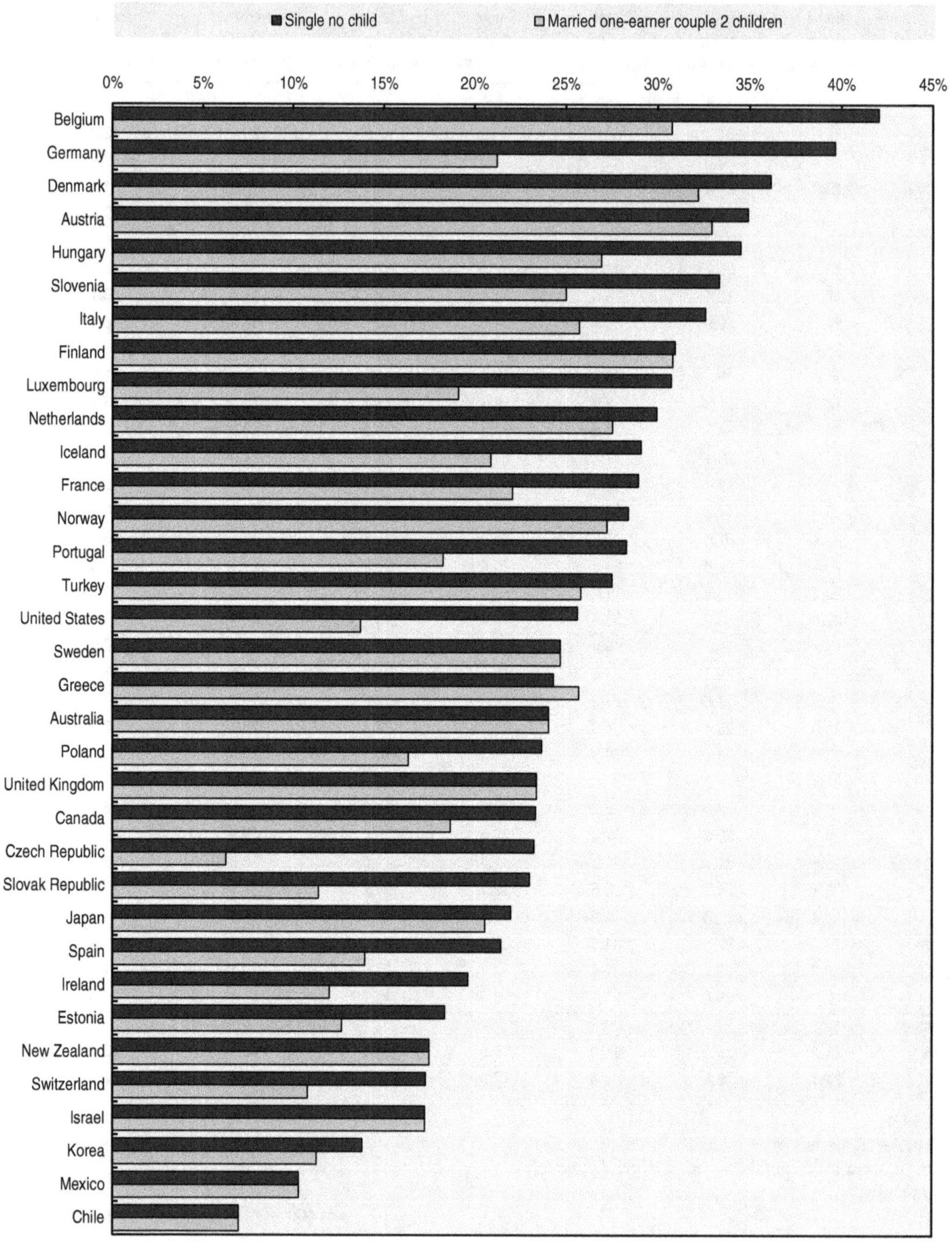

Note: The family type "single no child" corresponds to a wage level of 100% of average wage. The family type "married one earner couple 2 children" corresponds to a combined wage level of 100%-0% of average wage.

Source: Country submissions, *OECD Economic Outlook Volume* 2015 (No. 98).

StatLink http://dx.doi.org/10.1787/888933340437

Table 3.3. **Income tax plus employee contributions less cash benefits, 2015**

As % of gross wage earnings, by family-type and wage level

	Single no ch 67 (% AW)	Single no ch 100 (% AW)	Single no ch 167 (% AW)	Single 2 ch 67 (% AW)	Married 2 ch 100-0 (% AW)	Married 2 ch 100-33 (% AW)[2]	Married 2 ch 100-67 (% AW)[2]	Married no ch 100-33 (% AW)[2]
Australia	18.5	24.1	30.1	-7.4	12.9	18.1	21.9	19.7
Austria	29.0	34.9	39.4	8.9	21.4	20.6	25.3	29.6
Belgium	35.4	42.0	49.1	18.0	22.7	26.2	33.1	34.1
Canada	17.8	23.4	27.1	-18.6	9.0	14.6	18.1	20.0
Chile	7.0	7.0	7.9	6.1	7.0	4.7	6.6	7.0
Czech Republic	19.4	23.3	26.4	-1.1	1.7	9.9	13.5	20.2
Denmark	33.4	35.9	42.1	6.4	25.3	28.9	31.1	33.6
Estonia	17.0	18.4	19.6	-5.0	4.3	8.5	11.1	17.0
Finland	24.1	30.9	38.1	11.8	25.2	21.8	24.8	26.1
France	25.9	28.9	34.4	15.9	18.0	19.0	23.1	26.6
Germany	34.7	39.7	43.8	17.5	21.2	26.9	31.2	34.6
Greece	18.6	24.3	33.7	13.9	22.9	22.1	22.8	23.2
Hungary	34.5	34.5	34.5	6.5	16.9	21.2	23.9	34.5
Iceland	24.6	29.1	33.7	13.5	16.5	23.3	27.2	24.9
Ireland	13.2	19.7	32.2	-31.4	-0.3	5.2	11.2	12.2
Israel[1]	10.8	17.3	26.3	-1.6	14.5	11.8	11.1	13.9
Italy	23.4	32.6	40.0	3.0	20.6	20.0	24.3	25.8
Japan	20.4	22.0	25.8	13.3	15.8	17.5	18.5	21.1
Korea	10.2	13.8	17.2	8.4	11.3	11.0	11.1	12.5
Luxembourg	22.6	30.7	38.5	-4.3	5.6	10.6	17.0	20.7
Mexico	3.2	10.3	15.0	3.2	10.3	5.9	7.5	5.9
Netherlands	24.4	29.9	37.6	0.1	23.8	20.6	22.9	25.7
New Zealand	13.5	17.6	23.3	-14.4	4.9	12.0	16.5	16.2
Norway	25.0	28.4	34.9	12.0	23.0	22.2	24.5	25.4
Poland	22.2	23.7	24.9	11.3	16.4	18.5	20.2	22.2
Portugal	21.1	28.3	35.6	7.5	14.2	14.7	20.3	20.9
Slovak Republic	19.7	23.0	25.8	4.5	6.1	12.0	15.6	19.7
Slovenia	28.7	33.3	37.9	-4.4	11.4	19.6	24.1	30.5
Spain	16.8	21.5	27.7	1.4	14.0	16.3	17.3	17.7
Sweden	22.1	24.7	35.6	12.5	18.3	17.6	19.8	22.4
Switzerland	14.4	17.4	22.2	-1.3	4.2	7.4	10.8	15.0
Turkey	24.9	27.5	31.8	23.4	25.8	24.5	25.9	25.2
United Kingdom	19.2	23.4	29.8	-3.3	18.4	15.4	18.7	19.1
United States	22.9	25.6	31.1	3.9	13.7	17.6	20.0	22.8
Unweighted average								
OECD-Average	**21.1**	**25.5**	**31.0**	**3.8**	**14.6**	**16.7**	**19.7**	**21.9**
OECD-EU 21	**24.1**	**28.8**	**34.6**	**4.3**	**15.6**	**17.9**	**21.5**	**24.6**

Note: ch = children

Disclaimer: *http://oe.cd/disclaimer*

1. Information on data for Israel: *http://oe.cd/israel-disclaimer*.
2. Two-earner family.

StatLink http://dx.doi.org/10.1787/888933341295

Figure 3.3. **Income tax plus employee contributions less cash benefits, 2015**

As %jc of gross wage earnings, by family-type and wage level

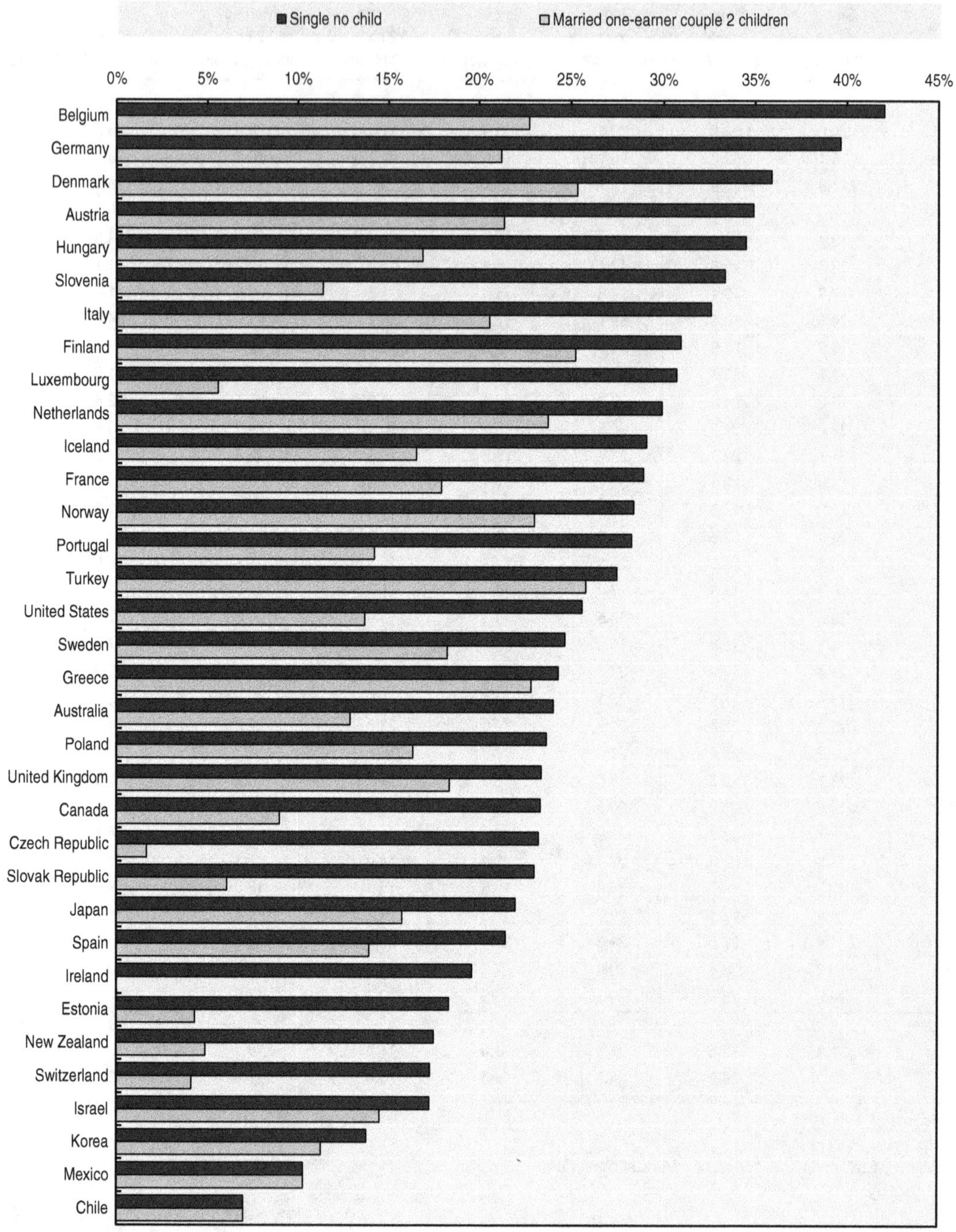

Note: The family type "single no child" corresponds to a wage level of 100% of average wage. The family type "married one earner couple 2 children" corresponds to a combined wage level of 100%-0% of average wage.

Source: OECD calculations based on country submissions and *OECD Economic Outlook, Volume 2015* (No. 98).

StatLink http://dx.doi.org/10.1787/888933340444

Table 3.4. **Income tax, by family-type and wage level, 2015**

As % of gross wage earnings

	Single no ch 67 (% AW)	Single no ch 100 (% AW)	Single no ch 167 (% AW)	Single 2 ch 67 (% AW)	Married 2 ch 100-0 (% AW)	Married 2 ch 100-33 (% AW)[2]	Married 2 ch 100-67 (% AW)[2]	Married no ch 100-33 (% AW)[2]
Australia	18.5	24.1	30.1	18.5	24.1	19.7	21.9	19.7
Austria	11.0	16.8	23.2	8.1	14.9	12.0	14.2	12.3
Belgium	21.5	28.1	35.1	16.1	16.8	21.5	23.9	23.3
Canada	11.8	15.8	22.2	4.2	11.1	12.7	14.0	12.8
Chile	0.0	0.0	0.9	0.0	0.0	0.0	0.0	0.0
Czech Republic	8.4	12.3	15.4	-5.3	-4.7	2.3	5.2	9.2
Denmark	33.8	36.1	42.1	32.2	32.2	34.0	35.2	34.0
Estonia	15.4	16.8	18.0	11.1	11.1	13.2	14.5	15.4
Finland	16.0	22.7	29.8	16.0	22.5	17.9	19.9	18.1
France	11.7	14.7	20.9	7.9	7.9	7.9	11.3	12.4
Germany	14.2	19.2	27.7	-2.8	1.0	6.6	11.0	14.1
Greece	3.1	8.8	18.2	3.1	10.2	7.7	8.2	7.7
Hungary	16.0	16.0	16.0	4.7	8.4	10.3	11.5	16.0
Iceland	24.1	28.7	33.5	24.1	20.5	24.3	26.9	24.3
Ireland	9.2	15.7	28.2	3.3	8.0	9.2	12.7	9.2
Israel[1]	4.9	9.4	16.8	0.0	9.4	7.1	5.6	7.1
Italy	13.9	23.1	30.4	6.2	16.2	12.8	16.5	16.3
Japan	6.1	7.7	12.4	6.1	6.3	6.8	7.1	6.8
Korea	1.8	5.4	10.0	0.0	2.9	2.6	2.8	4.1
Luxembourg	9.9	17.9	25.6	3.1	6.3	8.0	12.3	8.0
Mexico	2.0	8.9	13.5	2.0	8.9	4.6	6.2	4.6
Netherlands	7.1	16.7	28.4	5.6	16.1	12.8	12.2	13.3
New Zealand	13.5	17.6	23.3	14.9	17.6	16.2	16.5	16.2
Norway	16.8	20.2	26.7	13.3	19.0	17.2	18.8	17.2
Poland	4.4	5.9	7.1	-6.5	-1.5	0.7	2.4	4.4
Portugal	10.1	17.3	24.6	3.7	7.3	6.5	9.3	9.9
Slovak Republic	6.3	9.6	12.4	-0.9	-2.0	3.6	5.4	7.3
Slovenia	6.6	11.2	15.8	0.0	2.9	3.8	5.7	8.4
Spain	10.5	15.1	21.4	-5.0	7.6	10.0	11.0	11.4
Sweden	15.1	17.7	30.9	15.1	17.7	15.4	16.7	15.4
Switzerland	8.2	11.1	16.1	2.4	4.5	6.2	8.5	8.7
Turkey	9.9	12.5	16.8	8.4	10.8	9.5	10.9	10.2
United Kingdom	11.2	14.1	22.4	-3.8	14.1	11.1	13.0	11.1
United States	15.2	18.0	23.5	-3.8	6.1	9.9	12.3	15.2
Unweighted average								
OECD-Average	**11.4**	**15.7**	**21.8**	**5.9**	**10.4**	**10.7**	**12.5**	**12.5**
OECD-EU 21	**12.2**	**17.0**	**23.5**	**5.3**	**10.1**	**10.8**	**13.0**	**13.2**

Note: ch = children

Disclaimer: *http://oe.cd/disclaimer*

1. Information on data for Israel: *http://oe.cd/israel-disclaimer*.
2. Two-earner family.

StatLink http://dx.doi.org/10.1787/888933341307

Figure 3.4. **Income tax, by family-type, 2015**

As % of gross wage earnings

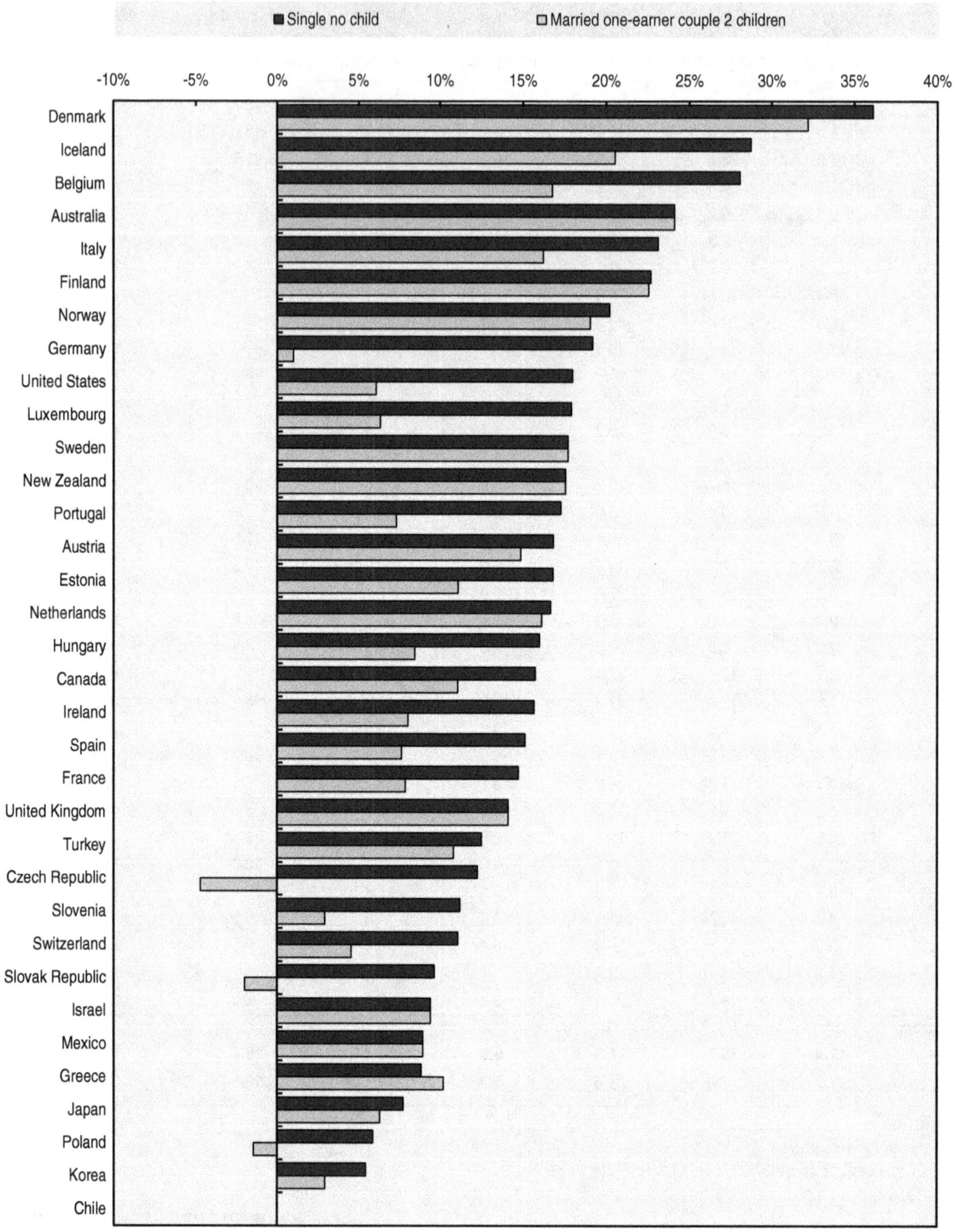

Note: The family type "single no child" corresponds to a wage level of 100% of average wage. The family type "married one earner couple 2 children" corresponds to a combined wage level of 100%-0% of average wage.

Source: OECD calculations based on country submissions and *OECD Economic Outlook, Volume 2015* (No. 98).

StatLink http://dx.doi.org/10.1787/888933340459

Table 3.5. **Employee contributions, 2015**

As % of gross wage earnings, by family-type and wage level

	Single no ch 67 (% AW)	Single no ch 100 (% AW)	Single no ch 167 (% AW)	Single 2 ch 67 (% AW)	Married 2 ch 100-0 (% AW)	Married 2 ch 100-33 (% AW)[2]	Married 2 ch 100-67 (% AW)[2]	Married no ch 100-33 (% AW)[2]
Australia	0.0	0.0	0.0	0.0	0.0	0.0	0.0	0.0
Austria	18.1	18.1	16.2	18.1	18.1	17.3	18.1	17.3
Belgium	13.9	14.0	14.0	13.9	14.0	10.8	14.0	10.8
Canada	7.2	7.6	4.9	7.2	7.6	7.2	7.5	7.2
Chile	7.0	7.0	7.0	7.0	7.0	7.0	7.0	7.0
Czech Republic	11.0	11.0	11.0	11.0	11.0	11.0	11.0	11.0
Denmark	0.0	0.0	0.0	0.0	0.0	0.0	0.0	0.0
Estonia	1.6	1.6	1.6	1.6	1.6	1.6	1.6	1.6
Finland	8.2	8.3	8.3	8.2	8.3	8.0	8.2	8.0
France	14.2	14.2	13.5	14.2	14.2	14.2	14.2	14.2
Germany	20.5	20.5	16.1	20.2	20.2	20.2	20.2	20.5
Greece	15.5	15.5	15.5	15.5	15.5	15.5	15.5	15.5
Hungary	18.5	18.5	18.5	18.5	18.5	18.5	18.5	18.5
Iceland	0.5	0.4	0.2	0.5	0.4	0.5	0.4	0.5
Ireland	4.0	4.0	4.0	4.0	4.0	3.0	4.0	3.0
Israel[1]	5.9	7.9	9.5	5.9	7.9	6.8	7.1	6.8
Italy	9.5	9.5	9.6	9.5	9.5	9.5	9.5	9.5
Japan	14.3	14.3	13.3	14.3	14.3	14.3	14.3	14.3
Korea	8.4	8.4	7.1	8.4	8.4	8.4	8.4	8.4
Luxembourg	12.7	12.8	12.9	12.7	12.8	12.7	12.8	12.7
Mexico	1.3	1.4	1.5	1.3	1.4	1.3	1.3	1.3
Netherlands	17.3	13.3	9.2	12.4	11.4	10.7	12.9	12.4
New Zealand	0.0	0.0	0.0	0.0	0.0	0.0	0.0	0.0
Norway	8.2	8.2	8.2	8.2	8.2	8.2	8.2	8.2
Poland	17.8	17.8	17.8	17.8	17.8	17.8	17.8	17.8
Portugal	11.0	11.0	11.0	11.0	11.0	11.0	11.0	11.0
Slovak Republic	13.4	13.4	13.4	13.4	13.4	12.4	13.4	12.4
Slovenia	22.1	22.1	22.1	22.1	22.1	22.1	22.1	22.1
Spain	6.4	6.4	6.3	6.4	6.4	6.4	6.4	6.4
Sweden	7.0	7.0	4.7	7.0	7.0	7.0	7.0	7.0
Switzerland	6.3	6.3	6.2	6.3	6.3	6.3	6.3	6.3
Turkey	15.0	15.0	15.0	15.0	15.0	15.0	15.0	15.0
United Kingdom	8.0	9.3	7.4	8.0	9.3	8.0	8.8	8.0
United States	7.7	7.7	7.7	7.7	7.7	7.7	7.7	7.7
Unweighted average								
OECD-Average	**9.8**	**9.8**	**9.2**	**9.6**	**9.7**	**9.4**	**9.7**	**9.5**
OECD-EU 21	**11.9**	**11.8**	**11.1**	**11.7**	**11.7**	**11.3**	**11.8**	**11.4**

Note: ch = children

Disclaimer: *http://oe.cd/disclaimer*

1. Information on data for Israel: *http://oe.cd/israel-disclaimer*.
2. Two-earner family.

StatLink http://dx.doi.org/10.1787/888933341313

Figure 3.5. **Employee contributions, 2015**

As % of gross wage earnings, by family-type

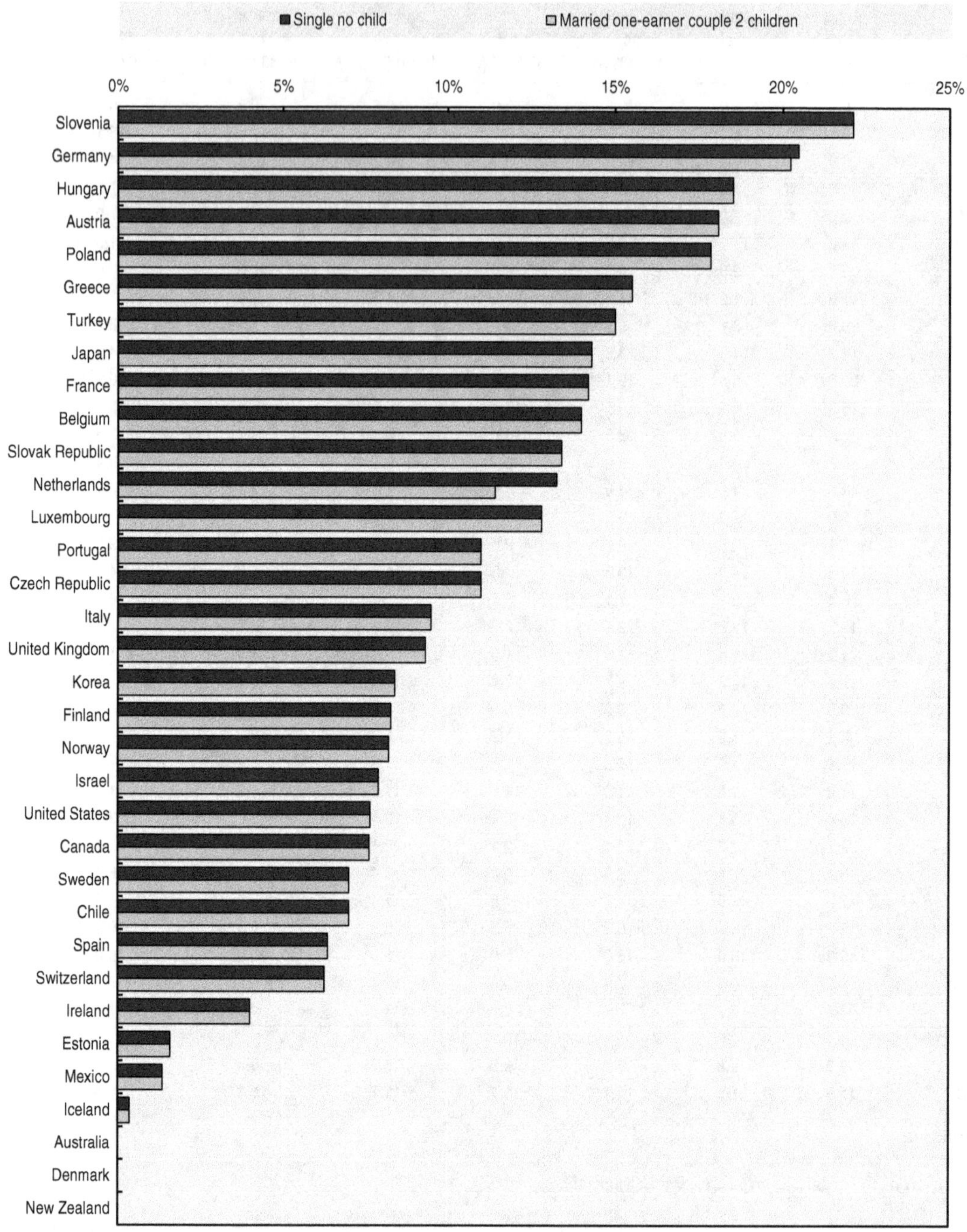

Note: The family type "single no child" corresponds to a wage level of 100% of average wage. The family type "married one earner couple 2 children" corresponds to a combined wage level of 100%-0% of average wage.

Source: OECD calculations based on country submissions and *OECD Economic Outlook, Volume 2015* (No. 98).

StatLink http://dx.doi.org/10.1787/888933340464

Table 3.6. **Marginal rate of income tax plus employee and employer contributions less cash benefits, 2015**

As % of labour costs, by family-type and wage level

	Single no ch 67 (% AW)	Single no ch 100 (% AW)	Single no ch 167 (% AW)	Single 2 ch 67 (% AW)	Married 2 ch 100-0 (% AW)	Married 2 ch 100-33 (% AW)[2]	Married 2 ch 100-67 (% AW)[2]	Married no ch 100-33 (% AW)[2]
Australia	39.6	42.4	42.4	58.5	61.3	70.7	42.4	42.4
Austria	56.8	60.5	42.2	56.8	60.5	60.5	60.5	60.5
Belgium	66.3	66.3	68.5	66.3	66.3	66.3	65.5	66.3
Canada	33.8	40.9	38.4	60.7	61.8	38.2	38.2	40.9
Chile	7.0	7.0	10.3	7.0	7.0	7.0	7.0	7.0
Czech Republic	48.6	48.6	48.6	48.6	48.6	48.6	48.6	48.6
Denmark	39.7	42.0	55.8	38.1	42.0	42.0	42.0	42.0
Estonia	41.2	41.2	41.2	41.2	41.2	41.2	41.2	41.2
Finland	54.5	55.5	58.5	54.5	56.2	56.2	56.2	55.5
France	67.2	59.3	59.8	57.5	43.5	43.5	56.4	56.4
Germany	55.6	60.2	44.3	53.6	52.3	55.3	57.7	55.6
Greece	47.1	47.6	54.8	47.1	47.6	47.6	47.6	47.6
Hungary	49.0	49.0	49.0	49.0	49.0	49.0	49.0	49.0
Iceland	42.5	42.5	48.3	51.4	51.4	47.8	47.8	42.5
Ireland	37.7	55.8	55.8	67.9	37.7	37.7	37.7	37.7
Israel[1]	31.0	37.5	46.9	17.9	37.5	37.5	37.5	37.5
Italy	56.0	56.0	63.3	57.1	57.1	57.1	56.6	56.0
Japan	32.8	37.0	35.3	32.8	37.0	37.0	37.0	37.0
Korea	25.4	29.2	31.9	17.0	29.2	29.2	29.2	29.2
Luxembourg	46.2	55.5	55.5	50.4	39.4	44.5	53.0	44.5
Mexico	17.5	25.2	28.4	17.5	25.2	25.2	25.2	25.2
Netherlands	46.7	46.7	52.1	49.0	46.7	46.7	46.7	46.7
New Zealand	17.5	30.0	33.0	38.8	51.3	51.3	30.0	30.0
Norway	42.7	50.6	53.3	42.7	50.6	50.6	50.6	50.6
Poland	37.2	37.2	37.2	37.2	37.2	37.2	37.2	37.2
Portugal	53.9	53.9	60.8	39.8	39.8	39.8	51.1	53.9
Slovak Republic	46.5	46.5	46.5	46.5	46.5	46.5	46.5	46.5
Slovenia	43.6	51.0	60.4	32.9	43.6	43.6	43.6	51.0
Spain	45.6	49.9	38.0	42.0	45.6	49.9	49.9	49.9
Sweden	45.5	48.3	67.3	45.5	48.3	48.3	48.3	48.3
Switzerland	26.3	31.8	35.9	18.9	22.1	26.1	29.4	26.9
Turkey	42.8	42.8	47.8	42.8	42.8	42.8	42.8	42.8
United Kingdom	40.2	40.2	49.0	76.3	40.2	40.2	40.2	40.2
United States	34.3	43.6	43.6	50.4	34.3	34.3	34.3	34.3
Unweighted average								
OECD-Average	**41.7**	**45.1**	**47.2**	**44.5**	**44.1**	**44.1**	**43.7**	**43.6**
OECD-EU 21	**48.8**	**51.0**	**52.8**	**50.4**	**47.1**	**47.7**	**49.3**	**49.3**

Note: ch = children

It is assumed that gross earnings of the principal earner in the household rise. The outcome may differ if the wage of the spouse goes up, especially if partners are taxed individually.

Disclaimer: *http://oe.cd/disclaimer*

1. Information on data for Israel: *http://oe.cd/israel-disclaimer*.
2. Two-earner family.

StatLink http://dx.doi.org/10.1787/888933341329

Figure 3.6. **Marginal rate of income tax plus employee and employer contributions less cash benefits, 2015**

As % of labour costs, by family-type

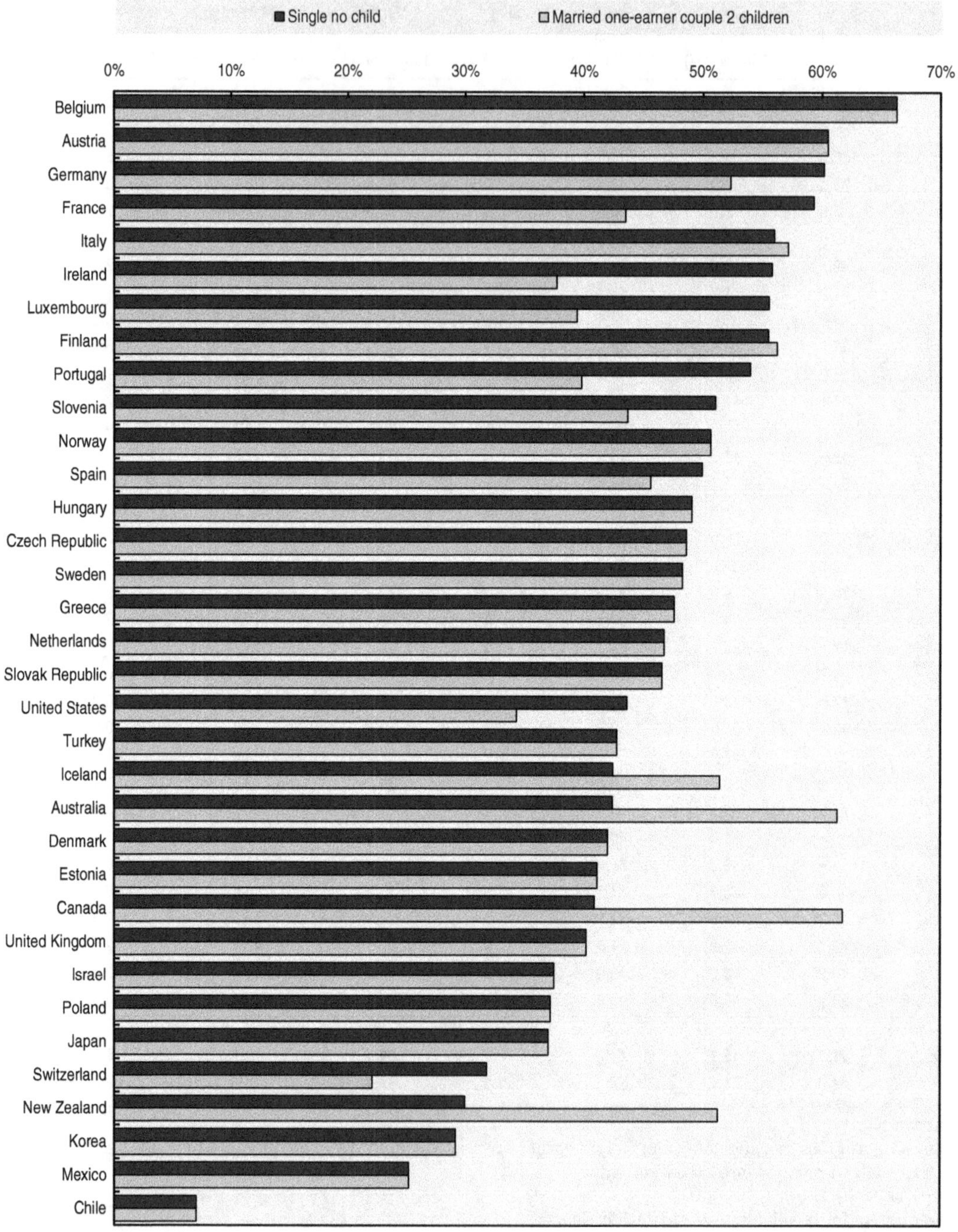

Note: The family type "single no child" corresponds to a wage level of 100% of average wage. The family type "married one earner couple 2 children" corresponds to a combined wage level of 100%-0% of average wage.

Source: OECD calculations based on country submissions and *OECD Economic Outlook, Volume 2015* (No. 98).

StatLink http://dx.doi.org/10.1787/888933340476

Table 3.7. **Marginal rate of income tax plus employee contributions less cash benefits, 2015**

As % of gross wage earnings, by family-type and wage level

	Single no ch 67 (% AW)	Single no ch 100 (% AW)	Single no ch 167 (% AW)	Single 2 ch 67 (% AW)	Married 2 ch 100-0 (% AW)	Married 2 ch 100-33 (% AW)[2]	Married 2 ch 100-67 (% AW)[2]	Married no ch 100-33 (% AW)[2]
Australia	36.0	39.0	39.0	56.0	59.0	69.0	39.0	39.0
Austria	44.4	49.1	37.9	44.4	49.1	49.1	49.1	49.1
Belgium	55.0	55.0	59.8	55.0	55.0	55.0	53.9	55.0
Canada	25.5	35.1	35.4	55.8	58.0	32.1	32.1	35.1
Chile	7.0	7.0	10.3	7.0	7.0	7.0	7.0	7.0
Czech Republic	31.1	31.1	31.1	31.1	31.1	31.1	31.1	31.1
Denmark	39.7	42.0	55.8	38.1	42.0	42.0	42.0	42.0
Estonia	21.3	21.3	21.3	21.3	21.3	21.3	21.3	21.3
Finland	44.0	45.2	48.9	44.0	46.1	46.1	46.1	45.2
France	39.9	43.9	42.6	22.1	22.1	22.1	39.9	39.9
Germany	47.1	52.5	44.3	44.7	43.1	46.7	49.5	47.0
Greece	34.1	34.7	43.7	34.1	34.7	34.7	34.7	34.7
Hungary	34.5	34.5	34.5	34.5	34.5	34.5	34.5	34.5
Iceland	38.2	38.2	44.4	47.8	47.8	43.9	43.9	38.2
Ireland	31.0	51.0	51.0	64.4	31.0	31.0	31.0	31.0
Israel[1]	26.0	33.0	43.0	12.0	33.0	33.0	33.0	33.0
Italy	41.8	41.8	51.5	43.4	43.4	43.4	42.6	41.8
Japan	22.7	27.6	31.2	22.7	27.6	27.6	27.6	27.6
Korea	17.7	21.9	27.9	8.4	21.9	21.9	21.9	21.9
Luxembourg	39.6	50.1	50.1	44.4	32.0	37.7	47.2	37.7
Mexico	12.1	19.5	22.9	12.1	19.5	19.5	19.5	19.5
Netherlands	41.2	41.2	52.1	43.8	41.2	41.2	41.2	41.2
New Zealand	17.5	30.0	33.0	38.8	51.3	51.3	30.0	30.0
Norway	35.2	44.2	47.2	35.2	44.2	44.2	44.2	44.2
Poland	26.7	26.7	26.7	26.7	26.7	26.7	26.7	26.7
Portugal	43.0	43.0	51.5	25.5	25.5	25.5	39.5	43.0
Slovak Republic	29.9	29.9	29.9	29.9	29.9	29.9	29.9	29.9
Slovenia	34.6	43.1	54.0	22.1	34.6	34.6	34.6	43.1
Spain	29.3	34.9	38.0	24.6	29.3	34.9	34.9	34.9
Sweden	28.4	32.0	57.0	28.4	32.0	32.0	32.0	32.0
Switzerland	21.7	27.6	32.2	13.8	17.2	21.5	25.0	22.3
Turkey	32.8	32.8	38.7	32.8	32.8	32.8	32.8	32.8
United Kingdom	32.0	32.0	42.0	73.0	32.0	32.0	32.0	32.0
United States	29.3	39.3	39.3	46.6	29.3	29.3	29.3	29.3
Unweighted average								
OECD-Average	**32.1**	**36.2**	**40.2**	**34.8**	**34.8**	**34.8**	**34.7**	**34.5**
OECD-EU 21	**36.6**	**39.8**	**44.0**	**37.9**	**35.1**	**35.8**	**37.8**	**37.8**

Note: ch = children

It is assumed that gross earnings of the principal earner in the household rise. The outcome may differ if the wage of the spouse goes up, especially if partners are taxed individually.

Disclaimer: *http://oe.cd/disclaimer*

1. Information on data for Israel: *http://oe.cd/israel-disclaimer*.
2. Two-earner family.

StatLink http://dx.doi.org/10.1787/888933341336

Figure 3.7. **Marginal rate of income tax plus employee contributions less cash benefits, 2015**

As % of gross wage earnings, by family-type

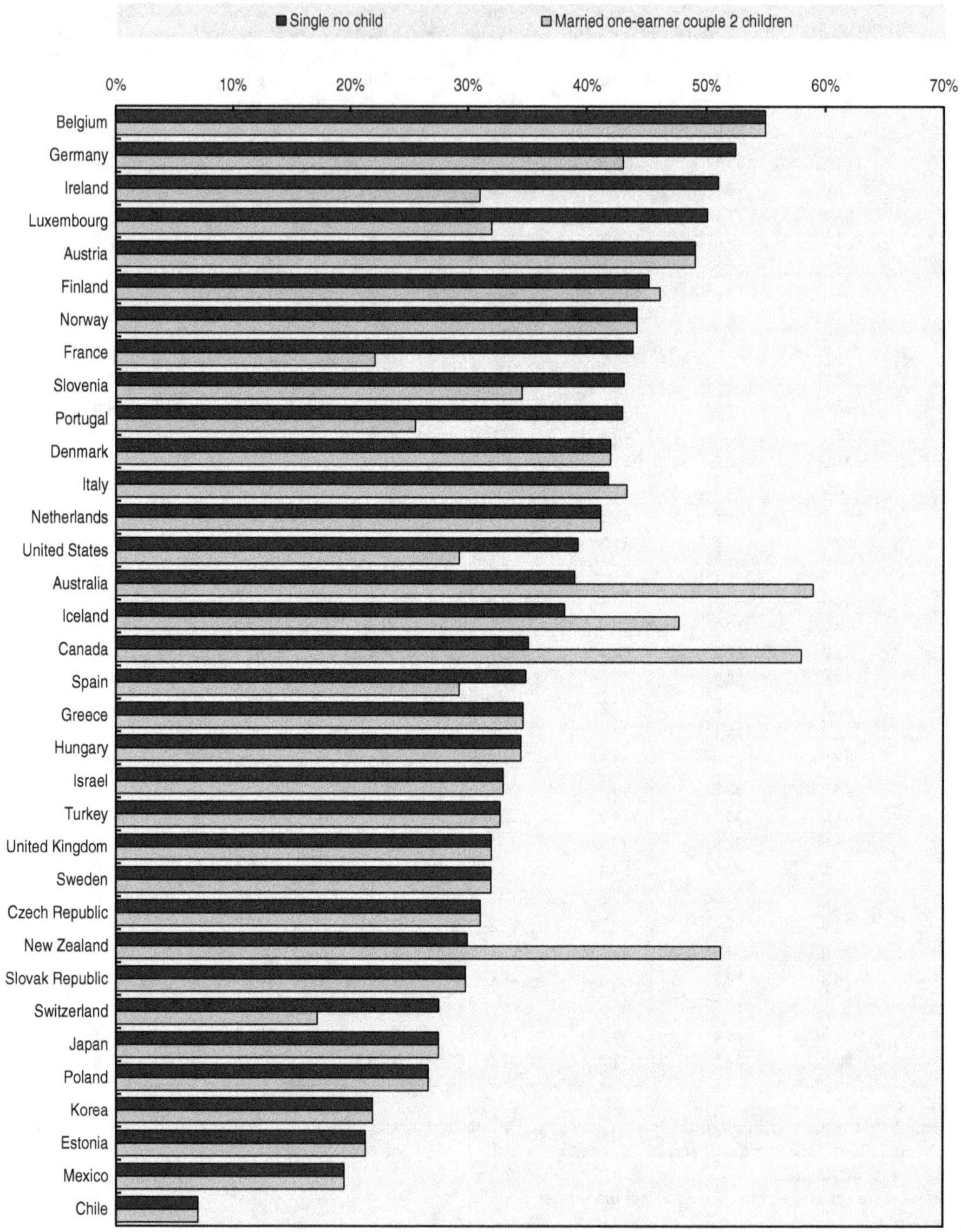

Note: The family type "single no child" corresponds to a wage level of 100% of average wage. The family type "married one earner couple 2 children" corresponds to a combined wage level of 100%-0% of average wage.

Source: OECD calculations based on country submissions and *OECD Economic Outlook, Volume 2015* (No. 98).

StatLink http://dx.doi.org/10.1787/888933340488

Table 3.8. **Increase in net income after an increase of 1 currency unit in gross wages, 2015**

By family-type and wage level (%)

	Single no ch 67 (% AW)	Single no ch 100 (% AW)	Single no ch 167 (% AW)	Single 2 ch 67 (% AW)	Married 2 ch 100-0 (% AW)	Married 2 ch 100-33 (% AW)[2]	Married 2 ch 100-67 (% AW)[2]	Married no ch 100-33 (% AW)[2]
Australia	0.79	0.80	0.87	0.41	0.47	0.38	0.78	0.76
Austria	0.78	0.78	1.03	0.61	0.65	0.64	0.68	0.72
Belgium	0.70	0.78	0.79	0.55	0.58	0.61	0.69	0.68
Canada	0.91	0.85	0.89	0.37	0.46	0.80	0.83	0.81
Chile	1.00	1.00	0.98	0.99	1.00	0.98	1.00	1.00
Czech Republic	0.86	0.90	0.94	0.68	0.70	0.76	0.80	0.86
Denmark	0.91	0.91	0.76	0.66	0.78	0.82	0.84	0.87
Estonia	0.95	0.97	0.98	0.75	0.82	0.86	0.89	0.95
Finland	0.74	0.79	0.83	0.64	0.72	0.69	0.72	0.74
France	0.81	0.79	0.88	0.93	0.95	0.96	0.78	0.82
Germany	0.81	0.79	0.99	0.67	0.72	0.73	0.73	0.81
Greece	0.81	0.86	0.85	0.77	0.85	0.84	0.85	0.85
Hungary	1.00	1.00	1.00	0.70	0.79	0.83	0.86	1.00
Iceland	0.82	0.87	0.84	0.60	0.63	0.73	0.77	0.82
Ireland	0.80	0.61	0.72	0.27	0.69	0.73	0.78	0.79
Israel[1]	0.83	0.81	0.77	0.87	0.78	0.76	0.75	0.78
Italy	0.76	0.86	0.81	0.58	0.71	0.71	0.76	0.78
Japan	0.97	0.93	0.93	0.89	0.86	0.88	0.89	0.92
Korea	0.92	0.91	0.87	1.00	0.88	0.88	0.88	0.89
Luxembourg	0.78	0.72	0.81	0.53	0.72	0.70	0.64	0.79
Mexico	0.91	0.90	0.91	0.91	0.90	0.86	0.87	0.86
Netherlands	0.78	0.84	0.77	0.56	0.77	0.74	0.76	0.79
New Zealand	0.95	0.85	0.87	0.54	0.51	0.55	0.84	0.84
Norway	0.86	0.78	0.81	0.74	0.73	0.72	0.74	0.75
Poland	0.94	0.96	0.98	0.83	0.88	0.90	0.92	0.94
Portugal	0.72	0.80	0.75	0.81	0.87	0.87	0.76	0.72
Slovak Republic	0.87	0.91	0.95	0.74	0.75	0.80	0.83	0.87
Slovenia	0.92	0.85	0.74	0.75	0.74	0.81	0.86	0.82
Spain	0.85	0.83	0.86	0.76	0.82	0.78	0.79	0.79
Sweden	0.92	0.90	0.67	0.82	0.83	0.83	0.85	0.88
Switzerland	0.92	0.88	0.87	0.85	0.86	0.85	0.84	0.91
Turkey	0.90	0.93	0.90	0.88	0.91	0.89	0.91	0.90
United Kingdom	0.84	0.89	0.83	0.26	0.83	0.80	0.84	0.84
United States	0.92	0.82	0.88	0.56	0.82	0.86	0.88	0.92
Unweighted average								
OECD-Average	**0.86**	**0.85**	**0.86**	**0.69**	**0.76**	**0.78**	**0.81**	**0.84**
OECD-EU 21	**0.84**	**0.85**	**0.85**	**0.66**	**0.77**	**0.78**	**0.79**	**0.83**

Note: ch = children

Net income is calculated as gross earnings minus personal income tax and employees' social security contributions plus family benefits. The increase reported in the Table represents a form of elasticity. In a proportional tax system the elasticity would equal 1. The more progressive the system at these income levels, the lower is the elasticity.

Disclaimer: *http://oe.cd/disclaimer*

1. Information on data for Israel: *http://oe.cd/israel-disclaimer*.
2. Two-earner family. Assumes a rise in the labour costs associated with the principal earner in the household.

StatLink http://dx.doi.org/10.1787/888933341344

Table 3.9. **Increase in net income after an increase of 1 currency unit in gross labour cost, 2015**

By family-type and wage level (%)

	Single no ch 67 (% AW)	Single no ch 100 (% AW)	Single no ch 167 (% AW)	Single 2 ch 67 (% AW)	Married 2 ch 100-0 (% AW)	Married 2 ch 100-33 (% AW)[2]	Married 2 ch 100-67 (% AW)[2]	Married no ch 100-33 (% AW)[2]
Australia	0.79	0.80	0.87	0.41	0.47	0.38	0.78	0.76
Austria	0.78	0.78	1.21	0.61	0.65	0.64	0.68	0.72
Belgium	0.67	0.75	0.80	0.53	0.57	0.58	0.67	0.64
Canada	0.90	0.86	0.92	0.37	0.47	0.81	0.85	0.83
Chile	1.00	1.00	0.98	0.99	1.00	0.98	1.00	1.00
Czech Republic	0.86	0.90	0.94	0.68	0.70	0.76	0.80	0.86
Denmark	0.92	0.91	0.77	0.67	0.78	0.83	0.85	0.89
Estonia	0.95	0.97	0.98	0.75	0.82	0.86	0.89	0.95
Finland	0.74	0.79	0.83	0.64	0.72	0.69	0.72	0.74
France	0.58	0.79	0.88	0.66	0.95	0.91	0.77	0.78
Germany	0.81	0.79	1.14	0.67	0.72	0.73	0.73	0.81
Greece	0.81	0.86	0.85	0.77	0.85	0.84	0.85	0.85
Hungary	1.00	1.00	1.00	0.70	0.79	0.83	0.86	1.00
Iceland	0.82	0.87	0.84	0.60	0.63	0.73	0.77	0.82
Ireland	0.80	0.61	0.72	0.27	0.69	0.72	0.78	0.78
Israel[1]	0.81	0.80	0.77	0.84	0.77	0.74	0.74	0.76
Italy	0.76	0.86	0.81	0.58	0.71	0.71	0.76	0.78
Japan	0.97	0.93	1.00	0.89	0.86	0.88	0.89	0.92
Korea	0.92	0.91	0.90	1.00	0.88	0.88	0.88	0.89
Luxembourg	0.78	0.72	0.81	0.53	0.72	0.70	0.64	0.79
Mexico	0.97	0.93	0.93	0.97	0.93	0.91	0.91	0.91
Netherlands	0.77	0.84	0.82	0.56	0.77	0.74	0.76	0.79
New Zealand	0.95	0.85	0.87	0.54	0.51	0.55	0.84	0.84
Norway	0.86	0.78	0.81	0.74	0.73	0.72	0.74	0.75
Poland	0.94	0.96	0.98	0.83	0.88	0.90	0.92	0.94
Portugal	0.72	0.80	0.75	0.81	0.87	0.87	0.76	0.72
Slovak Republic	0.87	0.91	0.95	0.74	0.75	0.78	0.83	0.86
Slovenia	0.92	0.85	0.74	0.75	0.74	0.81	0.86	0.82
Spain	0.85	0.83	1.11	0.76	0.82	0.78	0.79	0.79
Sweden	0.92	0.90	0.67	0.82	0.83	0.83	0.85	0.88
Switzerland	0.92	0.88	0.88	0.85	0.86	0.85	0.84	0.91
Turkey	0.90	0.93	0.90	0.88	0.91	0.89	0.91	0.90
United Kingdom	0.81	0.86	0.81	0.25	0.81	0.77	0.81	0.81
United States	0.93	0.83	0.89	0.56	0.83	0.87	0.90	0.93
Unweighted average								
OECD-Average	**0.85**	**0.85**	**0.89**	**0.68**	**0.76**	**0.78**	**0.81**	**0.84**
OECD-EU 21	**0.82**	**0.84**	**0.88**	**0.65**	**0.77**	**0.78**	**0.79**	**0.82**

Note: ch = children

Net income is calculated as gross earnings minus personal income tax and employees' social security contributions plus family benefits. The increase reported in the Table represents a form of elasticity. In a proportional tax system the elasticity would equal 1. The more progressive the system at these income levels, the lower is the elasticity.

Disclaimer: *http://oe.cd/disclaimer*

1. Information on data for Israel: *http://oe.cd/israel-disclaimer*.
2. Two-earner family. Assumes a rise in the labour costs associated with the principal earner in the household.

StatLink http://dx.doi.org/10.1787/888933341351

Table 3.10a. **Annual gross wage and net income, single person, 2015**

In US dollars using PPP, by family-type and wage level

	Single no ch 67 (% AW)		Single no ch 100 (% AW)		Single no ch 167 (% AW)		Single 2 ch 67 (% AW)	
	Total gross earnings before taxes	Net income after taxes	Total gross earnings before taxes	Net income after taxes	Total gross earnings before taxes	Net income after taxes	Total gross earnings before taxes	Net income after taxes
Australia	37 467	30 523	55 921	42 456	93 388	65 311	37 467	40 249
Austria	35 888	25 472	53 565	34 869	89 453	54 182	35 888	32 691
Belgium	38 302	24 730	57 166	33 132	95 468	48 569	38 302	31 418
Canada	27 952	22 979	41 719	31 968	69 671	50 775	27 952	33 157
Chile	12 956	12 049	19 338	17 984	32 294	29 730	12 956	12 163
Czech Republic	16 403	13 214	24 482	18 781	40 884	30 082	16 403	16 591
Denmark	36 188	24 097	54 013	34 619	90 201	52 220	36 188	33 864
Estonia	16 086	13 350	24 010	19 587	40 096	32 250	16 086	16 897
Finland	31 827	24 154	47 503	32 805	79 331	49 090	31 827	28 064
France	30 889	22 892	46 103	32 762	76 992	50 490	30 889	25 968
Germany	40 191	26 248	59 987	36 194	100 177	56 271	40 191	33 169
Greece	22 958	18 677	34 266	25 927	57 224	37 944	22 958	19 757
Hungary	16 286	10 668	24 308	15 922	40 594	26 589	16 286	15 229
Iceland	34 291	25 849	51 181	36 295	85 473	56 658	34 291	29 668
Ireland	27 506	23 875	41 054	32 976	68 560	46 454	27 506	36 140
Israel[1]	22 941	20 472	34 241	28 313	57 182	42 132	22 941	23 317
Italy	27 638	21 180	41 250	27 808	68 888	41 343	27 638	26 818
Japan	31 628	25 172	47 205	36 810	78 833	58 517	31 628	27 435
Korea	31 682	28 448	47 286	40 748	78 968	65 417	31 682	29 026
Luxembourg	40 744	31 526	60 812	42 134	101 556	62 459	40 744	42 511
Mexico	8 620	8 342	12 865	11 539	21 485	18 267	8 620	8 342
Netherlands	40 781	30 840	60 867	42 650	101 648	63 399	40 781	40 752
New Zealand	26 460	22 886	39 493	32 558	65 953	50 580	26 460	30 282
Norway	40 336	30 244	60 203	43 104	100 540	65 493	40 336	35 490
Poland	17 177	13 357	25 637	19 561	42 814	32 157	17 177	15 237
Portugal	19 894	15 705	29 692	21 290	49 585	31 935	19 894	18 405
Slovak Republic	14 582	11 710	21 764	16 748	36 347	26 977	14 582	13 921
Slovenia	20 542	14 639	30 660	20 439	51 202	31 814	20 542	21 437
Spain	26 485	22 030	39 529	31 037	66 014	47 737	26 485	26 117
Sweden	31 274	24 364	46 678	35 147	77 953	50 238	31 274	27 355
Switzerland	46 824	40 076	69 887	57 756	116 711	90 744	46 824	47 423
Turkey	17 371	13 040	25 926	18 793	43 297	29 539	17 371	13 303
United Kingdom	34 458	27 840	51 431	39 381	85 889	60 276	34 458	35 598
United States	34 146	26 330	50 964	37 899	85 110	58 625	34 146	32 821
Unweighted average								
OECD-Average	**28 199**	**21 970**	**42 088**	**30 882**	**70 288**	**47 478**	**28 199**	**27 077**
OECD-EU 21	**27 910**	**20 979**	**41 656**	**29 227**	**69 566**	**44 404**	**27 910**	**26 569**

Note: ch = children

Disclaimer: *http://oe.cd/disclaimer*

1. Information on data for Israel: *http://oe.cd/israel-disclaimer*.

StatLink http://dx.doi.org/10.1787/888933341364

Table 3.10b. **Annual gross wage and net income, married couple, 2015**

In US dollars using PPP, by family-type and wage level

	Married 2 ch 100-0 (% AW)		Married 2 ch 100-33 (% AW)[2]		Married 2 ch 100-67 (% AW)[2]		Married no ch 100-33 (% AW)[2]	
	Total gross earnings before taxes	Net income after taxes	Total gross earnings before taxes	Net income after taxes	Total gross earnings before taxes	Net income after taxes	Total gross earnings before taxes	Net income after taxes
Australia	55 921	48 699	74 375	60 905	93 388	72 980	74 375	59 737
Austria	53 565	42 125	71 241	56 586	89 453	66 797	71 241	50 155
Belgium	57 166	44 177	76 031	56 114	95 468	63 839	76 031	50 090
Canada	41 719	37 951	55 487	47 382	69 671	57 067	55 487	44 407
Chile	19 338	17 984	25 719	24 507	32 294	30 148	25 719	23 919
Czech Republic	24 482	24 070	32 560	29 347	40 884	35 371	32 560	25 971
Denmark	54 013	40 325	71 837	51 085	90 201	62 122	71 837	47 680
Estonia	24 010	22 966	31 933	29 203	40 096	35 629	31 933	26 511
Finland	47 503	35 511	63 179	49 397	79 331	59 665	63 179	46 690
France	46 103	37 826	61 317	49 684	76 992	59 225	61 317	45 008
Germany	59 987	47 265	79 782	58 350	100 177	68 939	79 782	52 178
Greece	37 692	29 077	50 131	39 047	62 946	48 578	50 131	38 507
Hungary	24 308	20 207	32 330	25 461	40 594	30 874	32 330	21 176
Iceland	51 181	42 717	68 071	52 225	85 473	62 213	68 071	51 154
Ireland	41 054	41 163	54 601	51 766	68 560	60 914	54 601	47 948
Israel[1]	34 241	29 262	45 540	40 166	57 182	50 857	45 540	39 217
Italy	41 250	32 763	54 863	43 866	68 888	52 134	54 863	40 714
Japan	47 205	39 750	62 783	51 819	78 833	64 245	62 783	49 556
Korea	47 286	41 951	62 891	55 970	78 968	70 169	62 891	55 044
Luxembourg	60 812	57 416	80 880	72 344	101 556	84 333	80 880	64 110
Mexico	12 865	11 539	17 111	16 097	21 485	19 881	17 111	16 097
Netherlands	60 867	46 404	80 953	64 262	101 648	78 392	80 953	60 129
New Zealand	39 493	37 551	52 526	46 223	65 953	55 078	52 526	44 000
Norway	60 203	46 345	80 071	62 307	100 540	75 887	80 071	59 768
Poland	25 637	21 440	34 097	27 780	42 814	34 171	34 097	26 527
Portugal	29 692	25 464	39 490	33 677	49 585	39 514	39 490	31 241
Slovak Republic	21 764	20 440	28 947	25 466	36 347	30 669	28 947	23 256
Slovenia	30 660	27 176	40 778	32 773	51 202	38 878	40 778	28 321
Spain	39 529	34 004	52 574	44 002	66 014	54 564	52 574	43 253
Sweden	46 678	38 138	62 082	51 146	77 953	62 502	62 082	48 155
Switzerland	69 887	66 987	92 949	86 064	116 711	104 134	92 949	79 040
Turkey	25 926	19 231	34 482	26 047	43 297	32 096	34 482	25 785
United Kingdom	51 431	41 950	68 403	57 899	85 889	69 790	68 403	55 331
United States	50 964	43 973	67 782	55 863	85 110	68 114	67 782	52 299
Unweighted average								
OECD-Average	**42 189**	**35 701**	**56 112**	**46 319**	**70 456**	**55 876**	**56 112**	**43 323**
OECD-EU 21	**41 819**	**34 758**	**55 619**	**45 203**	**69 838**	**54 138**	**55 619**	**41 569**

Note: ch = children

Disclaimer: *http://oe.cd/disclaimer*

1. Information on data for Israel: *http://oe.cd/israel-disclaimer*.
2. Two-earner family.

StatLink http://dx.doi.org/10.1787/888933341371

Table 3.11a. **Annual labour costs and net income, single person, 2015**

In US dollars using PPP, by family-type and wage level

	Single no ch 67 (% AW)		Single no ch 100 (% AW)		Single no ch 167 (% AW)		Single 2 ch 67 (% AW)	
	Total gross labour costs before taxes	Net income after taxes	Total gross labour costs before taxes	Net income after taxes	Total gross labour costs before taxes	Net income after taxes	Total gross labour costs before taxes	Net income after taxes
Australia	39 703	30 523	59 258	42 456	98 962	65 311	39 703	40 249
Austria	46 270	25 472	69 060	34 869	113 346	54 182	46 270	32 691
Belgium	48 925	24 730	74 137	33 132	123 537	48 569	48 925	31 418
Canada	31 302	22 979	46 759	31 968	76 194	50 775	31 302	33 157
Chile	12 956	12 049	19 338	17 984	32 294	29 730	12 956	12 163
Czech Republic	21 980	13 214	32 805	18 781	54 785	30 082	21 980	16 591
Denmark	36 649	24 097	54 473	34 619	90 662	52 220	36 649	33 864
Estonia	21 524	13 350	32 125	19 587	53 649	32 250	21 524	16 897
Finland	39 167	24 154	58 458	32 805	97 624	49 090	39 167	28 064
France	40 496	22 892	63 562	32 762	110 493	50 490	40 496	25 968
Germany	47 958	26 248	71 579	36 194	115 572	56 271	47 958	33 169
Greece	28 597	18 677	42 681	25 927	71 278	37 944	28 597	19 757
Hungary	20 928	10 668	31 236	15 922	52 164	26 589	20 928	15 229
Iceland	36 860	25 849	55 015	36 295	91 874	56 658	36 860	29 668
Ireland	30 463	23 875	45 467	32 976	75 930	46 454	30 463	36 140
Israel[1]	23 976	20 472	36 094	28 313	60 699	42 132	23 976	23 317
Italy	36 504	21 180	54 484	27 808	90 988	41 343	36 504	26 818
Japan	36 386	25 172	54 308	36 810	89 931	58 517	36 386	27 435
Korea	34 956	28 448	52 173	40 748	86 125	65 417	34 956	29 026
Luxembourg	45 739	31 526	68 267	42 134	114 007	62 459	45 739	42 511
Mexico	9 814	8 342	14 375	11 539	23 649	18 267	9 814	8 342
Netherlands	44 674	30 840	66 838	42 650	108 342	63 399	44 674	40 752
New Zealand	26 460	22 886	39 493	32 558	65 953	50 580	26 460	30 282
Norway	45 580	30 244	68 030	43 104	113 610	65 493	45 580	35 490
Poland	20 059	13 357	29 939	19 561	49 998	32 157	20 059	15 237
Portugal	24 618	15 705	36 744	21 290	61 362	31 935	24 618	18 405
Slovak Republic	19 132	11 710	28 555	16 748	47 687	26 977	19 132	13 921
Slovenia	23 850	14 639	35 596	20 439	59 446	31 814	23 850	21 437
Spain	34 403	22 030	51 348	31 037	85 490	47 737	34 403	26 117
Sweden	41 101	24 364	61 345	35 147	102 445	50 238	41 101	27 355
Switzerland	49 751	40 076	74 255	57 756	123 890	90 744	49 751	47 423
Turkey	20 410	13 040	30 463	18 793	50 874	29 539	20 410	13 303
United Kingdom	37 615	27 840	56 929	39 381	96 143	60 276	37 615	35 598
United States	37 353	26 330	55 457	37 899	92 215	58 625	37 353	32 821
Unweighted average								
OECD-Average	**32 828**	**21 970**	**49 137**	**30 882**	**81 800**	**47 478**	**32 828**	**27 077**
OECD-EU 21	**33 840**	**20 979**	**50 744**	**29 227**	**84 521**	**44 404**	**33 840**	**26 569**

Note: ch = children

Disclaimer: *http://oe.cd/disclaimer*

1. Information on data for Israel: *http://oe.cd/israel-disclaimer.*

StatLink http://dx.doi.org/10.1787/888933341380

Table 3.11b. **Annual labour costs and net income, married couple, 2015**

In US dollars using PPP, by family-type and wage level

	Married 2 ch 100-0 (% AW)		Married 2 ch 100-33 (% AW)[2]		Married 2 ch 100-67 (% AW)[2]		Married no ch 100-33 (% AW)[2]	
	Total gross labour costs before taxes	Net income after taxes	Total gross labour costs before taxes	Net income after taxes	Total gross labour costs before taxes	Net income after taxes	Total gross labour costs before taxes	Net income after taxes
Australia	59 258	48 699	78 814	60 905	98 962	72 980	78 814	59 737
Austria	69 060	42 125	91 850	56 586	115 330	66 797	91 850	50 155
Belgium	74 137	44 177	95 730	56 114	123 062	63 839	95 730	50 090
Canada	46 759	37 951	62 104	47 382	78 061	57 067	62 104	44 407
Chile	19 338	17 984	25 719	24 507	32 294	30 148	25 719	23 919
Czech Republic	32 805	24 070	43 631	29 347	54 785	35 371	43 631	25 971
Denmark	54 473	40 325	72 758	51 085	91 123	62 122	72 758	47 680
Estonia	32 125	22 966	42 726	29 203	53 649	35 629	42 726	26 511
Finland	58 458	35 511	77 749	49 397	97 624	59 665	77 749	46 690
France	63 562	37 826	79 951	49 684	104 058	59 225	79 951	45 008
Germany	71 579	47 265	95 200	58 350	119 537	68 939	95 200	52 178
Greece	46 950	29 077	62 443	39 047	78 406	48 578	62 443	38 507
Hungary	31 236	20 207	41 543	25 461	52 164	30 874	41 543	21 176
Iceland	55 015	42 717	73 169	52 225	91 874	62 213	73 169	51 154
Ireland	45 467	41 163	60 166	51 766	75 930	60 914	60 166	47 948
Israel[1]	36 094	29 262	47 783	40 166	60 070	50 857	47 783	39 217
Italy	54 484	32 763	72 463	43 866	90 988	52 134	72 463	40 714
Japan	54 308	39 750	72 229	51 819	90 694	64 245	72 229	49 556
Korea	52 173	41 951	69 390	55 970	87 129	70 169	69 390	55 044
Luxembourg	68 267	57 416	90 796	72 344	114 007	84 333	90 796	64 110
Mexico	14 375	11 539	19 530	16 097	24 189	19 881	19 530	16 097
Netherlands	66 838	46 404	88 723	64 262	111 512	78 392	88 723	60 129
New Zealand	39 493	37 551	52 526	46 223	65 953	55 078	52 526	44 000
Norway	68 030	46 345	90 480	62 307	113 610	75 887	90 480	59 768
Poland	29 939	21 440	39 819	27 780	49 998	34 171	39 819	26 527
Portugal	36 744	25 464	48 869	33 677	61 362	39 514	48 869	31 241
Slovak Republic	28 555	20 440	37 260	25 466	47 687	30 669	37 260	23 256
Slovenia	35 596	27 176	47 343	32 773	59 446	38 878	47 343	28 321
Spain	51 348	34 004	68 293	44 002	85 752	54 564	68 293	43 253
Sweden	61 345	38 138	81 588	51 146	102 445	62 502	81 588	48 155
Switzerland	74 255	66 987	98 759	86 064	124 005	104 134	98 759	79 040
Turkey	30 463	19 231	40 516	26 047	50 874	32 096	40 516	25 785
United Kingdom	56 929	41 950	74 645	57 899	94 545	69 790	74 645	55 331
United States	55 457	43 973	74 157	55 863	92 810	68 114	74 157	52 299
Unweighted average								
OECD-Average	**49 262**	**35 701**	**65 257**	**46 319**	**82 174**	**55 876**	**65 257**	**43 323**
OECD-EU 21	**50 948**	**34 758**	**67 312**	**45 203**	**84 924**	**54 138**	**67 312**	**41 569**

Note: ch = children

Disclaimer: *http://oe.cd/disclaimer*

1. Information on data for Israel: *http://oe.cd/israel-disclaimer*.
2. Two-earner family.

StatLink http://dx.doi.org/10.1787/888933341393

PART I

Chapter 4

Graphical exposition of the 2015 tax burden

The chapter presents a graphical exposition of the tax burdens on labour income in 2015 for gross wage earnings ranging from 50% to 250% of the average wage. These are illustrated in separate graphs for each of four family types and each OECD member country. The family types are single taxpayers without children; single parents with two children; one-earner married couples without children and one-earner married couples with two children.

The graphs are divided in two sets showing the average and the marginal tax wedge components as percentage of total labour costs (central and local income taxes; employee and employer social security contributions and family benefits). The graphs also show the net personal average and marginal tax rates.

The graphs in this section show the tax burden on labour income in 2015 for gross wage earnings between 50% and 250% of the average wage (AW). For each OECD member country, there are separate graphs for four family types: single taxpayers without children, single parents with two children, one-earner married couples without children and one-earner married couples with two children. The net personal average and marginal tax rates ([the change in] personal income taxes and employee social security contributions net of cash benefits as a percentage of [the change in] gross wage earnings) are included in the graphs that show respectively the average and the marginal tax wedge.*

The graphs illustrate the relative importance of the different components of the tax wedges; central government income taxes, local government income taxes, employee social security contributions, employer social security contributions (including payroll taxes where applicable) and family benefits as a percentage of total labour costs. It should be noted that a decreasing share in total labour costs implies that the values of tax payments less benefits are not increasing as rapidly as the corresponding total labour costs. It does not necessarily imply that the values of payments less benefits are decreasing in cash terms.

Low-income households are treated favourably by the tax-benefit system in many OECD countries. Negative central government income taxes are observed in the Czech Republic, Germany, Poland, the Slovak Republic and the United Kingdom because of non-wastable child tax credits; in Canada because of the non-wastable working income tax benefit; in Israel because of the non-wastable earned income tax credit for families with children; in Italy because of the Fiscal Bonus targeting low income workers; in Luxembourg and Spain because of non-wastable tax credits for single parents; in Mexico because of the non-wastable employment subsidy credit; in Sweden because of the non-wastable earned income tax credit and in the United States because of the non-wastable earned income credit and the child tax credit.

When cash benefits are also taken into account, single parents and/or one-earner married couples with 2 children do not pay income taxes and employee social security contributions up to income levels between 50% and 85% of the AW in 17 OECD member countries. The net personal average tax rate for single parents with two children becomes positive at 87% of the AW in Canada, 91% of the AW in New Zealand and 97% of the AW in Ireland. The corresponding measure for one-earner married couples with 2 children becomes positive at 87% of the AW in Canada, 91% of the AW in New Zealand, 95% of the AW in the Czech Republic and at 102% of the AW level in Ireland.

* The marginal tax wedges in the graphs are calculated in a slightly different manner than the marginal tax rates that are included in the rest of the Taxing Wages publication. In Taxing Wages, marginal rates are usually calculated by increasing gross earnings by one currency unit (except for the spouse in the one-earner married couple whose earnings increase by 33% of the average wage). However, the "+1 currency unit" approach requires the calculation of marginal rates for every single currency unit within the income range included in the graphs. It otherwise would not be correct to draw a line through the different data points because the data for the income levels in between the different points would be missing. In order to reduce the required number of calculations, the marginal rates that are shown in the graphs are calculated by increasing gross earnings by 1 percentage point – each line in the graph therefore consists of 200 data points – instead of 1 currency unit.

There are large variations in cash benefits levels across OECD countries. They represent about a quarter or more of total labour costs for low-income single parents and/ or one-earner married couples with two children in Australia, Canada, Denmark, Ireland, New Zealand and Slovenia.

The marginal tax wedge is relatively flat across the earnings distribution in some countries because of the flat social security contribution and personal income tax rates. Single taxpayers without children face a flat marginal tax wedge over the 50% - 250% of AW income range in Hungary (49.0%), the Czech Republic (48.6%) and Estonia (41.2%). The tax wedge is also relatively constant in Chile, Iceland, Turkey and the United Kingdom. In Chile, it is 7.0% on earnings below 118% of the AW and then 10.2% on higher earnings up to 250% of the AW. In Iceland, the marginal tax wedge is 42.5% on earnings from 52% to 139% of the AW and then 48.3% on earnings above 140% of the AW up to 250% of the AW. In Turkey, it is 42.8% on earnings below 106% of the AW and 47.8% on earnings between 107% and 250% of the AW. In the United Kingdom, it is 40.2% on earnings below 117% of the AW and then 49.0% on earnings between 118% and 250% of the AW.

Social security contributions are levied at flat rates in many OECD countries. Some countries have an earnings ceiling above which no additional social security contributions have to be paid. Within the income range of 50% to 250% of the AW, the marginal employer social security rates fall to zero as a result of income ceilings in Germany, Luxembourg, the Netherlands and Spain and to a large extent in the United States (the rate drops from 7.65% to 1.45% on earnings above USD 118 500). The marginal employee social security rates fall to zero in Austria, Canada, Germany, the Netherlands, Spain and Sweden. They also fall to a large extent in Luxembourg (employee social security contributions drop to 1.9% on earnings above EUR 115 377.84); the United Kingdom (employee national insurance contributions drop to 2% of earnings above GBP 42 385); and the United States (the rate drops from 7.65% to 1.45% on earnings above USD 118 500).

Taxpayers in some OECD countries experience declining marginal social security contribution rates as percentage of total labour costs over some parts of the earnings range as income increases. This can be observed for single taxpayers without children in Austria, Belgium, Canada, France, Germany, Japan, Korea, the Netherlands, Poland, the Slovak Republic and Switzerland.

Taxpayers face marginal tax rates and wedges of about 80% or more in several of OECD countries at particular earnings levels. This is the case for low-income taxpayers without children in Austria, Belgium, France, Greece, Ireland, Italy, Mexico, Portugal and Slovenia. They also apply to families with children in Australia, Austria, Belgium, Canada, Chile, the Czech Republic, France, Greece, Ireland, Italy, Japan, Luxembourg, Mexico, Poland, Portugal, the Slovak Republic, Slovenia and Spain. In many countries, these high marginal tax rates are partly the result, as income rises, in reductions in benefits, allowances or tax credits that are targeted at low-income taxpayers.

The zigzag movement in the marginal tax burdens observed in some of the graphs arises when the changes in taxes, social security contributions, and/or cash benefits for small rises in income vary over the income range in a non-continuous way. This is the case because of rounding rules in Germany, Luxembourg, Sweden and Switzerland; the discrete characteristics of the income tax credit in Greece; and of the PAYE (Pay As You Earn) tax credit, the spouse tax credit and the child transfers in Italy; and in the United States because of the truncation of gross earnings in the calculation of the child tax credit.

Australia 2015: Average tax wedge decomposition

By level of gross earnings expressed as a % of the average wage

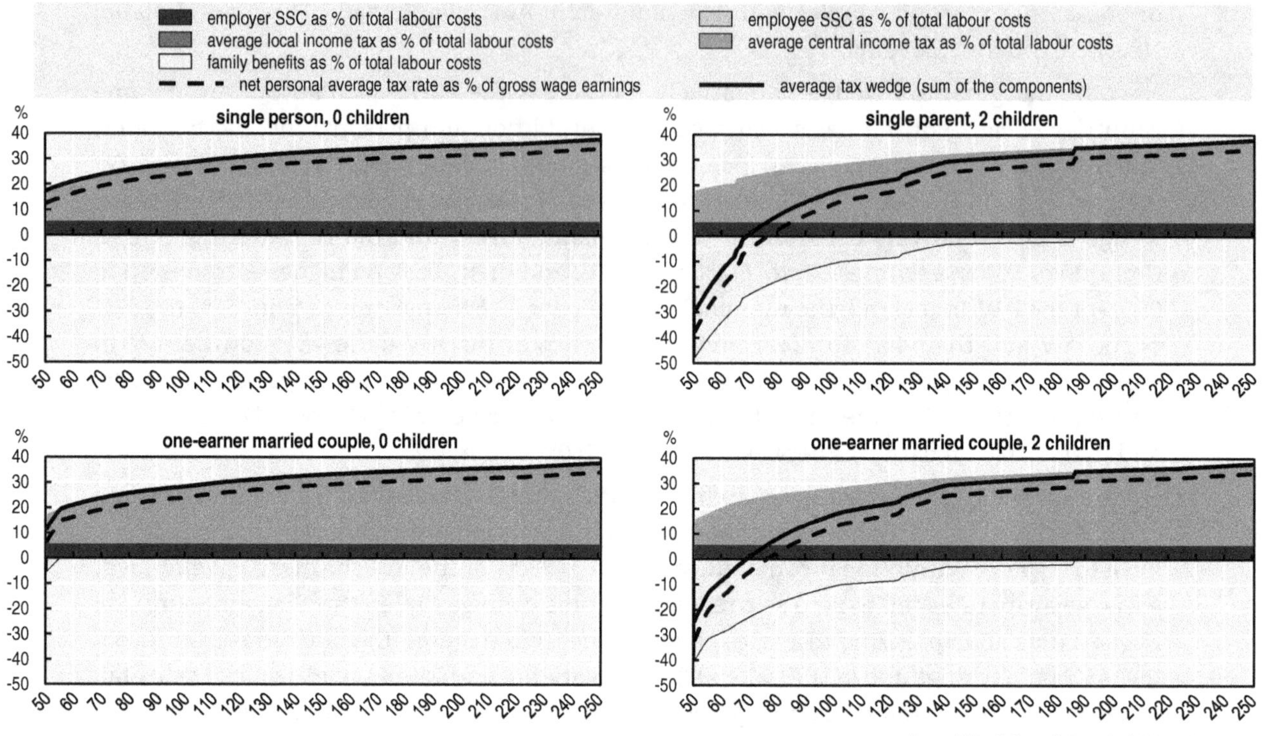

StatLink http://dx.doi.org/10.1787/888933340497

Australia 2015: Marginal tax wedge decomposition

By level of gross earnings expressed as a % of the average wage

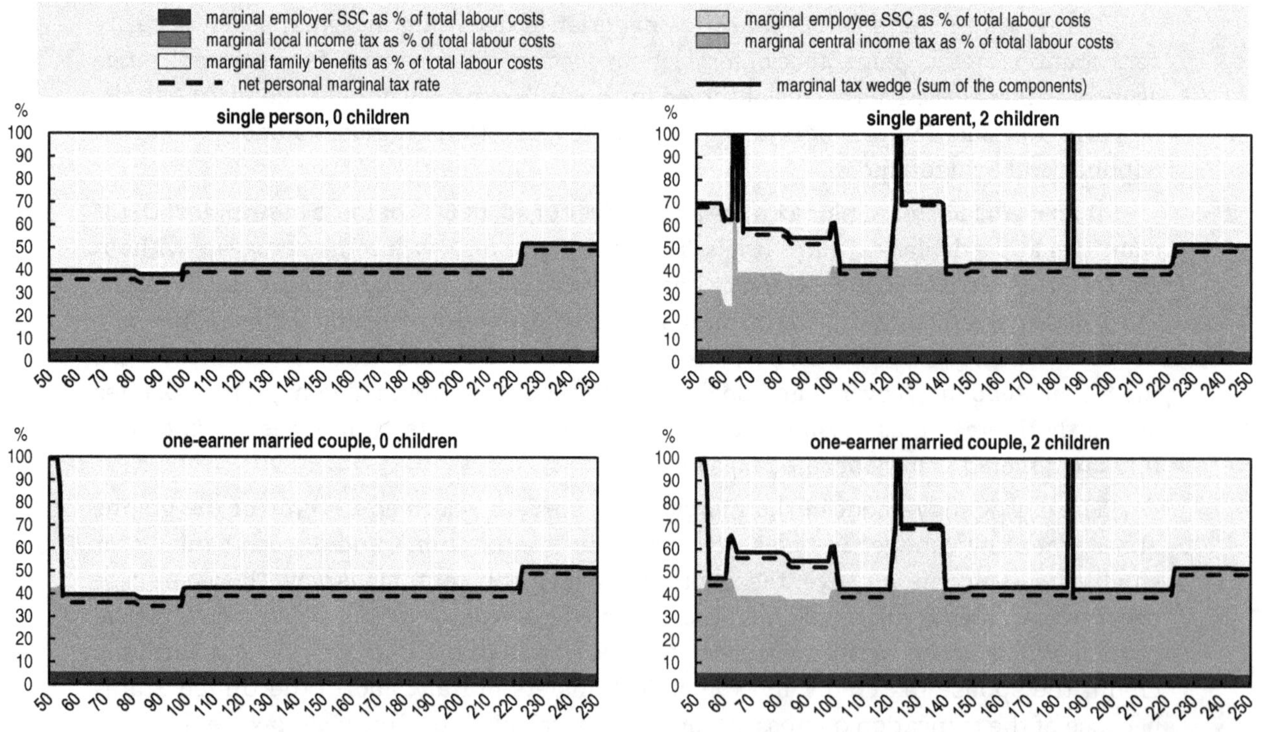

StatLink http://dx.doi.org/10.1787/888933340500

Austria 2015: Average tax wedge decomposition

By level of gross earnings expressed as a % of the average wage

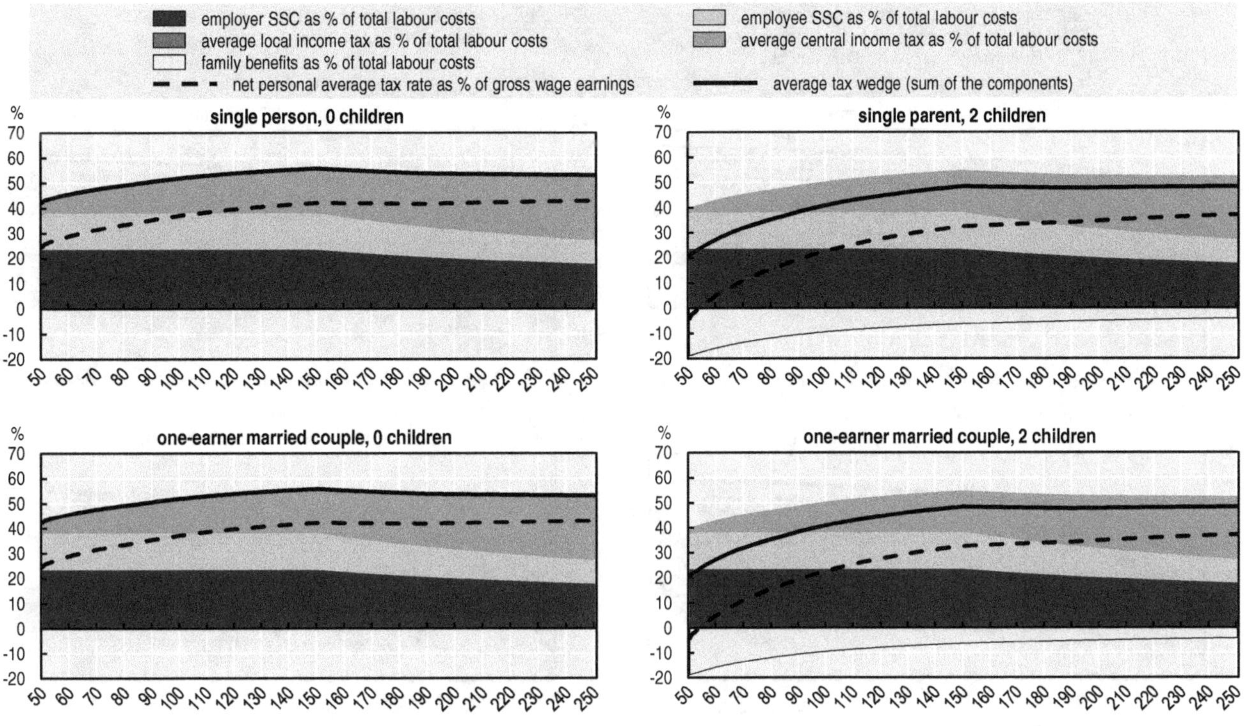

StatLink http://dx.doi.org/10.1787/888933340514

Austria 2015: Marginal tax wedge decomposition

By level of gross earnings expressed as a % of the average wage

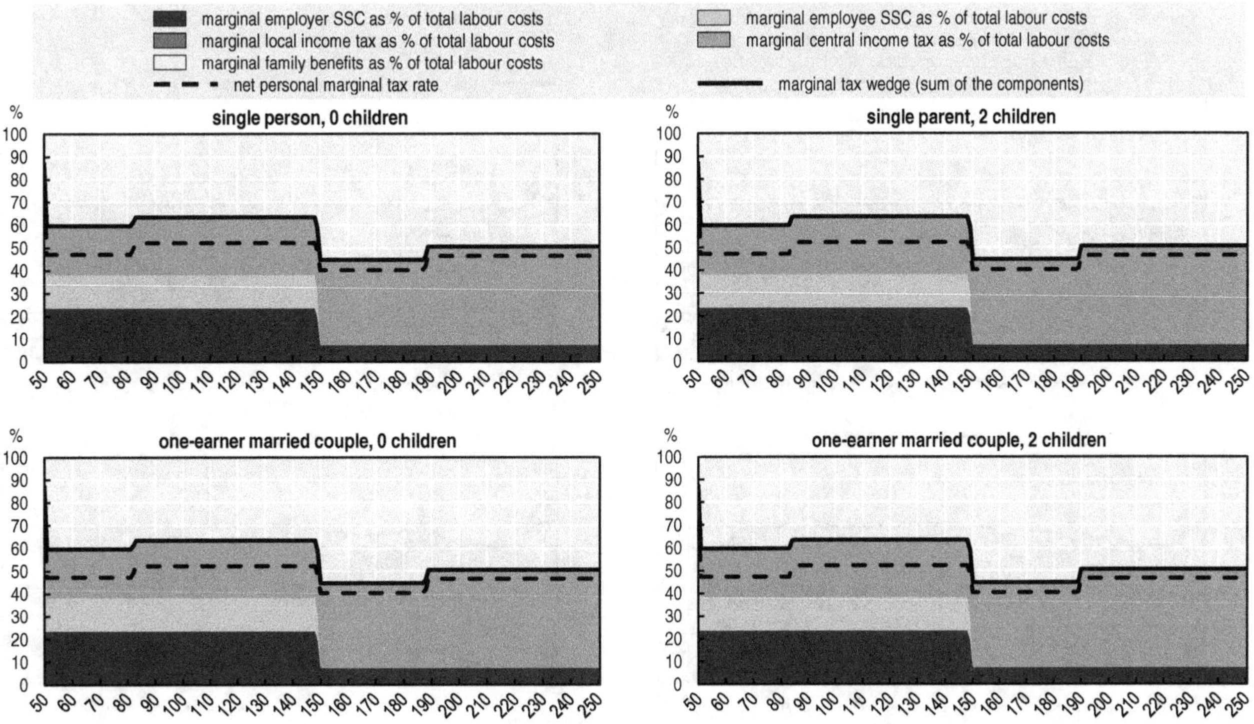

StatLink http://dx.doi.org/10.1787/888933340529

Belgium 2015: Average tax wedge decomposition

By level of gross earnings expressed as a % of the average wage

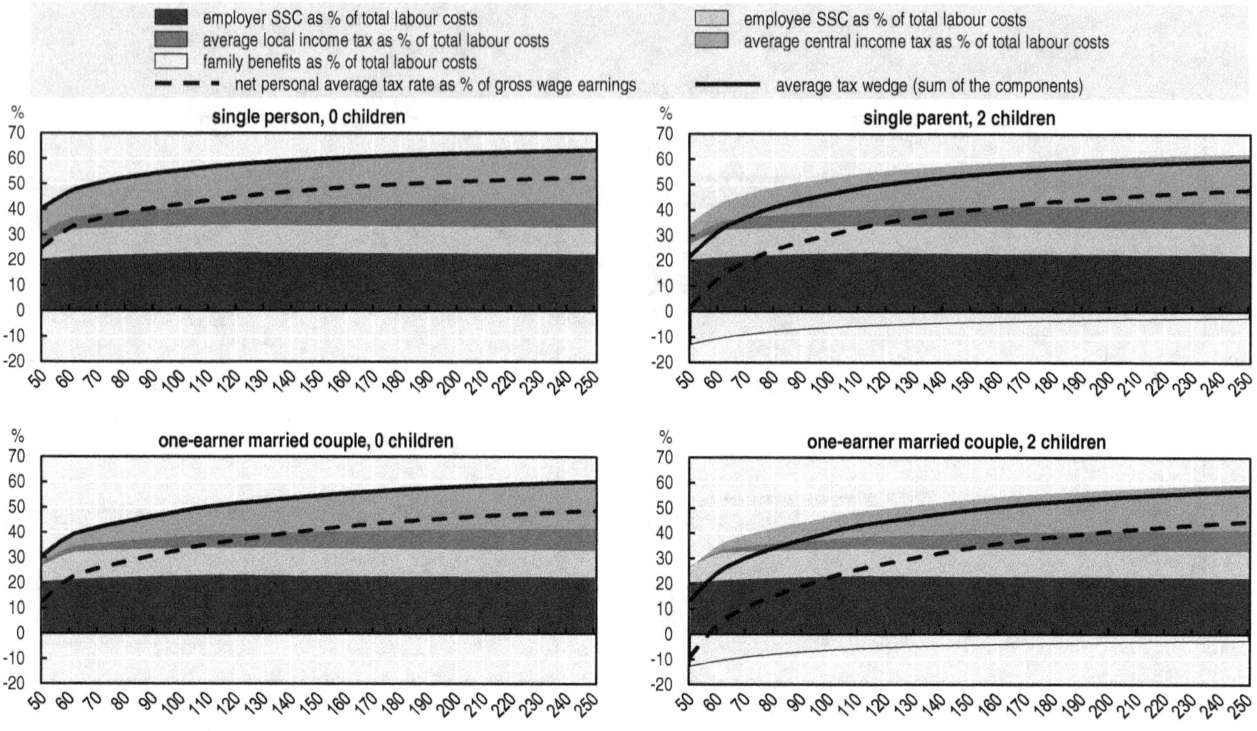

StatLink http://dx.doi.org/10.1787/888933340537

Belgium 2015: Marginal tax wedge decomposition

By level of gross earnings expressed as a % of the average wage

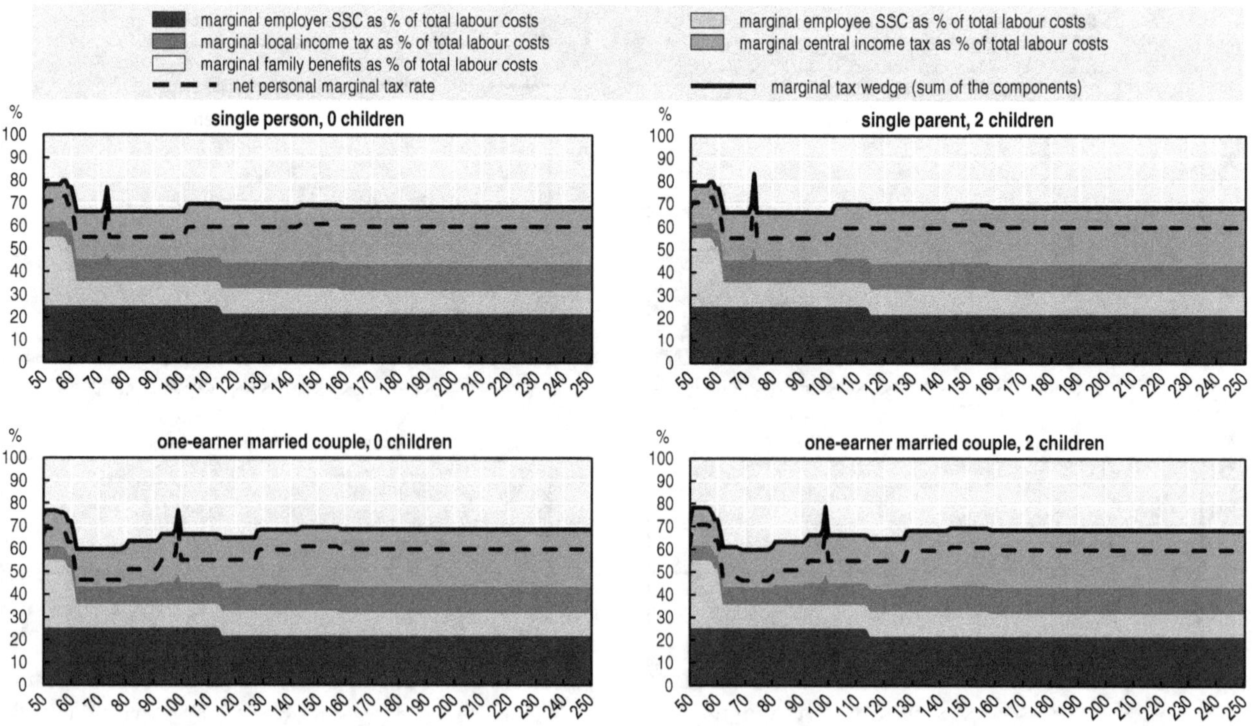

StatLink http://dx.doi.org/10.1787/888933340543

Canada 2015: Average tax wedge decomposition

By level of gross earnings expressed as a % of the average wage

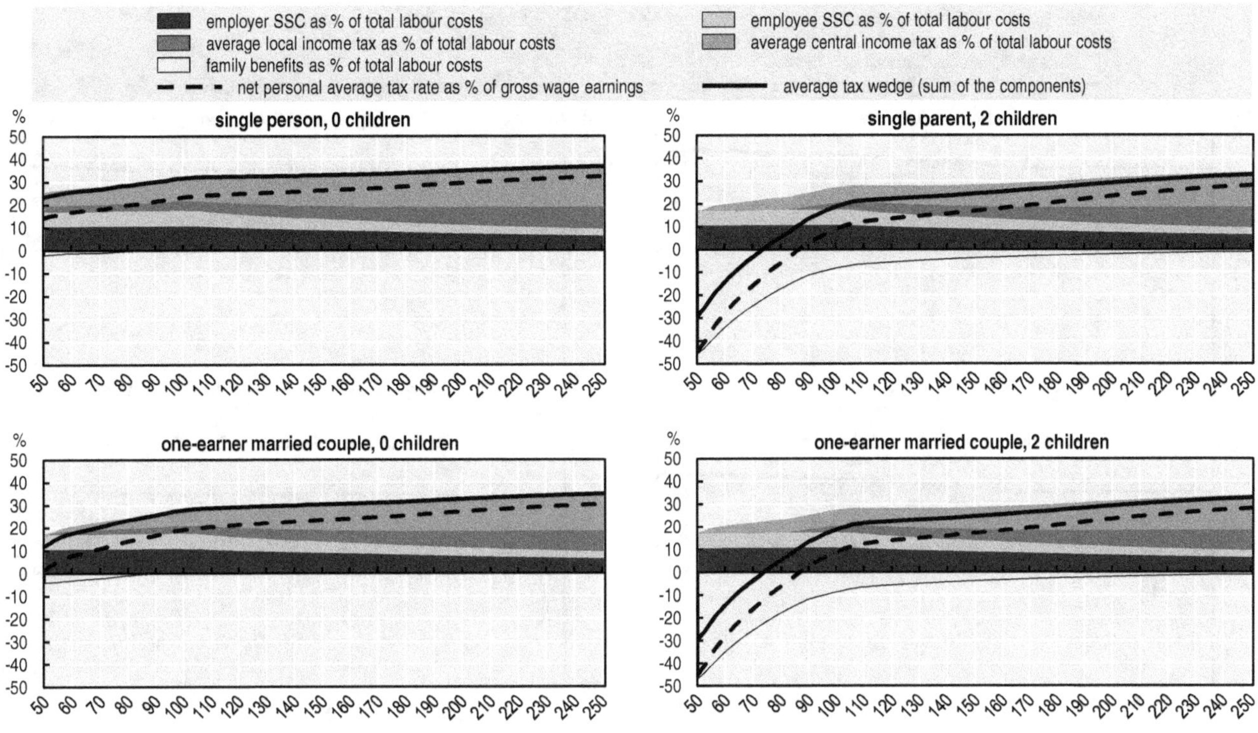

StatLink http://dx.doi.org/10.1787/888933340558

Canada 2015: Marginal tax wedge decomposition

By level of gross earnings expressed as a % of the average wage

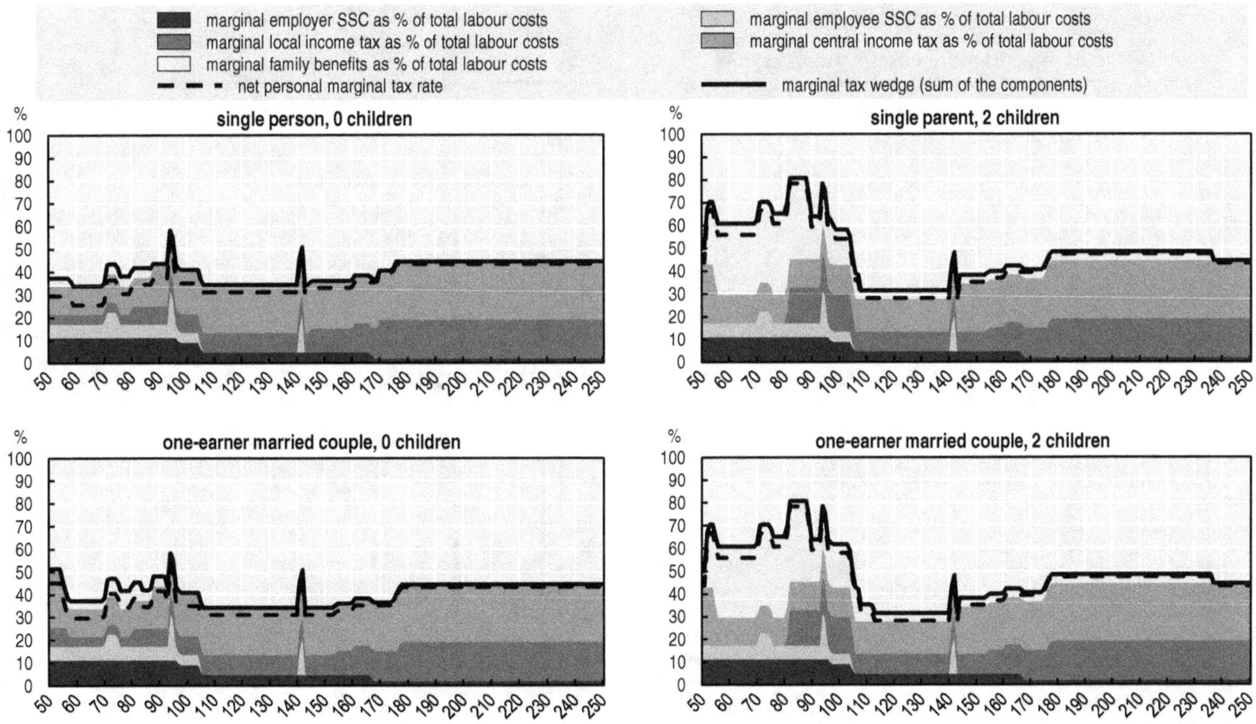

StatLink http://dx.doi.org/10.1787/888933340565

Chile 2015: Average tax wedge decomposition

By level of gross earnings expressed as a % of the average wage

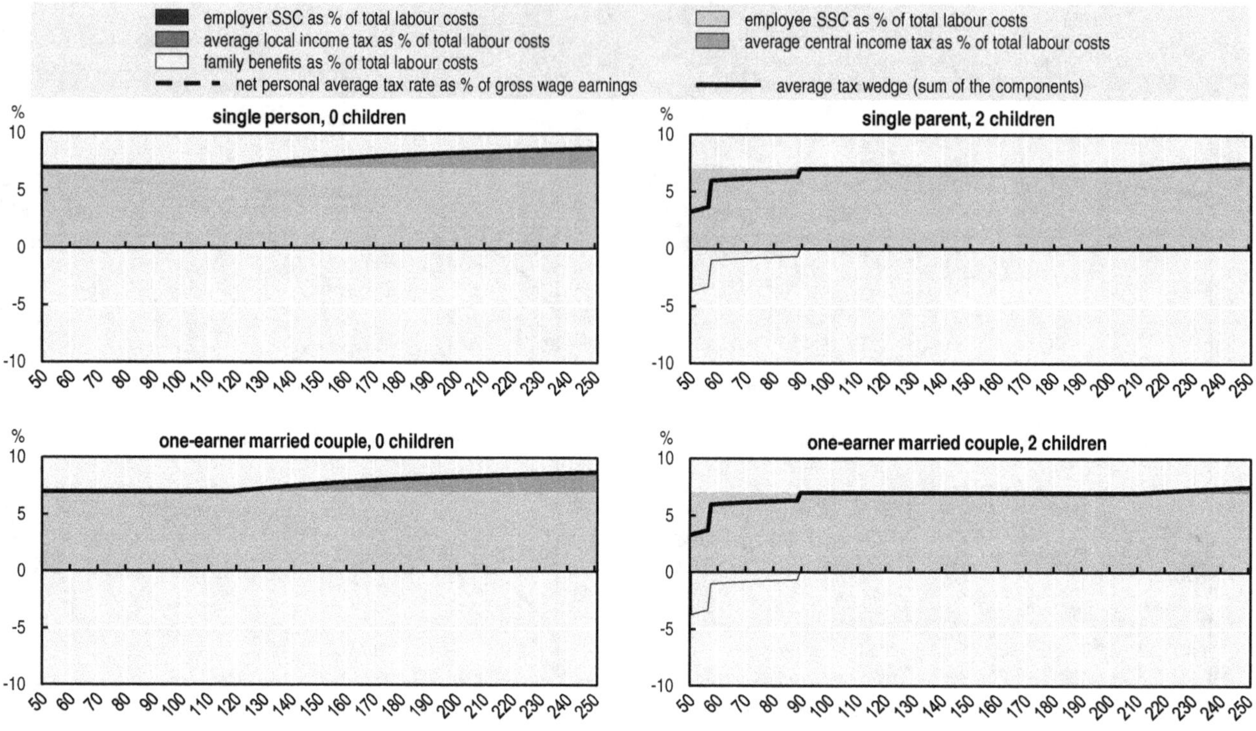

StatLink http://dx.doi.org/10.1787/888933340576

Chile 2015: Marginal tax wedge decomposition

By level of gross earnings expressed as a % of the average wage

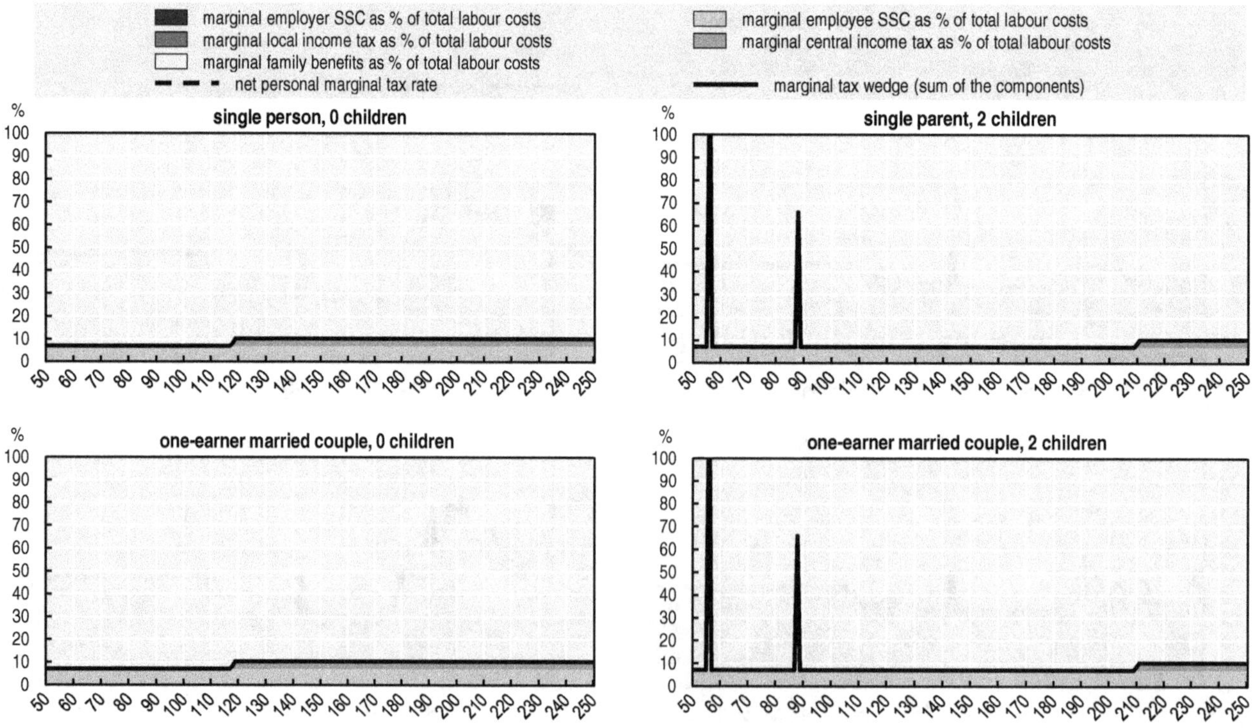

StatLink http://dx.doi.org/10.1787/888933340581

Czech Republic 2015: Average tax wedge decomposition

By level of gross earnings expressed as a % of the average wage

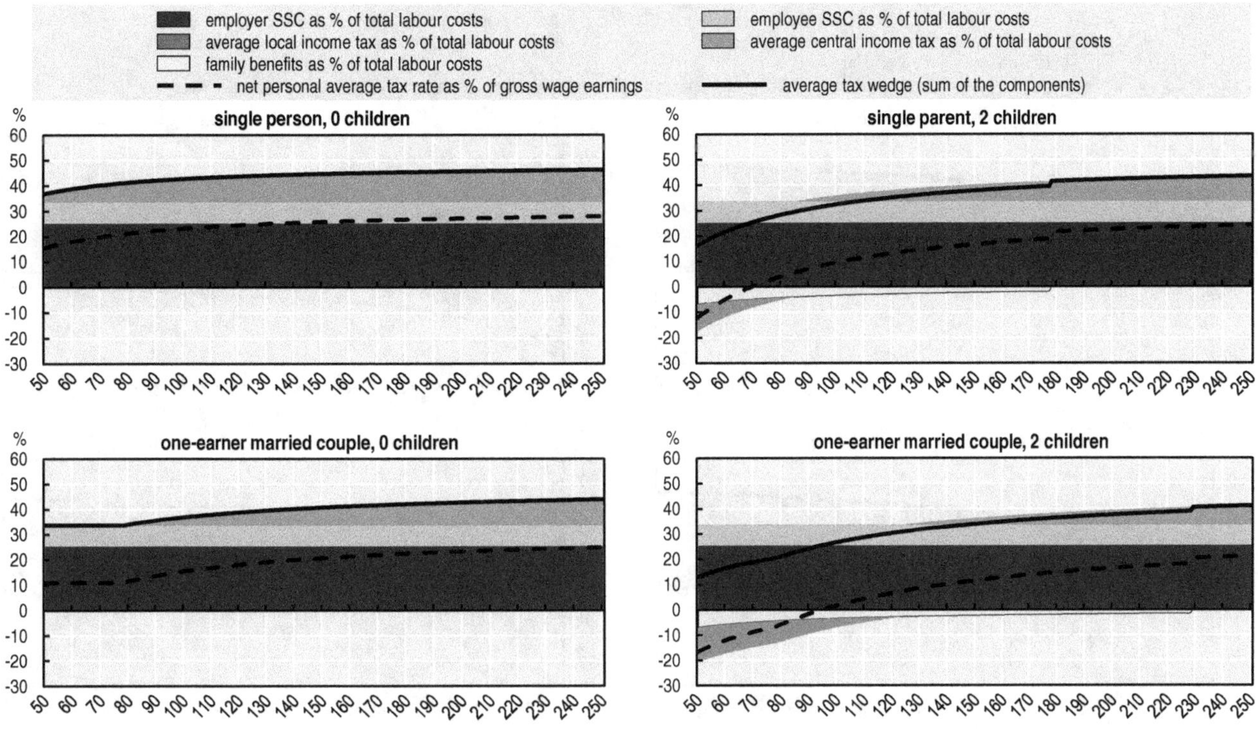

StatLink http://dx.doi.org/10.1787/888933340593

Czech Republic 2015: Marginal tax wedge decomposition

By level of gross earnings expressed as a % of the average wage

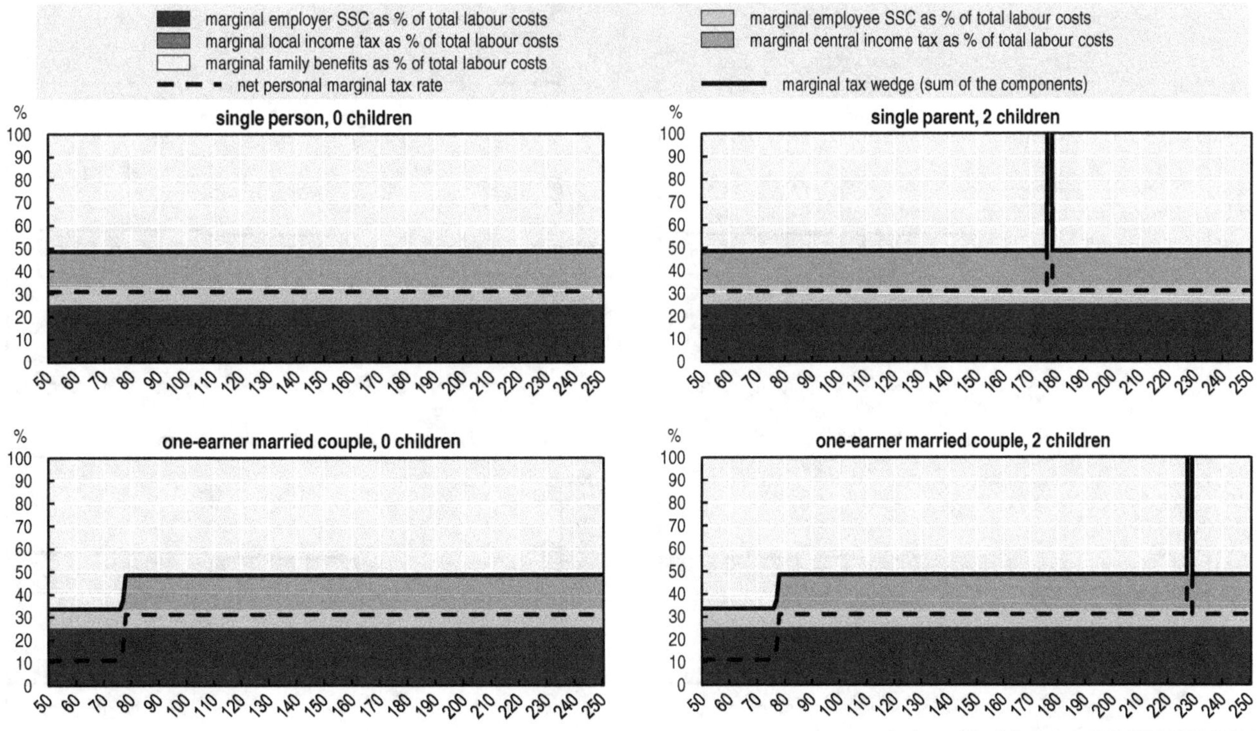

StatLink http://dx.doi.org/10.1787/888933340608

Denmark 2015: Average tax wedge decomposition

By level of gross earnings expressed as a % of the average wage

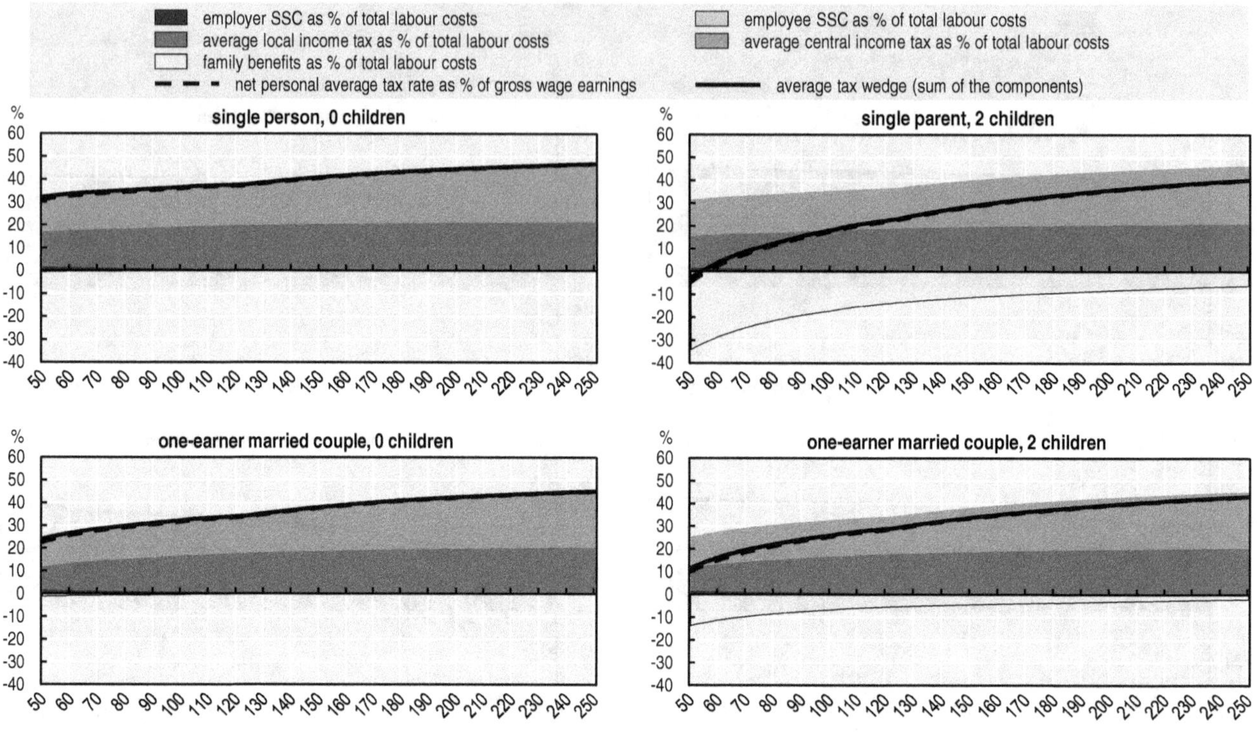

StatLink http://dx.doi.org/10.1787/888933340616

Denmark 2015: Marginal tax wedge decomposition

By level of gross earnings expressed as a % of the average wage

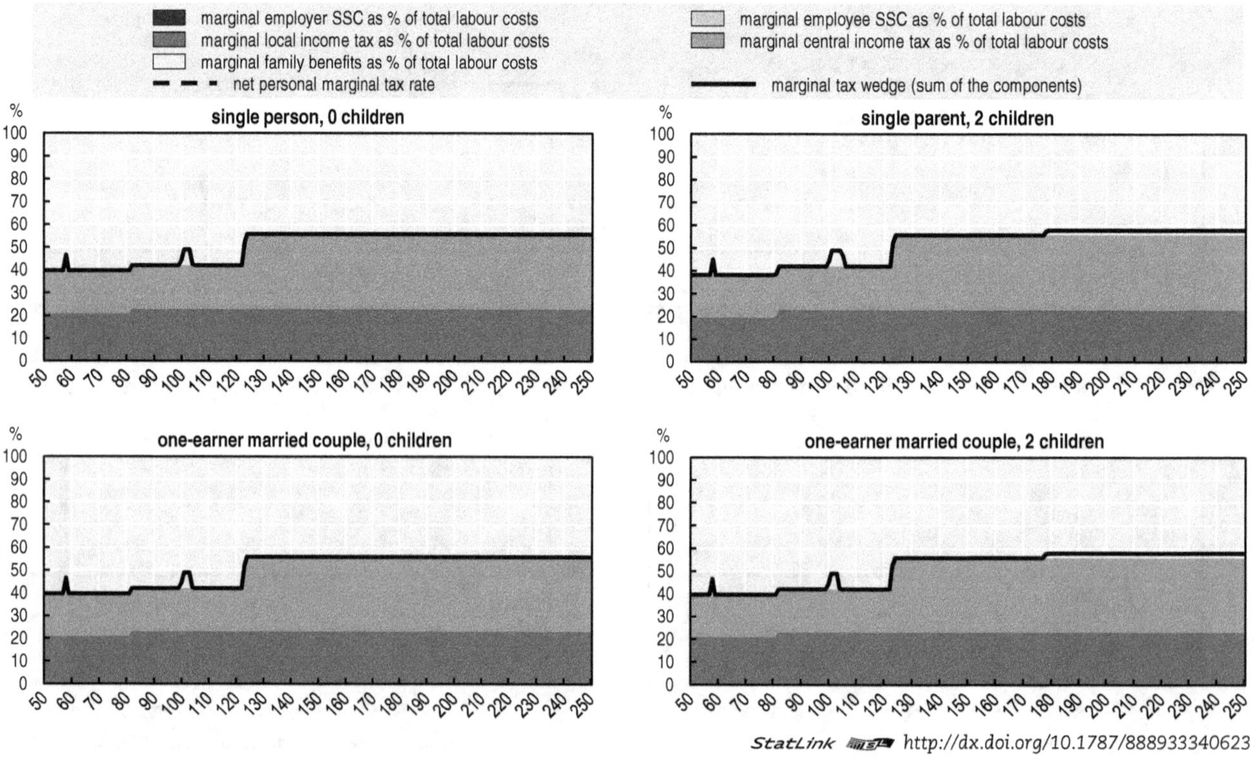

StatLink http://dx.doi.org/10.1787/888933340623

Estonia 2015: Average tax wedge decomposition

By level of gross earnings expressed as a % of the average wage

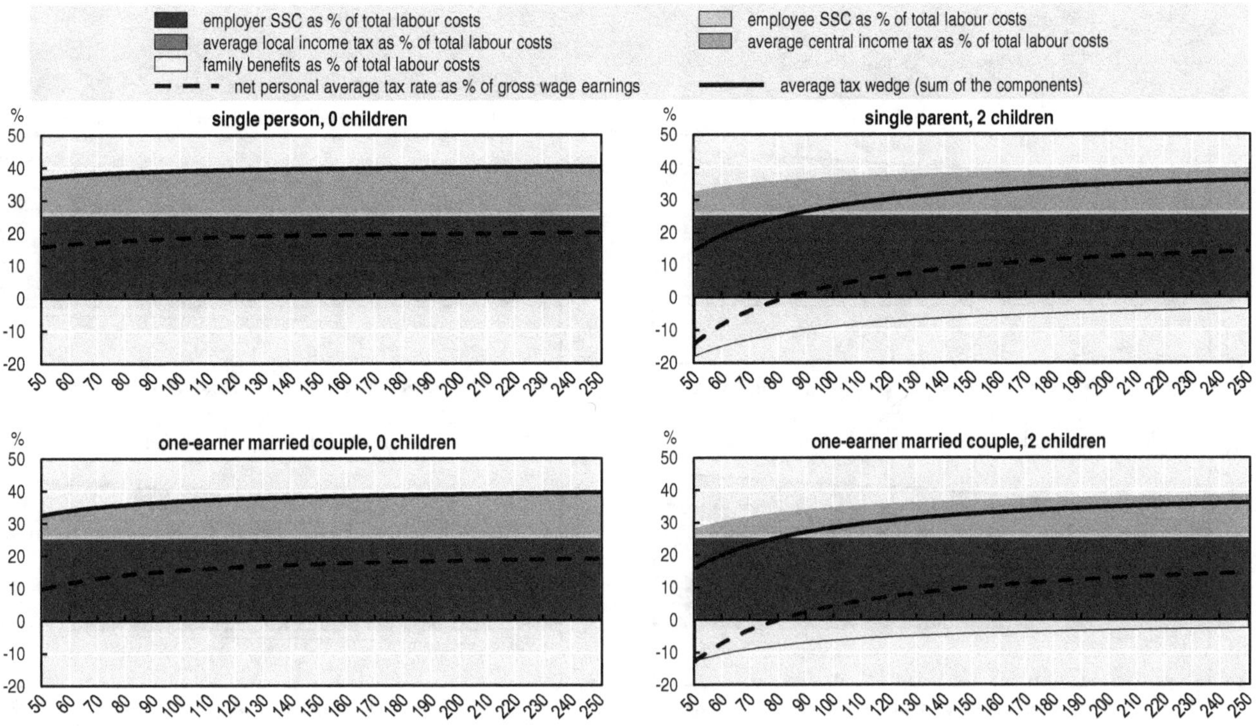

StatLink http://dx.doi.org/10.1787/888933340636

Estonia 2015: Marginal tax wedge decomposition

By level of gross earnings expressed as a % of the average wage

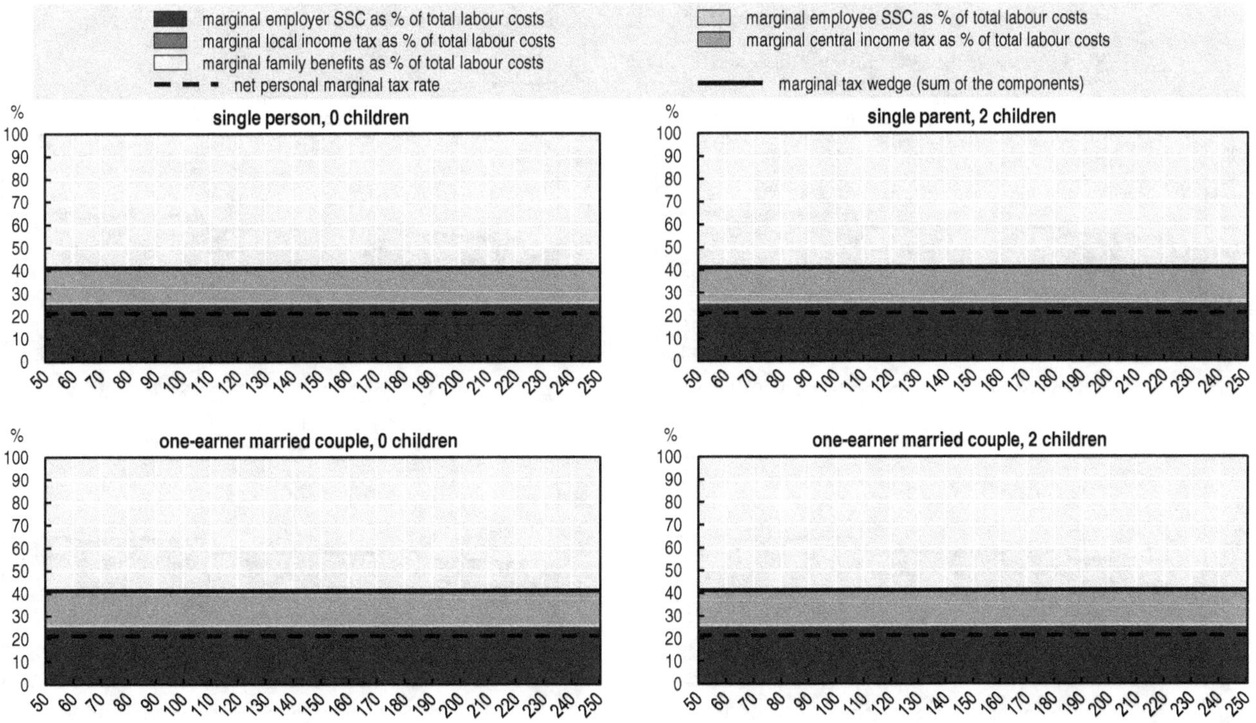

StatLink http://dx.doi.org/10.1787/888933340644

Finland 2015: Average tax wedge decomposition

By level of gross earnings expressed as a % of the average wage

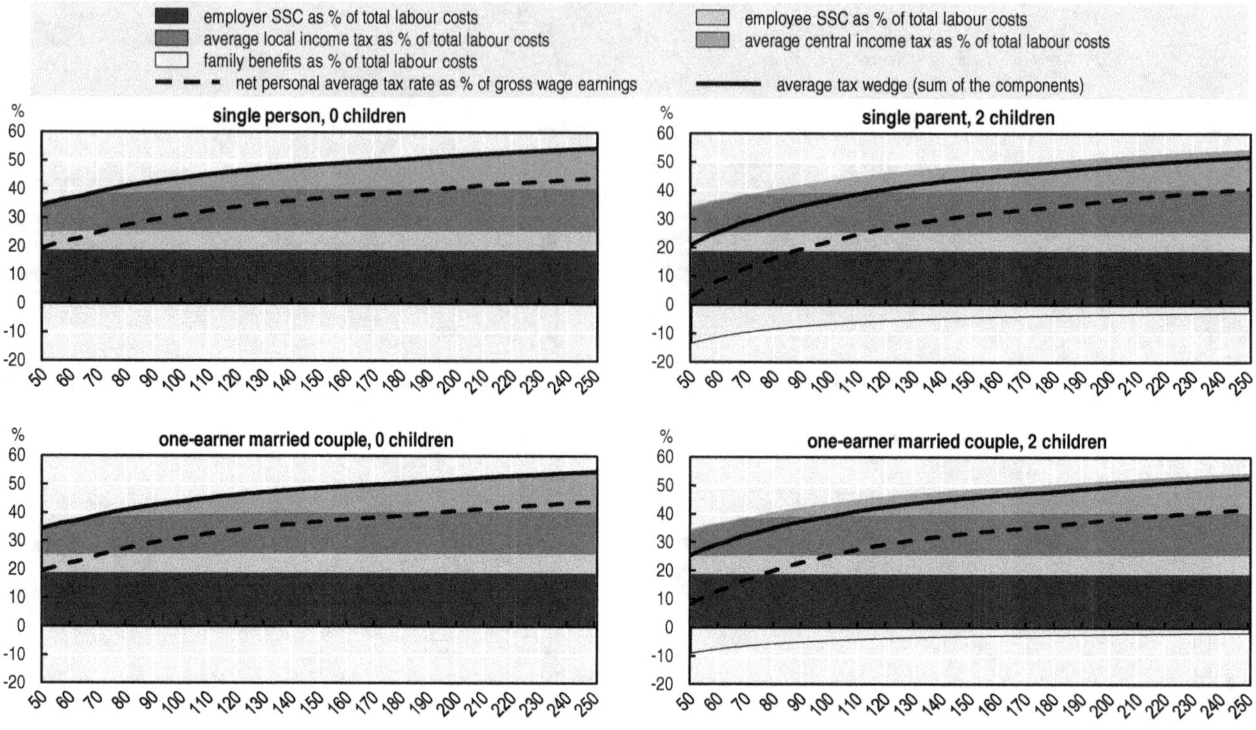

StatLink http://dx.doi.org/10.1787/888933340655

Finland 2015: Marginal tax wedge decomposition

By level of gross earnings expressed as a % of the average wage

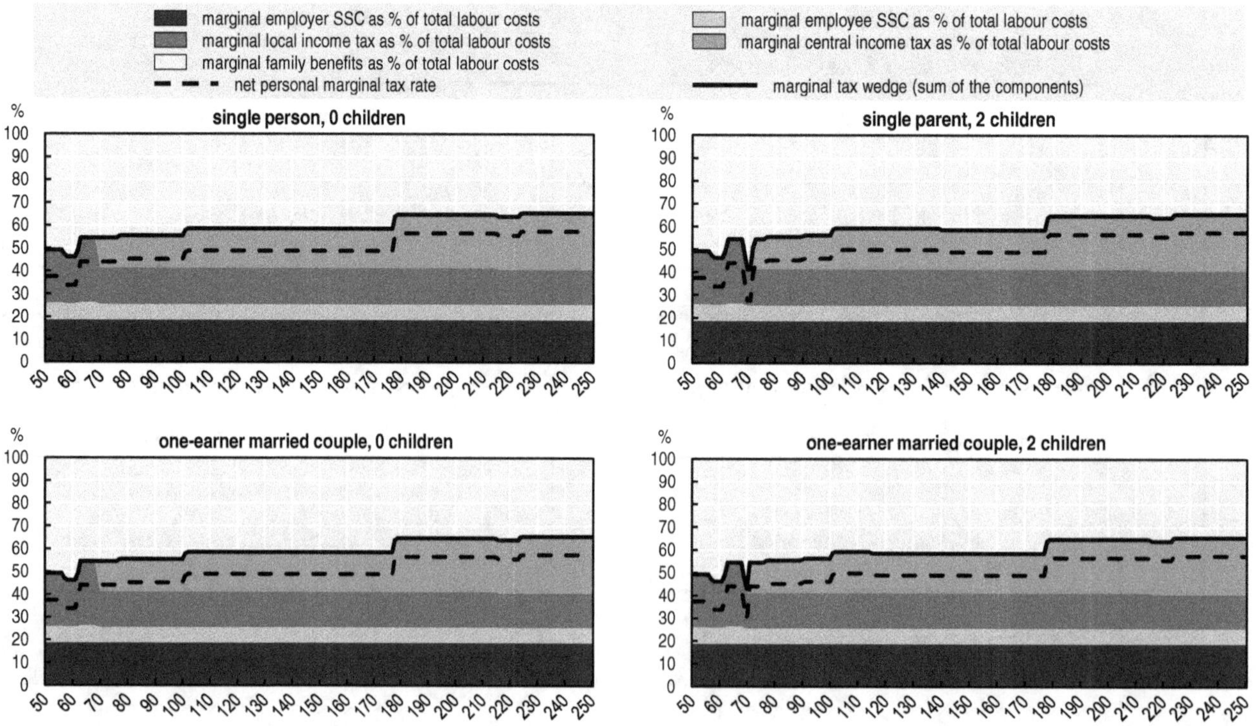

StatLink http://dx.doi.org/10.1787/888933340664

France 2015: Average tax wedge decomposition

By level of gross earnings expressed as a % of the average wage

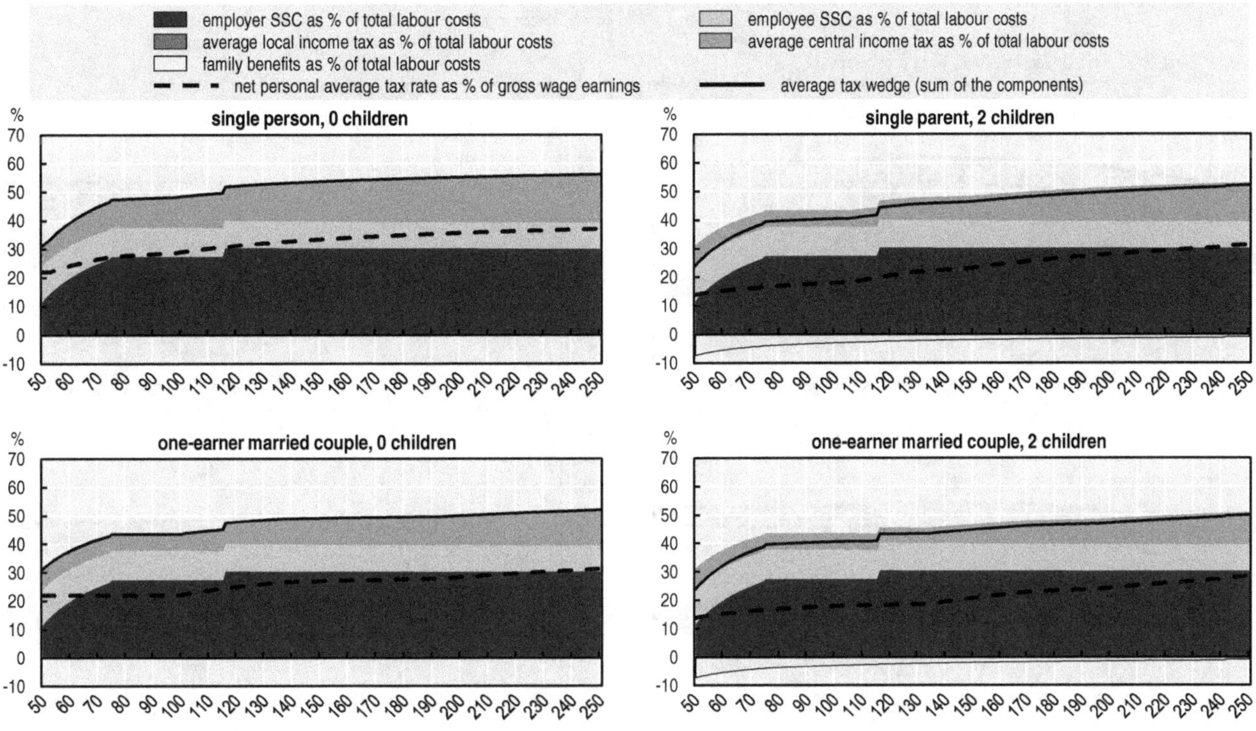

StatLink http://dx.doi.org/10.1787/888933340673

France 2015: Marginal tax wedge decomposition

By level of gross earnings expressed as a % of the average wage

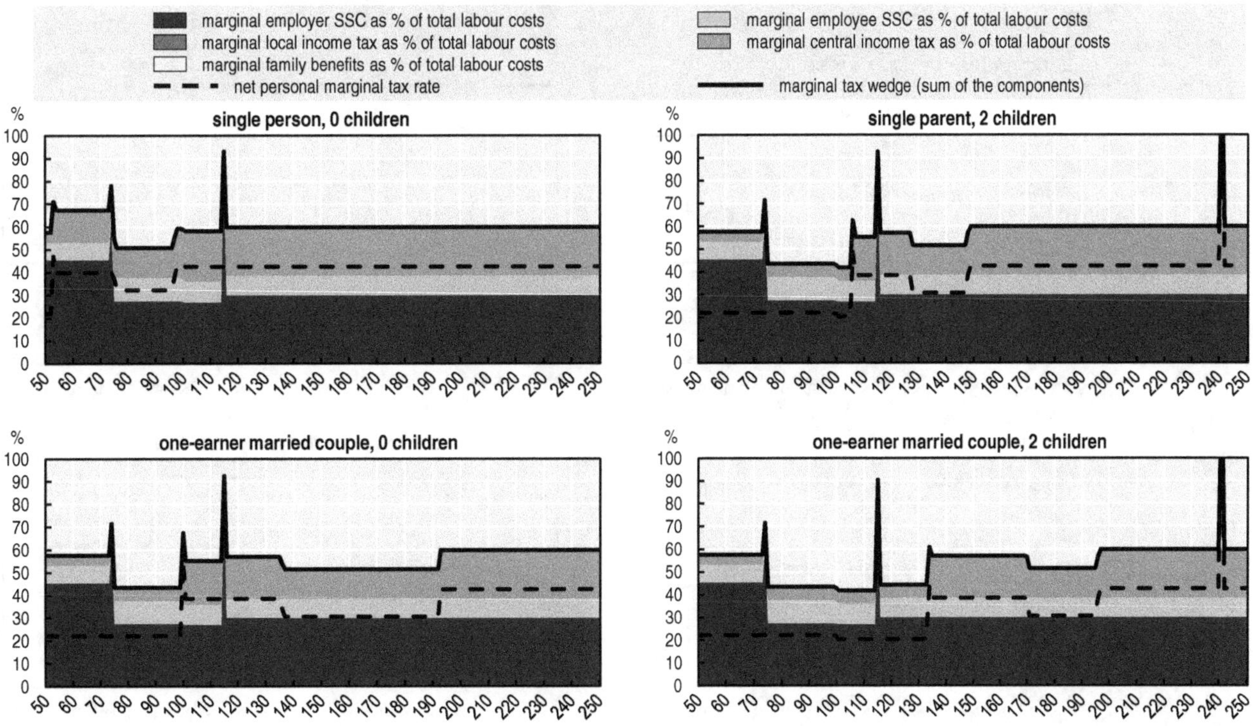

StatLink http://dx.doi.org/10.1787/888933340685

Germany 2015: Average tax wedge decomposition

By level of gross earnings expressed as a % of the average wage

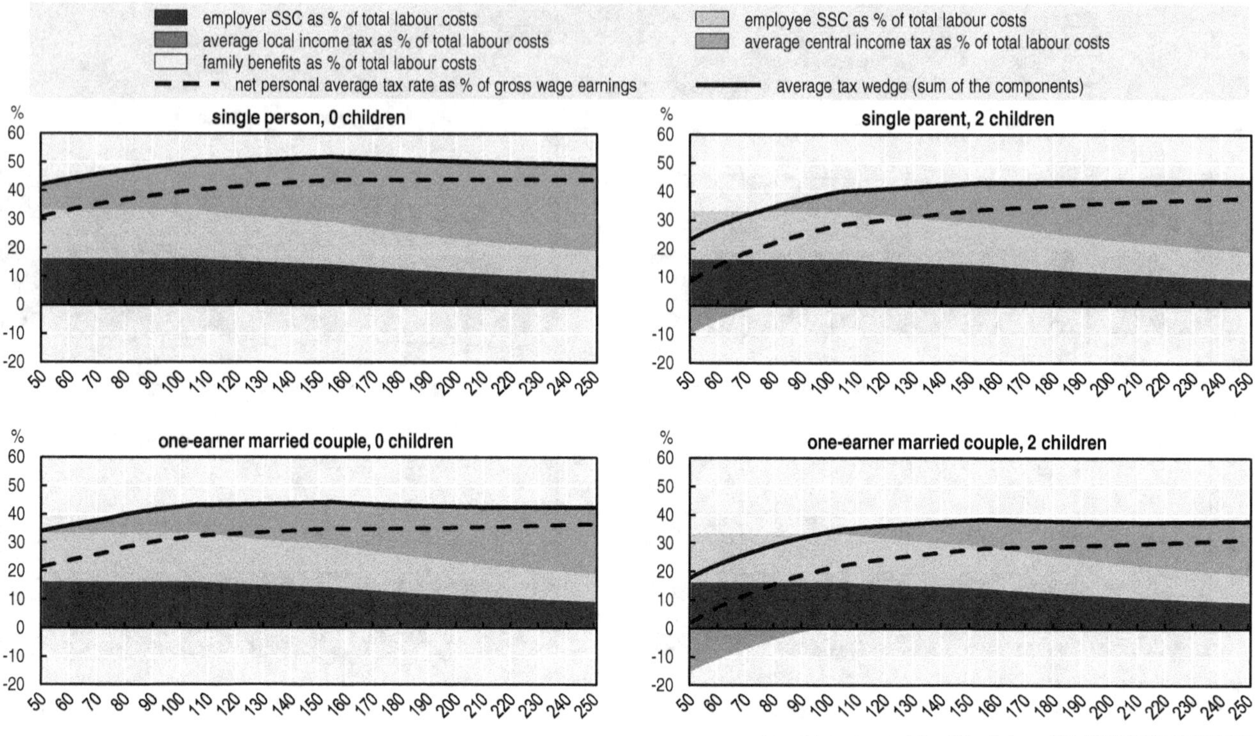

StatLink http://dx.doi.org/10.1787/888933340697

Germany 2015: Marginal tax wedge decomposition

By level of gross earnings expressed as a % of the average wage

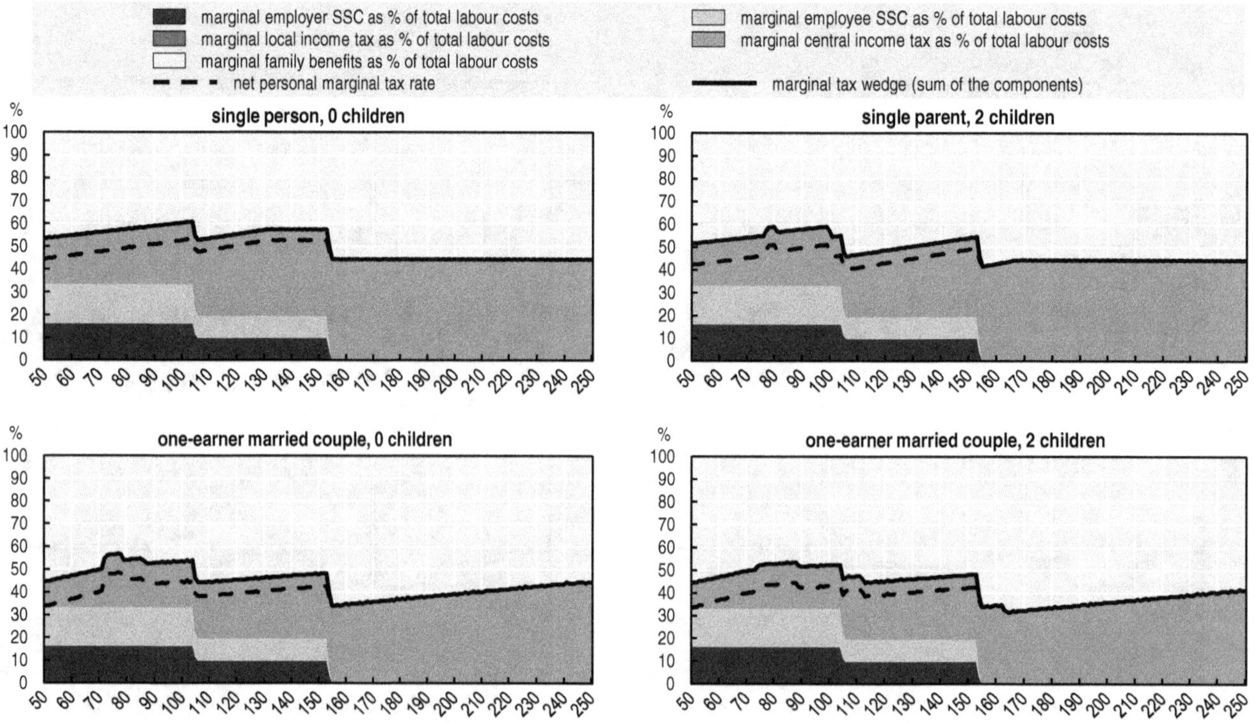

StatLink http://dx.doi.org/10.1787/888933340709

Greece 2015: Average tax wedge decomposition

By level of gross earnings expressed as a % of the average wage

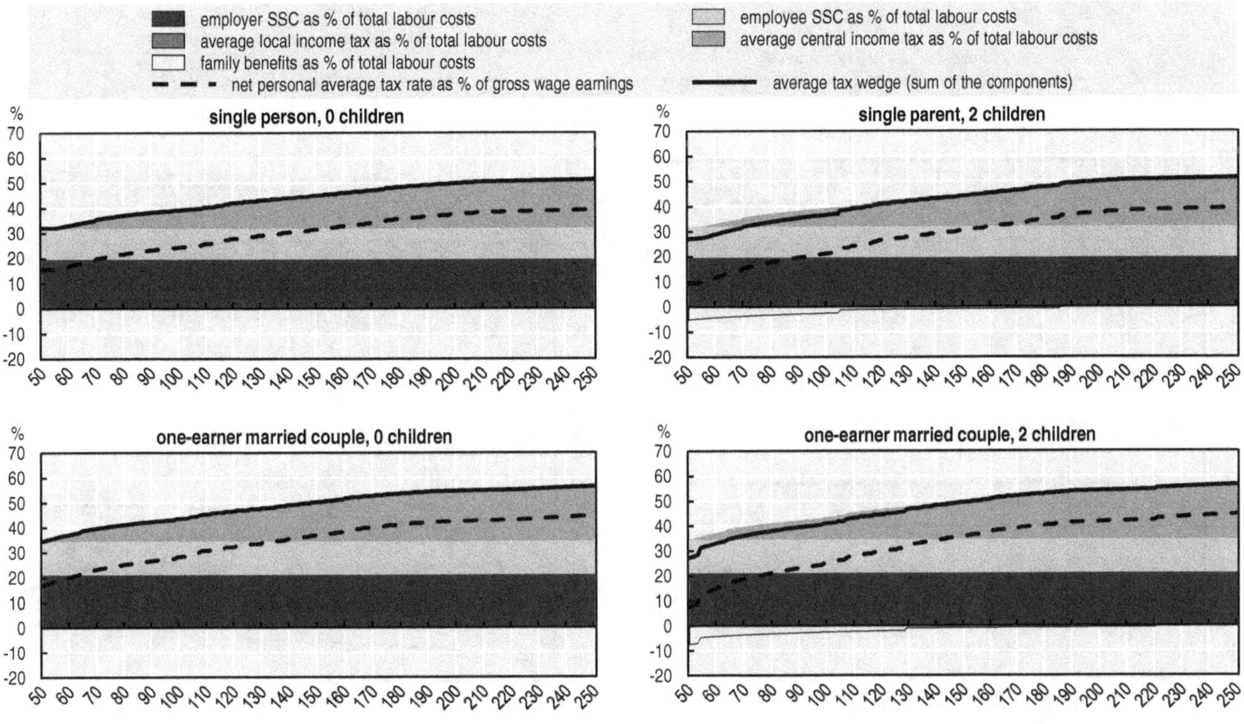

StatLink http://dx.doi.org/10.1787/888933340711

Greece 2015: Marginal tax wedge decomposition

By level of gross earnings expressed as a % of the average wage

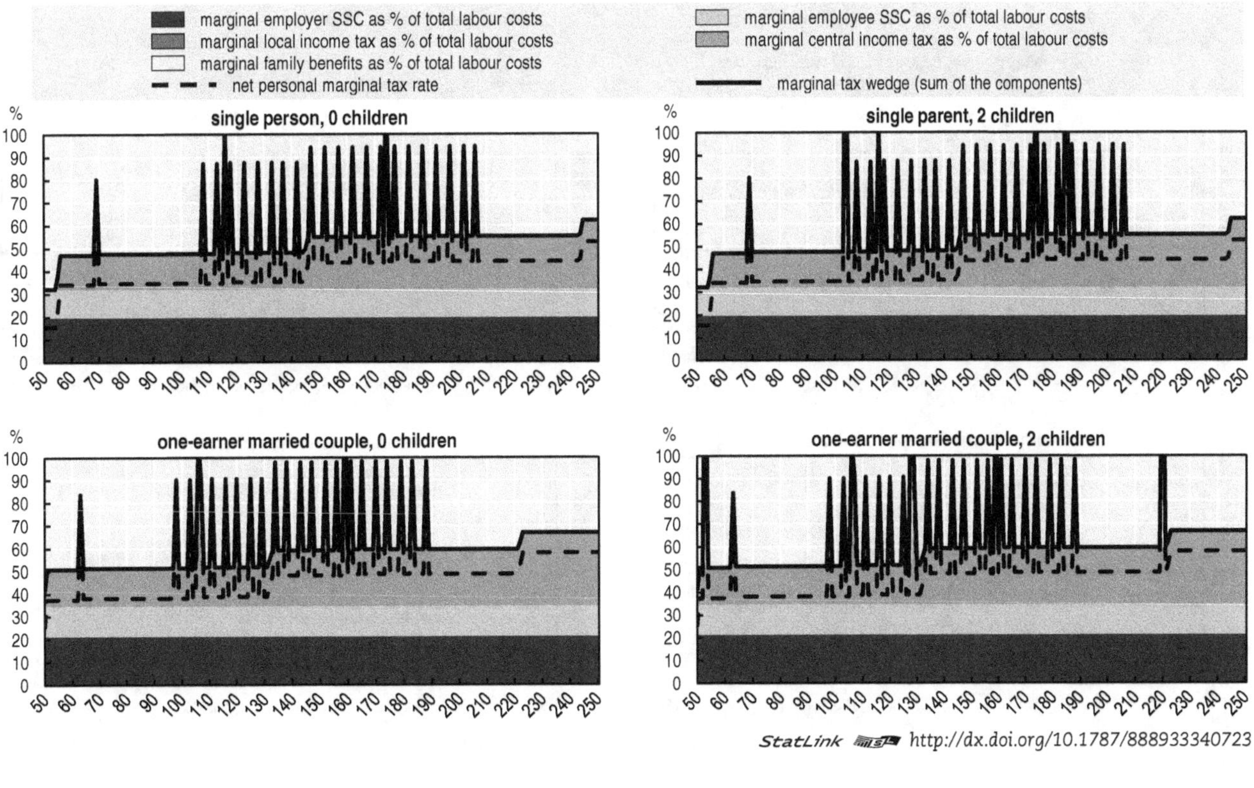

StatLink http://dx.doi.org/10.1787/888933340723

Hungary 2015: Average tax wedge decomposition

By level of gross earnings expressed as a % of the average wage

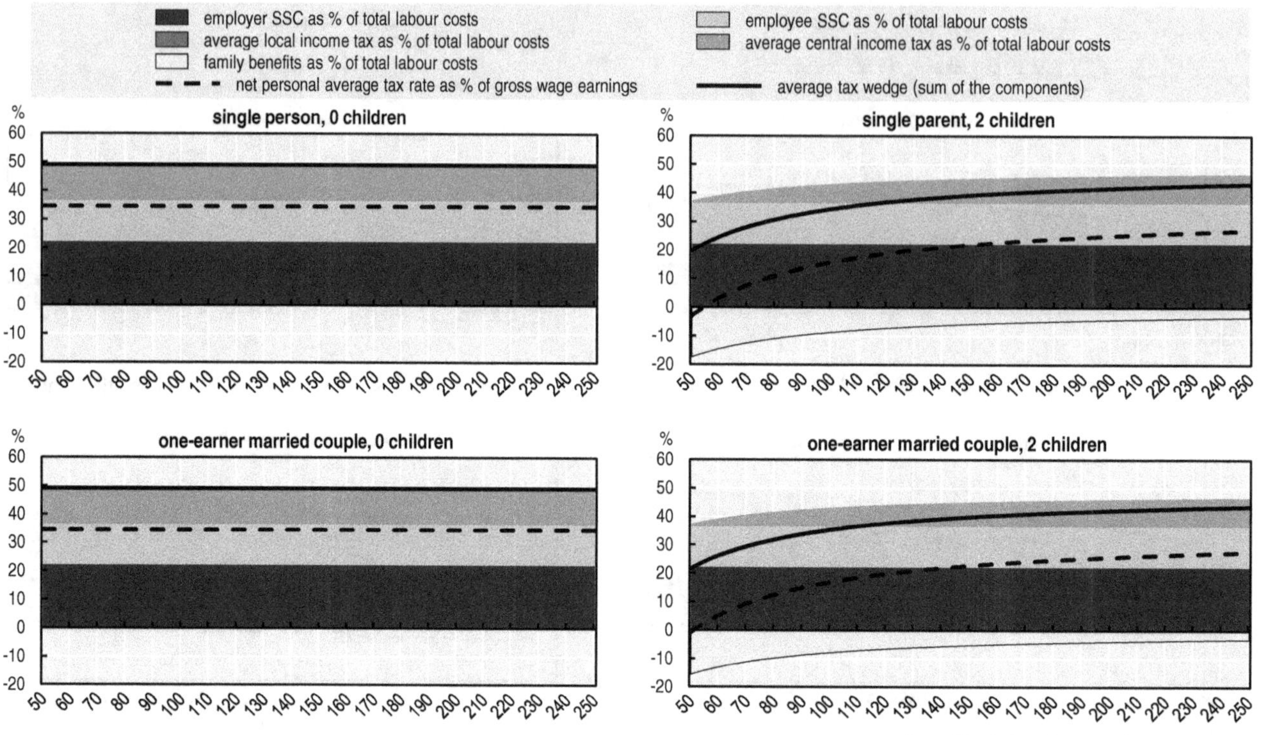

StatLink http://dx.doi.org/10.1787/888933340738

Hungary 2015: Marginal tax wedge decomposition

By level of gross earnings expressed as a % of the average wage

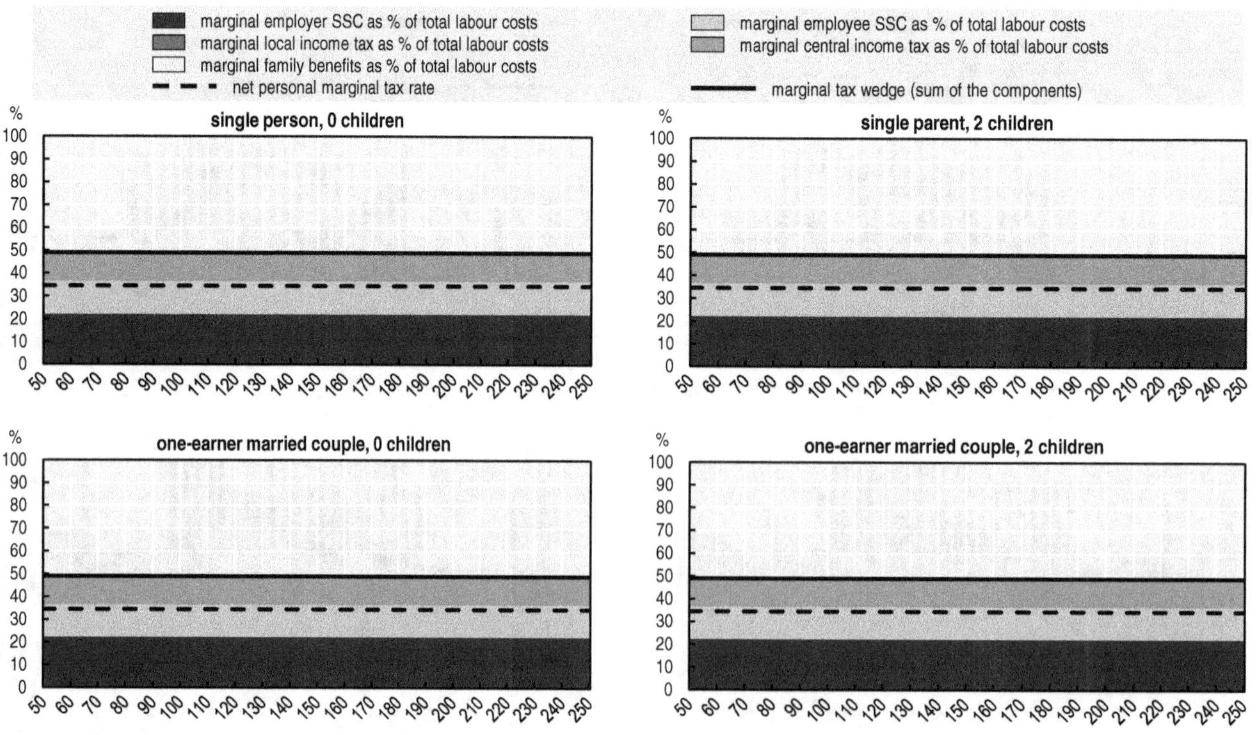

StatLink http://dx.doi.org/10.1787/888933340748

Iceland 2015: Average tax wedge decomposition

By level of gross earnings expressed as a % of the average wage

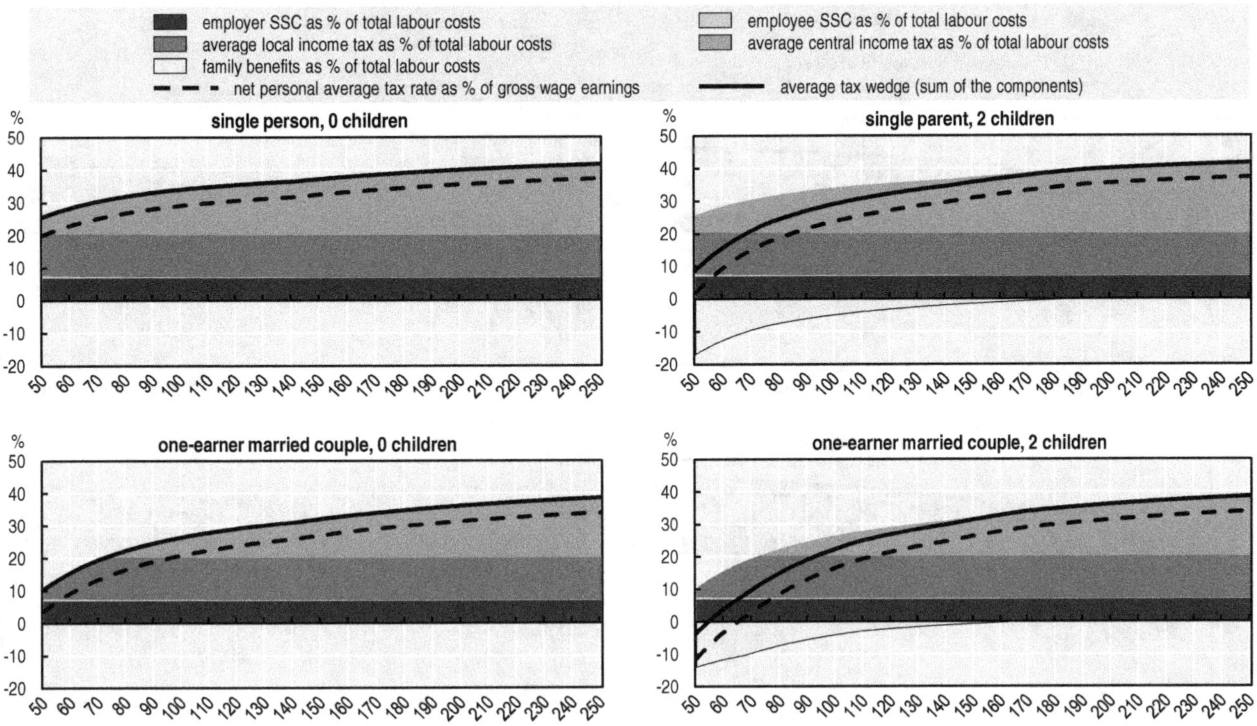

StatLink http://dx.doi.org/10.1787/888933340752

Iceland 2015: Marginal tax wedge decomposition

By level of gross earnings expressed as a % of the average wage

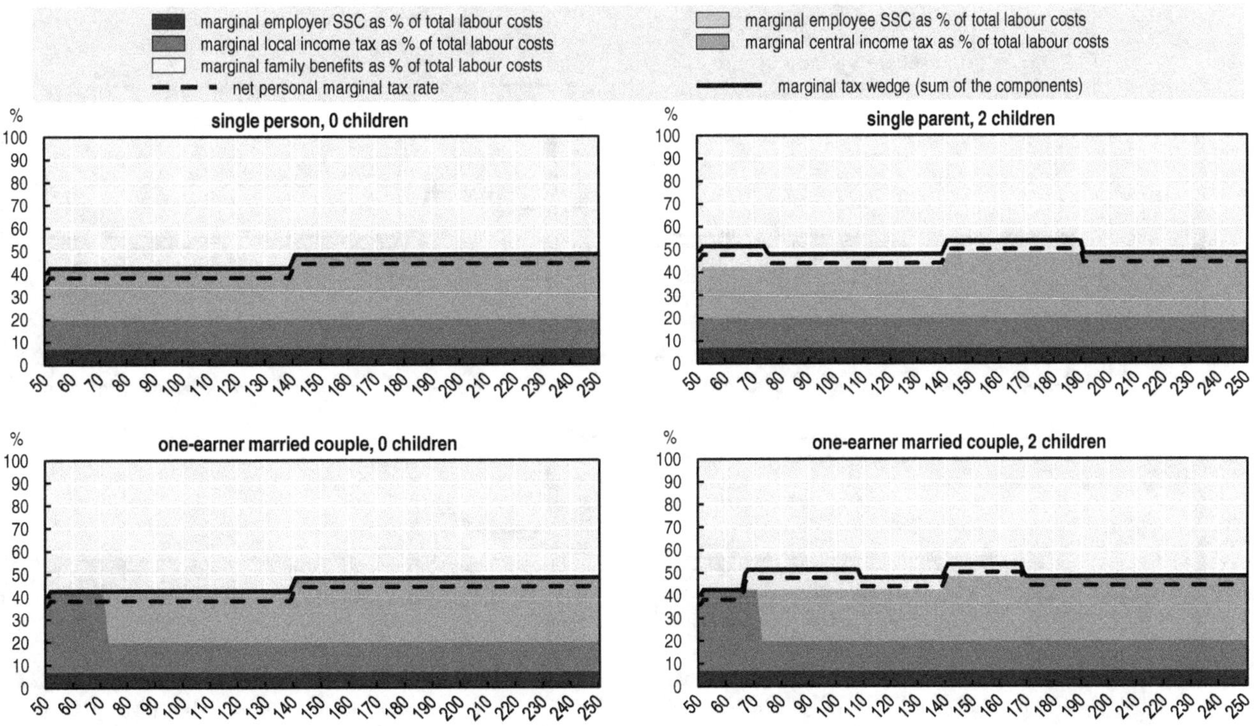

StatLink http://dx.doi.org/10.1787/888933340761

Ireland 2015: Average tax wedge decomposition

By level of gross earnings expressed as a % of the average wage

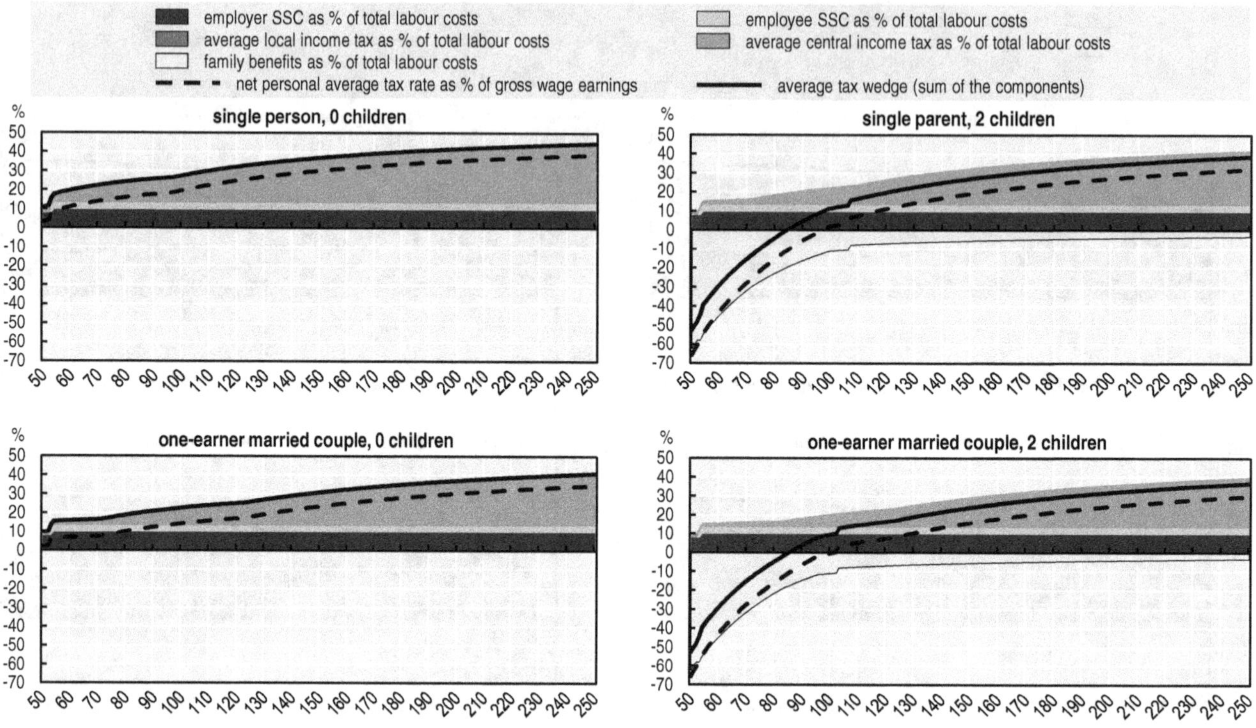

StatLink http://dx.doi.org/10.1787/888933340774

Ireland 2015: Marginal tax wedge decomposition

By level of gross earnings expressed as a % of the average wage

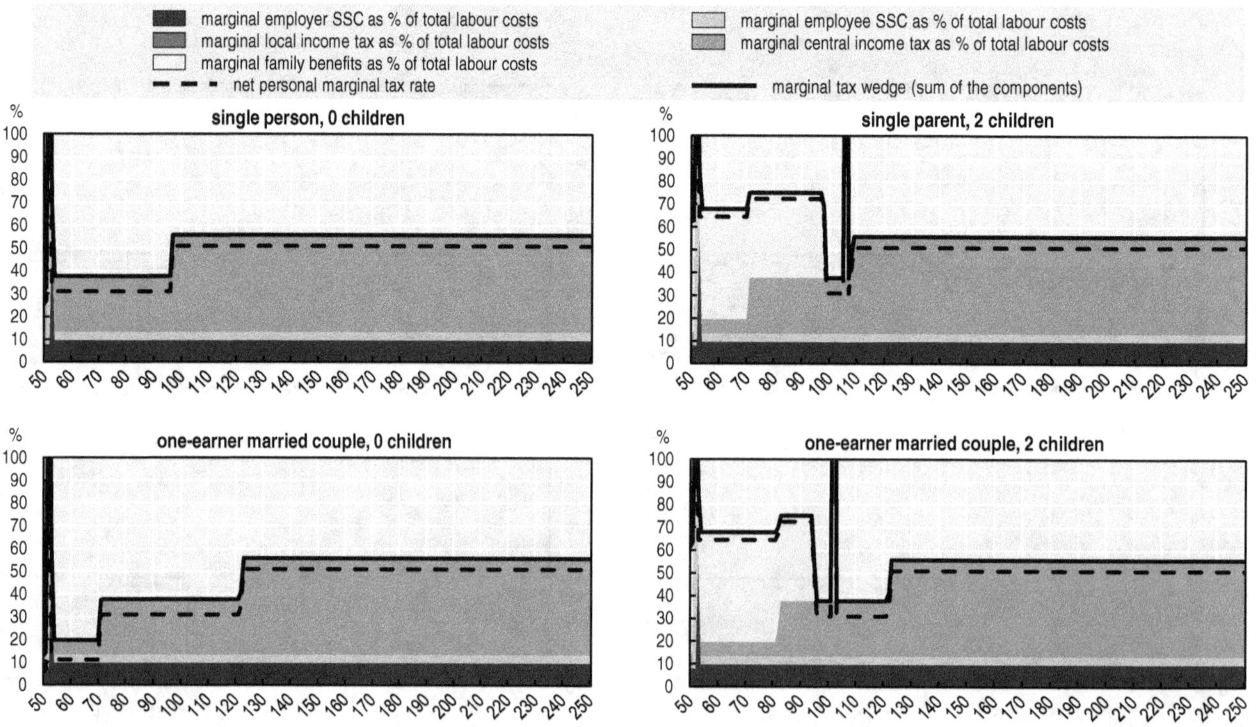

StatLink http://dx.doi.org/10.1787/888933340783

Israel 2015: Average tax wedge decomposition

By level of gross earnings expressed as a % of the average wage

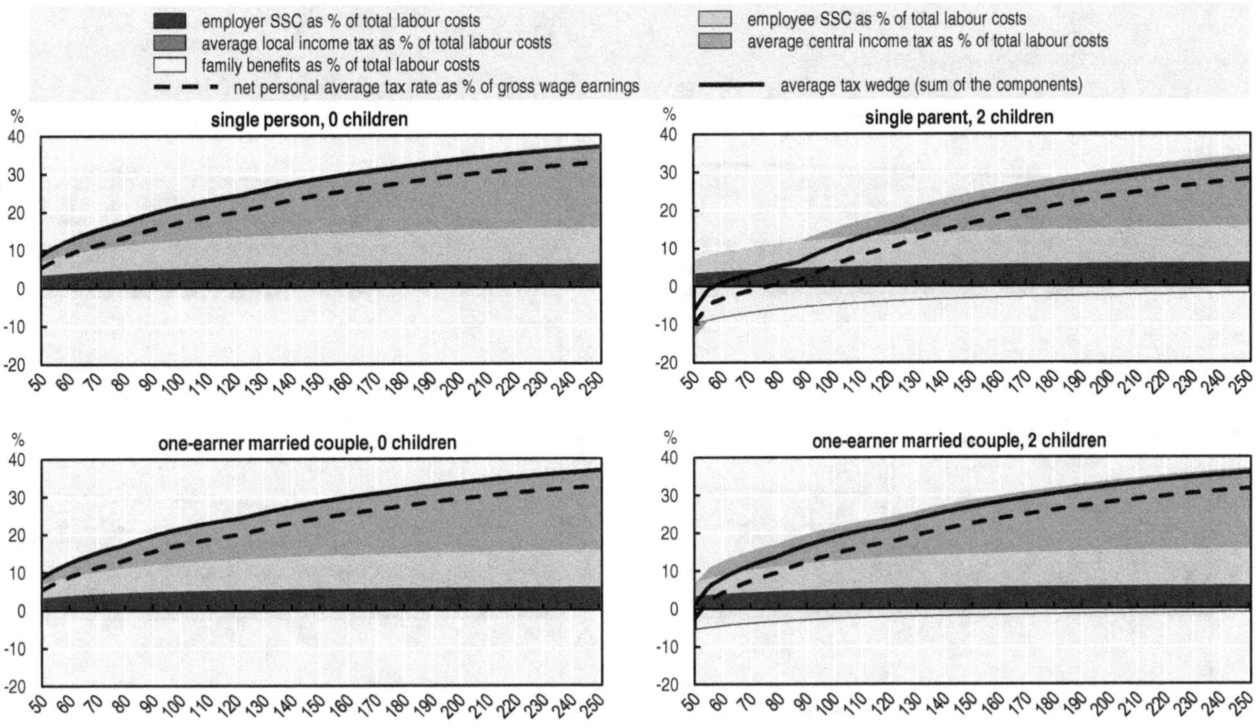

StatLink http://dx.doi.org/10.1787/888933340791

Israel 2015: Marginal tax wedge decomposition

By level of gross earnings expressed as a % of the average wage

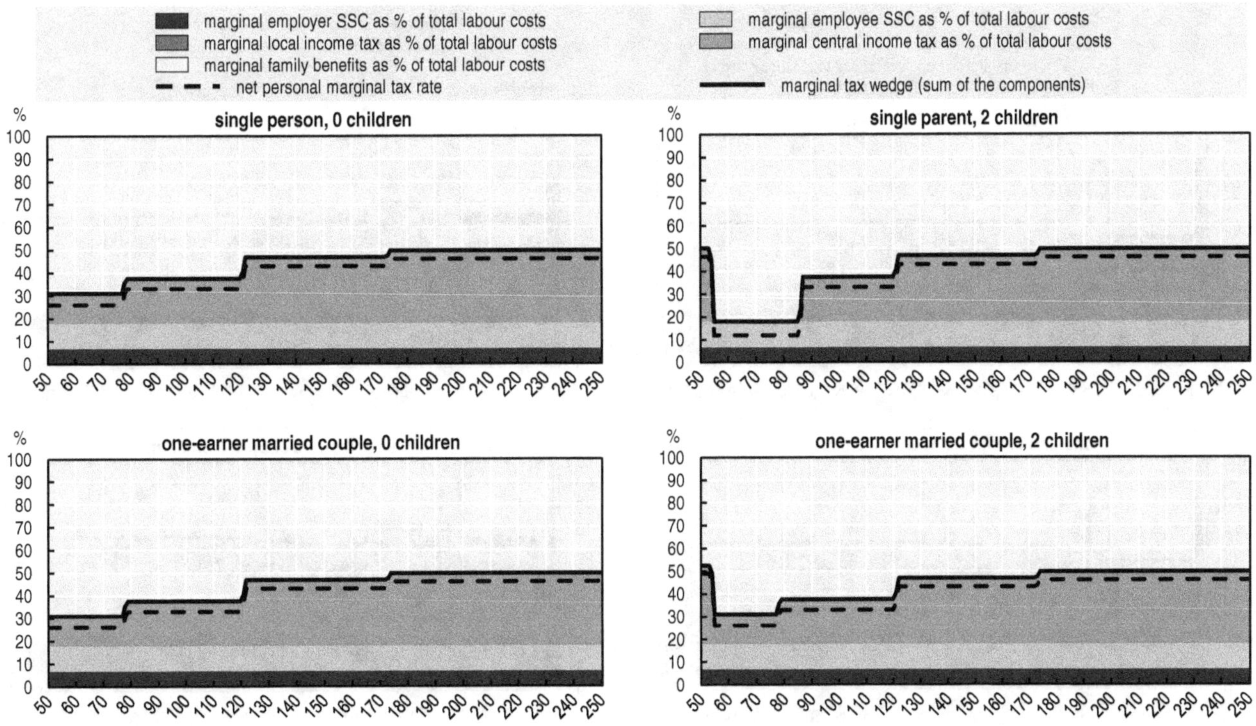

StatLink http://dx.doi.org/10.1787/888933340805

Italy 2015: Average tax wedge decomposition

By level of gross earnings expressed as a % of the average wage

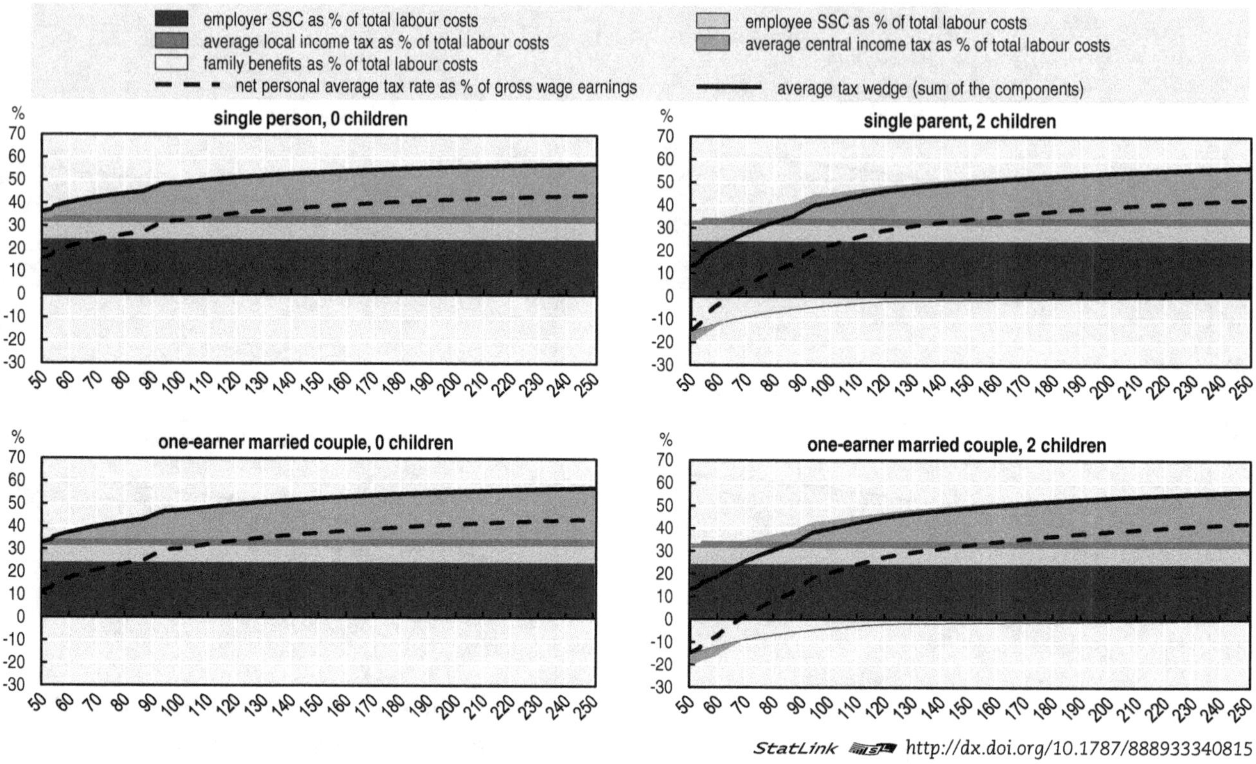

StatLink http://dx.doi.org/10.1787/888933340815

Italy 2015: Marginal tax wedge decomposition

By level of gross earnings expressed as a % of the average wage

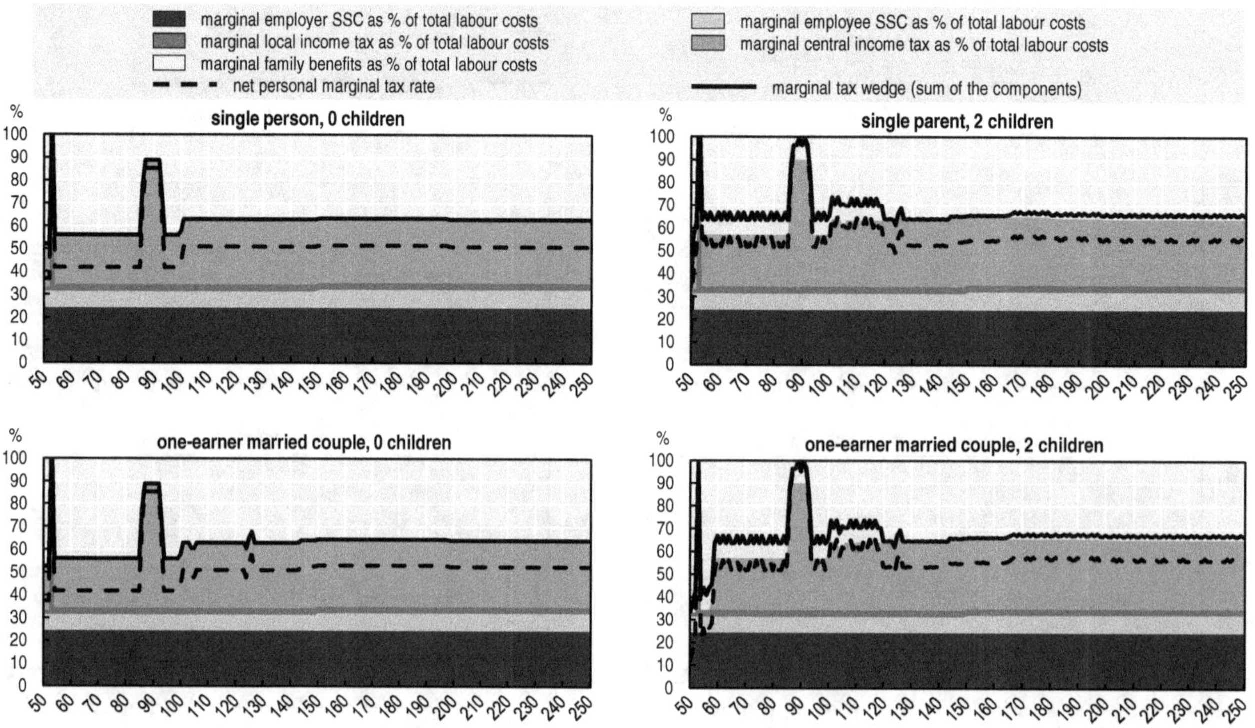

StatLink http://dx.doi.org/10.1787/888933340820

Japan 2015: Average tax wedge decomposition

By level of gross earnings expressed as a % of the average wage

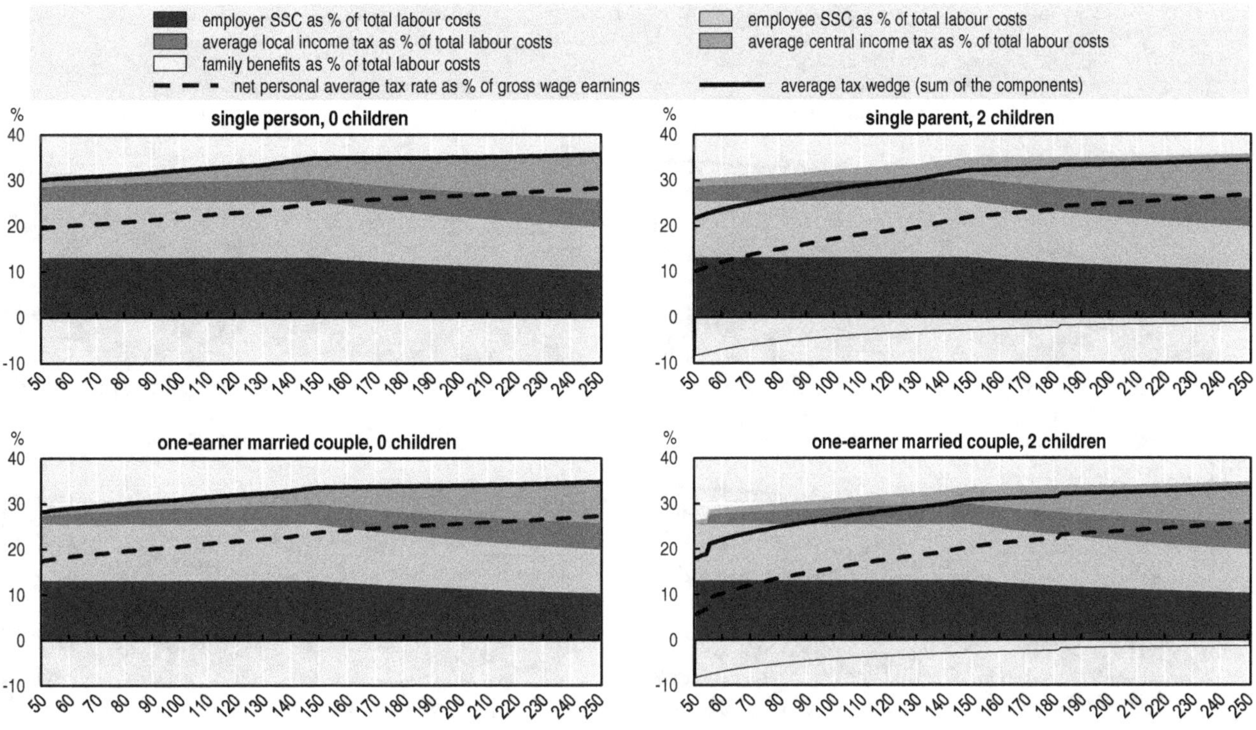

StatLink http://dx.doi.org/10.1787/888933340834

Japan 2015: Marginal tax wedge decomposition

By level of gross earnings expressed as a % of the average wage

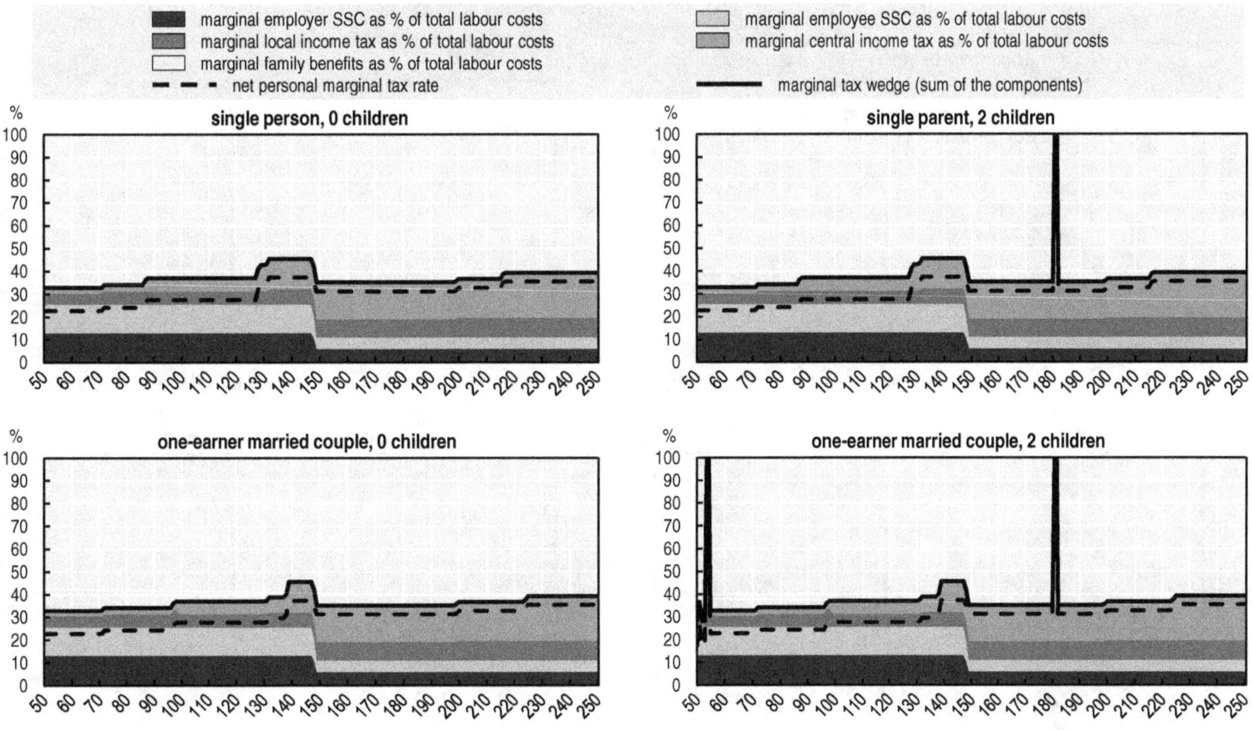

StatLink http://dx.doi.org/10.1787/888933340840

Korea 2015: Average tax wedge decomposition

By level of gross earnings expressed as a % of the average wage

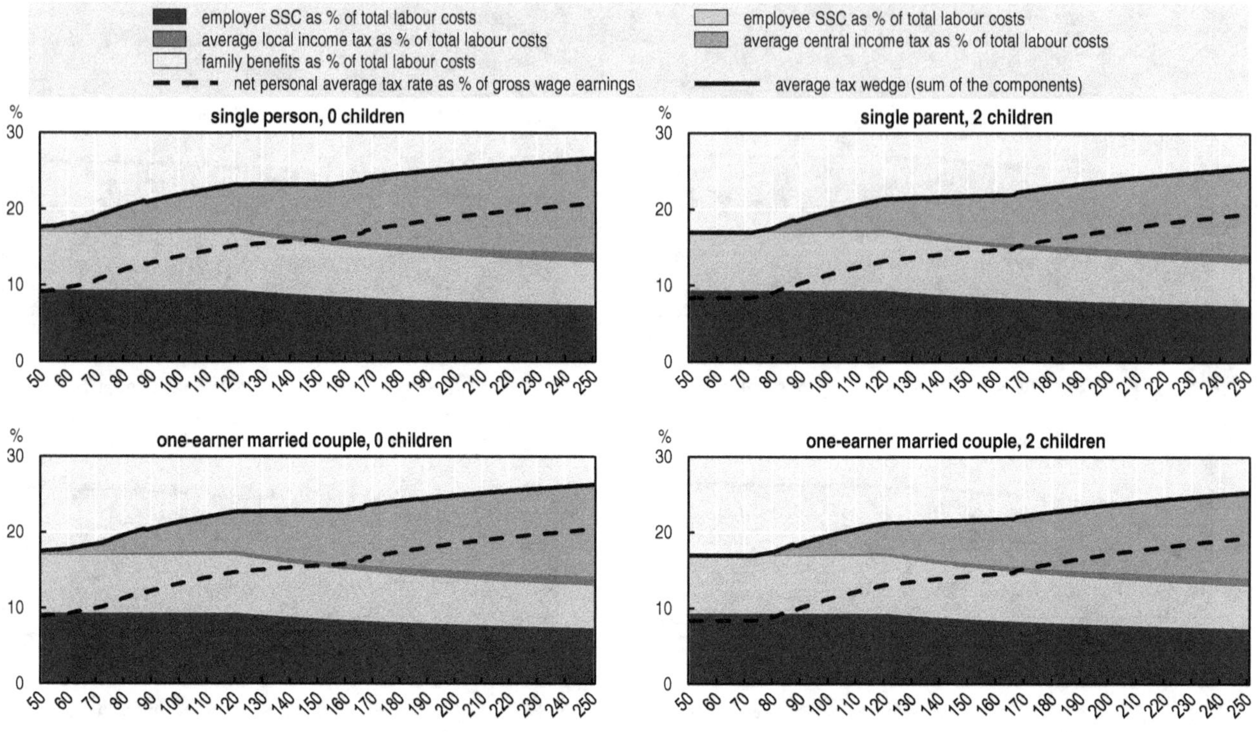

StatLink http://dx.doi.org/10.1787/888933340857

Korea 2015: Marginal tax wedge decomposition

By level of gross earnings expressed as a % of the average wage

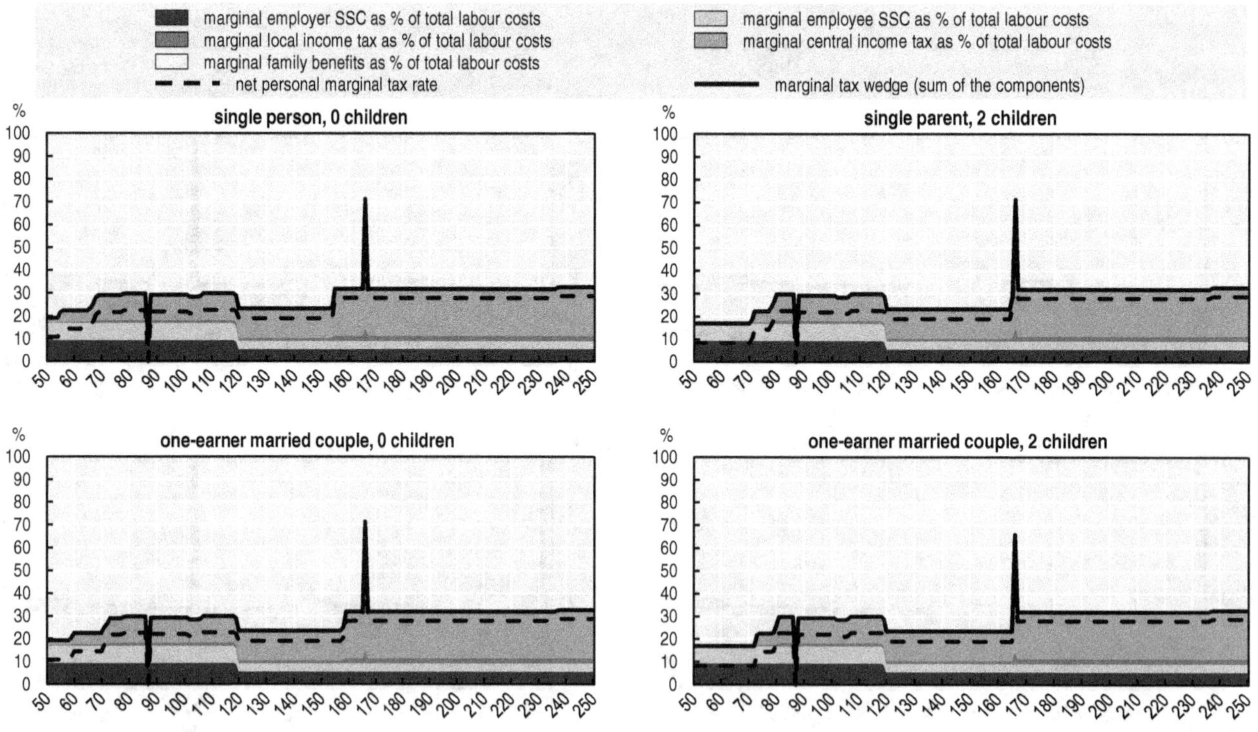

StatLink http://dx.doi.org/10.1787/888933340862

Luxembourg 2015: Average tax wedge decomposition

By level of gross earnings expressed as a % of the average wage

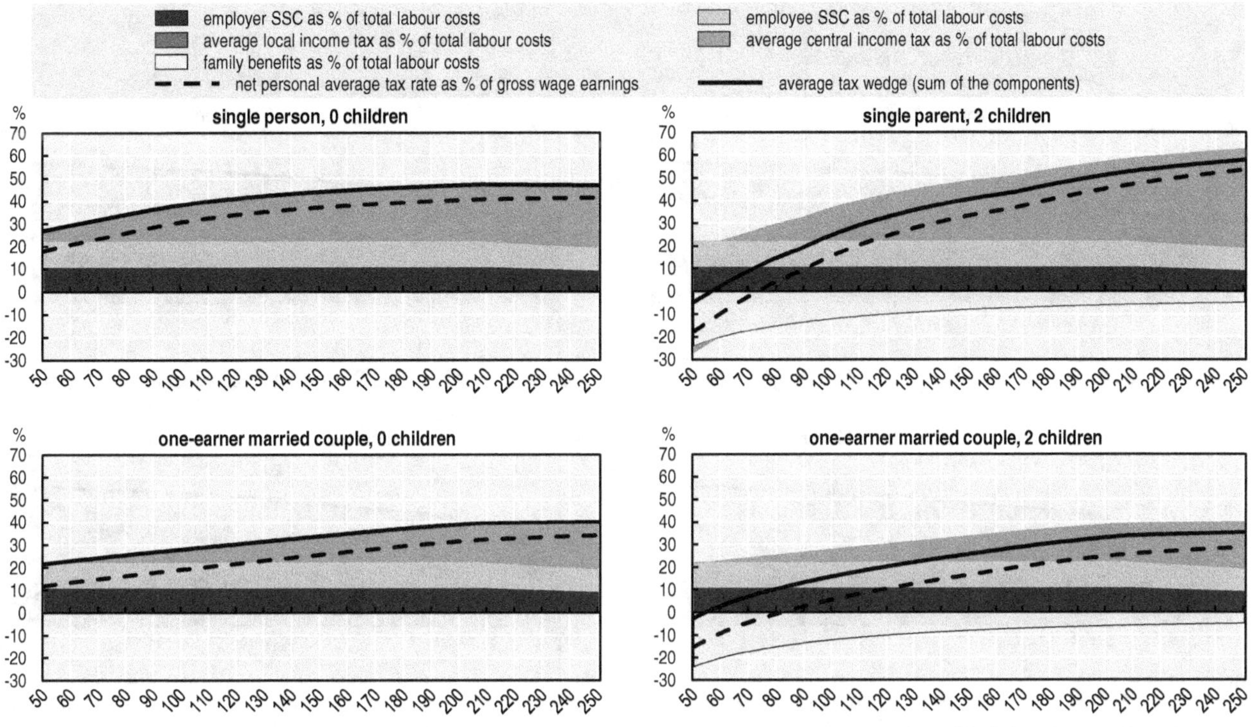

StatLink http://dx.doi.org/10.1787/888933340873

Luxembourg 2015: Marginal tax wedge decomposition

By level of gross earnings expressed as a % of the average wage

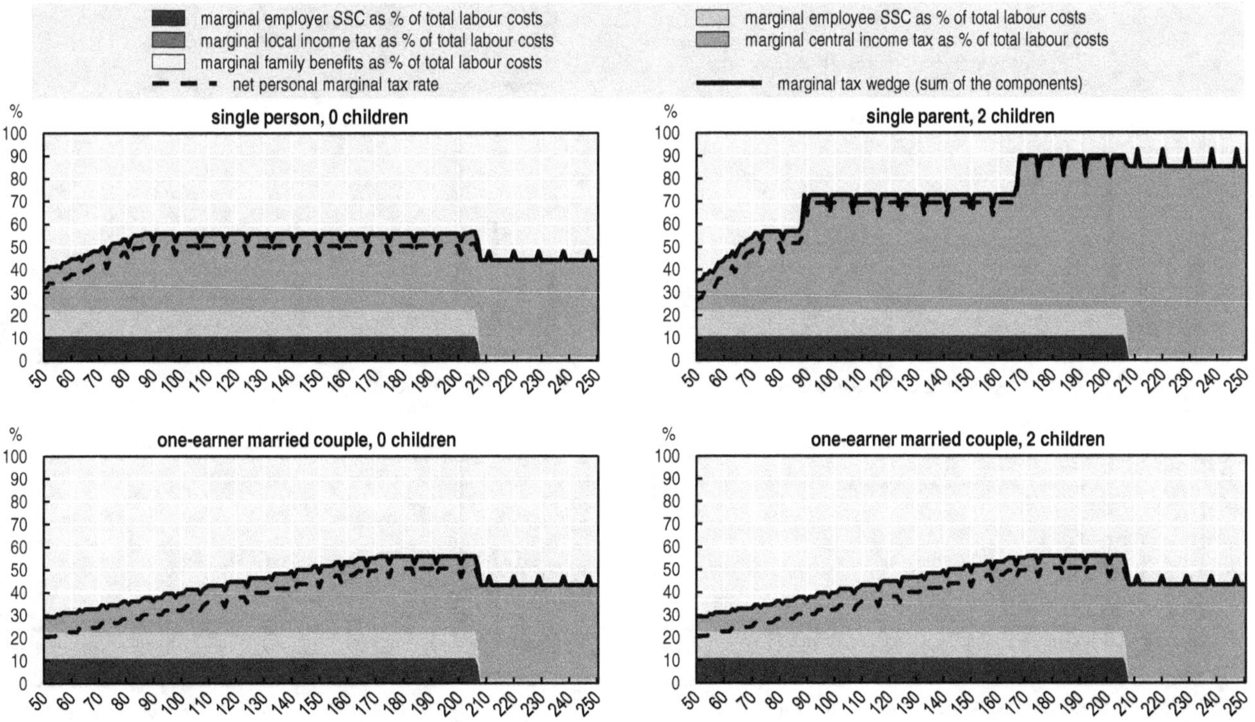

StatLink http://dx.doi.org/10.1787/888933340885

Mexico 2015: Average tax wedge decomposition

By level of gross earnings expressed as a % of the average wage

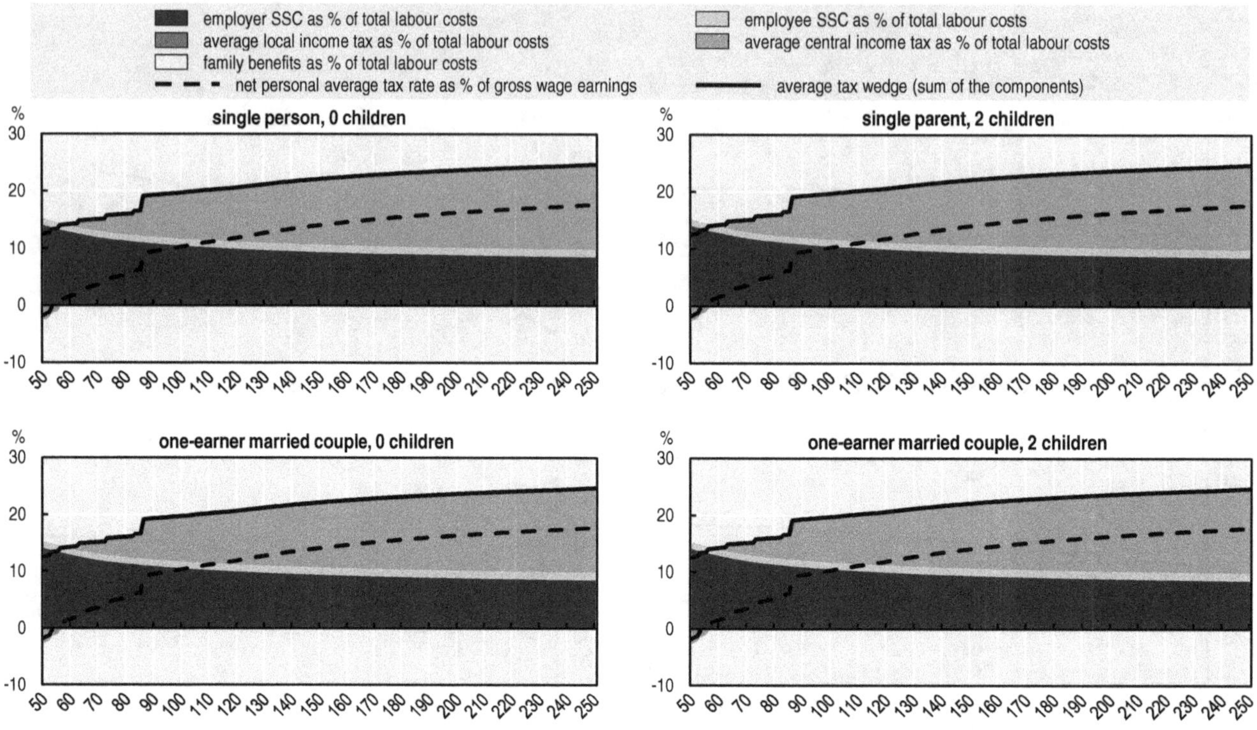

StatLink http://dx.doi.org/10.1787/888933340890

Mexico 2015: Marginal tax wedge decomposition

By level of gross earnings expressed as a % of the average wage

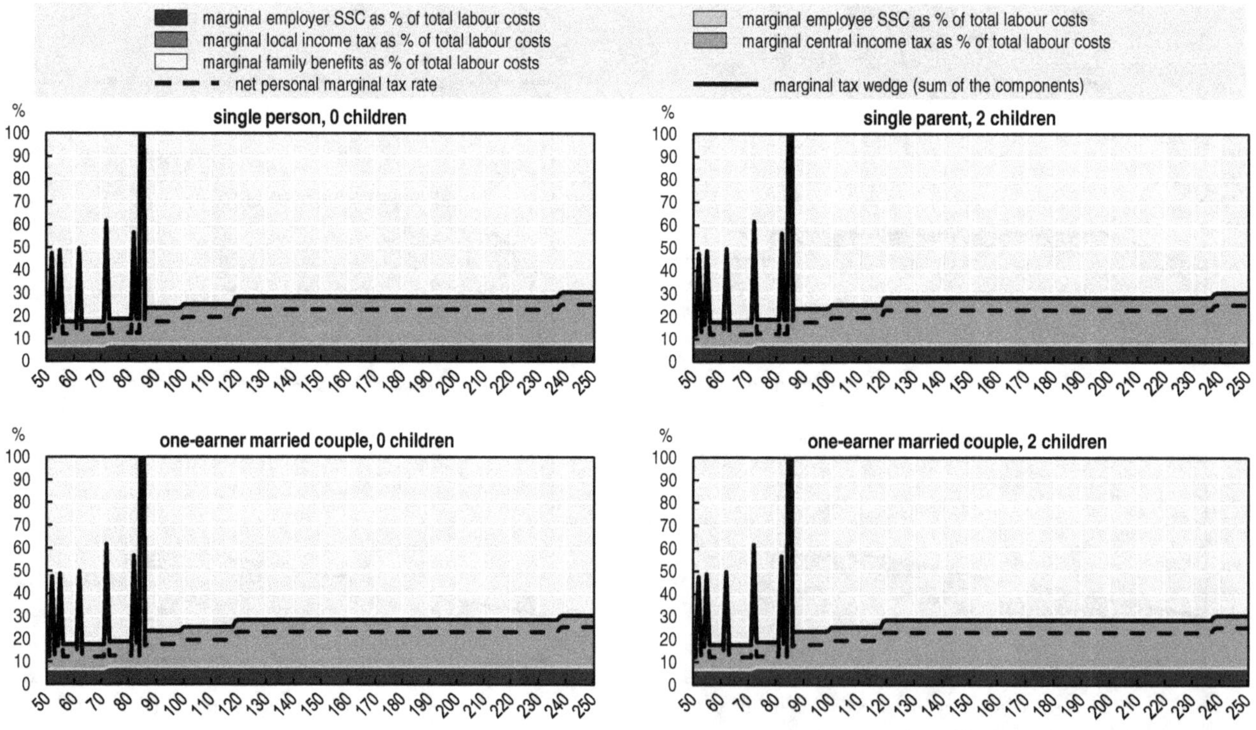

StatLink http://dx.doi.org/10.1787/888933340907

Netherlands 2015: Average tax wedge decomposition

By level of gross earnings expressed as a % of the average wage

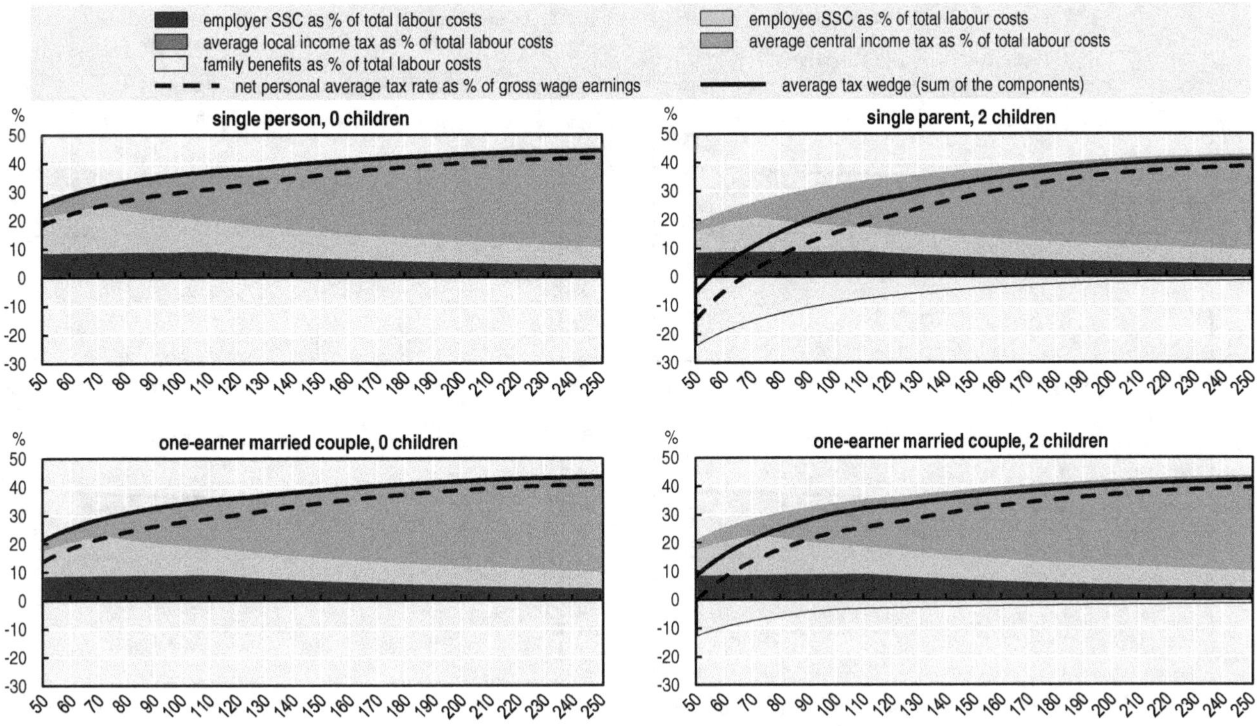

StatLink http://dx.doi.org/10.1787/888933340919

Netherlands 2015: Marginal tax wedge decomposition

By level of gross earnings expressed as a % of the average wage

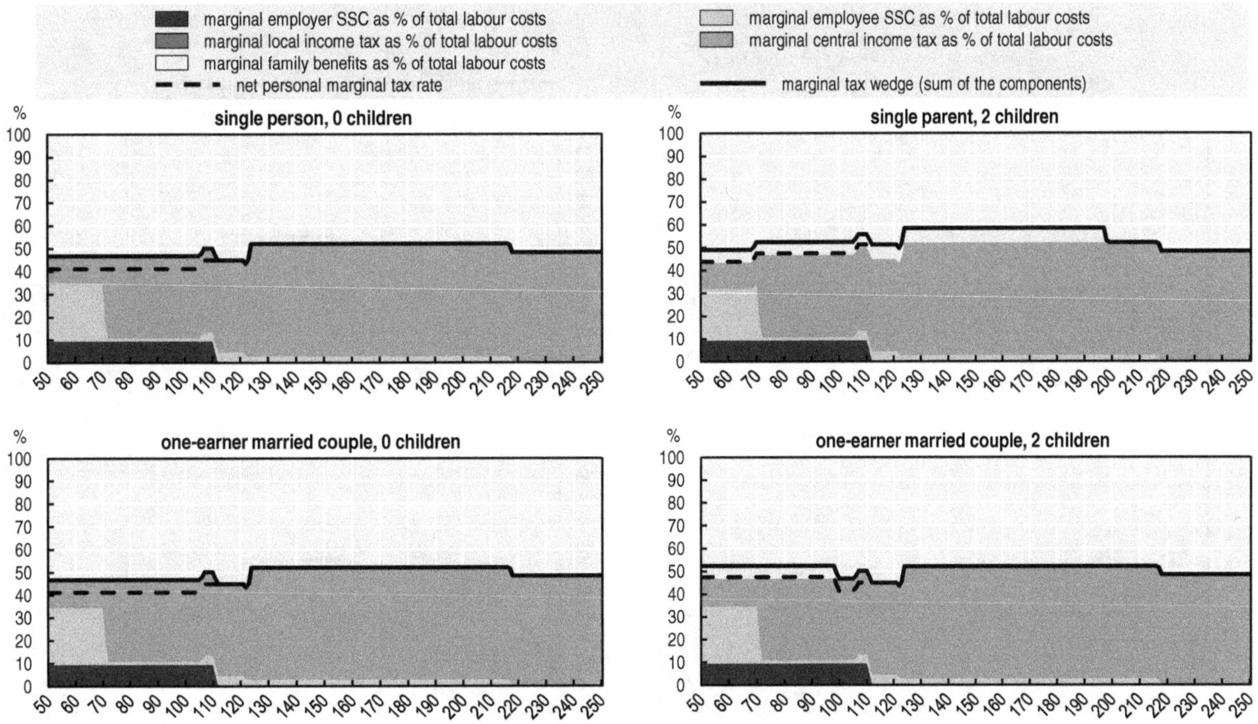

StatLink http://dx.doi.org/10.1787/888933340922

New Zealand 2015: Average tax wedge decomposition

By level of gross earnings expressed as a % of the average wage

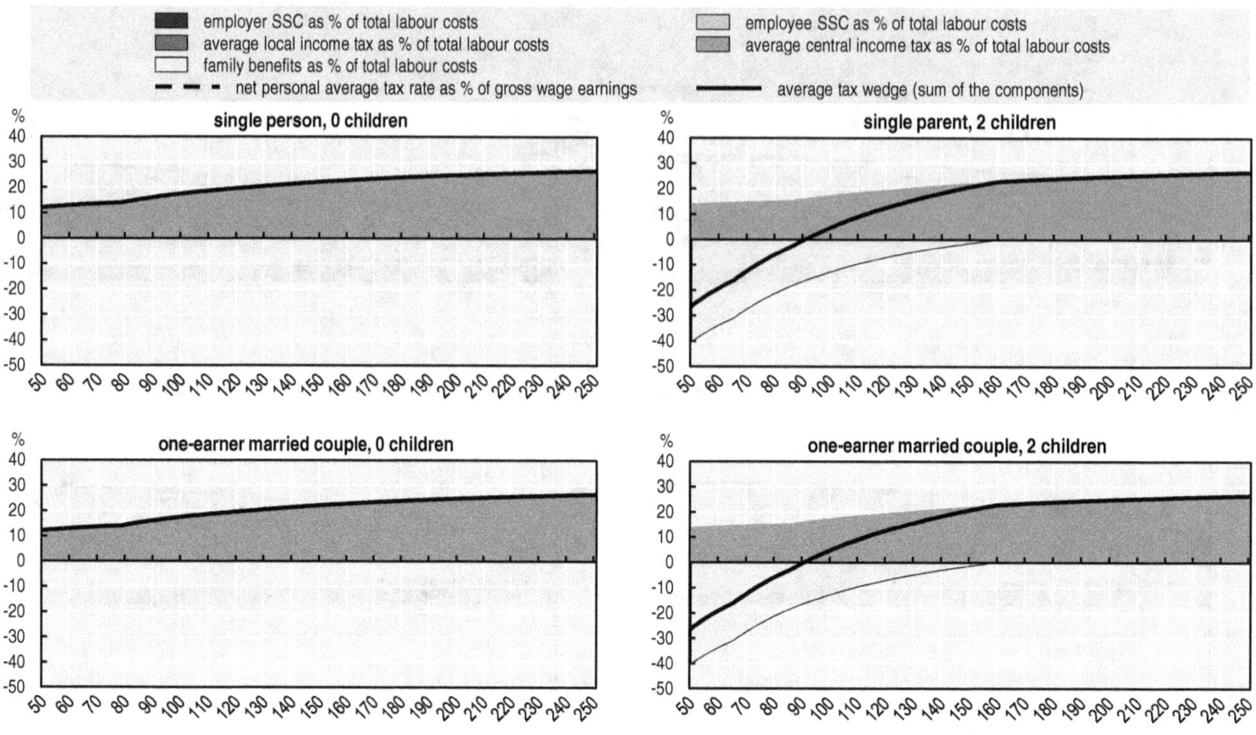

StatLink http://dx.doi.org/10.1787/888933340930

New Zealand 2015: Marginal tax wedge decomposition

By level of gross earnings expressed as a % of the average wage

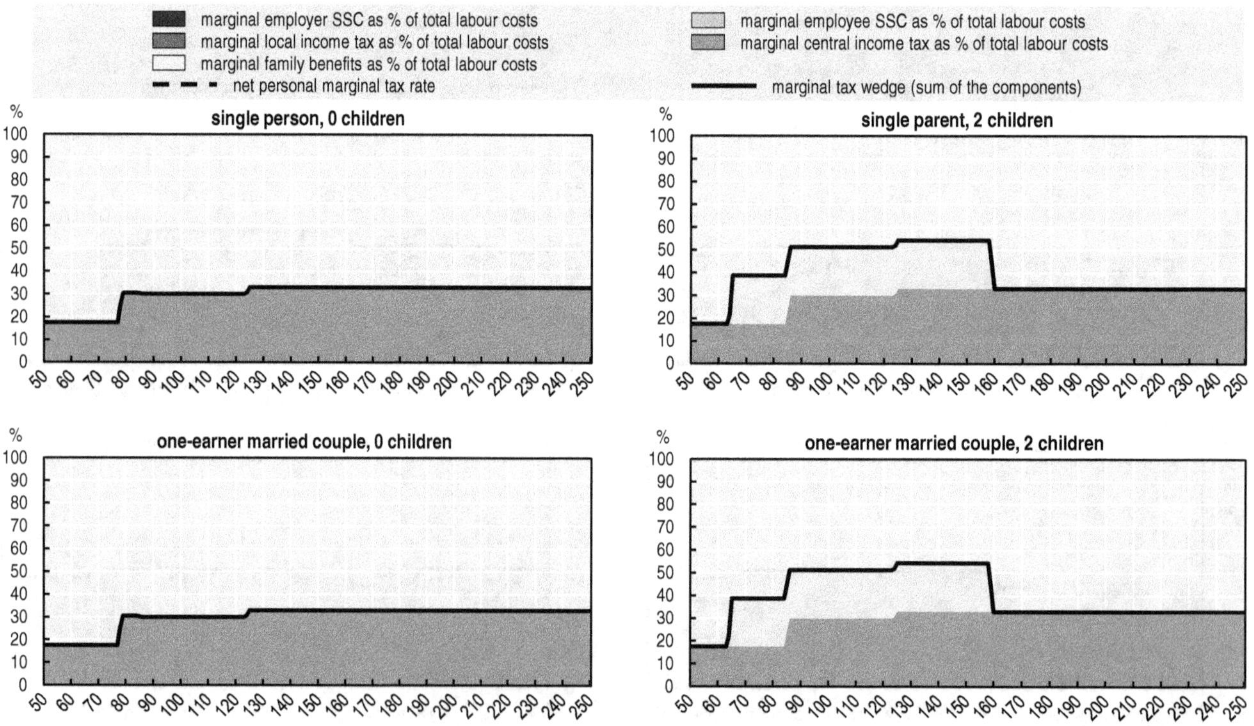

StatLink http://dx.doi.org/10.1787/888933340941

Norway 2015: Average tax wedge decomposition

By level of gross earnings expressed as a % of the average wage

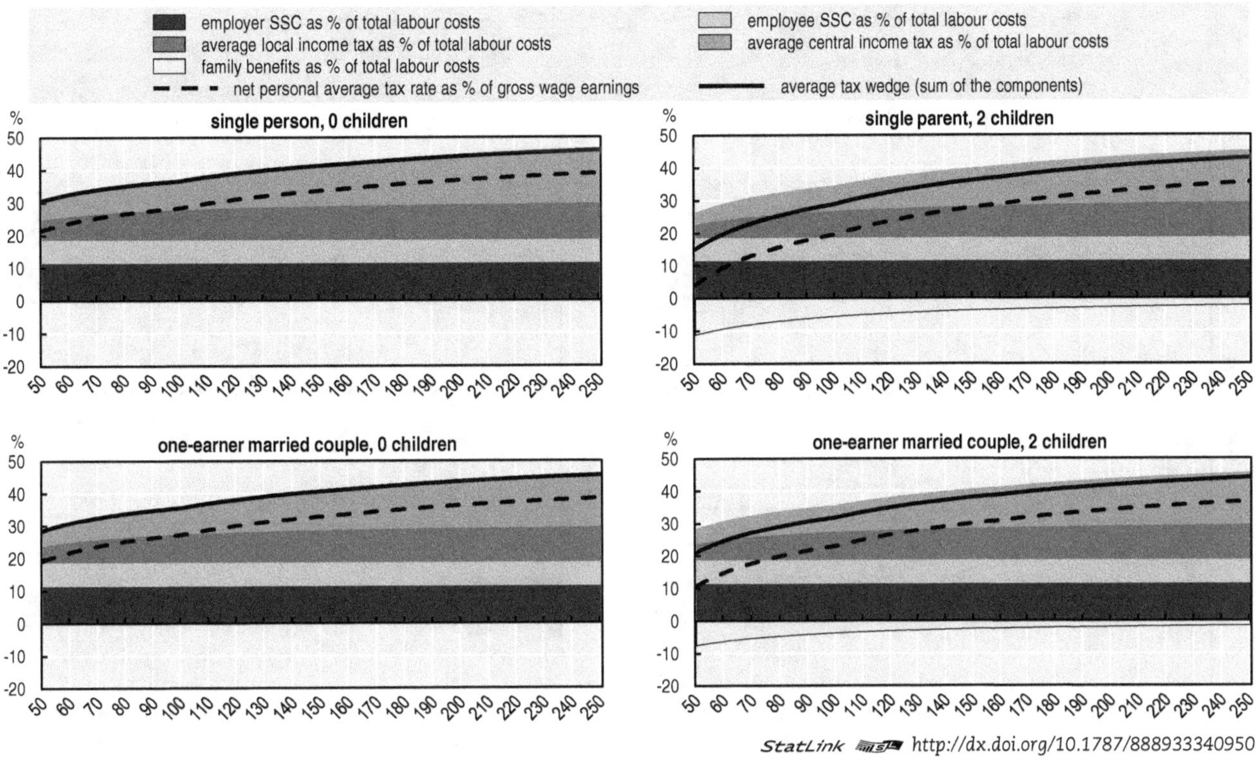

StatLink http://dx.doi.org/10.1787/888933340950

Norway 2015: Marginal tax wedge decomposition

By level of gross earnings expressed as a % of the average wage

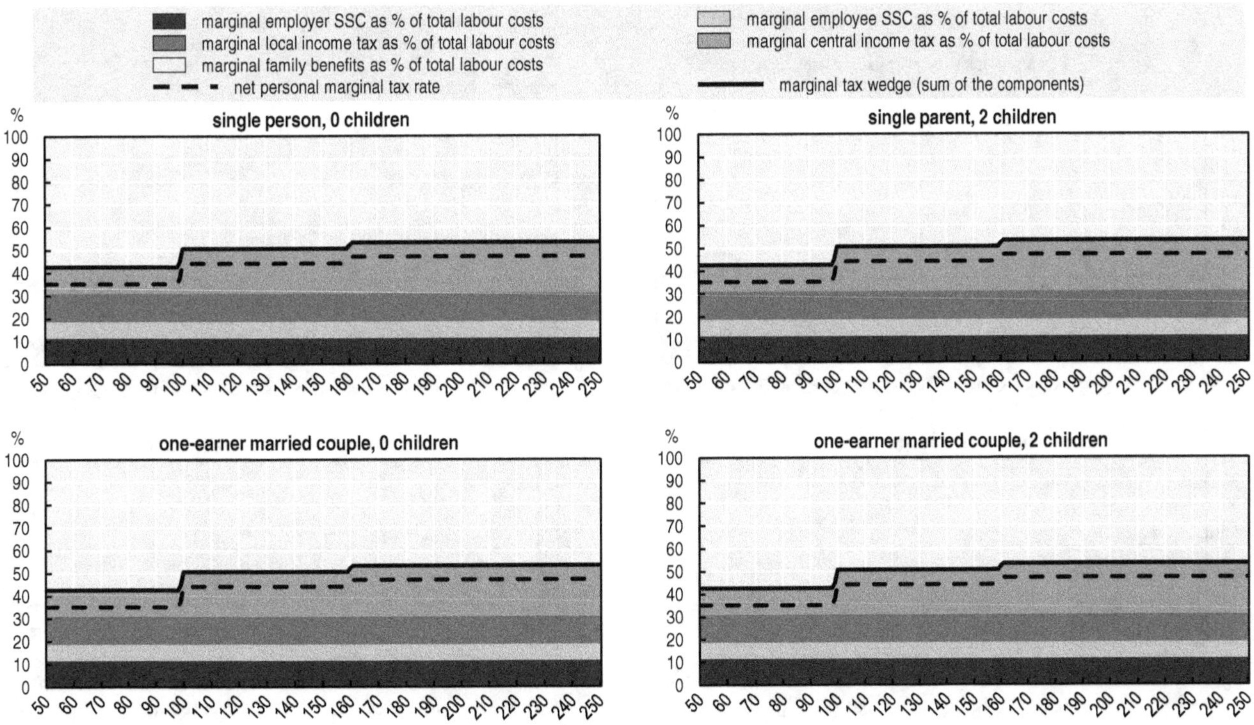

StatLink http://dx.doi.org/10.1787/888933340969

Poland 2015: Average tax wedge decomposition

By level of gross earnings expressed as a % of the average wage

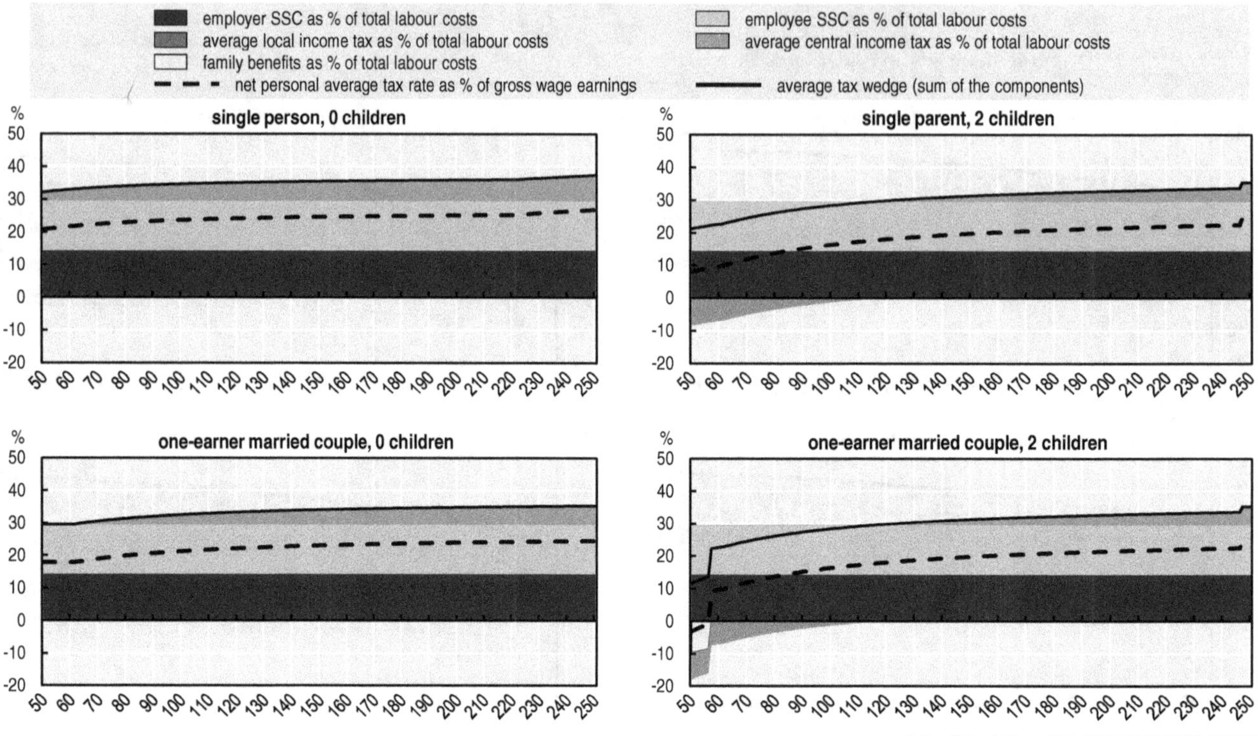

StatLink http://dx.doi.org/10.1787/888933340973

Poland 2015: Marginal tax wedge decomposition

By level of gross earnings expressed as a % of the average wage

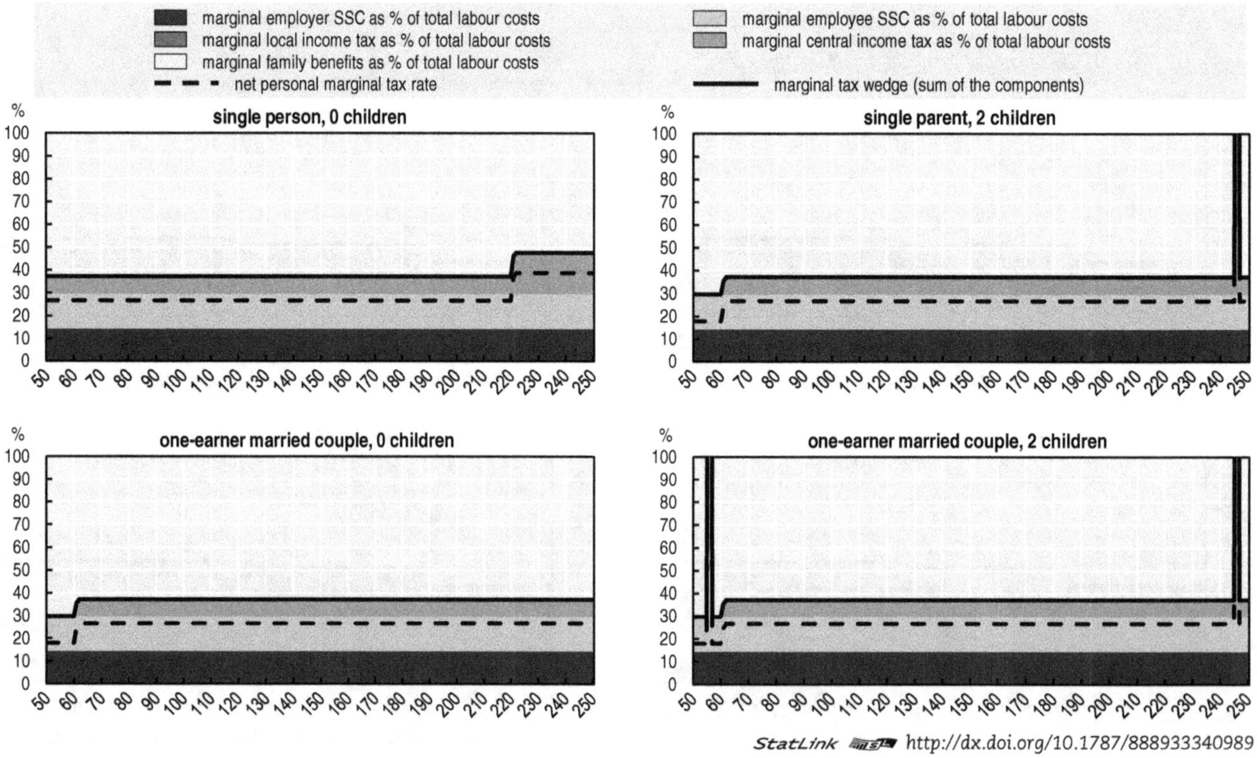

StatLink http://dx.doi.org/10.1787/888933340989

Portugal 2015: Average tax wedge decomposition

By level of gross earnings expressed as a % of the average wage

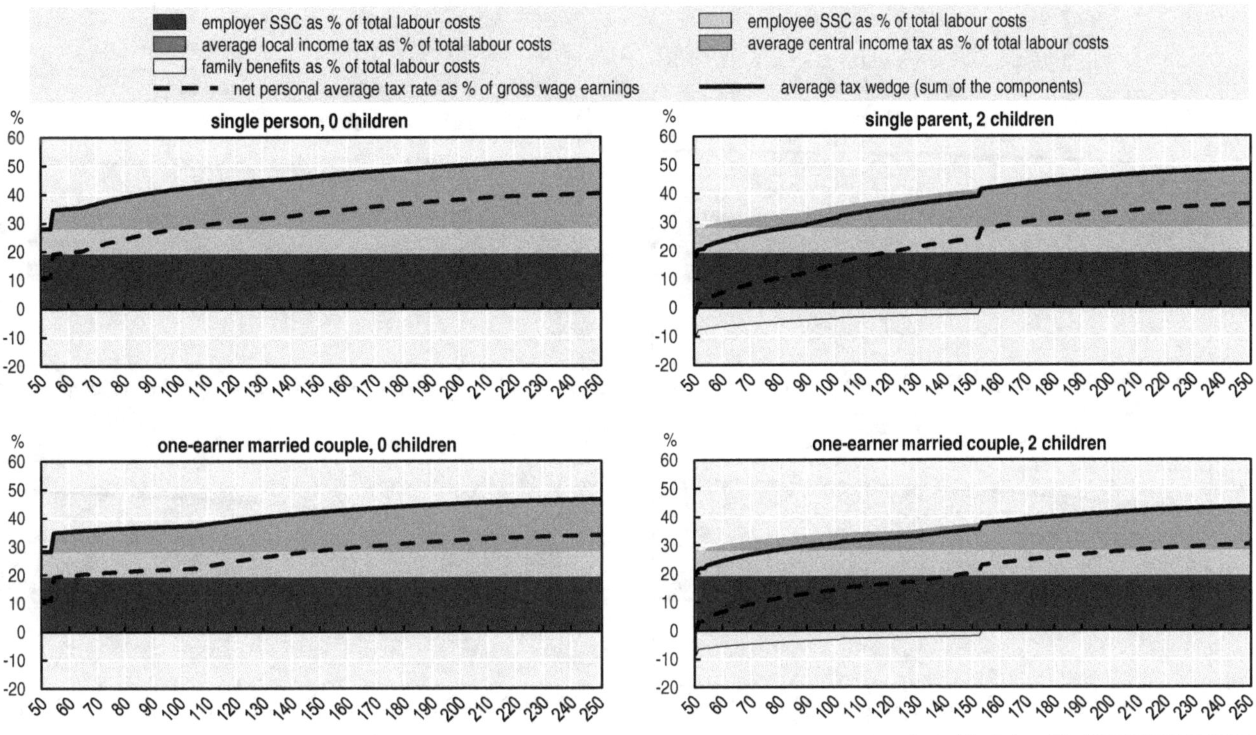

StatLink http://dx.doi.org/10.1787/888933340994

Portugal 2015: Marginal tax wedge decomposition

By level of gross earnings expressed as a % of the average wage

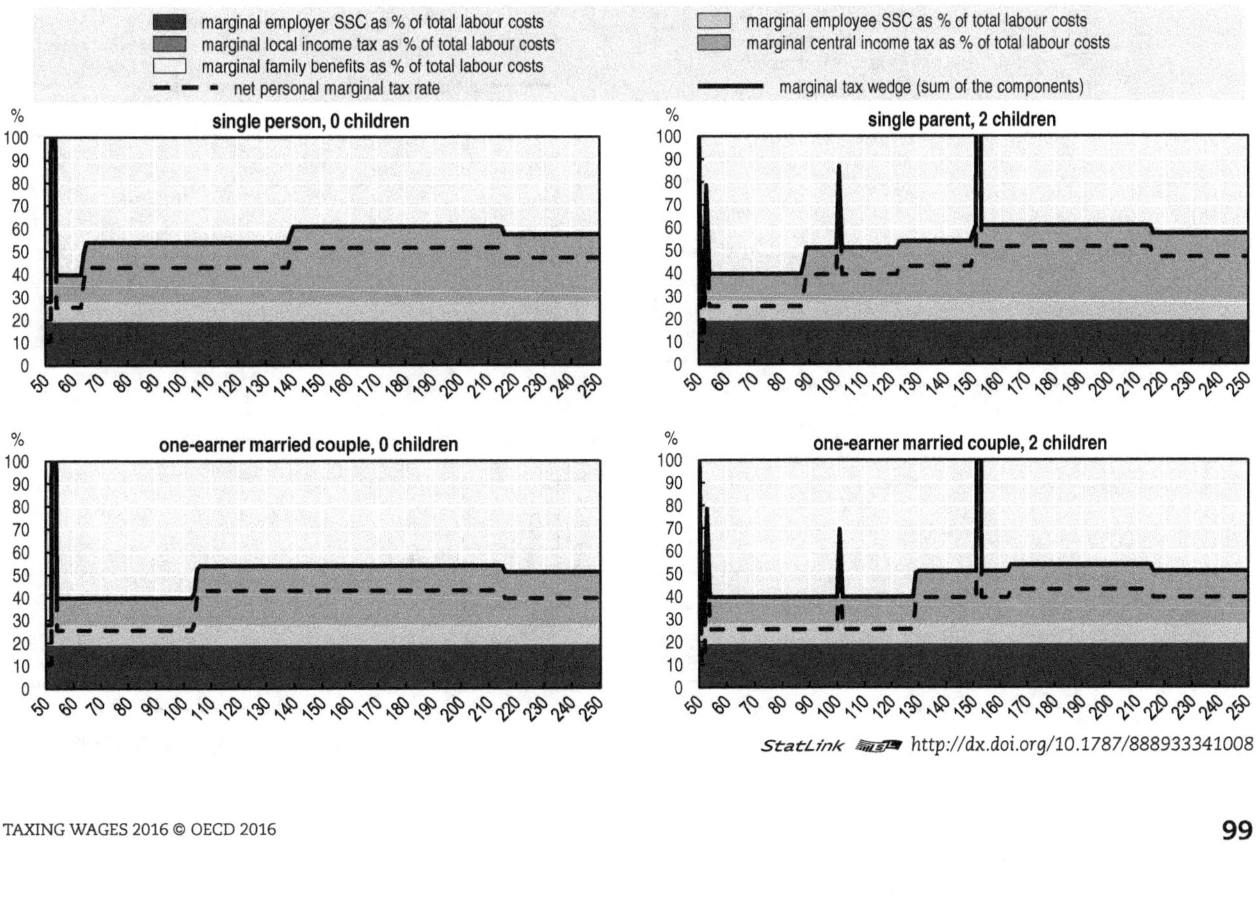

StatLink http://dx.doi.org/10.1787/888933341008

Slovak Republic 2015: Average tax wedge decomposition

By level of gross earnings expressed as a % of the average wage

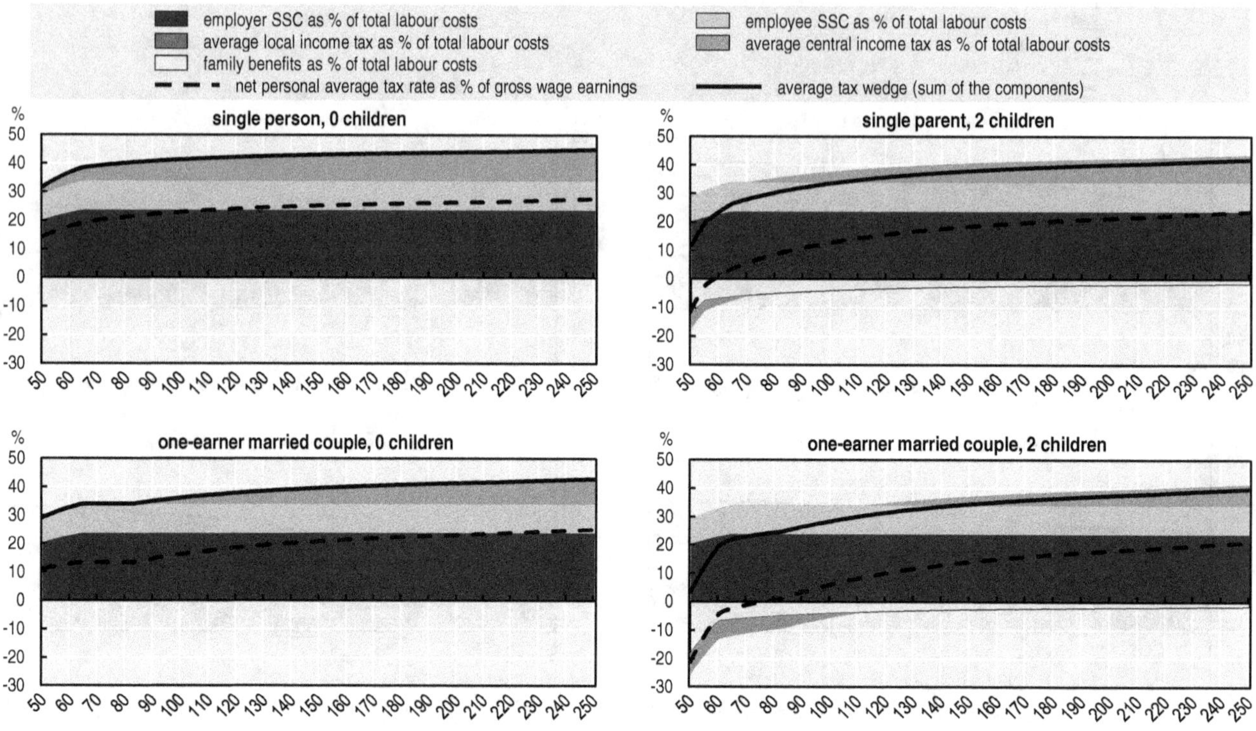

StatLink http://dx.doi.org/10.1787/888933341019

Slovak Republic 2015: Marginal tax wedge decomposition

By level of gross earnings expressed as a % of the average wage

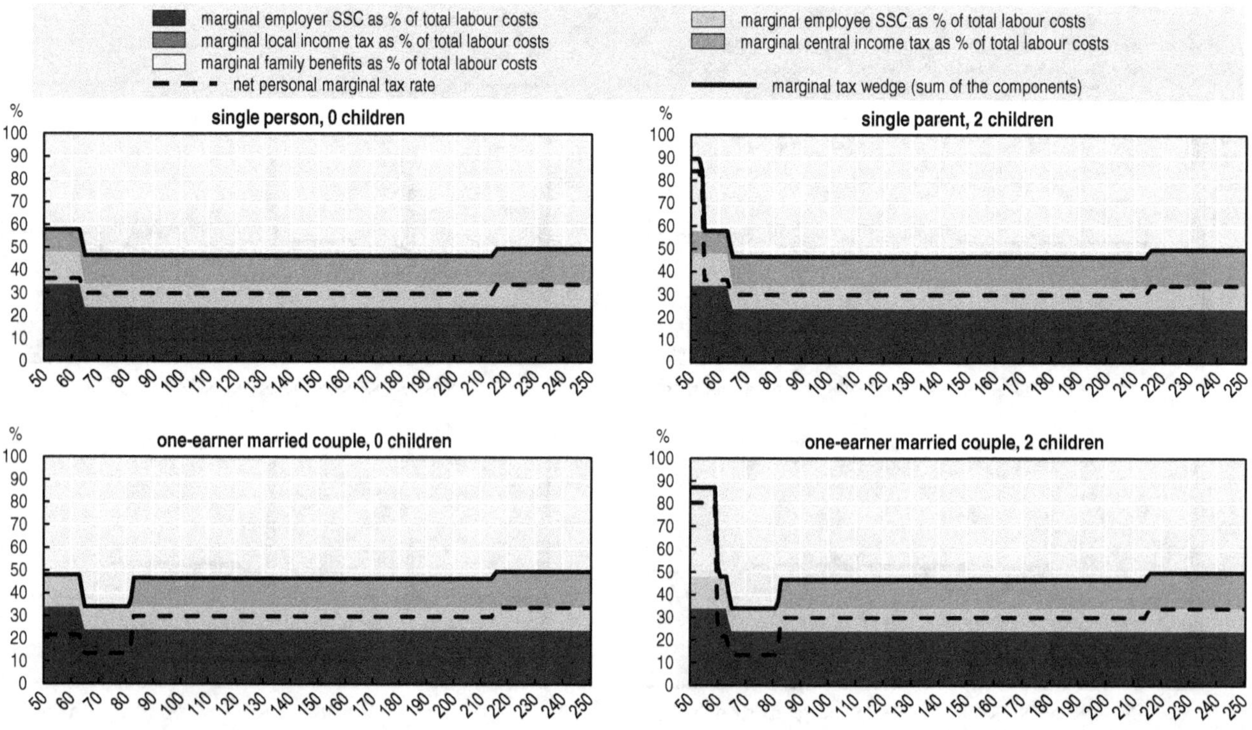

StatLink http://dx.doi.org/10.1787/888933341021

Slovenia 2015: Average tax wedge decomposition

By level of gross earnings expressed as a % of the average wage

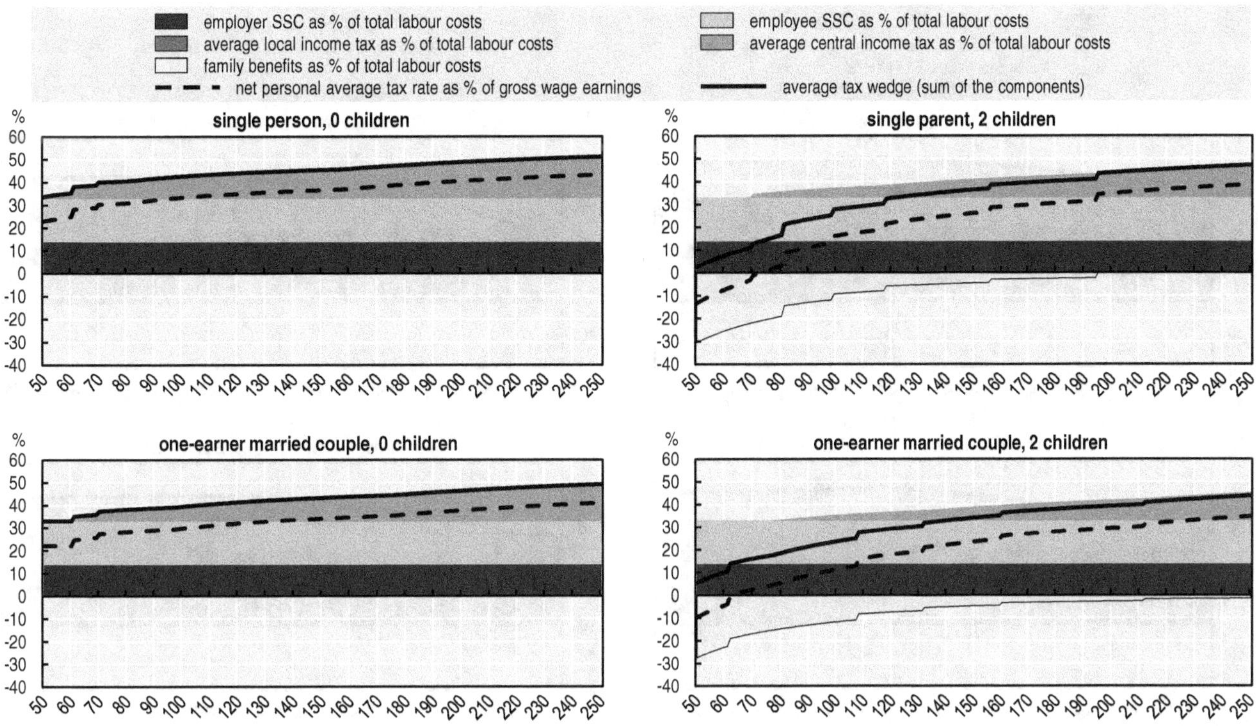

StatLink http://dx.doi.org/10.1787/888933341034

Slovenia 2015: Marginal tax wedge decomposition

By level of gross earnings expressed as a % of the average wage

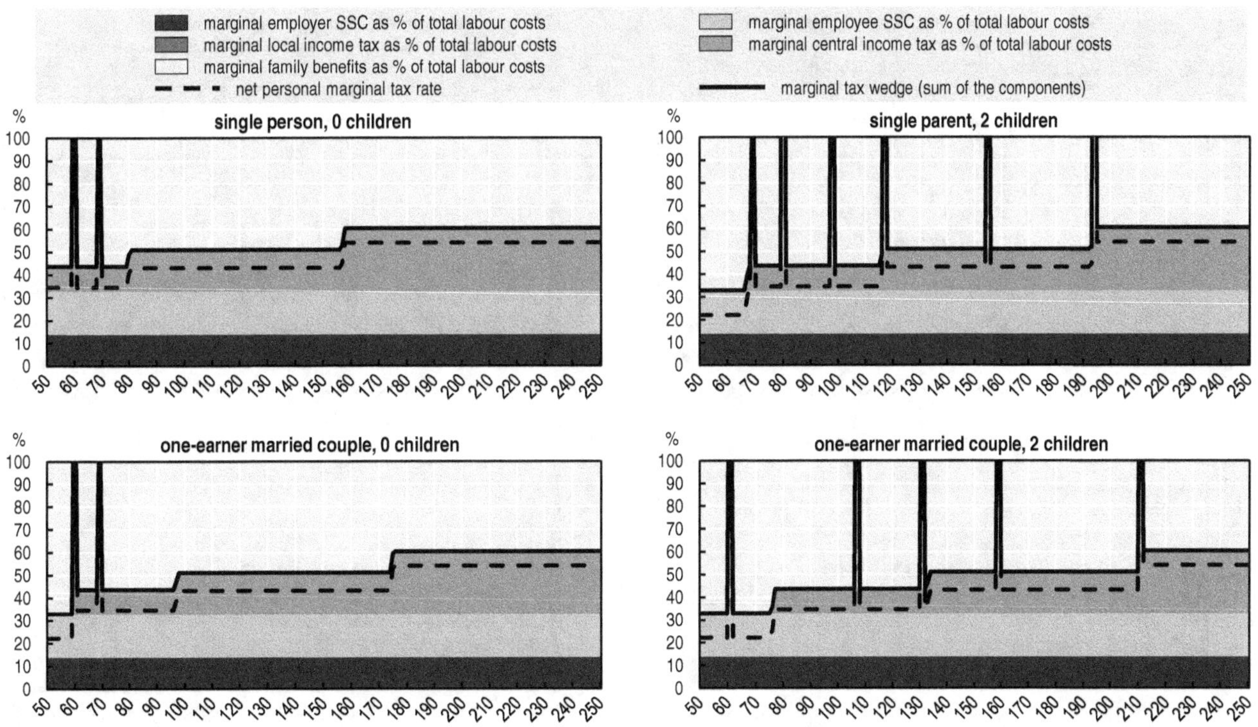

StatLink http://dx.doi.org/10.1787/888933341043

Spain 2015: Average tax wedge decomposition

By level of gross earnings expressed as a % of the average wage

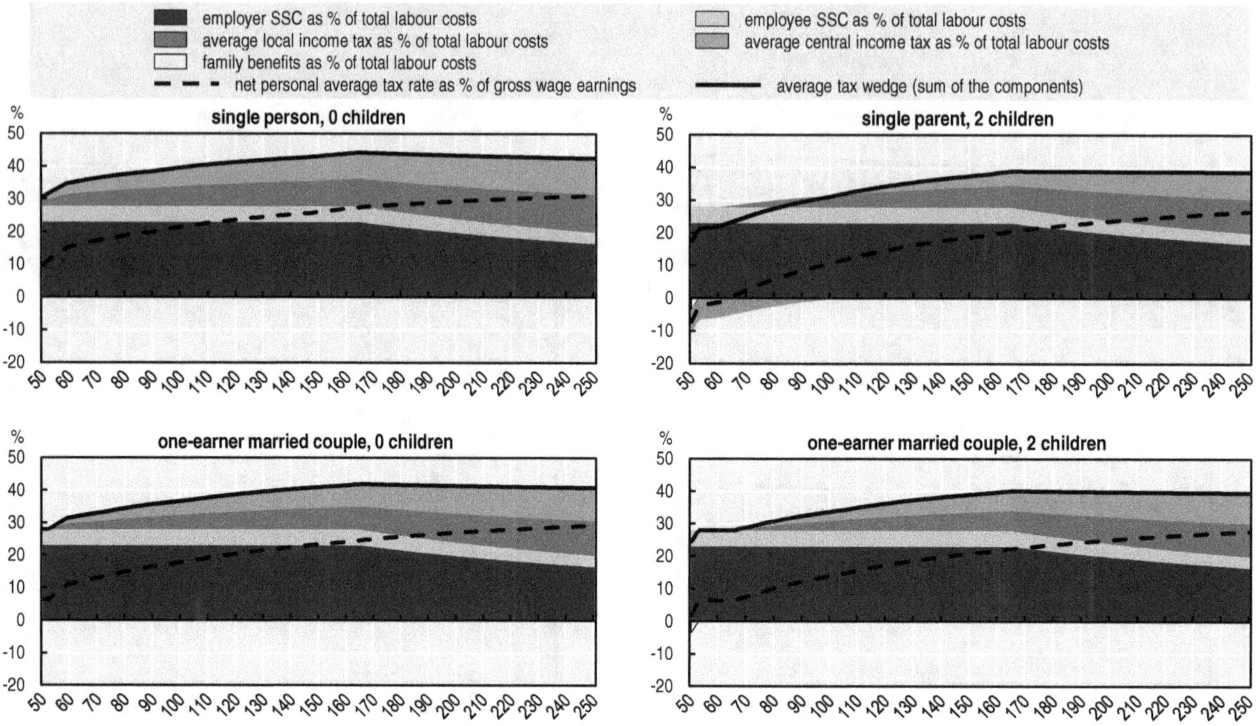

StatLink http://dx.doi.org/10.1787/888933341052

Spain 2015: Marginal tax wedge decomposition

By level of gross earnings expressed as a % of the average wage

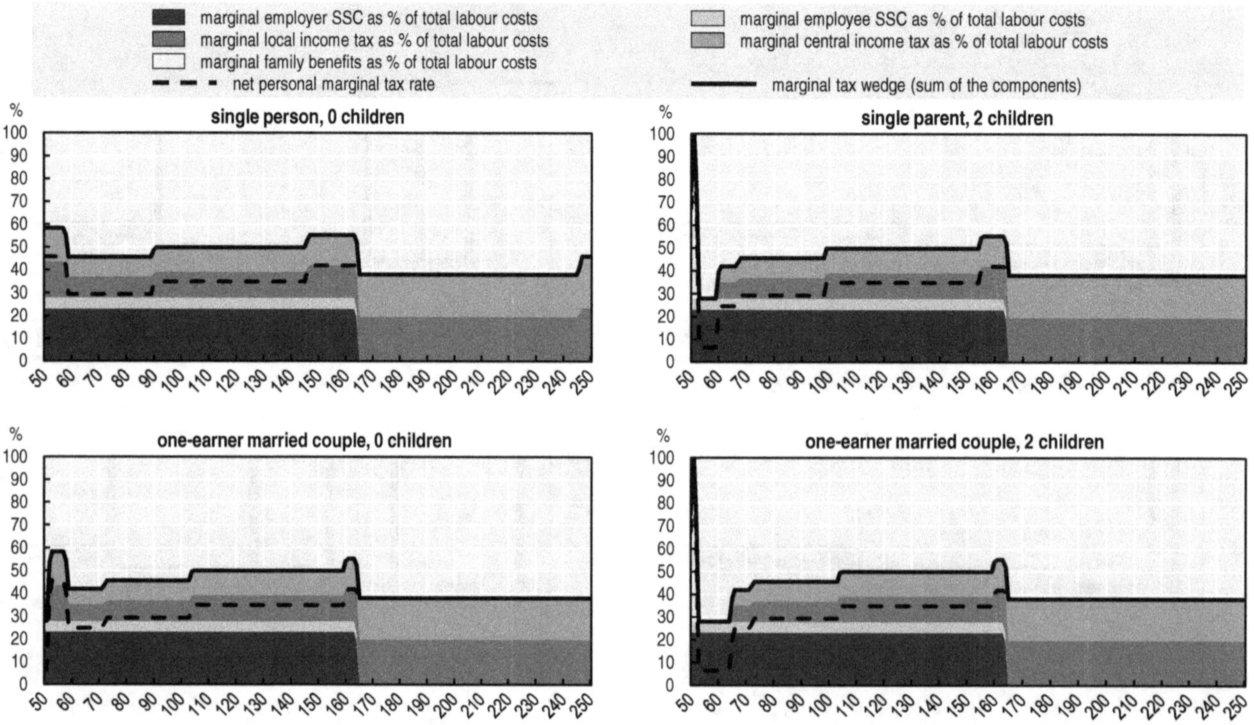

StatLink http://dx.doi.org/10.1787/888933341064

Sweden 2015: Average tax wedge decomposition

By level of gross earnings expressed as a % of the average wage

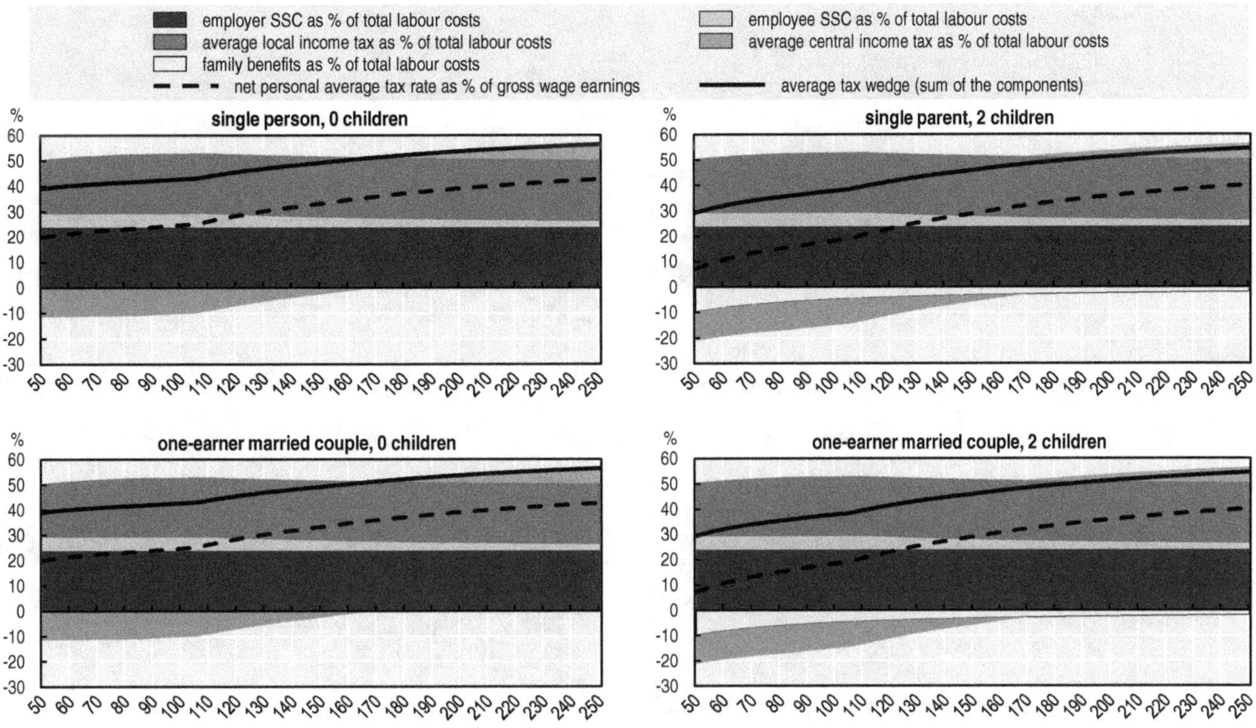

StatLink http://dx.doi.org/10.1787/888933341078

Sweden 2015: Marginal tax wedge decomposition

By level of gross earnings expressed as a % of the average wage

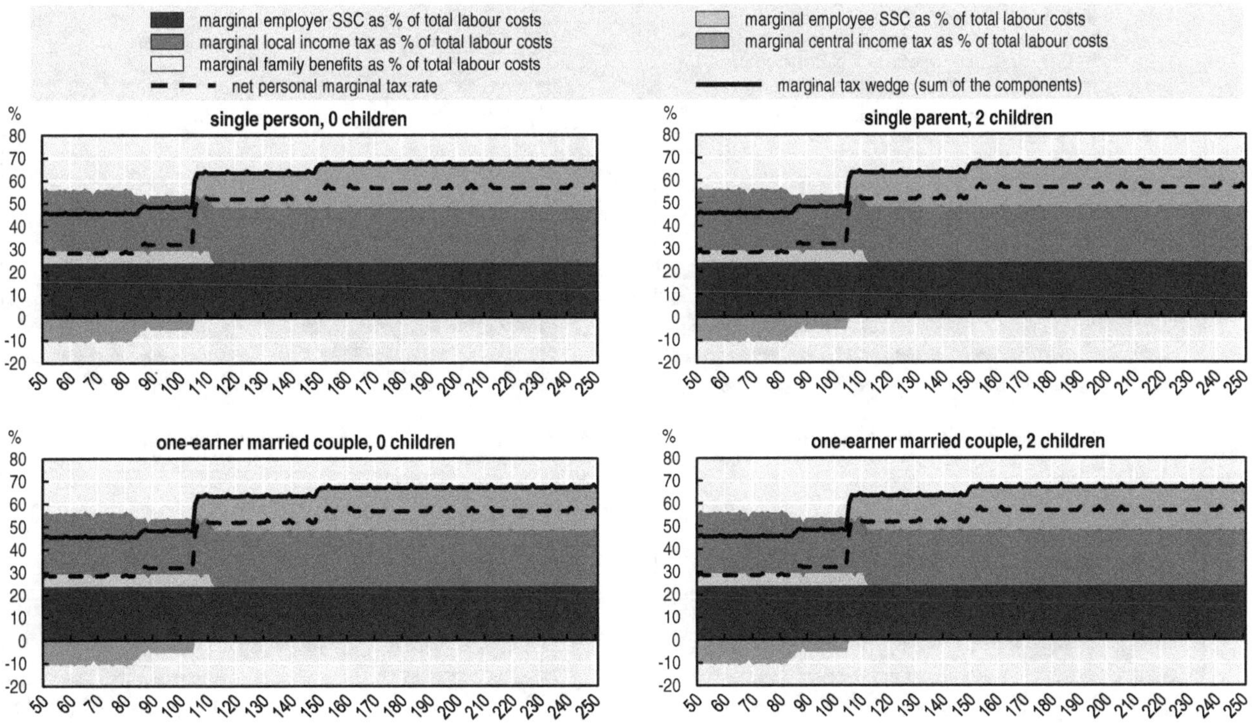

StatLink http://dx.doi.org/10.1787/888933341083

Switzerland 2015: Average tax wedge decomposition

By level of gross earnings expressed as a % of the average wage

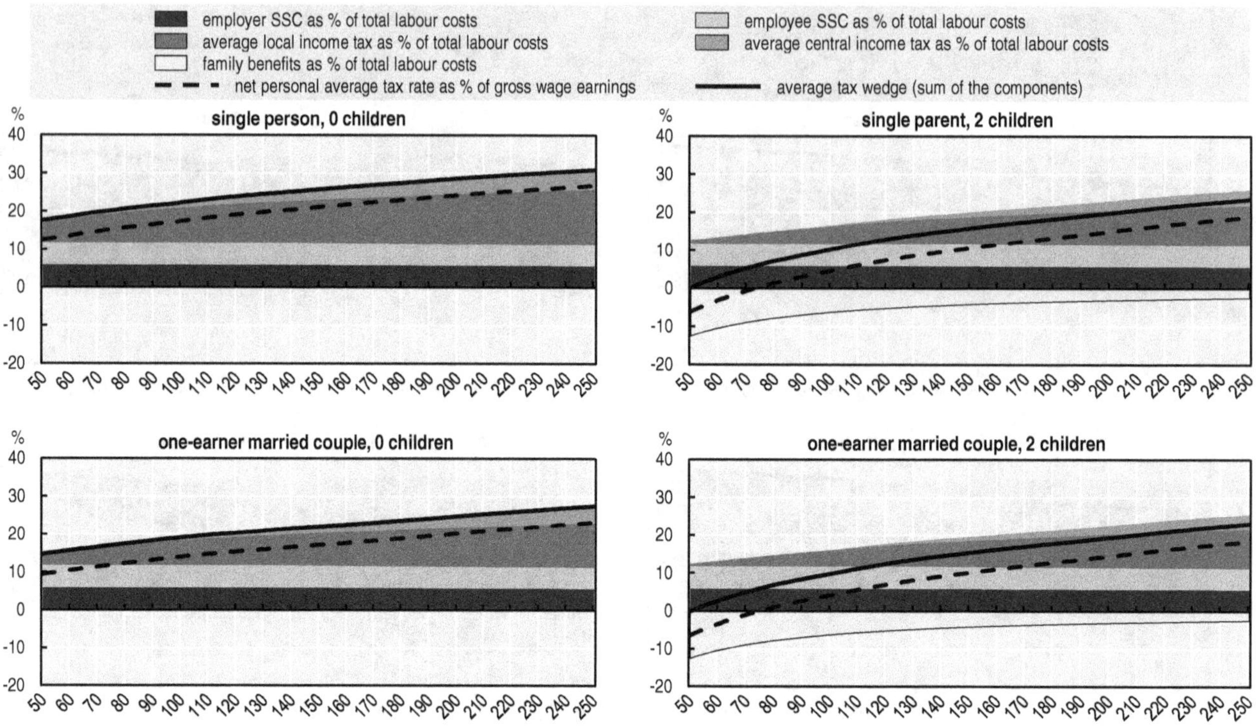

StatLink http://dx.doi.org/10.1787/888933341091

Switzerland 2015: Marginal tax wedge decomposition

By level of gross earnings expressed as a % of the average wage

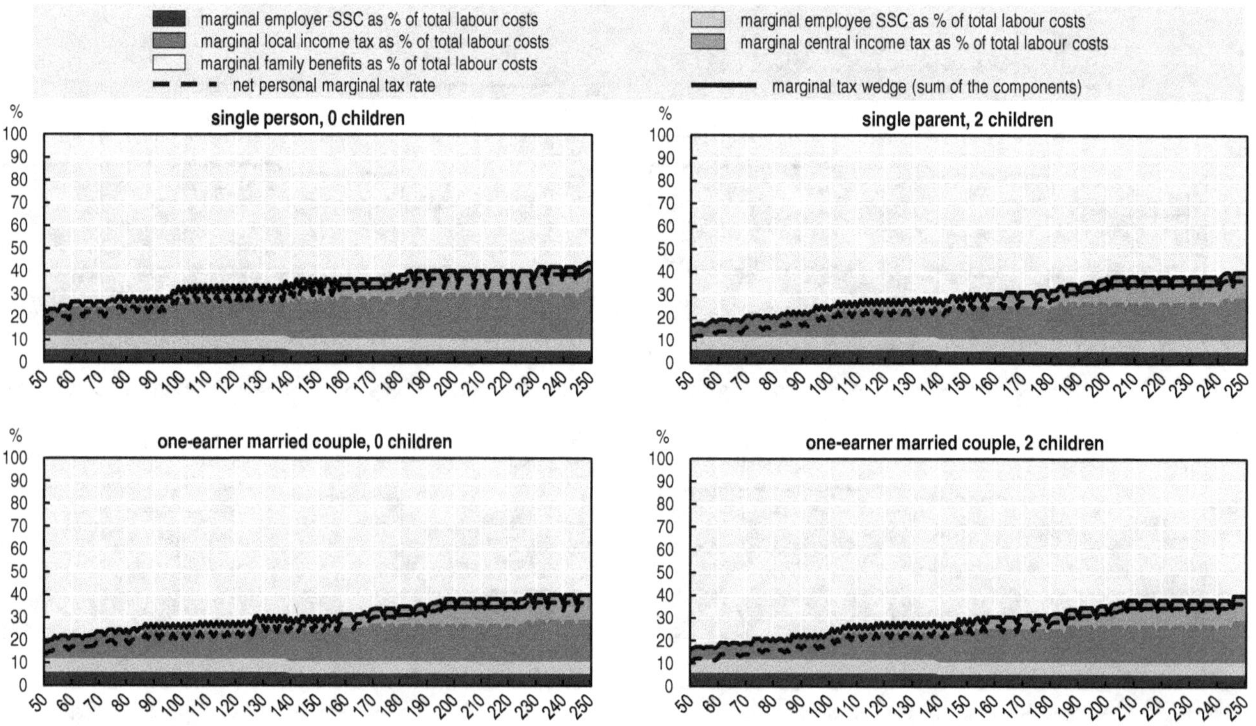

StatLink http://dx.doi.org/10.1787/888933341102

Turkey 2015: Average tax wedge decomposition

By level of gross earnings expressed as a % of the average wage

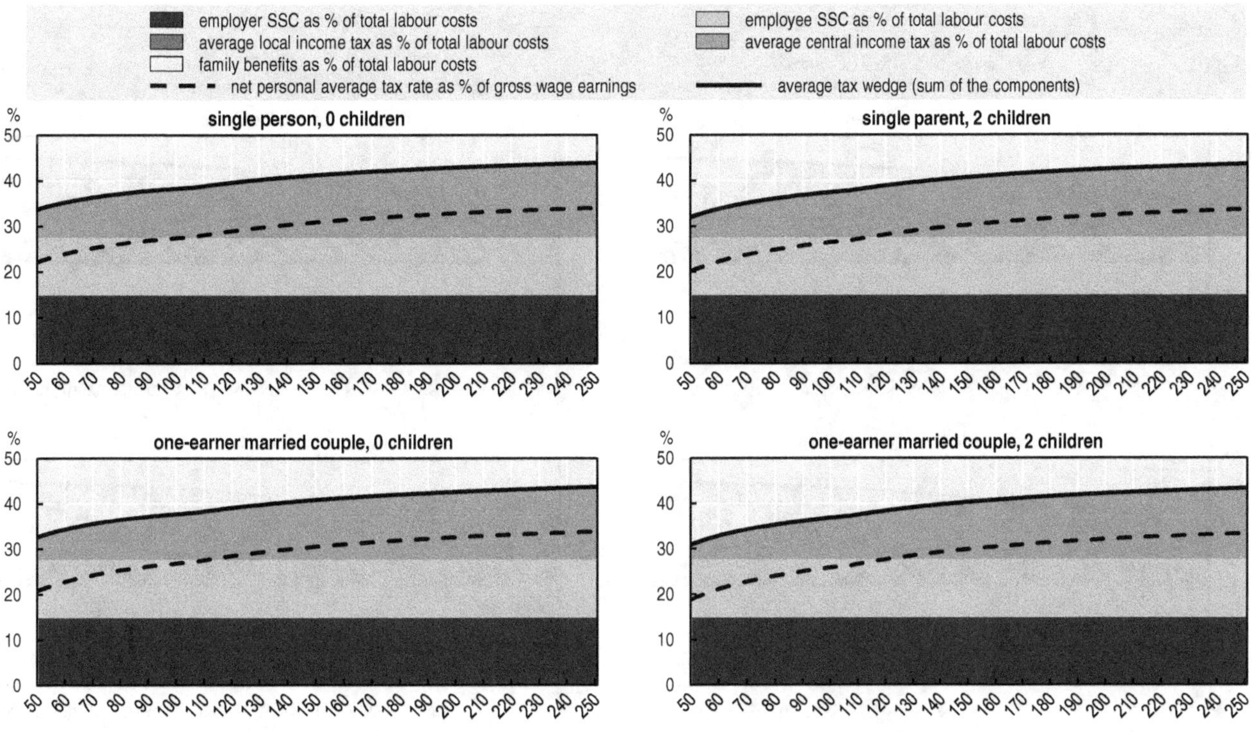

StatLink http://dx.doi.org/10.1787/888933341115

Turkey 2015: Marginal tax wedge decomposition

By level of gross earnings expressed as a % of the average wage

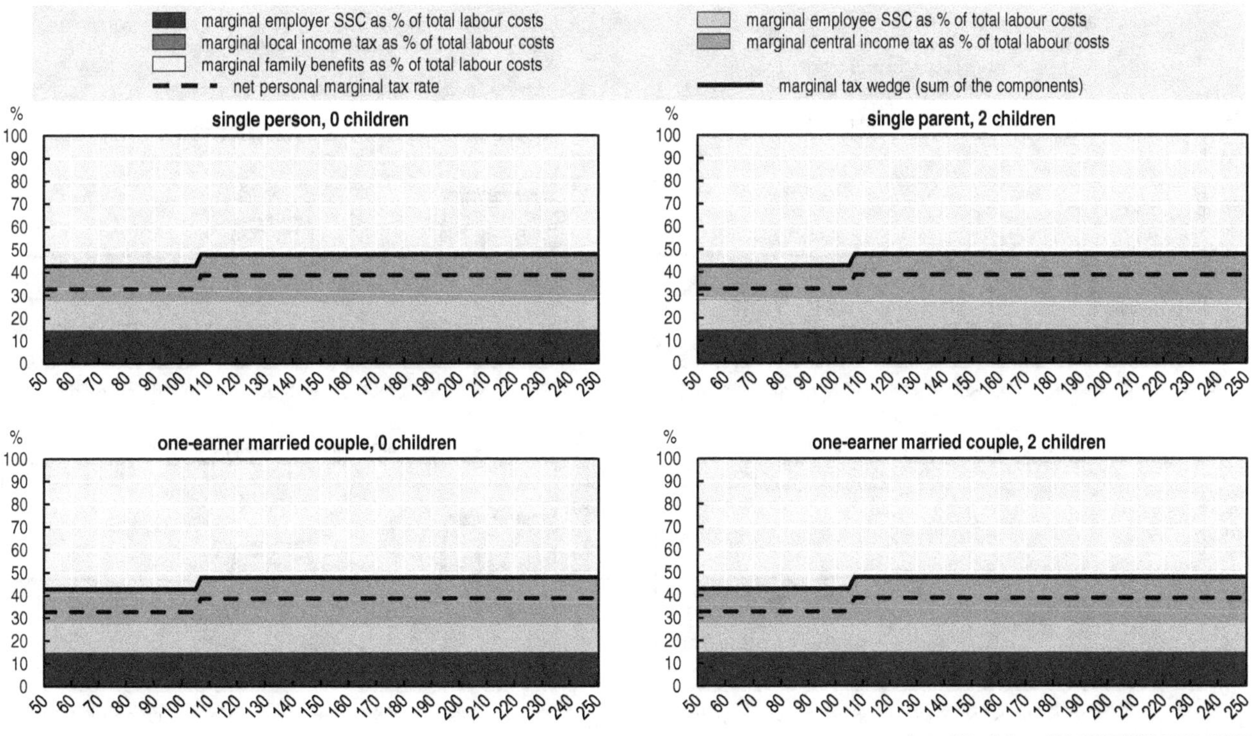

StatLink http://dx.doi.org/10.1787/888933341127

United Kingdom 2015: Average tax wedge decomposition

By level of gross earnings expressed as a % of the average wage

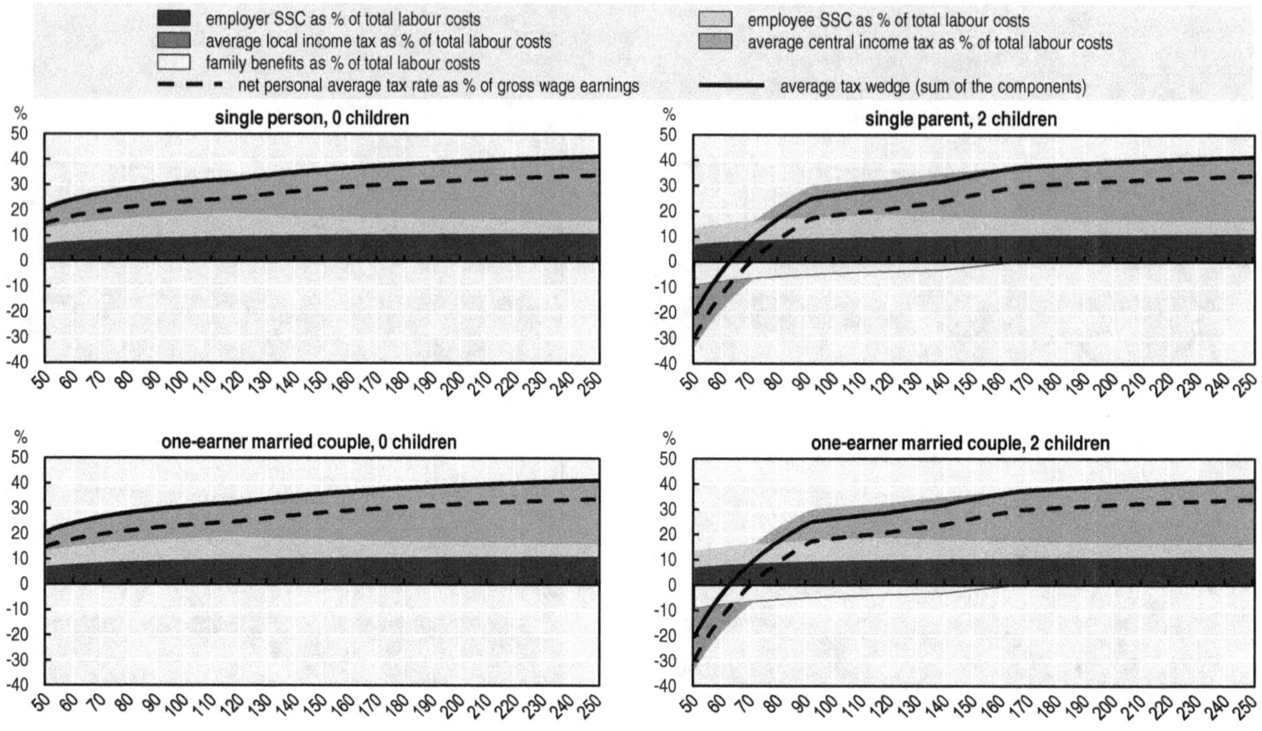

StatLink http://dx.doi.org/10.1787/888933341138

United Kingdom 2015: Marginal tax wedge decomposition

By level of gross earnings expressed as a % of the average wage

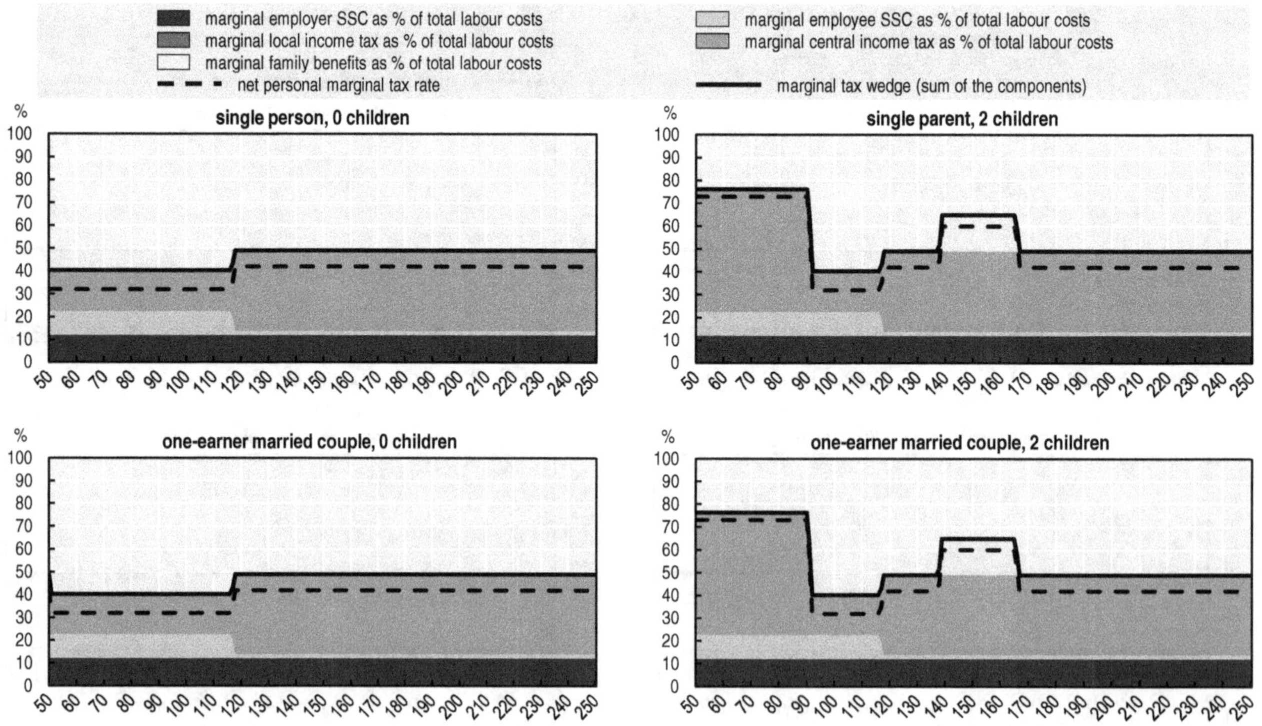

StatLink http://dx.doi.org/10.1787/888933341147

United States 2015: Average tax wedge decomposition

By level of gross earnings expressed as a % of the average wage

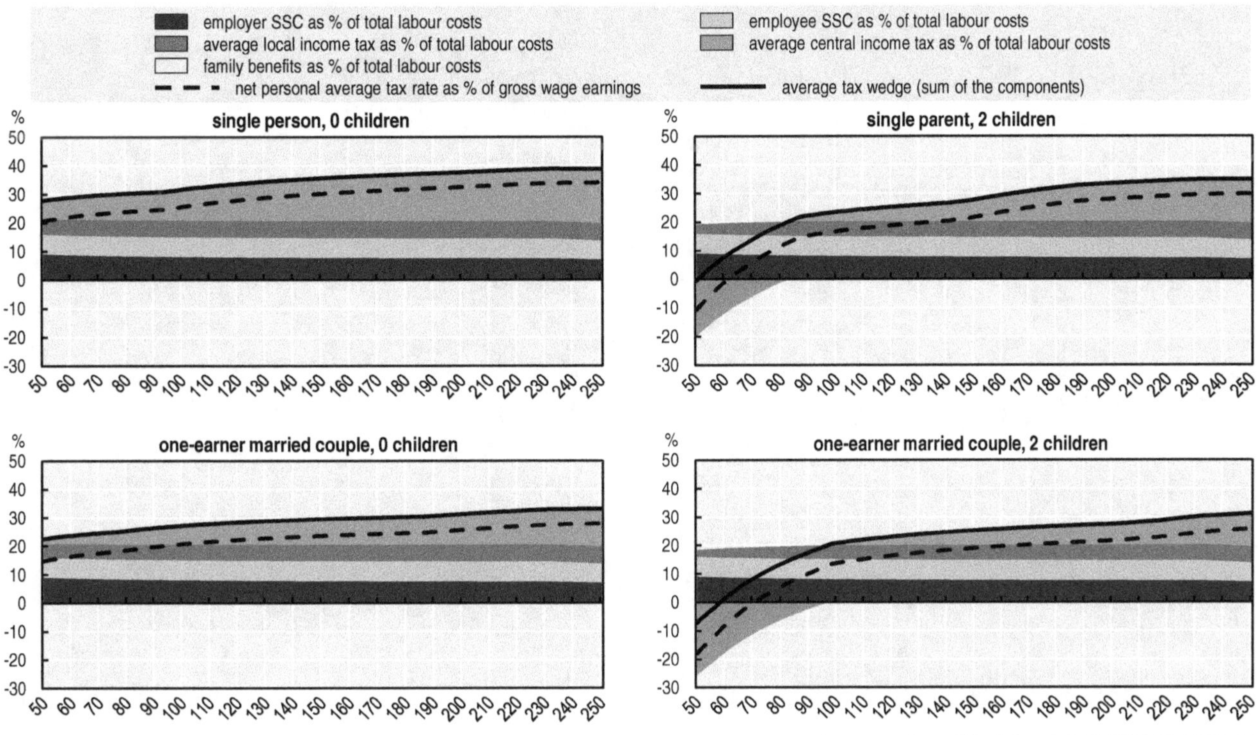

StatLink http://dx.doi.org/10.1787/888933341157

United States 2015: Marginal tax wedge decomposition

By level of gross earnings expressed as a % of the average wage

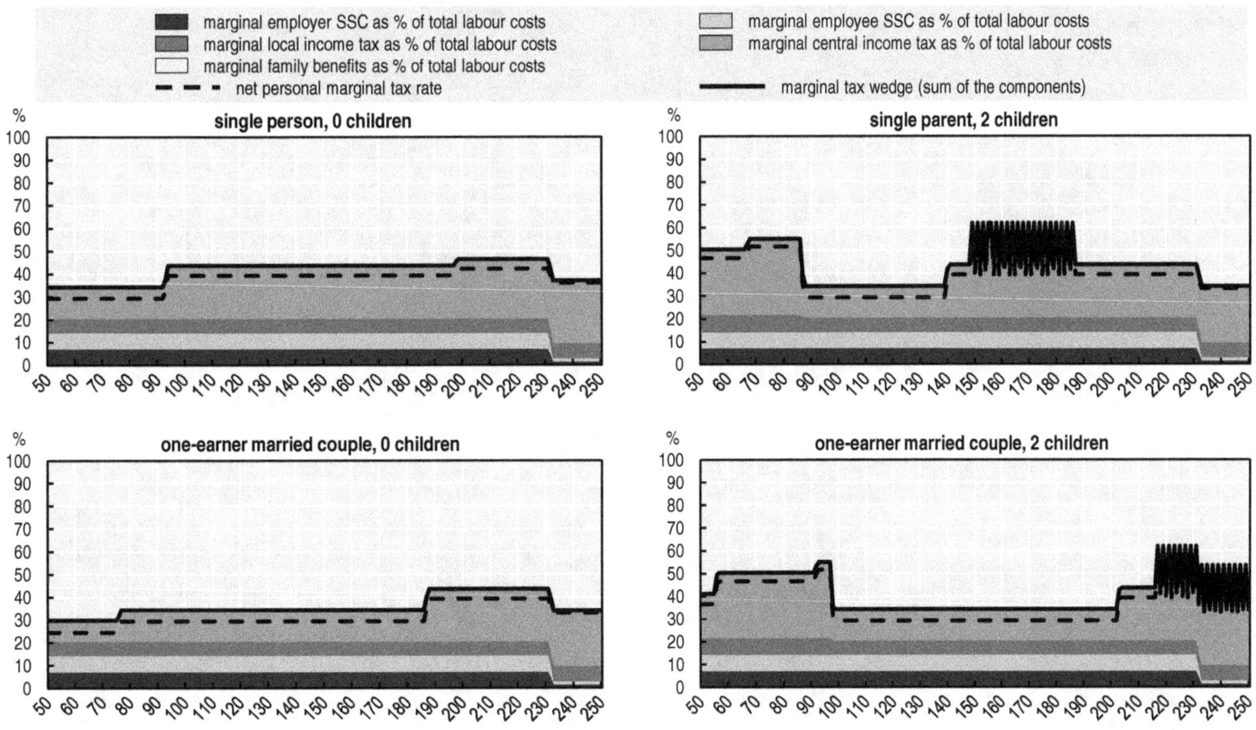

StatLink http://dx.doi.org/10.1787/888933341161

PART I

Chapter 5

2014 tax burdens (and changes to 2015)

The chapter presents the results of tax burden measures on labour income for the eight model family types for 2014. The chapter includes Tables 5.1 to 5.11 that show a number of measures for the average tax burdens (tax wedge, personal tax rate, net personal tax rate, personal income tax rate and employee social security contribution rate) and marginal rates (tax wedge and net personal tax rate). The results for two measures of tax progressivity are also considered: tax elasticity on gross earnings and labour costs.

The table formats are identical to Tables 3.1 to 3.11 that are discussed in Chapter 3 on tax burden results on labour income for 2015. The chapter compares the two sets of tables and analyses the changes in tax burden between 2014 and 2015.

The following commentary on the changes in tax burdens and marginal tax rates between 2014 and 2015 focuses on two of the eight family-types – single employees without children at the average wage level (column 2 of the tables) and one-earner married families with two children at the average wage level (column 5). Comparisons with the columns 1, 3-4 and 6-8 of the tables give corresponding results for the six other family-types. Generally, only those changes exceeding 1 percentage point for average effective rates and 5 percentage points for marginal effective rates are flagged.

Table 5.1 presents the total tax wedge, income tax plus employee and employer's social security contributions less cash benefits by family-type as a percentage of total labour costs (gross wage plus employers' social security contributions [including payroll taxes]). In the majority of countries, changes in the gap between total labour costs and the corresponding net take-home pay in 2015 as compared with 2014 were within plus or minus one percentage point.

Comparing column 2 in Tables 3.1 and 5.1, the OECD average tax wedge remained unchanged for a single average worker between 2014 and 2015. It fell by more than one percentage point in Greece (-1.2 percentage points) and Spain (-1.1 percentage point). There were no increases of more than one percentage point across the OECD member countries.

For one-earner married couples (comparing column 5 of Tables 3.1 and 5.1) the OECD average tax wedge remained also unchanged during this period. The wedge increased by more than one percentage point in two countries: Iceland (1.5 percentage points) and New Zealand (1.1 percentage point) and decreased by more than one percentage point in Estonia (-4.4 percentage points), Greece (-1.3 percentage points) and Spain (-1.1 percentage points).

Table 5.2 shows the combined burden of income tax and employee social security contributions in the form of personal average tax rates as a percentage of gross wage earnings. For single persons on average earnings, this increased by more than one percentage point between 2014 and 2015 in Portugal (1.1 percentage points) and decreased by more than one percentage point in Spain (-1.5 percentage points) and Estonia (-1.2 percentage points). For one-earner married couples with 2 children, it increased by more than one percentage point in Canada (2.2 percentage points), Italy and Portugal (both 1.1 percentage point) and decreased by more than one percentage point in Spain (-1.4 percentage points) and Estonia (-1.1 percentage points).

Table 5.3 provides the combined burden of income tax and employee social security contributions less the amount of cash family benefits (net personal average tax rate). Comparing column 2 of Tables 3.3 and 5.3, for single persons at average earnings, there were changes of more than one percentage point between 2014 and 2015 in Spain (-1.5 percentage points), Estonia (-1.2 percentage points) and Portugal (+1.1 percentage points). Comparing column 5 of Tables 3.3 and 5.3, increases in the net personal average tax rate of one-earner married couples exceeding one percentage point occurred in Iceland

(1.6 percentage points), Italy (1.2 percentage points), New Zealand and Portugal (both 1.1 percentage points). It decreased by more than one percentage point in Estonia (-5.7 percentage points) and Spain (-1.4 percentage points).

Table 5.4 presents information on income tax due as a percentage of gross wage earnings. In most OECD member countries, the income tax for single persons at average earnings changed only slightly between 2014 and 2015 and the OECD average income tax increased by 0.1 percentage point. Comparing column 2 of Tables 3.4 and 5.4, the income tax rate increased by more than one percentage point in the Netherlands (1.4 percentage points) and Portugal (1.1 percentage points) and decreased by more than one percentage point in Spain (-1.5 percentage points). The OECD average income tax rate for the one-earner married couple with two children increased by 0.1 percentage point during this period. The income tax rate increased by more than one percentage point in Canada (2.3 percentage points), in Italy, the Netherlands and Portugal (all three by 1.1 percentage points). It decreased by more than one percentage point only in Spain (-1.5 percentage points).

Table 5.5 shows information on employee social security contributions as a percentage of gross wage earnings. Comparing columns 2 and 5 of Tables 3.5 and 5.5, the only change of more than one percentage point across the OECD member countries between 2014 and 2015 was in the Netherlands (-1.8 percentage points for the single persons on average earnings and -1.5 percentage points for the one-earner married couple with two children). The OECD average remained unchanged for the two family-types during this period.

Table 5.6 shows the marginal tax wedge (rate of income tax plus employee and employer social security contributions and payroll taxes where applicable minus benefits) in 2014. Comparing columns 2 and 5 respectively in Tables 3.6 and 5.6, changes between 2014 and 2015 in the marginal wedge were generally within the range of plus or minus five percentage points. There were changes of more than five percentage points in three OECD countries for the one-earner married couple with two children at the average wage level: the Netherlands (-9.4 percentage points), Poland (+7.6 percentage points) and Australia (+7.1 percentage points). There were no changes of more than five percentage points for single persons on average earnings.

Table 5.7 presents the marginal rate of income tax plus employee social security contributions minus benefits by family-type and wage level. Comparing columns 2 and 5 respectively in Tables 3.7 and 5.7, the pattern of changes between 2014 and 2015 in the marginal rate were similar to that for the tax wedge discussed above. The examples of changes outside the range of plus or minus five percentage points were in the Netherlands (-10.3 percentage points), Poland (+8.9 percentage points), Australia (+7.5 percentage points) and Spain (-5.1 percentage points) for the one-earner couple at the average wage level with two children.

Table 5.8 shows the increase in net income (in per cent) after an increase of one currency unit in gross wage earnings for 2014.[1] Table 5.9 provides the percentage increase in net income given an increase in one currency unit of gross labour costs for the same year.[2] The results shown in these two tables are directly dependent upon the marginal and average tax rates that have been discussed in the paragraphs above. Tables 5.10 and 5.11 report background information on levels of labour costs plus gross and net wages in 2014.

Notes

1. The reported elasticities in Table 5.8 are calculated as (100-METR)/(100-AETR), where METR is the marginal rate of income tax plus employee social security contributions less cash benefits reported in Table 5.7 and AETR is the average rate plus employee social security contributions less cash benefits reported in Table 5.3.
2. The reported elasticities in Table 5.9 are calculated as (100-METR)/(100-AETR), where METR is the marginal rate of income tax plus employee and employer social security contributions less cash benefits reported in Table 5.6 and AETR is the average rate plus employee and employer social security contributions less cash benefits reported in Table 5.1.

Table 5.1. **Income tax plus employee and employer contributions less cash benefits, 2014**

As % of labour costs, by family-type and wage level

	Single no ch 67 (% AW)	Single no ch 100 (% AW)	Single no ch 167 (% AW)	Single 2 ch 67 (% AW)	Married 2 ch 100-0 (% AW)	Married 2 ch 100-33 (% AW)[2]	Married 2 ch 100-67 (% AW)[2]	Married no ch 100-33 (% AW)[2]
Australia	22.4	27.7	33.4	-1.8	17.4	20.9	25.5	23.5
Austria	44.9	49.4	52.0	29.2	38.9	38.5	42.0	45.5
Belgium	49.9	55.6	60.8	36.1	40.6	41.7	48.4	48.1
Canada	26.5	31.6	33.3	-4.7	19.3	24.2	27.3	28.4
Chile	7.0	7.0	7.9	6.1	7.0	4.7	6.6	7.0
Czech Republic	39.6	42.6	45.0	24.7	26.6	32.8	35.4	40.3
Denmark	34.1	36.2	42.3	7.2	25.6	29.5	31.6	34.3
Estonia	38.9	40.0	40.9	27.4	32.9	35.2	36.6	38.9
Finland	38.2	43.7	49.5	27.5	38.7	36.2	38.5	40.0
France	45.1	48.4	54.3	36.7	40.5	37.5	43.6	44.4
Germany	45.1	49.3	51.4	31.2	33.7	38.5	42.1	45.0
Greece	35.8	40.5	48.3	32.1	39.4	38.7	39.3	39.6
Hungary	49.0	49.0	49.0	26.4	34.8	38.3	40.5	49.0
Iceland	29.3	33.7	38.1	18.1	20.9	27.7	31.6	29.5
Ireland	22.0	27.9	39.5	-19.6	9.7	14.6	20.2	20.9
Israel[1]	14.2	21.1	30.0	2.9	18.7	15.8	15.1	17.6
Italy	42.3	48.2	53.8	26.7	38.9	39.5	42.3	43.9
Japan	30.6	32.0	34.7	24.3	26.5	28.0	28.9	31.1
Korea	18.5	21.7	23.5	16.9	19.4	19.2	19.3	20.5
Luxembourg	30.5	37.6	44.6	6.1	15.2	19.6	25.3	28.8
Mexico	14.7	19.5	22.6	14.7	19.5	17.3	17.6	17.3
Netherlands	31.4	36.8	41.9	11.0	31.0	28.2	30.2	32.8
New Zealand	13.4	17.2	23.1	-15.8	3.8	11.1	16.3	16.0
Norway	33.8	36.9	42.5	22.0	32.0	31.3	33.4	34.1
Poland	33.3	34.6	35.6	29.6	29.6	30.0	31.5	33.3
Portugal	34.9	41.2	47.5	25.1	29.8	30.9	36.8	34.8
Slovak Republic	38.6	41.3	43.4	26.9	28.1	33.4	35.5	39.3
Slovenia	38.6	42.5	46.4	9.9	23.5	30.7	34.5	40.1
Spain	37.3	40.7	45.0	30.6	34.9	36.5	37.6	37.5
Sweden	40.5	42.5	50.6	33.0	37.4	36.9	38.7	40.7
Switzerland	19.4	22.2	26.7	4.6	9.7	12.8	16.0	19.9
Turkey	35.8	38.1	41.5	34.4	36.6	35.4	36.6	36.1
United Kingdom	26.2	31.0	37.3	4.7	26.4	22.6	26.3	26.1
United States	29.5	31.6	36.4	12.0	20.6	24.6	26.6	29.5
Unweighted average								
OECD-Average	**32.1**	**35.9**	**40.4**	**17.5**	**26.7**	**28.3**	**31.1**	**32.8**
OECD-EU 21	**37.9**	**41.9**	**46.6**	**22.0**	**31.2**	**32.9**	**36.0**	**38.2**

Note: ch = children

Disclaimer: *http://oe.cd/disclaimer*

1. Information on data for Israel: *http://oe.cd/israel-disclaimer*.
2. Two-earner family.

StatLink http://dx.doi.org/10.1787/888933341408

Table 5.2. **Income tax plus employee contributions, 2014**

As % of gross wage earnings, by family-type and wage level

	Single no ch 67 (% AW)	Single no ch 100 (% AW)	Single no ch 167 (% AW)	Single 2 ch 67 (% AW)	Married 2 ch 100-0 (% AW)	Married 2 ch 100-33 (% AW)[2]	Married 2 ch 100-67 (% AW)[2]	Married no ch 100-33 (% AW)[2]
Australia	17.7	23.4	29.4	17.7	23.4	19.0	21.1	19.0
Austria	28.8	34.7	39.2	25.9	32.7	29.3	32.0	29.6
Belgium	35.9	42.4	49.2	30.4	31.1	32.7	38.3	34.6
Canada	19.0	23.4	27.1	8.7	16.5	18.3	20.3	19.9
Chile	7.0	7.0	7.9	7.0	7.0	7.0	7.0	7.0
Czech Republic	19.1	23.1	26.3	6.1	6.3	13.5	16.3	20.1
Denmark	33.6	35.9	41.9	32.0	32.0	33.8	35.0	33.8
Estonia	18.2	19.6	20.8	13.8	13.8	15.9	17.3	18.2
Finland	23.9	30.7	37.9	23.9	30.7	26.1	28.0	26.1
France	26.7	28.6	34.2	21.6	21.9	20.7	25.6	26.6
Germany	34.5	39.5	43.8	17.9	21.0	26.6	31.0	34.4
Greece	19.2	25.1	34.9	19.2	26.4	23.8	24.4	23.8
Hungary	34.5	34.5	34.5	22.8	26.6	28.6	29.8	34.5
Iceland	23.9	28.6	33.4	23.9	19.9	24.2	26.7	24.2
Ireland	13.6	20.2	33.0	8.0	12.2	12.8	17.1	12.8
Israel[1]	10.5	17.0	26.0	5.8	17.0	13.7	12.5	13.7
Italy	23.8	31.6	39.0	16.1	24.6	22.4	25.5	25.9
Japan	20.2	21.8	25.6	20.2	20.4	20.9	21.2	20.9
Korea	10.1	13.6	16.6	8.3	11.1	10.8	11.0	12.3
Luxembourg	22.0	30.0	37.9	15.1	18.5	20.0	24.3	20.0
Mexico	3.0	10.1	14.8	3.0	10.1	5.7	7.3	5.7
Netherlands	24.7	30.5	38.1	11.5	27.9	24.1	25.6	26.3
New Zealand	13.4	17.2	23.1	14.8	17.2	16.0	16.3	16.0
Norway	25.2	28.7	35.0	21.6	27.5	25.6	27.3	25.6
Poland	22.1	23.6	24.8	17.8	17.8	18.3	20.0	22.1
Portugal	19.5	27.2	35.0	14.6	17.2	17.2	21.8	19.3
Slovak Republic	19.5	22.9	25.7	12.1	11.1	16.7	18.6	20.4
Slovenia	28.7	33.2	37.7	22.1	24.9	25.8	27.7	30.5
Spain	18.5	23.0	28.7	9.8	15.4	17.5	19.0	18.9
Sweden	21.8	24.4	35.1	21.8	24.4	22.1	23.4	22.1
Switzerland	14.4	17.3	22.2	8.6	10.8	12.4	14.7	14.9
Turkey	24.5	27.3	31.3	23.0	25.5	24.1	25.5	24.9
United Kingdom	19.5	23.6	29.8	3.5	23.6	19.4	21.9	19.4
United States	22.9	25.6	31.1	3.7	13.6	17.5	19.9	22.8
Unweighted average								
OECD-Average	**21.2**	**25.5**	**30.9**	**15.7**	**20.0**	**20.1**	**22.2**	**21.9**
OECD-EU 21	**24.2**	**28.8**	**34.6**	**17.4**	**21.9**	**22.3**	**24.9**	**24.7**

Note: ch = children

Disclaimer: *http://oe.cd/disclaimer*

1. Information on data for Israel: *http://oe.cd/israel-disclaimer.*
2. Two-earner family.

StatLink http://dx.doi.org/10.1787/888933341416

Table 5.3. **Income tax plus employee contributions less cash benefits, 2014**

As % of gross wage earnings, by family-type and wage level

	Single no ch 67 (% AW)	Single no ch 100 (% AW)	Single no ch 167 (% AW)	Single 2 ch 67 (% AW)	Married 2 ch 100-0 (% AW)	Married 2 ch 100-33 (% AW)[2]	Married 2 ch 100-67 (% AW)[2]	Married no ch 100-33 (% AW)[2]
Australia	17.7	23.4	29.4	-7.9	12.4	16.1	21.1	19.0
Austria	28.8	34.7	39.2	8.6	21.1	20.6	25.1	29.6
Belgium	35.9	42.4	49.2	18.3	22.9	26.6	33.5	34.6
Canada	17.8	23.4	27.1	-17.2	9.6	15.2	18.6	19.9
Chile	7.0	7.0	7.9	6.1	7.0	4.7	6.6	7.0
Czech Republic	19.1	23.1	26.3	-1.0	1.6	10.0	13.4	20.1
Denmark	33.1	35.6	41.9	5.8	24.8	28.5	30.8	33.3
Estonia	18.2	19.6	20.8	2.7	10.0	13.1	15.1	18.2
Finland	23.9	30.7	37.9	10.7	24.6	21.5	24.3	26.1
France	26.7	28.6	34.2	15.4	17.8	17.6	23.1	26.6
Germany	34.5	39.5	43.8	17.9	21.0	26.6	31.0	34.4
Greece	19.2	25.1	34.9	14.5	23.6	22.8	23.6	23.8
Hungary	34.5	34.5	34.5	5.4	16.2	20.7	23.5	34.5
Iceland	23.9	28.6	33.4	11.9	14.9	22.2	26.4	24.2
Ireland	13.6	20.2	33.0	-32.4	-0.0	5.9	11.6	12.8
Israel[1]	10.5	17.0	26.0	-1.3	14.5	11.8	11.0	13.7
Italy	23.8	31.6	39.0	3.2	19.4	20.1	23.8	25.9
Japan	20.2	21.8	25.6	13.0	15.6	17.3	18.3	20.9
Korea	10.1	13.6	16.6	8.3	11.1	10.8	11.0	12.3
Luxembourg	22.0	30.0	37.9	-5.4	4.8	9.7	16.1	20.0
Mexico	3.0	10.1	14.8	3.0	10.1	5.7	7.3	5.7
Netherlands	24.7	30.5	38.1	2.4	24.1	21.2	23.4	26.3
New Zealand	13.4	17.2	23.1	-15.8	3.8	11.1	16.3	16.0
Norway	25.2	28.7	35.0	11.9	23.2	22.3	24.7	25.6
Poland	22.1	23.6	24.8	17.8	17.8	18.3	20.0	22.1
Portugal	19.5	27.2	35.0	7.4	13.1	14.5	21.8	19.3
Slovak Republic	19.5	22.9	25.7	4.1	5.6	12.6	15.4	20.4
Slovenia	28.7	33.2	37.7	-4.6	11.2	19.5	24.0	30.5
Spain	18.5	23.0	28.7	9.8	15.4	17.5	19.0	18.9
Sweden	21.8	24.4	35.1	11.9	17.8	17.1	19.4	22.1
Switzerland	14.4	17.3	22.2	-1.4	4.1	7.3	10.7	14.9
Turkey	24.5	27.3	31.3	23.0	25.5	24.1	25.5	24.9
United Kingdom	19.5	23.6	29.8	-4.0	18.6	15.6	18.9	19.4
United States	22.9	25.6	31.1	3.7	13.6	17.5	19.9	22.8
Unweighted average								
OECD-Average	**21.1**	**25.4**	**30.9**	**4.3**	**14.6**	**16.7**	**19.8**	**21.9**
OECD-EU 21	**24.2**	**28.8**	**34.6**	**5.2**	**15.8**	**18.1**	**21.7**	**24.7**

Note: ch = children

Disclaimer: *http://oe.cd/disclaimer*

1. Information on data for Israel: *http://oe.cd/israel-disclaimer*.
2. Two-earner family.

StatLink http://dx.doi.org/10.1787/888933341427

Table 5.4. **Income tax, 2014**

As % of gross wage earnings, by family-type and wage level

	Single no ch 67 (% AW)	Single no ch 100 (% AW)	Single no ch 167 (% AW)	Single 2 ch 67 (% AW)	Married 2 ch 100-0 (% AW)	Married 2 ch 100-33 (% AW)[2]	Married 2 ch 100-67 (% AW)[2]	Married no ch 100-33 (% AW)[2]
Australia	17.7	23.4	29.4	17.7	23.4	19.0	21.1	19.0
Austria	10.7	16.6	23.2	7.8	14.6	12.0	14.0	12.3
Belgium	22.0	28.4	35.2	16.5	17.1	21.9	24.3	23.8
Canada	11.8	15.7	22.2	1.5	8.8	11.1	12.8	12.8
Chile	0.0	0.0	0.9	0.0	0.0	0.0	0.0	0.0
Czech Republic	8.1	12.1	15.3	-4.9	-4.7	2.5	5.3	9.1
Denmark	33.6	35.9	41.9	32.0	32.0	33.8	35.0	33.8
Estonia	16.2	17.6	18.8	11.8	11.8	13.9	15.3	16.2
Finland	16.0	22.7	29.8	16.0	22.7	18.3	20.0	18.3
France	12.6	14.6	20.8	7.6	7.9	6.7	11.5	12.6
Germany	14.1	19.0	27.5	-2.2	0.8	6.4	10.8	14.0
Greece	3.2	9.1	18.9	3.2	10.4	7.8	8.4	7.8
Hungary	16.0	16.0	16.0	4.3	8.1	10.1	11.3	16.0
Iceland	23.3	28.2	33.2	23.3	19.5	23.6	26.3	23.6
Ireland	9.6	16.2	29.0	4.0	8.2	9.8	13.1	9.8
Israel[1]	4.7	9.1	16.4	0.0	9.1	6.9	5.5	6.9
Italy	14.4	22.1	29.4	6.6	15.1	12.9	16.0	16.4
Japan	6.1	7.7	12.4	6.1	6.3	6.8	7.1	6.8
Korea	1.7	5.3	9.6	0.0	2.7	2.5	2.6	4.0
Luxembourg	9.7	17.7	25.5	2.8	6.2	7.8	12.1	7.8
Mexico	1.8	8.8	13.3	1.8	8.8	4.4	6.0	4.4
Netherlands	5.3	15.3	27.5	3.0	15.0	11.7	10.9	12.0
New Zealand	13.4	17.2	23.1	14.8	17.2	16.0	16.3	16.0
Norway	17.0	20.5	26.8	13.4	19.3	17.4	19.1	17.4
Poland	4.3	5.8	7.0	0.0	0.0	0.4	2.1	4.2
Portugal	8.5	16.2	24.0	3.6	6.2	6.2	10.8	8.3
Slovak Republic	6.1	9.5	12.3	-1.3	-2.3	3.3	5.2	7.0
Slovenia	6.6	11.1	15.6	0.0	2.8	3.7	5.6	8.4
Spain	12.2	16.6	22.5	3.5	9.1	11.1	12.7	12.5
Sweden	14.8	17.4	30.4	14.8	17.4	15.1	16.4	15.1
Switzerland	8.1	11.1	16.0	2.4	4.5	6.1	8.4	8.7
Turkey	9.5	12.3	16.3	8.0	10.5	9.1	10.5	9.9
United Kingdom	11.5	14.3	22.3	-4.4	14.3	11.5	13.2	11.5
United States	15.2	18.0	23.4	-4.0	5.9	9.8	12.2	15.2
Unweighted average								
OECD-Average	**11.3**	**15.6**	**21.6**	**6.2**	**10.3**	**10.6**	**12.4**	**12.4**
OECD-EU 21	**12.2**	**16.9**	**23.5**	**5.9**	**10.1**	**10.8**	**13.0**	**13.2**

Note: ch = children

Disclaimer: *http://oe.cd/disclaimer*

1. Information on data for Israel: *http://oe.cd/israel-disclaimer*.
2. Two-earner family.

StatLink http://dx.doi.org/10.1787/888933341438

Table 5.5. **Employee contributions, 2014**

As % of gross wage earnings, by family-type and wage level

	Single no ch 67 (% AW)	Single no ch 100 (% AW)	Single no ch 167 (% AW)	Single 2 ch 67 (% AW)	Married 2 ch 100-0 (% AW)	Married 2 ch 100-33 (% AW)[2]	Married 2 ch 100-67 (% AW)[2]	Married no ch 100-33 (% AW)[2]
Australia	0.0	0.0	0.0	0.0	0.0	0.0	0.0	0.0
Austria	18.1	18.1	16.0	18.1	18.1	17.3	18.1	17.3
Belgium	13.9	14.0	14.0	13.9	14.0	10.8	14.0	10.8
Canada	7.2	7.6	4.9	7.2	7.6	7.2	7.5	7.2
Chile	7.0	7.0	7.0	7.0	7.0	7.0	7.0	7.0
Czech Republic	11.0	11.0	11.0	11.0	11.0	11.0	11.0	11.0
Denmark	0.0	0.0	0.0	0.0	0.0	0.0	0.0	0.0
Estonia	2.0	2.0	2.0	2.0	2.0	2.0	2.0	2.0
Finland	7.9	8.0	8.1	7.9	8.0	7.8	8.0	7.8
France	14.1	14.1	13.4	14.1	14.1	14.1	14.1	14.1
Germany	20.4	20.4	16.3	20.2	20.2	20.2	20.2	20.4
Greece	16.0	16.0	16.0	16.0	16.0	16.0	16.0	16.0
Hungary	18.5	18.5	18.5	18.5	18.5	18.5	18.5	18.5
Iceland	0.6	0.4	0.2	0.6	0.4	0.6	0.5	0.6
Ireland	4.0	4.0	4.0	4.0	4.0	3.0	4.0	3.0
Israel[1]	5.8	7.9	9.5	5.8	7.9	6.8	7.1	6.8
Italy	9.5	9.5	9.6	9.5	9.5	9.5	9.5	9.5
Japan	14.1	14.1	13.2	14.1	14.1	14.1	14.1	14.1
Korea	8.3	8.3	7.0	8.3	8.3	8.3	8.3	8.3
Luxembourg	12.2	12.3	12.4	12.2	12.3	12.2	12.3	12.2
Mexico	1.3	1.4	1.5	1.3	1.4	1.3	1.3	1.3
Netherlands	19.5	15.1	10.6	8.5	12.9	12.4	14.7	14.3
New Zealand	0.0	0.0	0.0	0.0	0.0	0.0	0.0	0.0
Norway	8.2	8.2	8.2	8.2	8.2	8.2	8.2	8.2
Poland	17.8	17.8	17.8	17.8	17.8	17.8	17.8	17.8
Portugal	11.0	11.0	11.0	11.0	11.0	11.0	11.0	11.0
Slovak Republic	13.4	13.4	13.4	13.4	13.4	13.4	13.4	13.4
Slovenia	22.1	22.1	22.1	22.1	22.1	22.1	22.1	22.1
Spain	6.4	6.4	6.3	6.4	6.4	6.4	6.4	6.4
Sweden	7.0	7.0	4.7	7.0	7.0	7.0	7.0	7.0
Switzerland	6.3	6.3	6.2	6.3	6.3	6.3	6.3	6.3
Turkey	15.0	15.0	15.0	15.0	15.0	15.0	15.0	15.0
United Kingdom	8.0	9.3	7.5	8.0	9.3	7.9	8.8	7.9
United States	7.7	7.7	7.7	7.7	7.7	7.7	7.7	7.7
Unweighted average								
OECD-Average	**9.8**	**9.8**	**9.3**	**9.5**	**9.7**	**9.5**	**9.8**	**9.6**
OECD-EU 21	**12.0**	**11.9**	**11.2**	**11.5**	**11.8**	**11.4**	**11.8**	**11.5**

Note: ch = children

Disclaimer: *http://oe.cd/disclaimer*

1. Information on data for Israel: *http://oe.cd/israel-disclaimer*.
2. Two-earner family.

StatLink http://dx.doi.org/10.1787/888933341443

Table 5.6. Marginal rate of income tax plus employee and employer contributions less cash benefits, 2014

As % of labour costs, by family-type and wage level

	Single no ch 67 (% AW)	Single no ch 100 (% AW)	Single no ch 167 (% AW)	Single 2 ch 67 (% AW)	Married 2 ch 100-0 (% AW)	Married 2 ch 100-33 (% AW)[2]	Married 2 ch 100-67 (% AW)[2]	Married no ch 100-33 (% AW)[2]
Australia	39.1	37.7	42.0	58.0	54.2	66.0	37.7	37.7
Austria	56.9	60.6	42.2	56.9	60.6	60.6	60.6	60.6
Belgium	66.3	66.3	68.5	66.3	66.3	66.3	65.5	66.3
Canada	33.8	40.9	38.4	60.7	61.8	38.2	38.2	40.9
Chile	7.0	7.0	10.2	7.0	7.0	7.0	7.0	7.0
Czech Republic	48.6	48.6	48.6	48.6	48.6	48.6	48.6	48.6
Denmark	39.5	41.8	55.6	37.9	41.8	41.8	41.8	41.8
Estonia	42.2	42.2	42.2	42.2	42.2	42.2	42.2	42.2
Finland	54.3	55.2	58.2	54.3	55.2	55.2	55.2	55.2
France	62.6	59.3	59.9	57.0	43.5	58.3	50.9	50.9
Germany	55.5	59.9	44.3	53.8	52.2	55.2	57.5	55.4
Greece	48.0	48.7	56.0	48.0	48.7	48.7	48.7	48.7
Hungary	49.0	49.0	49.0	49.0	49.0	49.0	49.0	49.0
Iceland	42.5	42.5	48.3	51.4	51.4	47.9	47.9	42.5
Ireland	37.7	56.7	56.7	67.9	37.7	37.7	37.7	37.7
Israel[1]	30.7	37.2	46.6	17.6	37.2	37.2	37.2	37.2
Italy	55.3	55.3	62.6	56.5	56.5	56.5	55.9	55.3
Japan	32.6	36.8	35.3	32.6	36.8	36.8	36.8	36.8
Korea	22.3	29.2	31.9	16.9	29.2	29.2	29.2	29.2
Luxembourg	45.8	55.1	55.1	50.0	39.0	44.1	50.8	44.1
Mexico	17.5	23.4	28.4	17.5	23.4	23.4	23.4	23.4
Netherlands	46.4	49.7	51.9	49.4	56.1	49.7	49.7	49.7
New Zealand	17.5	30.0	33.0	38.8	51.3	51.3	30.0	30.0
Norway	42.7	50.6	53.3	42.7	50.6	50.6	50.6	50.6
Poland	37.2	37.2	37.2	29.6	29.6	37.2	37.2	37.2
Portugal	53.9	53.9	60.8	51.1	39.8	51.1	51.1	53.9
Slovak Republic	46.5	46.5	46.5	46.5	46.5	46.5	46.5	46.5
Slovenia	43.6	51.0	60.4	32.9	43.6	43.6	43.6	51.0
Spain	45.7	49.5	40.0	53.0	49.5	49.5	49.5	49.5
Sweden	45.5	48.2	67.2	45.5	48.2	48.2	48.2	48.2
Switzerland	26.3	31.9	35.9	18.9	22.1	26.1	29.4	26.9
Turkey	42.8	42.8	47.8	42.8	42.8	42.8	42.8	42.8
United Kingdom	40.2	40.2	49.0	76.3	40.2	40.2	40.2	40.2
United States	34.3	43.6	43.6	50.4	34.3	34.3	34.3	34.3
Unweighted average								
OECD-Average	**41.5**	**45.0**	**47.3**	**44.9**	**44.0**	**44.7**	**43.4**	**43.3**
OECD-EU 21	**48.6**	**51.2**	**53.0**	**51.1**	**47.4**	**49.1**	**49.1**	**49.1**

Note: ch = children

It is assumed that gross earnings of the principal earner in the household rise. The outcome may differ if the wage of the spouse goes up, especially if partners are taxed individually.

Disclaimer: *http://oe.cd/disclaimer*

1. Information on data for Israel: *http://oe.cd/israel-disclaimer*.
2. Two-earner family.

StatLink http://dx.doi.org/10.1787/888933341458

Table 5.7. Marginal rate of income tax plus employee contributions less cash benefits, 2014

As % of gross wage earnings, by family-type and wage level

	Single no ch 67 (% AW)	Single no ch 100 (% AW)	Single no ch 167 (% AW)	Single 2 ch 67 (% AW)	Married 2 ch 100-0 (% AW)	Married 2 ch 100-33 (% AW)[2]	Married 2 ch 100-67 (% AW)[2]	Married no ch 100-33 (% AW)[2]
Australia	35.5	34.0	38.5	55.5	51.5	64.0	34.0	34.0
Austria	44.4	49.1	37.9	44.4	49.1	49.1	49.1	49.1
Belgium	55.0	55.0	59.8	55.0	55.0	55.0	53.9	55.0
Canada	25.5	35.1	35.4	55.8	58.0	32.1	32.1	35.1
Chile	7.0	7.0	10.2	7.0	7.0	7.0	7.0	7.0
Czech Republic	31.1	31.1	31.1	31.1	31.1	31.1	31.1	31.1
Denmark	39.5	41.8	55.6	37.9	41.8	41.8	41.8	41.8
Estonia	22.6	22.6	22.6	22.6	22.6	22.6	22.6	22.6
Finland	43.7	44.9	48.6	43.7	44.9	44.9	44.9	44.9
France	32.1	43.8	42.5	21.9	21.9	42.3	32.1	32.1
Germany	46.9	52.2	44.3	44.9	42.9	46.5	49.3	46.8
Greece	34.5	35.3	44.6	34.5	35.3	35.3	35.3	35.3
Hungary	34.5	34.5	34.5	34.5	34.5	34.5	34.5	34.5
Iceland	38.2	38.2	44.4	47.8	47.8	43.9	43.9	38.2
Ireland	31.0	52.0	52.0	64.4	31.0	31.0	31.0	31.0
Israel[1]	26.0	33.0	43.0	12.0	33.0	33.0	33.0	33.0
Italy	40.9	40.9	50.6	42.5	42.5	42.5	41.7	40.9
Japan	22.6	27.4	31.2	22.6	27.4	27.4	27.4	27.4
Korea	14.3	21.9	27.9	8.3	21.9	21.9	21.9	21.9
Luxembourg	39.1	49.6	49.6	43.9	31.5	37.2	44.8	37.2
Mexico	12.1	17.6	22.9	12.1	17.6	17.6	17.6	17.6
Netherlands	40.8	44.5	51.9	44.1	51.5	44.5	44.5	44.5
New Zealand	17.5	30.0	33.0	38.8	51.3	51.3	30.0	30.0
Norway	35.2	44.2	47.2	35.2	44.2	44.2	44.2	44.2
Poland	26.7	26.7	26.7	17.8	17.8	26.7	26.7	26.7
Portugal	43.0	43.0	51.5	39.5	25.5	39.5	39.5	43.0
Slovak Republic	29.9	29.9	29.9	29.9	29.9	29.9	29.9	29.9
Slovenia	34.6	43.1	54.0	22.1	34.6	34.6	34.6	43.1
Spain	29.5	34.4	40.0	38.9	34.4	34.4	34.4	34.4
Sweden	28.3	31.9	56.9	28.3	31.9	31.9	31.9	31.9
Switzerland	21.7	27.6	32.2	13.8	17.2	21.5	25.0	22.3
Turkey	32.8	32.8	38.7	32.8	32.8	32.8	32.8	32.8
United Kingdom	32.0	32.0	42.0	73.0	32.0	32.0	32.0	32.0
United States	29.3	39.3	39.3	46.6	29.3	29.3	29.3	29.3
Unweighted average								
OECD-Average	**31.7**	**36.1**	**40.3**	**35.4**	**34.7**	**35.7**	**34.2**	**34.1**
OECD-EU 21	**36.2**	**39.9**	**44.1**	**38.8**	**35.3**	**37.5**	**37.4**	**37.5**

Note: ch = children

It is assumed that gross earnings of the principal earner in the household rise. The outcome may differ if the wage of the spouse goes up, especially if partners are taxed individually.

Disclaimer: *http://oe.cd/disclaimer*

1. Information on data for Israel: *http://oe.cd/israel-disclaimer*.
2. Two-earner family.

StatLink http://dx.doi.org/10.1787/888933341469

Table 5.8. Increase in net income after an increase of 1 currency unit in gross wages, 2014

By family-type and wage level (%)

	Single no ch 67 (% AW)	Single no ch 100 (% AW)	Single no ch 167 (% AW)	Single 2 ch 67 (% AW)	Married 2 ch 100-0 (% AW)	Married 2 ch 100-33 (% AW)[2]	Married 2 ch 100-67 (% AW)[2]	Married no ch 100-33 (% AW)[2]
Australia	0.78	0.86	0.87	0.41	0.55	0.43	0.84	0.81
Austria	0.78	0.78	1.02	0.61	0.65	0.64	0.68	0.72
Belgium	0.70	0.78	0.79	0.55	0.58	0.61	0.69	0.69
Canada	0.91	0.85	0.89	0.38	0.47	0.80	0.83	0.81
Chile	1.00	1.00	0.97	0.99	1.00	0.98	1.00	1.00
Czech Republic	0.85	0.90	0.94	0.68	0.70	0.77	0.80	0.86
Denmark	0.90	0.90	0.77	0.66	0.77	0.81	0.84	0.87
Estonia	0.95	0.96	0.98	0.80	0.86	0.89	0.91	0.95
Finland	0.74	0.80	0.83	0.63	0.73	0.70	0.73	0.75
France	0.93	0.79	0.87	0.92	0.95	0.70	0.88	0.93
Germany	0.81	0.79	0.99	0.67	0.72	0.73	0.74	0.81
Greece	0.81	0.86	0.85	0.77	0.85	0.84	0.85	0.85
Hungary	1.00	1.00	1.00	0.69	0.78	0.83	0.86	1.00
Iceland	0.81	0.87	0.84	0.59	0.61	0.72	0.76	0.82
Ireland	0.80	0.60	0.72	0.27	0.69	0.73	0.78	0.79
Israel[1]	0.83	0.81	0.77	0.87	0.78	0.76	0.75	0.78
Italy	0.78	0.86	0.81	0.59	0.71	0.72	0.77	0.80
Japan	0.97	0.93	0.93	0.89	0.86	0.88	0.89	0.92
Korea	0.95	0.91	0.87	1.00	0.88	0.88	0.88	0.89
Luxembourg	0.78	0.72	0.81	0.53	0.72	0.70	0.66	0.79
Mexico	0.91	0.92	0.91	0.91	0.92	0.87	0.89	0.87
Netherlands	0.79	0.80	0.78	0.57	0.64	0.71	0.73	0.75
New Zealand	0.95	0.85	0.87	0.53	0.51	0.55	0.84	0.83
Norway	0.87	0.78	0.81	0.74	0.73	0.72	0.74	0.75
Poland	0.94	0.96	0.98	1.00	1.00	0.90	0.92	0.94
Portugal	0.71	0.78	0.75	0.65	0.86	0.71	0.77	0.71
Slovak Republic	0.87	0.91	0.94	0.73	0.74	0.80	0.83	0.88
Slovenia	0.92	0.85	0.74	0.75	0.74	0.81	0.86	0.82
Spain	0.87	0.85	0.84	0.68	0.78	0.79	0.81	0.81
Sweden	0.92	0.90	0.67	0.81	0.83	0.82	0.85	0.88
Switzerland	0.91	0.88	0.87	0.85	0.86	0.85	0.84	0.91
Turkey	0.89	0.92	0.89	0.87	0.90	0.89	0.90	0.90
United Kingdom	0.84	0.89	0.83	0.26	0.84	0.81	0.84	0.84
United States	0.92	0.82	0.88	0.55	0.82	0.86	0.88	0.92
Unweighted average								
OECD-Average	**0.86**	**0.86**	**0.86**	**0.69**	**0.77**	**0.77**	**0.82**	**0.84**
OECD-EU 21	**0.84**	**0.84**	**0.85**	**0.66**	**0.77**	**0.76**	**0.80**	**0.83**

Note: ch = children

Net income is calculated as gross earnings minus personal income tax and employees' social security contributions plus family benefits. The increase reported in the Table represents a form of elasticity. In a proportional tax system the elasticity would equal 1. The more progressive the system at these income levels, the lower is the elasticity.

Disclaimer: *http://oe.cd/disclaimer*

1. Information on data for Israel: *http://oe.cd/israel-disclaimer*.
2. Two-earner family. Assumes a rise in the labour costs associated with the principal earner in the household.

StatLink http://dx.doi.org/10.1787/888933341475

Table 5.9. Increase in net income after an increase of 1 currency unit in gross labour cost, 2014

By family-type and wage level (%)

	Single no ch 67 (% AW)	Single no ch 100 (% AW)	Single no ch 167 (% AW)	Single 2 ch 67 (% AW)	Married 2 ch 100-0 (% AW)	Married 2 ch 100-33 (% AW)[2]	Married 2 ch 100-67 (% AW)[2]	Married no ch 100-33 (% AW)[2]
Australia	0.78	0.86	0.87	0.41	0.55	0.43	0.84	0.81
Austria	0.78	0.78	1.20	0.61	0.65	0.64	0.68	0.72
Belgium	0.67	0.76	0.80	0.53	0.57	0.58	0.67	0.65
Canada	0.90	0.86	0.92	0.38	0.47	0.82	0.85	0.83
Chile	1.00	1.00	0.97	0.99	1.00	0.98	1.00	1.00
Czech Republic	0.85	0.90	0.94	0.68	0.70	0.77	0.80	0.86
Denmark	0.92	0.91	0.77	0.67	0.78	0.83	0.85	0.89
Estonia	0.95	0.96	0.98	0.80	0.86	0.89	0.91	0.95
Finland	0.74	0.80	0.83	0.63	0.73	0.70	0.73	0.75
France	0.68	0.79	0.88	0.68	0.95	0.67	0.87	0.88
Germany	0.81	0.79	1.15	0.67	0.72	0.73	0.74	0.81
Greece	0.81	0.86	0.85	0.77	0.85	0.84	0.85	0.85
Hungary	1.00	1.00	1.00	0.69	0.78	0.83	0.86	1.00
Iceland	0.81	0.87	0.84	0.59	0.61	0.72	0.76	0.82
Ireland	0.80	0.60	0.72	0.27	0.69	0.73	0.78	0.79
Israel[1]	0.81	0.80	0.76	0.85	0.77	0.75	0.74	0.76
Italy	0.78	0.86	0.81	0.59	0.71	0.72	0.77	0.80
Japan	0.97	0.93	0.99	0.89	0.86	0.88	0.89	0.92
Korea	0.95	0.91	0.89	1.00	0.88	0.88	0.88	0.89
Luxembourg	0.78	0.72	0.81	0.53	0.72	0.70	0.66	0.79
Mexico	0.97	0.95	0.93	0.97	0.95	0.93	0.93	0.93
Netherlands	0.78	0.80	0.83	0.57	0.64	0.70	0.72	0.75
New Zealand	0.95	0.85	0.87	0.53	0.51	0.55	0.84	0.83
Norway	0.87	0.78	0.81	0.74	0.73	0.72	0.74	0.75
Poland	0.94	0.96	0.98	1.00	1.00	0.90	0.92	0.94
Portugal	0.71	0.78	0.75	0.65	0.86	0.71	0.77	0.71
Slovak Republic	0.87	0.91	0.94	0.73	0.74	0.80	0.83	0.88
Slovenia	0.92	0.85	0.74	0.75	0.74	0.81	0.86	0.82
Spain	0.87	0.85	1.09	0.68	0.78	0.79	0.81	0.81
Sweden	0.92	0.90	0.67	0.81	0.83	0.82	0.85	0.88
Switzerland	0.91	0.88	0.88	0.85	0.86	0.85	0.84	0.91
Turkey	0.89	0.92	0.89	0.87	0.90	0.89	0.90	0.90
United Kingdom	0.81	0.87	0.81	0.25	0.81	0.77	0.81	0.81
United States	0.93	0.83	0.89	0.56	0.83	0.87	0.89	0.93
Unweighted average								
OECD-Average	**0.86**	**0.86**	**0.88**	**0.68**	**0.77**	**0.77**	**0.82**	**0.84**
OECD-EU 21	**0.83**	**0.84**	**0.88**	**0.65**	**0.77**	**0.76**	**0.80**	**0.82**

Note: ch = children

Net income is calculated as gross earnings minus personal income tax and employees' social security contributions plus family benefits. The increase reported in the Table represents a form of elasticity. In a proportional tax system the elasticity would equal 1. The more progressive the system at these income levels, the lower is the elasticity.

Disclaimer: *http://oe.cd/disclaimer*

1. Information on data for Israel: *http://oe.cd/israel-disclaimer*.
2. Two-earner family. Assumes a rise in the labour costs associated with the principal earner in the household.

StatLink http://dx.doi.org/10.1787/888933341482

Table 5.10a. **Annual gross wage and net income, single person, 2014**

In US dollars using PPP, by family-type and wage level

	Single no ch 67 (% AW)		Single no ch 100 (% AW)		Single no ch 167 (% AW)		Single 2 ch 67 (% AW)	
	Total gross earnings before taxes	Net income after taxes	Total gross earnings before taxes	Net income after taxes	Total gross earnings before taxes	Net income after taxes	Total gross earnings before taxes	Net income after taxes
Australia	36 191	29 773	54 016	41 401	90 207	63 676	36 191	39 040
Austria	35 497	25 279	52 980	34 606	88 477	53 802	35 497	32 448
Belgium	37 894	24 287	56 559	32 602	94 453	47 988	37 894	30 950
Canada	27 075	22 262	40 410	30 975	67 485	49 191	27 075	31 719
Chile	12 527	11 650	18 697	17 388	31 223	28 771	12 527	11 761
Czech Republic	15 933	12 891	23 780	18 298	39 713	29 276	15 933	16 084
Denmark	35 596	23 818	53 129	34 208	88 726	51 540	35 596	33 537
Estonia	15 318	12 532	22 863	18 373	38 180	30 232	15 318	14 910
Finland	31 219	23 758	46 595	32 291	77 814	48 343	31 219	27 869
France	30 525	22 381	45 560	32 508	76 086	50 049	30 525	25 818
Germany	39 455	25 842	58 889	35 645	98 344	55 248	39 455	32 382
Greece	22 522	18 208	33 614	25 194	56 136	36 546	22 522	19 260
Hungary	15 724	10 299	23 468	15 372	39 192	25 671	15 724	14 872
Iceland	33 763	25 682	50 392	35 967	84 155	56 029	33 763	29 758
Ireland	27 616	23 856	41 218	32 892	68 834	46 148	27 616	36 574
Israel[1]	22 857	20 455	34 116	28 314	56 973	42 184	22 857	23 162
Italy	27 207	20 720	40 608	27 780	67 815	41 391	27 207	26 348
Japan	31 815	25 374	47 486	37 113	79 301	58 981	31 815	27 666
Korea	31 473	28 303	46 975	40 564	78 448	65 418	31 473	28 848
Luxembourg	41 219	32 171	61 521	43 064	102 741	63 843	41 219	43 433
Mexico	8 726	8 464	13 025	11 704	21 751	18 534	8 726	8 464
Netherlands	40 439	30 437	60 356	41 951	100 794	62 394	40 439	39 480
New Zealand	25 850	22 384	38 582	31 928	64 432	49 570	25 850	29 930
Norway	38 516	28 800	57 486	40 998	96 002	62 362	38 516	33 947
Poland	16 498	12 853	24 623	18 812	41 121	30 913	16 498	13 557
Portugal	20 119	16 201	30 028	21 849	50 146	32 588	20 119	18 640
Slovak Republic	14 185	11 418	21 172	16 319	35 357	26 269	14 185	13 609
Slovenia	20 209	14 412	30 162	20 134	50 371	31 370	20 209	21 137
Spain	26 342	21 463	39 316	30 277	65 658	46 783	26 342	23 757
Sweden	30 657	23 970	45 756	34 598	76 413	49 565	30 657	26 997
Switzerland	45 659	39 099	68 148	56 354	113 808	88 543	45 659	46 283
Turkey	15 836	11 950	23 636	17 195	39 471	27 119	15 836	12 199
United Kingdom	33 707	27 146	50 309	38 435	84 015	58 940	33 707	35 057
United States	33 566	25 890	50 099	37 274	83 665	57 648	33 566	32 326
Unweighted average								
OECD-Average	**27 698**	**21 589**	**41 340**	**30 364**	**69 038**	**46 674**	**27 698**	**26 524**
OECD-EU 21	**27 518**	**20 664**	**41 072**	**28 819**	**68 590**	**43 757**	**27 518**	**26 034**

Note: ch = children

Disclaimer: *http://oe.cd/disclaimer*

1. Information on data for Israel: *http://oe.cd/israel-disclaimer*.

StatLink http://dx.doi.org/10.1787/888933341496

Table 5.10b. **Annual gross wage and net income, married couple, 2014**

In US dollars using PPP, by family-type and wage level

	Married 2 ch 100-0 (% AW)		Married 2 ch 100-33 (% AW)[2]		Married 2 ch 100-67 (% AW)[2]		Married no ch 100-33 (% AW)[2]	
	Total gross earnings before taxes	Net income after taxes	Total gross earnings before taxes	Net income after taxes	Total gross earnings before taxes	Net income after taxes	Total gross earnings before taxes	Net income after taxes
Australia	54 016	47 297	71 842	60 248	90 207	71 174	71 842	58 227
Austria	52 980	41 812	70 463	55 971	88 477	66 288	70 463	49 593
Belgium	56 559	43 587	75 223	55 228	94 453	62 855	75 223	49 220
Canada	40 410	36 529	53 746	45 601	67 485	54 919	53 746	43 032
Chile	18 697	17 388	24 866	23 697	31 223	29 148	24 866	23 126
Czech Republic	23 780	23 405	31 628	28 475	39 713	34 382	31 628	25 282
Denmark	53 129	39 930	70 662	50 546	88 726	61 437	70 662	47 136
Estonia	22 863	20 570	30 407	26 411	38 180	32 430	30 407	24 886
Finland	46 595	35 141	61 971	48 639	77 814	58 898	61 971	45 789
France	45 560	37 471	60 595	49 933	76 086	58 519	60 595	44 452
Germany	58 889	46 552	78 322	57 471	98 344	67 903	78 322	51 370
Greece	36 976	28 255	49 178	37 979	61 749	47 205	49 178	37 453
Hungary	23 468	19 668	31 213	24 741	39 192	29 967	31 213	20 444
Iceland	50 392	42 909	67 022	52 130	84 155	61 965	67 022	50 827
Ireland	41 218	41 225	54 820	51 563	68 834	60 860	54 820	47 801
Israel[1]	34 116	29 164	45 374	40 029	56 973	50 687	45 374	39 178
Italy	40 608	32 749	54 008	43 173	67 815	51 647	54 008	40 029
Japan	47 486	40 091	63 156	52 253	79 301	64 779	63 156	49 961
Korea	46 975	41 780	62 476	55 708	78 448	69 844	62 476	54 772
Luxembourg	61 521	58 577	81 823	73 853	102 741	86 170	81 823	65 427
Mexico	13 025	11 704	17 323	16 335	21 751	20 168	17 323	16 335
Netherlands	60 356	45 790	80 273	63 243	100 794	77 243	80 273	59 148
New Zealand	38 582	37 135	51 314	45 624	64 432	53 945	51 314	43 123
Norway	57 486	44 160	76 457	59 395	96 002	72 289	76 457	56 904
Poland	24 623	20 234	32 749	26 768	41 121	32 907	32 749	25 526
Portugal	30 028	26 080	39 937	34 150	50 146	39 228	39 937	32 231
Slovak Republic	21 172	19 977	28 158	24 616	35 357	29 928	28 158	22 426
Slovenia	30 162	26 798	40 116	32 283	50 371	38 294	40 116	27 888
Spain	39 316	33 249	52 291	43 148	65 658	53 180	52 291	42 428
Sweden	45 756	37 625	60 855	50 442	76 413	61 595	60 855	47 415
Switzerland	68 148	65 368	90 637	83 984	113 808	101 634	90 637	77 100
Turkey	23 636	17 609	31 435	23 848	39 471	29 393	31 435	23 599
United Kingdom	50 309	40 974	66 910	56 488	84 015	68 119	66 910	53 949
United States	50 099	43 287	66 632	54 975	83 665	67 018	66 632	51 426
Unweighted average								
OECD-Average	**41 439**	**35 120**	**55 114**	**45 557**	**69 204**	**54 883**	**55 114**	**42 574**
OECD-EU 21	**41 232**	**34 270**	**54 838**	**44 530**	**68 857**	**53 288**	**54 838**	**40 947**

Note: ch = children

Disclaimer: *http://oe.cd/disclaimer*

1. Information on data for Israel: *http://oe.cd/israel-disclaimer*.
2. Two-earner family.

StatLink http://dx.doi.org/10.1787/888933341505

Table 5.11a. **Annual labour costs and net income, single person, 2014**

In US dollars using PPP, by family-type and wage level

	Single no ch 67 (% AW)		Single no ch 100 (% AW)		Single no ch 167 (% AW)		Single 2 ch 67 (% AW)	
	Total gross labour costs before taxes	Net income after taxes	Total gross labour costs before taxes	Net income after taxes	Total gross labour costs before taxes	Net income after taxes	Total gross labour costs before taxes	Net income after taxes
Australia	38 346	29 773	57 233	41 401	95 578	63 676	38 346	39 040
Austria	45 836	25 279	68 412	34 606	112 086	53 802	45 836	32 448
Belgium	48 446	24 287	73 417	32 602	122 365	47 988	48 446	30 950
Canada	30 303	22 262	45 272	30 975	73 770	49 191	30 303	31 719
Chile	12 527	11 650	18 697	17 388	31 223	28 771	12 527	11 761
Czech Republic	21 350	12 891	31 865	18 298	53 215	29 276	21 350	16 084
Denmark	36 120	23 818	53 653	34 208	89 249	51 540	36 120	33 537
Estonia	20 526	12 532	30 636	18 373	51 162	30 232	20 526	14 910
Finland	38 418	23 758	57 340	32 291	95 758	48 343	38 418	27 869
France	40 758	22 381	63 010	32 508	109 535	50 049	40 758	25 818
Germany	47 061	25 842	70 240	35 645	113 632	55 248	47 061	32 382
Greece	28 379	18 208	42 357	25 194	70 737	36 546	28 379	19 260
Hungary	20 205	10 299	30 157	15 372	50 361	25 671	20 205	14 872
Iceland	36 325	25 682	54 217	35 967	90 543	56 029	36 325	29 758
Ireland	30 585	23 856	45 649	32 892	76 233	46 148	30 585	36 574
Israel[1]	23 854	20 455	35 872	28 314	60 272	42 184	23 854	23 162
Italy	35 935	20 720	53 634	27 780	89 570	41 391	35 935	26 348
Japan	36 546	25 374	54 546	37 113	90 381	58 981	36 546	27 666
Korea	34 712	28 303	51 809	40 564	85 489	65 418	34 712	28 848
Luxembourg	46 273	32 171	69 064	43 064	115 337	63 843	46 273	43 433
Mexico	9 926	8 464	14 544	11 704	23 934	18 534	9 926	8 464
Netherlands	44 348	30 437	66 353	41 951	107 467	62 394	44 348	39 480
New Zealand	25 850	22 384	38 582	31 928	64 432	49 570	25 850	29 930
Norway	43 523	28 800	64 960	40 998	108 483	62 362	43 523	33 947
Poland	19 266	12 853	28 755	18 812	48 021	30 910	19 266	13 557
Portugal	24 897	16 201	37 159	21 849	62 056	32 588	24 897	18 640
Slovak Republic	18 611	11 418	27 777	16 319	46 388	26 269	18 611	13 609
Slovenia	23 462	14 412	35 019	20 134	58 481	31 370	23 462	21 137
Spain	34 218	21 463	51 072	30 277	85 032	46 783	34 218	23 757
Sweden	40 289	23 970	60 132	34 598	100 421	49 565	40 289	26 997
Switzerland	48 513	39 099	72 408	56 354	120 812	88 543	48 513	46 283
Turkey	18 607	11 950	27 772	17 195	46 379	27 119	18 607	12 199
United Kingdom	36 788	27 146	55 681	38 435	94 039	58 940	36 788	35 057
United States	36 729	25 890	54 526	37 274	90 661	57 648	36 729	32 326
Unweighted average								
OECD-Average	**32 280**	**21 589**	**48 289**	**30 364**	**80 385**	**46 674**	**32 280**	**26 524**
OECD-EU 21	**33 418**	**20 664**	**50 066**	**28 819**	**83 388**	**43 757**	**33 418**	**26 034**

Note: ch = children

Disclaimer: *http://oe.cd/disclaimer*

1. Information on data for Israel: *http://oe.cd/israel-disclaimer.*

StatLink http://dx.doi.org/10.1787/888933341513

Table 5.11b. **Annual labour costs and net income, married couple, 2014**

In US dollars using PPP, by family-type and wage level

	Married 2 ch 100-0 (% AW)		Married 2 ch 100-33 (% AW)[2]		Married 2 ch 100-67 (% AW)[2]		Married no ch 100-33 (% AW)[2]	
	Total gross labour costs before taxes	Net income after taxes	Total gross labour costs before taxes	Net income after taxes	Total gross labour costs before taxes	Net income after taxes	Total gross labour costs before taxes	Net income after taxes
Australia	57 233	47 297	76 119	60 248	95 578	71 174	76 119	58 227
Austria	68 412	41 812	90 988	55 971	114 249	66 288	90 988	49 593
Belgium	73 417	43 587	94 772	55 228	121 863	62 855	94 772	49 220
Canada	45 272	36 529	60 126	45 601	75 575	54 919	60 126	43 032
Chile	18 697	17 388	24 866	23 697	31 223	29 148	24 866	23 126
Czech Republic	31 865	23 405	42 381	28 475	53 215	34 382	42 381	25 282
Denmark	53 653	39 930	71 709	50 546	89 773	61 437	71 709	47 136
Estonia	30 636	20 570	40 746	26 411	51 162	32 430	40 746	24 886
Finland	57 340	35 141	76 262	48 639	95 758	58 898	76 262	45 789
France	63 010	37 471	79 894	49 933	103 768	58 519	79 894	44 452
Germany	70 240	46 552	93 419	57 471	117 300	67 903	93 419	51 370
Greece	46 593	28 255	61 969	37 979	77 810	47 205	61 969	37 453
Hungary	30 157	19 668	40 108	24 741	50 361	29 967	40 108	20 444
Iceland	54 217	42 909	72 109	52 130	90 543	61 965	72 109	50 827
Ireland	45 649	41 225	60 407	51 563	76 233	60 860	60 407	47 801
Israel[1]	35 872	29 164	47 518	40 029	59 725	50 687	47 518	39 178
Italy	53 634	32 749	71 334	43 173	89 570	51 647	71 334	40 029
Japan	54 546	40 091	72 546	52 253	91 092	64 779	72 546	49 961
Korea	51 809	41 780	68 906	55 708	86 521	69 844	68 906	54 772
Luxembourg	69 064	58 577	91 855	73 853	115 337	86 170	91 855	65 427
Mexico	14 544	11 704	19 754	16 335	24 470	20 168	19 754	16 335
Netherlands	66 353	45 790	88 074	63 243	110 701	77 243	88 074	59 148
New Zealand	38 582	37 135	51 314	45 624	64 432	53 945	51 314	43 123
Norway	64 960	44 160	86 396	59 395	108 483	72 289	86 396	56 904
Poland	28 755	20 234	38 244	26 768	48 021	32 907	38 244	25 526
Portugal	37 159	26 080	49 422	34 150	62 056	39 228	49 422	32 231
Slovak Republic	27 777	19 977	36 944	24 616	46 388	29 928	36 944	22 426
Slovenia	35 019	26 798	46 575	32 283	58 481	38 294	46 575	27 888
Spain	51 072	33 249	67 926	43 148	85 290	53 180	67 926	42 428
Sweden	60 132	37 625	79 976	50 442	100 421	61 595	79 976	47 415
Switzerland	72 408	65 368	96 302	83 984	120 921	101 634	96 302	77 100
Turkey	27 772	17 609	36 936	23 848	46 379	29 393	36 936	23 599
United Kingdom	55 681	40 974	73 004	56 488	92 469	68 119	73 004	53 949
United States	54 526	43 287	72 919	54 975	91 255	67 018	72 919	51 426
Unweighted average								
OECD-Average	**48 413**	**35 120**	**64 171**	**45 557**	**80 777**	**54 883**	**64 171**	**42 574**
OECD-EU 21	**50 268**	**34 270**	**66 477**	**44 530**	**83 820**	**53 288**	**66 477**	**40 947**

Note: ch = children

Disclaimer: *http://oe.cd/disclaimer*

1. Information on data for Israel: *http://oe.cd/israel-disclaimer*.
2. Two-earner family.

StatLink http://dx.doi.org/10.1787/888933341525

PART II

Tax burden trends 2000-15

This section presents detailed results of the evolution of the tax burden between 2000 and 2015. It provides information for each of the OECD countries on the income taxes paid by workers, their social security contributions, the family benefits they receive in the form of cash transfers as well as the social security contributions and payroll taxes paid by their employers over this period.

PART II

Chapter 6

Evolution of the tax burden (2000-15)

The chapter presents the evolution of the tax burdens on labour income between 2000 and 2015. The chapter contains Tables 6.1 to 6.8 each corresponding to a particular model family type and divided into three parts: Part A. tables containing the (average) tax wedge comprising income taxes plus employee and employer social security contributions (including any applicable payroll taxes) less cash benefits; Part B. tables providing the (average) burden of personal income taxes; and the Part C. tables depicting the (average) burden of income taxes plus employee social security contributions less cash benefits (net personal average tax rates).

Historical trends

The evolution of the tax burden for the eight family types over the period 2000 to 2015 is presented in Tables 6.1 to 6.8 in the last section of this chapter titled "Tables showing income taxes, social security contributions and cash benefits". Each of the Tables 1 to 8 corresponds to a particular family type and each is divided into three parts.

The discussion focuses on the main observable trends over the period and highlights selected important year-to-year changes.

Important trends

The OECD average tax wedge, the income tax burden and the net tax burden (personal income tax plus social security contributions less cash benefits) have all declined between 2000 and 2015 for each of the selected family types.

The reductions over the period in the OECD average tax wedge ranged from 0.7 percentage points (for single persons on average earnings) to 1.4 percentage points (for single parents at 67% of the average wage).

The decrease in the OECD average income tax burden ranges from 0.2 percentage points (for single persons on average earnings) to 1.5 percentage points (for single parents at 67% of the AW).

The OECD net personal average tax burden has also declined for all family types in the period considered. The reduction ranges from 0.3 percentage points (for the one-earner couple at the average wage level with two children) to 0.9 percentage points (for single parents at 67% of the average wage and two-earner married couples with two children where one spouse is earning the average wage and the other 33% of it).

Tax wedge

Focusing on the overall (average) tax wedge (a. tables), there are ten OECD member countries with a reduction of more than five percentage points between 2000 and 2015 for at least one of the family types – Australia, Canada, Denmark, Hungary, Ireland, Israel, the Netherlands, New Zealand, Sweden and the United Kingdom.

The largest decline is observed in Ireland where single parents have benefited from a reduction in the wedge of 17.9 percentage points. Married couples with two children on average earnings and 133% of it in Ireland also enjoyed reductions of 6.0 and 6.3 percentage points respectively. In the Netherlands single persons at 67% of the average wage level with and without children enjoyed reductions of 17.6 and 11.3 percentage points in the wedge respectively.

A reduction of seven percentage points or more in the tax wedge for at least one family-type was observed in six other countries – Denmark, Hungary, Israel, New Zealand, Sweden and the United Kingdom. In Denmark, the largest decrease was for the single person earning 167% of the average wage (-7.6 percentage points). In Hungary, there were reductions of between 2.4 and 10.2 percentage points over the range of family types. The largest decreases were for single workers earning 167% of the average wage (-10.2 percentage points) and the one-earner married couples with 2 children at average earnings (-8.6 percentage points). In Israel, the tax wedge decreased by more than 7 percentage points for single persons without children earning 67% of the average wage (-8.6 percentage points), the average wage level (-8.0 percentage points) and 167% of it (-7.5 percentage points). In New Zealand, single parents earning 67% of the average wage level (-11.4 percentage points) benefited most from the reduction in the tax wedge. In Sweden, all but one of the families enjoyed a reduction in the tax wedge of 6 to 8 percentage points, the exception being the single workers earning 167% of the average wage level (-4.7 percentage points). It is interesting to note that in Iceland the single worker earning 167% of the average wage level enjoyed a reduction in the tax wedge (-1.3 percentage points), while the tax burden increased by more than 5 percentage points for all the other family types and notably by 13.6 percentage points for the single parents earning 67% of the average wage.

The tax wedge has decreased for all family types in twelve of the OECD member countries (Australia, Belgium, Canada, Denmark, Germany, Hungary, Israel, New Zealand, Poland, Slovenia, Sweden and Switzerland) while it has increased across all family types in five countries (Austria, Japan, Korea, Luxembourg and Mexico).

Average income tax rate

Between 2000 and 2015, the average income tax burden (b. tables) has decreased for all family types in thirteen of the OECD member countries: Belgium, Canada, Estonia, Finland, Germany, Hungary, Israel, New Zealand, Slovenia, Sweden, Switzerland, Turkey and the United Kingdom. The most significant reductions affecting all of the family types are noted in Sweden where all the family types enjoyed decreases of around 9-10 percentage points except the single taxpayer earning 167% of the average wage where the decrease was -5.4 percentage points. In Estonia, the average income tax burden has decreased by more than 6 percentage points for all families with children, with single parents at 67% of the average wage enjoying an income tax reduction of 8.8 percentage points. In Hungary, there were significant decreases of 14 percentage points for the single persons earning 167% of the average wage and 10 percentage points for the one-earner married couples with children earning the average wage. In Israel, the average income tax rate decreased by 6 to around 10 percentage points in all family types except for single parents at 67% of the average wage who had a reduction of 1.1 percentage points. Other decreases of more than 5 percentage points were observed in Finland (for married couples at 133% of the average wage with and without children by -5.5 and -5.3 percentage points respectively), New Zealand (-5.1 percentage points for the single worker earning 67% of the average wage without children), and the United Kingdom where there was a reduction of 12.4 percentage points for the single parent at 67% of the average wage. Reductions of less than 5 percentage points in average income tax rates are observed for all family types in Belgium, Canada, Germany, Slovenia, Switzerland and Turkey.

There are thirteen other OECD member countries with reductions in the personal income tax in some family types: Australia, the Czech Republic, France, Iceland, Ireland, Italy, Korea, Luxembourg, Norway, Poland, the Slovak Republic, Spain and the United States. In three of those countries the reductions in average income tax rates exceeded six percentage points: the Czech Republic (-8.7 percentage points for the one-earner married couple with children at the average wage level and -7.6 percentage points for the single parent earning 67% of the average), the Slovak Republic (-6.8 percentage points for the one-earner married couple at the average wage level with children) and Poland (-6.5 percentage points for the single parent earning 67% of the average wage).

At the other extreme, the personal income tax burden has increased across all family types in seven OECD member countries: Austria, Denmark, Greece, Japan, Mexico, the Netherlands and Portugal. In Mexico the increases were in the range 5 to 8 percentage points for each family type. In the Netherlands, there were increases of 11.3 percentage points for the one-earner married couple with two children and 7.1 percentage points for the single person on average earnings. In contrast, in Chile the average income tax burden slightly increased only in the case of the single worker earning 167% of the average wage (0.4 percentage points). The average income tax rates stayed constant for the other family types since they do not pay income taxes.

Net personal average tax rate

The *net* tax burden takes into account personal income taxes and employee social security contributions as well as cash benefits (c. tables). It decreased between 2000 and 2015 for all family types in nine OECD countries: Australia, Canada, Denmark, Germany, Israel, New Zealand, Poland, Sweden and Switzerland. Of these, the most significant reductions were observed in Sweden, ranging from -9.9 percentage points (the two-earning married couple without children where the spouse is earning 33% of the average wage) to -5.5 percentage points (single taxpayer earning 167% of the average wage). Significant reductions were also observed in Israel for all but one family type (reductions ranging between 6.0 and 8.8 percentage points), the exception being single parents earning 67% of the average wage where the reduction was only 0.1 percentage points. In New Zealand, the net personal average tax rate significantly decreased for half of the family types, notably by 11.4 percentage points for the single parents and 8.7 percentage points for the one-earner married couple with two children at the average wage level. In Denmark, the tax burden also significantly declined for half of the family types by percentage points ranging from 5.1 to 7.8. The largest decrease was observed for the single workers at 167% of the average wage.

The net personal average tax rate also decreased strongly in Ireland for most families with children and especially for single parents at 67% of the average wage (-22.1 percentage points). There were also substantial changes for the latter in the Netherlands and the United Kingdom (-14.4 percentage points and -11.0 respectively). There are five other OECD member countries with reductions in the net personal average tax rate exceeding five percentage points in some family types: Australia, Canada, Estonia, Hungary and Spain. In Australia, there were reductions of 5.5 percentage points for the one-earner married couple with two children and 5.3 percentage points for the single parent. For the latter, the net tax burden declined by 5.4 percentage points in Spain. A significant decrease was observed in Hungary for the single worker at 167% of the average wage (-8.3 percentage points). In Canada, the single parent and the one-earner couple at the average wage level experienced a decrease of more than 5 percentage points (-6.8 and –5.2 percentage points respectively). In Estonia, the married couples with children had their net tax burden decreased by more than 5 percentage points: 6.3 percentage points for the one-earner couple at the average wage level, 5.9 percentage points for the two-earner couple at 133% of the average wage and 5.7 percentage points for the two-earner couple at 167% of the average wage.

Between 2000 and 2015, an increase of five or more percentage points in the net tax burden for one or more family types was only observed in nine countries. In six of these countries, Austria, the Czech Republic, Iceland, Mexico, Norway and the Slovak Republic, the single parents earning 67% of the average wage saw increases of between 6 and 17 percentage points. There were increases of similar size for other family types in five countries. For example, in Mexico there were increases of between 7 and 8 percentage points for each of the other family types except the single person earning 167% of the average wage (+4.9 percentage points). The net personal average tax rate increased by 7.0 percentage points for the one-earner married couple with children in the Czech Republic and the single worker on 167% of the average wage in Portugal.

Progressivity

The discussion of the 2015 results in Part I of this publication gave some consideration to their use in assessing the progressivity of personal income taxes and the results presented in Part II can also be used to look at the evolution of this measure.

The degree of progressivity of the personal income tax system can be assessed by comparing the burden faced by single persons earning 67% of the average wage with that faced by their counterparts earning 167% of the average wage. Hence Table 6.1b is compared with Table 6.3b. For all OECD countries (except Hungary and Mexico) and for all years between 2000 and 2015 the lower paid worker always pays a lower percentage of income in personal income tax than the higher paid worker. In Hungary, the exceptions are that the levels are the same for both workers from 2013 onwards.

On average, the progressivity of the personal income taxes has not changed very much in OECD countries. On average (excluding Mexico), the single worker earning 67% of the average wage level paid 51% of the tax burden of the worker earning 167% of the average wage level in both 2000 and 2015.

Comparing the situation in each OECD country, personal income taxes have become more progressive in sixteen countries. The most significant changes were in New Zealand where the burdens on lower paid worker fell from 77% to 58%; and in Sweden, where it fell from about 68% to 49%.

Personal income taxes have become slightly less progressive (using this measure) in fifteen OECD countries: Australia, Austria, Denmark, Estonia, Greece, Hungary, Iceland, Korea, the Netherlands, Norway, Poland, Portugal, the Slovak Republic, Spain and the United States. The most significant change occurred in Hungary where the ratio rose from about 58% of the higher paid worker in 2000 to be at the same level from 2013 onwards.

Families

The results presented in Tables 6.5 and 6.2 can be used to compare the tax burdens faced by a one-earner married couple with two children at the average wage level and the single worker without children at the same income level. Focusing on the net tax burden (personal income tax plus employee social security contributions less cash benefits which can be found in Part c of the Tables), one observes that the OECD average fiscal savings for the married couple compared with the single worker were the same in 2000 and 2015.

The savings for the one-earner married couple have increased in fifteen countries and declined in seventeen others. There were three countries where the fiscal savings have increased by more than 5 percentage points; in New Zealand increasing by 6.9 percentage points from 5.8% to 12.7% of income and in Portugal and Ireland where the increases were of 5.3 and 5.1 percentage points respectively. There were corresponding reductions of more than 5 percentage points in the Czech Republic where the fiscal savings decreased by 6.2 percentage points from 27.8% to 21.6% of income and in Norway and the Netherlands where the declines were of 6.0 and 5.1 percentage points respectively.

Tables showing the income taxes, social security contributions and cash benefits

The evolution of the income taxes, social security contributions and cash benefits for the eight family types across the OECD over the period 2000 to 2015 is presented in Tables 6.1 to 6.8. Each of the Tables 1 to 8 corresponds to a particular family type and each is divided into three parts.

- Part a. tables containing the (average) tax wedge comprising income taxes plus employee and employer social security contributions (including any applicable payroll taxes) less cash benefits,
- Part b. tables providing the (average) burden of personal income taxes, and the
- Part c. tables depicting the (average) burden of income taxes plus employee social security contributions less cash benefits (*net* personal average tax rates).

Tables 6.9 and 6.10 show the average gross and net earnings of a single individual between 2000 and 2015 in US dollar using purchasing power parities of national currencies and in national currencies.

Table 6.1a. Income tax plus employee and employer contributions less cash benefits, single persons at 67% of average earnings

Tax burden as a % of labour costs, single persons without children

	2000	2005	2008	2009	2010	2011	2012	2013	2014	2015
Australia	25.9	25.1	22.0	20.8	21.0	20.7	21.7	21.9	22.4	23.1
Austria	43.2	43.3	44.5	43.3	43.5	43.9	44.2	44.6	44.9	45.0
Belgium	51.4	49.4	50.3	50.0	50.4	50.6	50.5	50.0	49.9	49.5
Canada	27.7	27.4	26.6	26.1	25.8	26.0	26.2	26.3	26.5	26.6
Chile	7.0	7.0	7.0	7.0	7.0	7.0	7.0	7.0	7.0	7.0
Czech Republic	41.3	42.0	40.1	38.8	39.0	39.7	39.4	39.4	39.6	39.9
Denmark	38.1	36.1	35.9	35.4	34.2	34.5	34.6	34.2	34.1	34.3
Estonia	39.8	38.1	37.1	37.8	38.7	39.0	39.2	38.8	38.9	38.0
Finland	42.7	39.3	38.7	37.2	36.8	36.8	36.8	37.6	38.2	38.3
France	43.9	46.5	46.6	46.6	46.8	47.0	47.0	45.6	45.1	43.5
Germany	47.6	47.3	46.5	45.9	44.9	45.6	45.5	45.1	45.1	45.3
Greece	36.0	35.5	36.3	36.6	35.8	40.0	39.8	37.0	35.8	34.7
Hungary	51.4	43.1	46.8	46.2	43.8	45.2	47.9	49.0	49.0	49.0
Iceland	23.8	28.3	27.6	26.1	28.4	29.4	29.3	29.7	29.3	29.9
Ireland	18.2	16.9	15.1	16.2	16.8	20.0	20.8	21.8	22.0	21.6
Israel[1]	23.2	18.1	15.5	14.5	14.1	13.9	13.8	13.6	14.2	14.6
Italy	43.6	42.5	43.3	43.5	44.0	44.5	44.7	44.9	42.3	42.0
Japan	23.4	26.5	28.0	27.8	28.9	29.5	29.9	30.2	30.6	30.8
Korea	15.0	15.7	17.4	16.9	17.4	17.8	18.0	18.4	18.5	18.6
Luxembourg	29.8	27.3	28.2	27.4	27.7	29.5	29.2	30.1	30.5	31.1
Mexico	7.6	10.1	11.0	11.9	12.9	13.2	13.6	14.4	14.7	15.0
Netherlands	42.3	41.7	34.1	33.3	33.6	33.5	33.5	32.2	31.4	31.0
New Zealand	18.6	18.8	18.1	15.5	14.3	13.0	13.1	13.3	13.4	13.5
Norway	35.1	34.3	34.2	34.1	34.1	34.3	34.2	34.1	33.8	33.6
Poland	34.6	35.1	31.4	31.1	31.3	31.6	32.9	33.1	33.3	33.4
Portugal	33.2	32.1	32.2	31.9	32.2	32.3	32.6	35.2	34.9	36.2
Slovak Republic	40.6	34.9	36.1	34.4	34.7	36.1	36.9	38.5	38.6	38.8
Slovenia	42.6	41.8	40.3	39.7	38.6	38.7	38.6	38.5	38.6	38.6
Spain	34.9	35.7	34.1	34.4	36.5	36.8	37.2	37.2	37.3	36.0
Sweden	48.6	46.6	42.6	41.3	40.7	40.7	40.8	40.9	40.5	40.7
Switzerland	20.2	19.5	19.1	19.1	19.3	19.6	19.4	19.4	19.4	19.4
Turkey[2]	39.1	42.0	36.1	34.1	34.4	34.5	34.6	34.9	35.8	36.1
United Kingdom	29.1	30.6	29.7	29.1	29.4	28.5	27.9	26.8	26.2	26.0
United States	29.0	28.7	27.4	28.0	28.3	27.8	27.8	29.4	29.5	29.5
Unweighted average										
OECD-Average	**33.2**	**32.6**	**31.8**	**31.2**	**31.3**	**31.8**	**32.0**	**32.2**	**32.1**	**32.1**
OECD-EU 21	**39.7**	**38.4**	**37.6**	**37.2**	**37.1**	**37.8**	**38.1**	**38.1**	**37.9**	**37.7**

Disclaimer: *http://oe.cd/disclaimer*

1. Information on data for Israel: *http://oe.cd/israel-disclaimer*.
2. Wage figures are based on the old definition of average worker (ISIC D, rev3.) for years 2000 to 2006.

StatLink http://dx.doi.org/10.1787/888933341536

Table 6.1b. **Income tax, single persons at 67% of average earnings**

Tax burden as a % of gross wage earnings, single persons without children

	2000	2005	2008	2009	2010	2011	2012	2013	2014	2015
Australia	21.1	20.6	17.3	15.8	16.0	16.0	17.1	17.3	17.7	18.5
Austria	7.6	8.8	10.4	8.7	9.0	9.5	9.9	10.4	10.7	11.0
Belgium	22.8	21.8	22.2	21.9	22.5	22.6	22.5	22.1	22.0	21.5
Canada	15.0	13.0	12.4	11.9	11.5	11.6	11.6	11.6	11.8	11.8
Chile	0.0	0.0	0.0	0.0	0.0	0.0	0.0	0.0	0.0	0.0
Czech Republic	8.3	9.2	6.7	6.9	7.2	8.2	7.8	7.8	8.1	8.4
Denmark	28.9	27.5	35.4	34.8	34.0	34.2	34.2	33.8	33.6	33.8
Estonia	19.9	16.4	15.5	14.9	14.8	15.2	15.5	16.0	16.2	15.4
Finland	20.9	18.6	17.8	16.5	15.7	15.5	14.9	15.9	16.0	16.0
France	12.5	12.3	12.2	12.2	12.2	12.4	12.6	12.6	12.6	11.7
Germany	16.3	15.0	15.4	14.8	13.8	13.9	14.1	14.1	14.1	14.2
Greece	2.3	1.4	2.4	2.8	1.8	6.6	6.1	3.2	3.2	3.1
Hungary	17.6	8.8	11.1	11.8	10.8	12.1	16.0	16.0	16.0	16.0
Iceland	20.0	24.0	23.1	20.8	21.5	22.6	23.1	23.7	23.3	24.1
Ireland	11.2	5.3	3.2	4.5	5.1	8.6	9.4	9.4	9.6	9.2
Israel[1]	12.1	6.6	5.7	5.0	4.4	4.4	4.4	4.2	4.7	4.9
Italy	15.2	14.3	15.6	15.9	16.6	17.2	17.5	17.7	14.4	13.9
Japan	5.5	5.3	6.3	6.3	6.1	6.1	6.1	6.1	6.1	6.1
Korea	0.8	1.0	1.7	1.3	1.4	1.4	1.5	1.8	1.7	1.8
Luxembourg	10.3	7.3	8.2	6.9	7.3	7.8	8.2	9.3	9.7	9.9
Mexico	-5.7	-3.2	-2.5	-1.4	-0.4	0.0	0.4	1.4	1.8	2.0
Netherlands	5.3	4.2	5.2	5.4	5.3	5.3	5.3	5.7	5.3	7.1
New Zealand	18.6	18.8	18.1	15.5	14.3	13.0	13.1	13.3	13.4	13.5
Norway	19.0	17.9	18.0	17.8	17.8	17.9	17.8	17.8	17.0	16.8
Poland	2.5	2.2	3.4	3.1	3.3	3.6	3.8	4.0	4.3	4.4
Portugal	6.4	5.0	5.1	4.7	5.1	5.2	5.6	8.8	8.5	10.1
Slovak Republic	6.0	4.4	5.9	3.8	4.2	5.9	5.9	5.9	6.1	6.3
Slovenia	10.2	8.1	8.0	7.9	6.6	6.7	6.6	6.5	6.6	6.6
Spain	8.6	9.7	7.9	8.4	11.2	11.5	12.0	12.1	12.2	10.5
Sweden	24.7	22.2	17.0	15.9	15.0	15.1	15.2	15.3	14.8	15.1
Switzerland	8.4	8.5	8.2	8.2	8.3	8.3	8.1	8.1	8.1	8.2
Turkey[2]	13.2	14.5	8.2	8.2	8.6	8.7	8.8	9.2	9.5	9.9
United Kingdom	15.1	15.5	14.6	14.2	14.4	13.5	13.1	12.0	11.5	11.2
United States	15.0	14.3	15.1	13.6	13.8	15.2	15.3	15.1	15.2	15.2
Unweighted average										
OECD-Average	**12.2**	**11.2**	**11.0**	**10.6**	**10.6**	**11.1**	**11.3**	**11.4**	**11.3**	**11.4**
OECD-EU 21	**13.0**	**11.3**	**11.6**	**11.2**	**11.2**	**11.9**	**12.2**	**12.3**	**12.2**	**12.2**

Disclaimer: *http://oe.cd/disclaimer*

1. Information on data for Israel: *http://oe.cd/israel-disclaimer*.
2. Wage figures are based on the old definition of average worker (ISIC D, rev3.) for years 2000 to 2006.

StatLink http://dx.doi.org/10.1787/888933341549

Table 6.1c. **Income tax plus employee contributions less cash benefits, single persons at 67% of average earnings**

Tax burden as a % of gross wage earnings, single persons without children

	2000	2005	2008	2009	2010	2011	2012	2013	2014	2015
Australia	21.1	20.6	17.3	15.8	16.0	16.0	17.1	17.3	17.7	18.5
Austria	25.6	26.8	28.5	26.7	27.0	27.6	28.0	28.5	28.8	29.0
Belgium	35.8	35.1	36.1	35.8	36.4	36.5	36.4	36.0	35.9	35.4
Canada	19.5	19.0	18.2	17.7	17.4	17.4	17.5	17.6	17.8	17.8
Chile	7.0	7.0	7.0	7.0	7.0	7.0	7.0	7.0	7.0	7.0
Czech Republic	20.8	21.7	19.2	17.9	18.2	19.2	18.8	18.8	19.1	19.4
Denmark	37.8	35.5	35.4	34.8	33.5	33.7	33.7	33.3	33.1	33.4
Estonia	19.9	17.4	16.1	16.7	17.6	18.0	18.3	18.0	18.2	17.0
Finland	27.8	24.8	23.9	22.7	22.7	22.6	22.4	23.4	23.9	24.1
France	25.9	25.9	25.9	25.9	25.9	26.1	26.3	26.4	26.7	25.9
Germany	36.8	36.4	36.1	35.4	34.3	34.8	34.9	34.5	34.5	34.7
Greece	18.2	17.4	18.4	18.8	17.8	22.8	22.6	19.7	19.2	18.6
Hungary	30.1	22.3	28.1	28.8	27.8	29.6	34.5	34.5	34.5	34.5
Iceland	20.2	24.2	23.8	21.6	22.2	23.3	23.8	24.3	23.9	24.6
Ireland	11.2	8.0	6.0	7.2	7.9	11.4	12.3	13.4	13.6	13.2
Israel[1]	19.4	13.4	11.8	10.9	10.4	10.3	10.2	10.0	10.5	10.8
Italy	24.4	23.5	25.1	25.4	26.1	26.7	27.0	27.2	23.8	23.4
Japan	15.5	17.1	18.5	18.5	19.1	19.5	19.8	20.0	20.2	20.4
Korea	7.5	8.1	9.3	8.9	9.2	9.5	9.7	10.0	10.1	10.2
Luxembourg	21.8	19.0	20.2	19.1	19.4	20.8	20.4	21.5	22.0	22.6
Mexico	-4.4	-1.9	-1.2	-0.1	0.8	1.3	1.7	2.6	3.0	3.2
Netherlands	32.9	32.0	27.7	27.1	27.1	27.1	26.8	26.2	24.7	24.4
New Zealand	18.6	18.8	18.1	15.5	14.3	13.0	13.1	13.3	13.4	13.5
Norway	26.8	25.7	25.8	25.6	25.6	25.7	25.6	25.6	25.2	25.0
Poland	23.7	24.2	21.2	20.9	21.1	21.5	21.6	21.8	22.1	22.2
Portugal	17.4	16.0	16.1	15.7	16.1	16.2	16.6	19.8	19.5	21.1
Slovak Republic	18.0	17.8	19.3	17.2	17.6	19.3	19.3	19.3	19.5	19.7
Slovenia	32.3	30.2	30.1	30.0	28.7	28.8	28.7	28.6	28.7	28.7
Spain	15.0	16.1	14.2	14.8	17.5	17.9	18.4	18.5	18.5	16.8
Sweden	31.7	29.2	23.9	22.9	22.0	22.1	22.2	22.4	21.8	22.1
Switzerland	14.9	14.6	14.2	14.3	14.4	14.6	14.3	14.4	14.4	14.4
Turkey[2]	27.2	29.5	23.2	23.2	23.6	23.7	23.8	24.2	24.5	24.9
United Kingdom	22.8	23.8	22.9	22.4	22.6	21.7	21.2	20.0	19.5	19.2
United States	22.6	22.0	20.7	21.3	21.5	20.9	20.9	22.8	22.9	22.9
Unweighted average										
OECD-Average	**21.9**	**21.2**	**20.6**	**20.2**	**20.3**	**20.8**	**21.0**	**21.2**	**21.1**	**21.1**
OECD-EU 21	**25.2**	**24.0**	**23.5**	**23.2**	**23.2**	**24.0**	**24.3**	**24.4**	**24.2**	**24.1**

Disclaimer: *http://oe.cd/disclaimer*

1. Information on data for Israel: *http://oe.cd/israel-disclaimer*.
2. Wage figures are based on the old definition of average worker (ISIC D, rev3.) for years 2000 to 2006.

StatLink http://dx.doi.org/10.1787/888933341553

Table 6.2a. Income tax plus employee and employer contributions less cash benefits, single persons at 100% of average earnings

Tax burden as a % of labour costs, single persons without children

	2000	2005	2008	2009	2010	2011	2012	2013	2014	2015
Australia	31.0	28.5	26.9	26.7	26.8	26.7	27.3	27.4	27.7	28.4
Austria	47.3	48.1	49.0	47.9	48.2	48.5	48.8	49.2	49.4	49.5
Belgium	57.1	55.5	55.9	55.7	55.9	56.1	56.0	55.7	55.6	55.3
Canada	32.9	31.9	31.3	30.5	30.4	30.7	30.8	31.0	31.6	31.6
Chile	7.0	7.0	7.0	7.0	7.0	7.0	7.0	7.0	7.0	7.0
Czech Republic	42.6	43.7	43.4	42.0	42.1	42.6	42.5	42.4	42.6	42.8
Denmark	42.1	38.8	38.9	37.5	36.4	36.6	36.7	36.4	36.2	36.4
Estonia	41.3	39.9	38.4	39.2	40.1	40.3	40.4	39.9	40.0	39.0
Finland	47.5	44.4	43.8	42.5	42.3	42.3	42.5	43.1	43.7	43.9
France	50.4	50.5	49.8	49.8	49.9	50.0	50.1	48.9	48.4	48.5
Germany	52.9	52.1	51.3	50.8	49.1	49.7	49.6	49.2	49.3	49.4
Greece	39.1	41.2	41.5	41.3	40.1	43.2	42.9	41.6	40.5	39.3
Hungary	54.7	51.1	54.1	53.1	46.6	49.5	49.5	49.0	49.0	49.0
Iceland	28.8	32.1	30.9	30.5	33.4	34.1	33.8	34.1	33.7	34.0
Ireland	28.9	23.5	22.3	24.7	25.8	25.8	26.9	27.6	27.9	27.5
Israel[1]	29.6	25.5	22.9	21.3	20.7	20.8	20.4	20.4	21.1	21.6
Italy	47.1	45.9	46.6	46.8	47.2	47.6	47.7	47.8	48.2	49.0
Japan	24.7	27.7	29.5	29.2	30.2	30.8	31.3	31.6	32.0	32.2
Korea	16.4	17.3	20.0	19.5	20.1	20.5	21.0	21.5	21.7	21.9
Luxembourg	35.8	33.4	34.7	33.9	34.3	36.3	36.0	37.2	37.6	38.3
Mexico	12.7	14.7	15.1	15.3	16.0	18.7	19.0	19.3	19.5	19.7
Netherlands	40.0	38.9	39.2	38.0	38.1	38.0	38.8	37.0	36.8	36.2
New Zealand	19.4	20.0	20.5	18.1	17.0	15.9	16.4	16.9	17.2	17.6
Norway	38.6	37.2	37.6	37.3	37.3	37.6	37.4	37.3	36.9	36.6
Poland	36.5	37.1	33.2	32.7	32.9	33.1	34.3	34.4	34.6	34.7
Portugal	37.3	36.8	36.9	36.5	37.1	38.0	37.6	41.4	41.2	42.1
Slovak Republic	41.9	38.0	38.8	37.7	37.9	38.8	39.6	41.1	41.3	41.3
Slovenia	46.3	45.6	42.9	42.2	42.5	42.6	42.5	42.4	42.5	42.6
Spain	38.6	39.0	38.0	38.3	39.7	40.0	40.6	40.7	40.7	39.6
Sweden	50.1	48.1	44.8	43.2	42.8	42.8	42.9	43.0	42.5	42.7
Switzerland	22.9	22.2	21.9	22.0	22.1	22.3	22.1	22.1	22.2	22.2
Turkey[2]	40.4	42.8	38.7	36.7	37.0	37.0	37.1	37.4	38.1	38.3
United Kingdom	32.6	33.9	32.8	32.4	32.6	32.5	32.1	31.4	31.0	30.8
United States	30.8	30.4	30.1	30.3	30.7	29.9	29.8	31.5	31.6	31.7
Unweighted average										
OECD-Average	**36.6**	**36.0**	**35.6**	**35.0**	**35.0**	**35.5**	**35.6**	**35.8**	**35.9**	**35.9**
OECD-EU 21	**43.3**	**42.2**	**41.7**	**41.3**	**41.0**	**41.6**	**41.8**	**41.9**	**41.9**	**41.8**

Disclaimer: *http://oe.cd/disclaimer*

1. Information on data for Israel: *http://oe.cd/israel-disclaimer*.
2. Wage figures are based on the old definition of average worker (ISIC D, rev3.) for years 2000 to 2006.

StatLink http://dx.doi.org/10.1787/888933341567

Table 6.2b. **Income tax, single persons at 100% of the average earnings**

Tax burden as a % of gross wage earnings, single persons without children

	2000	2005	2008	2009	2010	2011	2012	2013	2014	2015
Australia	26.6	24.2	22.5	22.1	22.3	22.3	23.0	23.1	23.4	24.1
Austria	12.9	15.0	16.2	14.7	15.0	15.5	15.9	16.3	16.6	16.8
Belgium	29.0	28.0	28.5	28.3	28.7	28.8	28.7	28.4	28.4	28.1
Canada	19.2	16.3	16.1	15.2	15.1	15.3	15.3	15.3	15.7	15.8
Chile	0.0	0.0	0.0	0.0	0.0	0.0	0.0	0.0	0.0	0.0
Czech Republic	10.0	11.5	11.1	11.3	11.5	12.1	11.9	11.9	12.1	12.3
Denmark	32.9	30.5	38.6	37.2	36.3	36.4	36.5	36.1	35.9	36.1
Estonia	21.9	18.8	17.3	16.8	16.7	16.9	17.1	17.5	17.6	16.8
Finland	26.9	24.7	24.2	23.0	22.3	22.2	21.8	22.5	22.7	22.7
France	15.7	15.3	14.1	14.1	14.2	14.2	14.5	14.6	14.6	14.7
Germany	22.7	20.8	21.2	20.6	18.7	18.9	19.0	19.0	19.0	19.2
Greece	6.1	8.8	9.1	8.8	7.2	10.8	10.1	9.1	9.1	8.8
Hungary	23.2	20.1	21.3	20.8	14.4	17.6	16.6	16.0	16.0	16.0
Iceland	25.3	28.0	26.8	25.7	27.1	27.9	28.2	28.6	28.2	28.7
Ireland	17.2	12.2	10.8	13.5	14.7	14.7	15.9	15.8	16.2	15.7
Israel[1]	18.0	13.3	11.2	9.7	9.0	9.1	8.7	8.6	9.1	9.4
Italy	19.9	18.8	20.0	20.2	20.7	21.3	21.5	21.6	22.1	23.1
Japan	7.0	6.7	8.0	7.9	7.6	7.6	7.6	7.6	7.7	7.7
Korea	2.3	2.8	4.6	4.1	4.5	4.4	4.9	5.2	5.3	5.4
Luxembourg	17.0	14.2	15.3	14.0	14.6	15.3	15.8	17.2	17.7	17.9
Mexico	1.0	3.2	3.8	4.1	4.8	7.9	8.2	8.5	8.8	8.9
Netherlands	9.6	11.2	15.5	16.6	16.2	16.4	17.0	15.7	15.3	16.7
New Zealand	19.4	20.0	20.5	18.1	17.0	15.9	16.4	16.9	17.2	17.6
Norway	22.9	21.2	21.8	21.5	21.5	21.6	21.4	21.4	20.5	20.2
Poland	4.8	4.5	5.5	5.0	5.1	5.4	5.5	5.6	5.8	5.9
Portugal	11.4	10.8	11.0	10.5	11.2	12.3	11.8	16.5	16.2	17.3
Slovak Republic	7.8	8.4	9.4	8.0	8.3	9.4	9.4	9.4	9.5	9.6
Slovenia	13.5	12.6	11.0	10.8	11.2	11.3	11.1	11.0	11.1	11.2
Spain	13.5	13.9	12.9	13.4	15.4	15.7	16.5	16.6	16.6	15.1
Sweden	26.7	24.2	19.9	18.4	17.8	17.9	17.9	18.1	17.4	17.7
Switzerland	11.3	11.5	11.1	11.2	11.3	11.2	11.0	11.0	11.1	11.1
Turkey[2]	14.7	15.5	11.3	11.3	11.6	11.6	11.8	12.0	12.3	12.5
United Kingdom	17.4	17.6	16.4	16.1	16.2	15.6	15.4	14.6	14.3	14.1
United States	17.3	16.6	17.7	16.5	17.0	18.0	18.0	17.8	18.0	18.0
Unweighted average										
OECD-Average	**16.0**	**15.3**	**15.4**	**15.0**	**14.9**	**15.3**	**15.4**	**15.6**	**15.6**	**15.7**
OECD-EU 21	**17.2**	**16.3**	**16.6**	**16.3**	**16.0**	**16.6**	**16.7**	**16.8**	**16.9**	**17.0**

Disclaimer: *http://oe.cd/disclaimer*

1. Information on data for Israel: *http://oe.cd/israel-disclaimer*.
2. Wage figures are based on the old definition of average worker (ISIC D, rev3.) for years 2000 to 2006.

StatLink http://dx.doi.org/10.1787/888933341575

Table 6.2c. **Income tax plus employee contributions less cash benefits, single persons at 100% of average earnings**

Tax burden as a % of gross wage earnings, single persons without children

	2000	2005	2008	2009	2010	2011	2012	2013	2014	2015
Australia	26.6	24.2	22.5	22.1	22.3	22.3	23.0	23.1	23.4	24.1
Austria	31.0	33.0	34.3	32.8	33.1	33.6	33.9	34.4	34.7	34.9
Belgium	43.0	42.0	42.5	42.3	42.7	42.8	42.7	42.4	42.4	42.0
Canada	25.1	23.9	23.4	22.5	22.4	22.5	22.6	22.7	23.4	23.4
Chile	7.0	7.0	7.0	7.0	7.0	7.0	7.0	7.0	7.0	7.0
Czech Republic	22.5	24.0	23.6	22.3	22.5	23.1	22.9	22.9	23.1	23.3
Denmark	41.9	38.5	38.6	37.2	35.9	36.1	36.1	35.8	35.6	35.9
Estonia	21.9	19.8	17.9	18.6	19.5	19.7	19.9	19.5	19.6	18.4
Finland	33.9	31.0	30.4	29.3	29.4	29.4	29.4	30.1	30.7	30.9
France	29.2	28.9	27.8	27.8	27.8	27.9	28.2	28.4	28.6	28.9
Germany	43.2	42.2	41.9	41.2	39.2	39.8	39.8	39.4	39.5	39.7
Greece	22.0	24.8	25.1	24.8	23.2	27.0	26.6	25.6	25.1	24.3
Hungary	35.7	33.6	38.3	37.8	31.4	35.1	35.1	34.5	34.5	34.5
Iceland	25.4	28.2	27.2	26.2	27.6	28.4	28.7	29.1	28.6	29.1
Ireland	20.3	15.2	13.9	16.7	17.9	17.8	19.1	19.8	20.2	19.7
Israel[1]	26.1	21.3	19.3	17.7	17.0	17.0	16.6	16.4	17.0	17.3
Italy	29.0	28.0	29.5	29.7	30.2	30.8	31.0	31.1	31.6	32.6
Japan	17.0	18.5	20.2	20.0	20.6	21.0	21.3	21.5	21.8	22.0
Korea	9.0	9.9	12.1	11.7	12.3	12.5	13.0	13.5	13.6	13.8
Luxembourg	28.7	25.9	27.4	26.2	26.8	28.4	28.1	29.5	30.0	30.7
Mexico	2.5	4.7	5.2	5.4	6.1	9.3	9.6	9.8	10.1	10.3
Netherlands	33.6	32.5	32.8	31.8	31.7	31.7	32.2	31.2	30.5	29.9
New Zealand	19.4	20.0	20.5	18.1	17.0	15.9	16.4	16.9	17.2	17.6
Norway	30.7	29.0	29.6	29.3	29.3	29.4	29.2	29.2	28.7	28.4
Poland	25.9	26.5	23.3	22.8	23.0	23.2	23.3	23.4	23.6	23.7
Portugal	22.4	21.8	22.0	21.5	22.2	23.3	22.8	27.5	27.2	28.3
Slovak Republic	19.8	21.8	22.8	21.4	21.7	22.8	22.8	22.8	22.9	23.0
Slovenia	35.6	34.7	33.1	32.9	33.3	33.4	33.2	33.1	33.2	33.3
Spain	19.8	20.3	19.3	19.8	21.7	22.0	22.9	22.9	23.0	21.5
Sweden	33.7	31.2	26.9	25.4	24.8	24.8	24.9	25.1	24.4	24.7
Switzerland	17.8	17.5	17.1	17.3	17.4	17.5	17.2	17.3	17.3	17.4
Turkey[2]	28.7	30.5	26.3	26.3	26.6	26.6	26.8	27.0	27.3	27.5
United Kingdom	25.8	26.9	25.6	25.2	25.4	25.1	24.7	24.0	23.6	23.4
United States	24.9	24.3	23.9	24.2	24.6	23.6	23.6	25.5	25.6	25.6
Unweighted average										
OECD-Average	**25.9**	**25.3**	**25.0**	**24.6**	**24.5**	**25.0**	**25.1**	**25.4**	**25.4**	**25.5**
OECD-EU 21	**29.5**	**28.7**	**28.4**	**28.0**	**27.8**	**28.5**	**28.6**	**28.7**	**28.8**	**28.8**

Disclaimer: *http://oe.cd/disclaimer*

1. Information on data for Israel: *http://oe.cd/israel-disclaimer*.
2. Wage figures are based on the old definition of average worker (ISIC D, rev3.) for years 2000 to 2006.

StatLink http://dx.doi.org/10.1787/888933341581

Table 6.3a. **Income tax plus employee and employer contributions less cash benefits, single persons at 167% of average earnings**

Tax burden as a % of labour costs, single persons without children

	2000	2005	2008	2009	2010	2011	2012	2013	2014	2015
Australia	38.8	36.1	32.7	32.6	32.4	32.2	33.1	33.2	33.4	34.0
Austria	50.4	51.4	51.8	51.2	51.4	51.5	51.4	51.9	52.0	52.2
Belgium	62.6	60.9	61.1	60.9	61.0	61.1	61.0	60.8	60.8	60.7
Canada	35.2	33.2	32.9	32.6	32.7	32.8	33.0	33.1	33.3	33.4
Chile	7.5	7.0	7.0	7.0	7.6	7.7	7.9	7.8	7.9	7.9
Czech Republic	44.8	46.1	46.1	44.6	44.7	45.0	44.9	44.9	45.0	45.1
Denmark	50.0	47.7	48.1	47.0	43.1	43.5	43.7	42.9	42.3	42.4
Estonia	42.5	41.4	39.5	40.3	41.2	41.3	41.4	40.8	40.9	39.9
Finland	53.2	50.3	49.5	48.3	48.2	48.3	48.5	48.9	49.5	49.7
France	52.5	53.3	53.4	53.6	53.6	53.8	54.0	54.1	54.3	54.3
Germany	56.2	54.9	53.1	53.1	51.5	51.3	51.3	51.3	51.4	51.3
Greece	45.1	48.0	46.4	46.0	45.6	48.6	48.2	49.3	48.3	46.8
Hungary	59.2	56.7	59.1	58.3	53.1	51.6	50.7	49.0	49.0	49.0
Iceland	39.6	37.0	33.6	34.1	37.8	38.4	38.3	38.6	38.1	38.3
Ireland	39.4	34.9	33.1	35.2	36.4	38.0	38.9	39.2	39.5	38.8
Israel[1]	38.1	34.6	32.2	30.0	29.5	29.2	28.6	29.2	30.0	30.6
Italy	51.1	50.7	51.8	52.0	52.5	53.0	53.2	53.3	53.8	54.6
Japan	28.5	30.3	32.5	32.3	33.3	33.8	34.2	34.5	34.7	34.9
Korea	20.5	21.4	22.6	21.8	21.7	22.2	22.6	23.0	23.5	24.0
Luxembourg	44.1	40.7	41.7	41.4	41.6	43.7	43.3	44.4	44.6	45.2
Mexico	19.5	21.9	20.6	20.9	21.4	21.6	22.0	22.2	22.6	22.8
Netherlands	44.9	42.4	42.5	41.8	41.8	41.8	42.5	41.9	41.9	41.5
New Zealand	24.2	25.8	26.3	24.6	23.3	22.0	22.4	22.8	23.1	23.3
Norway	45.2	43.9	43.2	43.0	43.0	43.2	43.1	43.0	42.5	42.4
Poland	38.1	38.7	35.1	34.1	34.2	34.3	35.5	35.5	35.6	35.7
Portugal	42.3	42.3	42.6	42.2	43.1	44.6	43.6	47.7	47.5	48.0
Slovak Republic	45.2	40.2	40.7	40.1	40.3	40.8	41.6	43.3	43.4	43.4
Slovenia	51.0	52.3	48.3	47.1	47.6	47.7	47.5	46.1	46.4	46.5
Spain	41.0	42.4	41.4	41.6	42.4	42.5	43.5	44.3	45.0	44.2
Sweden	55.7	54.7	52.8	51.2	51.0	50.9	50.7	50.8	50.6	51.0
Switzerland	27.4	26.6	26.4	26.5	26.6	26.8	26.7	26.7	26.7	26.8
Turkey[2]	35.0	44.6	41.1	39.2	39.8	40.0	40.2	40.6	41.5	41.9
United Kingdom	35.8	37.7	37.5	36.9	37.2	37.9	37.8	37.6	37.3	37.3
United States	37.1	35.5	35.5	35.6	35.9	34.7	34.6	36.3	36.4	36.4
Unweighted average										
OECD-Average	**41.2**	**40.8**	**40.1**	**39.6**	**39.6**	**39.9**	**40.0**	**40.3**	**40.4**	**40.4**
OECD-EU 21	**47.9**	**47.0**	**46.5**	**46.0**	**45.8**	**46.2**	**46.3**	**46.6**	**46.6**	**46.5**

Disclaimer: *http://oe.cd/disclaimer*

1. Information on data for Israel: *http://oe.cd/israel-disclaimer*.
2. Wage figures are based on the old definition of average worker (ISIC D, rev3.) for years 2000 to 2006.

StatLink http://dx.doi.org/10.1787/888933341593

Table 6.3b. **Income tax, single persons at 167% of average earnings**

Tax burden as a % of gross wage earnings, single persons without children

	2000	2005	2008	2009	2010	2011	2012	2013	2014	2015
Australia	34.9	32.2	28.7	28.3	28.2	28.2	29.2	29.2	29.4	30.1
Austria	20.4	22.1	23.1	22.0	22.2	22.5	22.8	23.0	23.2	23.2
Belgium	36.0	34.8	35.3	35.2	35.5	35.5	35.5	35.2	35.2	35.1
Canada	25.6	22.3	22.3	21.6	21.7	21.8	21.8	21.8	22.2	22.2
Chile	0.5	0.0	0.0	0.0	0.6	0.7	0.9	0.8	0.9	0.9
Czech Republic	13.0	14.8	14.8	14.8	14.9	15.3	15.2	15.2	15.3	15.4
Denmark	40.9	39.5	47.9	46.8	42.9	43.2	43.4	42.5	41.9	42.1
Estonia	23.6	20.8	18.7	18.3	18.2	18.3	18.4	18.7	18.8	18.0
Finland	34.0	31.9	31.2	30.0	29.5	29.4	29.0	29.6	29.8	29.8
France	21.2	20.0	20.2	20.3	20.3	20.5	20.8	20.8	20.8	20.9
Germany	31.7	28.9	29.2	28.6	27.1	27.5	27.6	27.5	27.5	27.7
Greece	13.8	17.5	15.4	14.8	14.4	17.7	16.9	18.8	18.9	18.2
Hungary	30.3	28.1	28.2	27.6	22.8	20.3	18.1	16.0	16.0	16.0
Iceland	36.6	33.3	29.8	29.7	32.1	32.7	33.2	33.6	33.2	33.5
Ireland	28.7	24.7	22.6	24.7	26.0	27.8	28.8	28.7	29.0	28.2
Israel[1]	26.3	21.9	19.2	16.9	16.4	16.0	15.4	15.7	16.4	16.8
Italy	25.3	25.1	26.8	27.1	27.7	28.3	28.5	28.7	29.4	30.4
Japan	11.1	10.8	12.8	12.4	12.0	12.0	12.2	12.1	12.4	12.4
Korea	6.7	8.1	9.3	8.6	8.6	8.5	8.8	9.2	9.6	10.0
Luxembourg	26.2	22.4	23.1	22.3	22.6	23.6	23.9	25.2	25.5	25.6
Mexico	8.0	11.8	11.2	11.5	11.9	12.3	12.7	13.0	13.3	13.5
Netherlands	25.4	25.1	27.9	28.8	28.4	28.6	29.2	28.2	27.5	28.4
New Zealand	24.2	25.8	26.3	24.6	23.3	22.0	22.4	22.8	23.1	23.3
Norway	30.4	28.7	28.1	27.9	27.9	28.0	27.8	27.8	26.8	26.7
Poland	6.6	6.4	7.7	6.5	6.6	6.8	6.8	6.9	7.0	7.1
Portugal	17.6	17.6	18.0	17.4	18.5	20.4	19.2	24.2	24.0	24.6
Slovak Republic	12.4	11.7	12.3	11.4	11.6	12.3	12.3	12.2	12.3	12.4
Slovenia	19.1	18.8	16.7	16.5	17.0	17.2	17.0	15.4	15.6	15.8
Spain	18.5	18.9	18.6	19.2	20.6	21.0	22.5	22.5	22.5	21.4
Sweden	36.3	35.3	32.8	31.1	30.9	30.8	30.5	30.6	30.4	30.9
Switzerland	16.2	16.4	16.0	16.1	16.3	16.1	16.0	16.0	16.0	16.1
Turkey[2]	18.0	17.7	14.2	14.2	14.9	15.1	15.3	15.9	16.3	16.8
United Kingdom	23.1	24.1	23.2	21.9	22.4	22.4	22.6	22.6	22.3	22.4
United States	24.3	22.5	23.3	22.6	22.9	23.5	23.5	23.4	23.4	23.5
Unweighted average										
OECD-Average	**22.6**	**21.8**	**21.6**	**21.2**	**21.1**	**21.4**	**21.4**	**21.6**	**21.6**	**21.8**
OECD-EU 21	**24.0**	**23.3**	**23.5**	**23.1**	**22.9**	**23.3**	**23.3**	**23.5**	**23.5**	**23.5**

Disclaimer: *http://oe.cd/disclaimer*

1. Information on data for Israel: *http://oe.cd/israel-disclaimer*.
2. Wage figures are based on the old definition of average worker (ISIC D, rev3.) for years 2000 to 2006.

StatLink http://dx.doi.org/10.1787/888933341600

Table 6.3c. **Income tax plus employee contributions less cash benefits, single persons at 167% of average earnings**

Tax burden as a % of gross wage earnings, single persons without children

	2000	2005	2008	2009	2010	2011	2012	2013	2014	2015
Australia	34.9	32.2	28.7	28.3	28.2	28.2	29.2	29.2	29.4	30.1
Austria	36.3	38.3	39.0	38.1	38.3	38.5	38.6	39.0	39.2	39.4
Belgium	50.1	48.8	49.3	49.2	49.5	49.6	49.5	49.2	49.2	49.1
Canada	29.3	27.2	27.0	26.5	26.6	26.7	26.8	26.8	27.1	27.1
Chile	7.5	7.0	7.0	7.0	7.6	7.7	7.9	7.8	7.9	7.9
Czech Republic	25.5	27.3	27.3	25.8	25.9	26.3	26.2	26.2	26.3	26.4
Denmark	49.9	47.5	47.9	46.8	42.9	43.2	43.4	42.5	41.9	42.1
Estonia	23.6	21.8	19.3	20.1	21.0	21.1	21.2	20.7	20.8	19.6
Finland	41.1	38.3	37.4	36.4	36.6	36.6	36.7	37.3	37.9	38.1
France	33.1	33.0	33.2	33.4	33.4	33.6	33.9	34.0	34.2	34.4
Germany	48.8	46.9	45.7	45.5	43.8	43.8	43.8	43.7	43.8	43.8
Greece	29.7	33.5	31.4	30.8	30.4	34.0	33.4	35.3	34.9	33.7
Hungary	42.8	41.6	45.2	44.6	39.8	37.8	36.6	34.5	34.5	34.5
Iceland	36.7	33.4	30.1	30.0	32.4	33.0	33.5	33.9	33.4	33.7
Ireland	32.1	27.9	25.9	28.2	29.6	31.3	32.3	32.7	33.0	32.2
Israel[1]	35.0	30.8	28.8	26.5	26.0	25.6	24.9	25.2	26.0	26.3
Italy	34.5	34.3	36.4	36.6	37.3	37.9	38.1	38.3	39.0	40.0
Japan	21.1	21.9	24.2	24.0	24.5	24.8	25.1	25.3	25.6	25.8
Korea	13.4	14.7	15.8	15.1	15.0	15.3	15.7	16.2	16.6	17.2
Luxembourg	37.9	34.2	35.3	34.6	34.9	36.8	36.3	37.6	37.9	38.5
Mexico	10.1	13.5	12.7	13.0	13.4	13.8	14.1	14.4	14.8	15.0
Netherlands	40.6	38.3	38.5	37.9	37.7	37.8	38.3	38.4	38.1	37.6
New Zealand	24.2	25.8	26.3	24.6	23.3	22.0	22.4	22.8	23.1	23.3
Norway	38.2	36.5	35.9	35.7	35.7	35.8	35.6	35.6	35.0	34.9
Poland	27.8	28.3	25.5	24.3	24.5	24.6	24.7	24.7	24.8	24.9
Portugal	28.6	28.6	29.0	28.4	29.5	31.4	30.2	35.2	35.0	35.6
Slovak Republic	24.4	24.8	25.4	24.6	24.8	25.4	25.5	25.6	25.7	25.8
Slovenia	41.2	40.9	38.8	38.6	39.1	39.3	39.1	37.5	37.7	37.9
Spain	24.4	25.1	24.6	25.2	26.5	26.8	28.3	28.5	28.7	27.7
Sweden	41.1	40.0	37.5	35.8	35.6	35.5	35.3	35.4	35.1	35.6
Switzerland	22.7	22.3	22.0	22.1	22.2	22.3	22.2	22.2	22.2	22.2
Turkey[2]	26.9	32.7	29.2	29.2	29.9	30.1	30.3	30.9	31.3	31.8
United Kingdom	28.8	30.5	30.3	29.7	30.0	30.4	30.4	30.1	29.8	29.8
United States	31.9	30.1	30.1	30.3	30.6	29.1	29.2	31.0	31.1	31.1
Unweighted average										
OECD-Average	**31.6**	**31.1**	**30.6**	**30.2**	**30.2**	**30.5**	**30.5**	**30.8**	**30.9**	**31.0**
OECD-EU 21	**35.3**	**34.8**	**34.4**	**34.0**	**33.9**	**34.4**	**34.4**	**34.6**	**34.7**	**34.6**

Disclaimer: *http://oe.cd/disclaimer*

1. Information on data for Israel: *http://oe.cd/israel-disclaimer*.
2. Wage figures are based on the old definition of average worker (ISIC D, rev3.) for years 2000 to 2006.

StatLink http://dx.doi.org/10.1787/888933341615

Table 6.4a. **Income tax plus employee and employer contributions less cash benefits, single parent at 67% of average earnings**

Tax burden as a % of labour costs, single parent with two children

	2000	2005	2008	2009	2010	2011	2012	2013	2014	2015
Australia	4.0	-3.2	-4.9	-7.2	-6.5	-5.7	-3.2	-2.6	-1.8	-1.4
Austria	25.2	25.7	28.4	25.5	26.1	27.2	28.0	28.8	29.2	29.3
Belgium	36.4	35.4	35.9	35.7	36.8	37.0	36.9	36.2	36.1	35.8
Canada	-0.4	-0.9	-6.1	-9.7	-7.4	-7.0	-6.5	-6.1	-4.7	-5.9
Chile	2.8	3.0	3.2	3.3	6.0	6.0	6.1	6.1	6.1	6.1
Czech Republic	12.7	17.8	15.1	15.6	15.8	25.4	24.2	24.1	24.7	24.5
Denmark	12.3	10.1	11.3	10.6	9.0	9.7	9.7	9.2	7.2	7.6
Estonia	18.5	21.8	18.7	22.7	24.1	25.2	26.3	26.6	27.4	21.5
Finland	28.3	26.6	26.9	25.6	25.5	25.7	25.6	26.8	27.5	28.3
France	34.5	38.0	38.6	38.5	38.8	38.9	38.9	37.3	36.7	35.9
Germany	31.8	33.5	33.2	31.2	29.8	31.0	31.2	30.9	31.2	30.8
Greece	35.4	35.2	35.3	35.7	34.4	38.8	38.6	33.4	32.1	30.9
Hungary	34.0	26.1	29.9	29.8	27.4	20.2	23.0	25.5	26.4	27.2
Iceland	5.9	14.8	14.9	12.2	16.7	19.0	17.0	19.0	18.1	19.5
Ireland	-0.7	-19.2	-25.1	-29.4	-27.8	-26.2	-21.9	-20.7	-19.6	-18.6
Israel[1]	3.3	4.6	2.5	1.8	1.6	0.8	0.5	1.2	2.9	2.7
Italy	29.5	27.5	26.4	26.9	28.1	29.0	29.4	29.0	26.7	26.5
Japan	21.0	22.5	21.9	21.5	18.6	19.8	23.5	23.8	24.3	24.6
Korea	14.4	15.3	16.6	16.3	16.7	17.1	17.3	17.5	16.9	17.0
Luxembourg	4.4	3.1	2.2	-0.4	0.6	3.1	3.5	5.1	6.1	7.1
Mexico	7.6	10.1	11.0	11.9	12.9	13.2	13.6	14.4	14.7	15.0
Netherlands	26.4	22.9	13.8	11.4	12.2	12.1	12.2	11.3	11.0	8.8
New Zealand	-3.0	-6.2	-17.3	-17.1	-17.7	-18.3	-18.2	-16.9	-15.8	-14.4
Norway	16.4	18.8	20.6	20.6	20.9	21.6	21.7	22.0	22.0	22.1
Poland	27.7	33.2	28.4	28.4	28.4	28.4	29.6	29.6	29.6	24.0
Portugal	26.6	23.6	22.8	19.5	20.6	22.3	23.1	25.5	25.1	25.2
Slovak Republic	25.3	21.1	24.2	21.6	21.9	23.6	24.5	26.4	26.9	27.2
Slovenia	13.4	14.9	13.7	12.5	12.4	12.8	13.0	13.1	9.9	10.1
Spain	28.6	30.0	28.4	28.4	29.2	29.9	30.3	30.4	30.6	24.1
Sweden	39.9	38.4	34.1	33.0	32.3	32.6	32.9	33.2	33.0	33.4
Switzerland	6.5	6.1	3.1	4.4	4.7	5.0	5.0	4.6	4.6	4.7
Turkey[2]	39.1	42.0	34.8	32.7	33.0	33.1	33.2	33.6	34.4	34.8
United Kingdom	15.3	13.7	11.6	8.5	9.3	7.1	6.7	5.7	4.7	5.4
United States	10.7	7.7	7.6	7.4	8.9	8.9	9.8	11.3	12.0	12.1
Unweighted average										
OECD-Average	**18.6**	**18.1**	**16.5**	**15.6**	**16.0**	**16.7**	**17.2**	**17.5**	**17.5**	**17.1**
OECD-EU 21	**24.1**	**22.8**	**21.6**	**20.5**	**20.7**	**21.6**	**22.2**	**22.3**	**22.0**	**21.2**

Disclaimer: *http://oe.cd/disclaimer*

1. Information on data for Israel: *http://oe.cd/israel-disclaimer*.
2. Wage figures are based on the old definition of average worker (ISIC D, rev3.) for years 2000 to 2006.

StatLink http://dx.doi.org/10.1787/888933341624

Table 6.4b. **Income tax, single parent at 67% of average earnings**

Tax burden as a % of gross wage earnings, single parent with two children

	2000	2005	2008	2009	2010	2011	2012	2013	2014	2015
Australia	15.5	20.6	17.3	14.0	14.3	14.3	15.4	17.3	17.7	18.5
Austria	5.8	5.8	7.7	5.4	5.8	6.4	6.9	7.5	7.8	8.1
Belgium	16.7	16.3	16.8	16.4	17.2	17.3	17.2	16.7	16.5	16.1
Canada	6.6	5.0	1.4	0.5	1.0	1.1	1.1	1.1	1.5	4.2
Chile	0.0	0.0	0.0	0.0	0.0	0.0	0.0	0.0	0.0	0.0
Czech Republic	2.3	1.1	-5.0	-4.4	-4.9	-3.6	-5.4	-5.4	-4.9	-5.3
Denmark	28.9	27.5	35.4	34.8	34.0	34.2	34.2	33.8	32.0	32.2
Estonia	19.9	16.4	4.7	9.2	9.3	10.0	10.6	11.3	11.8	11.1
Finland	20.9	18.6	17.8	16.5	15.7	15.5	14.9	15.9	16.0	16.0
France	7.1	7.2	7.4	7.4	7.5	7.5	7.6	7.6	7.6	7.9
Germany	-2.6	-1.5	-0.2	-2.6	-4.0	-3.2	-2.7	-2.6	-2.2	-2.8
Greece	1.4	1.0	1.2	1.7	0.0	5.1	4.5	3.2	3.2	3.1
Hungary	10.3	0.9	11.1	11.8	10.8	0.0	3.4	3.8	4.3	4.7
Iceland	20.0	24.0	23.1	20.8	21.5	22.6	23.1	23.7	23.3	24.1
Ireland	2.3	0.0	0.0	1.7	2.0	3.8	4.0	4.0	4.0	3.3
Israel[1]	1.1	0.0	0.0	0.0	0.0	0.0	0.0	0.0	0.0	0.0
Italy	10.0	6.4	8.0	8.5	9.3	10.2	10.6	9.8	6.6	6.2
Japan	2.8	2.6	3.1	2.9	2.7	4.1	6.1	6.1	6.1	6.1
Korea	0.1	0.6	0.9	0.6	0.7	0.7	0.8	0.7	0.0	0.0
Luxembourg	0.0	0.0	3.1	-0.8	-0.3	0.3	0.9	2.2	2.8	3.1
Mexico	-5.7	-3.2	-2.5	-1.4	-0.4	0.0	0.4	1.4	1.8	2.0
Netherlands	3.0	2.5	3.5	3.5	3.5	3.5	3.3	3.3	3.0	5.6
New Zealand	18.6	18.8	18.1	17.2	15.9	14.5	14.6	14.8	14.8	14.9
Norway	13.3	14.1	14.4	14.1	14.1	14.2	14.0	14.0	13.4	13.3
Poland	0.0	0.0	0.0	0.0	0.0	0.0	0.0	0.0	0.0	-6.5
Portugal	3.4	1.0	0.8	0.1	0.6	0.6	1.2	3.9	3.6	3.7
Slovak Republic	3.3	-2.7	-1.7	-4.0	-3.5	-1.6	-1.7	-1.7	-1.3	-0.9
Slovenia	3.4	0.5	1.1	1.0	0.0	0.0	0.0	0.0	0.0	0.0
Spain	0.4	2.2	0.4	0.7	1.7	2.6	3.1	3.3	3.5	-5.0
Sweden	24.7	22.2	17.0	15.9	15.0	15.1	15.2	15.3	14.8	15.1
Switzerland	4.0	4.2	3.4	3.3	3.4	3.2	2.8	2.4	2.4	2.4
Turkey[2]	13.2	14.5	6.6	6.6	7.0	7.0	7.2	7.6	8.0	8.4
United Kingdom	8.6	4.5	2.0	-0.7	-0.0	-2.3	-2.6	-3.7	-4.4	-3.8
United States	-5.0	-8.7	-5.5	-8.8	-7.4	-5.5	-4.4	-4.5	-4.0	-3.8
Unweighted average										
OECD-Average	**7.5**	**6.5**	**6.2**	**5.6**	**5.7**	**5.8**	**6.1**	**6.3**	**6.2**	**5.9**
OECD-EU 21	**8.1**	**6.2**	**6.2**	**5.8**	**5.7**	**5.8**	**6.0**	**6.1**	**5.9**	**5.3**

Disclaimer: *http://oe.cd/disclaimer*

1. Information on data for Israel: *http://oe.cd/israel-disclaimer*.
2. Wage figures are based on the old definition of average worker (ISIC D, rev3.) for years 2000 to 2006.

StatLink http://dx.doi.org/10.1787/888933341638

Table 6.4c. **Income tax plus employee contributions less cash benefits, single parent at 67% of average earnings**

Tax burden as a % of gross wage earnings, single parent with two children

	2000	2005	2008	2009	2010	2011	2012	2013	2014	2015
Australia	-2.1	-9.4	-11.2	-14.0	-13.2	-12.0	-9.3	-8.6	-7.9	-7.4
Austria	2.0	4.1	7.7	3.8	4.6	6.0	7.0	8.1	8.6	8.9
Belgium	16.1	17.1	17.7	17.6	18.9	19.1	19.0	18.4	18.3	18.0
Canada	-11.8	-12.6	-18.2	-22.2	-19.6	-19.5	-19.1	-18.8	-17.2	-18.6
Chile	2.8	3.0	3.2	3.3	6.0	6.0	6.1	6.1	6.1	6.1
Czech Republic	-17.9	-11.0	-14.6	-13.1	-12.9	0.0	-1.6	-1.7	-1.0	-1.1
Denmark	11.9	9.3	10.5	9.8	8.0	8.6	8.5	7.8	5.8	6.4
Estonia	-8.5	-4.4	-8.4	-3.5	-2.1	-0.5	0.9	1.6	2.7	-5.0
Finland	9.7	8.9	9.4	8.5	8.9	9.0	8.7	10.1	10.7	11.8
France	13.5	14.1	14.8	14.6	14.8	14.8	15.0	15.1	15.4	15.9
Germany	17.9	19.7	20.2	17.8	16.2	17.4	17.8	17.6	17.9	17.5
Greece	17.3	17.0	17.2	17.7	16.0	21.3	21.0	15.1	14.5	13.9
Hungary	5.0	-1.0	5.4	7.0	6.7	-2.5	3.2	4.2	5.4	6.5
Iceland	1.4	9.9	10.4	6.8	9.5	12.0	10.5	12.8	11.9	13.5
Ireland	-9.3	-32.0	-38.5	-43.3	-41.5	-39.8	-35.0	-33.7	-32.4	-31.4
Israel[1]	-1.5	-0.8	-1.8	-2.2	-2.6	-3.4	-3.6	-3.0	-1.3	-1.6
Italy	5.5	3.5	2.9	3.5	5.1	6.2	6.8	6.2	3.2	3.0
Japan	12.8	12.6	11.7	11.4	7.5	8.4	12.5	12.6	13.0	13.3
Korea	6.8	7.7	8.5	8.2	8.5	8.7	8.9	9.0	8.3	8.4
Luxembourg	-6.4	-8.0	-8.8	-12.0	-10.9	-8.8	-8.4	-6.5	-5.4	-4.3
Mexico	-4.4	-1.9	-1.2	-0.1	0.8	1.3	1.7	2.6	3.0	3.2
Netherlands	14.5	10.0	5.4	3.1	3.6	3.8	3.4	3.4	2.4	0.1
New Zealand	-3.0	-6.2	-17.3	-17.1	-17.7	-18.3	-18.2	-16.9	-15.8	-14.4
Norway	5.7	8.1	10.4	10.5	10.8	11.4	11.5	11.9	11.9	12.0
Poland	15.5	22.0	17.8	17.8	17.8	17.8	17.8	17.8	17.8	11.3
Portugal	9.1	5.5	4.5	0.3	1.7	3.8	4.9	7.8	7.4	7.5
Slovak Republic	-3.1	0.4	4.4	1.0	1.5	3.5	3.5	3.4	4.1	4.5
Slovenia	-2.1	-2.0	-1.2	-1.6	-1.7	-1.3	-1.0	-0.8	-4.6	-4.4
Spain	6.8	8.6	6.8	7.0	8.1	8.9	9.5	9.6	9.8	1.4
Sweden	20.1	18.4	12.8	12.0	11.1	11.4	11.8	12.2	11.9	12.5
Switzerland	0.3	0.4	-2.7	-1.3	-1.1	-0.9	-0.9	-1.4	-1.4	-1.3
Turkey[2]	27.2	29.5	21.6	21.6	22.0	22.0	22.2	22.6	23.0	23.4
United Kingdom	7.7	5.3	3.0	-0.2	0.6	-1.8	-2.0	-3.1	-4.0	-3.3
United States	2.6	-1.0	-1.0	-1.2	0.2	0.2	1.3	3.1	3.7	3.9
Unweighted average										
OECD-Average	**4.8**	**4.3**	**3.0**	**2.1**	**2.5**	**3.3**	**3.9**	**4.3**	**4.3**	**3.8**
OECD-EU 21	**6.0**	**5.0**	**4.2**	**3.2**	**3.6**	**4.6**	**5.3**	**5.4**	**5.2**	**4.3**

Disclaimer: *http://oe.cd/disclaimer*

1. Information on data for Israel: *http://oe.cd/israel-disclaimer*.
2. Wage figures are based on the old definition of average worker (ISIC D, rev3.) for years 2000 to 2006.

StatLink http://dx.doi.org/10.1787/888933341646

Table 6.5a. **Income tax plus employee and employer contributions less cash benefits, married couple at 100% of average earnings**

Tax burden as a % of labour costs, one-earner married couple with two children

	2000	2005	2008	2009	2010	2011	2012	2013	2014	2015
Australia	23.4	17.0	14.9	14.2	14.6	15.2	16.8	16.9	17.4	17.8
Austria	35.2	36.3	38.2	36.0	36.4	37.3	37.9	38.6	38.9	39.0
Belgium	42.6	40.3	40.6	40.4	41.2	41.4	41.3	40.7	40.6	40.4
Canada	23.1	21.2	19.0	16.6	17.7	18.1	18.4	18.6	19.3	18.8
Chile	6.1	6.1	6.2	6.2	6.3	7.0	7.0	7.0	7.0	7.0
Czech Republic	22.0	27.0	20.8	20.9	21.1	26.8	26.1	26.1	26.6	26.6
Denmark	28.8	27.0	27.4	26.9	25.4	25.9	26.2	25.8	25.6	26.0
Estonia	32.8	30.7	26.8	29.8	31.0	31.8	32.4	32.4	32.9	28.5
Finland	40.3	38.0	38.4	37.2	37.1	37.2	37.3	38.1	38.7	39.3
France	41.3	42.2	42.5	42.7	42.9	43.0	43.1	41.1	40.5	40.5
Germany	35.3	35.4	35.1	33.5	32.6	33.8	34.0	33.6	33.7	34.0
Greece	40.7	42.5	41.8	41.6	40.4	44.2	43.9	40.5	39.4	38.1
Hungary	43.9	40.6	43.9	43.2	36.7	33.0	34.2	34.2	34.8	35.3
Iceland	13.1	19.6	18.4	15.0	19.2	21.3	19.6	21.3	20.9	22.4
Ireland	15.5	5.7	3.8	2.8	4.7	5.6	8.0	9.3	9.7	9.5
Israel[1]	25.5	22.9	20.0	18.3	17.5	17.1	16.6	17.0	18.7	18.9
Italy	39.3	36.3	36.6	36.9	37.8	38.5	38.8	38.4	38.9	39.9
Japan	21.0	23.9	24.0	23.6	22.1	23.1	25.7	26.0	26.5	26.8
Korea	15.7	16.2	17.8	17.1	17.8	18.0	18.5	19.1	19.4	19.6
Luxembourg	11.7	9.0	11.2	11.1	11.6	13.7	13.6	14.6	15.2	15.9
Mexico	12.7	14.7	15.1	15.3	16.0	18.7	19.0	19.3	19.5	19.7
Netherlands	29.9	29.7	30.3	29.7	30.8	31.1	32.4	30.9	31.0	30.6
New Zealand	13.6	12.8	0.7	-0.3	-0.9	-1.1	0.6	2.4	3.8	4.9
Norway	28.4	29.6	30.8	30.6	30.7	31.2	31.1	31.2	32.0	31.9
Poland	30.1	33.8	28.4	28.4	28.4	28.4	29.6	29.6	29.6	28.4
Portugal	30.2	27.5	26.3	25.4	26.3	27.3	27.9	30.2	29.8	30.7
Slovak Republic	30.8	22.1	25.3	22.8	22.9	24.9	25.8	27.6	28.1	28.4
Slovenia	25.0	24.2	23.1	22.1	22.9	23.2	23.2	23.2	23.5	23.7
Spain	32.3	33.4	32.0	32.4	34.0	34.3	34.7	34.8	34.9	33.8
Sweden	44.3	42.6	39.2	37.7	37.2	37.4	37.6	37.9	37.4	37.8
Switzerland	11.7	11.4	9.2	10.1	10.3	10.3	10.1	9.7	9.7	9.8
Turkey[2]	40.4	42.8	37.2	35.2	35.4	35.5	35.6	35.8	36.6	36.9
United Kingdom	27.8	27.9	26.9	26.2	26.5	26.4	27.5	26.8	26.4	26.3
United States	21.2	18.2	17.1	17.4	18.5	18.5	18.6	20.3	20.6	20.7
Unweighted average										
OECD-Average	**27.5**	**26.7**	**25.6**	**24.9**	**25.1**	**25.8**	**26.3**	**26.4**	**26.7**	**26.7**
OECD-EU 21	**32.4**	**31.1**	**30.4**	**29.9**	**29.9**	**30.7**	**31.2**	**31.2**	**31.2**	**31.1**

Disclaimer: *http://oe.cd/disclaimer*

1. Information on data for Israel: *http://oe.cd/israel-disclaimer*.
2. Wage figures are based on the old definition of average worker (ISIC D, rev3.) for years 2000 to 2006.

StatLink http://dx.doi.org/10.1787/888933341654

Table 6.5b. **Income tax, married couple at 100% of average earnings**

Tax burden as a % of gross wage earnings, one-earner married couple with two children

	2000	2005	2008	2009	2010	2011	2012	2013	2014	2015
Australia	25.6	24.2	22.5	20.9	21.1	21.1	21.8	23.1	23.4	24.1
Austria	11.7	13.0	14.4	12.5	12.8	13.3	13.8	14.3	14.6	14.9
Belgium	18.9	16.5	17.3	17.0	17.7	17.8	17.7	17.2	17.1	16.8
Canada	15.0	11.7	9.8	8.2	8.5	8.7	8.8	8.8	8.8	11.1
Chile	0.0	0.0	0.0	0.0	0.0	0.0	0.0	0.0	0.0	0.0
Czech Republic	4.0	1.0	-5.8	-5.1	-5.3	-4.2	-5.2	-5.2	-4.7	-4.7
Denmark	26.3	25.3	33.4	32.7	32.1	32.4	32.5	32.2	32.0	32.2
Estonia	17.9	13.8	6.4	9.2	9.2	9.9	10.5	11.3	11.8	11.1
Finland	26.9	24.7	24.2	23.0	22.3	22.2	21.8	22.5	22.7	22.5
France	7.3	7.9	7.9	8.3	8.3	8.4	8.5	7.9	7.9	7.9
Germany	1.5	0.9	2.1	0.2	-0.6	0.1	0.6	0.6	0.8	1.0
Greece	8.2	10.4	9.5	9.2	7.7	12.0	11.4	10.4	10.4	10.2
Hungary	18.4	14.9	21.3	20.8	14.4	8.5	8.2	7.8	8.1	8.4
Iceland	16.1	19.8	19.3	15.8	17.0	18.5	19.1	19.9	19.5	20.5
Ireland	7.0	4.0	2.4	5.0	6.2	7.0	8.0	7.9	8.2	8.0
Israel[1]	18.0	13.3	11.2	9.7	9.0	9.1	8.7	8.6	9.1	9.4
Italy	15.6	11.5	12.8	13.2	13.9	14.7	15.0	14.6	15.1	16.2
Japan	2.9	3.5	4.3	4.1	3.9	4.9	6.2	6.1	6.3	6.3
Korea	1.5	1.5	2.2	1.4	1.9	1.7	2.1	2.5	2.7	2.9
Luxembourg	2.3	0.2	5.3	4.2	4.5	4.9	5.2	5.9	6.2	6.3
Mexico	1.0	3.2	3.8	4.1	4.8	7.9	8.2	8.5	8.8	8.9
Netherlands	4.8	10.9	15.1	16.3	15.9	16.2	16.8	15.3	15.0	16.1
New Zealand	19.4	20.0	20.5	18.4	17.0	15.9	16.4	16.9	17.2	17.6
Norway	18.1	18.7	19.3	19.0	19.0	19.1	18.9	18.9	19.3	19.0
Poland	1.0	0.7	0.0	0.0	0.0	0.0	0.0	0.0	0.0	-1.5
Portugal	6.2	3.7	3.2	2.8	3.3	3.4	3.9	6.3	6.2	7.3
Slovak Republic	4.8	-4.4	-2.8	-5.2	-5.1	-2.7	-2.7	-2.8	-2.3	-2.0
Slovenia	4.8	2.0	2.6	2.5	2.9	3.0	2.8	2.7	2.8	2.9
Spain	5.2	6.6	5.2	5.8	7.9	8.3	8.9	9.0	9.1	7.6
Sweden	26.7	24.2	19.9	18.4	17.8	17.9	17.9	18.1	17.4	17.7
Switzerland	6.2	6.6	5.8	5.8	5.9	5.4	4.9	4.5	4.5	4.5
Turkey[2]	14.7	15.5	9.5	9.5	9.8	9.8	9.9	10.2	10.5	10.8
United Kingdom	17.4	15.8	14.7	14.5	14.6	14.0	15.4	14.6	14.3	14.1
United States	6.8	3.3	5.0	2.5	3.6	5.6	5.8	5.7	5.9	6.1
Unweighted average										
OECD-Average	**11.2**	**10.1**	**10.1**	**9.5**	**9.5**	**9.8**	**10.0**	**10.1**	**10.3**	**10.4**
OECD-EU 21	**11.3**	**9.7**	**10.0**	**9.8**	**9.5**	**9.9**	**10.0**	**10.0**	**10.1**	**10.1**

Disclaimer: *http://oe.cd/disclaimer*

1. Information on data for Israel: *http://oe.cd/israel-disclaimer*.
2. Wage figures are based on the old definition of average worker (ISIC D, rev3.) for years 2000 to 2006.

StatLink http://dx.doi.org/10.1787/888933341669

Table 6.5c. **Income tax plus employee contributions less cash benefits, married couple at 100% of average earnings**

Tax burden as a % of gross wage earnings, one-earner married couple with two children

	2000	2005	2008	2009	2010	2011	2012	2013	2014	2015
Australia	18.4	12.0	9.8	8.7	9.3	10.1	11.9	12.0	12.4	12.9
Austria	15.1	17.8	20.3	17.4	17.9	19.0	19.8	20.7	21.1	21.4
Belgium	23.7	22.1	22.6	22.4	23.6	23.7	23.6	23.0	22.9	22.7
Canada	14.2	12.0	9.7	7.0	8.2	8.5	8.7	8.8	9.6	9.0
Chile	6.1	6.1	6.2	6.2	6.3	7.0	7.0	7.0	7.0	7.0
Czech Republic	-5.3	1.4	-6.9	-6.0	-5.7	1.9	1.0	0.9	1.6	1.7
Denmark	28.5	26.5	27.0	26.4	24.9	25.3	25.5	25.1	24.8	25.3
Estonia	10.6	7.5	2.5	6.1	7.3	8.3	9.1	9.4	10.0	4.3
Finland	24.8	23.2	23.6	22.7	23.0	23.1	23.0	23.9	24.6	25.2
France	16.1	16.9	17.4	17.6	17.7	17.8	18.0	17.5	17.8	18.0
Germany	22.0	22.0	22.5	20.6	19.6	20.8	21.0	20.8	21.0	21.2
Greece	24.1	26.4	25.5	25.2	23.7	28.2	27.9	24.1	23.6	22.9
Hungary	20.5	19.5	24.6	24.7	18.7	14.0	15.4	15.4	16.2	16.9
Iceland	8.9	15.0	14.0	9.7	12.2	14.5	13.3	15.2	14.9	16.5
Ireland	5.4	-4.4	-6.6	-7.6	-5.5	-4.5	-1.8	-0.4	-0.0	-0.3
Israel[1]	21.8	18.5	16.2	14.5	13.6	13.2	12.6	12.9	14.5	14.5
Italy	18.6	15.2	16.3	16.7	17.8	18.8	19.1	18.7	19.4	20.6
Japan	12.9	14.2	14.0	13.8	11.3	12.2	15.0	15.1	15.6	15.8
Korea	8.2	8.7	9.8	9.0	9.7	9.8	10.3	10.8	11.1	11.3
Luxembourg	1.9	-1.2	1.3	0.8	1.5	3.1	3.0	4.1	4.8	5.6
Mexico	2.5	4.7	5.2	5.4	6.1	9.3	9.6	9.8	10.1	10.3
Netherlands	22.4	22.3	23.0	22.6	23.6	24.0	25.1	24.5	24.1	23.8
New Zealand	13.6	12.8	0.7	-0.3	-0.9	-1.1	0.6	2.4	3.8	4.9
Norway	19.3	20.3	21.9	21.7	21.8	22.2	22.1	22.2	23.2	23.0
Poland	18.4	22.7	17.8	17.8	17.8	17.8	17.8	17.8	17.8	16.4
Portugal	13.6	10.3	8.8	7.7	8.8	10.1	10.8	13.7	13.1	14.2
Slovak Republic	4.4	1.7	5.8	2.5	2.6	5.2	5.1	5.0	5.6	6.1
Slovenia	10.1	9.1	9.9	9.6	10.4	10.8	10.8	10.8	11.2	11.4
Spain	11.5	13.0	11.5	12.2	14.2	14.7	15.2	15.3	15.4	14.0
Sweden	26.0	24.0	19.4	18.1	17.4	17.7	17.9	18.3	17.8	18.3
Switzerland	5.9	6.1	3.7	4.7	4.9	4.7	4.5	4.1	4.1	4.2
Turkey[2]	28.7	30.5	24.5	24.5	24.8	24.8	24.9	25.2	25.5	25.8
United Kingdom	20.6	20.2	19.0	18.4	18.7	18.3	19.7	19.0	18.6	18.4
United States	14.4	10.9	9.8	10.1	11.2	11.2	11.4	13.3	13.6	13.7
Unweighted average										
OECD-Average	**14.9**	**14.4**	**13.3**	**12.7**	**12.8**	**13.7**	**14.1**	**14.3**	**14.6**	**14.6**
OECD-EU 21	**15.9**	**15.1**	**14.5**	**14.1**	**14.2**	**15.1**	**15.6**	**15.6**	**15.8**	**15.6**

Disclaimer: *http://oe.cd/disclaimer*

1. Information on data for Israel: *http://oe.cd/israel-disclaimer*.
2. Wage figures are based on the old definition of average worker (ISIC D, rev3.) for years 2000 to 2006.

StatLink http://dx.doi.org/10.1787/888933341670

Table 6.6a. **Income tax plus employee and employer contributions less cash benefits, married couple with two children at 100% and 33% of average earnings**

Tax burden as a % of labour costs

	2000	2005	2008	2009	2010	2011	2012	2013	2014	2015
Australia	24.6	20.8	19.1	18.0	18.0	17.9	18.8	19.9	20.9	22.7
Austria	36.3	37.3	38.7	36.4	36.7	37.4	37.8	38.3	38.5	38.4
Belgium	44.3	41.3	41.6	41.5	42.2	42.4	42.4	41.9	41.7	41.4
Canada	26.9	25.2	23.9	23.0	23.2	23.4	23.7	24.0	24.2	23.7
Chile	4.8	4.9	4.5	4.5	4.8	4.8	4.8	4.8	4.7	4.7
Czech Republic	31.0	35.1	30.5	30.2	30.3	33.2	32.6	32.5	32.8	32.7
Denmark	33.0	31.0	31.3	30.7	29.5	29.9	30.1	29.7	29.5	29.8
Estonia	35.6	33.9	30.4	33.1	34.1	34.5	35.0	34.8	35.2	31.7
Finland	39.3	36.6	36.4	35.2	35.0	35.0	34.9	35.6	36.2	36.5
France	40.5	40.3	39.4	40.4	40.6	40.7	41.0	39.4	37.5	37.9
Germany	41.2	40.8	40.3	39.0	37.7	38.6	38.7	38.3	38.5	38.7
Greece	39.1	40.5	40.0	39.8	38.9	42.4	42.2	39.8	38.7	37.5
Hungary	44.8	40.0	42.8	42.1	36.4	34.4	35.4	36.2	38.3	38.7
Iceland	20.2	26.3	24.6	22.5	26.2	27.7	26.9	28.0	27.7	28.6
Ireland	20.3	9.6	7.3	8.7	10.6	12.3	13.4	14.4	14.6	14.0
Israel[1]	21.7	19.6	16.8	15.5	14.9	13.5	13.0	13.2	15.8	15.9
Italy	41.1	38.3	38.6	38.9	39.6	40.2	40.5	40.3	39.5	39.5
Japan	22.4	24.7	25.2	24.9	24.0	25.1	27.2	27.5	28.0	28.3
Korea	15.3	16.0	17.6	17.1	17.8	18.0	18.6	19.0	19.2	19.3
Luxembourg	15.8	13.8	15.8	15.4	15.9	18.0	17.9	19.0	19.6	20.3
Mexico	9.8	12.2	13.1	13.5	14.1	16.3	16.7	17.0	17.3	17.6
Netherlands	34.3	32.2	30.2	29.2	29.5	29.5	29.8	28.7	28.2	27.6
New Zealand	18.5	19.2	9.2	8.0	7.4	7.0	8.6	10.0	11.1	12.0
Norway	30.8	31.3	31.6	31.5	31.6	32.0	31.8	31.7	31.3	31.1
Poland	32.1	35.1	28.4	28.4	28.4	28.4	29.6	29.6	30.0	30.2
Portugal	30.6	28.6	28.4	27.7	28.2	28.4	28.9	31.2	30.9	31.1
Slovak Republic	35.1	28.2	30.1	26.7	27.2	29.4	30.3	33.0	33.4	31.7
Slovenia	33.7	32.3	30.7	30.0	30.4	30.6	30.6	30.5	30.7	30.8
Spain	35.0	35.3	34.4	34.6	35.7	35.9	36.4	36.4	36.5	35.6
Sweden	44.7	42.5	38.8	37.3	36.8	36.9	37.1	37.4	36.9	37.3
Switzerland	14.6	14.1	12.4	13.1	13.3	13.3	13.1	12.8	12.8	12.9
Turkey[2]	39.7	42.4	36.2	34.1	34.3	34.4	34.4	34.7	35.4	35.7
United Kingdom	25.5	25.9	25.2	24.4	24.7	24.8	24.4	23.3	22.6	22.4
United States	25.0	22.7	21.0	22.6	23.0	22.6	22.7	24.3	24.6	24.7
Unweighted average										
OECD-Average	**29.6**	**28.8**	**27.5**	**27.0**	**27.1**	**27.6**	**27.9**	**28.2**	**28.3**	**28.3**
OECD-EU 21	**34.9**	**33.3**	**32.3**	**31.9**	**31.8**	**32.5**	**32.8**	**32.9**	**32.9**	**32.6**

Disclaimer: *http://oe.cd/disclaimer*

1. Information on data for Israel: *http://oe.cd/israel-disclaimer*.
2. Wage figures are based on the old definition of average worker (ISIC D, rev3.) for years 2000 to 2006.

StatLink http://dx.doi.org/10.1787/888933341684

Table 6.6b. **Income tax, married couple with two children at 100% and 33% of average earnings**

Tax burden as a % of gross wage earnings

	2000	2005	2008	2009	2010	2011	2012	2013	2014	2015
Australia	22.0	21.0	18.9	17.3	17.4	17.4	18.1	18.7	19.0	19.7
Austria	9.4	11.0	12.0	10.5	10.7	11.1	11.4	11.7	12.0	12.0
Belgium	24.0	21.9	22.6	22.3	22.9	22.8	22.6	22.1	21.9	21.5
Canada	16.3	13.5	12.1	11.0	11.1	11.2	11.2	11.2	11.1	12.7
Chile	0.0	0.0	0.0	0.0	0.0	0.0	0.0	0.0	0.0	0.0
Czech Republic	5.2	5.1	2.5	2.8	2.5	3.2	2.3	2.2	2.5	2.3
Denmark	28.8	27.5	35.5	34.9	34.1	34.3	34.4	34.0	33.8	34.0
Estonia	19.9	16.3	10.0	12.0	12.0	12.5	13.0	13.6	13.9	13.2
Finland	23.4	21.0	20.2	19.1	18.4	18.2	17.4	18.2	18.3	17.9
France	8.9	7.7	6.3	7.7	7.8	7.9	8.3	8.3	6.7	7.9
Germany	8.6	7.3	8.2	6.7	5.4	5.9	6.3	6.3	6.4	6.6
Greece	6.2	7.8	7.1	6.9	5.8	9.8	9.2	7.8	7.8	7.7
Hungary	15.8	11.2	16.1	15.9	10.8	7.3	10.1	9.9	10.1	10.3
Iceland	19.9	23.9	23.0	20.7	21.7	22.8	23.2	23.8	23.6	24.3
Ireland	12.6	6.7	4.6	6.4	7.5	8.8	9.6	9.6	9.8	9.2
Israel[1]	13.5	10.0	8.4	7.3	6.8	5.8	5.4	5.0	6.9	7.1
Italy	14.2	10.8	12.0	12.4	13.2	13.9	14.2	14.0	12.9	12.8
Japan	4.4	4.2	5.0	4.9	4.7	5.6	6.7	6.6	6.8	6.8
Korea	1.1	1.4	2.0	1.5	1.9	1.7	2.2	2.5	2.5	2.6
Luxembourg	3.8	2.2	6.4	5.2	5.6	6.0	6.4	7.4	7.8	8.0
Mexico	-4.0	-1.4	-0.4	0.0	0.7	3.2	3.6	4.0	4.4	4.6
Netherlands	7.8	8.5	11.8	12.6	12.3	12.4	12.9	12.1	11.7	12.8
New Zealand	18.5	19.2	19.1	17.2	15.9	14.8	15.2	15.7	16.0	16.2
Norway	19.1	19.1	19.0	18.7	18.7	18.8	18.5	18.4	17.4	17.2
Poland	2.4	2.2	0.0	0.0	0.0	0.0	0.0	0.0	0.4	0.7
Portugal	5.7	3.7	3.4	2.9	3.3	3.3	3.9	6.5	6.2	6.5
Slovak Republic	4.6	1.4	2.0	-1.7	-1.0	1.6	1.7	2.9	3.3	3.6
Slovenia	6.8	4.3	3.6	3.6	3.8	3.8	3.7	3.7	3.7	3.8
Spain	8.7	9.2	8.2	8.7	10.2	10.4	11.0	11.1	11.1	10.0
Sweden	25.3	22.3	17.5	16.1	15.4	15.5	15.6	15.8	15.1	15.4
Switzerland	7.6	7.8	7.2	7.2	7.3	6.8	6.5	6.1	6.1	6.2
Turkey[2]	14.0	15.0	8.2	8.2	8.5	8.5	8.6	8.9	9.1	9.5
United Kingdom	15.1	14.1	13.3	12.9	13.1	13.4	13.0	11.9	11.5	11.1
United States	10.5	7.7	9.1	7.7	8.1	9.6	9.7	9.6	9.8	9.9
Unweighted average										
OECD-Average	**11.8**	**10.7**	**10.4**	**10.0**	**9.9**	**10.3**	**10.5**	**10.6**	**10.6**	**10.7**
OECD-EU 21	**12.3**	**10.6**	**10.6**	**10.4**	**10.2**	**10.6**	**10.8**	**10.9**	**10.8**	**10.8**

Disclaimer: *http://oe.cd/disclaimer*

1. Information on data for Israel: *http://oe.cd/israel-disclaimer*.
2. Wage figures are based on the old definition of average worker (ISIC D, rev3.) for years 2000 to 2006.

StatLink http://dx.doi.org/10.1787/888933341697

Table 6.6c. **Income tax plus employee contributions less cash benefits, married couple with two children at 100% and 33% of average earnings**

Tax burden as a % of gross wage earnings

	2000	2005	2008	2009	2010	2011	2012	2013	2014	2015
Australia	19.8	16.0	14.2	12.7	12.9	13.0	13.9	15.1	16.1	18.1
Austria	16.5	19.1	20.9	17.9	18.3	19.1	19.7	20.3	20.6	20.6
Belgium	29.3	26.7	26.8	26.6	27.5	27.5	27.4	26.8	26.6	26.2
Canada	18.6	16.6	15.3	14.2	14.4	14.6	14.8	14.9	15.2	14.6
Chile	4.8	4.9	4.5	4.5	4.8	4.8	4.8	4.8	4.7	4.7
Czech Republic	6.9	12.4	6.2	6.5	6.6	10.5	9.6	9.6	10.0	9.9
Denmark	32.7	30.4	30.7	30.1	28.7	29.0	29.1	28.7	28.5	28.9
Estonia	14.4	11.8	7.2	10.1	11.2	12.0	12.6	12.7	13.1	8.5
Finland	23.5	21.3	21.2	20.3	20.4	20.4	20.1	20.9	21.5	21.8
France	18.8	17.9	16.8	18.1	18.2	18.4	18.8	19.0	17.6	19.0
Germany	29.1	28.5	28.6	27.1	25.7	26.5	26.7	26.4	26.6	26.9
Greece	22.1	23.8	23.1	22.9	21.8	26.0	25.7	23.3	22.8	22.1
Hungary	20.5	18.0	22.8	23.0	18.3	15.8	20.2	20.2	20.7	21.2
Iceland	16.4	22.1	20.6	17.8	19.9	21.4	21.2	22.4	22.2	23.3
Ireland	11.4	0.4	-2.1	-0.6	1.5	3.4	4.6	5.6	5.9	5.2
Israel[1]	17.8	15.0	13.1	11.8	11.1	9.7	9.2	9.2	11.8	11.8
Italy	21.0	17.8	18.9	19.3	20.2	21.0	21.4	21.2	20.1	20.0
Japan	14.4	15.1	15.4	15.2	13.5	14.5	16.7	16.8	17.3	17.5
Korea	7.8	8.5	9.6	9.1	9.7	9.8	10.3	10.7	10.8	11.0
Luxembourg	6.3	3.9	6.3	5.6	6.3	7.9	7.8	9.1	9.7	10.6
Mexico	-2.6	0.0	1.0	1.4	2.0	4.5	4.9	5.3	5.7	5.9
Netherlands	26.6	24.2	23.3	22.5	22.6	22.7	22.7	22.3	21.2	20.6
New Zealand	18.5	19.2	9.2	8.0	7.4	7.0	8.6	10.0	11.1	12.0
Norway	21.9	22.3	22.8	22.7	22.8	23.0	22.8	22.8	22.3	22.2
Poland	20.8	24.1	17.8	17.8	17.8	17.8	17.8	17.8	18.3	18.5
Portugal	14.1	11.7	11.4	10.5	11.2	11.4	12.1	14.8	14.5	14.7
Slovak Republic	10.4	9.4	11.7	7.5	8.1	10.9	10.9	12.1	12.6	12.0
Slovenia	21.2	19.5	18.9	18.8	19.2	19.4	19.4	19.3	19.5	19.6
Spain	15.1	15.6	14.6	15.0	16.5	16.8	17.4	17.4	17.5	16.3
Sweden	26.5	23.9	18.9	17.6	16.9	17.1	17.3	17.7	17.1	17.6
Switzerland	9.0	8.9	7.1	7.8	8.0	7.9	7.7	7.3	7.3	7.4
Turkey[2]	28.0	30.0	23.2	23.2	23.5	23.5	23.6	23.9	24.1	24.5
United Kingdom	18.8	18.7	17.9	17.2	17.5	17.7	17.3	16.2	15.6	15.4
United States	18.2	15.4	13.6	15.3	15.7	15.2	15.4	17.3	17.5	17.6
Unweighted average										
OECD-Average	**17.6**	**16.9**	**15.6**	**15.2**	**15.3**	**15.9**	**16.2**	**16.5**	**16.7**	**16.7**
OECD-EU 21	**19.3**	**18.1**	**17.2**	**16.9**	**16.9**	**17.7**	**18.0**	**18.2**	**18.1**	**17.9**

Disclaimer: *http://oe.cd/disclaimer*

1. Information on data for Israel: *http://oe.cd/israel-disclaimer*.
2. Wage figures are based on the old definition of average worker (ISIC D, rev3.) for years 2000 to 2006.

StatLink http://dx.doi.org/10.1787/888933341707

Table 6.7a. **Income tax plus employee and employer contributions less cash benefits, married couple at 100% and 67% of average earnings**

Tax burden as a % of labour costs, two-earner married couple with two children

	2000	2005	2008	2009	2010	2011	2012	2013	2014	2015
Australia	26.7	23.6	23.0	22.4	23.8	24.3	25.0	25.2	25.5	26.3
Austria	39.0	40.1	41.6	39.7	40.1	40.7	41.2	41.7	42.0	42.1
Belgium	50.9	48.3	48.5	48.3	48.9	49.1	49.0	48.5	48.4	48.1
Canada	29.7	28.4	27.3	26.6	26.5	26.8	27.0	27.2	27.3	26.9
Chile	5.3	5.4	5.5	5.5	6.6	6.6	6.6	6.6	6.6	6.6
Czech Republic	36.3	38.9	34.5	34.2	34.3	35.5	35.1	35.1	35.4	35.4
Denmark	36.5	33.3	33.4	32.9	31.6	32.0	32.1	31.8	31.6	31.8
Estonia	37.4	35.9	32.6	34.7	35.8	36.2	36.6	36.3	36.6	33.6
Finland	41.3	38.6	38.5	37.2	37.0	37.0	37.1	37.9	38.5	38.9
France	43.3	44.7	45.1	45.1	45.3	45.4	45.6	44.1	43.6	43.3
Germany	45.4	44.8	44.2	43.0	41.5	42.3	42.4	42.0	42.1	42.3
Greece	39.4	40.7	40.6	40.5	39.3	43.0	42.8	40.4	39.3	38.0
Hungary	47.0	41.6	45.1	44.4	39.6	37.9	39.6	40.1	40.5	40.8
Iceland	25.4	30.3	28.2	26.9	30.4	31.6	30.9	31.8	31.6	32.3
Ireland	21.8	14.6	12.9	14.6	16.2	17.8	18.8	19.9	20.2	19.8
Israel[1]	21.6	18.5	16.0	14.8	14.4	14.1	13.8	14.1	15.1	15.3
Italy	44.2	41.7	41.7	41.9	42.5	43.0	43.2	43.1	42.3	42.7
Japan	22.9	25.4	26.2	25.9	25.4	26.4	28.2	28.5	28.9	29.2
Korea	15.5	16.1	17.8	17.3	17.9	18.2	18.6	19.1	19.3	19.5
Luxembourg	21.5	19.2	21.2	20.8	21.4	23.4	23.4	24.7	25.3	26.0
Mexico	10.6	12.9	13.4	14.0	14.7	16.5	16.8	17.3	17.6	17.8
Netherlands	38.1	36.6	33.6	31.7	31.9	31.8	32.1	30.6	30.2	29.7
New Zealand	19.0	19.6	15.7	14.7	13.9	13.2	14.7	15.9	16.3	16.5
Norway	33.0	32.8	33.5	33.3	33.4	33.7	33.7	33.7	33.4	33.2
Poland	35.8	36.3	28.8	28.7	29.1	29.5	30.9	31.1	31.5	31.7
Portugal	33.0	32.0	32.2	31.2	32.5	34.3	34.5	37.0	36.8	35.6
Slovak Republic	36.9	31.1	33.0	31.2	31.5	32.7	33.6	35.2	35.5	35.7
Slovenia	37.1	36.2	34.9	34.2	34.0	34.1	34.3	34.4	34.5	34.6
Spain	35.4	36.1	34.6	34.9	36.7	37.0	37.5	37.6	37.6	36.4
Sweden	46.0	44.2	40.5	39.1	38.6	38.7	38.8	39.1	38.7	39.0
Switzerland	17.7	17.2	15.7	16.2	16.4	16.4	16.3	16.0	16.0	16.0
Turkey[2]	39.9	42.5	37.1	35.1	35.4	35.4	35.6	35.8	36.6	36.9
United Kingdom	28.4	29.9	28.6	28.0	28.4	28.1	27.7	26.8	26.3	26.2
United States	26.9	25.0	23.7	24.9	25.3	24.6	24.7	26.3	26.6	26.6
Unweighted average										
OECD-Average	**32.0**	**31.2**	**30.3**	**29.8**	**30.0**	**30.5**	**30.8**	**31.0**	**31.1**	**31.0**
OECD-EU 21	**37.8**	**36.4**	**35.5**	**35.1**	**35.0**	**35.7**	**36.0**	**36.1**	**36.0**	**35.8**

Disclaimer: *http://oe.cd/disclaimer*

1. Information on data for Israel: *http://oe.cd/israel-disclaimer*.
2. Wage figures are based on the old definition of average worker (ISIC D, rev3.) for years 2000 to 2006.

StatLink http://dx.doi.org/10.1787/888933341714

Table 6.7b. **Income tax, married couple at 100% and 67% of average earnings**

Tax burden as a % of gross wage earnings, two-earner married couple with two children

	2000	2005	2008	2009	2010	2011	2012	2013	2014	2015
Australia	23.8	22.8	20.4	18.8	19.1	19.7	20.6	20.8	21.1	21.9
Austria	10.8	12.5	13.9	12.0	12.3	12.8	13.2	13.6	14.0	14.2
Belgium	26.4	24.0	24.5	24.2	24.8	24.9	24.7	24.4	24.3	23.9
Canada	17.5	14.9	13.8	13.0	12.8	12.9	13.0	13.0	12.8	14.0
Chile	0.0	0.0	0.0	0.0	0.0	0.0	0.0	0.0	0.0	0.0
Czech Republic	6.8	7.1	4.6	5.0	4.9	5.6	5.0	4.9	5.3	5.2
Denmark	31.3	28.9	36.8	36.2	35.4	35.5	35.6	35.2	35.0	35.2
Estonia	21.1	17.8	12.2	13.8	13.7	14.1	14.5	15.0	15.3	14.5
Finland	24.5	22.2	21.6	20.4	19.7	19.5	19.0	19.9	20.0	19.9
France	10.8	10.8	11.0	11.1	11.1	11.2	11.5	11.5	11.5	11.3
Germany	13.8	12.1	12.9	11.6	9.9	10.3	10.6	10.6	10.8	11.0
Greece	6.5	8.1	8.0	7.8	6.3	10.5	9.9	8.4	8.4	8.2
Hungary	18.0	12.4	17.2	17.2	13.0	10.0	11.3	11.1	11.3	11.5
Iceland	23.2	26.4	25.3	23.8	24.8	25.8	26.1	26.6	26.3	26.9
Ireland	14.5	9.4	7.7	9.9	10.8	12.2	12.9	12.9	13.1	12.7
Israel[1]	12.5	7.9	6.7	5.8	5.4	5.5	5.2	5.1	5.5	5.6
Italy	16.8	14.0	15.4	15.7	16.3	17.0	17.3	17.0	16.0	16.5
Japan	4.9	4.7	5.7	5.6	5.5	6.2	7.0	7.0	7.1	7.1
Korea	1.3	1.5	2.2	1.6	2.0	1.9	2.2	2.5	2.6	2.8
Luxembourg	8.2	6.2	10.0	8.8	9.3	9.8	10.3	11.6	12.1	12.3
Mexico	-1.7	0.6	1.3	1.9	2.7	4.7	5.1	5.6	6.0	6.2
Netherlands	7.9	8.3	11.2	11.9	11.7	11.8	12.1	11.3	10.9	12.2
New Zealand	19.0	19.6	19.5	17.9	16.5	15.3	15.7	16.0	16.3	16.5
Norway	20.6	19.9	20.3	20.0	20.0	20.1	19.9	19.9	19.1	18.8
Poland	3.8	3.6	0.5	0.4	0.8	1.2	1.5	1.8	2.1	2.4
Portugal	8.1	7.3	7.2	6.5	7.3	7.7	7.9	11.0	10.8	9.3
Slovak Republic	5.8	4.0	4.9	3.2	3.5	5.0	5.0	4.9	5.2	5.4
Slovenia	8.1	5.9	6.1	6.0	5.7	5.7	5.6	5.5	5.6	5.7
Spain	9.3	10.2	8.5	9.1	11.5	11.8	12.5	12.6	12.7	11.0
Sweden	25.9	23.4	18.7	17.4	16.7	16.8	16.8	17.0	16.4	16.7
Switzerland	9.8	10.1	9.4	9.4	9.5	9.1	8.8	8.5	8.4	8.5
Turkey[2]	14.1	15.1	9.4	9.4	9.7	9.8	9.9	10.2	10.5	10.9
United Kingdom	16.5	16.8	15.4	15.1	15.4	14.7	14.4	13.6	13.2	13.0
United States	12.8	10.5	11.7	10.5	10.9	12.0	12.2	12.1	12.2	12.3
Unweighted average										
OECD-Average	**13.3**	**12.3**	**12.2**	**11.8**	**11.7**	**12.1**	**12.3**	**12.4**	**12.4**	**12.5**
OECD-EU 21	**14.1**	**12.6**	**12.8**	**12.5**	**12.4**	**12.8**	**12.9**	**13.0**	**13.0**	**13.0**

Disclaimer: *http://oe.cd/disclaimer*

1. Information on data for Israel: *http://oe.cd/israel-disclaimer*.
2. Wage figures are based on the old definition of average worker (ISIC D, rev3.) for years 2000 to 2006.

StatLink http://dx.doi.org/10.1787/888933341726

Table 6.7c. Income tax plus employee contributions less cash benefits, married couple at 100% and 67% of average earnings

Tax burden as a % of gross wage earnings, two-earner married couple with two children

	2000	2005	2008	2009	2010	2011	2012	2013	2014	2015
Australia	22.0	19.0	18.3	17.4	19.0	19.7	20.6	20.8	21.1	21.9
Austria	20.1	22.6	24.7	22.2	22.6	23.4	24.0	24.7	25.1	25.3
Belgium	35.0	33.0	33.3	33.1	33.9	34.1	33.9	33.5	33.5	33.1
Canada	21.6	20.0	19.0	18.1	18.1	18.2	18.4	18.5	18.6	18.1
Chile	5.3	5.4	5.5	5.5	6.6	6.6	6.6	6.6	6.6	6.6
Czech Republic	14.0	17.5	11.6	11.8	12.0	13.6	13.1	13.0	13.4	13.5
Denmark	36.2	32.8	33.0	32.4	31.0	31.3	31.4	31.0	30.8	31.1
Estonia	16.8	14.4	10.1	12.6	13.7	14.3	14.8	14.7	15.1	11.1
Finland	26.0	23.8	23.7	22.7	22.9	22.9	22.8	23.7	24.3	24.8
France	21.4	21.7	22.1	22.2	22.2	22.4	22.7	22.8	23.1	23.1
Germany	34.3	33.3	33.3	31.9	30.1	30.9	31.1	30.8	31.0	31.2
Greece	22.4	24.1	24.0	23.8	22.3	26.7	26.4	24.1	23.6	22.8
Hungary	24.3	20.6	26.0	26.3	22.3	20.2	23.1	23.1	23.5	23.9
Iceland	21.9	26.3	24.3	22.4	24.4	25.7	25.6	26.5	26.4	27.2
Ireland	13.6	5.4	3.5	5.4	7.2	9.0	10.0	11.3	11.6	11.2
Israel[1]	17.7	13.8	12.2	11.1	10.5	10.3	9.9	10.0	11.0	11.1
Italy	25.2	22.4	22.9	23.3	24.0	24.7	25.0	24.8	23.8	24.3
Japan	14.9	15.9	16.5	16.3	15.1	16.0	17.8	17.9	18.3	18.5
Korea	8.0	8.6	9.8	9.3	9.8	9.9	10.4	10.8	11.0	11.1
Luxembourg	12.6	10.0	12.4	11.6	12.3	14.0	13.9	15.5	16.1	17.0
Mexico	-0.3	2.0	2.6	3.2	4.0	6.1	6.4	6.9	7.3	7.5
Netherlands	30.1	28.3	26.8	25.0	24.9	25.0	25.0	24.3	23.4	22.9
New Zealand	19.0	19.6	15.7	14.7	13.9	13.2	14.7	15.9	16.3	16.5
Norway	24.4	24.0	24.9	24.8	24.8	25.1	25.0	25.1	24.7	24.5
Poland	25.0	25.6	18.3	18.2	18.6	19.0	19.3	19.6	20.0	20.2
Portugal	17.0	15.9	16.2	14.9	16.5	18.7	18.9	22.0	21.8	20.3
Slovak Republic	12.9	13.0	15.4	13.2	13.6	15.1	15.1	15.0	15.4	15.6
Slovenia	25.1	23.5	23.7	23.6	23.4	23.5	23.7	23.8	24.0	24.1
Spain	15.6	16.6	14.9	15.5	17.8	18.2	18.9	18.9	19.0	17.3
Sweden	28.3	26.1	21.2	20.0	19.3	19.5	19.6	19.9	19.4	19.8
Switzerland	12.3	12.2	10.6	11.2	11.3	11.2	11.0	10.7	10.7	10.8
Turkey[2]	28.1	30.1	24.4	24.4	24.7	24.8	24.9	25.2	25.5	25.9
United Kingdom	21.5	22.7	21.3	20.7	21.1	20.6	20.3	19.4	18.9	18.7
United States	20.5	18.2	16.8	18.2	18.5	17.7	17.8	19.7	19.9	20.0
Unweighted average										
OECD-Average	**20.4**	**19.7**	**18.8**	**18.4**	**18.6**	**19.2**	**19.5**	**19.7**	**19.8**	**19.7**
OECD-EU 21	**22.7**	**21.6**	**20.9**	**20.5**	**20.6**	**21.3**	**21.6**	**21.7**	**21.7**	**21.5**

Disclaimer: *http://oe.cd/disclaimer*

1. Information on data for Israel: *http://oe.cd/israel-disclaimer*.
2. Wage figures are based on the old definition of average worker (ISIC D, rev3.) for years 2000 to 2006.

StatLink http://dx.doi.org/10.1787/888933341739

Table 6.8a. Income tax plus employee and employer contributions less cash benefits, married couple without children at 100% and 33% of average earnings

Tax burden as a % of labour costs

	2000	2005	2008	2009	2010	2011	2012	2013	2014	2015
Australia	27.4	25.5	23.5	23.1	23.1	22.9	23.5	23.2	23.5	24.2
Austria	44.7	45.1	45.7	44.4	44.5	44.8	45.1	45.3	45.5	45.4
Belgium	51.2	47.9	48.3	48.1	48.5	48.7	48.7	48.2	48.1	47.7
Canada	30.0	28.8	28.1	27.3	27.2	27.5	27.7	27.9	28.4	28.5
Chile	7.0	7.0	7.0	7.0	7.0	7.0	7.0	7.0	7.0	7.0
Czech Republic	41.3	42.6	41.4	39.9	40.0	40.4	40.3	40.2	40.3	40.5
Denmark	38.1	36.1	36.0	35.5	34.3	34.6	34.8	34.4	34.3	34.5
Estonia	39.8	38.1	37.0	38.0	38.8	39.0	39.2	38.8	38.9	38.0
Finland	44.7	41.3	40.5	39.2	38.9	38.9	38.8	39.4	40.0	39.9
France	45.3	45.0	46.0	46.1	46.1	46.2	46.4	44.9	44.4	43.7
Germany	47.5	47.2	46.4	45.9	44.8	45.5	45.4	45.0	45.0	45.2
Greece	38.9	40.4	40.5	40.2	39.4	42.7	42.5	40.6	39.6	38.3
Hungary	52.7	47.8	50.4	49.5	43.8	46.8	47.4	47.7	49.0	49.0
Iceland	23.7	28.2	27.6	26.0	28.6	29.6	29.4	29.9	29.5	30.1
Ireland	23.5	17.4	15.6	17.3	18.2	19.4	20.2	20.7	20.9	20.3
Israel[1]	24.8	21.6	19.0	17.7	17.4	17.3	17.0	17.0	17.6	17.9
Italy	44.0	42.4	43.2	43.4	43.9	44.4	44.6	44.8	43.9	43.8
Japan	24.0	27.0	28.6	28.3	29.4	30.0	30.4	30.7	31.1	31.4
Korea	15.8	16.7	19.0	18.6	19.2	19.6	20.0	20.4	20.5	20.7
Luxembourg	27.4	25.6	26.6	25.9	26.2	27.9	27.6	28.4	28.8	29.4
Mexico	9.8	12.2	13.1	13.5	14.1	16.3	16.7	17.0	17.3	17.6
Netherlands	38.0	36.9	34.7	33.9	34.2	34.1	34.7	33.5	32.8	32.2
New Zealand	18.5	19.2	19.1	16.9	15.9	14.8	15.2	15.7	16.0	16.2
Norway	36.0	35.4	35.1	34.9	34.8	35.1	34.8	34.7	34.1	33.9
Poland	34.6	35.1	31.3	31.0	31.3	31.5	32.9	33.0	33.3	33.4
Portugal	33.8	32.4	32.1	31.8	32.2	32.2	32.6	35.0	34.8	36.1
Slovak Republic	40.7	35.3	36.0	33.1	33.6	35.7	36.6	39.1	39.3	37.6
Slovenia	44.5	43.3	40.4	39.9	40.1	40.2	40.1	40.0	40.1	40.2
Spain	36.1	36.3	35.5	35.7	36.8	37.0	37.5	37.5	37.5	36.7
Sweden	49.1	46.6	43.0	41.5	41.0	41.0	41.1	41.3	40.7	41.0
Switzerland	20.8	20.2	19.6	19.7	19.8	20.2	19.9	19.9	19.9	20.0
Turkey[2]	39.7	42.4	36.8	34.8	35.0	35.1	35.1	35.4	36.1	36.4
United Kingdom	29.1	30.5	29.6	29.1	29.3	28.4	27.8	26.7	26.1	25.9
United States	29.5	28.7	27.4	28.0	28.3	27.8	27.7	29.3	29.5	29.5
Unweighted average										
OECD-Average	**33.9**	**33.1**	**32.5**	**31.9**	**31.9**	**32.4**	**32.6**	**32.7**	**32.8**	**32.7**
OECD-EU 21	**40.2**	**38.7**	**38.1**	**37.6**	**37.4**	**38.1**	**38.3**	**38.3**	**38.2**	**38.0**

Disclaimer: *http://oe.cd/disclaimer*

1. Information on data for Israel: *http://oe.cd/israel-disclaimer*.
2. Wage figures are based on the old definition of average worker (ISIC D, rev3.) for years 2000 to 2006.

StatLink http://dx.doi.org/10.1787/888933341746

Table 6.8b. Income tax, married couple without children at 100% and 33% of average earnings

Tax burden as a % of gross wage earnings

	2000	2005	2008	2009	2010	2011	2012	2013	2014	2015
Australia	22.8	21.0	18.9	18.2	18.3	18.3	18.9	18.7	19.0	19.7
Austria	9.4	11.0	12.0	10.9	11.1	11.4	11.7	12.1	12.3	12.3
Belgium	25.9	23.8	24.4	24.2	24.7	24.6	24.5	24.0	23.8	23.3
Canada	16.3	13.5	13.1	12.1	12.1	12.3	12.3	12.3	12.8	12.8
Chile	0.0	0.0	0.0	0.0	0.0	0.0	0.0	0.0	0.0	0.0
Czech Republic	8.3	10.0	8.4	8.5	8.6	9.1	8.9	8.9	9.1	9.2
Denmark	28.8	27.5	35.5	34.9	34.1	34.3	34.4	34.0	33.8	34.0
Estonia	19.9	16.3	15.4	14.9	14.8	15.1	15.5	15.9	16.2	15.4
Finland	23.4	21.0	20.2	19.1	18.4	18.2	17.4	18.2	18.3	18.1
France	11.9	10.7	12.1	12.2	12.2	12.3	12.5	12.6	12.6	12.4
Germany	16.2	14.9	15.3	14.7	13.7	13.9	14.0	14.0	14.0	14.1
Greece	5.9	7.7	7.8	7.5	6.3	10.1	9.6	7.8	7.8	7.7
Hungary	19.4	15.2	16.1	15.9	10.8	14.1	16.5	16.0	16.0	16.0
Iceland	19.9	23.9	23.0	20.7	21.7	22.8	23.2	23.8	23.6	24.3
Ireland	12.6	6.7	4.6	6.4	7.5	8.8	9.6	9.6	9.8	9.2
Israel[1]	13.5	10.0	8.4	7.3	6.8	6.8	6.6	6.4	6.9	7.1
Italy	15.7	14.2	15.5	15.8	16.4	17.1	17.3	17.6	16.4	16.3
Japan	6.1	5.8	7.1	6.9	6.7	6.6	6.7	6.6	6.8	6.8
Korea	1.7	2.1	3.4	3.1	3.4	3.4	3.7	4.0	4.0	4.1
Luxembourg	7.7	5.5	6.4	5.2	5.6	6.0	6.4	7.4	7.8	8.0
Mexico	-4.0	-1.4	-0.4	0.0	0.7	3.2	3.6	4.0	4.4	4.6
Netherlands	7.8	8.6	11.9	12.7	12.4	12.5	13.0	12.5	12.0	13.3
New Zealand	18.5	19.2	19.1	16.9	15.9	14.8	15.2	15.7	16.0	16.2
Norway	20.1	19.1	19.0	18.7	18.7	18.8	18.5	18.4	17.4	17.2
Poland	2.4	2.2	3.3	3.0	3.3	3.6	3.8	4.0	4.2	4.4
Portugal	7.1	5.3	5.0	4.6	5.0	5.1	5.5	8.6	8.3	9.9
Slovak Republic	6.2	4.9	5.9	2.2	2.9	5.5	5.5	6.7	7.0	7.3
Slovenia	11.9	10.4	8.2	8.2	8.4	8.5	8.4	8.3	8.4	8.4
Spain	10.1	10.5	9.7	10.1	11.6	11.8	12.4	12.5	12.5	11.4
Sweden	25.3	22.3	17.5	16.1	15.4	15.5	15.6	15.8	15.1	15.4
Switzerland	9.1	9.3	8.7	8.8	8.9	8.9	8.6	8.7	8.7	8.7
Turkey[2]	14.0	15.0	9.1	9.1	9.3	9.3	9.4	9.7	9.9	10.2
United Kingdom	15.1	15.4	14.6	14.2	14.3	13.4	13.0	11.9	11.5	11.1
United States	15.5	14.3	15.1	13.6	13.8	15.2	15.2	15.1	15.2	15.2
Unweighted average										
OECD-Average	**13.1**	**12.2**	**12.2**	**11.7**	**11.6**	**12.1**	**12.3**	**12.4**	**12.4**	**12.5**
OECD-EU 21	**13.9**	**12.6**	**12.8**	**12.4**	**12.3**	**12.9**	**13.1**	**13.3**	**13.2**	**13.2**

Disclaimer: *http://oe.cd/disclaimer*

1. Information on data for Israel: *http://oe.cd/israel-disclaimer*.
2. Wage figures are based on the old definition of average worker (ISIC D, rev3.) for years 2000 to 2006.

StatLink http://dx.doi.org/10.1787/888933341756

Table 6.8c. **Income tax plus employee contributions less cash benefits, married couple without children at 100% and 33% of average earnings**

Tax burden as a % of gross wage earnings

	2000	2005	2008	2009	2010	2011	2012	2013	2014	2015
Australia	22.8	21.0	18.9	18.2	18.3	18.3	18.9	18.7	19.0	19.7
Austria	27.5	29.1	30.0	28.2	28.4	28.8	29.1	29.4	29.6	29.6
Belgium	38.1	35.0	35.2	34.9	35.5	35.4	35.3	34.8	34.6	34.1
Canada	22.0	20.6	20.0	19.0	19.0	19.1	19.2	19.3	19.9	20.0
Chile	7.0	7.0	7.0	7.0	7.0	7.0	7.0	7.0	7.0	7.0
Czech Republic	20.8	22.5	20.9	19.5	19.6	20.1	19.9	19.9	20.1	20.2
Denmark	37.8	35.5	35.5	34.9	33.6	33.8	33.9	33.5	33.3	33.6
Estonia	19.9	17.3	16.0	16.6	17.6	17.9	18.3	17.9	18.2	17.0
Finland	30.4	27.3	26.3	25.2	25.3	25.2	24.8	25.6	26.1	26.1
France	25.3	24.3	25.8	25.9	25.9	26.0	26.3	26.4	26.6	26.6
Germany	36.7	36.3	36.0	35.3	34.2	34.7	34.8	34.4	34.4	34.6
Greece	21.8	23.7	23.8	23.5	22.3	26.3	26.1	24.3	23.8	23.2
Hungary	31.9	28.7	33.1	32.9	27.8	31.6	35.0	34.5	34.5	34.5
Iceland	20.1	24.1	23.7	21.5	22.4	23.5	23.9	24.5	24.2	24.9
Ireland	15.0	9.0	7.0	8.8	9.9	11.2	12.0	12.6	12.8	12.2
Israel[1]	21.1	17.1	15.4	14.2	13.7	13.7	13.4	13.2	13.7	13.9
Italy	24.9	23.3	25.0	25.3	25.9	26.6	26.8	27.1	25.9	25.8
Japan	16.1	17.7	19.3	19.1	19.6	20.1	20.4	20.5	20.9	21.1
Korea	8.4	9.2	11.0	10.7	11.2	11.4	11.9	12.3	12.3	12.5
Luxembourg	19.2	17.1	18.4	17.3	17.7	19.1	18.6	19.6	20.0	20.7
Mexico	-2.6	0.0	1.0	1.4	2.0	4.5	4.9	5.3	5.7	5.9
Netherlands	30.8	29.4	28.3	27.7	27.7	27.7	28.0	27.5	26.3	25.7
New Zealand	18.5	19.2	19.1	16.9	15.9	14.8	15.2	15.7	16.0	16.2
Norway	27.9	26.9	26.8	26.5	26.5	26.6	26.3	26.2	25.6	25.4
Poland	23.6	24.1	21.2	20.8	21.1	21.4	21.6	21.8	22.1	22.2
Portugal	18.1	16.3	16.0	15.6	16.0	16.1	16.5	19.6	19.3	20.9
Slovak Republic	18.2	18.3	19.3	15.6	16.3	18.9	18.9	20.1	20.4	19.7
Slovenia	34.0	32.5	30.3	30.3	30.5	30.6	30.5	30.4	30.5	30.5
Spain	16.5	16.8	16.1	16.5	17.9	18.1	18.8	18.8	18.9	17.7
Sweden	32.3	29.3	24.5	23.1	22.4	22.5	22.6	22.8	22.1	22.4
Switzerland	15.6	15.4	14.8	14.9	15.0	15.2	14.9	14.9	14.9	15.0
Turkey[2]	28.0	30.0	24.1	24.1	24.3	24.3	24.4	24.7	24.9	25.2
United Kingdom	22.7	23.8	22.9	22.3	22.6	21.6	21.1	19.9	19.4	19.1
United States	23.1	22.0	20.6	21.2	21.5	20.9	20.9	22.7	22.8	22.8
Unweighted average										
OECD-Average	**22.7**	**22.1**	**21.6**	**21.0**	**21.0**	**21.6**	**21.8**	**21.9**	**21.9**	**21.9**
OECD-EU 21	**26.0**	**24.7**	**24.4**	**23.8**	**23.7**	**24.5**	**24.7**	**24.8**	**24.7**	**24.6**

Note: Disclaimer: http://oe.cd/disclaimer

1. Information on data for Israel: http://oe.cd/israel-disclaimer.
2. Wage figures are based on the old definition of average worker (ISIC D, rev3.) for years 2000 to 2006.

StatLink http://dx.doi.org/10.1787/888933341765

Table 6.9. **Annual average gross and net wage earnings, single individual no children, 2000-15**

In US dollars using PPP

	2000		2005		2008		2009		2010		2011		2012		2013		2014		2015	
	gross	net	gross	net	gross	net	gross	net	gross	net	gross	net	gross	net	gross	net	gross	net	gross	net
Australia	31 591	23 189	37 866	28 695	40 783	31 587	44 094	34 368	44 401	34 507	46 261	35 957	48 085	37 048	53 500	41 140	54 016	41 401	55 921	42 456
Austria	33 034	22 805	38 385	25 704	43 705	28 730	44 801	30 112	45 788	30 645	47 511	31 571	49 636	32 791	52 226	34 270	52 980	34 606	53 565	34 869
Belgium	35 525	20 246	40 766	23 648	46 592	26 795	49 096	28 333	50 873	29 141	53 148	30 386	55 262	31 659	56 647	32 629	56 559	32 602	57 166	33 132
Canada	29 360	21 990	32 533	24 774	34 760	26 634	35 344	27 396	36 398	28 249	36 671	28 406	37 715	29 189	39 446	30 501	40 410	30 975	41 719	31 968
Chile	9 672	8 995	10 363	9 638	12 300	11 439	12 682	11 794	15 409	14 330	16 678	15 510	17 909	16 656	18 139	16 869	18 697	17 388	19 338	17 984
Czech Republic	11 325	8 778	15 301	11 623	19 117	14 598	20 275	15 756	20 605	15 978	22 039	16 949	22 600	17 427	23 388	18 039	23 780	18 298	24 482	18 781
Denmark	33 507	19 477	37 287	22 949	44 844	27 555	46 846	29 432	48 527	31 092	50 859	32 513	51 509	32 892	53 018	34 049	53 129	34 208	54 013	34 619
Estonia	8 638	6 742	12 559	10 073	18 302	15 032	18 093	14 734	18 550	14 936	19 780	15 881	20 953	16 780	22 094	17 788	22 863	18 373	24 010	19 587
Finland	26 503	17 524	32 834	22 640	40 727	28 362	42 556	30 100	43 278	30 544	44 335	31 312	45 379	32 048	46 496	32 483	46 595	32 291	47 503	32 805
France	28 452	20 156	33 055	23 512	38 062	27 487	39 635	28 599	40 516	29 233	42 041	30 298	42 754	30 707	44 994	32 237	45 560	32 508	46 103	32 762
Germany	35 584	20 211	44 643	25 797	50 514	29 374	50 161	29 492	52 437	31 880	55 218	33 269	56 388	33 963	57 507	34 833	58 889	35 645	59 987	36 194
Greece	23 153	18 052	30 673	23 078	34 001	25 471	35 286	26 530	34 446	26 439	33 408	24 400	33 377	24 495	33 634	25 040	33 614	25 194	34 266	25 927
Hungary	10 071	6 473	14 121	9 369	18 049	11 144	19 399	12 074	20 036	13 747	21 196	13 756	22 342	14 493	23 213	15 204	23 468	15 372	24 308	15 922
Iceland	32 174	23 989	41 785	30 019	46 397	33 754	40 598	29 945	39 893	28 883	41 766	29 913	44 527	31 765	49 025	34 782	50 392	35 967	51 181	36 295
Ireland	22 885	18 231	28 670	24 298	34 208	29 438	35 640	29 706	38 349	31 502	38 774	31 856	40 868	33 070	41 171	33 019	41 218	32 892	41 054	32 976
Israel[1]	27 778	20 526	27 734	21 841	30 832	24 889	30 263	24 905	30 575	25 376	31 790	26 371	32 500	27 093	32 786	27 417	34 116	28 314	34 241	28 313
Italy	26 379	18 717	28 212	20 310	34 030	23 981	35 172	24 719	36 222	25 272	37 556	26 005	39 006	26 933	40 233	27 715	40 608	27 780	41 250	27 808
Japan	32 181	26 721	38 431	31 322	42 654	34 021	41 802	33 423	42 757	33 936	44 869	35 433	46 928	36 912	47 065	36 935	47 486	37 113	47 205	36 810
Korea	26 564	24 187	36 557	32 944	42 837	37 635	41 722	36 844	43 934	38 534	43 081	37 703	45 400	39 487	46 309	40 068	46 975	40 564	47 286	40 748
Luxembourg	38 180	27 236	44 146	32 717	51 910	37 691	53 108	39 172	53 582	39 239	56 651	40 557	57 493	41 323	60 063	42 325	61 521	43 064	60 812	42 134
Mexico	7 977	7 779	9 807	9 349	10 943	10 376	11 446	10 823	11 434	10 733	11 910	10 808	12 117	10 959	12 341	11 127	13 025	11 704	12 865	11 539
Netherlands	35 749	23 730	43 185	29 145	51 222	34 401	52 768	35 991	53 264	36 403	55 749	38 075	57 012	38 679	59 671	41 059	60 356	41 951	60 867	42 650
New Zealand	24 185	19 501	25 771	20 609	29 866	23 740	31 739	26 002	32 105	26 650	33 242	27 967	34 285	28 667	37 725	31 354	38 582	31 928	39 493	32 558
Norway	32 694	22 658	42 545	30 197	50 687	35 684	50 925	36 015	52 365	37 041	54 654	38 590	55 845	39 536	57 965	41 040	57 486	40 998	60 203	43 104
Poland	12 528	9 282	14 921	10 970	18 158	13 928	18 701	14 439	20 059	15 451	21 193	16 281	22 169	17 002	23 431	17 942	24 623	18 812	25 637	19 561
Portugal	15 613	12 108	20 519	16 049	24 000	18 727	24 648	19 358	26 190	20 376	26 160	20 071	28 861	22 286	30 280	21 968	30 028	21 849	29 692	21 290
Slovak Republic	9 605	7 706	12 114	9 477	16 559	12 781	17 686	13 902	18 290	14 330	18 500	14 281	19 112	14 756	20 101	15 527	21 172	16 319	21 764	16 748
Slovenia	16 731	10 782	21 225	13 857	24 858	16 642	24 943	16 727	26 388	17 604	27 561	18 352	28 553	19 061	29 501	19 738	30 162	20 134	30 660	20 439
Spain	23 598	18 914	26 953	21 483	32 289	26 058	34 052	27 311	34 575	27 062	36 245	28 256	37 437	28 879	38 641	29 786	39 316	30 277	39 529	31 037
Sweden	28 860	19 127	33 640	23 149	40 175	29 361	40 625	30 307	40 962	30 816	42 505	31 944	44 534	33 445	45 703	34 229	45 756	34 598	46 678	35 147
Switzerland	39 390	32 371	45 686	37 687	53 651	44 461	55 277	45 738	56 399	46 594	60 246	49 705	65 520	54 223	67 869	56 139	68 148	56 354	69 887	57 756
Turkey[2]	19 612	13 977	18 946	13 167	16 755	12 346	17 998	13 265	19 177	14 080	19 869	14 577	21 416	15 687	22 851	16 677	23 636	17 195	25 926	18 793
United Kingdom	39 176	29 065	47 682	34 879	51 290	38 168	50 893	38 049	49 653	37 046	48 713	36 501	50 105	37 713	50 725	38 568	50 309	38 435	51 431	39 381
United States	33 129	24 877	37 637	28 502	43 196	32 857	44 295	33 588	45 665	34 429	46 895	35 811	47 746	36 460	48 774	36 359	50 099	37 274	50 964	37 899
OECD Average	25 335	18 415	30 193	22 161	35 020	25 791	35 743	26 498	36 638	27 176	37 928	27 973	39 348	28 998	40 853	30 020	41 401	30 408	42 151	30 928

1. Information on data for Israel: http://oe.cd/israel-disclaimer
2. Wage figures are based on the old definition of average worker (ISIC D, rev3.) for years 2000 to 2006.

StatLink http://dx.doi.org/10.1787/888933341236

Table 6.10. **Annual average gross and net wage earnings, single individual no children, 2000-15 (national currency)**

	2000		2005		2008		2009		2010		2011		2012		2013		2014		2015	
	gross	net	gross	net	gross	net	gross	net	gross	net	gross	net	gross	net	gross	net	gross	net	gross	net
Australia	41 322	30 332	52 572	39 840	60 321	46 720	63 546	49 529	66 724	51 856	69 903	54 334	74 057	57 059	77 574	59 652	79 409	60 863	80 774	61 325
Austria	29 732	20 526	34 025	22 784	37 258	24 492	37 832	25 428	38 504	25 770	39 693	26 376	40 708	26 893	41 940	27 521	42 814	27 965	43 484	28 307
Belgium	31 644	18 035	36 673	21 273	40 698	23 405	42 149	24 324	43 423	24 873	44 636	25 520	45 886	26 288	46 197	26 609	46 451	26 776	46 693	27 062
Canada	36 038	26 992	39 483	30 066	42 907	32 877	42 516	32 955	44 400	34 459	45 469	35 221	46 940	36 329	47 946	37 074	49 821	38 188	50 877	38 986
Chile	2770 353	2576 428	3458 172	3216 100	4218 584	3923 283	4478 647	4165 142	5508 104	5122 537	5804 093	5397 806	6218 613	5783 310	6604 419	6142 110	7019 299	6527 948	7556 043	7027 120
Czech Republic	160 922	124 729	219 050	166 403	272 651	208 198	281 887	219 060	287 320	222 803	295 273	227 083	302 500	233 263	301 868	232 827	308 688	237 526	317 924	243 889
Denmark	281 700	163 750	320 300	197 131	359 300	220 779	367 051	230 604	376 073	240 954	386 457	247 052	391 951	250 287	393 463	252 688	397 600	256 000	405 876	260 145
Estonia	3 931	3 068	6 304	5 056	10 045	8 250	9 492	7 729	9 712	7 820	10 368	8 324	11 004	8 813	11 732	9 446	12 338	9 915	12 926	10 545
Finland	26 362	17 431	32 086	22 125	37 372	26 026	38 444	27 191	39 395	27 804	40 243	28 422	41 413	29 247	42 447	29 654	43 035	29 824	43 536	30 065
France	26 712	18 923	30 521	21 710	33 580	24 250	34 132	24 628	34 693	25 032	35 497	25 582	36 274	26 053	36 842	26 396	37 307	26 619	37 792	26 856
Germany	34 400	19 539	38 700	22 363	41 000	23 842	40 600	23 871	41 736	25 374	43 300	26 088	44 300	26 682	44 700	27 075	45 700	27 662	47 042	28 383
Greece	15 693	12 236	21 902	16 478	23 835	17 856	24 619	18 510	24 156	18 541	23 391	17 084	22 240	16 322	20 682	15 397	20 450	15 327	20 296	15 357
Hungary	1086 240	698 166	1815 852	1204 835	2336 124	1442 307	2436 408	1516 415	2512 020	1723 560	2645 712	1717 097	2840 112	1842 297	2934 744	1922 257	3054 276	2000 551	3172 122	2077 740
Iceland	2 712 000	2 022 102	4 140 000	2 974 230	5 448 000	3 963 490	5 076 000	3 744 125	5 256 000	3 805 407	5 628 000	4 030 857	6 120 000	4 365 845	6 660 000	4 725 047	6 960 000	4 967 661	7 440 480	5 276 383
Ireland	22 008	17 532	28 963	24 547	32 550	28 011	31 802	26 507	32 308	26 540	32 264	26 508	33 819	27 366	33 754	27 071	34 178	27 275	34 847	27 991
Israel[1]	95 664	70 691	103 087	81 180	119 233	96 250	120 028	98 777	121 581	100 905	125 405	104 026	128 550	107 163	128 664	107 597	134 748	111 832	137 958	114 075
Italy	21 550	15 291	24 450	17 602	26 845	18 918	27 419	19 270	28 243	19 705	28 872	19 991	29 440	20 328	30 013	20 675	30 400	20 797	30 710	20 702
Japan	4 987 116	4 140 942	4 978 855	4 057 883	4 983 948	3 975 163	4 828 001	3 860 274	4 773 076	3 788 423	4 821 385	3 807 417	4 893 341	3 848 998	4 835 595	3 794 828	4 972 455	3 886 313	5 005 807	3 903 446
Korea	19849 729	18073 190	28840 599	25990 086	33658 172	29570 496	34410 564	30387 885	36929 183	32390 144	36816 740	32220 027	38811 570	33756 834	40353 852	34915 409	41428 224	35774 131	42162 723	36332 932
Luxembourg	35 875	25 591	42 067	31 176	47 043	34 156	48 183	35 540	49 387	36 167	50 674	36 278	51 971	37 354	53 630	37 792	54 920	38 443	55 553	38 490
Mexico	48 607	47 400	69 895	66 631	81 740	77 504	85 043	80 412	87 672	82 301	91 386	82 933	95 224	86 121	98 922	89 190	103 246	92 777	105 924	95 005
Netherlands	31 901	21 176	38 700	26 118	43 146	28 977	44 412	30 292	45 215	30 901	46 287	31 612	47 263	32 065	48 194	33 162	49 155	34 165	49 235	34 499
New Zealand	34 923	28 159	39 559	31 635	44 521	35 389	46 653	38 221	48 007	39 850	49 395	41 557	51 278	42 875	53 234	44 244	54 733	45 293	56 110	46 257
Norway	298 385	206 788	378 498	268 644	443 613	312 312	456 214	322 642	471 669	333 640	491 064	346 725	504 528	357 179	524 501	371 355	537 195	383 117	552 012	395 224
Poland	23 061	17 085	27 889	20 505	33 711	25 857	34 878	26 929	36 482	28 105	38 731	29 754	40 205	30 835	41 652	31 896	44 083	33 679	45 521	34 733
Portugal	10 922	8 470	14 042	10 983	15 581	12 158	15 613	12 262	16 542	12 870	16 208	12 435	17 040	13 158	17 653	12 807	17 411	12 669	17 280	12 390
Slovak Republic	5 048	4 050	6 856	5 364	8 820	6 808	9 043	7 108	9 325	7 306	9 592	7 405	9 810	7 574	10 001	7 725	10 422	8 034	10 616	8 170
Slovenia	8 894	5 732	12 981	8 475	15 769	10 557	16 079	10 783	16 915	11 284	17 373	11 568	17 538	11 707	17 673	11 824	17 948	11 981	18 109	12 072
Spain	17 319	13 882	20 616	16 433	23 252	18 765	24 164	19 380	24 786	19 400	25 515	19 892	25 894	19 975	26 027	20 062	26 191	20 169	26 259	20 618
Sweden	263 581	174 686	315 492	217 096	352 470	257 589	362 291	270 277	368 208	277 001	376 309	282 810	387 960	291 356	398 220	298 247	408 188	308 651	421 364	317 267
Switzerland	72 910	59 918	79 620	65 679	83 088	68 856	83 974	69 483	85 068	70 280	86 305	71 205	89 364	73 955	89 743	74 233	89 779	74 241	90 286	74 614
Turkey[2]	5 545	3 952	15 737	10 937	14 913	10 989	16 421	12 102	18 026	13 235	19 708	14 458	21 973	16 094	24 674	18 007	27 487	19 996	32 048	23 231
United Kingdom	24 910	18 481	30 334	22 189	33 382	24 841	33 391	24 964	34 297	25 589	34 083	25 538	34 864	26 241	35 088	26 678	35 182	26 878	36 017	27 578
United States	33 129	24 877	37 637	28 502	43 196	32 857	44 295	33 588	45 665	34 429	46 895	35 811	47 746	36 460	48 774	36 359	50 099	37 274	50 964	37 899

Note: The annual average gross wage earnings in euro area countries are expressed in euros for all years.

1. Information on data for Israel: *http://oe.cd/israel-disclaimer*
2. Wage figures are based on the old definition of average worker (ISIC D, rev3.) for years 2000 to 2006.

StatLink http://dx.doi.org/10.1787/888933341243

PART III

Country details, 2015

This part of the publication provides the individual country details for 2015 that lie behind the comparative analysis. For each country, a table of detailed country results is followed by a description of the tax/benefit system.

All thirty four country tables in this part of the report have a similar format. The left hand page of each table specifies the tax-benefit position of single persons in four cases, which differ by wage level and the presence of children (0/2). The right hand page of the table specifies the tax-benefit position of married couples, again discerning between four cases, which now differ by wage level, the presence of children (0/2) and one-/two earner situations.

All tables start with gross wage earnings (line 1) and derive taxable income for the personal income tax levied by central government (line 4), taking into account a number of standard tax allowances (line 2) and taxable cash transfers (line 3). Taxable income allows one to determine central government income tax paid (line 7); including reductions in the form of tax credits (line 6). Total payments to general government (line 10) also include state and local income taxes (line 8) and employees' compulsory social security contributions (line 9). Take-home pay (line 12) is calculated as gross wage earnings less all payments to general government, plus universal cash transfers received from general government (line 11).

Line 13 reports employers' compulsory social security contributions (including payroll taxes).

Average tax rate (line 14) are then calculated as:

- *the share of income tax in gross wage earnings;*
- *the share of employees' social security contributions in gross wage earnings;*
- *the share of income tax and employees' social security contributions minus benefits in gross wage earnings; and,*
- *the share of income tax and all social security contributions minus benefits in gross labour costs.*

Marginal tax rates (line 15) are calculated similarly as:

- *the increase in income tax and employees' contributions minus benefits as a share of the related increase in gross wage earnings (both for the principal earner and the spouse); and,*
- *the increase in tax and all social security contributions minus benefits as a share of the related increase in gross labour costs (both for the principal earner and the spouse).*

Taxing Wages 2016

Australia
(2014-15 income tax year)

This chapter includes data on the income taxes paid by workers, their social security contributions, the family benefits they receive in the form of cash transfers as well as the social security contributions and payroll taxes paid by their employers. Results reported include the marginal and average tax burden for eight different family types.

Methodological information is available for personal income tax systems, compulsory social security contributions to schemes operated within the public sector, universal cash transfers as well as recent changes in the tax/benefit system. The methodology also includes the parameter values and tax equations underlying the data.

Australia 2015

The tax/benefit position of single persons

		Wage level (per cent of average wage)	67	100	167	67
		Number of children	none	none	none	2
1.	**Gross wage earnings**		54 119	80 774	134 893	54 119
	Principal Gross wage earnings		54 119	80 774	134 893	54 119
	Spouse Gross wage earnings		0	0	0	0
2.	**Standard tax allowances**					
	Basic allowance					
	Married or head of family					
	Dependent children					
	Deduction for social security contributions and income taxes					
	Work-related expenses					
	Other					
		Total	0	0	0	0
3.	**Tax credits or cash transfers included in taxable income**		0	0	0	0
4.	**Central government taxable income (1 - 2 + 3)**		54 119	80 774	134 893	54 119
5.	**Central government income tax liability (exclusive of tax credits)**					
	Income tax		9 136	17 833	37 857	9 136
	Medicare Levy		1 082	1 615	2 698	1 082
	Temporary Budget Repair Levy		0	0	0	0
		Total	10 218	19 449	40 555	10 218
6.	**Tax credits**					
	Basic credit		188	0	0	188
	Married or head of family		0	0	0	0
	Children					
	Other					
		Total	188	0	0	188
7.	**Central government income tax finally paid (5-6)**		10 030	19 449	40 555	10 030
8.	**State and local taxes**		0	0	0	0
9.	**Employees' compulsory social security contributions**		0	0	0	0
10.	**Total payments to general government (7 + 8 + 9)**		10 030	19 449	40 555	10 030
11.	**Cash transfers from general government**					
	For head of family		0	0	0	0
	For two children		0	0	0	14 048
		Total	0	0	0	14 048
12.	**Take-home pay (1-10+11)**		44 089	61 325	94 337	58 137
13.	**Employers' payroll tax**		3 230	4 820	8 050	3 230
14.	**Average rates**					
	Income tax		18.5%	24.1%	30.1%	18.5%
	Employees' social security contributions		0.0%	0.0%	0.0%	0.0%
	Total payments less cash transfers		18.5%	24.1%	30.1%	-7.4%
	Total tax wedge including employer payroll taxes		23.1%	28.4%	34.0%	-1.4%
15.	**Marginal rates**					
	Total payments less cash transfers: Principal earner		36.0%	39.0%	39.0%	56.0%
	Total payments less cash transfers: Spouse		n.a.	n.a.	n.a.	n.a.
	Total tax wedge: Principal earner		39.6%	42.4%	42.4%	58.5%
	Total tax wedge: Spouse		n.a.	n.a.	n.a.	n.a.

Australia 2015

The tax/benefit position of married couples

			100-0	100-33	100-67	100-33
		Wage level (per cent of average wage)	100-0	100-33	100-67	100-33
		Number of children	2	2	2	none
1.	**Gross wage earnings**		80 774	107 429	134 893	107 429
	Principal Gross wage earnings		80 774	80 774	80 774	80 774
	Spouse Gross wage earnings		0	26 655	54 119	26 655
2.	**Standard tax allowances**					
	Basic allowance					
	Married or head of family					
	Dependent children					
	Deduction for social security contributions and income taxes					
	Work-related expenses					
	Other					
		Total	0	0	0	0
3.	**Tax credits or cash transfers included in taxable income**		0	0	0	0
4.	**Central government taxable income (1 - 2 + 3)**		80 774	107 429	134 893	107 429
5.	**Central government income tax liability (exclusive of tax credits)**					
	Income tax		17 833	19 440	26 969	19 440
	Medicare Levy		1 615	2 149	2 698	2 149
	Temporary Budget Repair Levy		0	0	0	0
		Total	19 449	21 588	29 667	21 588
6.	**Tax credits**					
	Basic credit		0	445	188	445
	Married or head of family		0	0	0	0
	Children					
	Other					
		Total	0	445	188	445
7.	**Central government income tax finally paid (5-6)**		19 449	21 143	29 479	21 143
8.	**State and local taxes**		0	0	0	0
9.	**Employees' compulsory social security contributions**		0	0	0	0
10.	**Total payments to general government (7 + 8 + 9)**		19 449	21 143	29 479	21 143
11.	**Cash transfers from general government**					
	For head of family		0	0	0	0
	For two children		9 017	1 687	0	0
		Total	9 017	1 687	0	0
12.	**Take-home pay (1-10+11)**		70 342	87 973	105 414	86 286
13.	**Employers' payroll tax**		4 820	6 411	8 050	6 411
14.	**Average rates**					
	Income tax		24.1%	19.7%	21.9%	19.7%
	Employees' social security contributions		0.0%	0.0%	0.0%	0.0%
	Total payments less cash transfers		12.9%	18.1%	21.9%	19.7%
	Total tax wedge including employer payroll taxes		17.8%	22.7%	26.3%	24.2%
15.	**Marginal rates**					
	Total payments less cash transfers: Principal earner		59.0%	69.0%	39.0%	39.0%
	Total payments less cash transfers: Spouse		33.9%	51.0%	36.0%	21.0%
	Total tax wedge: Principal earner		61.3%	70.7%	42.4%	42.4%
	Total tax wedge: Spouse		37.6%	53.8%	39.6%	25.4%

The national currency is the Australian dollar (AUD). For the 2014-15 income tax year AUD 1.33 was equal to USD 1. The average worker earned AUD 80 774 in 2014-15.

1. Personal income tax system

1.1. *Federal income tax*

1.1.1. *Tax unit*

Members of the family are taxed separately.

1.1.2. *Tax allowances and credits*

1.1.2.1. Standard tax reliefs

- *Basic reliefs:* Income earned up to AUD 18 200 by resident taxpayers is subject to tax at a zero rate.
- *Standard marital status reliefs:* The Dependent Spouse Tax Offset has been abolished for the 2014-15 income year and beyond.
- *Relief(s) for children:* See Section 4.2 for more detail on the Baby Bonus.
- *Relief for social security contributions* and other taxes: No such contributions are levied.
- *Reliefs for low income earners:* A tax offset worth a maximum of AUD 445 is available for low income earners called the Low Income Tax Offset. Taxpayers whose taxable income was less than AUD 37 000 in 2014-15 are eligible to receive the full amount of the offset. The offset is reduced by AUD 0.015 for every AUD 1 by which a taxpayer's taxable income exceeds AUD 37 000 and is no longer available once a taxpayer's taxable income exceeds AUD 66 667.
- *Relief for mature age workers:* The Mature Age Worker Tax Offset has been abolished for the 2014-15 income year and beyond.
- *Relief for recipients of certain social security benefits:* The Beneficiary Tax Offset is available for those who receive certain taxable social security benefits called "rebatable benefits". It is calculated to ensure that a person who receives a rebatable benefit does not pay any tax on that income. The amount of the Beneficiary Tax Offset available to an individual is determined by the total amount of the rebatable benefit(s) they receive in an income year.
- *Relief for taxpayers who maintain a dependant who is genuinely unable to work:* A taxpayer who maintains a dependant who is genuinely unable to work due to invalidity or carer obligations may be eligible for the Dependent (Invalid and Carer) Tax Offset. This tax offset is worth a maximum of AUD 2 537 in 2014-15. To qualify for the offset, the combined adjusted taxable income of the taxpayer and their spouse (where one exists) should not exceed AUD 150 000. The amount of offset that may be received is reduced by AUD 1 for every AUD 4 by which the dependant's adjusted taxable income exceeds AUD 282 and is no longer available once the dependant's adjusted taxable income exceeds AUD 10 430.

- There are also tax rebates to ensure that taxpayers in receipt of a taxable Australian Government pension, as well as Australians who are of Age Pension age and who meet all of the Age Pension eligibility criteria except the income and/or asset tests, pay less tax. The Senior Australian and Pensioner Tax Offset is worth up to AUD 2 230 for a single taxpayer, up to AUD 1 602 for each member of a senior couple not separated by illness and AUD 2 040 for each member of a senior couple separated by illness. The offset is withdrawn at the rate of AUD 0.125 for every dollar that a recipient's income exceeds their effective tax-free threshold. For a single taxpayer, this means that the offset is withdrawn from AUD 32 279 and is no longer available once income reaches AUD 50 119. For members of a couple not separated by illness, the offset is withdrawn from a combined income of AUD 57 948 and is no longer available once combined income reaches AUD 83 580.
- *Other:* No other standard relief available.

1.1.2.2. Main non-standard tax reliefs applicable to an average worker include:

- *Relief for superannuation:* Contributions to a low-income spouse's superannuation attract an 18% rebate up to a maximum rebate of AUD 540. In 2014-15, eligible individuals with incomes not exceeding AUD 37 000 effectively have the tax paid on their concessional contributions refunded, up to a maximum of AUD 500.
- *Relief for private health insurance:* For the 2014-15 income year, there are different rebate amounts depending on age and income. For individuals below 65 years without dependants and with annual income for surcharge purposes below AUD 90 000 the rebate is 29.04% from 1 July 2014 to 31 March 2015 and 27.82 from 1 April 2015 of the cost of cover for eligible private health care. For families (couples and individuals with at least one dependent child) below 65 years with annual income for surcharge purposes below AUD 180 000, the rebate is 29.04% from 1 July 2014 to 31 March 2015 and from 1 April 2015 27.82% of the cost of cover for eligible private health care. The threshold is increased by AUD 1 500 for each dependent child after the first.
- The rebate percentages are reduced for individuals and families with annual incomes above these amounts. The rebate percentages are also higher for individuals and families aged 65 years or more.
- *Relief for medical expenses:* In 2014-15, there is an offset for annual net out-of-pocket medical expenses. Eligibility for the offset is based on annual income. This offset is being phased out, so for the 2014-15 income year, it is only available to individuals who claimed the offset in 2012-13 and 2013-14, or who have medical expenses relating to disability aids, attendant care or aged care. Single taxpayers with an adjusted taxable income (ATI) of AUD 90 000 or less, and families with ATI below AUD 180 000 (plus AUD 1 500 for each additional dependent child after the first), are able to claim 20% of medical expenses over AUD 2 218. Single taxpayers and families with incomes above these respective amounts are able to claim 10% of medical expenses over AUD 5 233.
- Other non-standard reliefs provided as deductions are:
    - subscriptions paid in respect of membership of a trade, business or professional association or union;
    - charitable contributions of AUD 2 or more to specified funds, authorities and institutions, including public benevolent institutions, approved research institutes for scientific research, building funds for schools conducted by non-profit organisations etc.; and

- work-related expenses including cost of replacement of tools of trade, cost of provision and of cleaning protective clothing and footwear, travelling between jobs or travelling in the course of employment.

1.1.3. *Tax schedule*

General rates of tax – resident individuals

Taxable income (AUD)		Tax at general rates on total taxable income
Not less than	Not more than	
0	18 200	NIL
18 201	37 000	NIL + 19c for each AUD in excess of AUD 18 200
37 001	80 000	AUD 3 572 + 32.50c for each AUD in excess of AUD 37 000
80 001	180 000	AUD 17 547 + 37c for each AUD in excess of AUD 80 000
180 001 and over		AUD 54 547 + 45c for each AUD in excess of AUD 180 000

For the income years 2014-15, 2015-16 and 2016-17 there will be a Temporary Budget Repair Levy imposed on high income earners. The levy is applied at the rate of 2.0% of an individual's taxable income above AUD 180 000.

To nominally contribute towards the cost of basic medical and hospital care a Medicare Levy is imposed on the taxable incomes of resident taxpayers. In 2014-15 the levy applied at the rate of 2.0% of the taxable income of an individual.

Certain thresholds are applied before the levy is imposed. In 2014-15, an individual taxpayer was not liable for the levy where their taxable income did not exceed AUD 20 896. A taxpayer in a couple or sole parent family who is not receiving Parenting Payment, (see section 4.2), does not pay the levy if the taxable family income does not exceed AUD 35 261. The threshold is increased by AUD 3 238 for each dependent child. Where an individual's taxable income exceeds AUD 20 896, or a family's income exceeds AUD 35 261 (plus AUD 3 238 for each dependent child), the levy shades in at a rate of 10% of the excess of taxable income over the threshold, until the levy is equal to 2.0% of the individual's or family's taxable income.

For 2014-15, individual senior Australians of Age Pension age were not liable to pay the levy where their taxable income did not exceed AUD 33 044. Where taxable income exceeded AUD 33 044 but did not exceed AUD 40 349, the levy liability was equal to 10% of the excess of taxable income over AUD 33 044. Pensioner families (including couples and sole parents on Parenting Payment) and senior Australian families of Age Pension age, did not become liable to pay any Medicare levy until their combined income in 2014-15 exceeded AUD 46 000 (plus AUD 3 238 for each dependent child).

Individual taxpayers who had income for surcharge purposes greater than AUD 90 000 in 2014-15 (or if a couple had a combined income greater than AUD 180 000) but who did not have a complying private health care policy, were liable for the Medicare levy surcharge, which is applied as a flat rate on their taxable income. The surcharge rates are 1%, 1.25% and 1.5% depending on the taxpayer's taxable income above these thresholds. However, affected taxpayers typically purchase a complying policy as the cost of such a policy is generally less than the surcharge. The surcharge is therefore not included in this publication.

1.2. *State and local income taxes*

In Australia no states or territories levy a tax based on a resident's income.

2. Social security contributions

2.1. *Employees' contributions*

None. There is, however, a Medicare Levy which is based upon taxable income. See Section 1.13.

2.2. *Employers' contributions*

No contributions are collected from employers or employees specifically for pensions, sickness, unemployment or work injury benefits, family allowances or other benefits.

Part of Australia's retirement income system is the provision of compulsory employer contributions (the Superannuation Guarantee system). In 2014-15 the Superannuation Guarantee required employers to pay 9. 5% on top of employees' gross ordinary time earnings to an approved superannuation fund, provided they earn more than AUD 450 per month (they may also choose to make contributions for workers earning less than this threshold). This threshold is not indexed. There is also a limit to the Superannuation Guarantee. In each quarter any earnings beyond a threshold are not covered by the Superannuation Guarantee. This threshold is indexed to a measure of average earnings. In the 2014-15 tax year this threshold was AUD 49 430 per quarter. The Superannuation Guarantee rate will remain at 9.5% until 2020-21.

These contributions are not reflected in the "Taxing Wages" calculations because they are not a form of taxation (they are not an unrequited transfer to general government). While employers are legislatively required to make contributions to approved superannuation funds legislated, superannuation funds are private, although subject to regulation. Employers' contributions are generally made to individual accounts and form part of employees' personal superannuation assets. Some defined benefit schemes for public sector employees and private defined benefit schemes also exist. The employee may take superannuation benefits as either a lump sum payment or pension on retirement. Accordingly, superannuation contributions are reflected in the Non-Tax Compulsory Payment calculations.

3. Other taxes

3.1. *Pay-roll tax*

Australian State Governments levy pay-roll taxes on wages, cash or in kind, provided by larger employers to their employees. The rates of pay-roll tax, thresholds and deductions differ between States. In New South Wales, the State with the largest population, the pay-roll tax rate in 2014-15 was 5.45% for employers with total Australian wages in excess of AUD 750 000. Employers are entitled to an exemption from tax, or a pro-rated pay-roll tax threshold, on wages paid in New South Wales up to a maximum of AUD 750 000. The exempt amount is reduced based on the proportion of the employer's New South Wales pay-roll to its total Australian pay-roll.

4. Universal cash transfers

4.1. *Transfers related to marital status*

There are no cash transfers made on a universal basis to married couples.

4.2. *Transfers related to dependent children*

- Family Tax Benefit (FTB) Part A is paid to a parent, guardian or an approved care organisation to help families meet the costs of raising children. For 2014-15, the base rate of FTB(A) is payable where the combined "adjusted" taxable income of parents does not exceed AUD 94 316 plus AUD 3 796 for each child after the first. The payment shades out at the rate of AUD 0.30 per AUD 1 of income over the ceiling. The base rate of payment is AUD 2 204.60 (this figure includes an end of year supplement) for a dependent child aged under 15 and for dependent full time students aged 16 to 19 (Note from 1 May 2014 eligibility was limited to children up to 15 years and 16-19 years and in full time secondary school). The base rate of payment is increased by a Large Family Supplement (LFS) for families with three or more children. The LFS is payable at a rate of AUD 321.20 for the third and each subsequent child.
- A higher FTB(A) benefit is available for lower income earners, and the value of this benefit is dependent on the age and number of children. For 2014-15 families may receive a maximum payment of AUD 5 336.30 (this figure includes an end of year supplement) for each child aged under 13 years and AUD 6 723.30 (this figure includes an end of year supplement) for each child aged 13 to 15 years and for each child aged 16-19 in full time secondary school. The higher benefit is also boosted by the LFS for families with three or more children. For 2014-15, the higher benefit tapers out at the rate of AUD 0.20 for each dollar of income over AUD 50 151 until the base payment is reached. However, people receiving any social security allowances or pensions automatically qualify for the maximum higher benefit. The attached calculations assume each dependant is between 5 and 12 years of age.
- Family Tax Benefit Part B (FTB[B]) is targeted at single income couple and sole parent families. Eligibility for FTB(B) is contingent upon having a FTB child under the age of 15 or a qualifying dependent full-time student up to of the end of the calendar year they turn 18. There are two separate income tests applied to the parent(s). The parent earning the higher amount (or the sole parent, in the case of single parent families) must earn AUD 150 000 or less for the financial year for the family to be eligible. A secondary earner income threshold is also applied to the parent earning the lower amount. For 2014-15, this threshold is AUD 5 329, above which the entitlement is reduced by AUD 0.20 for each dollar of income. There is no secondary earner income test applied to sole parents. For 2014-15, the maximum payment is AUD 3 091.55 if the youngest dependent child is aged between 5 and 15 (or up to 18 years if the dependent child is a full-time student), and AUD 4 274.15 if there is a child under 5 years. The attached calculations assume each dependant is between 5 and 12 years of age.
- Recipients of the Family Tax Benefit may elect to receive the benefit in fortnightly instalments or as an end of year lump sum payment.
- A Newborn Supplement and Newborn Upfront Payment may be paid to families for each baby born from 1 March 2014. To be eligible families will need to be eligible for Family Tax Benefit Part A and not be accessing Parental Leave Pay for that child. For multiple births, Parental Leave Pay may be payable for one child and Newborn Supplement for the other child or children. The value of the payment in 2014-15 is up to AUD 2 056.45 for the first child (and all multiple births) and up to AUD 1 028.15 for subsequent children. This supplement and upfront payment replace the previous Baby Bonus.

- On 1 January 2011 Australia's first Paid Parental Leave (PPL) scheme commenced. PPL provides the primary carer of a child with 18 weeks' pay at the national minimum wage (AUD 640.90 per week before tax in 2014-15), in the year following the child's birth or adoption. The primary carer must have worked for at least 10 of the 13 months prior to the birth or adoption, and for at least 330 hours in that 10 month period. The primary carer's adjusted taxable income must be AUD 150 000 or less in the financial year prior to the date of claim or date of birth or adoption. PPL and Baby Bonus cannot be paid for the same child. A person cannot claim FTB(B) or the dependent spouse, child housekeeper and housekeeper tax offsets while they are receiving PPL.
- Child Care Benefit (CCB) is a means-tested payment which assists families with the cost of approved child care. In 2014-15 CCB is payable to eligible families with incomes up to AUD 149 597 for one child in care, with the income limit rising for each additional child in care. Families with annual incomes under AUD 42 997 receive the maximum rate of CCB, which is AUD 4.10 per hour for a non-school child in care. CCB is payable for a maximum of 50 hours per week. To receive more than 24 hours of CCB per week both parents must be participating in work, training or study activities for at least 15 hours per week. The attached calculations assume no child care usage.
- Child Care Rebate (CCR) is an additional payment aimed at promoting workforce participation. CCR is not means tested. It pays 50% of out-of-pocket child care expenses (after any CCB), up to an annual cap of AUD 7 500 per child in 2014-15. Families have to participate in work, training or study related commitments at some time during a week or have an exemption. No minimum number of hours is required.
- Parenting Payment is a taxable payment payable to partnered and sole parents for low income families with a qualifying child under six and eight years of age respectively. In 2014-15 the maximum annual amount of Parenting Payment (Partnered) (PP[P]) was AUD 12 098. Only one parent in a couple can be entitled to PP(P). The maximum annual amount of Parenting Payment (Single) (PP[S]) was AUD 18 721. These payments are subject to income and assets tests. The Parenting Payment (Partnered) tapers out at a rate of AUD 0.50 per AUD 1 of income over AUD 2 600 up to AUD 6 500 and reduces at a rate of AUD 0.60 per AUD 1 for income over AUD 6 500. Under the PP(P) income test, a spouse receives a reduced Parenting Payment, tapering at a rate of AUD 0.60, when the higher earning partner's income exceeds AUD 23 673. If the spouse has little or no income (less than AUD 2 600 per annum), he or she would not receive any Parenting Payment when the higher earning partner's income exceeds AUD 43 836. PP(S) reduces by AUD 0.40 for each AUD 1 of income above AUD 4 799.60 plus AUD 639.60 for each child other than the first. A sole parent with two qualifying dependants may be entitled to some taxable PP(S) in 2014-15 where private income does not exceed AUD 51 602. The attached calculations assume dependants are aged six and seven.
- The Newstart allowance is a taxable payment payable to single persons and partnered individuals who are unemployed. It is also payable to a member of a couple if their youngest child is aged six years or more and to single parents if their youngest child is aged eight years or more. It is conditional on recipients fulfilling a personal Employment Pathway Plan, which typically involves taking part in activities such as job seeking and training. In 2014-15 the Newstart allowance for singles without dependants was AUD 13 400 and for partnered individuals was AUD 12 098. These payments taper out at a rate of AUD 0.50 per AUD 1 for incomes between AUD 2 600 and AUD 6 500, and reduce

at a rate of AUD 0.60 per AUD for incomes over AUD 6 500. The Newstart allowance for partnered individuals reduces by AUD 0.60 for each AUD 1 of their partner's income above AUD 23 673. For single principal carers with dependent child(ren), it reduces at a rate of AUD 0.40 per AUD 1 for incomes over AUD 2 600.

- A non-taxable supplementary payment called Pharmaceutical Allowance (PA) is payable to eligible persons; for example, persons who receive the PP(S). PA is added to the maximum basic rate of PP(S) before a person's PP(S) entitlement is calculated. Anyone with a PP(S) entitlement, after PA has been added, receives the full amount of PA. For 2014-15, the payment is AUD 161.20.
- A Telephone Allowance is available on a quarterly basis to eligible individuals, including individuals who receive PP(S) or PA if their PP(S) entitlement is reduced to 0. The basic rate of the Telephone Allowance is AUD 108.06 for 2014-15, with a higher rate of AUD 161.29 available for recipients of Disability Support Pension who are under the age of 21 and where a home internet service is connected in the individual's or partner's name. The attached calculations assume the standard rate is applicable.

4.2. Other transfers

Single Income Family Supplement

- The Single Income Family Supplement (SIFS) is a non-taxable payment for households with one main income earner.
- The SIFS phases in at a rate of AUD 0.025 for every AUD 1 above AUD 68 000 until it reaches AUD 300. Once the main earner's income exceeds AUD 120 000 the SIFS reduces by AUD 0.01 for every AUD 1. If there is a secondary earner, every AUD of their income above AUD 16 000, reduces the SIFS by AUD 0.15.

Schoolkids Bonus

- Parents or carers eligible for FTB Part A are eligible to receive Schoolkids Bonus. In 2014-15, the Bonus was worth AUD 422 for each child in primary school and AUD 842 for each child in secondary school. From 1 January 2015, the Schoolkids Bonus was limited to families and individuals with an income of AUD 100 000 per year or less.

Income Support Bonus

- The Income Support Bonus is a non-taxable payment made to recipients of eligible social security benefits. In 2014-15, single persons received AUD 218.60 and each member of a couple received AUD 182.20.

5. Recent changes in the tax/benefit system

Energy Supplement

- From 1 July 2013, the Clean Energy Supplement was available for recipients of Family Tax Benefit payments. Previously these recipients were paid the Clean Energy Advance. The Clean Energy Supplement has been renamed to the Energy Supplement.

6. Memorandum items

6.1. Identification of an average worker

The source of the information used in replying to the questionnaire was the Australian Bureau of Statistics publication *Average Weekly Earnings – Australia*, catalogue number

6302.0. The survey is now conducted on a biannual basis (it was previously conducted on a quarterly basis up to the June 2012 quarter) and is based on a representative sample of employers in each industry. As a result of this change in frequency, average weekly earnings for the 2013-14 income tax year have been calculated as the average of the two biannual figures (November 2013 and May 2014 [released in August 2014]).

In August 2009 the Australian Bureau of Statistics redesigned the survey and replaced the industry classification based on the 1993 edition of the Australian and New Zealand Standard Industrial Classification (ANZSIC), which had been in use since 1994, with the 2006 edition of ANZSIC. The 2006 edition of ANZSIC was developed to provide a more contemporary industrial classification system, taking into account issues such as changes in the structure and composition of the economy, changing user demands and compatibility with major international classification standards. Accordingly, the average wage figure for 2010 and later years is inconsistent with that provided for previous years.

All wage and salary earners who received pay for the reference period are represented in the Survey of Average Weekly Earnings (AWE), except:

- members of the Australian permanent defence forces;
- employees of enterprises primarily engaged in agriculture, forestry and fishing;
- employees of private households;
- employees of overseas embassies, consulates, etc.;
- employees based outside Australia; and
- employees on workers' compensation who are not paid through the payroll.

Also excluded are the following persons who are not regarded as employees for the purposes of this survey:

- casual employees who did not receive pay during the reference period;
- employees on leave without pay who did not receive pay during the reference period;
- employees on strike, or stood down, who did not receive pay during the reference period;
- directors who are not paid a salary;
- proprietors/partners of unincorporated businesses;
- self-employed persons such as subcontractors, owner/drivers, consultants;
- persons paid solely by commission without a retainer; and
- employees paid under the Paid Parental Leave Scheme.

The sample for the AWE survey, like most ABS business surveys, is selected from the ABS Business Register which is primarily based on registrations with the Australian Taxation Office's (ATO) Pay As You Go Withholding (PAYGW) scheme (and prior to 1 June 2000 the Group Employer (GE) scheme). The population is updated quarterly to take account of:

- new businesses;
- businesses which have ceased employing;
- changes in employment levels;
- changes in industry; and
- other general business changes.

Earnings comprise weekly ordinary time earnings and weekly overtime earnings.

Weekly ordinary time earnings refers to one week's earnings of employees for the reference period attributable to award, standard or agreed hours of work. It is calculated before taxation and any other deductions (e.g. superannuation, board and lodging) have been made. Included in ordinary time earnings are award, workplace and enterprise bargaining payments, and other agreed base rates of pay, over award and over agreed payments, penalty payments, shift and other allowances; commissions and retainers; bonuses and similar payments related to the reference period; payments under incentive or piecework; payments under profit sharing schemes normally paid each pay period; payment for leave taken during the reference period; all workers' compensation payments made through the payroll; and salary payments made to directors. Excluded are overtime payments, retrospective pay, pay in advance, leave loadings, severance, termination and redundancy payments, and other payments not related to the reference period.

Weekly overtime earnings refers to payment for hours in excess of award, standard or agreed hours of work.

6.2. Employers' contribution to private health and pension scheme

In Australia very few employers make any contributions towards health schemes for their employees, especially where the employee is at a wage level comparable to that of an average production worker.

From a survey of employment benefits conducted by the Australian Bureau of Statistics, the findings of which were published in 2001 as *Superannuation, Australia 2000* (ABS Catalogue No. 6360.0), it was estimated that 98% of all employed persons with leave entitlements were covered by a superannuation scheme.

2015 parameter values

Average earnings/yr	Ave_earn	80 774	
Low Income Tax Offset	low_inc_cr	445	
	low_inc_lim	37 000	
	low_inc_redn	0.015	
Tax schedule	tax_sch	0.000	18 200
		0.190	37 000
		0.325	80 000
		0.370	180 000
		0.450	
Medicare levy	medic_rate	0.02	
exemption limits	sing_lim	20 896	
married	m_lim	35 261	
sing parent receiving PPS	SAPTO_lim	46 000	
+ per child	ch_lim	3 238	
shading-in rate	shade_rate	0.1	
Temporary Budget Repair Levy	TBRL_rate	0.02	
income threshold	TBRL_lim	180 000	
Part A FTB max	FTB_A_max	5 336.3	
Part A FTB basic	FTB_A_base	2 204.6	
part A income limit 1	FTB_A_lim1	50 151	
part A income limit 2	FTB_A_lim2	94 316	
reduction rate 1	FTB_A_taper1	0.2	
reduction rate 2	FTB_A_taper2	0.3	
additional limit2 per extra child	FTB_A_child	3 796	
Large family supplement	FTB_A_large	321.2	
Part A FTB Clean Energy Advance (CEA) max	FTB_A_CEA_max	0	
Part A FTB CEA basic	FTB_A_CEA_basic	0	
Part A FTB Clean Energy Supplement (CES) max	FTB_A_CES_max	91.25	
Part A FTB CES basic	FTB_A_CES_basic	36.5	
Part B FTB	FTB_B	3 091.55	
part B partner income limit	FTB_B_lim	5 329	
reduction rate	FTB_B_taper	0.2	
Income limit (primary earner)	FTB_B_lim_p	150 000	
Part B FTB CEA no child <5 years old	FTB_B_CEA_5	0	
Part B FTB CES no child <5 years old	FTB_B_CES_5	51.1	
Single Income Family Supplement max rate	SIFS_max	300	
Single Income Family Supplement phase-in threshold	SIFS_in_lim_pr	68 000	
Single Income Family Supplement taper in Rate –primary earner	SIFS_in_taper_pr	0.025	
Single Income Family Supplement phase-out threshold (primary earner)	SIFS_out_lim_pr	120 000	
Single Income Family Supplement taper out rate (primary earner)	SIFS_out_taper_pr	0.01	
Single Income Family Supplement phase out threshold (secondary earner)	SIFS_out_lim_sec	16 000	
Single income family supplement phase out taper –secondary earner	SIFS_out_taper_sec	0.15	
Parenting payment single	PPS	18 721.04	
reduction rate	PPS_taper	0.4	
income limit	PPS_lim	4 799.6	
additional limit per child	PPS_ch_lim	639.6	
Parenting payment single CEA	PPS_CEA	0	
Parenting payment single Clean Energy Supplement (CES)	PPS_CES	311.48	
Pharmaceutical allowance	PA	161.2	
State pay-roll tax rate (NSW)	Pay_roll_rate	0.0545	
Additional parameters			
Newstart allowance single rate	NSAS	13 400.14	
Newstart allowance single CEA	NSAS_CEA	0	
Newstart allowance single CES	NSAS_CES	228.28	
Newstart allowance partnered rate	NSAP	12 098.58	
Newstart allowance partnered CEA	NSAP_CEA	0	
Newstart allowance partnered CES	NSAP_CES	204.88	
reduction rate 1	NSA_taper1	0.5	
reduction rate 2	NSA_taper2	0.6	
income limit 1	NSA_lim1	2 600	
income limit 2	NSA_lim2	6 500	
Senior Australian and Pensioner Tax Offset	SAPTO	2 230	
Senior Australian and Pensioner Tax Offset single threshold	SAPTO_thresh	32 279	
Senior Australian and Pensioner Tax Offset taper rate	SAPTO_taper	0.125	
SchoolKids Bonus	SKB	422	
	SKB_lim	100 000	
Telephone allowance	Tele_A	108.06	
Flood levy	tax_flo		
Income Support Bonus – Single	ISB_s	218.6	
Income Support Bonus – partnered	ISB_p	182.2	

2015 tax equations

The equations for the Australian system in 2015 are mostly repeated for each individual of a married couple. However, the spouse credit is relevant only to the calculation for the principal earner and the calculation of the Medicare levy uses shading-in rules which depend on the levels of earnings of the spouses. The basis of calculation is shown by the Range indicator in the table below.

The functions which are used in the equations (Taper, MIN, Tax etc) are described in the technical note about tax equations. Variable names are defined in the table of parameters above, within the equations table, or are the standard variables "married" and "children". A reference to a variable with the affix "_total" indicates the sum of the relevant variable values for the principal and spouse. And the affixes "_princ" and "_spouse" indicate the value for the principal and spouse respectively. Where the calculation for one earner takes into account variables for the other earner, the affix "_oth" is used. Equations for a single person are as shown for the principal, with "_spouse" values taken as 0.

	Line in country table and intermediate steps	Variable name	Range	Equation
1.	Earnings	earn		
2.	Allowances	tax_al	B	0
3.	Credits in taxable income:			
	Credits in taxable income of principal	taxbl_cr_princ	P	IF(AND(Children>0,Married=0),Taper(PPS,earn_princ,PPS_lim+PPS_ch_lim*(Children-1),PPS_taper),IF(AND(Children=0,Married=0),taper2(NSAS,earn_princ,NSA_lim1,NSA_lim2,NSA_taper1,NSA_taper2),IF(Married>0,taper3(NSAP,earn_princ,earn_spouse,NSA_lim1,NSA_lim2,NSA_taper1,NSA_taper2,0),,0)))
	Credits in taxable income of spouse	taxbl_cr_spouse	S	IF(AND(Children>0,Married=0),0,IF(AND(Children=0,Married=0),0,IF(Married>0,taper3(NSAP,earn_spouse,earn_princ,NSA_lim1,NSA_lim2,NSA_taper1,NSA_taper2,0),0)))
4.	CG taxable income	tax_inc	B	earn+taxbl_cr
5.	CG tax before credits			
	Medicare Levy	med_levy	B	medicare(tax_inc,sing_lim,m_lim,SAPTO_lim,ch_lim,shade_rate,medic_rate,Married,tax_inc_oth,Children)
	Temporary Budget Repair Levy	TBRL	B	TBRL_rate*Positive(tax_inc-TBRL_lim)
	Tax liability	liab	P	Tax(tax_inc, tax_sch)
6.	Tax credits :			
	Low income credit	low_cr	B	Taper(low_inc_cr,tax_inc,low_inc_lim,low_inc_redn)
	Senior Australian and Pensioner Tax Offset	sap_cr	P	IF(AND(taxbl_cr_princ>0,NOT(AND(Children>0,Married=0))),Tax(taxbl_cr_princ,tax_sch),IF(taxbl_cr_princ>0,Taper(SAPTO,tax_inc,SAPTO_thresh,SAPTO_taper),0)
	Beneficiary tax offset	ben_cr	B	IF(AND(taxbl_cr>0, NOT(AND(Children>0, Married=0))), Tax(taxbl_cr, tax_sch), 0)
	Total	tax_cr	B	low_cr+sap_cr+ben_cr
7.	CG tax	CG_tax	B	Positive(liab-tax_cr) + med_levy + TBRL
8.	State and local taxes	local_tax	B	0
9.	Employees' soc security	SSC	B	0
11.	Cash transfers:			
	Family Tax Benefit (Part A)	ftbA	P	IF(PA>0,((FTB_A_max+FTB_A_CES_max)*Children+IF(Children>2,(Children-2)*FTB_A_large,0)),MAX(((FTB_A_max+FTB_A_CES_max)*Children+IF(Children>2,(Children-2)*FTB_A_large,0)-Positive((princ_earn+taxbl_cr+spouse_earn+taxbl_cr_spouse)-FTB_A_lim1)*FTB_A_taper1), Positive((FTB_A_base+FTB_A_CES_basic)*Children+IF(Children>2,(Children-2)* FTB_A_large,0)-Positive((princ_earn+taxbl_cr+spouse_earn+taxbl_cr_spouse)-(FTB_A_lim2+(Positive(Children-1))*FTB_A_child))*FTB_A_taper2)))

	Line in country table and intermediate steps	Variable name	Range	Equation
	Family Tax Benefit (Part B)	ftbB	J	IF(earn_princ<FTB_B_lim_p,IF(Children>0,Taper(FTB_B+FTB_B_CES_5, earn_spouse+taxbl_cr_spouse,FTB_B_lim,FTB_B_taper),0),0)
	Pharmaceutical Allowance	PA	J	AND(Children>0,Married=0)*IF(Taper(PPS+PA+PPS_CES,earn_princ, PPS_lim+PPS_ch_lim*(Children-1),PPS_taper)>0,PA,0)
	Clean Energy Advance	CEA	J	IF(AND(Children>0,Married=0,Taper(PPS+PPS_CES,earn_princ,PPS_lim+PPS_ch_lim*(Children-1),PPS_taper)>0),PPS_CEA,IF(AND(Children=0,Married=0,taper2(NSAS+NSAS_CES,earn_princ,NSA_lim1,NSA_lim2,NSA_taper1,NSA_taper2)>0),NSAS_CEA,IF(AND(Married>0,taper3(NSAP,earn_spouse,earn_princ,NSA_lim1,NSA_lim2,NSA_taper1,NSA_taper2,NSAP_CES)>0),NSAP_CEA)))+IF(AND(taxbl_cr_princ>0,Married>0,taper2(NSAP+NSAP_CES,earn_princ,NSA_lim1,NSA_lim2,NSA_taper1,NSA_taper2)>0),NSAP_CEA,0)+IF(AND(ftbA>0,ftbA>FTB_A_base*Children+IF(Children>2,(Children-2)*FTB_A_large,0)),FTB_A_CEA_max*Children,0)+IF(AND(ftbA>0,ftbA<=FTB_A_base*Children+IF(Children>2,(Children-2)*FTB_A_large,0)),FTB_A_CEA_basic*Children,0)+IF(ftbB>0,FTB_B_CEA_5,0)
	Clean Energy Supplement	CES	J	IF(AND(Children>0,Married=0,Taper(PPS+PPS_CES,earn_princ,PPS_lim+PPS_ch_lim*(Children-1),PPS_taper)>0), MAX(0,Taper(PPS+PPS_CES,earn_princ,PPS_lim+PPS_ch_lim*(Children-1),PPS_taper)-Taper(PPS, earn_princ,PPS_lim+PPS_ch_lim*(Children-1),PPS_taper)),IF(AND(Children>0, Married=0Taper(PPS+PPS_CES,earn_princ,PPS_lim+PPS_ch_lim*(Children-1),PPS_taper)=0), 0,IF(AND(Children=0,Married=0,taper2(NSAS+NSAS_CES,earn_princ,NSA_lim1,NSA_lim2,NSA_taper1,NSA_taper2)>0),taper2(NSAS+NSAS_CES,earn_princ,NSA_lim1,NSA_lim2,NSA_taper1,NSA_taper2)-taper2(NSAS,earn_princ,NSA_lim1, NSA_lim2,NSA_taper1,NSA_taper2),IF(AND(Married>0,taper3(NSAP,earn_spouse, earn_princ,NSA_lim1,NSA_lim2,NSA_taper1,NSA_taper2,NSAP_CES)>0),taper3(NSAP,earn_spouse,earn_princ,NSA_lim1,NSA_lim2,NSA_taper1,NSA_taper2,NSAP_CES)-taper3(NSAP,earn_spouse,earn_princ,NSA_lim1,NSA_lim2, NSA_taper1,NSA_taper2,NSAP_CES-NSAP_CES)))))+IF(AND(Married>0, ,taper2(NSAP+NSAP_CES,earn_princ,NSA_lim1,NSA_lim2,NSA_taper1,NSA_taper2)>0), max(0, taper2(NSAP+NSAP_CES,earn_princ,NSA_lim1, NSA_lim2,NSA_taper1,NSA_taper2)- taper2(NSAP,earn_princ,NSA_lim1, NSA_lim2,NSA_taper1,NSA_taper2)),0)
	SchoolKids Bonus	SKB	J	IF(earn_princ+earn_spouse+taxbl_cr_princ+taxbl_cr_spouse<SKB_lim, IF(FTB Part A>0,SKB*Children,0),0)
	Single Income Family Supplement	SIFS	J	sifs(tax_inc_princ,tax_inc_spouse,ftbA+ftbB,SIFS_max,SIFS_in_lim_pr,SIFS_in_taper_pr,SIFS_out_lim_pr,SIFS_out_taper_pr,SIFS_out_lim_sec,SIFS_out_taper_sec)
	Income support bonus	ISB	B	IF(AND(Married=0,(taxbl_cr_princ+earn_princ+PA)>0),ISB_s,IF(AND(Married>0,taper3(NSAP, taxbl_cr_princ, earn_princ,NSA_lim1,NSA_lim2,NSA_taper1,NSA_taper2,NSAP_CES)>0),ISB_p,0))+IF(AND(Married>0,taper2(NSAP+NSAP_CES,earn_princ,NSA_lim1,NSA_lim2,NSA_taper1,NSA_taper2)>0),ISB_p,0)
	Telephone Allowance	TeleA	P	IF(Married=0,IF(Children>0,IF(Taper(PPS+PA+PPS_CES,earn_princ,PPS_lim+PPS_ch_lim*(Children-1),PPS_taper)>0,Tele_A,0),0),0)
		cash_trans	J	ftbA+ftbB+taxbl_cr_princ+PA+taxbl_cr_spouse+Tele_A +CEA=CES+SKB+SIFS+ISB
13.	Employer's State pay-roll tax	tax_empr	B	earn*Pay_roll_rate

Key to range of equation B calculated separately for both principal earner and spouse P calculated for principal only (value taken as 0 for spouse calculation) J calculated once only on a joint basis. Key refers to an optimisation of benefits i.e. Parenting payment for principal and Newstart allowance for spouse versus Parenting payment for spouse and Newstart allowance for principal.

Taxing Wages 2016

Austria

This chapter includes data on the income taxes paid by workers, their social security contributions, the family benefits they receive in the form of cash transfers as well as the social security contributions and payroll taxes paid by their employers. Results reported include the marginal and average tax burden for eight different family types.

Methodological information is available for personal income tax systems, compulsory social security contributions to schemes operated within the government sector, universal cash transfers as well as recent changes in the tax/benefit system. The methodology also includes the parameter values and tax equations underlying the data.

Austria 2015

The tax/benefit position of single persons

	Wage level (per cent of average wage)		67	100	167	67
	Number of children		none	none	none	2
1.	**Gross wage earnings**		29 134	43 484	72 618	29 134
2.	**Standard tax allowances**					
	Basic allowance		60	60	60	60
	Married or head of family					
	Dependent children		0	0	0	440
	Deduction for social security contributions and income taxes		5 261	7 852	11 755	5 261
	Work-related expenses		132	132	132	132
	Other		620	620	620	620
		Total	6 073	8 664	12 567	6 513
3.	**Tax credits or cash transfers included in taxable income**		0	0	0	0
4.	**Central government taxable income (1 - 2 + 3)**		23 061	34 820	60 051	22 621
5.	**Central government income tax liability (exclusive of tax credits)**		3 540	7 670	17 222	3 380
6.	**Tax credits**					
	Basic credit		0	0	0	0
	Married or head of family		0	0	0	669
	Children					
	Other		345	345	345	345
		Total	345	345	345	1 014
7.	**Central government income tax finally paid (5-6)**		3 195	7 325	16 877	2 366
8.	**State and local taxes**		0	0	0	0
9.	**Employees' compulsory social security contributions**					
	Gross earnings		5 261	7 852	11 755	5 261
	Taxable income					
		Total	5 261	7 852	11 755	5 261
10.	**Total payments to general government (7 + 8 + 9)**		8 456	15 177	28 633	7 627
11.	**Cash transfers from general government**					
	For head of family					
	For two children		0	0	0	5 031
		Total	0	0	0	5 031
12.	**Take-home pay (1-10+11)**		20 678	28 307	43 985	26 539
13.	**Employer's wage dependent contributions and taxes**					
	Employer's compulsory social security contributions		6 243	9 318	13 950	6 243
	payroll taxes		2 185	3 261	5 446	2 185
		Total	8 428	12 579	19 396	8 428
14.	**Average rates**					
	Income tax		11.0%	16.8%	23.2%	8.1%
	Employees' social security contributions		18.1%	18.1%	16.2%	18.1%
	Total payments less cash transfers		29.0%	34.9%	39.4%	8.9%
	Total tax wedge including employer's social security contributions		45.0%	49.5%	52.2%	29.3%
15.	**Marginal rates**					
	Total payments less cash transfers: Principal earner		44.4%	49.1%	37.9%	44.4%
	Total payments less cash transfers: Spouse		n.a.	n.a.	n.a.	n.a.
	Total tax wedge: Principal earner		56.8%	60.5%	42.2%	56.8%
	Total tax wedge: Spouse		n.a.	n.a.	n.a.	n.a.

Austria 2015

The tax/benefit position of married couples

			100-0	100-33	100-67	100-33
	Wage level (per cent of average wage)					
	Number of children		2	2	2	none
1.	**Gross wage earnings**		43 484	57 833	72 618	57 833
2.	**Standard tax allowances**					
	Basic allowance		60	120	120	120
	Married or head of family					
	Dependent children		440	440	528	0
	Deduction for social security contributions and income taxes		7 852	10 013	13 113	10 013
	Work-related expenses		132	264	264	264
	Other		620	1 240	1 240	1 240
		Total	9 104	12 077	15 265	11 637
3.	**Tax credits or cash transfers included in taxable income**		0	0	0	0
4.	**Central government taxable income (1 - 2 + 3)**		34 380	45 757	57 353	46 197
5.	**Central government income tax liability (exclusive of tax credits)**		7 480	7 480	11 000	7 670
6.	**Tax credits**					
	Basic credit		0	0	0	0
	Married or head of family		669	0	0	0
	Children					
	Other		345	690	690	690
		Total	1 014	690	690	690
7.	**Central government income tax finally paid (5 - 6)**		6 466	6 915	10 310	7 105
8.	**State and local taxes**		0	0	0	0
9.	**Employees' compulsory social security contributions**					
	Gross earnings		7 852	10 013	13 113	10 013
	Taxable income					
		Total	7 852	10 013	13 113	10 013
10.	**Total payments to general government (7 + 8 + 9)**		14 318	16 928	23 423	17 118
11.	**Cash transfers from general government**					
	For head of family					
	For two children		5 031	5 031	5 031	0
		Total	5 031	5 031	5 031	0
12.	**Take-home pay (1-10+11)**		34 197	45 937	54 226	40 716
13.	**Employer's wage dependent contributions and taxes**					
	Employer's compulsory social security contributions		9 318	12 393	15 561	12 393
	Payroll taxes		3 261	4 338	5 446	4 338
		Total	12 579	16 730	21 007	16 730
14.	**Average rates**					
	Income tax		14.9%	12.0%	14.2%	12.3%
	Employees' social security contributions		18.1%	17.3%	18.1%	17.3%
	Total payments less cash transfers		21.4%	20.6%	25.3%	29.6%
	Total tax wedge including employer's social security contributions		39.0%	38.4%	42.1%	45.4%
15.	**Marginal rates**					
	Total payments less cash transfers: Principal earner		49.1%	49.1%	49.1%	49.1%
	Total payments less cash transfers: Spouse		18.2%	15.1%	44.4%	15.1%
	Total tax wedge: Principal earner		60.5%	60.5%	60.5%	60.5%
	Total tax wedge: Spouse		36.5%	34.1%	56.8%	34.1%

The Austrian currency is the Euro (EUR). In 2015, EUR 0.90 was equal to USD 1. In that year, the average worker in Austria earned EUR 43 484 (Secretariat estimate).

1. Personal income tax

1.1. *Central government income tax*

1.1.1. *Tax unit*

Each person is taxed separately.

1.1.2. *Tax allowances*

1.1.2.1. Standard tax reliefs

- Work related expenses: a minimum allowance of EUR 132 is available to all employees.
- Minimum allowance for special expenses of EUR 60.
- Social security contributions and connected contributions (see Section 2).
- Children allowance of EUR 220 for one or EUR 132 for both parents per child. The parents have the choice between these opportunities.

1.1.2.2. Non-standard tax reliefs

- Mainly work-related expenses ("Werbungskosten").
- Traffic relief according to the distance between home/address and working place.

  The following allowances are deductible from income (EUR per year):

	Public transport	
	Available	Not available
More than 2 km	0	372
More than 20 km	696	1 476
More than 40 km	1 356	2 568
More than 60 km	2 016	3 672

- Special expenses allowance ("Sonderausgaben"): some personal expenses (for example, life insurance premiums, and expenses for the purchase of residence including repayments of housing loans) are partly deductible from income. The allowance is limited to EUR 2 920 per taxpayer or EUR 5 840 for sole earners or parents. A quarter of "Sonderausgaben" can be deducted up to a taxable income of EUR 36 400, whereas between EUR 36 400 and EUR 60 000 the deductible amount is (linearly) reduced to EUR 60. Unless higher special expenses can be proved, a standard deduction for "Sonderausgaben" of EUR 60 is granted (see Section 1.121). Grants to non-profit charitable organisations up to 10% of taxable income are deductible. Additionally, contributions to the church are deductible up to an amount of EUR 400.

- Tax-free supplements exist for dirty, hard, dangerous, night, weekend and holiday work and overtime. The supplement for 10 hours of overtime up to EUR 86 per month is tax free, the other supplements are tax free up to EUR 360 (EUR 540 for night workers) per month.

1.1.3. *Rate schedule*

The new tax schedule has a zero-zone up to EUR 11 000 and shows tax formulas for three tax brackets. The effective marginal tax rates resulting from these formulas are:

Income (EUR) up to	Marginal rate %
11 000	0
25 000	36.5
60 000	43.21429
Above	50

There is a special taxation other than the normal tax schedule for Christmas and leave bonus to the extent that their sum does not exceed two average monthly payments (1/6 of current income). If these bonuses before deduction of SSC are below EUR 2 100 p.a., no tax is calculated. Otherwise the tax amount is calculated according to the following formula:

Income from Christmas and leave bonus (EUR) up to	Marginal rate %
620	0
25 000	6
50 000	27
83 333	37.5
Above	50

In case of bonuses up to EUR 25 000 the tax amount is 30% of the bonus (net of SSC) exceeding EUR 2 000 instead of the formula above, if this results to a lower tax amount. So the break-even is at EUR 2 345 a month.

1.1.4. *Tax credits*

Tax credits are available as follows:

- Employee's tax credit of EUR 54. In the overall tax calculation, negative tax is possible but is limited to 20% of social security contributions respectively to a maximum of EUR 220. For employees with a traffic allowance (see 1.12.2) the maximum is EUR 450 and the percentage increases to 36%.
- Traffic (commuting) tax credit EUR 291.
- Additional traffic tax credit in case of entitlement to traffic relief according to the distance between home/address and working place (see 1.12.2). In this case employees are entitled to an additional traffic tax credit of EUR 2 per km distance from home to working place.
- Sole earner's and sole parent's tax credit for families with children. The sole earner's credit is not given when a spouse's income exceeds EUR 6 000. This tax credit is EUR 494

for one child and increases by EUR 175 for the second and by EUR 220 for the third and every additional child. This tax credit is non-wastable and can be paid out as a negative income tax (in addition to the negative tax permitted in respect of the Employee's tax credit).

- Children's tax credit EUR 700.8 (58.40 per month) per child. As this tax credit is paid together with children allowances and not connected with income tax assessment, it is treated as a transfer in this Report (similar treatment as in *Revenue Statistics*).
- Tax credit for retired persons. The tax credit amounts to EUR 764 for sole earners with income up to EUR 19 930 and if the spouse's income does not exceed EUR 2 200. Otherwise the tax credit is EUR 400. The tax credit is linearly reduced to 0 between EUR 17 000 (EUR 19 930 for sole earners) and EUR 25 000 of income. In the overall tax calculation, negative tax is possible but is limited to 20% of social security contributions respectively to a maximum of EUR 55.

1.2. State and local income taxes

None.

2. Compulsory social security contributions to schemes operated within the government sector

2.1. Employee and employer social security contributions

	Ceilings (EUR)		Rates (%)	
	Regular wage per month	Christmas and leave bonus	Employee[2]	Employer[3]
Health insurance	4 650	9 300	3.95	3.70
Unemployment insurance	4 650	9 300	4	3.00
Pension insurance	4 650	9 300	10.25	12.55
Accident insurance	4 650	9 300	–	1.30
Contribution to the labour chamber	4 650	1	0.50	–
Contribution for the promotion of residential building	4 650	1	0.50	0.50
Addition to secure wage payments in the case of bankruptcy	4 650	9 300	–	0.45

1. No contributions on Christmas and leave bonus. In Revenue Statistics, the contribution to the labour chamber is accounted under Taxes on Income of Individuals (1110) the total of the contribution for the promotion of residential buildings is included in Taxes on payroll (3000).
2. There is a threshold for employee contributions of EUR 405.98 per month.
3. A new program has been introduced as of 1January, 2004 for severance payments. Employers are required to pay 1.53% of gross wages for those whose employment starts after 1 January, 2003 or where the employer and employee opt to participate in the new program. This contribution is seen as a non-tax compulsory wage-related payment.
4. Employees' unemployment insurance rate is reduced for low earnings. In 2015, it is zero for monthly earnings up to EUR 1 280, 1% up to EUR 1 396 , 2% up to EUR 1 571 and 3% above.

2.2. Payroll taxes

There are two payroll taxes which are levied on employers for all private sector employees with a monthly gross wage total of more than EUR 1 095: the contribution to the Family Burden Equalisation Fund (4.5%) and the Community Tax (3%). The wage-dependant part of the contribution to the Entrepreneurs' Chamber (listed under heading 1000, taxes on profits, in the *Revenue Statistics*) which is levied, together with the contributions to the Family Burden Equalisation Fund, at different rates depending upon the Länder Chamber (the average rate is approximately 0.4%) is not taken into account. The contribution for the promotion of residential buildings (listed under heading 3000, taxes on payroll, in *Revenue Statistics*) is included in the social security contributions shown above as it is levied by the Health Insurance Companies on monthly income (current) along with the other social security contribution amounts.

3. Universal cash transfers

3.1. *Amount for marriage*

No recurrent payments.

3.2. *Amount for children*

A family allowance is granted for each child. The monthly payment is EUR 109.70 for the first child, EUR 123.10 for the second, EUR 146.10 for the third and EUR 161.90 for each subsequent child. It is increased by EUR 7.60 for children above 3 years, EUR 26.50 for children above 10 years of age and by EUR 49.20 for students (above 19). In the calculation the weighted average is applied. Parents of children under the age of 3 years are entitled to a childcare transfer, introduced in 2002. Beginning 2010, the flexibility of the childcare transfer was increased significantly. The entitled parent can choose between following alternatives: EUR 14.53 per day until the 36th month of birth, EUR 20.80 (24 months), EUR 26.60 (18 months) or EUR 33.00 (14 months). Additionally instead of the fix amounts the entitled person can opt for 80% of the last net-earning, limited to EUR 2 000 a month (14 months). The children's tax credit (EUR 50.90 monthly, see § 1.14) is paid out together with the family allowance and therefore treated as a transfer.

There is a supplement to the family allowance of EUR 20.00 per month for the third and every additional child, if the family taxable income (i.e. the sum of the tax base for the progressive income tax schedule) of the preceding year did not exceed EUR 55 000. This supplement is paid out on application after an assessment of the very year.

An additional family allowance ("13th allowance") of EUR 100 is given for children in the age between 6 and 16 every September.

4. Main changes in tax/benefit systems since 1994

In 1994, a major tax reform took effect. Most measures concerned the taxation of firms. For employees the following points are important. The general tax credit was increased by ATS 3 840, i.e. ATS 320 per month. For employees with low income a negative income tax option was introduced (the negative income tax is limited to the wage earners tax credit, but it cannot exceed 10% of social security contributions).

In 1995, family allowances were reduced by ATS 100 per month (ATS 1 200 per year).

In 1996, a consolidation package was introduced, some measures of which took effect already in 1996. The deductibility of special expenses was reduced (half to quarter) and abolished for incomes exceeding ATS 700 000. Tax free overtime supplements were limited to ATS 590 per month. The general tax credit was linearly reduced to zero for income between ATS 200 000 and ATS 500 000 and there was a change in the deductibility of social security contributions on non-current wages and salaries.

The family package of 1998 brought an increase of ATS 1 500 in the family allowances and the children's tax credits each in 1999. A supplement of ATS 2 400 in 1999 and ATS 4 800 in 2000 for the 3rd etc. child for families earning less than ATS 504 000 was introduced. The sole earner's or sole parent's tax credit negative tax limit was abolished.

For 2000 and the following years, there was an additional increase in the sum of family allowances and children's tax credits of ATS 3 000, but the differentiation according to the number of children was transferred to the allowances, i.e. from 2000 onwards there is a unique annual tax credit of ATS 8 400 per child.

The tax reform of 1999, effective from the beginning of 2000, brought a reduction in the tax schedule and an increase of the general tax credit leading to a (linearly increasing) tax reduction between ATS 4 000 and 7 000 p.a. The maximum reduction is reached at a gross income near the ceiling for social security contributions. The reform also included a number of other measures which concerned mainly enterprise taxation.

The budget consolidation measures for 2001 included an abolition of the general tax credit for incomes exceeding ATS 487 400, the halving of the employee's tax credit to ATS 750 and a phasing-out of the pensioner's tax credit for income between ATS 230 000 and 300 000. The adaptation of the tax laws to the Euro did not bring any substantive changes. In 2004 (effective), the family allowances for children above three years of age were increased by EUR 7.30 per month.

In 2004, the first step of a comprehensive tax reform came into force. The general tax credit was increased from EUR 887 to EUR 1 264 and the phasing-out rules were considerably simplified and made uniform for all groups of taxpayers.

The tax reform in 2005 brought a new income tax schedule. Apart from the top rate of 50% for income exceeding EUR 51 000, it shows the average rates for two amounts of income. The tax amounts for incomes between these amounts have to be calculated by linear interpolation. The formulas that have to be applied are shown in the tax law. The tax reform included some measures which were made retrospective for 2004. These measures are the increase of the sole earner and the single parent tax credit depending on the number of children (together with a higher earnings limit for the spouse of a single earner) and an increase of the traffic reliefs by about 15%. The maximum deductible amount for church contributions was increased as well. In 2006, the traffic reliefs were again increased by about 10%.

In 2007, the traffic allowances were increased by 10% (effective from 1st July), the maximum negative tax for employees with traffic allowances was increased from EUR 110 to EUR 240 (for 2008 and 2009). For 2008, the family allowances for the third and subsequent children were increased. In 2008, the unemployment insurance contributions of low-earning employees were reduced (effective from 1st July). In 2008 up to monthly earnings of EUR 1 100 the rate was zero, for earnings below EUR 1 200 the contribution was 1%, below EUR 1 350 2% and above the current rate of 3%. These income limits are increased according to the raise of the ceiling levels of social security contributions every year.

In September 2008, the parliament decided some measures to compensate for the strong increase of food and energy prices: inter alia, the tax exemption of overtime supplements was increased and a 13th payment of children allowances introduced.

The tax reform 2009 (effective from 1st January) brought an increase of the zero bracket (from EUR 10 000 to EUR 11 000), a reduction of the income tax rates (except the top rate), an upward shift of the top rate bracket (from EUR 51 000 to EUR 60 000) and several measures for families with children: children allowance (EUR 220 or EUR 132 each parent p.a.), deductibility of cost for child care (up to EUR 2 300 p.a. per child), tax-free payments (up to EUR 500 p.a.) from employers to their employees for child care and an increase of the children tax credit.

Starting with 2013 a progressive rate schedule is applied to Christmas and leave bonus instead of a flat rate regime of 6% (see 1.13)

In 2015 the negative tax credit for employee is increased and a negative tax credit for pensioners introduced.

5. Memorandum items

5.1. *Calculation of earnings data*

- Sector used: All private employees except apprentices employed full-time for the whole year
- Geographical coverage: Whole country
- Sex: Male and Female
- Earnings base:
  - Items excluded: Unemployment compensation
    Sickness compensation
  - Items included: Vacation payments
    Overtime payments
    Recurring cash payments
    Fringe benefits (taxable value)
- Basic method of calculation used: Average annual earnings
- Income tax year ends: 31 December

Period to which the earnings calculation refers to: one year.

2015 parameter values

Average earnings/yr	Ave_earn	43 484	Secretariat estimate
Non current income as %	non_cur_pc	14.286%	
Tax free inc on non-current	Bonus	620	
Ceiling for taxing non-current income	nonc_ceil	2 000	
Tax schedule for nci exc. 25000	nci_sch	0	25 000
		0.21	50 000
		0.2975	83 333
		0.44	
Work related	work_rel	132	
Allowance f."Special expenses"	Basic_al	60	
Children allowance for 2 earning parents	Child_al_2	132	
Children allowance for sole earner/parent	Child_al_1	220	
Tax free inc.	tax_free	0%	
Basic tax credit	basic_cr		
Employee's tax credit	wage_cr	54	
Max. neg. employee's tax credit	neg_wage_cr	220	
Max. neg. employee's tax credit rate	neg_wage_cr_rate	20%	
Traffic (commuting) tax credit	traffic_cr	291	
Sole earner's (parent's) tax credit	sole_cr	0	
Children suppl.to SETC: 1st child	dsole1_cr	494	
2nd child	dsole2_cr	175	
3rd+ child	dsole3_cr	220	
Spouse income not more than	sole_lim0	0	
Spouse with children	sole_lim1	6 000	
Tax on non-current income	non_cur_rate	6%	
Altern.tax on non-current income	alt_nonc_rate	30%	
Income tax schedule	Tax_sch	0	11 000
		0.365	25 000
		0.43214	60 000
		0.5	
Ceiling f. soc. security contributions	SSC_ceil	4 650	
lower limit	SSC_low	405.98	
Employees' contr. rates	health_rate	3.95%	
	unemp_rate	0%	1 280
		1%	1 396
		2%	1 571
		3%	
	Pension_rate	10.25%	
Sum without unempl. and others	empl_14	14.20%	
	others_rate	1%	
Employers' contr.rates	health_empr	3.70%	
	unemp_empr	3%	
	Pension_empr	12.55%	
	accident_empr	1.30%	
	payinsur_empr	0.45%	
Sum without others	empr_14	21.00%	
	others_empr	0.50%	
Payroll taxes	payroll_rate	7.50%	
Child benefit: 1st child	CB_1	1 316.40	
2nd child	CB_2	1 477.20	
3rd child	CB_3	1 753.20	
4th+ child	CB_4	1 942.80	
suppl.>3years	CB03sppl	91.20	
suppl.>10years	CB10sppl	318.00	
suppl >19years	CB19sppl	590.40	
5 years<suppl<17years	CB5to17	100.0	
Child tax credit	child_cr_1	700.8	

2015 Tax equations

The equations for the Austrian system are, in principle, on an individual basis. The only variable which is dependent on the marital status is the head of family (sole earner) tax credit which is also given to single people with children. For the Christmas and leave bonus (both amounting to one monthly wage or salary) there are special rules for the calculation of social security contributions (separate ceilings and slightly lower rate) and wage tax (reduced flat rate). The income tax schedule and the tax credits are applied only for "current pays". The children tax credit is in principle given to the mother (as a negative tax together with "family allowances" = transfer for children). The sole earner and the employee tax credit are connected with negative income tax rules. Therefore, the tax finally paid may be different from tax liability minus tax credits.

Bn	Variable	Code for docn equations	Excel-Function
3	earnings (%AW)	percent	0, 1/3, 2/3, 1 or 5/3 in Taxing Wages output tables (but model can be applied to all earnings levels)
4	number of children	child	0 or 2 in Taxing Wages output tables
5	Gross earnings	earn	=Ave_earn*percent
6	Current income	cearn	=(1-non_cur_pc)*earn
7	Basic allowance	allow	=(earn>14*SSC_low)*Basic_al
8	SSC on curr.inc.	SSCc	=(empl_14+unemp(earn,unemp_rate)+others_rate)* MIN(12*SSC_ceil;cearn)*(cearn>12*SSC_low)
9	Work related expenses	work_rel	=work_rel
10	Tax-free income	taxfrinc	=tax_free*earn
11	Child allowance	Child_al_princ Child_al_spouse	IF(cearn_spouse-allow_spouse-SSCc_spouse-work_rel_spouse-taxfrinc_spouse-11945<0,Child_al_1, Child_al_2)*child IF(Child_al_princ=child*Child_al_2, Child_al_2, 0)*Child
12	Tax base for schedule	ctbase	=(earn>14*SSC_low)*(cearn-allow-SSCc-work_rel-taxfrinc-child_al*child)
13	Gross tax on current income	gtaxcur	=Tax(ctbase;tax_sch)
14	Basic tax credit	btaxcr	=0
15	Married or head of family	headcr	=(earn_sp<IF(child>0;sole_lim1;sole_lim0))*(sole_cr+(child>0)*dsole1_cr+(child >1)*dsole2_cr+(child>2)*(child-2)*dsole3_cr
16	Other	othcr	=min(wage_cr;20%*SSC)+traffic_cr
17	Interm. tax on current income	itcur	=gtaxcur-btaxcr-headcr-othcr
18	Net tax on current income	ntaxcur	=IF(itcur>-headcr; itcur;MAX(-neg_wage_cr_rate*SSC-(child>0)*headcr; -neg_wage_cr-(child>0)*headcr))
19	Non current income	ncearn	=earn-cearn
20	SSC on non-curr. inc.	SSCnc	=(health_rate+unemp(earn,unemp_rate)+pension_rate)* MIN(2*SSC_ceil;ncearn)*(ncearn>2*SSC_low)
21	Non current income-SSC	ncearn_adj1	=ncearn-SSCnc
22	of which tax free	taxfree	=MIN(bonus;ncearn_adj)
23	Non-curr. tax base	ncearn_adj2	=ncearn_adj-taxfree
24	Tax schedule for nci exc. 25000	nci_sch	=Positive(MINA(ncearn_adj1-nonc_ceil)*alt_nonc_rate;ncearn_adj2*non_cur_rate))+MAX(0;Tax(ncearn_adj1; nci_sch))
25	Taxable income	taxinc	=ctbase+ncearn_adj2
26	Tax liability excl. tax credits	inctax_ex	=gtaxcur+taxnc
27	Income tax finally paid	inctax	=ntaxcur+taxnc
28	Employee's SSC	SSC	=SSCc+SSCnc
29	Employer's SSC	SSCf	=((empr_14+others_empr)*MIN(12*SSC_ceil;cearn)+empr_14*MIN(12*SSC_ceil ;ncearn))
30	Pay-roll taxes	payroll	=payroll_rate*earn

Bn	Variable	Code for docn equations	Excel-Function
31	Cash transfers	cash	=IF(child=0;0;IF(child=2;CB_1+CB_2+child*CB10sppl+child*(child_cr_1+CB5to17)))
32	Take-home pay		=earn-inctax-SSC+cash
33	Wage cost		=earn+SSCf+payroll

unemp is a Visual Basic Function which chooses lower unemployment SSC rates for low earnings.
Key to range of equation B calculated separately for both principal earner and spouse P calculated for principal only (value taken as 0 for spouse calculation) J calculated once only on a joint basis.

Belgium

This chapter includes data on the income taxes paid by workers, their social security contributions, the family benefits they receive in the form of cash transfers as well as the social security contributions and payroll taxes paid by their employers. Results reported include the marginal and average tax burden for eight different family types.

Methodological information is available for personal income tax systems, compulsory social security contributions to schemes operated within the government sector, universal cash transfers as well as recent changes in the tax/ benefit system. The methodology also includes the parameter values and tax equations underlying the data.

Belgium 2015

The tax/benefit position of single persons

	Wage level (per cent of average wage)	67	100	167	67
	Number of children	none	none	none	2
1.	**Gross wage earnings**	31 284	46 693	77 977	31 284
2.	**Standard tax allowances**				
	Basic allowance				
	Married or head of family				
	Dependent children				
	Deduction for social security contributions and income taxes	4 089	6 103	10 192	4 089
	Work-related expenses	3 156	3 557	4 090	3 156
	Other				
	Total	7 244	9 660	14 282	7 244
3.	**Tax credits or cash transfers included in taxable income**	0	0	0	0
4.	**Central government taxable income (1 - 2 + 3)**	24 040	37 033	63 695	24 040
5.	**Central government income tax liability (exclusive of tax credits)**	8 109	13 956	27 246	8 109
6.	**Tax credits**				
	Basic credit	0	0	0	0
	Married or head of family	1 845	1 773	1 773	2 232
	Children	0	0	0	1 201
	Other				
	Total	1 845	1 773	1 773	3 433
7.	**Central government income tax finally paid (5-6)**	4 636	9 017	18 853	3 461
8.	**State and local taxes**	2 098	4 080	8 531	1 566
9.	**Employees' compulsory social security contributions**				
	Gross earnings	4 089	6 103	10 192	4 089
	Taxable income	262	431	731	262
	Total	4 351	6 533	10 923	4 351
10.	**Total payments to general government (7 + 8 + 9)**	11 085	19 631	38 307	9 378
11.	**Cash transfers from general government**				
	For head of family				
	For two children	0	0	0	3 756
	Total	0	0	0	3 756
12.	**Take-home pay (1-10+11)**	20 199	27 062	39 670	25 662
13.	**Employer's compulsory social security contributions**	8 677	13 862	22 927	8 677
14.	**Average rates**				
	Income tax	21.5%	28.1%	35.1%	16.1%
	Employees' social security contributions	13.9%	14.0%	14.0%	13.9%
	Total payments less cash transfers	35.4%	42.0%	49.1%	18.0%
	Total tax wedge including employer's social security contributions	49.5%	55.3%	60.7%	35.8%
15.	**Marginal rates**				
	Total payments less cash transfers: Principal earner	55.0%	55.0%	59.8%	55.0%
	Total payments less cash transfers: Spouse	n.a.	n.a.	n.a.	n.a.
	Total tax wedge: Principal earner	66.3%	66.3%	68.5%	66.3%
	Total tax wedge: Spouse	n.a.	n.a.	n.a.	n.a.

Belgium 2015

The tax/benefit position of married couples

		Wage level (per cent of average wage)	100-0	100-33	100-67	100-33
		Number of children	2	2	2	none
1.	**Gross wage earnings**		46 693	62 102	77 977	62 102
2.	**Standard tax allowances**					
	Basic allowance					
	Married or head of family					
	Dependent children					
	Deduction for social security contributions and income taxes		6 103	6 103	10 192	6 103
	Work-related expenses		3 557	6 160	6 713	6 160
	Other					
		Total	9 660	12 263	16 905	12 263
3.	**Tax credits or cash transfers included in taxable income**		0	0	0	0
4.	**Central government taxable income (1 - 2 + 3)**		37 033	49 838	61 072	49 838
5.	**Central government income tax liability (exclusive of tax credits)**		11 986	17 403	22 066	17 403
6.	**Tax credits**					
	Basic credit		0	331	0	331
	Married or head of family		3 618	3 618	3 618	3 618
	Children		1 083	1 083	1 083	0
	Other					
		Total	4 701	5 031	4 701	3 948
7.	**Central government income tax finally paid (5-6)**		5 392	9 070	12 852	9 872
8.	**State and local taxes**		2 440	4 254	5 816	4 617
9.	**Employees' compulsory social security contributions**					
	Gross earnings		6 103	6 103	10 192	6 103
	Taxable income		431	597	731	597
		Total	6 533	6 700	10 923	6 700
10.	**Total payments to general government (7 + 8 + 9)**		14 365	20 024	29 590	21 188
11.	**Cash transfers from general government**					
	For head of family					
	For two children		3 756	3 756	3 756	0
		Total	3 756	3 756	3 756	0
12.	**Take-home pay (1-10+11)**		36 083	45 833	52 143	40 913
13.	**Employer's compulsory social security contributions**		13 862	16 089	22 538	16 089
14.	**Average rates**					
	Income tax		16.8%	21.5%	23.9%	23.3%
	Employees' social security contributions		14.0%	10.8%	14.0%	10.8%
	Total payments less cash transfers		22.7%	26.2%	33.1%	34.1%
	Total tax wedge including employer's social security contributions		40.4%	41.4%	48.1%	47.7%
15.	**Marginal rates**					
	Total payments less cash transfers: Principal earner		55.0%	55.0%	53.9%	55.0%
	Total payments less cash transfers: Spouse		36.7%	40.8%	53.9%	40.8%
	Total tax wedge: Principal earner		66.3%	66.3%	65.5%	66.3%
	Total tax wedge: Spouse		44.7%	60.5%	65.5%	60.5%

The national currency is the euro. In 2015, EUR 0.90 was equal to USD 1. The Secretariat has estimated that in that same year the average worker earned EUR 46 693 (Secretariat estimate).

1. Personal income tax system

1.1. *Federal government income tax*

1.1.1. *Tax unit*

Spouses are taxed separately. As from 2004, the principle of separate taxation applies to all categories of income. A non-earning spouse is taxed separately on a notional share of income that can be transferred to him or her (see "non-earning spouse allowance", below). Married couples nonetheless file joint income tax returns.

1.1.2. *Tax allowances*

1.1.2.1. Deduction of social security contributions

Unless stated otherwise, social insurance contributions are deductible from gross income.

1.1.2.2. Work-related expenses

Salaried employees and self-employed professionals are entitled to a standard deduction for work-related expenses. This deduction may under no circumstances exceed respectively EUR 4 090 per spouse for salaried employees and EUR 3 960 per spouse for self-employed professionals and is computed as follows:

The lump-sum deduction for business expenses for employees has been increased as of income year 2015, with also a new maximum amount. The lump-sum deduction for business expenses for self-employed professionals remains unchanged.

For salaried employees:

Gross earnings less social insurance contributions (EUR)	Rate (%)
Below 5 760	29.35
Between 5 760 and 11 380	10.50
Between 11 380 and 19 390	8
Above 19 390	3

For self-employed professionals:

Gross earnings less social insurance contributions (EUR)	Rate (%)
Below 5 730	28.70
Between 5 730 and 11 380	10
Between 11 380 and 18 940	5
Above 18 940	3

Paid company directors are also entitled to a standard deduction for work-related expenses; this is equal to 3% of gross income (less social insurance contributions) and may not exceed EUR 2 380 per spouse.

An additional allowance may be granted to wage-earners if their workplace is more than a certain distance from their home.

Actual expenses incurred in order to acquire or retain earned income are deductible if they exceed the standard deduction. The deductibility of certain categories of work-related expenses (cars, clothing, restaurant meals and business gifts) is limited, however. Taxpayers who report actual expenses may deduct EUR 0.15 per kilometre, up to 100 km per single journey, for travel between their home and their workplace by means other than private car.

1.1.2.3. Non-earning spouse allowance (*quotient conjugal*)

A notional amount of income can be transferred between spouses if one of them earns no more than 30% of the couple's combined earned income. In this case, the amount transferred is limited to 30% of aggregate net earned income, less the individual income of the spouse to whom the notional share is transferred. This allowance is limited to EUR 10 230.

1.1.2.4. Exempt income

The base amount is:

Taxable income (S)	Fixed amount	Variable amount
0-26 360	7 380	0
26 360-26 650	7 090	26 650-S
26 650 and up	7 090	0

These amounts vary with regards to the family situation. Additional exemptions for dependent children (a handicapped child counts as two children):

- 1 child 1 510
- 2 children 3 880
- 3 children 8 700
- 4 children 14 060
- > 4 children 5 370 per additional child

Dependent child exemptions in excess of available income give rise to a reimbursable tax credit. This reimbursable tax credit is calculated at the marginal rate for the spouse with the highest income and capped at EUR 430 per dependent child.

Additional special exemptions are also granted for certain household members (in euro):

- Other dependants 1 510
- Handicapped spouse 1 510
- Other handicapped dependants 1 510
- Widow(er) with dependent child(ren) 1 510
- Single father or mother 1 510

These additional exemptions are applied first to the taxable income of the spouse having the most income, with any remainder then being applied to the income of the other spouse.

The basic exemption plus any additional exemptions for dependants and single parents is applied against each bracket from the bottom up; in other words, the lowest brackets are depleted first.

1.1.2.5. Schedule

Taxable income (EUR)	Marginal rate (%)
0-8 710	25
8 710-12 400	30
12 400-20 660	40
20 660-37 870	45
37 870-and above	50

The basic exemption plus any additional exemptions is applied from the bottom up.

1.2. Regional and local government taxes

With the implementation of the sixth state reform, the Flemish Region, the Walloon Region and the Brussels-Capital Region have been delegated several important competences with regard to the individual income tax. As a result of this reform, as from 1 July 2014, the regional competences are:

- the possibility to levy surcharges on the federal PIT (the supplementary regional tax on the personal income tax). The surcharge may be proportional or vary with income but there are limits to ensure that the tax remains progressive);
- to grant (on the result of the surcharges) tax discounts;
- to grant tax reductions, tax increases and tax credits;
- to regulate exclusively some tax reductions.

Under the new tax model, the assumed federal income tax amount must first be calculated. The taxable base is reduced by the exempt income (see 1.124), the tax credits for pensions, unemployment, sickness and other social benefits and the tax credit for income taxed abroad. Additionally, it is reduced by the tax due on passive income for which the Federal State remains exclusively competent.

The remaining PIT liability is than split between the central government and the Regions according to a ratio of 0.7401 /0.2599.

Subsequently, the Regions are allowed to levy a proportional surcharge on this reduced federal income tax. This surcharge may, within certain limits and given the matters for which the Regions are competent, vary per tax bracket. The actual rate is set at 35.117% (0.2599/(1-0.2599).

The starting point for the calculation of the municipal (and agglomeration) surcharges is the individual income tax ("impôt total", i.e. the sum of federal PIT and regional PIT), before taking into account the surcharge resulting from insufficient prepayments, the foreign tax credit, federal and regional reimbursable tax credits (among others for children and for low-income workers), prepayments and withholding taxes. The rate of this local surtax is set by each municipality, and there is no upper limit. An additional surcharge of 1% is levied in the Brussels-Capital Region, in addition to the municipal surcharge.

The calculation of the regional and local surtax for the average worker study assumes that the worker lives in the Region of Brussels-Capital. The weighted average local surtax of the 19 municipalities which form the Brussels-Capital Region is 7.5%.

1.3. Tax credits

Refundable tax credit for low-income workers

A refundable tax credit is intended for low-income workers and company managers (subject to the employees' social security system) entitled to the employment bonus.

The refundable tax credit amounts to 14.40% / 17.81% as of 1 August 2015 of the "employment bonus" which is actually granted on remunerations earned during the taxable period. It cannot exceed EUR 310/EUR 360 as of 1 August 2015 per taxable period.

1.4. Rebate on the wage withholding tax

Employers benefit from a rebate on the wage withholding tax, at the rate of 1%. The rebate does not affect the PIT liability of the employee and the amount of the withholding tax he may credit on its PIT liability: it just reduces the amount of withholding tax paid by the employer to the tax administration. This means that the rebate operates like a wage subsidy, or like a negative payroll tax. The rebate is a standard one: it applies in an unconditional way to any wage earners in sectors C-K.

For employers who are either considered as small companies, as defined in article 15 of the Belgian Corporation Code, or natural persons meeting *mutatis mutandis* the criteria set out in the same article 15, the rate has been increased to 1.12%.

2. Compulsory social security contributions to schemes operated within the government sector

2.1. Rates and ceiling

a. Payroll deductions

The rates of employer and employee contributions are set by law. The applicable rates (in %) are as follows (for businesses having 20 or more employees):

2015	Employee	Employer	Total
Unemployment	0.87	3.16	4.03
Health insurance indemnities	1.15	2.35	3.5
Health care	3.55	3.8	7.35
Placement services		0.05	0.05
Family allowances		7	7
Pensions	7.50	8.86	16.36
Child care		0.05	0.05
Work-related illnesses		1.01	1.01
Work-related accidents		0.32	0.32
Education leave		0.05	0.05
Business closures		0.41	0.41
Wage restraint		7.59	7.59
Total	13.07	34.65	47.72

Vacation pay is not subject to the social security contributions applicable to salaries, but a social security levy of 13.07% is deducted when the money is attributed.

b. Reduction of employer contributions

The schedule applicable as from 01.01.2014 is as follows:

Gross annual earnings (S) in EUR	Fixed amount	Variable amount
0-22 241.96	1 850.4	0.162 (22 241.96-S)
22 241.96-53 604.28	1 850.4	0
53 604.28 and up	1 850.4	0.06 (S-53 604.28)

c. Reduction of individual social security contributions

A reduction of individual social security contributions is granted monthly for low-income earners, depending on wage level. The schedule below is restated in annual terms.

The schedule applicable as from 01.01.2014 is as follows:

Gross annual salary (S) in EUR	Reduction in Euros
0 < S < 18 021.84	2 207.64
18 021.84 < S < 28 624.92	Min (2 207.64, (2 208-0.2082 (S-18 021.84))
S > 28 624.92	0

The schedule applicable as from 01.08.2015 is as follows:

Gross annual salary (S) in EUR	Reduction in Euros
0 < S < 18 562.44	2 279.76
18 562.44 < S < 28 956.00	Min (2 279.76, (2 279.76-0.2193 (S-18 562.44))
S > 28 956.00	0

d. Special social security contribution

All persons totally or partially subject to the social security scheme for salaried workers are liable for this special contribution. In theory, the amount of the contribution is determined according to aggregate household income. Aggregate household income is equal to combined gross earnings less ordinary social security contributions and work-related expenses. The amount of the contribution is as follows:

Taxable income (EUR)	Amount due on the lower limit	% above the lower limit
from 0 to 18 592.02	0	0
from 18 592.02 to 21 070.96	0	9
from 21 070.96 to 60 161.85	223.10	1.3
60 161.85 and above	731.29	0

e. Work accidents

All employers are required to insure their employees against accidents that occur in the workplace or while travelling to or from the workplace. The insurance is written by a private company. The usual premiums are approximately 1% of gross pay for office workers and 3.3% for labourers. The premiums are based on capped gross wages: in 2011 these premiums apply to gross wages (including holiday pay and extra-legal remunerations) with a minimum of EUR 6 068 and a maximum of EUR 37 546 (EUR 5 949 and EUR 36 810 respectively in 2010). Higher rates apply in certain industries in which risks are greater. The premium rate for construction workers, for example, varies between 7% and 8%.

2.2. *Deductions according to family status or gender*

None.

3. Universal cash transfers

Family allowances are granted for children. The annual amounts of these benefits (in euro) are as follows:

	< 5 years	5-6 years	7-10 years	11-12 years	12-16 years	17-18 years	> 18 years
1st child	1 103.36	1 126.36	1 315.12	1 332.12	1 430.76	1 450.76	1 494.76
2nd child	2 024.60	2 047.60	2 423.92	2 440.92	2 639.64	2 659.64	2 815.76
3rd child	3 012.92	3 035.92	3 412.24	3 429.24	3 627.96	3 647.96	3 804.08

To determine the resources available to the average worker, the Taxing Wages calculations assume that one child was between seven and ten years of age and that the other child was between eleven and twelve years of age.

4. Main changes in the tax/benefit system

None.

2015 parameter values

	Ave_earn	46 693	Secretariat estimate		
Work-related expenses	work_rel_max	4 090			
	work_rel_sch	0.2935	5 760		
		0.1050	11 380		
		0.08	19 390		
		0.03			
Tax credits (exempt income)	single_cr	7 090			
	Married_cr	7 090			
	Supp_cr_base	290			
	supp_cr_thrsh1	26 360			
One child	child_cr1	1 510			
Two children	child_cr2	3 880			
Single parents	s_parent_cr	1 510			
Maximum Child Credit Payment	child_cr_max	430			
Basic Credit	basic_cr_base	0			
	basic_cr_thrsh1	4 960			
	basic_cr_thrsh2	6 620			
	basic_cr_thrsh3	16 560			
	basic_cr_thrsh4	21 520			
Income tax schedule		tax_rate1			
	tax_sch	0.25	8 710		
		0.30	12 400		
		0.40	20 660		
		0.45	37 870		
		0.50			
	quote_max	10 230			
	quote_rate	0.3			
Regional tax	red_rate	0.2599			
	reg_tax_rate	0.35117			
Local tax	local_rate	0.065			
	add_local_rate	0.01			
Unemployment	unemp_rate	0.0087			
Medical care	med_rate	0.0115			
Sickness	sickness_rate	0.0355			
Pension	pension_rate	0.0750			
Employee contribution	SSC_rt	0.1307			
	SSC_redn	0	0	2 237.69	0
	(annual)	18 247.09	18 247.09	2 237.69	0.2128
		28 762.87	18 247.09	2 237.69	0.2128
		28 762.87	0	0	0
		99 999 999	0	0	
Special annual contribution	SSC_special	0.000	18 592.02		
		0.090	21 070.96		
		0.013	60 161.85		
		0.000			
Employer contributions	SSC_empr_rt	0.3465			
	SSC_empr_redn	0	1 850.40	0.1620	22 241.96
		22 241.96	1 850.40	0	53 604.28
		53 604.28	1 850.40	-0.06	53 604.28
		9 999 999	0	0	
Structural reduction on the withholding tax on wages	PrP_redn	0.01			
Low-income credit	LIC_rate	0.1582			
	LIC_max	330.83			
Child benefit (age 7-10)	CB_1	1 332.12			
second child (age 7-10)	CB_2	2 423.92			
third child (age 7-10)	CB_3	3 412.24			

2015 tax equations

The equations for the Belgian system in 2015 are mostly calculated on an individual basis. But central government tax for a married couple is calculated on two bases and the lower value is used. One of the bases takes account of the combined income of the couple. Also, tax credits may be used against the tax liability of the secondary earner if the principal earner is unable to use them.

The functions which are used in the equations (Taper, Tax etc.) are described in the technical note about tax equations. Variable names are defined in the table of parameters above or are the standard variables "married" and "children". A reference to a variable with the affix "_total" indicates the sum of the relevant variable values for the principal and spouse. And the affixes "_princ" and "_spouse" indicate the value for the principal and spouse respectively. Equations for a single person are as shown for the principal with "_spouse" values taken as 0.

	Line in country table and intermediate steps	Variable name	Range	Equation
1.	Earnings	earn		
2.	Allowances:	tax_al	B	MIN(work_rel_max, Tax(earn-SSC, work_rel_sch))+SSC
3.	Credits in taxable income	taxbl_cr	B	0
4.	CG taxable income	tax_inc_int	B	earn-tax_al
	Quote part	Q	J	IF(married, Positive(MIN(tax_inc_int_total*quote_rate, quote_max)-tax_inc_int_spouse), 0)
	CG adjusted taxable income - principal	tax_inc_adj_princ	P	Positive(tax_inc_int_princ – Q)
	CG adjusted taxable income - spouse	tax_inc_adj_spouse	S	Positive(tax_inc_int_spouse + Q)
5.	CG tax before credits	CG_tax_excl	J	Tax(tax_inc_adj, tax_sch)
6.	Calculation of credits			
	Child exemption amount	child_ex_inc	P	(children=1)*child_cr1+(children=2)*child_cr2
	Family exemption amount	fam_ex_inc	B	IF(Married,married_cr,single_cr+(Children>0)*s_parent_cr)+IF(tax_inc_adj<=0,0,IF(tax_inc_adj<=supp_cr_thrsh1,supp_cr_base,MAX(0,supp_cr_base+supp_cr_thrsh1-tax_inc_adj)))
	Initial exempt income - principal	ex_inc_int_princ	P	child_ex_inc+fam_ex_inc_princ
	Initial exempt income - spouse	ex_inc_int_spouse	S	fam_ex_inc_spouse
	Transferable amount	ex_inc_tran	J	married*IF(ex_inc_int_princ<tax_inc_adj_princ, MIN(MAX((ex_inc_int_spouse-tax_inc_adj_spouse), 0), tax_inc_adj_princ-ex_inc_int_princ), -(MIN(MAX((ex_inc_int_princ-tax_inc_adj_princ), 0), MAX(0, tax_inc_adj_spouse-ex_inc_int_spouse))))
	Final exempt income - principal	ex_inc_fin_princ	P	ex_inc_int_princ+ex_inc_tran
	Final exempt income - spouse	ex_inc_fin_spouse	S	ex_inc_int_spouse-ex_inc_tran
	Tax credits	tax_credits	J	Tax(ex_inc_fin, tax_sch)
	Basic Credit	basic_cr	B	basic_cr_base*IF(tax_inc<=basic_cr_thrsh1, 0, IF(tax_inc<=basic_cr_thrsh2, (tax_inc-basic_cr_thrsh1)/(basic_cr_thrsh2-basic_cr_thrsh1), IF(tax_inc<=basic_cr_thrsh3, 1, IF(tax_inc<=basic_cr_thrsh4, (basic_cr_thrsh4-tax_inc)/(basic_cr_thrsh4-basic_cr_thrsh3), 0)))) +IF(tax_inc=0;0;MIN(LIC_rate*(MIN(VLOOKUP(earn, SSC_redn,3), VLOOKUP(earn, SSC_redn, 3)-VLOOKUP(earn, SSC_redn, 4)*(earn-VLOOKUP(earn, SSC_redn, 2)))));LIC_max))

	Line in country table and intermediate steps	Variable name	Range	Equation
7.	CG tax			
	Tax prior to non-wasteable credits	CG_tax_init	B	Positive(CG_tax_incl-tax_credits) *(1-red_rate)
	Non-wasteable child credit	child_credit_nw	J	MIN(Tax(MIN((children=1)*child_cr1+(children=2)*Parameters!child_cr2), (positive(ex_inc_int-tax_inc_int), tax_sch), children*child_cr_max)
	Final CG tax	CG_tax_final	J	CG_tax_init-basic_cr_total-child_credit_nw
8.	State and local taxes			
	Regional tax	regional_tax	B	CG_tax_init*reg_tax_rate
	Local tax	local_tax	J	(local_rate+add_local_rate)*(CG_tax_init+regional_tax)
9.	Employees' soc security	SSC	B	Positive((earn)*SSC_rt-MIN(VLOOKUP(earn, SSC_redn,3), VLOOKUP(earn, SSC_redn, 3)-VLOOKUP(earn, SSC_redn, 4)*(earn-VLOOKUP(earn, SSC_redn, 2))))
		SSC_special	J	positive(Tax(tax_inc_total, SSC_special)
		SSC_total		SSC+SSC_special
11.	Cash transfers	cash_trans	J	(Children>0)*CB_1+(Children>1)*CB_2
13.	Employer's soc security	empr_sch	B	Positive(earn*(SSC_empr_rt- PrP_redn)-(VLOOKUP(earn, SSC_empr_redn, 2)-VLOOKUP(earn, SSC_empr_redn, 3)*(earn-VLOOKUP(earn, SSC_empr_redn, 1))))

Key to range of equation B calculated separately for both principal earner and spouse P calculated for principal only (value taken as 0 for spouse calculation) J calculated once only on a joint basis.

Canada

This chapter includes data on the income taxes paid by workers, their social security contributions, the family benefits they receive in the form of cash transfers as well as the social security contributions and payroll taxes paid by their employers. Results reported include the marginal and average tax burden for eight different family types.

Methodological information is available for personal income tax systems, compulsory social security contributions to schemes operated within the government sector, universal cash transfers as well as recent changes in the tax/benefit system. The methodology also includes the parameter values and tax equations underlying the data.

Canada 2015

The tax/benefit position of single persons

	Wage level (per cent of average wage)	67	100	167	67
	Number of children	none	none	none	2
1.	**Gross wage earnings**	34 088	50 877	84 965	34 088
2.	**Standard tax allowances**				
	Basic allowance				
	Married or head of family				
	Dependent children				
	Deduction for social security contributions and income taxes				
	Work-related expenses				
	Other				
	Total	0	0	0	0
3.	**Tax credits or cash transfers included in taxable income**	0	0	0	1 440
4.	**Central government taxable income (1 - 2 + 3)**	34 088	50 877	84 965	35 528
5.	**Central government income tax liability (exclusive of tax credits)**	5 113	8 064	15 563	5 329
6.	**Tax credits**				
	Basic credit	1 871	1 871	1 871	2 087
	Married or head of family	0	0	0	1 483
	Children	0	0	0	0
	Other(CPP & EI)	323	491	512	323
	Total	2 194	2 362	2 383	3 893
7.	**Central government income tax finally paid (5-6)**	2 919	5 702	13 181	1 436
8.	**State and local taxes**	1 115	2 314	5 703	0
9.	**Employees' compulsory social security contributions**				
	Gross earnings	2 155	3 276	3 411	2 155
	Taxable income (Provincial Health Care Levy)	300	600	750	300
	Total	2 455	3 876	4 161	2 455
10.	**Total payments to general government (7 + 8 + 9)**	6 488	11 891	23 044	3 891
11.	**Cash transfers from general government**				
	For head of family	424	0	0	479
	For two children	0	0	0	9 760
	Total	424	0	0	10 239
12.	**Take-home pay (1-10+11)**	28 023	38 986	61 921	40 436
13.	**Employer's compulsory social security contributions**	4 085	6 146	7 955	4 085
14.	**Average rates**				
	Income tax	11.8%	15.8%	22.2%	4.2%
	Employees' social security contributions	7.2%	7.6%	4.9%	7.2%
	Total payments less cash transfers	17.8%	23.4%	27.1%	-18.6%
	Total tax wedge including employer's social security contributions	26.6%	31.6%	33.4%	-5.9%
15.	**Marginal rates**				
	Total payments less cash transfers: Principal earner	25.5%	35.1%	35.4%	55.8%
	Total payments less cash transfers: Spouse	n.a.	n.a.	n.a.	n.a.
	Total tax wedge: Principal earner	33.8%	40.9%	38.4%	60.7%
	Total tax wedge: Spouse	n.a.	n.a.	n.a.	n.a.

Canada 2015

The tax/benefit position of married couples

	Wage level (per cent of average wage)	100-0	100-33	100-67	100-33
	Number of children	2	2	2	none
1.	**Gross wage earnings**	50 877	67 667	84 965	67 667
2.	**Standard tax allowances**				
	Basic allowance				
	Married or head of family				
	Dependent children				
	Deduction for social security contributions and income taxes				
	Work-related expenses				
	Other				
	Total	0	0	0	0
3.	**Tax credits or cash transfers included in taxable income**	1 440	1 440	1 440	0
4.	**Central government taxable income (1 - 2 + 3)**	52 317	69 107	86 405	67 667
5.	**Central government income tax liability (exclusive of tax credits)**	8 280	10 798	13 393	10 582
6.	**Tax credits**				
	Basic credit	1 871	3 742	3 742	3 742
	Married or head of family	1 915	432	432	0
	Children	0	0	0	0
	Other(CPP & EI)	491	637	815	637
	Total	4 278	4 812	4 989	4 379
7.	**Central government income tax finally paid (5-6)**	4 002	5 987	8 404	6 203
8.	**State and local taxes**	1 642	2 605	3 501	2 459
9.	**Employees' compulsory social security contributions**				
	Gross earnings	3 276	4 249	5 431	4 249
	Taxable income (Provincial Health Care Levy)	600	600	900	600
	Total	3 876	4 849	6 331	4 849
10.	**Total payments to general government (7 + 8 + 9)**	9 520	13 441	18 236	13 512
11.	**Cash transfers from general government**				
	For head of family	0	0	0	0
	For two children	4 925	3 557	2 865	0
	Total	4 925	3 557	2 865	0
12.	**Take-home pay (1-10+11)**	46 282	57 784	69 594	54 155
13.	**Employer's compulsory social security contributions**	6 146	8 070	10 231	8 070
14.	**Average rates**				
	Income tax	11.1%	12.7%	14.0%	12.8%
	Employees' social security contributions	7.6%	7.2%	7.5%	7.2%
	Total payments less cash transfers	9.0%	14.6%	18.1%	20.0%
	Total tax wedge including employer's social security contributions	18.8%	23.7%	26.9%	28.5%
15.	**Marginal rates**				
	Total payments less cash transfers: Principal earner	58.0%	32.1%	32.1%	35.1%
	Total payments less cash transfers: Spouse	31.5%	34.2%	29.5%	30.2%
	Total tax wedge: Principal earner	61.8%	38.2%	38.2%	40.9%
	Total tax wedge: Spouse	38.5%	41.5%	37.3%	38.0%

The national currency is the Canadian dollar (CAD). In 2015, CAD 1.28 was equal to USD 1. In that year, the average worker earned CAD 50 877.

1. Personal income tax systems

1.1. *Central/federal government income taxes*

1.1.1. *Tax unit*

Under the present system, tax is levied on individuals separately; certain tax reliefs depend on family circumstances.

1.1.2. *Tax allowances and credits*

1.1.2.1. Standard credits

- *Basic personal amount:* All taxpayers qualify for a basic personal tax credit of CAD 1 699.05.
- *Credit for Spouse or Eligible Dependant:* A taxpayer supporting a spouse or other eligible dependant receives a tax credit of CAD 1 699.05 which is reduced by 15 cents for each dollar of the dependant's income.
- *Social security contributions:* Taxpayers are entitled to claim 15% of their contributions to the Canada or Quebec Pension Plans (to a maximum credit of CAD 2 479.95 for the Canada Pension Plan and to a maximum credit of CAD 2 630.25 for the Quebec Pension Plan) and their Employment Insurance premiums (to a maximum credit of CAD 930.60 outside Quebec; the Employment Insurance premium rate is lower for Quebec residents, who also pay into the Quebec Parental Insurance Plan; the maximum combined credit for a Quebec resident is CAD 1 148.65).
- *Working Income Tax Benefit (WITB):* The WITB provides a non-wastable tax credit equal to 25% of each dollar of earned income in excess of CAD 3 000 to a maximum credit of CAD 1 015 for single individuals without dependents and CAD 1 844 for families (couples and single parents). The credit is reduced by 15% of net family income in excess of CAD 11 525 for single individuals and CAD 15 915 for families. This is the default national design; provinces may choose to propose jurisdiction-specific changes to this design, subject to certain principles.
- *Canada Employment Tax Credit:* A tax credit of up to CAD 171.90 on employment income.

1.1.2.2. Main non-standard tax reliefs applicable to an average worker:

A number of non-standard tax reliefs are available to the average worker in Canada. The main ones are:

- *Medical expenses credit:* Taxpayers are entitled to a 15-per-cent tax credit for an amount of eligible medical expenses that exceeds the lesser of 3% of net income or CAD 2 208.
- *Charitable donations credit:* The credit is 15% on the first CAD 200 of eligible charitable donations and 29% on eligible donations in excess of CAD 200. Eligible donations are those made to registered charities, to a maximum of 75% of net income.

- *Registered pension plan contributions:* Employees who are members of a registered pension plan are entitled to deduct their contributions to the plan in respect of current and/or past service. Generally, employee contributions to a defined benefit registered pension plan are not subject to any limit; however, limits apply to the benefits that a plan may provide. Individuals can deduct their contributions to a defined contribution registered pension plan up to a limit of 18% of earned income, to a maximum of CAD 25 370.
- *Registered retirement savings plan (RRSP) premiums:* Individuals can deduct their contributions to an RRSP up to a limit of 18% of the previous year's earned income, to a maximum of CAD 24 930 a year, unless they are also accruing benefits under a registered pension plan or a deferred profit sharing plan. Members of those other plans are limited to RRSP contributions of 18% of the previous year's earned income to a maximum of CAD 24 930, minus a pension adjustment amount based on pension benefits accrued in the previous year.
- *Union and professional dues:* Individuals with annual dues paid to a trade union or an association of public servants or paying dues required to maintain a professional status recognised by statute are allowed to deduct such fees in computing taxable income.
- *Moving expenses:* Eligible moving expenses are deductible from income if the taxpayer moves at least 40 kilometres closer to a new place of employment.
- *Child care expenses:* A portion of child care expenses is deductible if incurred for the purpose of earning business or employment income, studying or taking an occupational training course or carrying on research for which a grant is received. The lower-income spouse must generally claim the deduction. The amount of the deduction is limited to the least of:
  1. the expenses incurred for the care of a child;
  2. two-thirds of the taxpayer's earned income; and
  3. CAD 8 000 for each child who is under age seven, and CAD 5 000 per child between seven and sixteen years of age. The amount for a disabled child under seventeen is CAD 11 000.
- *Family Tax Cut:* Couples with minor children can notionally transfer up to CAD 50 000 of taxable income from the higher-income spouse to a spouse in a lower tax bracket. The value of the tax relief is capped at CAD 2 000.

1.1.3. *Tax schedule*

2015 Federal income tax rates

Taxable income (CAD)	Rate (%)
0-44 701	15
44 701-89 401	22
89 401-138 586	26
138 586 and over	29

1.2. *State and local income taxes*

1.2.1. *General description*

All provinces and territories levy their own personal income taxes. All, with the exception of Quebec, have a tax collection agreement with the federal government, and thus use the federal definition of taxable income. They are free to determine their own tax brackets, rates and credits. Quebec collects its own personal income tax and is free to determine all of the tax parameters, including taxable income. In practice, its definition of taxable income is broadly similar to the federal definition.

1.2.2. Tax regime selected for this study

The calculation of provincial tax for the average worker study assumes the worker lives in Ontario, the most populous of the 10 provinces and 3 territories. The main features of the Ontario tax system relevant to this report are summarised below:

Tax schedule

Income bracket	Rate (%)
CAD 0 to CAD 40 922	5.05
CAD 40 922 to CAD 81 847	9.15
CAD 81 847 to CAD 150 000	11.16
CAD 150 000 to CAD 220 000	12.16
Over CAD 220 000	13.16

Surtax

Provincial tax after accounting for wastable credits	Surtax rate
Amounts exceeding CAD 4 418	20% of the excess amount
Amounts exceeding CAD 5 654	36% of the excess amount

Wastable tax credits

- A basic tax credit of CAD 498.08.
- A maximum credit of CAD 422.94 for a dependant spouse or eligible dependant that is withdrawn as the income of the spouse or eligible dependant exceeds CAD 837 and is completely withdrawn when the income of the spouse is at least CAD 9 212.
- 5.05% of contributions made to the Canada Pension Plan and of Employment Insurance premiums.

Tax reduction

An earner is entitled to claim a tax reduction where the initial entitlement is equal to CAD 228 plus CAD 421 for each dependent child under the age of 19. Where someone has a spouse, only the spouse with the higher net income can claim the dependent child tax reduction. If this amount is greater or equal to the liable provincial tax, then no tax is due. If the amount is less than the liable tax, then the actual tax reduction is equal to twice the initial entitlement amount less the liable tax (if this calculation is zero or negative, the reduction is equal to zero).

2. Compulsory social security contributions to schemes operated within the government sector

2.1. Employees' contributions

2.1.1. Pensions

Generally, all employees are eligible for coverage under the Canada Pension Plan (Québec Pension Plan in the province of Québec). For 2015, all employees are required to contribute to the Canada Pension Plan at a rate of 4.95% of income up to a maximum contribution of CAD 2 479.95 (the contribution rate is 5.25% of income for the Québec Pension Plan up to a maximum contribution of CAD 2 630.25). Income subject to contributions is earnings (wages and salaries) less a CAD 3 500 basic exemption. The maximum contribution of CAD 2 479.95 is reached at an earnings level of CAD 53 600 i.e. (CAD 53 600-CAD 3 500) × 0.0495 = CAD 2 479.95. For employees, each contribution to the CPP or QPP gives rise to a tax credit equal to 15% of the contributed amount. Employers are also required to contribute to the Canada Pension Plan on behalf of their employees at the same rate and can deduct their contributions from taxable income (refer § 2.21).

Self-employed persons must also contribute to the Canada Pension Plan (Québec Pension Plan in the province of Québec) on their own behalf. However, the self-employed are required to contribute at the combined employer/employee rate of 9.90% of earnings up to a maximum of CAD 4 959.90 (10.5% of earnings up to a maximum of CAD 5 260.50 in Quebec). The self-employed can deduct the employer portion of their contribution from income, equal to 50% of the total contribution or CAD 2 479.95 (2 630.25 in Quebec). The remaining 50%, representing the employee portion, is then claimed as a tax credit at 15%.

2.1.2. *Sickness*

There is no national sickness benefit plan administered by the federal government. However, all provinces have provincially-administered health care insurance plans. Three provinces, Quebec, Ontario, and British Columbia, levy health premiums on individuals separately from the personal income tax to help finance their health programmes.

In the case of Ontario, the premium is determined based on taxable income. Individuals who earn up to CAD 20 000 are exempt. The premium is phased in with a number of different rates to a maximum of CAD 900 for taxable income levels greater than CAD 200 600. The following table provides further details on the structure that is applicable in 2015.

The Ontario Health Premium

Taxable income	Fixed component (CAD)	Variable component
0-CAD 20 000	0	
CAD 20 000-CAD 25 000	0	6% of the taxable income in excess of CAD 20 000
CAD 25 000-CAD 36 000	300	
CAD 36 000-CAD 38 500	300	6% of the taxable income in excess of CAD 36 000
CAD 38 500-CAD 48 000	450	
CAD 48 000-CAD 48 600	450	25% of the taxable income in excess of CAD 48 000
CAD 48 600-CAD 72 000	600	
CAD 72 000-CAD 72 600	600	25% of the amount of taxable income in excess of CAD 72 600
CAD 72 600-CAD 200 000	750	
CAD 200 000-CAD 200 600	750	25% of the amount of taxable income in excess of CAD 200 000
Over CAD 200 600	900	

2.1.3. *Unemployment*

In general, all employees are eligible for Employment Insurance. Eligibility to receive benefits is determined by insurable hours worked (with a minimum entry threshold of 420 to 700 hours, depending on region and the unemployment rate at the time the claim for benefits starts). For 2015, employees outside Quebec are required to contribute at the rate of 1.88% of insurable earnings. Insurable earnings are earnings (wages and salaries) up to a maximum of CAD 49 500 per year. The maximum employee contribution is therefore

CAD 930.60 per year. Employment insurance contributions give rise to a tax credit equal to 15% of the amount contributed. Employers are also required to contribute to the plan (see Section 2.23).

Quebec residents contribute to Employment Insurance at a rate of 1.53%; the same earnings ceiling applies. They also contribute to the Quebec Parental Insurance Plan at a rate of 0.559% of insurable earnings; maximum insurance earnings for 2015 are CAD 70 000. For a Quebec resident, the maximum employee contribution (Employment Insurance plus Quebec Parental Insurance Plan) is CAD 1 148.65.

2.1.4. *Work injury*

See Section 2.24.

2.2. *Employers' contributions*

2.2.1. *Pensions*

Employers are required to contribute to the Canada Pension Plan on behalf of their employees an amount equal to their employees' contributions. Thus, employers also contribute at the rate of 4.95% of earnings (less the CAD 3 500 earnings exemption) to a maximum of CAD 2 479.95. For the Quebec Pension Plan, the contribution rate is 5.25% of earnings, to a maximum of CAD 2 630.25.

2.2.2. *Sickness*

There is no national sickness benefit plan administered by the federal government. However, all provinces have provincially-administered health care insurance plans. Three provinces levy a special tax on employer payrolls to finance health services (Québec and Ontario) or health services and education (Manitoba). These payroll taxes are deductible from the employer's income subject to tax. In the case of the province of Ontario, employers pay a 1.95% Employer Health Tax on the value of their payroll that exceeds CAD 450 000.

2.2.3. *Unemployment*

Employers are required to contribute to the employment insurance scheme. The general employer contribution is 1.4 times the employee contribution, that is, 2.63% of insurable earnings (outside Quebec). Premiums are adjusted for employers who provide sick pay superior to payments provided under the employment insurance regime. All employment insurance contributions are deductible from the employer's income subject to tax.

2.2.4. *Work injury*

There is no national work injury benefit plan administered by the federal government. However, employers are required to contribute to a provincial workers' compensation plan which pays benefits to workers (or their families in case of death) for work-related illness or injury. The employer contribution rates, which vary by industry and province, are related to industry experience of work-related illness and injury. Premiums are deductible from the employer's income subject to tax. In the case of Ontario, employers broadly corresponding to industry Sectors B-N inclusive pay, on average, 2.96% of the wages paid to each employee to a maximum of CAD 85 200.

3. Universal cash transfers

3.1. *Transfers related to marital status*

None.

3.2. *Transfers for dependent children*

3.2.1. *Federal*

The Canada Child Tax Benefit (CCTB) provides CAD 1 500per child under age 18 plus a CAD 105 supplement for the 3rd child and each additional child. This basic benefit is reduced by 4% of family net income in excess of CAD 45 602 for families with two or more children and 2% for families with one child. In addition, a National Child Benefit supplement (NCBs) is provided to low-income families with children. The maximum NCBs is CAD 2 325 for one child, plus CAD 2 056 for a second child, plus CAD 1 956 for the third and each additional child. The NCBs is phased out based on family net income in excess of CAD 26 545. The reduction rates are 12.2% for families with one child, 23.0% for families with two children and 33.3% for larger families.

The Universal Child Care Benefit (UCCB) provides all families with CAD 1 920 for each child under age six and CAD 720 for each child age six to seventeen. Amounts received under the UCCB are taxable in the hands of the lower-income spouse but are not used to reduce other income-tested benefits such as the CCTB. In the case of single parents, the UCCB can be taxable in the hands of the eligible dependant.

The Goods and Services Tax Credit provides a relief of CAD 278 for each adult 19 years of age or older and CAD 146 for each dependent child under the age of 19. Single tax filers without children and with an employment income higher than CAD 9 011 receive an additional CAD 146 that is phased in at a rate of 2%. Single tax filers with children receive an additional CAD 146 that is not subject to phase-in. The credit received for the first dependent child of a single parent is also increased from CAD 146 to CAD 278. The total amount is reduced at a rate of five percent of net family income over CAD 36 180. The amount is paid directly to families.*

3.2.2. *Provincial*

For each child under eighteen, qualifying families can receive up to CAD 1 363 from the Ontario Child Benefit (OCB). The benefit is withdrawn at a rate of 8% of family income that exceeds CAD 20 811.

Ontario has a Sales Tax Credit that provides a relief of up to CAD 293 for each adult and each child. It is reduced by 4% of adjusted family net income over CAD 22 502for single people and over CAD 28 127for families. The amount is paid directly to families.

* The payments that relate to income from the 2015 tax year are payable between July 2016 and June 2017. The amounts shown in this Report assume indexation of 2.0% for the 2015 tax year (and 2016-17 benefit year); the actual indexation parameter will be announced in December 2015.

4. Main changes in the tax/benefit system since 2009

5. Memorandum items

5.1. *Identification of an average worker*

The earnings data refer to production workers in the industries B to N. To obtain the annual average wage figure, the average weekly earnings for the year for employees (including overtime) are multiplied by 52.

5.2. *Employer contributions to private health and pension schemes*

These do exist but no information is available on the amounts involved.

2015 parameter values

Average earnings/yr	Ave_earn	50 877	Secretariat estimate
Tax credits	Basic_cred	1 699.05	
Spouse	Spouse_cred	1 699.05	
withdrawal rate	Sp_crd_wth	0.15	
Threshold	Sp_crd_thrsh	0	
Canada Employment Tax Credit	Empl_crd	171.90	
Family Tax Cut Maximum Credit	iscrmax	2 000	
Family Tax Cut Transfer Limit	inctrflm	50 000	
Canada Child Tax Benefit	Ch_credit	1 500	
Child under 7	Ch_crd_und7	0	
additional for 3rd+	Ch_crd_3rd	105	
reduction rate: 1 child	Ch_crd_red1	0.02	
reduction. rate: 2 or more	Ch_crd_red2	0.04	
Threshold	Ch_crd_thrsh	45 602	
Universal Child Care Benefit (ages 6-17)	UCCB_6_17	720	
National Child Benefit Supplement	WIS_crd_1st	2 325	
	WIS_crd_2nd	2 056	
	WIS_crd_3rd	1 956	
threshold to start phase-out	WIS_phout_st	26 545	
threshold to end phase-out	WIS_phout_end	45 602	
reduction rate	WIS_redn1	0.122	
	WIS_redn2	0.230	
	WIS_redn3	0.333	
Working Income Tax Benefit	WITB_phzin_thrsh	3 000	
WITB–Phase-in Rate	WITB_phzn_rt	0.25	
WITB–Maximum Credit (per Adult/Equiv.)	WITB_max	1 015	
WITB–Addl. Maximum Credit (Fam.)	WITB_max_fam	829	
WITB–Reduction Rate	WITB_phzout_rt	0.15	
WITB–Threshold	WITB_phzout_thrsh	11 525	
WITB–Addl. Threshold (Fam.)	WITB_phzn_thrsh_fam	4 390	
Federal tax schedule	Fed_sch	0.15	44 701
		0.22	89 401
		0.26	138 586
		0.29	
High-income surtax rate	H_sur_rate	0	
threshold	H_sur_thrsh	18 500	
Canada pension plan rate	CPP_rate	0.0495	
exemption	CPP_ex	3 500	
max contrib.	CPP_max	2 479.95	
Unemployment ins.rate	Unemp_rate	0.0188	
max contrib.	Unemp_max	930.60	
tax credit rate	Unemp_crd_rate	0.15	
employer contrib. mult.	Unemp_emplr	1.4	
GST adult credit	GST_crd_ad	278	
child credit	GST_crd_ch	146	
threshold	GST_crd_thrsh	36 180	
reduction rate	GST_crd_redn	0.05	
single supplement	GST_crd_sgsp	146	
single supplement eligibility threshold	GST_sgsp_thrsh	9 011	
single supplement phase-in rate	GST_sgsp_rate	0.02	
Province: Ontario			
Tax Credits	P_basic_crd	498.08	
Spouse	P_spouse_crd	422.94	
withdrawal rate	P_sp_crd_wd	0.0505	
threshold	P_sp_crd_thr	837	
% of BFT	P_pct_bft	0.375	

2015 parameter values

Unemployment tax credit rate	P_unem_tc_rt	0.0505		
Surtax rate 1	P_sur_rt1	0.20		
threshold	P_sur_thr1	4 418		
rate 2	P_sur_rt2	0.36		
threshold	P_sur_thr2	5 654		
Tax reduction	P_tax_red	228		
amount per dependent	P_tr_chld	421		
amount per disabled dep	P_tr_dis_ch	421		
Provincial tax schedule	Prov_sch	0.0505	40 922	
		0.0915	81 847	
		0.1116	150 000	
		0.1216	220 000	
		0.1316		
Ontario Child Benefit	P_ch_amt	1 363		
amount per child	P_ch_thresh	20 811		
threshold	P_ch_redn_rate	0.08		
reduction rate				
Sales tax credits				
sales tax credit adult	P_sales_cred	293		
sales tax credit child	P_salcr_chd	293		
threshold	P_ps_thresh	22 502		
threshold seniors/families	P_ps_thr_sen	28 127		
reduction rate	P_ps_red_rt	0.04		
reduction rate seniors	P_ps_rr_sen	0.04		
Ontario Health Premium	P_hlth_sch	20 000	0	0
		25 000	0.06	0
		36 000	0	300
		38 500	0.06	300
		48 000	0	450
		48 600	0.25	450
		72 000	0	600
		72 600	0.25	600
		200 000	0	750
		200 600	0.25	750
maximum	P_hlth_max	900		
Employer Health Tax	emp_healthtax	0.0195		
Employer Workers Compensation Levy	emp_workcomp	0.0296		
Employer Workers Compensation Levy Ceiling	emp_workcomp_ceil	85 200		
Maximum number of children under the age of 7	children_und7_max	1		

2015 Tax equations

The equations for the Canadian system are mostly repeated for each individual of a married couple. But the spouse credit is relevant only to the calculation for the principal earner and the non-wastable credits are calculated only once. This is shown by the Range indicator in the table below.

The functions which are used in the equations (Taper, MIN, Tax etc) are described in the technical note about tax equations. Variable names are defined in the table of parameters above, within the equations table, or are the standard variables "married" and "children". A reference to a variable with the affix "_total" indicates the sum of the relevant variable values for the principal and spouse. And the affixes "_princ" and "_spouse" indicate the value for the principal and spouse, respectively. Equations for a single person are as shown for the principal, with "_spouse" values taken as 0.

	Line in country table and intermediate steps	Variable name	Range	Equation
1.	Earnings	earn		
2.	Allowances	tax_al	B	0
3.	Credits in taxable income	taxbl_cr		
	Universal Child Care Benefit (6-17)	Spouse_UCCB	S	UCCB_6_17*Children
4.	CG taxable income	tax_inc	B	Earn
5.	CG tax before credits:	Basic_Fed_tax	B	Tax(earn, Fed_sch)
	Basic Federal tax	Basic_Fed_tax	B	Tax(earn, Fed_sch)
6.	Tax credits :			
	Basic credit	basic_cr	P	Basic_cred + Empl_crd
			S	(earn_spouse>0)*Empl_crd+IF(AND(Married=1,earn_spouse>0),Basic_cred,0)+IF (AND(Married=0,tax_inc_spouse>0),Basic_cred-Taper(Spouse_cred,tax_inc_spouse,Sp_crd_thrsh,Sp_crd_wth),0)
	Spouse credit	spouse_cr	P	IF(OR(Married=1,Children>0),Taper(Spouse_cred, tax_inc_spouse, Sp_crd_thrsh,Sp_crd_wth), 0)
	Unemployment insurance	unemp_cr	B	Unemp_crd_rate*SSC
	Total (wastable) tax credits	tax_cr	B	basic_cr+spouse_cr+unemp_cr
	Working Income Tax Benefit	WITB	P	IF(Married>0,MAX(0,MIN(WITB_max+WITB_max_fam,(WITB_phzn_rt*MAX(0,earn_total-WITB_phzin_thrsh)))-MAX(0,WITB_phzout_rt*MAX(0,earn_total-(WITB_phzout_thrsh+WITB_phzn_thrsh_fam)))), IF(Children>0,MAX(0,MIN(WITB_max+WITB_max_fam,(WITB_phzn_rt*MAX(0,earn_total-WITB_phzin_thrsh)))-MAX(0,WITB_phzout_rt*MAX(0,earn_total-(WITB_phzout_thrsh+WITB_phzn_thrsh_fam)))), MAX(0,MIN(WITB_max,(WITB_phzn_rt*MAX(0,earn_total-WITB_phzin_thrsh)))-MAX(0,WITB_phzout_rt*MAX(0,earn_total-WITB_phzout_thrsh)))))
	Family Tax Cut	Iscrmax	P	(MIN(iscrmax,(Basic_Fed_tax+Basic_Fed_tax Spouse)-(Tax(tax_inc-ftc(tax_inc,tax_inc Spouse,inctrflm),Fed_sch)+Tax(tax_inc Spouse+ftc(tax_inc,tax_inc Spouse,inctrflm),Fed_sch)))+MAX(0,(SSC Spouse+(earn Spouse>0)*Empl_crd)-MAX(Basic_Fed_tax Spouse-Basic_cred,0)))*MIN(children,1)
7.	CG tax	CG_tax	B	Positive(Basic_Fed_tax-tax_cr)-WITB
8.	State and local taxes			
	Liable provincial tax	Prov_tax_sch	B	Tax(earn, Prov_sch)
	Provincial tax credits	Prov_tax_cred	P	P_basic_crd+P_unem_tc_rt*SSC_princ+IF(AND(Married=0, Children>0), P_spouse_crd, Married*Taper(P_spouse_crd, earn_spouse, P_sp_crd_thr, P_sp_crd_wd))
			S	=(earn_spouse>0)*(P_unem_tc_rt*SSC_spouse)+OR(Married=1,Children>0)*P_basic_crd

	Line in country table and intermediate steps	Variable name	Range	Equation
	Provincial surtax	Prov_surtax	B	P_sur_rt1*Positive(Prov_tax_sch-Prov_tax_cred-P_sur_thr1)+P_sur_rt2*Positive(Prov_tax_sch-Prov_tax_cred-P_sur_thr2)
	Provincial tax reduction	Prov_tax_redn	B	MAX(2*(P_tax_red+Children*P_tr_chld)-(Prov_tax_sch-Prov_tax_cred+Prov_surtax), 0)
	Provincial sales tax credit	Prov_tax_stcred	P	Taper(IF(Married=1, 2, 1)*P_sales_cred+Children*P_salcr_chd, earn_total, IF(Married+Children=0, P_ps_thresh,P_ps_thr_sen),P_ps_red_rt)
	Liable provincial tax	Prov_tax	B	Positive(Prov_tax_sch-Prov_tax_cred+Prov_surtax-Prov_tax_redn)
9.	Employees' soc security:			
	Canada Pension Plan	CPP	B	MIN(CPP_rate*Positive((earn-CPP_ex), CPP_max)
	Unemployment insurance	Unemp	B	MIN(Unemp_rate*earn, Unemp_max)
	State health premium	Prov_health	B	MIN(Hstep(tax_inc, P_hlth_sch), P_hlth_max)
	Total Employees'soc security	SSC	B	CPP+Unemp+Prov_health
11.	Cash transfers (nonwastable)			
	Child Tax Benefit	CTB	P	(Children>0)*(Taper(Children*Ch_credit +MAXA((Children-2), 0)*Ch_crd_3rd+MINA(Children, children_und7_max)*Ch_crd_und7, earn_total, Ch_crd_thrsh, IF(Children=1, Ch_crd_red1, Ch_crd_red2)))+MAXA(IF(Children>0, IF(Children<2, WIS_crd_1st, IF(Children<3, WIS_crd_1st+WIS_crd_2nd, WIS_crd_1st+WIS_crd_2nd+(Children-2)* WIS_crd_3rd)), 0)-MAXA((earn_total-WIS_phout_st), 0)*IF(Children=1, WIS_redn1, IF(Children=2, WIS_redn2, WIS_redn3)), 0)
	GST Credit – Total	GST_cr	P	Taper((GST_crd_ad+(Married=1)*(GST_crd_ad+Children*GST_crd_ch)+(Married =0)*(Children>0)*(GST_crd_ad+GST_crd_sgsp+Positive(Children-1)*GST_crd_ch)+(Married=0)*(Children=0)*Positive(MIN(GST_crd_sgsp, (earn_total-GST_sgsp_thrsh)*GST_sgsp_rate))), earn_total, GST_crd_thrsh, GST_crd_redn)
	GST Credit – Adult	GST_cr_adult	P	Taper((GST_crd_ad+(Married=1)*(GST_crd_ad)+(Married=0)*Positive(MIN(GST_crd_sgsp, (earn_total-GST_sgsp_thrsh)*GST_sgsp_rate))), earn_total, GST_crd_thrsh, GST_crd_redn)
	GST Credit – Child	GST_cr_child	P	GST_cr-GST_cr_adult
	Ontario child benefit	Prov_child_ben	P	Taper(Children*P_ch_amt,earn_total,P_ch_thresh,P_ch_redn_rate)
	Ontario sales tax credit	Prov_sales_cr	P	Taper(IF(Married=1,2,1)*P_sales_cred+Children*P_salcr_chd,earn_total, IF(Married+Children=0, P_ps_thresh,P_ps_thr_sen),P_ps_red_rt)
	Total Cash Transfers	Cash_tran	P	Spouse_UCCB+CTB+GST_cr+Prov_child_ben+ Prov_sales_cr
13.	Employer's soc security			
	Canada Pension Plan	CPP_empr	B	CPP
	Unemployment insurance	Unemp_empr	B	Unemp*Unemp_emplr
	Ontario Employers Health Tax	Health_empr	B	earn*emp_healthtax
	Ontario Workers Compensation	Comp_empr	B	MIN(earn, emp_workcomp_ceil)*emp_workcomp
	Total Employer's soc security	SSC_empr	B	CPP_empr+Unemp_empr+Health_empr+Comp_empr

Key to range of equation B calculated separately for both principal earner and spouse P calculated for principal only (value taken as 0 for spouse calculation) J calculated once only on a joint basis.

Taxing Wages 2016

Chile

This chapter includes data on the income taxes paid by workers, their social security contributions, the family benefits they receive in the form of cash transfers as well as the social security contributions and payroll taxes paid by their employers. Results reported include the marginal and average tax burden for eight different family types.

Methodological information is available for personal income tax systems, compulsory social security contributions to schemes operated within the government sector, universal cash transfers as well as recent changes in the tax/benefit system. The methodology also includes the parameter values and tax equations underlying the data.

Chile 2015

The tax/benefit position of single persons

			67	100	167	67
		Wage level (per cent of average wage)	67	100	167	67
		Number of children	none	none	none	2
1.	**Gross wage earnings**		5 062 549	7 556 043	12 618 592	5 062 549
2.	**Standard tax allowances**					
	Basic allowance		0	0	0	0
	Married or head of family					
	Dependent children					
	Deduction for social security contributions and income taxes		354 378	528 923	883 301	354 378
	Work-related expenses					
	Other		595 356	888 591	1 483 946	595 356
		Total	949 734	1 417 514	2 367 248	949 734
3.	**Tax credits or cash transfers included in taxable income**		0	0	0	0
4.	**Central government taxable income (1 - 2 + 3)**		4 112 815	6 138 529	10 251 344	4 112 815
5.	**Central government income tax liability (exclusive of tax credits)**		0	0	118 745	0
6.	**Tax credits**					
	Basic credit					
	Married or head of family					
	Children		0	0	0	225 536
	Other					
		Total	0	0	0	225 536
7.	**Central government income tax finally paid (5-6)**		0	0	118 745	0
8.	**State and local taxes**		0	0	0	0
9.	**Employees' compulsory social security contributions**					
	Gross earnings		354 378	528 923	883 301	354 378
	Taxable income					
		Total	354 378	528 923	883 301	354 378
10.	**Total payments to general government (7 + 8 + 9)**		354 378	528 923	1 002 047	354 378
11.	**Cash transfers from general government**					
	For head of family					
	For two children		0	0	0	44 556
		Total	0	0	0	44 556
12.	**Take-home pay (1-10+11)**		4 708 170	7 027 120	11 616 545	4 752 726
13.	**Employer's compulsory social security contributions**		0	0	0	0
14.	**Average rates**					
	Income tax		0.0%	0.0%	0.9%	0.0%
	Employees' social security contributions		7.0%	7.0%	7.0%	7.0%
	Total payments less cash transfers		7.0%	7.0%	7.9%	6.1%
	Total tax wedge including employer's social security contributions		7.0%	7.0%	7.9%	6.1%
15.	**Marginal rates**					
	Total payments less cash transfers: Principal earner		7.0%	7.0%	10.2%	7.0%
	Total payments less cash transfers: Spouse		n.a.	n.a.	n.a.	n.a.
	Total tax wedge: Principal earner		7.0%	7.0%	10.2%	7.0%
	Total tax wedge: Spouse		n.a.	n.a.	n.a.	n.a.

Chile 2015

The tax/benefit position of married couples

		Wage level (per cent of average wage)	100-0	100-33	100-67	100-33
		Number of children	2	2	2	none
1.	**Gross wage earnings**		7 556 043	10 049 537	12 618 592	10 049 537
2.	**Standard tax allowances**					
	Basic allowance		0	0	0	0
	Married or head of family					
	Dependent children					
	Deduction for social security contributions and income taxes		528 923	703 468	883 301	703 468
	Work-related expenses					
	Other		888 591	1 181 826	1 483 946	1 181 826
		Total	1 417 514	1 885 293	2 367 248	1 885 293
3.	**Tax credits or cash transfers included in taxable income**		0	0	0	0
4.	**Central government taxable income (1 - 2 + 3)**		6 138 529	8 164 244	10 251 344	8 164 244
5.	**Central government income tax liability (exclusive of tax credits)**		0	0	0	0
6.	**Tax credits**					
	Basic credit					
	Married or head of family					
	Children		225 536	225 536	225 536	0
	Other					
		Total	225 536	225 536	225 536	0
7.	**Central government income tax finally paid (5-6)**		0	0	0	0
8.	**State and local taxes**		0	0	0	0
9.	**Employees' compulsory social security contributions**					
	Gross earnings		528 923	703 468	883 301	703 468
	Taxable income					
		Total	528 923	703 468	883 301	703 468
10.	**Total payments to general government (7 + 8 + 9)**		528 923	703 468	883 301	703 468
11.	**Cash transfers from general government**					
	For head of family					
	For two children		0	229 692	44 556	0
		Total	0	229 692	44 556	0
12.	**Take-home pay (1-10+11)**		7 027 120	9 575 762	11 779 846	9 346 070
13.	**Employer's compulsory social security contributions**		0	0	0	0
14.	**Average rates**					
	Income tax		0.0%	0.0%	0.0%	0.0%
	Employees' social security contributions		7.0%	7.0%	7.0%	7.0%
	Total payments less cash transfers		7.0%	4.7%	6.6%	7.0%
	Total tax wedge including employer's social security contributions		7.0%	4.7%	6.6%	7.0%
15.	**Marginal rates**					
	Total payments less cash transfers: Principal earner		7.0%	7.0%	7.0%	7.0%
	Total payments less cash transfers: Spouse		-2.2%	7.0%	7.0%	7.0%
	Total tax wedge: Principal earner		7.0%	7.0%	7.0%	7.0%
	Total tax wedge: Spouse		-2.2%	7.0%	7.0%	7.0%

Chile's national currency is the peso (CLP). For 2015, the average exchange rate was CLP 654.32 to USD 1. That same year, the average worker in Chile earned CLP 7 556 043 (country estimate).

Taxes allowances and tax thresholds for the personal income tax system and upper earnings limits for social security contributions are determined using and expressed in CPI-indexed units. As of 31 December, 2015, the following currency values applied to these units:

Major revenue items	Unit	CLP	USD
Social security contributions	Unidad de Fomento[1] (UF)	25 629.09[1]	39.17
Monthly tax thresholds	Unidad Tributaria Mensual (UTM)	44 955	68.71
Annual tax thresholds	Unidad Tributaria Anual (UTA)	539 460	824.55

1. This amount is subject to daily adjustment in line with the CPI and is compared with monthly earnings in the assessment of social security contributions

1. Personal income tax system

1.1. *Central/federal government income taxes*

1.1.1. *Tax unit*

Each family member declares and pays taxes separately.

1.1.2. *Tax allowances and credits*

1.1.2.1. Standard tax reliefs

- Education tax credit: Parents with children attending preschool, primary, special or secondary education, with a total annual taxable income (both parents) of up to CLP 20 298 239 (UF 792), are entitled to a tax credit of CLP 112 768 (UF 4.4) per child, for expenses related to education. Children shall have a minimal school attendance of 85% and the school must be recognized by the State. This tax credit can be claimed by both parents, or only by one of them.
- *Relief for social security contributions:* Employee's compulsory social insurance contributions are deductible for income tax purposes regardless of whether they are paid to government or private health insurers. (See section 2.1 below).

1.1.2.2. Main non-standard tax reliefs

- *Voluntary contributions and APV (Voluntary Pension Fund Savings):* Voluntary contributions to pension funds and voluntary pension savings fund (APV) may be deducted from taxable income, with an annual upper limit of CLP 15 377 454 (UF 600.)
- *Mortgage Interest:* Taxpayers whose annual income falls below CLP 48 551 400 (UTA 90) may deduct from their taxable income 100% of interest paid within a year for mortgage loans. This percentage is reduced in the case of taxpayers with higher incomes up to

CLP 80 919 000 (UTA 150). This relief cannot be granted along-side the *DFL2 Housing Mortgage Loan Payments* benefit, and cannot exceed CLP 4 315 680 (UTA 8) per annum.

1.1.3. *Tax schedule*

Tax rates are applied on monthly income and these taxes are retained and paid by employers. In order to estimate taxes, tax rates are applied on an annual basis, on the annual average income.

Taxable income (UTA)	Taxable income (CLP thousands)	Tax rates
0-13.5	0-7 283	Exempt
13.5-30	7 283-16 184	4%
30-50	16 184-26 973	8%
50-70	26 973-37 762	13.5%
70-90	37 762-48 551	23%
90-120	48 551-64 735	30.4%
120-150	64 735-80 919	35.5%
150 and over	80 919 and over	40%

1.2. *State and local income taxes*

No taxes apply to income at state or local government level.

2. Compulsory social security contributions to schemes operated within the government sector

2.1. *Employees' contributions*

Employees have mandatorily to contribute 7% of their income to a health insurance plan subject to an upper earnings limit of CLP 22 012 186 (UF 73.2). They are free to choose whether to pay into a government-managed plan or alternatively to a private insurer* (Isapres). The public insurance is based on a joint system that, in general, operates on an equal basis for all its beneficiaries, irrespective of the risk and the amount of the individual contribution. Its financing is partly covered by the contributions and partly by way of a government subsidy. Premiums paid to the plans offered by Isapres are based on the contributors' individual risk and these plans are exclusively financed with the employees' contributions. Public insurance contributions are included in the modelling as the majority of employees pay into plans managed by the government sector.

Employee social security contributions in respect of pensions and unemployment are not classified as taxes in this report; though they are included in modelling as deductions for income tax.

- The mandatory contributions to pension funds and unemployment insurance plans are not classified as taxes, since the payments are made to private institutions. In 1980, the public social security system was replaced with a privately managed individual capitalisation system. This system is obligatory to all employees who have joined the labour force since 1983 and free-lance workers since 2012, and of a voluntary nature to all contributing to the former system. The contributions to the old government operated pension fund system are not included in the modelling because they relate to a minority

* Enrollment in the private health system during 2013 amounted to 18.2% of all beneficiaries.

of employees and the system will eventually disappear once the contributions and related benefit payments to those individuals remaining in it have ceased.

- The modelling allows that the contributions to pension funds and unemployment insurance managed by private institutions are deducted from gross income. In the case of their pension funds, these payments amount to 10% of their gross income, with an upper earnings limit of CLP 22 012 186 (UF 73.2). Added to that is an amount that varies depending on the managing company that covers the management of each pension fund account.* The monthly unemployment insurance premium is 0.6% of the employee's gross income, with an upper earnings limit of CLP 33 018 279 (UF 109.8) limit. Employees do not pay the monthly unemployment insurance premium when they have a fixed-term contract or after 11 years of labour relationship.
- There are also mandatory contributions to managed funds by members of the police force and the army which are classified as taxes but are not included in the modelling as they relate to a minority of the overall workforce.
- If the employee has a high risk job, he has to make an additional contribution of 2% (heavy work) or 1% (less heavy work) of his gross income to his pension fund account.

2.2. *Employers' contributions*

There are four categories of employer social security contribution, none of which are classified as tax revenues in this report.

- Employers make mandatory payments of 0.95% of their employees' gross income for an occupational accident and disease insurance policy subject to an upper earnings limit. For the majority of employees the payments are made to employers' associations of labour security which are private non-profit institutions. Those remaining are made to the Social Security Regularisation Unit (ISL). Although this latter organisation is controlled by the government, the funds are invested on the private institutions market. The employers also pay an additional contribution which depends on the activity and risk associated to the enterprise (it cannot exceed 3.4% of the employees' gross earnings). This additional contribution could be reduced, down to 0%, depending on the safety measures the employer implements in the enterprise. If health and safety conditions at work are not satisfactory, this additional contribution could be applied with a surcharge of up to 100%.
- In addition, employers make payments of 2.4% of each employee's income (0.8% after 11 years of labour relationship and 3% for fixed-term contracts) to finance unemployment insurance. These funds are managed privately.
- Employers have to pay a disability insurance of 1.15% of the employees' gross income, to the pension fund manager.
- If the employee has a high risk job, the employer has to pay 2% (heavy work) or 1% (less heavy work) of the employee's gross income to his pension fund account.

3. Universal cash transfers

3.1. *Marital status-related transfers*

No such transfers are paid.

* Average cost in 2015 was 1.16% of gross income.

3.2. *Transfers related to dependent children*

The "Family Allowance" is paid on a monthly basis to any employee making social security contributions who has dependent children. The definition of dependants includes:

- Adopted children as well as those born to the parents;
- Children up to the age of 18 or 24 years provided they are single and are regular students in an elementary, secondary, technical, specialised or higher education establishment and whose income is less than half the minimum wage for more than three months in each calendar year.
- The amount of the payment depends on the number of dependent children and the beneficiary's level of income according to the table below. The modelling assumes that the benefit is assessed on the spouse with the lower earning level where both spouses are working.

2015 Transfer by dependant

Annual income range (CLP)	Annual payment (CLP)
0-2 933 868	114 846
2 933 868-4 285 224	70 482
4 285 224 -6 683 496	22 278
6 683 496 and over	0

4. Memorandum items

4.1. *Identification of an average worker*

- The source of information is a survey conducted by the National Statistics Institute (INE) to determine the Salary and Labour Cost Index. This nationwide survey is carried out on a monthly sample and gathers information on salaries and labour costs. It applies to companies with at least 5-worker payrolls grouped in accordance with UN ISIC Rev. 3 international economic activity standard, covering workers in industry sectors C-O.*
- The average gross earnings was obtained by multiplying the average hourly wage by the average number of hours worked. It covers both full and part-time workers.

4.2. *Employers' contribution to private health and pension schemes*

- In Chile very few employers make any contributions towards health schemes for their employees, and the relevant information is not available.

* L(7522) and L(7523) are not included.

2015 parameter values

Average earnings/yr	Ave_earn	7 556 043	Country estimate
Allowances	Basic_al	0	
Income tax	Tax_sch	0	7 282 710
		0.04	16 183 000
		0.080	26 973 000
		0.135	37 762 200
		0.23	48 551 400
		0.304	64 735 200
		0.355	80 919 000
		0.4	
Education tax credit	edu_tax_cre	112 768	
	edu_tax_cre_lim	20 298 239	
Employees SSC	SSC_sch	0.07	22 012 186
Upper threshold		0	
Family allowance	CTR_child	0	114 846
Child element		2 933 868	70 482
		4 285 224	22 278
		6 683 496	0

2015 tax equations

The functions which are used in the equations (Taper, MIN, Tax etc) are described in the technical note about tax equations. Variable names are defined in the table of parameters above, within the equations table, or are the standard variables "married" and "children". A reference to a variable with the affix "_total" indicates the sum of the relevant variable values for the principal and spouse. And the affixes "_princ" and "_spouse" indicate the value for the principal and spouse, respectively. Equations for a single person are as shown for the principal, with "_spouse" values taken as 0.

	Line in country table and intermediate steps	Variable name	Range	Equation
1.	Earnings	earn		
2.	Allowances:	Tax_al	B	Min(Basic_al,earn)
3.	Credits in taxable income	taxbl_cr	B	0
4.	CG taxable income	tax_inc	B	Positive(earn-tax_al)
5.	CG tax before credits	CG_tax_excl	B	Tax(tax_inc, tax_sch)
6.	Tax credits :	tax_cr	P	IF(taxinc_princ+taxinc_spouse<=edu_tax_cre_lim,IF(taxinc_spouse =0,edu_tax_cre*Children,edu_tax_cre*Children*0.5),0)
			S	IF(AND(taxinc_princ+taxinc_spouse<=edu_tax_cre_lim,taxinc_spouse>0),edu_tax _cre*Children*0.5,0)
7.	CG tax	CG_tax	B	Positive(CG_tax_excl-tax_cr)
8.	State and local taxes	local_tax	B	0
9.	Employees' soc security	SSC	B	Tax(earn, SSC_sch)
11.	Family allowance	cash_trans	P/S	IF(Children=0,0, IF(earn_spouse>0, VLOOKUP (earn_spouse, CTR_child) , VLOOKUP (earn_princ, CTR_child)) * children)
13.	Employer's soc security	SSC_empr		0

Key to range of equation B calculated separately for both principal earner and spouse P calculated for principal only (value taken as 0 for spouse calculation) J calculated once only on a joint basis.

Czech Republic

This chapter includes data on the income taxes paid by workers, their social security contributions, the family benefits they receive in the form of cash transfers as well as the social security contributions and payroll taxes paid by their employers. Results reported include the marginal and average tax burden for eight different family types.

Methodological information is available for personal income tax systems, compulsory social security contributions to schemes operated within the government sector, universal cash transfers as well as recent changes in the tax/benefit system. The methodology also includes the parameter values and tax equations underlying the data.

Czech Republic 2015

The tax/benefit position of single persons

		Wage level (per cent of average wage)	67	100	167	67
		Number of children	none	none	none	2
1.	**Gross wage earnings**		213 009	317 924	530 933	213 009
2.	**Standard tax allowances**					
	Basic allowance		0	0	0	0
	Married or head of family		0	0	0	0
	Dependent children		0	0	0	0
	Deduction for social security contributions and income taxes		0	0	0	0
	Work-related expenses					
	Other					
		Total	0	0	0	0
3.	**Tax credits or cash transfers included in taxable income**		0	0	0	0
4.	**Central government taxable income (1 - 2 + 3 + 13)**		285 432	426 018	711 450	285 432
5.	**Central government income tax liability (exclusive of tax credits)**		42 815	63 903	106 717	42 815
6.	**Tax credits**					
	Basic credit					
	Married or head of family					
	Children					
	Other		24 840	24 840	24 840	54 048
		Total	24 840	24 840	24 840	54 048
7.	**Central government income tax finally paid (5-6)**		17 975	39 063	81 877	- 11 233
8.	**State and local taxes**		0	0	0	0
9.	**Employees' compulsory social security contributions**					
	Gross earnings		23 431	34 972	58 403	23 431
	Taxable income					
		Total	23 431	34 972	58 403	23 431
10.	**Total payments to general government (7 + 8 + 9)**		41 406	74 034	140 280	12 198
11.	**Cash transfers from general government**					
	For head of family					
	For two children		0	0	0	14 640
		Total	0	0	0	14 640
12.	**Take-home pay (1-10+11)**		171 603	243 889	390 653	215 451
13.	**Employer's compulsory social security contributions**		72 423	108 094	180 517	72 423
14.	**Average rates**					
	Income tax		8.4%	12.3%	15.4%	-5.3%
	Employees' social security contributions		11.0%	11.0%	11.0%	11.0%
	Total payments less cash transfers		19.4%	23.3%	26.4%	-1.1%
	Total tax wedge including employer's social security contributions		39.9%	42.8%	45.1%	24.5%
15.	**Marginal rates**					
	Total payments less cash transfers: Principal earner		31.1%	31.1%	31.1%	31.1%
	Total payments less cash transfers: Spouse		n.a.	n.a.	n.a.	n.a.
	Total tax wedge: Principal earner		48.6%	48.6%	48.6%	48.6%
	Total tax wedge: Spouse		n.a.	n.a.	n.a.	n.a.

Czech Republic 2015

The tax/benefit position of married couples

	Wage level (per cent of average wage)	100-0	100-33	100-67	100-33
	Number of children	2	2	2	none
1.	**Gross wage earnings**	317 924	422 839	530 933	422 839
2.	**Standard tax allowances**				
	Basic allowance	0	0	0	0
	Married or head of family	0	0	0	0
	Dependent children	0	0	0	0
	Deduction for social security contributions and income taxes	0	0	0	0
	Work-related expenses				
	Other				
	Total	0	0	0	0
3.	**Tax credits or cash transfers included in taxable income**	0	0	0	0
4.	**Central government taxable income (1 - 2 + 3 + 13)**	426 018	566 604	711 450	566 604
5.	**Central government income tax liability (exclusive of tax credits)**	63 903	84 991	106 717	84 991
6.	**Tax credits**				
	Basic credit				
	Married or head of family				
	Children				
	Other	78 888	54 048	54 048	24 840
	Total	78 888	54 048	54 048	24 840
7.	**Central government income tax finally paid (5-6)**	- 14 985	9 855	27 829	39 063
8.	**State and local taxes**	0	0	0	0
9.	**Employees' compulsory social security contributions**				
	Gross earnings	34 972	46 512	58 403	46 512
	Taxable income				
	Total	34 972	46 512	58 403	46 512
10.	**Total payments to general government (7 + 8 + 9)**	19 986	56 367	86 232	85 575
11.	**Cash transfers from general government**				
	For head of family				
	For two children	14 640	14 640	14 640	0
	Total	14 640	14 640	14 640	0
12.	**Take-home pay (1-10+11)**	312 577	381 112	459 341	337 264
13.	**Employer's compulsory social security contributions**	108 094	143 765	180 517	143 765
14.	**Average rates**				
	Income tax	-4.7%	2.3%	5.2%	9.2%
	Employees' social security contributions	11.0%	11.0%	11.0%	11.0%
	Total payments less cash transfers	1.7%	9.9%	13.5%	20.2%
	Total tax wedge including employer's social security contributions	26.6%	32.7%	35.4%	40.5%
15.	**Marginal rates**				
	Total payments less cash transfers: Principal earner	31.1%	31.1%	31.1%	31.1%
	Total payments less cash transfers: Spouse	34.7%	11.0%	31.1%	11.0%
	Total tax wedge: Principal earner	48.6%	48.6%	48.6%	48.6%
	Total tax wedge: Spouse	51.3%	33.6%	48.6%	33.6%

The national currency is the Czech koruna (CZK). In 2015, CZK 24.59 was equal to USD 1. In that year, the average worker earned CZK 317 924 (Secretariat estimate).

1. personal income tax system

1.1. *Central government income taxes*

1.1.1. *Tax unit*

- The tax unit is the individual.

1.1.2. *Tax allowances and tax credits*

1.1.2.1. Standard reliefs

- *Relief for social and health security contributions.* Employees' social security contributions (see Section 2.1) are not deductible for income tax purposes.

1.1.2.2. Main non-standard tax reliefs applicable to an AW

- *Charitable donations allowance:* A tax allowance of up to 10% of taxable income is available for donations made to municipalities or legal entities for the financing of social, health, cultural, humanitarian, religious, ecological and sport activities. The minimum limit for donations is the lesser of 2% of taxable income or CZK 1 000. A similar procedure shall apply for gratuitous performance to finance the removal of the consequences of a natural disaster occurring in the territory of an EU Member State, Norway or Iceland. The total deduction may not exceed 15% of the tax base. As gratuitous performance for healthcare purposes, the value of one blood donation from an unpaid donor is valued at a sum of CZK 2 000 and the value of an organ donation from a living donor is valued at a sum of CZK 20 000.
- *Interest payments:* Taxpayers may claim an allowance of up to CZK 300 000 for mortgage interest payments or other interest payments related to the purchase or the improvement of their house. The total sum of interest by which the tax base is reduced on all credits of payers in the same jointly managed household must not exceed CZK 300 000.
- *Supplementary pension scheme contributions:* In a period of taxation, the tax base may be reduced by a contribution, in the maximum total amount of CZK 12 000, paid by a taxpayer to their supplementary pension insurance with a State contribution under a contract on supplementary pension insurance with a State contribution entered into between the payer and a pension company; the sum that may be deducted in this manner equals the total amount of contributions paid by the payer for their supplementary pension insurance with a State contribution in the period of taxation, reduced by CZK 12 000.
- *Private life insurance premiums:* Taxpayers may claim an allowance of up to CZK 12 000 for premiums paid according to a contract between the taxpayer and an insurance company if the benefit (lump sum or recurrent pension) is paid out 60 months after the signature of the contract and in the year in which the taxpayer reaches the age of 60.

1.1.2.3. Tax schedule

From January 2008, a progressive system of taxation is replaced by a single rate of 15%. The tax base, reduced by the non-taxable part of the tax base (see 1.122 – Main non-standard tax reliefs), rounded down to whole hundreds of CZK is subject to tax at the rate of 15%. After that, tax credits (see 1.124) can be used to directly reduce a person's tax liability.

1.1.2.4. Tax credits

- Credit of CZK 24 840 per taxpayer, the tax shall not be reduced for a payer that receives a retirement pension from pension insurance or from foreign compulsory insurance of the same kind as of 1 January of the period of taxation.
- Credit of CZK 24 840 per spouse (husband or wife) living with a taxpayer in a common household provided that the spouse's own income does not exceed CZK 68 000 in the taxable period.
- Credit of CZK 13 404 for first child, credit of CZK 15 804 for second child, credit of CZK 17 004 for third and each additional child (irrespective of the child's own income) living with a taxpayer in a common household on the territory of a Member State of the EU, Norway or Iceland, if the child satisfies one or more of the following criteria:
  - age below 18 year of age,
  - age below 26 year of age and receiving full-time education,
  - age below 26 year of age and physically or mentally disabled provided that the child is not in receipt of a state disability payment

If the child is a "ZTP-P" card holder (the child with a certain type of disabilities), the tax credit is CZK 26 808. The taxpayer can claim the tax credit in the form of tax reliefs or tax bonuses or their combination.

- Credit of CZK 2 520 if the taxpayer is in receipt of a partial disability pension or is entitled to both an old-age pension and a partial disability pension
- Credit of CZK 5 040 it the taxpayer is in receipt of a full disability pension, or another type of pension conditional on his full disability pension, or if the taxpayer is entitled to both old-age pension and full disability pension or deemed to be fully disabled under statutory provisions, but his application for a full disability pension was rejected for reasons other than that he was not fully disabled (handicapped).
- Credit of CZK 16 140 if the taxpayer is a "ZTP-P" card holder.
- Credit of CZK 4 020 if the taxpayer takes part in a systematic educational or training programme under statutory provisions in order to prepare for his future vocation (profession) by means of such studies or prescribed training until completion of his/her 26 or 28 years (Ph.D. programme).
- New tax abatement (credit) which can be applied in case that a maintained child of a taxpayer is placing in a pre-school facility. The tax abatement can be applied in the amount of pre-school facility fees, which is really paid for maintained child, however at maximum up to the amount of minimum wage for a maintained child. Tax abatement may only be used if the maintained child lives with the taxpayer in a jointly managed household. Introduction of this relief is a part of the Act on provision of childcare in a child society.

The non-standard tax reliefs, tax abatement and special solidarity surcharge of 7 % for income from employment and entrepreneurship exceeding 48 times the average salary within the calendar year are not included in the tax equations underlying the Taxing Wages results.

1.2. *State and local income tax*

There are no regional or local income taxes.

2. Compulsory social security contributions to schemes operated within the government sector

The maximum annual earnings used to calculate social security contributions are 48 times the national average monthly wage. The maximum ceiling for social security contributions is CZK 1 277 328 for the year 2015. The maximum ceiling for health insurance has not existed since 2013.

2.1. *Employees' contributions*

Compulsory contributions of 11% of gross wages and salaries are paid by all employees into government operated schemes. The total is made up as follows (in %):

Health insurance	4.5
Social insurance	6.5

2.2. *Employers' contributions*

The total contribution for employers is 34% of gross earnings.

The contribution consists of the health insurance contribution (9% of gross wages and salaries) and social insurance (25%).

3. Universal cash transfers

3.1. *Transfers related to marital status*

None.

3.2. *Transfers for dependent children*

Non-taxable child allowances are the basic income-tested benefit provided to a dependent child with the objective to contribute to the coverage of costs incurred in his upbringing and sustenance. Entitlement to the child allowance is bound with certain income criteria. The central government pays this allowance in respect of each dependent child based on the family income level and provided that family's income does not exceed 2.4 times the relevant family's living minimum (LM). Family income includes the earnings of both parents net of income tax and the employees' social security and health insurance contributions. Child allowances are provided at three levels depending on the age of the child and are paid as follows:

Family income	Up to 2.4 LM
Age of child	Total payment CZK per month
Below 6 year of age	500
6-15 years	610
15-26 years	700

The monthly family's LM for the AW-type family with children can be calculated by summing the following amounts (in CZK):

Living minimum	
Basic personal requirement	
Single	3 410
First person in household	3 140
Second and other persons who are not a dependent child	2 830
Child aged below 6	1 740
Child aged between 6 and 15	2 140
Child aged between 15 and 26	2 450
Household expenses	
One person household	3 410
Two person household	5 970
Three person household	7 710
Four person household	9 850
Five person household	12 300

The LM is required by law. In case that family income (income of persons assessed together) don't achieve the amount of family's LM can be put in a request for state social support (housing benefit, family benefits, social assistance and other). The system applies the solidarity principle between the high-income families and low-income families, as well as between the childless families and those with children.

The term "social allowance" was abolished from 1 January 2012. However, this fact has no effect on the tax-benefit system for low-income families. The system of personalized payment was simplified and extended. For examples, in case of loss of income (social allowance) some people may put in a request for increase care allowance up to CZK 2 000. This allowance is addressed for recipients who are dependent children below 18 years of age and parent of dependent children below 18 years of age if the income of the family is under 2.0 family's living minimum. Protection in the housing sector is also addressed in the context of state social support system (housing allowances-benefit) and the system of assistance in material need as additional housing. Also foster care benefits create a separate benefit system; since 1 January 2013 they have ceased to be a component of the state social support system. These allowances (housing, care and foster care) are not included in the Taxing Wages models.

3.3. *Additional transfers*

Additional allowances (means-tested benefits in material need) are paid by the central government to low income families in adverse social and financial situation. The amount transferred is derived from the LM and varies according to total family income including family allowances and own efforts, opportunities and needs are taken into account. This allowance is not included in the computation.

4. Main changes in tax/benefit systems since 2015

In 2015, there were no changes that would have a significant effect on the current calculation of Taxing Wages.

List of main changes that have no impact on the current computation of TW:

- A new tax credit which can be applied in case that a child of a taxpayer visits a nursery school (preschool children, including kindergarten up to start school attendance) is introduced. The tax credit can be applied in the amount of nursery school fees really paid for child, however at maximum up to the amount of minimum salary for a child.

Introduction of this relief is a part of the Act on provision of childcare in a child society (see Chapter 1.124).

- Tax credit on second and third and next child has increased based on the Amendment (CZK 15 804 for second child, CZK 17.004 for third and each additional child) – see chapter 1.124.
- Change regarding obligation to file personal income tax return in case of taxpayers underlying to solidarity tax. Newly, the obligation to file the personal income tax return occurs only when an annual limit for solidarity tax application is exceeded.
- Based on ongoing amendments limitation of tax advantage of private life insurance in case of partial payment has been included in the Amendment. If a taxpayer receives compensation from his/her life insurance account before the given conditions are met, tax exemption of contributions paid by his/her employer as well as possibility to apply a tax deduction will be ceased. In such a case, the employee will be obliged to additionally taxations of this benefit through a personal income tax return. At the same time, tax advantage from life insurance will be newly applicable only in case of life insurance contracts allowing payments after meeting said conditions as of the moment of the contract's termination.
- As of 2015 notification obligation for taxpayers should be effective – individuals who receive tax exempted income of more than CZK 5mio. A taxpayer will be obliged to report such a situation to a tax administrator until deadline for filing the personal income tax return. There are penalties set by the Income Tax Act if the taxpayer breaches this obligation.
- In reaction to the Constitutional Court's case the Amendments again allows application of basic tax credit for working retirees. Based on this information the tax credit was applied retrospectively for 2013 and 2014. The impact of this application has no effect to the tax equations underlying the TW results but had impact on collection of IT in 2014 and 2015.
- A new tax abatement has no effect to the tax equations underlying the TW result but has impact on collection of IT in 2015

5. Memorandum items

5.1. *Identification of AW and valuation of earnings*

The Ministry of Finance estimates the average earnings of the AW based on the data supplied by the Czech Statistical Office. The calculation of the average earnings AW is made by CZ-NACE division, which is compatible with ISIC classifications Ver. 4.

5.2. *Employers' contributions to private pension, health and related schemes*

There are supplementary private pension schemes only, but employers' contributions vary. Relevant information is not available.

2015 parameter values

	Ave_earn	317 924	Secretariat estimate
Income tax rate	tax_rate	0.15	
Social security – social insurance	SSs_rate	0.065	
Social security – health insurance	SSh_rate	0.045	
Employers	SSC_empr_rate	0.34	
Child Tax credit - first child	child_cr_1	13 404	
- second child	child_cr_2	15 804	
- third child	child_cr_3	17 004	
Tax credit for individuals	tax_cr_base	24 840	
Tax credit for spouse	tax_cr_spo	24 840	
Tax credit for spouse income ceiling	Tax_cr_spo_inc_ceil	68 000	
Living minimum (LM)			
	basic_adult	3 410	
	basic_household	5 970	
	basic_child	2 140	
	house_exp	1	3 410
		2	5 970
		3	7 710
		4	9 850
		5	12 300
Cash transfers	transf_1	610	
Social security, social insurance – ceiling	soc_sec_si_ceil	1 277 328	

2015 tax equations

The equations for the Czech system are on an individual basis. But the spouse tax credit is relevant only to the calculation for the principal earner and cash transfers are calculated only once. This is shown by the Range indicator in the table below.

The functions which are used in the equations (Taper, MIN, Tax etc) are described in the technical note about tax equations. Variable names are defined in the table of parameters above, within the equations table, or are the standard variables "married" and "children". A reference to a variable with the affix "_total" indicates the sum of the relevant variable values for the principal and spouse. And the affixes "_princ" and "_spouse" indicate the value for the principal and spouse, respectively. Equations for a single person are as shown for the principal, with "_spouse" values taken as 0.

		Variable name	Range	Equation
1.	Earnings	earn	B	
2.	CG taxable income	tax_inc_princ	B	Earn+(earn*SSC_empr_rate)
3.	CG tax before credits			
	CG tax before credits principal	CG_tax_excl_princ	B	Tax(tax_inc_princ, tax_rate)
4.	Tax credits:			
	Tax credit for children	tax_cr_ch	P	If (number of children>3; (number of children - 3)*child_cr_3+child_cr_1+child_cr_2+child_cr_3; If (number of children>2;child_cr_1 +child_cr_2 + child_cr_3; If (number of children>1;child_cr_1+child_cr_2; If (number of children=0;0)))))
	Basic tax credit	tax_cr_bas	B	tax_cr_bas
	Tax credit for spouse	tax_cr_spouse	P	Married*tax_cr_spo
5.	CG tax			
	CG tax principal	CG_tax_princ	B	Max(CG_tax_excl_princ - tax_cr_bas_princ - tax_cr_spo , 0) - tax_cr_ch
6.	State and local taxes	local_tax	B	0
7.	Employees' social security	SSs SSh	B B	MIN(earn,soc_sec_si__ceil)*SSs_rate earn*SSh_rate
8.	Cash transfers			
	Net family income	net_inc	J	earn_total-CG_tax_total-SSC_total
9.	Living minimum (monthly)	LM	J	(1-Married)*basic_adult+Married*basic_household +Children*basic_child+ VLOOKUP((1+Married+Children), house_exp, 2, FALSE)
10.	Total cash transfers	cash_trans	J	Children*IF(net_inc<=(2.4)*LM*12, transf_1*12)
11.	Employer's social security	SSs_empr SSh_empr	B B	MIN(earn,soc_sec_sir_ceil)*SSs_empr_rate earn*SSh_empr_rate

Key to range of equation: B calculated separately for both principal earner and spouse; P calculated for principal only (value taken as 0 for spouse calculation); J calculated once only on a joint basis.

Denmark

This chapter includes data on the income taxes paid by workers, their social security contributions, the family benefits they receive in the form of cash transfers as well as the social security contributions and payroll taxes paid by their employers. Results reported include the marginal and average tax burden for eight different family types.

Methodological information is available for personal income tax systems, compulsory social security contributions to schemes operated within the government sector, universal cash transfers as well as recent changes in the tax/benefit system. The methodology also includes the parameter values and tax equations underlying the data.

Denmark 2015

The tax/benefit position of single persons

	Wage level (per cent of average wage)	67	100	167	67
	Number of children	none	none	none	2
1.	**Gross wage earnings**	271 937	405 876	677 813	271 937
2.	**Standard tax allowances**				
	Basic allowance				
	Married or head of family				
	Dependent children				
	Deduction for social security contributions and income taxes	21 755	32 470	54 225	21 755
	Work-related expenses	0	0	0	0
	Other				
	Total	21 755	32 470	54 225	21 755
3.	**Tax credits or cash transfers included in taxable income**	0	0	0	0
	Earnings tax credit deduction	21 891	26 800	26 800	36 575
	Total	- 21 891	- 26 800	- 26 800	- 36 575
4.	**Central government taxable income (1 - 2 + 3)**	228 291	346 606	596 788	213 606
5.	**Central government income tax liability (exclusive of tax credits)**	29 259	43 948	98 611	28 672
6.	**Tax credits**				
	Basic credit	5 243	5 243	5 243	5 243
	Married or head of family				
	Children				
	Other				
	Total	5 243	5 243	5 243	5 243
7.	**Central government income tax finally paid (5-6)**	45 771	71 175	147 593	45 184
8.	**State and local taxes**	46 045	75 510	137 816	42 388
9.	**Employees' compulsory social security contributions**				
	Gross earnings	0	0	0	0
	Taxable income				
	Total	0	0	0	0
10.	**Total payments to general government (7 + 8 + 9)**	91 817	146 686	285 409	87 572
11.	**Cash transfers from general government**				
	For head of family				
	For two children	0	0	0	68 708
	Green check	955	955	0	1 395
	Total	955	955	0	70 103
12.	**Take-home pay (1-10+11)**	181 075	260 145	392 404	254 468
13.	**Employer's compulsory social security contributions**	3 462	3 462	3 462	3 462
14.	**Average rates**				
	Income tax	33.8%	36.1%	42.1%	32.2%
	Employees' social security contributions	0.0%	0.0%	0.0%	0.0%
	Total payments less cash transfers	33.4%	35.9%	42.1%	6.4%
	Total tax wedge including employer's social security contributions	34.2%	36.4%	42.4%	7.6%
15.	**Marginal rates**				
	Total payments less cash transfers: Principal earner	39.7%	42.0%	55.8%	38.1%
	Total payments less cash transfers: Spouse	n.a.	n.a.	n.a.	n.a.
	Total tax wedge: Principal earner	39.7%	42.0%	55.8%	38.1%
	Total tax wedge: Spouse	n.a.	n.a.	n.a.	n.a.

Denmark 2015

The tax/benefit position of married couples

			100-0	100-33	100-67	100-33
		Wage level (per cent of average wage)	100-0	100-33	100-67	100-33
		Number of children	2	2	2	none
1.	**Gross wage earnings**		405 876	539 815	677 813	539 815
2.	**Standard tax allowances**					
	Basic allowance					
	Married or head of family					
	Dependent children					
	Deduction for social security contributions and income taxes		32 470	43 185	54 225	43 185
	Work-related expenses		0	0	0	0
	Other					
		Total	32 470	43 185	54 225	43 185
3.	**Tax credits or cash transfers included in taxable income**		0	0	0	0
	Earnings tax credit deduction		26 800	26 800	26 800	26 800
		Total	- 26 800	- 26 800	- 26 800	- 26 800
4.	**Central government taxable income (1 - 2 + 3)**		346 606	459 047	574 897	459 047
5.	**Central government income tax liability (exclusive of tax credits)**		43 948	58 315	73 207	58 315
6.	**Tax credits**					
	Basic credit		15 728	10 485	10 485	10 485
	Married or head of family					
	Children					
	Other					
		Total	15 728	10 485	10 485	10 485
7.	**Central government income tax finally paid (5-6)**		65 933	91 015	116 947	91 015
8.	**State and local taxes**		64 702	92 705	121 556	92 705
9.	**Employees' compulsory social security contributions**					
	Gross earnings		0	0	0	0
	Taxable income					
		Total	0	0	0	0
10.	**Total payments to general government (7 + 8 + 9)**		130 635	183 719	238 502	183 719
11.	**Cash transfers from general government**					
	For head of family					
	For two children		25 152	25 152	25 152	0
	Green check		2 630	2 630	2 350	2 190
		Total	27 782	27 782	27 502	2 190
12.	**Take-home pay (1-10+11)**		303 023	383 877	466 812	358 285
13.	**Employer's compulsory social security contributions**		3 462	6 924	6 924	6 924
14.	**Average rates**					
	Income tax		32.2%	34.0%	35.2%	34.0%
	Employees' social security contributions		0.0%	0.0%	0.0%	0.0%
	Total payments less cash transfers		25.3%	28.9%	31.1%	33.6%
	Total tax wedge including employer's social security contributions		26.0%	29.8%	31.8%	34.5%
15.	**Marginal rates**					
	Total payments less cash transfers: Principal earner		42.0%	42.0%	42.0%	42.0%
	Total payments less cash transfers: Spouse		39.6%	39.7%	39.7%	39.7%
	Total tax wedge: Principal earner		42.0%	42.0%	42.0%	42.0%
	Total tax wedge: Spouse		41.2%	39.7%	39.7%	39.7%

The national currency is the Kroner (DKK). In 2015, DKK 6.73 was equal to USD 1. In that year, the average worker earned DKK 405 876 (Secretariat estimate), which is calculated on the background of the extrapolated 2014 average worker income with the expected 2015 growth rate of wages on 2.1%.

1. Personal income tax system

In the Danish personal income tax system, the income of the individual taxpayer is split into three categories:

- *Personal income,* which consists of employment income, business income, pensions, unemployment benefits etc. and with fully deductibility of Labour Market Contributions.
- *Capital income* (e.g. interest income and some capital gains) is calculated as a net amount (the sum of positive and negative capital income net of interest expenses). Dividend income and the property value of owner-occupied dwellings are taxed at different tax rates.
- *Taxable income* – the aggregate of personal income and capital income less deductions (e.g. work-related expenses etc.).

All three categories are relevant for various tax rates, see Section 1.2.1.

The employees' social security contributions and their payments to labour market supplementary pension schemes (see Section 2.1) are not included in personal income (or taxable income).

Regarding the tax unit, the earned income of each spouse is taxed separately. However, as is mentioned in Section 1.2.1, some unutilised personal allowances can be transferred between them.

1.1. *Tax allowances and tax credits*

1.1.1. *Standard reliefs*

Wage or salary earners who make expenses in order to earn their income (e.g. transport expenses, trade union membership dues, unemployment premiums) can fully deduct these expenses from taxable income.

The tax credit scheme allows the taxpayer to deduct 8.05% of earned income to a maximum of DKK 26 800 in order to calculate taxable income. Single parents get an extra employment allowance of 5.40% in 2015 with a maximum allowance of DKK 17 900. The effective value of the credit is equal to the municipality tax (24.9%) plus the 4.0% health care tax rate that is paid to the state (28.91% on average) multiplied by the value of the deduction.

1.1.2. *Main non-standard tax reliefs applicable to an AW*

- *Interest payments* are fully deductible from capital income.

- The *non-standard deduction for wage and salary earners:* The actual costs that are made in order to acquire income are deductible from taxable income. The main items are:
  - Contributions paid to trade unions;
  - Transportation costs: Up to 24 km. per day: no deduction. 24-120 km.: DKK 2.05 per km. Above 120 km.: DKK 1.03 per km. as a standard, but transport from municipalities placed in the outskirts of the country gives a credit of DKK 2.05 also above 120 km;
  - Other costs above DKK 5 700.
- *Contributions/premiums* paid to *private pension saving plans* are in general deductible from personal income. From 1999 onwards, contributions/premiums paid to private pension saving plans with sum payments are no longer deductible from income subject to the top tax bracket rate. From 2013 onwards, contributions/premiums paid to private pension saving plans with sum payments are no longer deductible.
- Other reliefs:
  - Alimonies, if according to contract, are deductible from taxable income;
  - Contributions to certain non-profit institutions are deductible from taxable income (limit DKK 15 000);
  - Losses incurred from unincorporated business in earlier years are, in principle, deductible from personal income.

1.1.3. *Tax credits*

Each individual is granted a personal allowance, which is converted into a wastable tax credit by applying the marginal tax rate of the first bracket of the income tax schedule. For taxpayers who are 18 years of age or are older, the tax credit amounts to:

For central government income tax	8.08% of DKK 43 400 = DKK 3 507
For central government health care tax	4.00% of DKK 43 400 = DKK 1 736
For municipal income tax	24.91% of DKK 43 400 = DKK 10 808

Special personal allowance for an individual younger than 18: DKK 32 600.

If a married person cannot utilise the personal allowance, the unutilised part is transferred to the spouse.

1.2. *Central government income taxes*

1.2.1. *Tax schedule*

Individuals pay an 8% Labour Market Contribution (*Arbejdsmarkedsbidrag* in Danish), levied on the gross wage or other income from work before the deduction of any allowance.

Before 2008, the revenue was earmarked for certain social security expenditures through the Labour market Fund, but this system was abolished from 2008, and the tax enters the budget in the same way as any other income taxes. From 2011 the last links regarding social security of the tax were removed making all taxpayers working in Denmark pay the labour market contribution. The labour market contribution is thus treated as a PIT in Taxing Wages from 2008.

Low tax bracket to the central government is assessed on the aggregate of personal income and positive net capital income at the rate of 8.08%.

From 2010 and onwards the medium tax bracket was removed.

Top tax bracket to the central government is assessed on the excess of DKK 459 200 of the aggregate of personal income and positive net capital income in excess of DKK 41 400 at the rate of 15%. If a married individual cannot utilise the total allowance of DKK 459 200, the unutilised part is *not* transferred to the spouse.

If the marginal tax rate including local tax exceeds 51.95%, the top tax bracket rate is reduced by the difference between the marginal tax rate and 51.95%.

1.2.2. Health care tax

Central government levies an additional health care tax of 4%. The tax base is taxable income (see Section 1).

1.3. State and local income taxes

1.3.1. General description

Local income taxes are levied only by the municipalities. The rates vary across jurisdictions.

1.3.2. Tax base

The tax base is taxable income (see Section 1). Tax credit varies with tax rates. The average amount is given below.

1.3.3. Tax rates

Lowest rate: 22.5% (municipalities);

Highest rate: 27.8% (municipalities);

Average rate: 24.904% (municipalities);

The average rate is used in this study. It is applied to the tax base less personal allowances (see Section 1.1).

2. Compulsory social security contributions to schemes operated within the government sector

2.1. Employees' contributions

Employees make a fixed contribution of DKK 11 154 for unemployment insurance. From 1999 onwards, the contribution for unemployment insurance is split into two: one part consists of the contribution for unemployment insurance (DKK 3 972) while the other part consists of a voluntary contribution to an early retirement scheme (DKK 5 784). In addition an administration fee of DKK 1 398 on average is added.

Contributions to the unemployment funds are not mandatory. Nevertheless, these payments have up until the implementation of ESA 2010 and the major revision of the Danish national accounts in the autumn 2014 been defined as social security contributions and classified as taxes in the Danish national accounts because there is no direct link between what members pay to the schemes and what they receive and the funds are subsidized by the state. The contributions to the unemployment funds are no longer classified as taxes in the Danish national accounts.

In addition, there is a compulsory fixed contribution to a general Labour Market Supplementary Pension Scheme of DKK 1 080 for workers who work at least 117 hours per month (for workers who work less than 117 hours but not less than 78 hours, the rate is DKK 720; for workers who work less than 78 hours but not less than 39 hours, the rate is DKK 360); their employer makes a corresponding contribution that is double this amount. Under this scheme, each employee has a plan and it should be noted that the contribution that is ascribed to this plan is determined by the level of employment and does not necessarily relate to the actual amount described above. The employee contribution of DKK 1 080 is modelled as a standard tax relief from the personal income tax. As the employee and employer contribution is paid to a privately-managed pension scheme, these contributions are not considered to be taxes but rather as non-tax compulsory payments and are therefore not included in the tax calculations.

Also, all private sector employers contribute to Financing Contribution (DKK 644) and barsel.dk (DKK 750). Both of the payments are paid to privately managed funds. The Financing Contribution covers part of the Danish state's expenses to ATP-contributions as well as expenses to Employees' Guarantee Fund for the unemployed. Barsel.dk is a statutory scheme covering the part of the private sector labour market that is not covered by other approved maternity/paternity compensation schemes. Those contributions are considered as non-tax compulsory payments and not included in the tax calculations either.

2.2. *Employers' contributions*

It is compulsory for the employer to contribute to Employers' Reimbursement System (DKK 2 840), industrial injury tax (DKK 242) and Employees' Guarantee Fund (DKK 380).The employer also contributes to a Labour Market Supplementary Pension scheme, which in case of a full-time employee corresponds to a fixed amount of DKK 2 160 (being twice the fixed amount of DKK 1 080 mentioned in Section 2.1).

3. Universal cash transfers

The transfers for each dependent child are as follows:

Age group	Quarterly amount (DKK) for each child
0-2	4 443
3-6	3 519
7-17	2 769

The transfer is reduced when the income of a parent exceeds DKK 723 100. There are additional special amounts for single parents: the transfer for each dependent child is DKK 5 356 per year and a yearly transfer of DKK 5 460 regardless of the number of children. In addition, there is a state transfer of DKK 13 692 per year for each dependent child in case an 'absent parent' does not contribute (this amount) to the family. This transfer is included in this Report's calculations for single parents.

Individuals older than 18 years receive a "green check" of DKK 955; this amount is increased with DKK 220 per child for up to two children. Only one partner in a married couple receives the increased "green check" for children. The "green check" is nominally fixed and is phased out at a rate of 7.5% for income above DKK 374 800. If the yearly income of the individuals is lower than DKK 219 000 the individuals receive an "additional green check" of DKK 280.

4. Main changes in tax/benefit systems

From 2000 to 2002, the low tax bracket rate has been reduced from 7% to 5.5%. The low tax bracket is assessed on the aggregate of personal income and positive net capital income.

After the parliamentary elections in 2001, the Conservative/Liberal government adopted a tax freeze policy, which implied that tax rates could not be increased, either in nominal or relative terms, during that government term. Taxes were therefore not increased during the period 2002-05. After the parliamentary elections in February 2005, the Conservative/Liberal government and the tax freeze policy were confirmed.

In order to respect the "tax freeze", the low tax bracket has been reduced by 0.36% from 2004 to 2010 as a compensation for increases in local income taxes from 33.31% in 2004 to 33.66% in 2011.

In the spring of 2003, the government agreed with one of the opposition parties to implement a tax package. The aim of this package was to decrease the level of labour taxation in Denmark, and thereby to reduce the distortions in the labour market and to improve the incentives to work. The package contained two main elements: an increase of the threshold for the medium tax bracket of nearly DKK 50 000 and the introduction of a tax credit scheme whereby the taxpayer can deduct 2.5% of earned income to a maximum of DKK 7 500 (in 2007) in the calculation of taxable income.

Before 2004, a compulsory contribution of 1% of employees' gross earnings was paid to an individual Labour Market Supplementary Pension Scheme established for the employee – this contribution is not considered as a social security contribution but rather as savings being made by the individual. However, from 2004 to 2010, this contribution was suspended and finally abolished and the deposits paid out as of April 2010.

In September 2007, the tax cuts from the 2003-package was extended. The threshold for the medium tax bracket was to be raised with DKK 57 900 in 2009 to meet with the top tax bracket threshold. The deductible tax credit was increased to 4.0% of earned income in 2008 and to 4.25% in 2009; thus raising the maximum to 12 300 in 2008 and to 13 600 in 2009. The effective value of the credit and of the personal income allowance is equal to the local income tax rate, the church tax plus the health care tax rate (31.63% on average in 2013) multiplied by the value of the deduction.

From the 1st of January 2007 a Local Government Reform has come into force, which changes the structure of labour taxation. The reform however had only a minimal impact on the overall level of taxation. The number of municipalities has been cut from 270 to 98 and five regions have replaced the 14 counties. The regions will not impose taxes but will be financed through state subsidies and by contributions from the municipalities. The reform implied an increase in the average municipal tax rate from 22.1% in 2006 to 24.577% in 2007. Since then, there has been a further increase in the average municipal tax to 24.907% in 2013. The county tax has been replaced by a new health care tax of 8% which is levied by central government. The health care tax rate is decreased to 6% in 2013. The levels of taxation have thus been reduced from three to two: only the central and local governments now levy taxes.

In the spring of 2009, the government and one of the opposition parties agreed upon a major tax reform to be phased in from 2010 to 2019. The reform aims at reducing the high marginal tax rates on personal income and thus to stimulate labour supply in the medium to long-term. The reform decreases income taxes by DKK 29 billion in 2010. The tax reform is planned to be revenue neutral as a whole, but was underfinanced in the short run (2010-12) in order to stimulate the economy. The main measures taken in 2010 include the reduction of the rate of the bottom tax bracket from 5.26% to 3.67%, abolition of the medium tax bracket with the 6% rate altogether, and increase the top tax bracket threshold by DKK 28 800 to DKK 389 000. The reform will decrease the lowest marginal tax rate from 42.4% to 41.0% and the highest marginal tax rate on labour income from 63.0% to 56.1%. The marginal tax rate on positive net capital income (up to 51.5 after abolition of the middle tax bracket) is further reduced for the vast majority by introduction of an extra allowance of DKK 40 000 (DKK 80 000 for married couples) for positive net capital income in the top bracket tax.

The reform is partly financed by higher energy, transport and environmental taxes to support the energy and climate policy objectives of the government, and also by increases of excise rates on health-related goods (fat, candy, sugary drinks, tobacco). These increases are partly compensated by giving a "green check" to households (see Section 3). The tax reform is also partly financed by base broadening measures. The measures include a gradual reduction from 2012 to 2019 of the tax value (from 33.5% to 25.5%) of assessment oriented deductions and limitations of the tax deductibility of net interest payments over a nominal threshold of DKK 50 000 (DKK 100 000 for married couples). Also the deductibility of payments above DKK 100 000 a year to individual pension insurance schemes with less than life-long coverage has been limited, as well as tightening of the tax treatment of company cars and other fringe benefits. Furthermore, a 6% tax is imposed from 2011 on pension payments exceeding DKK 362 800.

To consolidate the budget, a *Fiscal Consolidation Agreement* was reached in May 2010, somewhat modifying the prescriptions of the Spring Package of 2009.

The specific provisions of the *Fiscal Consolidation Agreement* include:

- The suspension from 2011 until 2013 of automatic adjustments in various tax thresholds (including personal allowances).
- Postponing from 2011 to 2014 the increase of the threshold for the top income tax rate (15%) from DKK 389 900 to 409 100 (EUR 52 316 to 54 892). The increase was an element of the 2009 *tax reform*.
- The labour union membership fees' tax deductibility is limited to DKK 3 000 (EUR 403) from the year 2011. The threshold is not adjusted.
- From 2011, the annual amount of child allowance is limited to DKK 35 000 (EUR 4 696), irrespective of the number of children. This was abolished by the new government by 2012. Child allowances will be gradually reduced by 5% until 2013.

As part of the Finance Act 2012 it was decided to introduce an "additional green check" to people beyond 18 years with low income (less than DKK 212 000). The "additional green check" is DKK 280.

In June 2012 a tax reform was reached. Included in the reform were changes in the earned income tax credit and the top tax bracket. The earned income tax credit is gradually raised from 4.40% in 2012 to 10.65% in 2022 (6.95% in 2013) where the maximum limit of earned income tax credit is raised from DKK 14 100 in 2012 to DKK 34 100 in 2022 (DKK 22 300 in 2013). Furthermore, a special earned income tax credit for single parents was decided from 2014. This will be gradually introduced to the amount of 6.25% in 2022 with a maximum limit of DKK 20 000. In The Tax Reform 2012 it was also decided to gradually raise the top tax bracket from DKK 389 900 in 2012 to DKK 467 000 in 2022 (DKK 421 000 in 2013).

As part of the Finance Act 2013 an agreement, The Excise Duty and Competition Package, was reached. This agreement includes a decrease in the excise duty on electricity, an abolition of the fat tax and a planned expansion in the excise duty on sugar, which will reduce expenses of both consumers and companies. This was financed by an increase in the bottom tax rate of 0.19 percentage points and a reduction in the personal allowance by DKK 900 for all persons (under and over 18 years) introduced from the income year 2013. As a consequence the marginal tax ceiling was increased from 51.5% to 51.7%. It is estimated that the abolished excise duties and the increased income taxes will have similar effects on distribution and labour supply.

Certain elements of the tax reform from 2012 were accelerated in the 2014 Budget. The employment allowance is adjusted upwards to 7.65% (2014), 8.05% (2015), 8.3% (2016) and 8.75% (2017), with a simultaneous increase of the maximum allowance from DKK 25 000 in 2014 to DKK 28 600 in 2018. The extra employment allowance for single parents is increased to 5.40% in 2014 (instead of 2.60%) with a maximum allowance of DKK 17 700.

Growth Plan 2014 contained measures to reduce the public service obligation on electricity and roll back an increase in excise duty on fossil fuel. As part of the financing of Growth Plan 2014 the low tax bracket rate is increased by 0.28 percentage point over the next five years, including 0.25 percentage point in 2015, with a parallel increase in the tax ceiling. Also, the green check and the supplementary green check are reduced over the next five years, starting in 2015.

In the autumn 2014, the new ESA 2010 guidelines (European System of National and Regional Accounts) and a major revision of the Danish national accounts were implemented which changed the classification of a few taxes. For example, the church tax and contributions to the unemployment fund are no longer classified as taxes, but as volunteer contributions (see Section 2.1).

As part of the Finance Act 2015 the tax deductibility of labour union membership fees is increased from DKK 3 000 to DKK 6 000 in 2015.

5. Memorandum items

5.1. *Identification of an AW*

The AW is identified as an average worker employed at firms which are members of the Danish Employers' Confederation.

5.2. *Employers' contribution to private schemes*

The employer must provide his employees with work injuries' insurance.

Employees typically participate in a private occupational (labour market) pension scheme to which both the employee and the employer make contributions. The employee's contribution is deductible for income tax purposes and is treated in this Report as a non-standard tax relief. The employer's contribution is not included in the gross wage income of the employee.

2015 parameter values

Average earnings	Ave_earn	405 876
Central taxes	Health_tax_rate	0.04
	Low_rate	0.0808
	Medium_thrsh	0
	Medium_rate	0
	Top_thrsh	459 200
	Top_rate	0.15
	Marg_rate_ceil	0.5195
	Adj_top_rate	0.14966
	Temp_tax_rate	0.00
	Temp_tax_thrsh	0
	Personal_al	43 400
The green check	green_check	955
	1 child	220
	child max	440
	Green_check_thrsh	374 800
	Green_check_taper_rate	0.075
	Extra_green_check	280
	Extra_green_check_thrsh	219 000
Local taxes	gener_rate	0.24904
	church_rate	0
total local tax rate	Local_rates	0.24904
Earned income tax credit scheme	earncredit_rate	0.0805
	earncredit_max	26800
for single parents	Sing_par_earncredit_rate	0.054
	Sing_par_earncredit_max	17 900
Child transfers	Child_3to6	14 076
	Child_7to17	11 076
	Child_limit	723 100
	Child_red	0.02
for single parents	Sing_par_basic	5 460
	Sing_par_ch	19 048
Individual Labour Market Pension Scheme	Pension_rate	0
Employees soc. security:		
suppl. pension scheme	Pension	1 080
unempl. insurance	Unemp	0
Labour Market Contribution	Labour_market_rate	0.08
Employer soc. security:		
suppl. pension scheme	Pension_empr	2 160
contributions to ATP	SSC_ATP	3 462
SSC rate	SSC_empr	0.00
Financing Contribution	NTCP_FC	644
barsel.dk	NTCP_barsel	750

2015 tax equations

The equations for the Danish system in 2015 are mostly on an individual basis but there is an interaction in the calculation of Central Government tax between spouses and the child benefit is calculated only once. This is shown by the Range indicator in the table below.

The functions which are used in the equations (Taper, MIN, Tax etc) are described in the technical note about tax equations. Variable names are defined in the table of parameters above, within the equations table, or are the standard variables "married" and "children". A reference to a variable with the affix "_total" indicates the sum of the relevant variable values for the principal and spouse. And the affixes "_princ" and "_spouse" indicate the value for the principal and spouse, respectively. Equations for a single person are as shown for the principal, with "_spouse" values taken as 0.

	Line in country table and intermediate steps	Variable name	Range	Equation
1.	Earnings	earn		
2.	Allowances:	tax_al	B	Labour_market_contr+Pension_rate*earn
		earncredit	B	Min(earn*earncredit_rate, earncredit_max)+(Children>0)*(Married=0)* Min(earn*Sing_par_earncredit_rate; Sing_par_earncredit_max)
3.	Credits in taxable income	taxbl_cr	B	0
4.	CG taxable income	tax_inc	B	Positive(earn-tax_al-earncredit+taxbl_cr)
	Personal income	pers_inc	B	Positive(earn-pension-pension_rate*earn-Labour_market_contr)
5.	CG tax before credits	CG_tax_excl_princ	P	Low_rate*tax_inc_princ+Medium_rate*Positive(tax_inc_princ-Medium_thrsh-Married*Positive(Medium_thrsh-pers_inc_spouse))+Adj_top_rate*Positive (tax_inc_princ-Top_thrsh)
		CG_health_tax_excl_princ	P	Health_tax_rate*tax_inc_princ
		CG_tax_excl_spouse	S	Low_rate*tax_inc_spouse+Medium_rate*Positive(tax_inc_spouse-Medium_thrsh)+Adj_top_rate*Positive(tax_inc_spouse-Top_thrsh)
		CG_health_tax_excl_spouse	S	(Married=1)*Health_tax_rate*tax_inc_spouse
6.	Tax credits :	tax_cr_princ	P	Personal_al*Low_rate+Married*Positive(Personal_al-pers_inc_spouse)*Low_rate
		health_tax_cr_princ	P	Health_tax_rate*(Personal_al+Married*Positive(Personal_al-tax_inc_spouse))
		tax_cr_spouse	S	Personal_al*Low_rate
		health_tax_cr_spouse	S	(Married=1)*Health_tax_rate*Personal_al
	Labour Market Contribution	Labour_market_contr	B	Labour_market_rate*earn
7.	CG tax	CG_tax	B	Positive(CG_tax_excl-tax_cr)+Positive(CG_health_tax_excl-health_tax_cr)+Labour_market_contr
8.	State and local taxes	local_tax_princ	P	Positive((Local_rates)*(tax_inc_princ-Personal_al-Married*Positive(Personal_al-tax_inc_spouse)))
		local_tax_spouse	S	(Local_rates)*Positive(tax_inc_spouse-Personal_al)
9.	Employees' soc security contribution	SSC	B	(earn>0)*Unemp
10.	Total payments	tot_payments	J	Positive(CG_tax_total+local_tax_total+SSC_total)

	Line in country table and intermediate steps	Variable name	Range	Equation
11.	Cash transfers	cash_trans	J	Positive(((Children>0)*(Child_3to6+(Children>1)*(Children-1)*Child_7to17+(Married=0)*(Sing_par_basic+Children*Sing_par_ch)))-(Positive(earn_princ-Child_limit)*Child_red)-(Positive(earn_spouse-Child_limit)*Child_red))+IF(Married=1,(Taper(green_check,pers_inc_princ,Green_check_thrsh,Green_check_taper_rate)+Taper(green_check+MIN(Children*_1_child,child_max),pers_inc_spouse,Green_check_thrsh,Green_check_taper_rate)),Taper(green_check+MIN(Children*_1_child,child_max),pers_inc_princ, Green_check_thrsh,Green_check_taper_rate))+ IF(Married=1,(IF(pers_inc_princ<Extra_green_check_thrsh,Extra_green_check,0)+IF(pers_inc_spouse<Extra_green_check_thrsh,Extra_green_check,0)),IF(pers_inc_princ<Extra_green_check_thrsh,Extra_green_check,0))
13.	Employer's soc security	SSC_empr	B	SSC_empr*earn+SSC_ATP

Key to range of equation B calculated separately for both principal earner and spouse P calculated for principal only (value taken as 0 for spouse calculation) J calculated once only on a joint basis.

Taxing Wages 2016

Estonia

This chapter includes data on the income taxes paid by workers, their social security contributions, the family benefits they receive in the form of cash transfers as well as the social security contributions and payroll taxes paid by their employers. Results reported include the marginal and average tax burden for eight different family types.

Methodological information is available for personal income tax systems, compulsory social security contributions to schemes operated within the government sector, universal cash transfers as well as recent changes in the tax/benefit system. The methodology also includes the parameter values and tax equations underlying the data.

Estonia 2015

The tax/benefit position of single persons

		Wage level (per cent of average wage)	67	100	167	67
		Number of children	none	none	none	2
1.	**Gross wage earnings**		8 660	12 926	21 586	8 660
2.	**Standard tax allowances**					
	Basic allowance		1 848	1 848	1 848	3 696
	Married or head of family					
	Dependent children					
	Deduction for social security contributions and income taxes		139	207	345	139
	Work-related expenses		0	0	0	0
	Other					
		Total	1 987	2 055	2 193	3 835
3.	**Tax credits or cash transfers included in taxable income**		0	0	0	0
4.	**Central government taxable income (1 - 2 + 3)**		6 674	10 871	19 392	4 826
5.	**Central government income tax liability (exclusive of tax credits)**		1 335	2 174	3 878	965
6.	**Tax credits**					
	Basic credit					
	Married or head of family					
	Children		0	0	0	0
	Other					
		Total	0	0	0	0
7.	**Central government income tax finally paid (5-6)**		1 335	2 174	3 878	965
8.	**State and local taxes**		0	0	0	0
9.	**Employees' compulsory social security contributions**					
	Gross earnings		139	207	345	139
	Taxable income					
		Total	139	207	345	139
10.	**Total payments to general government (7 + 8 + 9)**		1 473	2 381	4 224	1 104
11.	**Cash transfers from general government**					
	For head of family					
	For two children		0	0	0	1 540
		Total	0	0	0	1 540
12.	**Take-home pay (1-10+11)**		7 187	10 545	17 362	9 097
13.	**Employer's compulsory social security contributions**		2 927	4 369	7 296	2 927
14.	**Average rates**					
	Income tax		15.4%	16.8%	18.0%	11.1%
	Employees' social security contributions		1.6%	1.6%	1.6%	1.6%
	Total payments less cash transfers		17.0%	18.4%	19.6%	-5.0%
	Total tax wedge including employer's social security contributions		38.0%	39.0%	39.9%	21.5%
15.	**Marginal rates**					
	Total payments less cash transfers: Principal earner		21.3%	21.3%	21.3%	21.3%
	Total payments less cash transfers: Spouse		n.a.	n.a.	n.a.	n.a.
	Total tax wedge: Principal earner		41.2%	41.2%	41.2%	41.2%
	Total tax wedge: Spouse		n.a.	n.a.	n.a.	n.a.

Estonia 2015

The tax/benefit position of married couples

			100-0	100-33	100-67	100-33
		Wage level (per cent of average wage)	100-0	100-33	100-67	100-33
		Number of children	2	2	2	none
1.	**Gross wage earnings**		12 926	17 191	21 586	17 191
2.	**Standard tax allowances**					
	Basic allowance		5 544	5 544	5 544	3 696
	Married or head of family					
	Dependent children					
	Deduction for social security contributions and income taxes		207	275	345	275
	Work-related expenses		0	0	0	0
	Other					
		Total	5 751	5 819	5 889	3 971
3.	**Tax credits or cash transfers included in taxable income**		0	0	0	0
4.	**Central government taxable income (1 - 2 + 3)**		7 175	11 372	15 696	13 220
5.	**Central government income tax liability (exclusive of tax credits)**		1 435	2 274	3 139	2 644
6.	**Tax credits**					
	Basic credit					
	Married or head of family					
	Children		0	0	0	0
	Other					
		Total	0	0	0	0
7.	**Central government income tax finally paid (5-6)**		1 435	2 274	3 139	2 644
8.	**State and local taxes**		0	0	0	0
9.	**Employees' compulsory social security contributions**					
	Gross earnings		207	275	345	275
	Taxable income					
		Total	207	275	345	275
10.	**Total payments to general government (7 + 8 + 9)**		1 642	2 549	3 485	2 919
11.	**Cash transfers from general government**					
	For head of family					
	For two children		1 080	1 080	1 080	0
		Total	1 080	1 080	1 080	0
12.	**Take-home pay (1-10+11)**		12 364	15 722	19 181	14 272
13.	**Employer's compulsory social security contributions**		4 369	5 811	7 296	5 811
14.	**Average rates**					
	Income tax		11.1%	13.2%	14.5%	15.4%
	Employees' social security contributions		1.6%	1.6%	1.6%	1.6%
	Total payments less cash transfers		4.3%	8.5%	11.1%	17.0%
	Total tax wedge including employer's social security contributions		28.5%	31.7%	33.6%	38.0%
15.	**Marginal rates**					
	Total payments less cash transfers: Principal earner		21.3%	21.3%	21.3%	21.3%
	Total payments less cash transfers: Spouse		21.3%	21.3%	21.3%	21.3%
	Total tax wedge: Principal earner		41.2%	41.2%	41.2%	41.2%
	Total tax wedge: Spouse		41.2%	41.2%	41.2%	41.2%

The Estonian currency is the Euro (EUR). In 2015, EUR 0.90 was equal to USD 1. In 2015, the average worker in Estonia earned EUR 12 925.62 (Country estimate).

1. Personal income tax system

1.1. *Central government income tax*

1.1.1. *Tax unit*

The tax unit is the family.

1.1.2. *Tax allowances*

1.1.2.1. Standard tax reliefs

- A *general (basic) allowance* of EUR 1 848 is deductible from individual income in 2015.
- A *child* allowance of EUR 1 848 is also deductible from income for each of the second and any subsequent children up to and including the age of 16.
- *Relief for social security contributions*: Employee's compulsory contributions for unemployment insurance are deductible for income tax purposes.
- *Tax credits*: None for employees

1.1.2.2. Non-standard tax reliefs applicable to income from employment

- *II pillar pension contributions*: In 2015, these represent voluntary payments to private funds for all employees and are paid at a rate of 2% or 3% of earnings.
- Occupational accident and illness benefits that are not paid as insurance benefits are deductible from taxable income within the limit of EUR 768 per year.
- *Housing loan interest, educational costs, gifts and donations* are deductible from taxable income within upper limits of EUR 1 920 and 50% of taxable income per year.
- *Voluntary pension contributions (III pillar)*: Contributions paid by a resident to the provider of a pension plan based in Estonia or in another EU Member State according to a pension plan that is approved and entered into a special register in accordance with the pension legislation are deductible from taxable income. In 2015 such deductions are subject to an annual limit of a sum equal to 15% and maximum of EUR 6 000 of the employee's, public servant`s or members of legal person management or control body income in a calendar year.

1.1.3. *Tax schedule*

The rate of 20% applies for all levels of taxable income.

1.2. *Regional and local income tax*

There are no regional or local income taxes.

2. Compulsory social security insurance system

The compulsory social security insurance system consists of three schemes as follows:

- pension insurance;
- health insurance;
- unemployment insurance.

2.1. *Employees' contributions*

Employees pay 1.6% of their earnings in contributions for unemployment insurance. The taxable base is the total amount of the gross wage or salary including vacation payments, fringe benefits and remuneration of expenses related to work above a certain threshold. The assessment period is the calendar month.

2.2. *Employers' contributions*

Social security insurance contributions are also paid by employers on behalf of their employees. The taxable base and the assessment period are the same as for employees' contributions. The employers' contribution rates are applied in two parts:

- Unemployment insurance – 0.8% of employee earnings.
- Pension and health insurance – as follows for monthly earnings above EUR 355.

Scheme name	Rate of contribution (%)
Pension insurance	20.00
Health insurance	13.00
Total	33.00

In addition there is a lump sum payment for each employee of EUR 117.15 per month (split between pensions and health insurance on a 20:13 basis).

3. Payroll tax

None.

4. Universal cash transfers

4.1. *Transfers related to marital status*

None.

4.2. *Transfers for dependent children*

Estonia's family benefits are designed to provide partial coverage of the costs families incur in caring for, raising and educating their children.

The state pays family benefits to all children until they reach the age of 16. Children enrolled in basic or secondary schools or vocational education institutions operating on the basis of basic education have the right to receive family benefits until the age of 19. Applications for the allowance are made on an annual basis and the payments are not taxable. The values of these benefits in 2015 are shown in the table below. The single parent child allowance is paid for each child.

In addition there are nine other types of family benefits for which payment depends on either the age of the child(ren) and/ or the status of the person(s) looking of them: maternity benefit; childbirth allowance; parental benefit; child care allowance; conscript's child allowance; child's school allowance, child allowance for a child under guardianship or foster care; start in independent life allowance; adoption allowance (single payment). These are not included in the modelling.

Type of benefit	Annual amount of benefit (in EUR)
Child allowance (paid until children turn 16 or until the end of the academic year in which they turn 19 if they continue studying).	
For the first and second child	540.00
For the third and any subsequent children	1 200.00
Single parent's child allowance	230.16
Parents allowance for families with seven or more children	2 024.88

5. Main changes in tax/benefit system since 2005

- The personal income tax rate was steadily reduced from 24% in 2005 to 21% in 2008. In 2015 it was reduced to 20%.
- The child tax allowance applied for the third and subsequent children for 2005 and the second and subsequent children in 2006 and 2007. It applied to all children in 2008 and then returned to the 2007 position in 2009.
- The employee unemployment contribution rate was reduced from 1% to 0.6% in 2006 and then raised in 2 stages to 2.8% at the end of 2009. The corresponding rates for employers were a reduction from 0.5 % to 0.3% in 2006 increasing to 1.4%. In 2013 the employee unemployment contribution rate was reduced from 2.8% to 2.0% and the corresponding rate for employers from 1.4% to 1.0%. In 2015 the employee unemployment contribution rate was reduced from 2.0% to 1.6% and the corresponding rate for employers from 1.0% to 0.8%.
- In addition to existing benefits, from July 1, 2013 the need-based child benefits were introduced. Need-based family benefit income threshold is based on Statistical Office relative poverty threshold published by the 1st of March in a year before current budget year. In 2015 the need-based threshold is EUR 329 in a month for the first household member. For every other at least 14-years old member the threshold is EUR 164.5 and for the younger members EUR 98.7 in a month. Need-based family benefit is in 2015 EUR 45 in a month for single child family and EUR 90 for families with two or more children.

6. Memorandum items

6.1. *Average gross annual wage earnings calculation*

In Estonia the gross earnings figures cover wages and salaries paid to individuals in formal employment including payment for overtime. They also include bonus payments and other payments such as pay for annual leave, paid leave up to seven days, public holidays, absences due to sickness for up to 30 days, job training, and slowdown through no fault of the person in formal employment.

The average gross wage earnings figures of all adult workers covering industry sectors B-N by NACE Rev. 2 are estimated with average wage growth rate forecast of Estonian Ministry of Finance.

6.2. Employer contributions to private pension and health schemes

Some employer contributions are made to private health and pension schemes but there is no relevant information available on the amounts that are paid.

2015 parameter values

Average earnings/yr	Ave_earn	12 926	Country estimate
Allowances	Basic_al	1 848	
	Child_al	1 848	
Income tax	Tax_rate	0.20	
Employers SSC	SSC_rate1	0.33	
	Threshold	4 260	
	lump_sum	1 405.8	
	SSC_rate2	0.008	
Employees SSC	SSC_rate3	0.016	
Child allowances			
First & second child	CA_first&second	540	
Other children	CA_others	1 200	
Additional for children of lone parents			
	CA_onepar	230.16	
Need-based child benefits			
one child	CB_1	540	
two or more children	CB_2	1 080	
Need-based family threshold			
first member	F_thrsh_1	3 948.00	
other members above 14	F_thrsh_2	1 974.00	
other members under 14	F_thrsh_3	1 184.40	
Days in tax year	numdays	365	

2015 tax equations

The equations for the Estonian system are mostly on an individual basis.

The functions which are used in the equations (Taper, MIN, Tax etc) are described in the technical note about tax equations. Variable names are defined in the table of parameters above, within the equations table, or are the standard variables "married" and "children". A reference to a variable with the affix "_total" indicates the sum of the relevant variable values for the principal and spouse. And the affixes "_princ" and "_spouse" indicate the value for the principal and spouse, respectively. Equations for a single person are as shown for the principal, with "_spouse" values taken as 0.

	Line in country table and intermediate steps	Variable name	Range	Equation
1.	Earnings	earn		
2.	Allowances:	tax_al	J	Min(Basic_al*(1+married)+SSC_empee+(children>1)*child_al*(Children-1),earn)
3.	Credits in taxable income	taxbl_cr	B	0
4.	CG taxable income	tax_inc	B	Positive(earn-tax_al)
5.	CG tax before credits	CG_tax_excl	B	Tax_inc*tax_rate
6.	Tax credits :	tax_cr	B	0
7.	CG tax	CG_tax	B	CG_tax_excl-tax_cr
8;	State and local taxes	local_tax	B	0
9.	Employees' soc security	SSC_empee	B	earn*SSC_rate3
11.	Cash transfers	cash_trans	J	IF(Children<3,CA_firstsecond*Children,(2*CA_firstsecond)+(CA_other*(Children-2)))+(Married=0)*Children*CA_onepar+IF((earn_total-CG_tax-SSC_empee)<(F_thrsh_1+(F_thrsh_2*Married=1)+ (F_thrsh_3*Children)),IF(Children>1, CB_2, CB_1),0)
13.	Employer's soc security	SSC_empr	B	IF(earn>0,IF(earn>threshold,earn*SSC_rate1,lump_sum),0)+earn*SSC_rate2

Key to range of equation B calculated separately for both principal earner and spouse P calculated for principal only (value taken as 0 for spouse calculation) J calculated once only on a joint basis.

Taxing Wages 2016

Finland

This chapter includes data on the income taxes paid by workers, their social security contributions, the family benefits they receive in the form of cash transfers as well as the social security contributions and payroll taxes paid by their employers. Results reported include the marginal and average tax burden for eight different family types.

Methodological information is available for personal income tax systems, compulsory social security contributions to schemes operated within the government sector, universal cash transfers as well as recent changes in the tax/benefit system. The methodology also includes the parameter values and tax equations underlying the data.

Finland 2015

The tax/benefit position of single persons

	Wage level (per cent of average wage)	67	100	167	67
	Number of children	none	none	none	2
1.	**Gross wage earnings**	29 169	43 536	72 705	29 169
2.	**Standard tax allowances**				
	Basic allowance				
	Married or head of family				
	Dependent children				
	Deduction for social security contributions and income taxes	2 080	3 104	5 184	2 080
	Work-related expenses	620	620	620	620
	Other				
	Total	2 700	3 724	5 804	2 700
3.	**Tax credits or cash transfers included in taxable income**	0	0	0	0
4.	**Central government taxable income (1 - 2 + 3)**	26 470	39 812	66 902	26 470
5.	**Central government income tax liability (exclusive of tax credits)**	851	3 186	8 990	851
6.	**Tax credits**				
	Basic credit	1 025	906	556	1 025
	Married or head of family				
	Children	0	0	0	200
	Other				
	Total	1 025	906	556	1 225
7.	**Central government income tax finally paid (5-6)**	143	2 423	8 577	143
8.	**State and local taxes**	4 510	7 449	13 084	4 510
9.	**Employees' compulsory social security contributions**				
	Gross earnings	2 080	3 104	5 184	2 080
	Taxable income	300	496	870	300
	Total	2 380	3 600	6 054	2 380
10.	**Total payments to general government (7 + 8 + 9)**	7 033	13 471	27 715	7 033
11.	**Cash transfers from general government**				
	For head of family				
	For two children	0	0	0	3 584
	Total	0	0	0	3 584
12.	**Take-home pay (1-10+11)**	22 137	30 065	44 990	25 721
13.	**Employer's compulsory social security contributions**	6 726	10 039	16 766	6 726
14.	**Average rates**				
	Income tax	16.0%	22.7%	29.8%	16.0%
	Employees' social security contributions	8.2%	8.3%	8.3%	8.2%
	Total payments less cash transfers	24.1%	30.9%	38.1%	11.8%
	Total tax wedge including employer's social security contributions	38.3%	43.9%	49.7%	28.3%
15.	**Marginal rates**				
	Total payments less cash transfers: Principal earner	44.0%	45.2%	48.9%	44.0%
	Total payments less cash transfers: Spouse	n.a.	n.a.	n.a.	n.a.
	Total tax wedge: Principal earner	54.5%	55.5%	58.5%	54.5%
	Total tax wedge: Spouse	n.a.	n.a.	n.a.	n.a.

Finland 2015

The tax/benefit position of married couples

			100-0	100-33	100-67	100-33
		Wage level (per cent of average wage)	100-0	100-33	100-67	100-33
		Number of children	2	2	2	none
1.	**Gross wage earnings**		43 536	57 903	72 705	57 903
2.	**Standard tax allowances**					
	Basic allowance					
	Married or head of family					
	Dependent children					
	Deduction for social security contributions and income taxes		3 104	4 128	5 184	4 128
	Work-related expenses		620	1 240	1 240	1 240
	Other					
		Total	3 724	5 368	6 424	5 368
3.	**Tax credits or cash transfers included in taxable income**		0	0	0	0
4.	**Central government taxable income (1 - 2 + 3)**		39 812	52 535	66 282	52 535
5.	**Central government income tax liability (exclusive of tax credits)**		3 186	3 186	4 036	3 186
6.	**Tax credits**					
	Basic credit		906	1 927	1 931	1 927
	Married or head of family					
	Children		62	162	162	0
	Other					
		Total	968	2 088	2 093	1 927
7.	**Central government income tax finally paid (5-6)**		2 361	2 454	2 504	2 516
8.	**State and local taxes**		7 449	7 939	11 958	7 939
9.	**Employees' compulsory social security contributions**					
	Gross earnings		3 104	4 128	5 184	4 128
	Taxable income		496	528	796	528
		Total	3 600	4 657	5 980	4 657
10.	**Total payments to general government (7 + 8 + 9)**		13 409	15 050	20 442	15 112
11.	**Cash transfers from general government**					
	For head of family					
	For two children		2 419	2 419	2 419	0
		Total	2 419	2 419	2 419	0
12.	**Take-home pay (1-10+11)**		32 546	45 272	54 683	42 791
13.	**Employer's compulsory social security contributions**		10 039	13 352	16 766	13 352
14.	**Average rates**					
	Income tax		22.5%	17.9%	19.9%	18.1%
	Employees' social security contributions		8.3%	8.0%	8.2%	8.0%
	Total payments less cash transfers		25.2%	21.8%	24.8%	26.1%
	Total tax wedge including employer's social security contributions		39.3%	36.5%	38.9%	39.9%
15.	**Marginal rates**					
	Total payments less cash transfers: Principal earner		46.1%	46.1%	46.1%	45.2%
	Total payments less cash transfers: Spouse		11.4%	22.4%	44.0%	22.4%
	Total tax wedge: Principal earner		56.2%	56.2%	56.2%	55.5%
	Total tax wedge: Spouse		28.0%	36.9%	54.5%	36.9%

The national currency is the Euro (EUR). In 2015, EUR 0.90 was equal to USD 1. In that year, the average worker earned EUR 43 536 (Secretariat estimate).

1. Personal income tax system

1.1. Central government income taxes

1.1.1. Tax unit

Spouses are taxed separately for earned income.

1.1.2. Standard tax allowances and tax credits

1.1.2.1. Standard reliefs

- *Work-related expenses:* A standard deduction for work-related expenses equal to the amount of wage or salary, with a maximum amount of EUR 620 is granted.
- *Tax credit*: An earned income tax credit is granted against the central government income tax. If the credit exceeds the amount of central government income tax, the excess credit is deductible from the municipal income tax and the health insurance contribution for medical care. The credit is calculated on the basis of taxpayers' income from work. The credit amounts to 8.6% of income exceeding EUR 2 500, until it reaches its maximum of EUR 1 025. The amount of the credit is reduced by 1.2% of the earned income minus work related expenses exceeding EUR 33 000. The credit is fully phased out when taxpayers' income is about EUR 119 000.
- *Child tax credit:* The credit is granted to taxpayers who have children in their care and custody according to the Population Register System records. It is given for four children at most. All parents and custodians get it regardless of which one of them has the child(ren) living with them. The size of the child tax credit depends on the number of children and whether the taxpayer has joint custody or single custody: for joint custody the credit is EUR 50 per year and child, and for single custody it is EUR 100 per year and child. If net taxable income exceeds EUR 36 000 per year (earned income and capital income combined), the credit is reduced. For the part of the income exceeding the threshold, the amount to be credited is phased out by a one percentage point rate. The child tax credit is will be in force from 2015 through 2017.

1.1.2.2. Main non-standard tax reliefs applicable to an AW

- *Interest:* Interest on loans associated with the earning of taxable income, 65% of the interest on loans for the purchase of owner-occupied dwellings, and student loans guaranteed by the state can be deducted against capital income. Of the excess of interest over capital income, 30% (32% for first-time homebuyers) can be credited against income tax up to a maximum of EUR 1 400.
- *Membership fees:* Membership fees paid to employees' organisations or trade unions.

- *Travelling expenses:* Travelling expenses from the place of residence to the place of employment using the cheapest means in excess of EUR 750 up to a maximum deduction of EUR 7 000.
- *Double housing expenses*: If the place of employment is located too far from home in order to commute (distance > 100 km), the taxpayer can deduct the costs of hiring a second dwelling located near the place of work up to EUR 250 per month. This deduction can be claimed only by one person per household.
- *Other work-related outlays:* Outlays for tools, professional literature, research equipment and scientific literature, and expenses incurred in scientific or artistic work (unless compensated by scholarships).

Travelling expenses and other work-related outlays are deductible only to the extent that their total amount exceeds the amount of the standard deduction for work-related expenses.

1.1.3. *Rate schedule*

Central government income tax:

Taxable income (EUR)	Tax on lower limit (EUR)	Tax on excess income in bracket (%)
16 500-24 700	8	6.5
24 700-40 300	541	17.5
40 300-71 400	3 271	21.5
71 400-90 000	9 957.5	29.75
90 000 and more	15 491	31.75

1.2. *Local income tax*

1.2.1. *Tax base and tax rates*

The tax base of the local income tax is taxable income as established for the income tax levied by central government.

Municipal tax is levied at flat rates. In 2015 the tax rate varies between 16.50 and 22.50%, the average rate being approximately 19.84%.

Municipal tax is not deductible against central government taxes. Work-related expenses and other non-standard deductions are deductible, as for purposes of the central government income tax.

1.2.2. *Tax allowances in municipal income taxation*

- An earned income tax allowance is calculated on the basis of taxpayer's income from work. The allowance amounts to 51% of income between EUR 2 500 and EUR 7 230 and 28% of the income exceeding EUR 7 230, until it reaches its maximum of EUR 3 570. The amount of the allowance is reduced by 4.5% on earned income minus work related expenses exceeding EUR 14 000.
- A basic tax allowance is granted on the basis of taxable income remaining after the other allowances have been subtracted. The maximum amount, EUR 2 970, is reduced by 18% on income exceeding the aforementioned amount.

2. Compulsory social security contributions to schemes operated within the government sector

2.1. Employee contributions

2.1.1. Rate and ceiling

In 2015, the rate of the health insurance contribution for medical care paid by an employee is 1.32%. The tax base for this contribution is net taxable income for municipal income tax purposes.

In addition there is an employees' pension insurance contribution which amounts to 5.70% of gross salary, an employees' unemployment insurance contribution equal to 0.65% of gross salary and a health insurance contribution for daily allowance equal to 0.78% of gross salary. For employees aged 53 and older, the pension insurance contribution amounts to 7.30% of gross salary. These contributions are deductible for income tax purposes.

2.1.2. Distinction by marital status or sex

The rates do not differ.

2.2. Employers' contributions

The average rate of the employers' social security contribution in 2015 is 23.06% of gross wage.

3. Universal cash transfers

3.1. Amount for marriage

None.

3.2. Amount for children

The central government pays in 2015 the following allowances (EUR):

For the first child	1 149.00
For the second child	1 269.6
For the third child	1 620.12
For the fourth child	1 855.68
Fifth and subsequent child	2 091.24

The child subsidy for a single parent is increased by an annual amount of EUR 582.6 for each child.

4. Main changes in the tax/benefit system since 2014

As a means to compensate low to middle income earners for a 8% cut in child benefits a temporary (2015-17) child tax credit was introduced. The credit is granted to taxpayers who have children in their care and custody. It is given for four children at most. For joint custody parents the credit is 50 EUR per year and child, and for single custody parents it is 100 EUR per year and child.

Adjustments for inflation and rise of earnings levels were, with exception of the two top brackets, made to the central government tax scale in 2015.

In 2014 the public broadcasting tax is 0.68% on taxable earned income, taxes of min. EUR 51 and max. EUR 143 will be collected.

The maximum amount of the earned income tax credit in state taxation was raised from EUR 1 010 to EUR 1 025.

The maximum amount of the basic allowance in municipal taxation was raised from EUR 2 930 to EUR 2 970.

Home-loan interest counts at 65%, down from 75%, as deductible/creditable interest.

5. Memorandum items

5.1. *Calculation of average gross annual wage*

The Finnish figures are generally calculated as follows:

- Gross annual earnings are calculated at an individual level on the basis of the hour's usually worked, average hourly pay for the fourth quarter, and the share of annual periodic bonuses.
- The earnings exclude sickness and unemployment compensations, but include all normal overtime compensations, bonuses, holiday remunerations and remunerations for public holidays.

5.2. *Employer contributions to private pension and health schemes*

No information is available.

2015 parameter values

Average earnings	Ave_earn	43 536	Secretariat estimate
Expenses	Work_exp_max	620	
	Work_exp_rate	1	
Allowances	al_SSC_rate	0.0713	
State tax	Tax_min	8	
Tax schedule	Tax_sch	0	16 500
		0.065	24 700
		0.175	40 300
		0.215	71 400
		0.2975	90 000
		0.3175	
Broadcasting tax	brdcst_tax_rate	0.0068	
	brdcst_tax_min	51	
	brdcst_tax_max	143	
Earned income tax credit	eitc_thrsh	2 500	
	eitc_rate	0.086	
	eitc_redn_thrsh	33 000	
	eitc_redn_rate	0.012	
	eitc_max	1 025	
Child tax credit	child_cr	50	
	child_thres	36 000	
	child_red	0.01	
Earned income tax allowance	al_thrsh	2 500	
	al_thrsh2	7 230	
	al_rate	0.51	
	al_rate2	0.28	
	al_redn_thrsh	14 000	
	al_redn_rate	0.045	
	al_max	3 570	
low income	SL_max	2 970	
	SL_rate	0.18	
Local intax	Local_rate	0.1984	
	Church_rate	0	
	Local_tot	0.1984	
Soc sec taxpayer	SSC_rate	0.0132	
soc.sec empr	SSC_empr	0.2306	
Cash transfer	ch_1	1 149.00	
	ch_2	1 269.60	
	ch_3	1 620.12	
	ch_4	1 855.68	
	ch_5	2 091.24	
	ch_small	0	
	ch_lone	582.6	

2015 tax equations

The equations for the Finnish system are mostly on an individual basis except for the child benefit which is calculated only once. This is shown by the Range indicator in the table below.

The functions which are used in the equations (Taper, MIN, Tax etc) are described in the technical note about tax equations.

Variable names are defined in the table of parameters above, within the equations table, or are the standard variables "married" and "children". A reference to a variable with the affix "_total" indicates the sum of the relevant variable values for the principal and spouse. And the affixes "_princ" and "_spouse" indicate the value for the principal and spouse, respectively. Equations for a single person are as shown for the principal, with "_spouse" values taken as 0.

	Line in country table and intermediate steps	Variable name	Range	Equation
1.	Earnings	earn		
	Work related expenses	work_rel	B	MIN(Work_exp_max, Work_exp_rate*earn)
	SSC deduction	SSC_al	B	earn*al_SSC_rate
2.	Allowances:	tax_al	B	work_rel+SSC_al
3.	Credits in taxable income	taxbl_cr	B	0
4.	CG taxable income	tax_inc	B	Positive(earn-tax_al)
5.	CG tax before credits	CG_tax_excl	B	=Tax(tax_inc, Tax_sch)+Tax_min* (tax_inc>Tax_thrsh)
6.	Tax credits :	tax_cr	B	MINA(eitc_max,eitc_rate*Positive(earn-eitc_thrsh))-MINA(eitc_max,eitc_redn_rate*Positive(earn-work_rel-eitc_redn_thrsh))
	Child tax credit	child_cr	P	taper(child_cr*(1+(married=0))*children,tax_inc_p,child_thres,child_red)
			S	If(tax_inc_s>0,taper(child_cr*children,tax_inc_s,child_thres,child_red),0)
		broadcasting_tax	B	IF((earn-work_rel)*brdcst_tax_rate<brdcst_tax_min,0,IF((earn-work_rel)*brdcst_tax_rate>brdcst_tax_max,brdcst_tax_max,(earn-work_rel)*brdcst_tax_rate))
7.	CG tax	CG_tax	B	Positive(CG_tax_excl - tax_cr-child_cr)+broadcasting_tax
	Earned income allowance	earninc_al	B	MIN(al_max, IF(earn>al_thrsh2, al_rate*(al_thrsh2-al_thrsh1)+al_rate2*(earn-al_thrsh2), Positive(earn-al_thrsh)))- MIN(al_max, al_redn_rate* Positive(earn-work_rel-al_redn_thrsh))
	Low income	low_inc	B	Positive(MIN(earn-work_rel-low_al-SSC_al, SL_max)- SL_rate*Positive(earn-work_rel- low_al-SSC_al-SL_max))
	Taxable income (local)	tax_inc_l	B	tax_inc-earninc_al-low_inc
8.	State and local taxes	local_tax	B	Positive(tax_inc_l*Local_tot-(local_tot/(local_tot+SSC_rate))*Positive(Tax_cr-CG_tax_excl))
9.	Employees' soc security	SSC	B	Positive(SSC_rate*tax_inc_l – (SSC_rate/(local_tot+SSC_rate))*Positive(Tax_cr-CG_tax_excl)) + SSC_al
11.	Cash transfers	cash_trans	J	(Children>0)*ch_1+(Children>1)*ch_2+ (Children>2)*ch_3+ (Children>3)*ch_4+ Positive(Children-4)*ch_4 +(Married=0)*Children*ch_lone
13.	Employer's soc security	SSC_empr	B	earn*SSC_empr

Key to range of equation B calculated separately for both principal earner and spouse P calculated for principal only (value taken as 0 for spouse calculation) J calculated once only on a joint basis.

France

This chapter includes data on the income taxes paid by workers, their social security contributions, the family benefits they receive in the form of cash transfers as well as the social security contributions and payroll taxes paid by their employers. Results reported include the marginal and average tax burden for eight different family types.

Methodological information is available for personal income tax systems, compulsory social security contributions to schemes operated within the government sector, universal cash transfers as well as recent changes in the tax/benefit system. The methodology also includes the parameter values and tax equations underlying the data.

France 2015

The tax/benefit position of single persons

		Wage level (per cent of average wage)	67	100	167	67
		Number of children	none	none	none	2
1.	**Gross wage earnings**		25 321	37 792	63 113	25 321
2.	**Standard tax allowances**					
	Basic allowance					
	Married or head of family					
	Dependent children					
	Deduction for social security contributions and income taxes		4 864	7 260	11 686	4 864
	Work-related expenses		2 046	3 053	5 143	2 046
	Other					
		Total	6 910	10 313	16 828	6 910
3.	**Tax credits or cash transfers included in taxable income**		0	0	0	0
4.	**Central government taxable income (1 - 2 + 3)**		18 411	27 479	46 285	18 411
5.	**Central government income tax liability (exclusive of tax credits)**		2 960	5 570	13 201	1 990
6.	**Tax credits**					
	Basic credit					
	Married or head of family					
	Children					
	Other		0	0	0	0
		Total	0	0	0	0
7.	**Central government income tax finally paid (5-6)**		2 960	5 570	13 201	1 990
8.	**State and local taxes**		0	0	0	0
9.	**Employees' compulsory social security contributions**					
	Gross earnings		3 596	5 366	8 523	3 596
	Taxable income					
		Total	3 596	5 366	8 523	3 596
10.	**Total payments to general government (7 + 8 + 9)**		6 555	10 936	21 725	5 586
11.	**Cash transfers from general government**					
	For head of family (Gross)					
	For two children (Gross)		0	0	0	1 560
	CRDS Deducted		0	0	0	- 8
		Total	0	0	0	1 552
12.	**Take-home pay (1-10+11)**		18 766	26 856	41 388	21 287
13.	**Employers' compulsory social security contributions**		7 875	14 312	27 462	7 875
14.	**Average rates**					
	Income tax		11.7%	14.7%	20.9%	7.9%
	Employees' social security contributions		14.2%	14.2%	13.5%	14.2%
	Total payments less cash transfers		25.9%	28.9%	34.4%	15.9%
	Total tax wedge including employer's social security contributions		43.5%	48.5%	54.3%	35.9%
15.	**Marginal rates**					
	Total payments less cash transfers: Principal earner		39.9%	43.9%	42.6%	22.1%
	Total payments less cash transfers: Spouse		n.a.	n.a.	n.a.	n.a.
	Total tax wedge: Principal earner		67.2%	59.3%	59.8%	57.5%
	Total tax wedge: Spouse		n.a.	n.a.	n.a.	n.a.

France 2015

The tax/benefit position of married couples

			Wage level (per cent of average wage)	100-0	100-33	100-67	100-33
			Number of children	2	2	2	none
1.	**Gross wage earnings**			37 792	50 264	63 113	50 264
2.	**Standard tax allowances**						
	Basic allowance						
	Married or head of family						
	Dependent children						
	Deduction for social security contributions and income taxes			7 260	9 656	12 124	9 656
	Work-related expenses			3 053	4 061	5 099	4 061
	Other						
			Total	10 313	13 717	17 223	13 717
3.	**Tax credits or cash transfers included in taxable income**			0	0	0	0
4.	**Central government taxable income (1 - 2 + 3)**			27 479	36 547	45 890	36 547
5.	**Central government income tax liability (exclusive of tax credits)**			2 970	3 951	7 154	6 232
6.	**Tax credits**						
	Basic credit						
	Married or head of family						
	Children						
	Other			0	0	0	0
			Total	0	0	0	0
7.	**Central government income tax finally paid (5-6)**			2 970	3 951	7 154	6 232
8.	**State and local taxes**			0	0	0	0
9.	**Employees' compulsory social security contributions**						
	Gross earnings			5 366	7 137	8 962	7 137
	Taxable income						
			Total	5 366	7 137	8 962	7 137
10.	**Total payments to general government (7 + 8 + 9)**			8 337	11 088	16 116	13 369
11.	**Cash transfers from general government**						
	For head of family (Gross)						
	For two children (Gross)			1 560	1 560	1 560	0
	CRDS Deducted			- 8	- 8	- 8	0
			Total	1 552	1 552	1 552	0
12.	**Take-home pay (1-10+11)**			31 007	40 728	48 549	36 894
13.	**Employers' compulsory social security contributions**			14 312	15 275	22 187	15 275
14.	**Average rates**						
	Income tax			7.9%	7.9%	11.3%	12.4%
	Employees' social security contributions			14.2%	14.2%	14.2%	14.2%
	Total payments less cash transfers			18.0%	19.0%	23.1%	26.6%
	Total tax wedge including employer's social security contributions			40.5%	37.9%	43.1%	43.7%
15.	**Marginal rates**						
	Total payments less cash transfers: Principal earner			22.1%	22.1%	39.9%	39.9%
	Total payments less cash transfers: Spouse			22.1%	22.1%	39.9%	39.9%
	Total tax wedge: Principal earner			43.5%	43.5%	56.4%	56.4%
	Total tax wedge: Spouse			27.6%	27.6%	67.2%	44.2%

The national currency is the euro (EUR). In 2015, EUR 0.90 equalled USD 1. In that year, the average worker earned EUR 37 792 (Secretariat estimate).

1. Personal income tax system

1.1. *Tax levied by the central government on 2015 income*

1.1.1. *Tax unit*

The tax unit is aggregate family income, but children over 18 are included only if their parents claim them as dependants. Other persons may be fiscally attached on certain conditions: unlike spouses, who are always taxed jointly, children over 18 and other members of the household may opt to be taxed separately. Beginning with the taxation of 2004 income, the law provides for joint taxation of partners in a French civil union (*pacte civil de solidarité*, or PACS), as soon as the PACS is signed. Reporting obligations for "PACSed" partners are similar to those of married couples.

Earned income is reported net of compulsory employer and employee payroll deductions, except for 2.4 percentage points' worth of CSG (*contribution sociale généralisée*) and the 0.5 % CRDS (*contribution pour le remboursement de la dette sociale*), which are not deductible from the income tax base.

1.1.2. *Tax reliefs and tax credits*

1.1.2.1. Standard tax reliefs

- Work-related expenses, corresponding to actual amounts or a standard allowance of 10% of net pay (with a minimum of EUR 426 and a ceiling of EUR 12 169 per earner).
- Family status: The "family quotient" (*quotient familial*) system takes a taxpayer's marital status and family responsibilities into account. It involves dividing net taxable income into a certain number of shares [two shares for a married (or "PACSed") couple, one share for a single person, one half-share for each dependent child, an additional half-share for the third and each subsequent dependent child, an additional half-share for single parent, and so on]: the total tax due is equal to the amount of tax corresponding to one share multiplied by the total number of shares. The tax benefit for a half-share is limited, however, to EUR 1 510 per half-share in excess of two shares for a couple, or one share for a single person, except for the first two half-shares granted for the first child of a single parent, in which case the maximum benefit is EUR 3 562.

1.1.2.2. Main non-standard reliefs available to the average worker

Certain expenditures to improve or maintain the taxpayer's primary residence, including outlays for heat insulation or heating adjustments, major capital expenditures and money spent to equip a home to produce energy from a renewable source (30% tax credits, subject to a multi-year maximum); compensatory allowances in case of divorce if paid in a lump sum (25% reduction, capped at EUR 30 500); child care costs for children under seven (50% reduction, up to annual expenditure of EUR 2 300); dependent children attending secondary school or in higher education; donations to charities or other organisations assisting those in needs; trade union dues, etc. The exemption of the employer's participation to the collective contracts of supplementary health cover is abolished in the budget act for 2014 (i.e. income earned in 2013).

1.1.2.3. Refundable tax credit: employment premium (*prime pour l'emploi*, or PPE)

This is a tax credit for households comprising wage-earners whose equivalent full-time net taxable earned income was between EUR 3 743 and EUR 26 572. The credit is determined in a multi-step calculation. First, the amount of the premium is calculated for each eligible wage-earner, and then the individual amounts are aggregated. The resulting amount may then be increased under certain conditions (dependent children or single-parent wage-earner). It is this final amount that is deducted from the family's tax liability. However, the credit is attributed only if the household's reference taxable income does not exceed the following limits: EUR 16 251 for a single person, EUR 25 231 for a single-parent family with two children, EUR 32 498 for a married or PACSed couple with no children, EUR 41 478 for a married or PACSed couple with two children. The credit was increased sharply, since the maximum individual amount was raised to EUR 960 in 2008. The PPE is not paid if it is less than EUR 30.

In the event of part-time work, the income used to compute the amount of the credit is converted to a full-time equivalent, and the resulting credit is then adjusted to the actual amount of time worked and increased The increase has been raised: in 2007 (2006 income), the PPE of persons whose work ratio is 50% (persons working half-time all year or full-time for six months) amounts to 92.5% of the PPE of persons working full-time all year, versus 82.5% in 2006.

The following table shows the applicable schedule for computing the employment premium by income level and type of family, as selected by the OECD:

Family status	Full-time equivalent annual earnings between	Amount of employment premium (PPE)	Increase for family responsibilities	
Single person with no children	EUR 3 743 < R < = EUR 12 475	R*7.7%		
	EUR 12 475 < R < = EUR 17 451	(EUR 17 451 -R) * 19.3 %		
			Childless	Two children
Two-earner couple (married/PACSed)	EUR 3 743 < R < = EUR 12 475	R*7.7%	-	EUR 72
	EUR 12 475 < R < = EUR 17 451	(EUR 17 451 -R) * 19.3 %	-	EUR 72
			Childless	Two children
Single-earner couple (married/PACSed)	EUR 3 743 < R < = EUR 12 475	R*7.7% + EUR 83	-	EUR 72
	EUR 12 475 < R < = EUR 17 451	(EUR 17 451 -R)*19.3%+ EUR 83	-	EUR 72
	EUR 17 451 < R < = EUR 24 950	EUR 83	-	EUR 36
	EUR 24 950 < R < = EUR 26 572	(EUR 26 572 -R)* 5.1%	-	EUR 36
Single-parent family with two children	EUR 3 743 < R < = EUR 12 475	R*7.7%	EUR 108	
	EUR 12 475 < R < = EUR 17 451	(EUR 17 451 -R) * 19.3 %	EUR 108	
	EUR 17 451 < R < = EUR 26 572	0	EUR 72	

The PPE is increased for dependants in a household, and whether a married/PACSed couple has one or two earners can also affect the amount of the credit (with the amount for single-earner couples increased by EUR 83). The PPE is increased by EUR 36 for each dependent child, except in special cases (*e.g.* single-earner married/PACSed PPE recipients in the top two income brackets).

For the seventh consecutive year, the government decided to continue the freeze on the PPE scale for 2014.

Since 2010 personal income tax, the PPE is partly replaced by a new cash transfer benefit implemented in July 2009: the RSA (active solidarity income). This cash transfer ensures households earn a minimum income that increases with the number of hours worked. The RSA is not assessed here because to do so the knowledge of every cash transfer of the households (such as cash transfers for housing, unemployment etc.) is needed. The RSA is designed to meet three goals:

- encourage people to enter or return to the labour market, by guaranteeing them a lasting improvement in income;
- reduce poverty by providing recipients with a decent income;
- improve social support and occupational reintegration.

The RSA is a benefit that supersedes two existing basic welfare payments, the so called "revenu minimum d'insertion" (minimum unemployment benefit – RMI) and the so called "allocation de parent isolé" (single-parent allowance – API). It also replaces temporary payments for welfare recipients who return to work ("prime de retour à l'emploi", "prime forfaitaire de retour à l'emploi" bonuses and the "intéressement proportionnel" system of benefits combined with part-time work). However, the eight family types studied here earn too high an income to benefit from this credit.

Starting from 2016, the PPE and the part of the RSA dedicated to workers ("RSA activité") will be replaced by the "prime d'activité". It will be a cash transfer benefit (as the RSA). It has not been included in the model as it concerns incomes earned starting from 2016. **In the model, the removal of the PPE is not compensated by the creation of the "prime d'activité".**

1.1.3. *Tax schedule*

	Fraction of taxable income (1 share, in Euros)	Rate (in %)
1st bracket	Up to 9 700	0
2nd bracket	From 9 700 to 26 791	14
3rd bracket	From 26 791 to 71 826	30
4th bracket	From 71 826 to 152 108	41
5th bracket	From 152 108	45

A special rebate for taxpayers with a low tax liability is applied to the amount of tax resulting from the above schedule before reductions and tax credits. To be eligible, the tax on the household's income must be less than EUR 1 553 for single households and less than 2 560 for the couples. The rebate is equal to the three-quarter of the difference between this ceiling and the amount of tax before the rebate. If the final tax is less than EUR 61, no tax is payable.

1.1.4. *Exceptional contribution on high revenues*

An exceptional contribution on high revenues is based on the reference taxable income ("revenu fiscal de référence"). The tax rates are 3% from EUR 250 000 to EUR 500 0000 (single person), 4% over EUR 500 0000 (single person), 3% from EUR 500 000 to EUR 1 000 000 (married couple or civil union) and 4% over EUR 1 000 000 (married couple or civil unions).

1.2. *Taxes levied by decentralised authorities*

Local taxes levied on working households are:

- Residency tax (*taxe d'habitation*), which is set by local authorities;
- Property taxes on developed and undeveloped land;
- There are common rules for each type of tax, to which certain municipalities make certain adjustments.

These local taxes, the rates of which vary widely, depending on the municipality, are not assessed here.

1.3. *Universal social contribution (contribution sociale généralisée, or CSG)*

The universal social contribution (CSG) was introduced on 1 February 1991. Since 1 January 1998, the rate of CSG has been 7.5%. This rate has been applied to a base of 98.25% as of 1 January 2012. The CSG is deductible against taxable income, but at a lower rate of 5.1%.

1.4. *Contribution to the reimbursement of social debt (contribution au remboursement de la dette sociale, or CRDS)*

The contribution to the reimbursement of social debt has been in effect since 1 February 1997. Like the universal social contribution, its base has passed to 98.25% of gross pay as of 1 January 2012. The rate is set at 0.5%. Unlike social security contributions, CRDS payments are not deductible from taxable income.

2. Compulsory social security contributions to schemes operated within the government sector

Some contributions are levied on a capped portion of monthly earnings. Since 1997, this ceiling has been adjusted once a year on 1 January. In January 2015, the ceiling was EUR 3 170 (or EUR 38 040 per year).

2.1. *Employee contributions*

2.1.1. *Pension*

- 6.85% on earnings up to the ceiling (6.80% in 2014).
- 0.30% on total earnings (0.25 in 2014).

2.1.2. *Illness, pregnancy, disability, death*

- 0.75% on total earnings.

2.1.3. *Unemployment*

- 2.4% on earnings up to 4 times the ceiling.

2.1.4. *Others*

- Supplemental pension* for non-managers: minimum 3.1% (3.05 in 2014) up to the ceiling and 8.1% between one and three times the ceiling; for managers, 3.23% (3.18 in 2014) up to the ceiling and 7.93% (7.88 in 2014) between one and four times the ceiling.**

* The social protection scheme is named ARRCO for non-managers and AGIRC for managers.

** Between four and eight times the ceiling, the repartition of the pension contributions between employee and employer contribution is not nationally decided.

- The AGFF (Association pour la gestion du fonds de financement) contribution replaces ASF (Association pour la gestion de la structure financière), which had previously been included in "unemployment" levies. The rate of this contribution for non-managerial workers is 0.8% of earnings up to the social security ceiling plus 0.9% of any income in excess of the ceiling but not exceeding triple the amount of the ceiling.

2.2. Employer contributions

2.2.1. Pensions

8.5% (8.45% in 2014) of gross pay, up to the ceiling, plus a 1.80% (1.75 in 2014) levy on total pay.

2.2.2. Illness, pregnancy, disability, death

12.8% of total earnings.

An additional contribution of 0.3% (contribution de solidarité autonomie – (CSA) is levied on total salary.

2.2.3. Unemployment

4% of earnings (4.5%, 5.5% or 7% for some temporary contracts), up to four times the ceiling; in addition, 0.3% up to four times the ceiling to endow the salary guarantee fund (AGS).

2.2.4. Work-related accidents

Contribution rates for work-related accidents vary by line of business and are published annually in the official gazette (*Journal officiel de la République française*). In 2015, the average rate is 2.44%.

2.2.5. Family allowances

5.25% of total pay. The rate has been reduced to 3.45% up to 1.6 times the minimum wage from 2015 with the responsibility pact.

2.2.6. Others

- Supplemental pension: for non-managers, 4.65% (4.58 in 2014) up to the ceiling and 12.15% (12.08 in 2014) between one and three times the ceiling; for managers, 4.87% up (4.80 in 2014) to the ceiling and 12.97% (12.90 in 2014) between one and four times the ceiling.
- The AGFF contribution is 1.2% for non-managers or managers up to the ceiling, 1.3% for non-managers between one and three times the ceiling and 1.3% for managers between one and four times the ceiling. In the table, this is combined with the rates for supplemental pensions.
- Others (construction, housing, apprenticeship, further training): 2.63% (3.23 in 2014) of pay (for enterprises with more than 20 employees). The transport tax is not included because it varies geographically.

2.2.7. Reduction of employer-paid social insurance contributions

Act No. 2003-47 of 17 January 2003 on salaries, working time and the development of employment (the "Fillon Act") amended how the reduction of contributions is calculated.

As a result, since 1 July 2005 the maximum reduction has been 26% (in companies with more than 20 employees) for a worker paid the minimum wage. It then declines gradually to zero at 160% of the annual minimum wage. It applies irrespective of the number of hours worked.

The Budget Act for 2007 (Article 41 V) bolsters this measure for very small enterprises with effect from 1 July 2007. For employers with between 1 and 19 employees, the maximum deduction was raised to 28.1% at the minimum wage, declining gradually – here too – to zero at 160% of the minimum wage.

In 1 January 2011 the "Fillon act" was modified and included an annualized calculation of the general tax reliefs of employer contributions. For part-time wage-earners, the relief is computed using an equivalent full-time salary and is then adjusted proportionally to the number of hours paid.

From 2015, the Responsibility Pact (Phase 1) includes new reductions of the labour cost: total exemption of all URSSAF employer contributions on the minimum wage (except unemployment contributions); reduction of 1.8 point on employer-paid contributions for family allowance (3.45% instead of 5.25% for salary up to 1.6 times the minimum wage). The gross annual minimum wage (for 1 820 hours) in 2015 was an estimated EUR 17 490.

2.2.8. Competitive tax credit (CICE – Crédit d'impôt pour la compétitivité et l'emploi)

As for 2014, the competitive tax credit (CICE – Crédit d'impôt pour la compétitivité et l'emploi) will benefit all businesses, regardless of their legal status or economic sector, that employ salaried workers and be liable for either corporation tax or income tax, based on actual profits.

The CICE is based on all wages paid to salaried employees in a given calendar year up to 2.5 times the minimum wage (without taking into account any overtime or additional hours worked). For part-time employees and seasonal workers, the minimum wage corresponding to the working hours stipulated in the contract shall be taken into account.

The rate of the tax credit shall be 6% for wages paid in 2015.

3. Universal cash transfers

Main family benefits (in respect of dependent children)

- Family allowances: monthly base for family allowances (BMAF) = EUR 406.21 as of 1 April 2015 (as of 1 April 2014). Rate: since 1 July 2015 the family allowances are subject to revenue conditions:
  - Up to 55 950 (+5 595 per child), the rate is 32% for two children and 41% per additional child. An extra amount of 16 % of the BMAF is reversed if the child is over 14 (the extra amount is not incorporated into the model).
  - Between 55 950 (+5 595 per child) and 78 300 (+5 595 per child), the above rates are divided by 2.
  - Beyond 78 300 (+5 595 per child), the above rates are divided by 4.
- ARS (Allocation de Rentrée Scolaire): The amount payable depends on the age of the child to reflect needs. The allowance is payable to families or persons with children aged 6 to 18 attending school, and whose income is below a certain level (not incorporated into the model).

Age of the child	Percentage of the BMAF in September 2014
6-10 years	89.72%
11-14 years	94.67%
15-18 years	97.95%

- Family supplement (Complément Familial): 41.65% of the BMAF at 1 January 2015. Subject to revenue ceilings, this is paid to families as of the third child and an extra amount (EUR 29.49/month) is reversed for families whose incomes are below the poverty line (the CF is not incorporated into the model).
- Early childhood benefit (not incorporated in the model) known as PAJE (Prestation d'Accueil du Jeune Enfant): subject to revenue ceilings. It includes:
  - A birth grant of EUR 918.5 received at the 7th month of pregnancy.
  - A benefit ("allocation de base") of 183.7 (or 91.8 depending on revenue) Euros a month from the birth of the child until three years of age.
- The CRDS is levied on family allowances at a rate of 0.5% (no deduction). The allowances mentioned above are after deduction of the CRDS.

4. Main changes in the tax system and social benefits regime since the taxation of 2014 income

- Tax system (2015 income)
- Creation of a new cash transfer benefit for low income workers ("*prime d'activité*") which replace the PPE and the RSA.*
- Extension of the rebate for taxpayers with a low tax liability.
- Social benefits regime
- Reduction of employer-paid contributions for family allowance (3.45% instead of 5.25% for salary up to 1.6 times the minimum wage).
- The modulation of family allowances based on income (divided by 2 or 4 for high-income families).

5. Memorandum items

To assess the degree of comparability between countries, the following additional information should be taken into account:

- Coverage is of the private and semi-public sectors of NACE sections C to K up to 2007 and NACE rev. 2 sections B to N from 2008.
- The category "employees" encompasses all full-time dependent employees (excluding apprentices and interns).
- The figures presented are obtained by applying income tax and social contribution scales to gross salaries as listed in annual social data reports (DADS) in NACE.

* In the model, for 2015 revenues, this reform only affects the income tax (no PPE in 2016) but not the benefits, since the "prime d'activité" will be served as from the beginning of 2016.

2015 parameter values

Average earnings/yr	Ave_earn	37 792	(Secretariat estimate)
Work expenses	work_rel_fl	426	
	work_rel_ceil	12 169	
	work_rel_rate	0.1	
Tax schedule	tax_sch	0	9 700
		0.14	26 791
		0.3	71 826
		0.41	152 108
		0.45	
	limit_demipart	1 510	
	limit_sp_demipart1	3 562	
Décote value	decote_sing	1 553	
	decote_mar	2 560	
	decote_pente	0.75	
	tax_min	61	
CEHR	cehr_rate1	0.03	
	cehr_rate2	0.04	
	cehr_ceil1	250 000	
	cehr_ceil2	500 000	
CSG+CRDS	CSG_CRDS_abat	0.0175	
	CSG_rat_noded	0.0240	
	CRDS_rat_noded	0.0050	
	CSG_CRDS_rat_noded	0.0290	
	CSG_rat_ded	0.0510	
	CRDS_special	0.0050	
Social security contributions	SSC_ceil	38 040	
	pension_rate	0.685	
	pension_rate2	0.003	
	sickness_rate	0.0075	
	unemp_rate	0.0240	
Extra pension (non-cadres) (incl. AGFF)	pens_rate_ex	0.0390	
	pens_rate_ex2	0.090	
Employer contributions	pens_empr1	0.0850	
	pens_empr2	0.0180	
Authonomous Solidarity Contribution	sickness_empr	0.1280	
	CSA	0.0030	
Unemployment (incl. "garantie de salaire")	unemp_empr	0.0430	
Accidents	accidents_empr	0.0244	
	SMIC	17 490.2	
Family Allowance	fam_empr	0.0525	
	fam_empr_2	0.0345	
Extra pension (incl. AGFF)	pens_empr_ex	0.0585	
	pens_empr_ex2	0.1345	
Others	others_empr	0.0263	
	others_empr2	0.0263	
Transitory Empl. SSC reduction rate	SSC_empr_redrate1	0	
Employer SSC reduction rate	SSC_empr_redrate2	0.6	
Employer SSC reduction maximum	SSC_empr_red_max	0.2835	
Employer SSC reduction SMIC reference	SSC_empr_SMIC_ref	1.6	
Child benefit (second child) before CRDS	CB_2	1 559.96	

2015 parameter values

third and subsequent before CRDS	CB_3	1 998.58
First ceiling for CB	CB_c1	55 950
Second ceiling for CB	CB_c2	78 300.00
Increase of ceiling per child	CB_ceiling_extra_child	5 595.00
Derivation of minimum income	SMIC_horaire	9.61
	SMIC_heures	1 820
	minrevtp	17 490.2
Taux de réduction CICE	cice_red	0.06
	cice_max	2.5

2015 tax equations

The equations for the French system are mostly calculated on a family basis. Variable names are defined in the table of parameters above, within the equations table, or are the standard variables "married" and "children". A reference to a variable with the affix "_total" indicates the sum of the relevant variable values for the principal and spouse. And the affixes "_princ" and "_spouse" indicate the value for the principal and spouse, respectively. Equations for a single person are as shown for the principal, with "_spouse" values taken as 0.

	Line in country table and intermediate steps	Variable name	Range	Equation
1.	Earnings	earn		
	Quotient for tax calculation	quotient	J	1+Married+IF(Children<3, Children/2, Children-1)+0.5*(Married=0)*(Children>0)
2.	Allowances:			
	CSG deductible	CSG_ded	B	CSG_rat_ded*((1-CSG_CRDS_abat)*MIN(earn;4*SSC_ceil)+Positive(earn-4*SSC_ceil))
	Salary net	earn_dec	B	earn-SSC-CSG_ded
	Work related	work_exp	B	MIN(work_rel_ceil, MAX(work_rel_rate* earn_dec, MIN(work_rel_fl, earn_dec)))
	Basic	basic_al	B	0
3.	Credits in taxable income	taxbl_cr	B	0
4.	CG taxable income	tax_inc	J	Positive(earn_dec_total-work_exp)
5.	CG tax before credits			
	Calculation according to schedule	sch_tax	J	MAX(quotient*Tax(tax_inc/quotient, tax_sch), IF(Married, 2*Tax(tax_inc/2, tax_sch)-limit_demipart*(quotient-2), Tax(tax_inc, tax_sch)-(Children>0)*(limit_sp_demipart1+limit_demipart*(quotient-2))))++cehr_rate1*MIN((cehr_ceil2-cehr_ceil1)*(1+Married);MAX(tax_inc-cehr_ceil1*(1+Married);0))+cehr_rate2 * MAX(tax_inc-cehr_ceil2*(1+Married);0)
	Adjusted for decote	adj_tax	J	SI(Married;Positive(MINA(tax_sch; (1+decote_pente)*tax_sch-decote_pente*decote_mar));Positive(MINA(tax_sch;(1+decote_pente)*tax_sch-decote_pente*decote_sing)))
	Tax liable	inc_tax	J	(adj_tax>=tax_min)*adj_tax
	CSG+CRDS (non-deductible)	CSG_CRDS_noded	B	CSG_CRDS_rat_nod*((1-CSG_CRDS_abat)*MIN(earn;4*SSC_ceil)+Positive(earn-4*SSC_ceil))
	CSG deductible	CSG_ded	B	CSG_rat_ded*((1-CSG_CRDS_abat)*MIN(earn;4*SSC_ceil)+Positive(earn-4*SSC_ceil))
6.	Tax credits :	tax_cr		0
7.	CG tax	CG_tax	J	inc_tax+CSG_CRDS_noded+CSG_ded-tax_cr
8.	State and local taxes	local_tax	J	0

	Line in country table and intermediate steps	Variable name	Range	Equation
9.	Employees' soc security	SSC	B	pension_rate*MINA(earn, SSC_ceil) +(sickness_rate+pension_rate2)*earn+ unemp_rate*MINA(earn, 4*SSC_ceil) +pens_rate_ex*MINA(earn, SSC_ceil)+ (earn>SSC_ceil)*pens_rate_ex2*MINA(earn-SSC_ceil, 3*SSC_ceil-SSC_ceil)
11.	Cash transfers	cash_transf_gross	J	IF(Children<2;0;(CB_2+(Children-2)*CB_3)*IF(tax_inc<=(CB_c1+CB_ceiling_ extra_child*Children);1;SI(tax_inc<=(CB_c2+CB_ceiling_extra_child*Children); 0,5+0,5/2;0,5+0,25/2)))
		crds_cash_transf	J	cash_transf_gross*-1*CRDS_special
		cash_transf_net	J	cash_transf_gross+crds_cash_transf
13.	Employer's soc security	SSC_empr_gross	B	(sickness_empr + CSA + pens_empr2 + accidents_empr+others_empr)*earn +pens_empr1*MINA(earn;SSC_ceil) +pens_empr_ex*MINA(earn;SSC_ceil) +pens_empr_ex2* MAX(MIN(earn;3*SSC_ceil) - SSC_ceil;0) +unemp_empr* MIN(earn;4*SSC_ceil)) + SI(earn<SSC_empr_SMIC_ref*SMIC; fam_empr_ 2*earn; fam_empr*earn)
		SSC_empr_ reduction	B	IF(OR(earn>SSC_empr_SMIC_ref*SMIC,earn=0),0,-MIN (SSC_empr_red_max* earn,(SSC_empr_red_max/ SSC_empr_redrate2)*(SSC_empr_SMIC_ref* minrevtp/earn-1)*earn)) - IF(earn<cice_max*minrevtp;earn*cice_red)
		SSC_empr_final	B	SSC_empr_gross+SSC_empr_reduction
	Memorandum item: Non-wastable tax credit			
	tax expenditure component	taxexp	P	tax_cr-transfer
	cash transfer component	transfer	P	IF(CG_tax<0,-CG_tax,0)

Key to range of equation B calculated separately for both principal earner and spouse P calculated for principal only (value taken as 0 for spouse calculation) J calculated once only on a joint basis.

Germany

This chapter includes data on the income taxes paid by workers, their social security contributions, the family benefits they receive in the form of cash transfers as well as the social security contributions and payroll taxes paid by their employers. Results reported include the marginal and average tax burden for eight different family types.

Methodological information is available for personal income tax systems, compulsory social security contributions to schemes operated within the government sector, universal cash transfers as well as recent changes in the tax/benefit system. The methodology also includes the parameter values and tax equations underlying the data.

Germany 2015

The tax/benefit position of single persons

		Wage level (per cent of average wage)	67	100	167	67
		Number of children	none	none	none	2.00
1.	**Gross wage earnings**		31 518	47 042	78 560	31 518
2.	**Standard tax allowances**					
	Basic allowance					
	Married or head of family		0	0	0	2 148
	Dependent children		0	0	0	0
	Deduction for social security contributions and income taxes		4 699	7 013	8 675	4 620
	Work-related expenses		1 000	1 000	1 000	1 000
	Other		36	36	36	36
		Total	5 735	8 049	9 711	7 804
3.	**Tax credits or cash transfers included in taxable income**		0	0	0	0
4.	**Central government taxable income (1 - 2 + 3)**		25 783	38 993	68 849	23 714
5.	**Central government income tax liability (exclusive of tax credits)**		4 481	9 027	21 790	3 644
6.	**Tax credits**					
	Basic credit					
	Married or head of family					
	Children		0	0	0	4 512
	Other					
		Total	0	0	0	4 512
7.	**Central government income tax finally paid (5-6)**		4 481	9 027	21 790	- 868
8.	**State and local taxes**		0	0	0	0
9.	**Employees' compulsory social security contributions**					
	Gross earnings		6 453	9 632	12 641	6 375
	Taxable income					
		Total	6 453	9 632	12 641	6 375
10.	**Total payments to general government (7 + 8 + 9)**		10 934	18 658	34 431	5 507
11.	**Cash transfers from general government**					
	For head of family					
	For two children		0	0	0	0
		Total	0	0	0	0
12.	**Take-home pay (1-10+11)**		20 584	28 383	44 129	26 012
13.	**Employers' compulsory social security contributions**		6 091	9 091	12 072	6 091
14.	**Average rates**					
	Income tax		14.2%	19.2%	27.7%	-2.8%
	Employees' social security contributions		20.5%	20.5%	16.1%	20.2%
	Total payments less cash transfers		34.7%	39.7%	43.8%	17.5%
	Total tax wedge including employer's social security contributions		45.3%	49.4%	51.3%	30.8%
15.	**Marginal rates**					
	Total payments less cash transfers: Principal earner		47.1%	52.5%	44.3%	44.7%
	Total payments less cash transfers: Spouse		n.a.	n.a.	n.a.	n.a.
	Total tax wedge: Principal earner		55.6%	60.2%	44.3%	53.6%
	Total tax wedge: Spouse		n.a.	n.a.	n.a.	n.a.

Germany 2015

The tax/benefit position of married couples

			100-0	100-33	100-67	100-33
	Wage level (per cent of average wage)		100-0	100-33	100-67	100-33
	Number of children		2	2	2	none
1.	**Gross wage earnings**		47 042	62 566	78 560	62 566
2.	**Standard tax allowances**					
	Basic allowance					
	Married or head of family		0	0	0	0
	Dependent children		0	0	0	0
	Deduction for social security contributions and income taxes		6 895	9 171	11 515	9 327
	Work-related expenses		1 000	2 000	2 000	2 000
	Other		72	72	72	72
		Total	7 967	11 243	13 587	11 399
3.	**Tax credits or cash transfers included in taxable income**		0	0	0	0
4.	**Central government taxable income (1 - 2 + 3)**		39 075	51 323	64 973	51 167
5.	**Central government income tax liability (exclusive of tax credits)**		4 974	8 666	13 121	8 837
6.	**Tax credits**					
	Basic credit					
	Married or head of family					
	Children		4 512	4 512	4 512	0
	Other					
		Total	4 512	4 512	4 512	0
7.	**Central government income tax finally paid (5-6)**		462	4 154	8 609	8 837
8.	**State and local taxes**		0	0	0	0
9.	**Employees' compulsory social security contributions**					
	Gross earnings		9 514	12 654	15 889	12 810
	Taxable income					
		Total	9 514	12 654	15 889	12 810
10.	**Total payments to general government (7 + 8 + 9)**		9 976	16 807	24 497	21 647
11.	**Cash transfers from general government**					
	For head of family					
	For two children		0	0	0	0
		Total	0	0	0	0
12.	**Take-home pay (1-10+11)**		37 066	45 758	54 063	40 919
13.	**Employers' compulsory social security contributions**		9 091	12 091	15 182	12 091
14.	**Average rates**					
	Income tax		1.0%	6.6%	11.0%	14.1%
	Employees' social security contributions		20.2%	20.2%	20.2%	20.5%
	Total payments less cash transfers		21.2%	26.9%	31.2%	34.6%
	Total tax wedge including employer's social security contributions		34.0%	38.7%	42.3%	45.2%
15.	**Marginal rates**					
	Total payments less cash transfers: Principal earner		43.1%	46.7%	49.5%	47.0%
	Total payments less cash transfers: Spouse		44.0%	46.7%	49.5%	47.0%
	Total tax wedge: Principal earner		52.3%	55.3%	57.7%	55.6%
	Total tax wedge: Spouse		53.1%	55.3%	57.7%	55.6%

The national currency is the Euro (EUR). In 2015, EUR 0.90 was equal to USD 1. The average worker earned EUR 47 042 (Secretariat estimate).

1. Personal income tax systems

1.1. *Central/federal government income taxes*

1.1.1. *Tax unit*

Spouses may choose between two options: Joint assessment or individual assessment. The vast majority of couples benefits financially from the joint assessment by minimizing the tax burden of the household. The income of dependent children is not assessable with that of the parents. The calculations in this Report are therefore based on the assumption of joint taxation for spouses.

1.1.2. *Tax allowances and tax credits:*

1.1.2.1. Standard reliefs and work-related expenses

- *Basic reliefs*: None.
- *Standard marital status reliefs*: In the case of joint assessment, specific allowances are doubled. The income tax liability for spouses who are assessed jointly is computed as follows:
  - *Splitting method*:
    - First step: Calculating the tax base: All incomes of the spouses are summed up and the sum is divided by two.
    - Second step: The tax rate is applied to this tax base.
    - Third step: The amount calculated in step 2 is doubled.
  - Results: Given the progressive income taxation the resulting tax liability for the household is lower than the sum of individual taxation. The household as a unit benefits from this solution otherwise both parts of the couple would opt out. Principal and second earners have the same average and marginal income tax rates.
  - The splitting effect decreases by increasing convergence of the incomes of principal earner and the spouse.
- *Relief(s) for children:* As of 1 January 2015, there are increased tax credits of EUR 2 256 for the first and the second child, of EUR 2 328 for the third child and of EUR 2 628 for the fourth and subsequent children. There is a tax allowance of EUR 2 256 for the subsistence of a child and an additional EUR 1 320 for minding and education or training needs (EUR 3 576). The amount of this allowance is doubled in case of jointly assessed parents. If the value of the tax credit is less than the relief calculated applying the tax allowances, the taxpayer obtains the tax allowance instead of the tax credit. It is also doubled for lone parents in cases where the other parent does not pay alimony. This is the assumption in the calculations presented in this Report.

- *Relief for lone parents*: As of 1 January 2015, taxpayers who live alone with at least one child that entitles them to the tax allowances or tax credits for children, receive an additional allowance of EUR 1 908 (formerly EUR 1 308). This additional allowance is increased by EUR 240 for each child in case of more than one child living in the household.
- *Reliefs for social security contributions and life insurance contributions:* Social security contributions and other expenses incurred in provision for the future (e.g. life insurance) are deductible up to specific ceilings. In 2005, a new calculation scheme came into force:
  - Step 1: all contributions made to pension funds (i.e. both employee's and employer's contributions) are added up. Step 2: the resulting amount is limited to EUR 20 000. Step 3: a certain percentage is applied to this amount (starting from 60% in 2005, this percentage will be increased by 2 percentage points each year; it will reach 100% in 2025). Step 4: the resulting amount, diminished by the (tax-free) contributions of the employer, is deductible from income.
  - The tax treatment of social security expenses (health, unemployment and care insurance) changed as of 1 January 2010. Employees' annual contributions to statutory health insurance excluding sickness benefit (assumed to amount to 96% of statutory health contributions) and employees' contributions to mandatory long-term care insurance are deductible from the tax base. In case these contributions do not exceed EUR 1 900/3 800 (single/married couples), contributions to unemployment insurance and other insurances premiums can be deducted in addition up to this ceiling.
  - If the resulting sum of deductible amounts according the legislation in force since 2005 is lower than the allowance calculated under the scheme that was valid up to 2004, the former regulations are applied in favour of the taxpayer (for more details on the old scheme: see 2005 edition and section 4. of this Report).
- *Work-related expenses:* EUR 1 000 lump-sum allowance per gainfully-employed person.
- *Special expenses:* Lump sum allowance (EUR 36/72 (singles/couples)) for special expenses, e.g. for tax accountancy. The actual expenses will be fully deductible from taxable income if the taxpayer proves that these expenses exceed the lump sum allowance.

1.1.2.2. Main non-standard tax reliefs applicable to an AW

- *Contributions to pensions, life insurance, superannuation schemes:* Other expenses than the compulsory contributions to social security are deductible as reliefs for (voluntary) social security contributions up to specific ceilings (see Section 1.121).
- *Medical expenses:* Partially deductible if not covered by insurance.
- *Other:* Work-related expenses that exceed the lump-sum allowance are fully deductible (no ceiling).

1.1.3. *Tax schedule*

The German tax schedule is formula-based. Taxable income is rounded down (to the EUR).

- X is the taxable income,
- T is the income tax liability,
- As of 1 January 2015 the following definitions are used in the income tax liability formulas:

$$Y = \frac{X - 8\,472}{10\,000}$$

$$Z = \frac{X - 13469}{10000}$$

The income tax liability (amounts in EUR) is calculated as follows:

1. T = 0 for X ≤ 8 472
2. T = (997.60 Y + 1 400) Y for 8 473 ≤ X ≤ 13 469
3. T = (228.74 Z + 2 397) Z + 948,68 for 13 470 ≤ X ≤ 52 881
4. T = 0.42 X 8 261,29 for 52 882 ≤ X ≤ 250 730
5. T = 0.45 X – 15 783,19 for 250 731 ≤ X

These formulas are used to calculate the income tax for single individuals and married couples too.

If families choose the option of being assessed separately these formulas are applied to the individual taxable income of the principal earner and the spouse. In the case of jointly assessed families these rates are applied to half of the joint taxable income (see point 1.1.2.1. Splitting method).

1.1.4. Solidarity surcharge

The solidarity surcharge is levied at 5.5% of the income tax liability subject to an exemption limit of EUR 972/1 944 (singles/couples). The income tax liability is calculated applying the tax allowance for children. If the income tax liability exceeds the exemption limit, the solidarity surcharge will be phased in at a higher rate of 20% of the difference between the income tax liability and the exemption limit until it equals 5.5% of the total liability.

1.2. State and local income taxes

None.

2. Compulsory social security contributions to schemes operated within the government sector

The amount of social security contributions depends on the wage and the insurance contribution rate. All contributions are subject to a contribution ceiling, i.e. the maximum income for which statutory insurance contributions are calculated. The contribution rates for pension, health, care and unemployment insurances are fixed by the government.

2.1. Employees' contributions

In general, earnings up to EUR 4 800 per year were free of employee social security contributions until 31 December 2012. As of 1 January 2013, some essential changes came into effect concerning minimally paid employment. The earnings limit increased from EUR 400 to EUR 450 per month. Persons whose mini-job started before 2013 and do not exceed the previous earnings limit of EUR 400 stay contribution-free in all classes of social insurance. Otherwise, persons who take up a new mini-job are generally subject to mandatory insurance coverage in the statutory pension scheme with the full pension contribution rate of 18.7% (in 2015). If the earnings are below the amount of EUR 175 (minimum contribution limit), a minimum contribution of EUR 32.73 has to be paid (18.7% of EUR 175). The employer's share amounts to 15% of the whole pay whereas the employee's part adds up to 3.7% (or the difference between minimum contribution and employer share). By applying for an exemption from obligatory insurance coverage the mini-job holder may reduce his share to EUR 0.

As of 1 April 2003, there was an additional concession for employees with monthly income between EUR 400.01 and EUR 800 per month (the so-called "sliding pay scale", EUR 4 800.12 and EUR 9 600 per year). Due to the new regulations mentioned above the earnings limits shifted to EUR 450.01 and EUR 850.00 per month (EUR 5 400.12 and EUR 10 200 per year). If the employee's income falls within this range, part of the income will be exempt from social insurance contributions. However, employers are still required to pay the regular contributions on the employee's earnings. The arrangement is purely intended to relieve the financial burden on employees. The employees' contributions to social insurance rise on a straight-line basis over the income band reaching the full rate at EUR 850 per month. Details on social security contributions for workers earning more than EUR 10 200 per year are provided below.

2.1.1. *Pensions*

Employers and employees pay each half of the contribution rate of 18.7% in 2015, that is 9.35% of the employee's gross wage earnings, up to a contribution ceiling of EUR 72 600.

2.1.2. *Sickness*

As of 1 January 2015, the applicable contribution rate is 14.6% on principle (portion of 7.3% for employers and employees). Depending on the financial situation of each sickness fund, employees are obliged to pay a supplementary contribution to the sickness fund. In 2015, this supplementary contribution amounts to 0.9% on average. Therefore, the contribution rate averages 8.2% for employees in 2015. The contribution ceiling in 2015 is EUR 49 500. While all calculations shown in this Report assume membership in the public health insurance, workers with earnings above the contribution ceiling may opt out of the mandatory public health insurance system and may choose a private insurance provider instead (those opting for a private health insurance provider are required to obtain private long-term care insurance as well).

2.1.3. *Unemployment*

Employees pay half of the insurance contributions; the employer pays the other half. In 2015, the contribution rate is 3.0% of assessable income. Employee and employer each pay 1.5%. The contribution ceiling is EUR 72 600.

2.1.4. *Care*

A long-term care insurance (a 1% contribution rate) went into effect on 1 January 1995. The rate was raised to 1.7% of the gross wage when home nursing care benefits were added six months later. As of 1 July 2008, the rate was increased to 1.95%. In 2013 and 2014, the contribution rate amounted to 2.05%. As of 1 January 2015, the contribution rate adds up to 2.35%. The employers pay half of the contributions for long-term care insurance. In other words, employers and employees both pay a rate of 1.175%. The assessable income is scaled according to the gross wage earnings but there is a contribution ceiling of EUR 49 500 in 2015.

As from 1 January 2005, child-raising is given special recognition in the law relating to statutory long-term care insurance. Childless contribution payers are required to pay a supplement of 0.25%, raising the contribution rate paid by a childless employee from 0.975% to 1.225% as of 1 July 2008. In 2013 and 2014, the contribution rate of a childless employee added up to 1.275%. As of 1 January 2015, the contribution rate amounts to 1.425% for a childless employee

2.1.5. *Work injury*

Employer only.

2.1.6. *Family allowances*

None.

2.1.7. *Others*

None.

2.2. *Employers' contributions*

See Section 2.1.

2.2.1.-2.2.4. *(Pensions, sickness, unemployment, care):*

See Section 2.1

2.2.5. *Work injury*

Germany has established a statutory occupational accident insurance. It is provided by industrial, agricultural and public-sector employers' liability insurance funds. This insurance protects employees and their families against the consequences of accidents at work and occupational illnesses. It is funded through the contributions paid by employers only. The amount of the employer's contributions depends on the sum total of employee's annual pay and the employer's respective hazard level. As it is not possible to identify a representative contribution rate, these amounts are not considered in this Report.

2.2.6. *Family allowances*

None.

2.2.7. *Others*

None.

3. Universal cash transfers

3.1. *Transfers related to marital status*

None.

3.2. *Transfers for dependent children*

None.

4. Main changes in tax/benefit systems since 1997

The following table shows changes in the tax credit and the tax allowance for children since 1997:

Year	Child credit				Child allowance
	First child	Second child	Third child	Fourth and subsequent children	
1997	1 350	1 350	1 841	2 147	3 534
1999	1 534	1 534	1 841	2 147	3 534

Year	Child credit				Child allowance
	First child	Second child	Third child	Fourth and subsequent children	
2000	1 657	1 657	1 841	2 147	5 080
2002	1 848	1 848	1 848	2 148	5 808
2009*	1 968	1 968	2 040	2 340	6 024
2010	2 208	2 208	2 280	2 580	7 008
2015	2 256	2 256	2 328	2 628	7 152

* plus EUR 100 one-off child credit payment for each child.

Up to 2004, the calculation of the relief for social security contributions and other expenses proceeded in three steps. First, EUR 3 068/6 136 (singles/couples) was deducted. These amounts were, however, lowered by 16% of gross wages (serving as a proxy for employers' social security contributions). This deduction was provided as a partial compensation for the self-employed which do not receive tax-free employers' social security contributions. Second, the remaining expenses were deductible up to EUR 1 334/2 668 (singles/couples). Third, half of the remaining expenses were deductible up to EUR 667/ 1 334 (singles/couples).

In 2004, the tax rate was reduced and the formula for calculating the income tax was changed. The relief for lone parents was reduced to EUR 1 308, the lump sum allowance for work related expenses was reduced to EUR 920.

As from 1 January 2005, the final stage of the 2000-tax reform came into effect. The bottom and top income tax rates were further reduced to 15% and 42%. Since 1998, both the bottom and top income tax rate have been reduced by about 11 percentage points while the personal allowance has been raised from EUR 6 322 to EUR 7 664. The tax cuts reduce the tax burden for all income taxpayers, affording the greatest relief to employees and families with low and medium incomes as well as to small- and medium-sized unincorporated businesses.

On 1 January 2005, the law regulating the taxation of pensions and pension expenses entered into force. The law provides a gradual transition to ex-post taxation of pensions paid by the statutory pensions insurance. In the long run, the tax treatment of capital-based employee pension schemes based on a contract between employer and employee will be reformed in the same way as the tax treatment in respect of the state pension scheme. In addition to the increased deductibility of contributions to the state and certain private pension schemes, the law contains rules which are intended to increase the attractiveness of private capital-based pension schemes and to encourage individuals to invest privately for their old-age pension.

Up to 30 June of 2005, employees paid half of the sickness insurance contributions; the employer paid the other half. As from 1 July 2005, members of the statutory health insurance scheme also pay an income-linked contribution of 0.9% to which employers do not contribute. As from 1 July 2005, all statutory health insurance funds have reduced their contribution rates by 0.9 percentage points.

In 2007, a new top income tax rate of 45% was introduced for taxable income above EUR 250 000 (EUR 500 000 for jointly assessed spouses).

In 2009, the bottom income tax rate was reduced to 14%. The basic allowance was increased to EUR 7 834. All thresholds were increased by EUR 400.

Since 1 January 2010, the basic allowance has been augmented to EUR 8 004 and all thresholds have been increased by EUR 330. Furthermore, new legislation improves the tax treatment of expenditure on health insurance and long-term care insurance. As of 1 January 2013, the basic allowance rose to EUR 8 130. As of 1 January 2014, the basic allowance was increased to EUR 8 354. As of 1 January 2015, the basic allowance amounts to EUR 8 472. The relief for lone parents now adds up to EUR 1 908. Lone parents are entitled to an extra allowance of EUR 240 for the second and each subsequent child.

5. Memorandum items

5.1. *Average gross annual earnings calculation*

- Source of calculation: Federal Statistical Office.
- Excluding sickness and unemployment, including normal overtime and bonuses.

5.2. *Employer's contributions to private pension, etc. schemes*

No information available, though such schemes do exist.

2015 parameter values

Average earnings/yr	Ave_earn	47 042	Secretariat estimate
Tax allowances	Child_al	7 152	
Lone Parents, first child	Lone_al	1 908	
Lone parents, subsequent child	Lone_al_add	240	
Work related	Work_rel_al	1 000	
SSC allowance	SSC_dn	1 500	
	SSC_dn_rt	0.16	
	SSC_dn_lim	1 334	
	SSC_dn_lump_rt	0.2	
Allow. for special expenses	SE_al	36	
Church tax rate	Ch_tax_rt	0	
Tax formula	Tax_rate2	0.42	
	Tax_rate3	0.45	
	Tax_thrsh1	8 472	
	Tax_thrsh2	13 469	
Top Rate Tax Reduction	Reduction	8 261.29	
	Reduction2	15 783.19	
Tax Equation Rates			
tax_eqn_rates	Squared	Single	Constant
z	228.74	2 397	948.68
y	997,60	1 400	0
Income tax rate stage	tax_first_stage	8 472	
	tax_second_stage	13 469	
	tax_third_stage	52 881	
	tax_fourth_stage	250 730	
Solidarity Surcharge	surcharge	0.055	
Solidarity Exemption Limit	surcharge_limit	972	
Alternative Surcharge Rate	surcharge_alt	0.2	
Child credit	Ch_cred		
	1. ch.	2 256	
	2. ch.	2 256	
	3.ch.	2 328	
	4.ch.	2 628	

Social security	Sickness	Pension	Unemployment	Care	Alternative employer rate	SSC Factor F
period_1	12	12	12	12	12	12
period_2	0	0	0	0		
sum (Month's)	12	12	12	12	12	12
employer_1	0.073	0.0935	0.015	0.01175	0.3	0.7585
employer_2	0	0	0	0		
employee_1	0.082	0.0935	0.015	0.01175	0.037	0.7585
employee_2	0	0	0	0		
childless_1	0.082	0.0935	0.015	0.01425	0.037	0.7585
childless_2	0	0	0	0		
ceil	49 500	72 600	72 600	49 500	2 100	
SSC Floor	SSC_floor	10 200				
Intermediate SSC Ceiling	SSC_floor1	5 400				

2015 tax equations

The equations for the German system in 2015 are mostly calculated on a family basis.

The standard functions which are used in the equations are described in the technical note about tax equations. The function acttax carries out a rounded calculation for the tables but the unrounded version purtax is used in calculating the marginal rates.

For a taxpayer with children, either the child allowance is given in the tax calculation or the cash transfer is given if this is more beneficial. In practice, therefore, it is necessary to make two calculations – with and without the child allowance. Nevertheless, the calculation of solidarity surcharge is always based on the calculation which does assume that the child tax allowance is given.

Variable names are defined in the table of parameters above, within the equations table, or are the standard variables "married" and "children". The affixes "_princ" and "_spouse" on Variable names in functions indicate that the values have to be calculated for the principal and spouse, respectively. The parameter year in function SSC_Allowance is the year for which you calculate the Allowance.

	Line in country table and intermediate steps	Variable name	Range	Equation
1.	Earnings	earn		
	Quotient for tax calculation	quotient	J	1+Married
2.	Allowances:			
	Children	children_al	J	Children*Child_al
	Lone parent	lone_allce	J	Children>0)*(Married=0)*Lone_al+(Children>0)*(Married=0)*(Children-1)*Lone_al_add
	Soc sec contributions	SSC_al	J	Function: SSC_Allowance(earn_princ, earn_spouse , SSC_princ + SSC_spouse , Quotient, SSC_dn, SSC_dn_rt, SSC_dn_lim, SSC_dn_lump_rt, If(Children>0; "employee"; "childless"), year, rounded)
	Work related	work_al	J	Work_rel_al+MIN(earn_spouse,Work_rel_al)
	Allow. for special expenses	SE_al	J	SE_al*quotient
	Total	tax_al	J	children_al+SSC_al+work_al+ lone_allce + SE_al
3.	Credits in taxable income	taxbl_cr	J	0
4.	CG taxable income	tax_inc	J	earn-tax_al
5.	CG tax before credits			
	adjusted taxable income	adj	J	tax_inc/quotient
	Formula based tax schedule	tax_formula	J	Function: acttax(taxinc, rate, reduction, threshold1, threshold2, threshold3, equationrate, tax_first_stage, tax_second_stage, tax_third_stage, tax_fourth_stage, rate2, reduction2)
	Adjust for the quotient	tax_adj	J	Quotient*tax_formula
	Include solidarity surcharge	sol_surch	J	MIN(tax_adj * surcharge, Positive(tax_adj - surcharge_limit*Quotient) * surcharge_alt)
	Tax paid	CG_tax_excl	J	tax_adj+sol_surch
6.	Tax credits :	tax_cr	J	0
7.	CG tax	CG_tax	J	CG_tax_excl
8.	State and local taxes	local_tax	J	0
9.	Employees' soc security	SSC	B	Function: SSC (earn_princ, If(Children>0; "employee"; "childless"), rounded) + SSC (earn_spouse, If(Children>0; "employee"; "childless"), rounded)
11.	Cash transfers	Cash_tran	J	Children*ch_cred
13.	Employer's soc security	SSC_empr	B	Function: SSC (earn_princ, "employer", rounded) + SSC (earn_spouse, "employer", rounded)

Key to range of equation B calculated separately for both principal earner and spouse P calculated for principal only (value taken as 0 for spouse calculation) J calculated once only on a joint basis.

Greece

This chapter includes data on the income taxes paid by workers, their social security contributions, the family benefits they receive in the form of cash transfers as well as the social security contributions and payroll taxes paid by their employers. Results reported include the marginal and average tax burden for eight different family types.

Methodological information is available for personal income tax systems, compulsory social security contributions to schemes operated within the government sector, universal cash transfers as well as recent changes in the tax/benefit system. The methodology also includes the parameter values and tax equations underlying the data.

Greece 2015

The tax/benefit position of single persons

		Wage level (per cent of average wage)	67	100	167	67
		Number of children	none	none	none	2
1.	**Gross wage earnings**		13 599	20 296	33 895	13 599
2.	**Standard tax allowances**					
	Basic allowance					
	Married or head of family					
	Dependent children					
	Deduction for social security contributions and income taxes		2 108	3 146	5 254	2 108
	Work-related expenses					
	Other					
		Total	2 108	3 146	5 254	2 108
3.	**Tax credits or cash transfers included in taxable income**		0	0	0	0
4.	**Central government taxable income (1 - 2 + 3)**		11 491	17 151	28 641	11 491
5.	**Central government income tax liability (exclusive of tax credits)**		2 528	3 773	6 665	2 528
6.	**Tax credits**					
	Basic credit		2 100	2 100	900	2 100
	Married or head of family					
	Children					
	Other					
		Total	2 100	2 100	900	2 100
7.	**Central government income tax finally paid**		428	1 793	6 166	428
8.	**State and local taxes**		0	0	0	0
9.	**Employees' compulsory social security contributions**					
	Gross earnings		2 108	3 146	5 254	2 108
	Taxable income					
		Total	2 108	3 146	5 254	2 108
10.	**Total payments to general government (7 + 8 + 9)**		2 536	4 939	11 420	2 536
11.	**Cash transfers from general government**					
	For head of family					
	For two children		0	0	0	640
		Total	0	0	0	640
12.	**Take-home pay (1-10+11)**		11 063	15 357	22 475	11 703
13.	**Employer's compulsory social security contributions**		3 340	4 985	8 325	3 340
14.	**Average rates**					
	Income tax		3.1%	8.8%	18.2%	3.1%
	Employees' social security contributions		15.5%	15.5%	15.5%	15.5%
	Total payments less cash transfers		18.6%	24.3%	33.7%	13.9%
	Total tax wedge including employer's social security contributions		34.7%	39.3%	46.8%	30.9%
15.	**Marginal rates**					
	Total payments less cash transfers: Principal earner		34.1%	34.7%	43.7%	34.1%
	Total payments less cash transfers: Spouse		n.a.	n.a.	n.a.	n.a.
	Total tax wedge: Principal earner		47.1%	47.6%	54.8%	47.1%
	Total tax wedge: Spouse		n.a.	n.a.	n.a.	n.a.

Greece 2015

The tax/benefit position of married couples

		Wage level (per cent of average wage)	100-0	100-33	100-67	100-33
		Number of children	2	2	2	none
1.	**Gross wage earnings**		22 326	29 694	37 285	29 694
2.	**Standard tax allowances**					
	Basic allowance					
	Married or head of family					
	Dependent children					
	Deduction for social security contributions and income taxes		3 461	4 603	5 779	4 603
	Work-related expenses					
	Other					
		Total	3 461	4 603	5 779	4 603
3.	**Tax credits or cash transfers included in taxable income**		0	0	0	0
4.	**Central government taxable income (1 - 2 + 3)**		18 866	25 091	31 505	25 091
5.	**Central government income tax liability (exclusive of tax credits)**		4 150	5 520	6 931	5 520
6.	**Tax credits**					
	Basic credit		2 000	4 100	4 100	4 100
	Married or head of family					
	Children					
	Other					
		Total	2 000	4 100	4 100	4 100
7.	**Central government income tax finally paid (5-6)**		2 282	2 282	3 052	2 282
8.	**State and local taxes**		0	0	0	0
9.	**Employees' compulsory social security contributions**					
	Gross earnings		3 461	4 603	5 779	4 603
	Taxable income					
		Total	3 461	4 603	5 779	4 603
10.	**Total payments to general government (7 + 8 + 9)**		5 743	6 885	8 831	6 885
11.	**Cash transfers from general government**					
	For head of family					
	For two children		640	320	320	0
		Total	640	320	320	0
12.	**Take-home pay (1-10+11)**		17 223	23 129	28 774	22 809
13.	**Employer's compulsory social security contributions**		5 483	7 293	9 157	7 293
14.	**Average rates**					
	Income tax		10.2%	7.7%	8.2%	7.7%
	Employees' social security contributions		15.5%	15.5%	15.5%	15.5%
	Total payments less cash transfers		22.9%	22.1%	22.8%	23.2%
	Total tax wedge including employer's social security contributions		38.1%	37.5%	38.0%	38.3%
15.	**Marginal rates**					
	Total payments less cash transfers: Principal earner		34.7%	34.7%	34.7%	34.7%
	Total payments less cash transfers: Spouse		20.3%	15.5%	34.7%	15.5%
	Total tax wedge: Principal earner		47.6%	47.6%	47.6%	47.6%
	Total tax wedge: Spouse		36.0%	32.2%	47.6%	32.2%

The national currency is the Euro (EUR). In 2015, EUR 0.90 was equal to USD 1. In 2015, the estimated gross earnings of the average worker are EUR 20 296 (Secretariat estimate).

1. Personal income tax system

1.1. Central government income tax

1.1.1. Tax unit

Individuals are subject to national income tax. Every individual who derives income from sources in Greece is subject to tax irrespective of his nationality, place of domicile or residence. Moreover, every individual with domicile in Greece (more than 183 days) is subject to tax on his/her worldwide income irrespective of the individual's nationality. Due consideration is given to bilateral conventions designed to obviate double taxation.

All individuals who have completed 18 years of age are obliged to file a tax return regardless of having taxable income or not. Regarding income derived by minor children, the parent who has the custody is liable for filing a tax return. The income of minor children is added to the income of the parent who has the custody and is taxed in the name of the parent who is in principle liable for tax filing. This provision does not apply to the following types of income, in respect of which the minor child has a personal tax obligation: a) employment income and b) pensions due to the death of his father or mother.The minimum imputed income, which is required to cover the taxpayer's main living expenses is EUR 3 000 for a single individual and EUR 5 000 for spouses.

Spouses file a joint return but each spouse is liable for the tax payable on his or her share of the joint income. Losses incurred by one spouse may not be set off against the income of the other spouse. Deductible personal expenses concerning both spouses and tax credits are apportioned to each spouse according to the income earned by each one of them. Spouses file a return separately if a) they have been divorced at the time of the tax filing or b) one of the spouses is bankrupt or has been subject to guardianship.Taxpayer's spouse can be considered as a dependent member, provided that he/she does not have any taxable income.

Single children under the age of 18, children who are adults up to 25 years old and study at the university, or serve their military service or are registered as unemployed to the Manpower Employment Organisation (OAED), taxpayers' ascendants and spouses' relatives (up to the 3rd degree) who are orphans are deemed to be borne by the taxpayer provided that they cohabit with the taxpayer and their annual taxable income does not exceed the amount of EUR 3 000 (alimony and disability benefits and similar allowances are not included). Single disabled children (> = 67 %) or spouses' disabled siblings (> = 67 %) are also considered as dependent members, except their annual income exceeds the amount of EUR 6 000 (alimony and disability benefits and similar allowances are not included).

1.1.2. *Tax allowances and tax credits*

1.1.2.1. Standard tax reliefs

- Social security contributions: all compulsory social security contributions and optional contributions to legally constituted funds are fully deductible from taxable gross income.

1.1.2.2. Deductions from the payable amount of tax, as calculated on the basis of the scale (Non-Standard tax credits):

A) The tax arising by the tax scale for employees and pensioners is reduced as following:

- by EUR 2 100 for annual income up to EUR 21 000;
- by the amount of EUR 100 per each EUR 1 000 of income and up to EUR 2 100 for annual income exceeding the amount of EUR 21 000;
- for income exceeding the amount of EUR 42 000, no tax deduction is granted.

The above tax deduction is granted under the condition of the on time submission of receipts/invoices for the purchase of goods and services equal to 10% of the taxable income and up to the amount of EUR 10 500. Should the value of invoices is less than the one required, a 22% penalty is imposed on the remaining amount.

B) The following tax credits are deducted from the payable amount of tax, as calculated on the basis of the scale after applying the above tax allowance:

- 10% of the expenses of medical and hospital care of the taxpayer and his/her dependents provided they are not covered by Social Security Funds and they exceed 5% of the taxable income. The total credit cannot exceed EUR 3 000.
- 10% of the expenses of medical and hospital care of the taxpayer and his dependents, provided they are not covered by Social Security Funds and they exceed 5% of the taxable income. The total credit cannot exceed EUR 3 000. Hospital expenses in respect of unmarried or widowed children who suffer from an incurable disease, who are mentally retarded or are blind and whose total annual income does not exceed EUR 6 000 are also included.

C) The amount of tax derived on the basis of all scales is reduced by EUR 200 for the taxpayer himself as well as for each dependent member, provided that the taxpayer or his dependents are handicapped (over 67 %) or handicapped soldiers or military personnel injured in the course of their duties or war victims or victims of terrorist attacksor in case they receive pension by the State as war victims or as handicapped.

Note: Taxpayers who reside abroad but derive taxable income from sources in Greece are not eligible for these deductions, with the exemptions of residents of the EU Member States who derive at least 90% of their total income from sources in Greece.

Spouses:

When the wife derives income taxable on the basis of the scale, then the following are deducted from her own payable amount of tax:

a) deductions related to medical and hospital expenses, donations and the lump sum of EUR 200 of the spouse;

b) deductions related to medical and hospital expenses of the spouse's children from a former marriage, her children born out of wedlock, her parents and orphaned relatives of first and second degree of kin.

If from the joint tax return submitted by the spouses no tax obligation arises for one of them, or the payable amount of tax is less than the sum of the deductions (medical and hospital expenses, lump sum of EUR 200) then the whole amount of the deductions or the ensuing difference is attributed to the payable tax of the other spouse.

1.1.2.3. Exemptions

Some forms of income, specified by Law are exempt from the tax.

Examples:

- on condition of reciprocity, income of all kinds derived abroad by foreign ambassadors and diplomatic representatives, consulate agents and employees of embassies and consulates that have the nationality of the represented State as well as by individuals working in the EU Institutions or other International Organizations;
- alimony received by the beneficiary according to the Court adjudication or notary Document;
- all forms of pensions and relief provided to war victims and their families, as well as to soldiers and military personnel injured in the course of their duties in times of peace;
- benefits and similar allowances provided to special categories of handicapped people;
- salaries, pensions etc. paid to handicapped people (over 80 %);
- unemployment benefits granted by the National Employment Organisation (OAED) provided that the total annual income of the beneficiary does not exceed the amount of EUR 10 000;
- the social solidarity benefit (E.K.A.S.) of pensioners;
- financial aid to recognised political refugees, to people residing temporarily in Greece for humanitarian reasons and to persons that have submitted the relevant application to the competent Greek authorities, paid by bodies carrying out refugee aid schemes financed by the UN and the EU;
- the benefit for hazardous labour provided to employees working in the armed forces, the police, the fire and port departments as well as the special allowance to medical, nursing and ambulance staff up to 65%;
- Individuals and entities that are defined as microenterprises according to the European Commission Recommendation 2003/361/EC of 6 May 2003 are exempt from income tax on profits derived from the disposal of generated electricity to Public Power Corporation SA or other supplier, following their inclusion in the "Special Programme for the Development of Photovoltaic Systems up to 10 kw".

1.1.2.4. Tax calculation

There are four categories of income:

a) Income from employment and pensions

b) Income from business activities, which also includes income from self-employed and agricultural activities as well

c) Income from capital and

d) Income from capital gain, which includes income deriving on transfer of real estate or securities.

Net income is computed separately within each category with tax rules that vary across income categories. Total taxable income is computed as the aggregate of the net results of all categories. Losses in one category may be set off against income of another category. If the declared income is not accepted as the base for the tax assessment, the tax authorities can base the assessment on the presumptive income, which is the minimum amount of income required to cover the taxpayer's main living expenses.

Employment income is subject to withholding tax. The tax is withheld by the employer and is calculated by applying the taxpayer's progressive income tax schedule. The employer calculates the withholding tax on the basis of the taxpayer's annual net salary (net of social security contributions). The withholding tax is then reduced by 1.5% of the total amount of taxes due. The resulting tax is the annual tax due, 1/14 of which constitutes the monthly withholding tax for the private sector's employees (every employee in the private sector receives 14 monthly salaries per year, i.e. 12 monthly wages plus 1 salary as Christmas bonus, ½ salary as Easter bonus and ½ salary as summer vacation bonus). For the employees of the public sector, the monthly withholding tax is calculated as 1/12 of the annual tax due, because of the fact that bonuses in the public sector have been eliminated. If the taxpayer's final tax liability (derived from the annual declared income) exceeds the aggregate of the amounts already withheld or prepaid, the remaining tax is generally payable in three equal bimonthly instalments. Any excess tax paid or withheld will be refunded.

Rate schedule

Depending on the income category the following tax schedules apply:

a) Tax schedule for salaried persons (employees & pensioners)

Income bracket (EUR)	Tax rate (%)	Tax bracket (EUR)	Total amount	
			Income (EUR)	Tax (EUR)
25 000	22%	5 500	25 000	5 500
17 000	32%	5 440	42 000	10 940
Excess	42%			

The above tax scale does not apply for employment income acquired by:

- Officers working in ships of the merchant marine, whose income is taxed at a 15% flat rate and
- Low-income crew working in ships of the merchant marine, whose income is taxed at a 10% flat rate.

The taxable income of the first bracket of the above scale is increased by 50% for taxpayers living in islands with less than 3 100 inhabitants.

For deductions see above: 1.1.2.2 Deductions from the payable amount of tax, as calculated on the basis of the scale

b) Tax schedule for non-salaried persons (self employed and personal businesses)

Income bracket (EUR)	Tax rate (%)	Tax bracket (EUR)	Total amount	
			Income (EUR)	Tax (EUR)
50 000	26%	13 000	50 000	13 000
Excess	33%			

For new personal business or new self-employed who started their entrepreneurship after 1 January 2013, the tax rate of the first income bracket of the above scale is decreased by 50% for income up to EUR 10 000 for the first three years of their business activity.

Profits derived from personal agricultural business are taxed at a 13% tax rate.

The taxable income of the first bracket of the above scale is increased by 50% for taxpayers living in islands with less than 3 100 inhabitants. This provision is valid until 31 December 2015

c) Tax schedule for special solidarity contribution

The Special Solidarity Contribution, which was first introduced by Art. 29 of Law 3986/ 2011 and applied for fiscal years 2010-2014, was effectively suspended at the end of 2014. It has subsequently been re-imposed on income derived during tax years 2015 and 2016. According to the Law 4334/2015, which has a retrospective effect and applies on income earned from 01/01/2015 onwards, the contribution's rates were revised as follows:

Net income (EUR)	Tax rate (%)
12 001-20 000.99	0.7
20 001-30 000.99	1.4
30 001-50 000.99	2
50 001-100 000.99	4
100 001-500 000	6
Above 500 000	8

These rates are imposed on the total net income and not progressively according to scale (steps): e.g.: net income EUR 50 000 *2% = EUR 1 000 for special solidarity contribution.

1.2. State and local income taxes

There are no local income taxes in Greece. Municipalities (the local authorities) receive 20% of the national income tax revenues.

2. Compulsory social security contributions to schemes operated within the government sector

The great majority of individuals who are employed in the private sector and render dependent personal services are principally, directly and compulsorily insured in the Social Insurance Organisation (IKA). Apart from the main contribution, IKA compulsorily collects contributions for other minor Funds created for the employee's benefit (Unemployment Benefits Funds, etc.). A subsidiary Social Insurance Fund (ETEA) for employees who are principally insured in IKA has been established since2012.

The average rates of contributions payable by white-collar employees as a percentage of gross earnings are as follows (%):

From 1 July, 2014:

	Employer	Employee	Total
1. Social Insurance Organisation (IKA)	17.88	9.22	27.10
2. Subsidiary Social Insurance Fund (ETEA)	3.00	3.00	6.00
3. Other Funds	3.68	3.28	6.96
Total	**24.56**	**15.50**	**40.06**

Higher contributions are due (18.95% paid by the employee and 26.71% paid by the employer) in case of blue-collar workers who are engaged in heavy work (unhealthy, dangerous, etc. work) as they are entitled to a pension five years earlier than the other workers. In the industrial sector, the employer pays an additional occupational risk contribution at a rate of 1% because these workers are more vulnerable to labour accidents and occupational diseases.

Contributions are calculated on the basis of the monthly salary or wages paid but within the limits specified in the National General Collective Labour Agreement. Monthly gross remuneration includes salaries and wages, fringe benefits and bonuses and any profit distributions to employees. From 2013 onwards, an equalized ceiling of EUR 5 546.80 applies for all categories of employees.

Self-employed individuals must make monthly compulsory lump-sum contributions to OAEE (Free Professional Social Insurance Organisation); these contributions depend on the number of years that the self-employed has been insured (for more details, see the explanatory annex to table III.3 of the OECD's Tax Database).

All these social security contributions are fully deductible for income tax purposes.

3. Universal cash transfers

3.1. *Transfers related to marital status*

According to the National General Collective Labour Agreement, a marriage allowance, which is set at a rate of 10% of the gross salary, is granted only to workers employed by employers that belong to the contracting employer organisations.* For public servants no marriage benefit is granted.

3.2. *Transfers for dependent children*

According to the Law 4093/2012 (as amended by Law 4144/2013, Law 4111/2013 and Law 4170/2013), the "Single children support allowance" replaced the previously existing family allowances and applies since 01/01/2013. The allowance's amount is calculated according to the number of dependent children as well as the income category of the household. More specifically the allowance provides for EUR 40/month per child.

Households that are entitled to the allowance are divided into four income categories according to their income:

- Income of < EUR 6 000: full allowance
- Income of EUR 6 001-12 000: 2/3 of the allowance
- Income of EUR 12 001-18 000: 1/3 of the allowance

where the income is calculated as the **net annual total family** income divided by the sum of family members (where the first spouse is weighted as 1, the 2nd spouse is weighted as 1/3 and each dependent child is weighted as 1/6).

For public servants, this benefit is limited to a flat gross monthly amount of EUR 50 for one child, EUR 70 for two children, EUR 120 for three children and EUR 170 for four children. The amount of EUR 170 is increased by EUR 70 per additional child.

* Namely the Hellenic Federation of Enterprises, the Hellenic Confederation of Professionals, Craftsmen and Merchants, the National Confederation of Hellenic Commerce and the Association of Greek Tourism Enterprises.

3.3. *Benefits for families with three or more children*

Law 4141/2013 (as amended by Law 4170/2013) introduced the "Special Allowance for families with three or more children", which is granted to families with three or more dependent children. The Special Allowance's amount is fixed to EUR 500/year per child, provided that the total income of the household does not exceed EUR 45 000 for families with three dependent children and EUR 48 000 for families with four dependent children, while in case of larger families the amount of EUR 45 000 is increased by EUR 4 000 per additional child.

Note 1: The Special allowance for families with three or more children is not included in the net, annual, family income and is exempt from income tax since 01-01-2013 (Law 4254/2014).

Note 2: Both Single children support allowance and the Special allowance for families with three or more children are exempt from Special Solidarity Contribution (Law 4254/2014).

4. Main changes in the tax/benefit system since 2014

The imposition of "Special Solidarity Contribution" was suspended for two more years. In addition, the applicable rates were revised.

5. Memorandum items

5.1. *Identification of an AW and method of calculations used*

Methodological note for the estimation of the average annual earnings per employee, for the period 2000-15.

Terminology and coverage

The average annual earnings below refer to full time employees for Sectors C to N of ISIC Rev. 3.1, before 2008, and for Sectors B to N including Division 95 and excluding Divisions 37, 39 and 75 of ISIC Rev. 4, for 2008 onwards.

Data sources

In the estimation procedure of the average annual earnings per employee, for the period 2000-14 the following data are taken into account:

- Annual earnings and number of employees, as derived from the **Structure of Earnings Survey** (SES), of the years 2002, 2006 and 2010.
- Hours worked and annual average number of employees, as derived from the **Labour Force Survey** (LFS), of the years 2000-14.
- Average annual earnings indices, as derived from the Indices on **Quarterly Labour Cost Survey**, of the years 2000-14.

Annual Gross earnings per full time employee 2000-13 Greece

Year	NACE Rev 2 classification
2000	15 693
2001	15 688
2002	**17 359**
2003	19 339
2004	21 669
2005	21 902
2006	**23 800**
2007	23 893
2008	23 835
2009	24 619
2010	**24 156**
2011	23 391
2012	22 240
2013	20 682
2014	20 450
2015	Will be available in September

Notes:

1. The Average gross Annual Earnings per **full time employee** for the period 2000 to 2014 **includes**:
   - the special payments for shift and night work, as well as work during weekends and holidays;
   - the total annual bonuses as well as those that are regularly paid on a monthly basis, the 13th salary (Christmas salary, where applicable) and 14th salary (Easter and vacation payments, where applicable);
   - the annual bonuses based on productivity;
   - the education and working time allowance;
   - the marriage and children allowance;

and excludes:
   - the annual payments in kind: foods, drinks, footwear, clothes, accommodation, business cars provided, mobile phone, etc.;
   - the annual premiums related to profit-sharing schemes.
2. The data for 2011 and onwards will be revised when the final results of the SES 2014 will be available.
3. The data for 2013 are revised with the final data from LFS and LCI.

Source: ELSTAT.

5.2. Main employers' contributions to private pension, health, and related schemes

Contributions to private pension and sickness schemes made by employers are not added to employees' gross earnings for tax purposes and are therefore not subject to tax. Since these contributions are not obligatory for employers, no data is provided by the National Statistical Service of Greece. Very few employers have adopted such additional insurance schemes.

2015 parameter values

Average earnings/yr	Ave_earn	20 296	Secretariat estimate
Tax credit	Child_cred	0	
Rates of family subsidies			
paid by employers	Wife_sub	0.1	
children (up to 3)	Child_sub	0	
Income tax schedule	Tax_sch	0.22	25 000
		0.32	42 000
		0.42	
Tax deduction	Tax_cred	2 100	
	Tax_cred_thrsh	21 000	
	Tax_red	100	
Solidarity contribution	Solidarity_sch	0	12 000
		0.007	20 000
		0.014	30 000
		0.02	50 000
		0.04	100 000
		0.06	500 000
		0.08	
Social security contributions	SSC_rate	0.155	
	SSC_rate_empr	0.2456	
	SSC_ceil	77 655.20	
	SSC_ceil_use	1	
Single children support allowance	Child_all	0	480
		6 000	320
		12 000	160
		18 000	0
	Spouse_weight	0.33	
	Child_weight	0.17	

2015 tax equations

The equations for the Greek system in 2015 are mostly on an individual basis. The level of gross earnings for the principal earner is increased by the spouse and child subsidy paid by the employer.

The functions which are used in the equations (Taper, MIN, Tax etc.) are described in the technical note about tax equations. Variable names are defined in the table of parameters above, within the equations table, or are the standard variables "married" and "children". A reference to a variable with the affix "_total" indicates the sum of the relevant variable values for the principal and spouse. And the affixes "_princ" and "_spouse" indicate the value for the principal and spouse, respectively. Equations for a single person are as shown for the principal, with "_spouse" values taken as 0.

	Line in country table and intermediate steps	Variable name	Range	Equation
1.	Earnings	earn_princ	P	Ave_earn*(1+Married*Wife_sub+ MIN(Children,3)*Child_sub)
		earn_spouse	S	Ave_earn*(1+Married*Wife_sub+ MIN(Children,3)*Child_sub)
2.	Allowances:	tax_al	B	SSC
3.	Credits in taxable income	taxbl_cr		0
4.	CG taxable income	tax_inc	B	Positive(earn-tax_al)
5.	CG tax before credits	CG_tax_excl	B	Tax(tax_inc,tax_sch)-Low_rate*Positive(MIN(Effect_low_band-Low_thrsh,tax_inc-Low_thrsh))
	Solidarity contribution	sol_contr	B	=Solidarity(earn-SSC,Solidarity_sch)
6.	Tax credits :	tax_cr	**B**	=Positive(tax_cred-(INT(Positive(earn-tax_cred_thrsh)/1000)*tax_cred_red))
7.	CG tax	CG_tax	B	Positive(CG_tax_excl-tax_cr)+sol_contr
8.	State and local taxes	local_tax	B	0
9.	Employees' soc security	SSC	B	IF(SSC_ceil_use=1,SSC_rate*MIN(earn,SSC_ceil),SSC_rate*earn)
11.	Cash transfers			
		fam_netinc	B	earn – CG_tax - SSC
		cash_trans	B	VLOOKUP(fam_netinc,Child_all,2)*Children
13.	Employer's soc security	SSC_empr	B	IF(SSC_ceil_use=1,SSC_rate_empr*MIN(earn,SSC_ceil),SSC_rate_empr*earn)

Key to range of equation B calculated separately for both principal earner and spouse P calculated for principal only (value taken as 0 for spouse calculation) J calculated once only on a joint basis.

Hungary

This chapter includes data on the income taxes paid by workers, their social security contributions, the family benefits they receive in the form of cash transfers as well as the social security contributions and payroll taxes paid by their employers. Results reported include the marginal and average tax burden for eight different family types.

Methodological information is available for personal income tax systems, compulsory social security contributions to schemes operated within the government sector, universal cash transfers as well as recent changes in the tax/benefit system. The methodology also includes the parameter values and tax equations underlying the data.

Hungary 2015

The tax/benefit position of single persons

	Wage level (per cent of average wage)	67	100	167	67
	Number of children	none	none	none	2
1.	**Gross wage earnings**	2 125 322	3 172 122	5 297 443	2 125 322
2.	**Standard tax allowances**				
	Basic allowance				
	Married or head of family				
	Dependent children	0	0	0	1 500 000
	Deduction for social security contributions and income taxes				
	Work-related expenses				
	Other				
	Total	0	0	0	1 500 000
3.	**Tax credits or cash transfers included in taxable income**	0	0	0	0
4.	**Central government taxable income (1 - 2 + 3)**	2 125 322	3 172 122	5 297 443	625 322
5.	**Central government income tax liability (exclusive of tax credits)**				
	Central government income tax liability (exclusive of tax credits)	340 051	507 539	847 591	100 051
	Total	340 051	507 539	847 591	100 051
6.	**Tax credits**				
	Basic credit	0	0	0	0
	Married or head of family				
	Children				
	Other				
	Total	0	0	0	0
7.	**Central government income tax finally paid (5-6)**	340 051	507 539	847 591	100 051
8.	**State and local taxes**	0	0	0	0
9.	**Employees' compulsory social security contributions**				
	Gross earnings	393 184	586 843	980 027	393 184
	Taxable income				
	Total	393 184	586 843	980 027	393 184
10.	**Total payments to general government (7 + 8 + 9)**	733 236	1 094 382	1 827 618	493 236
11.	**Cash transfers from general government**				
	For head of family				
	For two children	0	0	0	355 200
	Total	0	0	0	355 200
12.	**Take-home pay (1-10+11)**	1 392 086	2 077 740	3 469 825	1 987 286
13.	**Employer's wage dependent contributions and taxes**				
	Employer's compulsory social security contributions	573 837	856 473	1 430 310	573 837
	Payroll taxes	31 880	47 582	79 462	31 880
	Total	605 717	904 055	1 509 771	605 717
14.	**Average rates**				
	Income tax	16.0%	16.0%	16.0%	4.7%
	Employees' social security contributions	18.5%	18.5%	18.5%	18.5%
	Total payments less cash transfers	34.5%	34.5%	34.5%	6.5%
	Total tax wedge including employer's social security contributions	49.0%	49.0%	49.0%	27.2%
15.	**Marginal rates**				
	Total payments less cash transfers: Principal earner	34.5%	34.5%	34.5%	34.5%
	Total payments less cash transfers: Spouse	n.a.	n.a.	n.a.	n.a.
	Total tax wedge: Principal earner	49.0%	49.0%	49.0%	49.0%
	Total tax wedge: Spouse	n.a.	n.a.	n.a.	n.a.

Hungary 2015

The tax/benefit position of married couples

		Wage level (per cent of average wage)	100-0	100-33	100-67	100-33
		Number of children	2	2	2	none
1.	**Gross wage earnings**		3 172 122	4 218 922	5 297 443	4 218 922
2.	**Standard tax allowances**					
	Basic allowance					
	Married or head of family					
	Dependent children		1 500 000	1 500 000	1 500 000	0
	Deduction for social security contributions and income taxes					
	Work-related expenses					
	Other					
		Total	1 500 000	1 500 000	1 500 000	0
3.	**Tax credits or cash transfers included in taxable income**		0	0	0	0
4.	**Central government taxable income (1 - 2 + 3)**		1 672 122	2 718 922	3 797 443	4 218 922
5.	**Central government income tax liability (exclusive of tax credits)**					
	Central government income tax liability (exclusive of tax credits)		267 539	435 027	607 591	675 027
		Total	267 539	435 027	607 591	675 027
6.	**Tax credits**					
	Basic credit		0	0	0	0
	Married or head of family					
	Children					
	Other					
		Total	0	0	0	0
7.	**Central government income tax finally paid (5-6)**		267 539	435 027	607 591	675 027
8.	**State and local taxes**		0	0	0	0
9.	**Employees' compulsory social security contributions**					
	Gross earnings		586 843	780 501	980 027	780 501
	Taxable income					
		Total	586 843	780 501	980 027	780 501
10.	**Total payments to general government (7 + 8 + 9)**		854 382	1 215 528	1 587 618	1 455 528
11.	**Cash transfers from general government**					
	For head of family					
	For two children		319 200	319 200	319 200	0
		Total	319 200	319 200	319 200	0
12.	**Take-home pay (1-10+11)**		2 636 940	3 322 594	4 029 025	2 763 394
13.	**Employer's wage dependent contributions and taxes**					
	Employer's compulsory social security contributions		856 473	1 139 109	1 430 310	1 139 109
	Payroll taxes		47 582	63 284	79 462	63 284
		Total	904 055	1 202 393	1 509 771	1 202 393
14.	**Average rates**					
	Income tax		8.4%	10.3%	11.5%	16.0%
	Employees' social security contributions		18.5%	18.5%	18.5%	18.5%
	Total payments less cash transfers		16.9%	21.2%	23.9%	34.5%
	Total tax wedge including employer's social security contributions		35.3%	38.7%	40.8%	49.0%
15.	**Marginal rates**					
	Total payments less cash transfers: Principal earner		34.5%	34.5%	34.5%	34.5%
	Total payments less cash transfers: Spouse		34.5%	34.5%	34.5%	34.5%
	Total tax wedge: Principal earner		49.0%	49.0%	49.0%	49.0%
	Total tax wedge: Spouse		49.0%	49.0%	49.0%	49.0%

The national currency is the Forint (HUF). In 2015, HUF 279.19 was equal to USD 1. In 2015, the average worker earned HUF 3 172 122 (Secretariat estimate).

1. Personal income tax systems

1.1. *Central/federal government income taxes*

1.1.1. Tax unit

The tax unit is, in all cases, the separate individual. In exceptional cases, the employer can become subject to personal income tax, for instance in the case of benefits in kind.

1.1.2. Tax allowances and tax credits

1.1.2.1. Standard reliefs

- *Basic reliefs*: None.
- *Standard marital status reliefs*: None.
- *Employee Tax credit:* Since 1 January 2012 there is no employee tax credit.
- *Family tax allowance:* For families having children, the basis of income tax can be reduced by the family tax allowance, which amounts to HUF 62 500 per month/each dependent (for families having one or two children), or HUF 206 250 per month/each dependent (for families having at least three children). This tax allowance can be applied by a pregnant woman (or her husband) as from the 91st day after conception until birth of the child. The tax allowance may be claimed by one spouse or be split between the spouses. As of 1 January 2014 the family tax allowance was extended: families whose combined PIT base is not sufficient to claim the maximum amount of the family tax allowance can deduct the remaining sum from the 7% health insurance contribution and the 10% pension contribution. This measure does not affect the eligibility for social security benefits (pensions, healthcare, transfers, etc.).

1.1.2.2. Main non-standard tax reliefs

- *Trade Union membership dues:* Membership dues and contributions paid to trade unions and other corporate bodies of employees are deductible without any restriction.
- Tax credits are made available for physical disability or agricultural activities. Tax deduction is available for those having income from abroad.
- From 1 January 2015 for newly married couples (where it's the first marriage for at least one of the parties) the basis of income tax can be reduced by HUF 31,250 per month for one person of the couple for 24 months.

1.1.3. Tax schedule

The rate of personal income tax amounts to 16%.

1.2. *State and local income taxes*

In Hungary there is no local personal income tax system supplementing the central one.

2. Compulsory social security contributions to schemes operated within the government sector

2.1. Employees' contributions

2.1.1. Pensions

The rate of pension contribution amounts to 10% of gross earnings.

2.1.2. Sickness

The rate of health security contribution amounts to 7% of gross earnings.

2.1.3. Unemployment

The worker must pay, as employees' contribution, 1.5% of gross earnings.

2.1.4. Others

None. The average worker does not have any obligation to pay other contributions than the above mentioned. However, the contribution rates may be different for certain types of income or for certain groups of income recipients (e.g. employees with pensioner status). None of these exceptions are applicable to the workers taken into consideration in this report.

2.2. Employers' contributions

2.2.1. Pensions

None.

2.2.2. Sickness

None.

2.2.3. Unemployment

None.

2.2.4. Others

From 2012 the employers' social security contributions were merged into the new payroll tax, called social contribution tax. This change is of legal nature, the combined rate remains 27% while the revenue is divided among the pension, health care and labour-market funds (26% for pensions, 1% for health care).

The employer contributions also include a payroll tax: the training levy amounts to 1.5% of gross earnings.

From 1 January 2013, the Job Protection Act (JPA) introduced new targeted reliefs in the employers' contributions (social contribution tax and training levy) to incentivise the employment of the most disadvantageous groups on the labour market. From 1 July 2015 the JPA will be extended to agricultural occupations in the age group of 25-55 years. This measure reduces the standard rate of the employers' contributions up to a cap of HUF 100 000 per month. The JPA introduced a permanent reduction of the employers' tax rate by 14.5% for:

- employees under 25 years of age,
- employees over 55 years of age,

- employees working in elementary occupations.

It also introduced temporary reductions (28.5% in the first two years of the employment, and 14.5% in the third year) for:

- long term unemployed re-entering the labour market,
- people returning to work after child-care leave,
- career starters.

From 1st January 2015 the budgetary institutions are not eligible for the JPA tax allowances anymore.

The new targeted reliefs in the employers' contributions are not considered in the Taxing Wages model.

Social security contributions will have to be paid on other benefits than gross earnings (e.g. grants in kind) and payments (e.g. certain kind of contracts).

3. Universal cash transfers

3.1. *Transfers related to marital status*

None.

3.2. *Transfers for dependent children*

Effective from 1 January 2008:

Type of family	HUF per month
For a couple with one child	12 200
For a single earner with one child	13 700
For a couple with two children, per child	13 300
For a single earner with two children, per child	14 800
For a couple with 3 or more children, per child	16 000
For a single earner with 3 or more children, per child	17 000
For a couple with permanently sick and disabled child	23 300
For a single earner with permanently sick and disabled child	25 900

4. Main changes in the tax/benefit system since 2010

- The tax base correction was phased out in two steps.
- The employee tax credit was abolished.
- The employees' health care contribution was increased.
- The employers' social security contributions were merged into the social contribution tax (legal change only, rates and base remained unchanged).
- Health contributions on benefits in kind were increased.
- As a temporary measure, a wage compensation scheme was in effect in the form of an employers' SSC credit.
- Targeted employment incentives to boost the employment levels of groups at the margin of the labour force.
- The child tax allowance was extended in 2014 by allowing the deduction of the allowance from employees' SSC.

5. Memorandum items

5.1. *Employer contributions to private social security arrangements*

In Hungary the law dealing with the voluntary mutual insurance funds (like pension funds) was enacted on 6 December 1993. Based on the rules for 2011, the monthly contribution paid to a voluntary mutual pension fund by the employer of a private worker who participates in a voluntary mutual pension fund, limited to an amount below half of the mandatory minimum wage, is taxable according to an effective personal income tax rate of 19.04 (the nominal tax rate of 16% multiplied by 1.19)%. In the case of employers' contributions paid to health or mutual aid funds, the applicable limit is 30% of the mandatory minimum wage. Contributions in excess of these limits are taxable at an effective personal income tax rate of 19.04% and a health contribution of 27% is also payable on these amounts. Sponsor's donations paid by the employer to its employees' voluntary mutual insurance fund are taxable as well. In addition, employees can apply a 20% tax credit (with a limit of HUF 100 000 or 130 000 per year; in the case of payments simultaneously made to pension, health or mutual aid funds, the limit is HUF 120 000 or 150 000 per year) on these taxable payments. The tax authority pays the tax credit directly to a voluntary mutual insurance fund.

In general, insurance premiums (on the basis of which an employee is named as the recipient/beneficiary of insurance services) paid by the employer are taxable, and social security contributions plus training contribution are also payable. At the same time insurance premiums related to life insurance policy for accidental death, injury liability, or medical care insurance for full and permanent incapacity to work are exempted from taxation and any contributions.

As from 2008 employer pension institutions can be established. Based on the rules for 2011, the monthly contribution paid to an employer pension institution by the employer of a private worker, limited to an amount below half of the mandatory minimum wage, is taxable according to an effective personal income tax rate of 19.04%. Contributions in excess of this limit are taxable at an effective personal income tax rate of 19.04% and a health contribution of 27% is also payable on these amounts.

2015 parameter values

Average earnings/yr	Ave_earn	3 172 122	Secretariat estimate		
Child allowance (per child)	child_al	1	750 000		
		2	750 000		
		3	2 475 000		
		4	2 475 000		
Income tax schedule	tax_sch	0.16			
Social security contributions	SSC_unemp	0.015			
	SSC_p	0.1			
	SSC_h	0.07			
Payroll taxes	SSC_empr	0.27			
	payroll_rate	0.015			
		# of children	1	2	3+
Transfers for children	CB_rates	0	12 200	13 300	16 000
(monthly)		1	13 700	14 800	17 000

2015 tax equations

The equations for the Hungarian system in 2015 are mostly on an individual basis. But the child allowance can be split between the spouses and cash transfers are calculated only once. This is shown by the Range indicator in the table below.

The functions which are used in the equations (Taper, MIN, Tax etc) are described in the technical note about tax equations. Variable names are defined in the table of parameters above, within the equations table, or are the standard variables "married" and "children". A reference to a variable with the affix "_total" indicates the sum of the relevant variable values for the principal and spouse. And the affixes "_princ" and "_spouse" indicate the value for the principal and spouse, respectively. Equations for a single person are as shown for the principal, with "_spouse" values taken as 0.

	Line in country table and intermediate steps	Variable name	Range	Equation
1.	Earnings	earn		
2.	Allowances:			
	Children	child_al	P	IF(Children>0, Children*VLOOKUP(Children, child_al, 2), 0)
	Total	tax_al	B	child_al
3.	Credits in taxable income	taxbl_cr	B	0
4.	CG taxable income	tax_inc	P	MAX(0,earn -tax_al)
	CG taxable income	tax_inc	S	Positive(earn_spouse-Positive(tax_al-earn_spouse-SSC_deduction_princ/tax_sch))
5.	CG tax before credits	CG_tax_excl	B	tax_inc*tax_sch
7.	CG tax	CG_tax	B	CG_tax_excl-tax_cr
8.	State and local taxes	local_tax	B	0
	Child tax allowance (Employees' SSC)	SSC_child_cr	P	=MIN(earn_princ*(SSC_h+SSC_p),Positive(tax_al-earn_princ)*tax_sch)
	Child tax allowance (Employees' SSC)		S	=MIN(earn_spouse*(SSC_h+SSC_p),Positive(-earn_princ)*tax_sch)
9.	Employees' soc security	SSC	B	earn*(SSC_unemp+ SSC_h+SSC_p)-SSC_child_cr
11.	Cash transfers	cash_trans	J	Children*(VLOOKUP((1-Married), CB_rates, MIN(Children, 3)+1)*12)
13.	Employer's soc security	SSC_empr	B	earn*SSC_empr
	Employer's payroll taxes	Payroll	B	earn*payroll_rate

Key to range of equation B calculated separately for both principal earner and spouse P calculated for principal only (value taken as 0 for spouse calculation) J calculated once only.

Iceland

This chapter includes data on the income taxes paid by workers, their social security contributions, the family benefits they receive in the form of cash transfers as well as the social security contributions and payroll taxes paid by their employers. Results reported include the marginal and average tax burden for eight different family types.

Methodological information is available for personal income tax systems, compulsory social security contributions to schemes operated within the government sector, universal cash transfers as well as recent changes in the tax/benefit system. The methodology also includes the parameter values and tax equations underlying the data.

Iceland 2015

The tax/benefit position of single persons

		Wage level (per cent of average wage)	67	100	167	67
		Number of children	none	none	none	2
1.	**Gross wage earnings**		4 985 122	7 440 480	12 425 602	4 985 122
2.	**Standard tax allowances**					
	Basic allowance					
	Married or head of family					
	Dependent children					
	Deduction for social security contributions and income taxes		199 405	297 619	497 024	199 405
	Work-related expenses					
	Other					
		Total	199 405	297 619	497 024	199 405
3.	**Tax credits or cash transfers included in taxable income**		0	0	0	0
4.	**Central government taxable income (1 - 2 + 3)**		4 785 717	7 142 861	11 928 578	4 785 717
5.	**Central government income tax liability (exclusive of tax credits)**		1 120 270	1 716 628	3 050 377	1 120 270
6.	**Tax credits**					
	Basic credit		610 824	610 824	610 824	610 824
	Married or head of family					
	Children					
	Other					
		Total	610 824	610 824	610 824	610 824
7.	**Central government income tax finally paid (5-6)**		509 446	1 105 804	2 439 553	509 446
8.	**State and local taxes**		691 058	1 031 429	1 722 487	691 058
9.	**Employees' compulsory social security contributions**					
	Gross earnings		26 864	26 864	26 864	26 864
	Taxable income					
		Total	26 864	26 864	26 864	26 864
10.	**Total payments to general government (7 + 8 + 9)**		1 227 368	2 164 097	4 188 903	1 227 368
11.	**Cash transfers from general government**					
	For head of family					
	For two children		0	0	0	555 219
		Total	0	0	0	555 219
12.	**Take-home pay (1-10+11)**		3 757 754	5 276 383	8 236 699	4 312 973
13.	**Employer's compulsory social security contributions**		373 386	557 292	930 678	373 386
14.	**Average rates**					
	Income tax		24.1%	28.7%	33.5%	24.1%
	Employees' social security contributions		0.5%	0.4%	0.2%	0.5%
	Total payments less cash transfers		24.6%	29.1%	33.7%	13.5%
	Total tax wedge including employer's social security contributions		29.9%	34.0%	38.3%	19.5%
15.	**Marginal rates**					
	Total payments less cash transfers: Principal earner		38.2%	38.2%	44.4%	47.8%
	Total payments less cash transfers: Spouse		n.a.	n.a.	n.a.	n.a.
	Total tax wedge: Principal earner		42.5%	42.5%	48.3%	51.4%
	Total tax wedge: Spouse		n.a.	n.a.	n.a.	n.a.

Iceland 2015

The tax/benefit position of married couples

		100-0	100-33	100-67	100-33
	Wage level (per cent of average wage)	100-0	100-33	100-67	100-33
	Number of children	2	2	2	none
1.	**Gross wage earnings**	7 440 480	9 895 839	12 425 602	9 895 839
2.	**Standard tax allowances**				
	Basic allowance				
	Married or head of family				
	Dependent children				
	Deduction for social security contributions and income taxes	297 619	395 834	497 024	395 834
	Work-related expenses				
	Other				
	Total	297 619	395 834	497 024	395 834
3.	**Tax credits or cash transfers included in taxable income**	0	0	0	0
4.	**Central government taxable income (1 - 2 + 3)**	7 142 861	9 500 005	11 928 578	9 500 005
5.	**Central government income tax liability (exclusive of tax credits)**	1 716 628	2 255 471	2 836 898	2 255 471
6.	**Tax credits**				
	Basic credit	1 221 648	1 149 667	1 221 648	1 149 667
	Married or head of family				
	Children				
	Other				
	Total	1 221 648	1 149 667	1 221 648	1 149 667
7.	**Central government income tax finally paid (5-6)**	494 980	1 105 804	1 615 250	1 105 804
8.	**State and local taxes**	1 031 429	1 299 820	1 722 487	1 299 820
9.	**Employees' compulsory social security contributions**				
	Gross earnings	26 864	53 728	53 728	53 728
	Taxable income				
	Total	26 864	53 728	53 728	53 728
10.	**Total payments to general government (7 + 8 + 9)**	1 553 273	2 459 352	3 391 465	2 459 352
11.	**Cash transfers from general government**				
	For head of family				
	For two children	322 802	155 788	10 073	0
	Total	322 802	155 788	10 073	0
12.	**Take-home pay (1-10+11)**	6 210 009	7 592 275	9 044 211	7 436 487
13.	**Employer's compulsory social security contributions**	557 292	741 198	930 678	741 198
14.	**Average rates**				
	Income tax	20.5%	24.3%	26.9%	24.3%
	Employees' social security contributions	0.4%	0.5%	0.4%	0.5%
	Total payments less cash transfers	16.5%	23.3%	27.2%	24.9%
	Total tax wedge including employer's social security contributions	22.4%	28.6%	32.3%	30.1%
15.	**Marginal rates**				
	Total payments less cash transfers: Principal earner	47.8%	43.9%	43.9%	38.2%
	Total payments less cash transfers: Spouse	43.7%	41.6%	43.9%	35.8%
	Total tax wedge: Principal earner	51.4%	47.8%	47.8%	42.5%
	Total tax wedge: Spouse	47.6%	45.6%	47.8%	40.3%

The national currency is the Króna (plural: Krónur) (ISK). In 2015, ISK 131.90 was equal to USD 1. In 2015, the average worker is expected to earn ISK 7 440 480 (Secretariat estimate).*

1. Personal income tax system

1.1. Central government income taxes

1.1.1. Tax unit

Income is taxed on an individual basis, except for capital income of married couples which is taxed jointly.

1.1.2. Tax allowances and credits

1.1.2.1. Standard reliefs

- *Basic tax credit*: A fixed tax credit, amounting to ISK 610 824 in 2015, is granted to all individuals 16 years and older, regardless of their marital status. The tax credit is deducted from levied central and local government taxes. Unutilised tax credits or portions thereof are wastable, i.e. non-refundable and non-transferable between tax years.
- *Standard marital status relief:* Married couples may utilise up to 100% of each spouses' unutilised portion of his/her basic tax credit.
- *Relief(s) for children*: None.
- *Relief(s) for compulsory pension contributions:* The compulsory payment to pension funds amounts to 4% of wages and is deductible. In addition, an optional payment of up to 4% of wages may also be deducted. As the additional 4% contribution is optional, it is viewed as a non-standard relief in this Report.

1.1.2.2. Main non-standard tax reliefs applicable to an AW

- *Interest payment relief:* A fully refundable tax credit is granted to purchasers of personal dwellings (homes) to recuperate a part of mortgage-related interest expenses. The maximum tax-related interest credit in 2015 is ISK 400 000 for a single person, ISK 500 000 for a single parent and ISK 600 000 for a married couple. The following constraints apply to interest rebates: 1) they cannot exceed 7.0% of the remaining debt balance incurred in buying a home for one's own use. 2) The maximum amount of interest payments that qualify for an interest rebate calculation is ISK 800 000 for an individual, ISK 1 000 000 for a single parent and ISK 1 200 000 for a couple. 3) 8.5% of taxable income is subtracted from the interest expense. 4) The rebates begin to be curtailed at a net worth threshold of ISK 4 000 000 for a single individual and a single parent and ISK 6 500 000 for a couple and are eliminated altogether at a 60% higher amount, or ISK 6 400 000 and 10 400 000, respectively. (These amounts are based on income in the year 2015 but are paid out in 2016. These numbers are estimates; final figures will be available once the 2016 budget has been passed).

* The definition of average worker in Iceland includes workers in five categories. See Section 5.1.

1.1.3. *Tax schedule*

The income tax base is composed of *personal income* (e.g. wages, salaries, fringe benefits, pensions, etc.), which is taxed on an individual basis, and *capital income* which is taxed jointly for married couples.

The tax on personal income is triple-rated. The central government income tax rate in 2015 is 22.86% for income up to ISK 309 140 per month. A 25.3% tax rate applies to the next ISK 527 264 or up to ISK 836 404. For income exceeding ISK 836 404 the tax rate is 31.8%. The income tax rate applies to all personal income in excess of ISK 142 153 per month (ISK 1 705 836 per year). Tax relief is provided by the basic credit described in Section 1.121.

The tax on capital income is 20%. It is levied on all capital income of individuals, such as interest, dividends, rents etc. Interest income up to ISK 125 000 per year and 30% of income from rent of residential property is tax free.

1.2. *Local government income tax*

The local government income tax base is the same as the central government's personal income tax base.

The local governments' income tax is single-rated, but the rate varies between 12.44 and 14.52% between municipalities. The average rate in 2015 is 14.44%.

2. Compulsory social security contributions to schemes operated within the government sector

2.1. *Employees' contributions*

Fee to the Retiree Investment Fund: 16 to 70 year-old individuals are subject to a fixed tax of ISK 10 464 in 2015, provided the individual's taxable income is at least ISK 1 637 598 for the year. This tax will be collected in 2016.

Fee to the broadcast media: 16 to 70 year-old individuals with taxable income over ISK 1 637 598 for the year are subject to a fixed tax of ISK 16 400 in 2015, which will be collected in 2016.

These amounts are estimates and thus subject to change as the fees are payable in 2016.

2.2. *Employers' contributions*

Employers have to pay a social security tax on total wages of 7.49%. In addition, 0.65% is levied on the wages of fishermen as a premium for their government accident insurance. Furthermore, a new financial activities tax was introduced in 2012, which requires financial and insurance companies to pay an additional 5.5% payroll tax in 2015.

3. Universal cash transfers

3.1. *Marital status related transfers*

None.

3.2. *Transfers for dependent children*

Child benefits are granted for each child, subject to income thresholds. In 2014 they are as follows (in ISK per year):

For each child under the age of seven:	119 300
Children under the age of eighteen at the end of 2014:	
First child	199 839
Each additional child	237 949
Benefits for single parents:	
First child	332 950
Each additional child	341 541
Income threshold for benefit curtailment:	
For couples	4 800 000
For a single parent	2 400 000
Curtailment of benefits (children under the age of seven only):	
For each child	4%
Curtailment of benefits (all children under the age of eighteen):	
For one child	4%
For two children	6%
For three children or more	8%

Note that child benefits in this Report are based on income in the year 2015 but are paid out in 2016 (see also Section 4.4). These numbers are estimates and thus subject to change.

4. Main changes in the tax/benefit system since 1998

4.1. *The deductibility of the payment to pension funds*

All employees are required to participate in pension funds. The employee contribution is generally 4% of wages and the employer contribution was 6%, and increased to 8% as of beginning 2007. Both contributions are deductible from income before tax. In some cases, the contributions of employees and employers are higher. An optional, additional payment from employees of up to 4% of wages is also deductible and goes into an individual retirement account. However, from 2012 to mid-2014, this additional payment was temporarily set at 2 %.

This voluntary pension savings option was first introduced in 1999 in order to encourage personal saving. At the time the contribution rate was 2% for employees and 0.2% for employers. In May 2000 these rates were doubled to 4 and 0.4%, respectively, as noted above. In addition, some employers, such as the central government, have increased their employer counter-contribution by agreement with employees. The central government contributed 1% against a voluntary employee contribution of 4% in 2001 and 2% as of the beginning of 2002. All such contributions are tax-deductible, both with the employer and the employee at the time the contribution is made. The actual pension is taxed as personal income when it is drawn. As of the beginning of 2004, the employer option of deducting the above 0.4% against the social security tax was abolished. Since such employer counter-contributions had become part of wage agreements in most cases, it was no longer felt that such a tax incentive was needed.

4.2. *Central and local income tax rates in 1997-2015*

In 1997-07, the Government pursued a policy of reducing the marginal tax rate, as can been seen in the table below. This development was reversed in 2009 when income tax was raised by 1.35 percentage points in response to the Treasury's rising debt burden brought on by the economic crisis. At the beginning of 2010 the tax system was changed from single rated to triple rated. The tax rate was set at 24.1% for the first monthly ISK 200 000 but it was raised by 2.9% for the next ISK 450 000 and again by 6% for income in excess of ISK 650 000. In 2014, the rates are 22.86%, 25.3% and 31.8%, and the corresponding income thresholds are ISK 290 000 and 784 619 per month; see Section 1.13 for further details. From 1998 onwards, the central government and average local government personal income tax rates have been as follows:

	Central government general tax rate (%)	Municipal tax rate (%)	Total tax rate (%)	Central government surtax (%)
1998	27.41	11.61	39.02	7.00
1999	26.41	11.93	38.34	7.00
2000	26.41	11.96	38.37	7.00
2001	26.08	12.68	38.76	7.00
2002	25.75	12.79	38.54	7.00
2003	25.75	12.80	38.55	5.00
2004	25.75	12.83	38.58	4.00
2005	24.75	12.98	37.73	2.00
2006	23.75	12.97	36.72	0
2007	22.75	12.97	35.72	0
2008	22.75	12.97	35.72	0
2009	24.10	13.10	37.20	0
2010	24.10	13.12	37.32	2.90/6.00
2011	22.90	14.41	37.31	2.90/6.00
2012	22.90	14.44	37.34	2.90/6.00
2013	22.90	14.42	37.32	2.90/6.00
2014	22.86	14.44	37.30	2.44/6.50
2015	22.86	14.44	37.30	2.44/6.50

4.3. *A special tax on higher income*

In 1998, the special tax on higher income was raised by 2 percentage points, from 5 to 7%. For 2003-income, it was reduced back to 5%. It was reduced to 4% for 2004 income and to 2% for 2005-income. In the fiscal year 2006, the tax was abolished. In the latter half of 2009 the special tax on higher income was introduced again at 8%. In 2010 the tax system changed to triple-rated; see Sections 4.2 and 1.13.

4.4. *A revision of child benefit system*

Child benefits are granted for each child, subject to income thresholds. The amendments to tax legislation that came into effect in 2004 included a schedule for raising child benefits. As from 2007, the child benefits will be paid for children up to 18 years old instead of 16 years old. For 2008-15, benefits are as follows (in ISK per year):

	2008	2009	2010	2011	2012	2013	2014	2015
For all children under the age of seven	61 191	61 191	61 191	61 191	100 000	100 000	115 825	119 300
Children under the age of eighteen:								
First child	152 331	152 331	152 331	152 331	167 564	167 564	194 081	199 839
Each additional child	181 323	181 323	181 323	181 323	199 455	199 455	231 019	237 949
Benefits for single parents:								
First child	253 716	253 716	253 716	253 716	279 087	279 087	323 253	332 950
Each additional child	260 262	260 262	260 262	260 262	286 288	286 288	331 593	341 541
Income threshold for benefit curtailment:								
For couples	3 600 000	3 600 000	3 600 000	3 600 000	4 800 000	4 800 000	4 800 000	4 800 000
For a single parent	1 800 000	1 800 000	1 800 000	1 800 000	2 400 000	2 400 000	2 400 000	2 400 000

	2008	2009	2010	2011	2012	2013	2014	2015
Curtailment of benefits under the age of seven:								
For each child			3%	3%	3%	3%	4%	4%
Curtailment of benefits under the age of eighteen:								
For one child	2%	2%	3%	3%	3%	3%	4%	4%
For two children	5%	5%	5%	5%	5%	5%	6%	6%
For three children or more	7%	7%	7%	7%	7%	7%	8%	8%

The data for 2015 is subject to change as the benefits are not payable until 2016.

4.5. *A revision of interest rebates*

In 2004, the interest rebate was cut by 10%, effective for that year only. The ceiling on interest payments that qualify for the interest rebate was reduced from 7% to 5.5% in 2005 and the interest rate cut was reduced from 10% to 5%. As of the beginning of 2006, the ceiling was further reduced to 5%. In 2005 and again in 2007 the net worth ceiling was lifted considerably in reaction to the increase in net worth due to the house price boom in 2005-07. In 2008, as mortgage-related interest expenses surged, the ceiling on interest payments was raised back to 7% and the maximum rebate amount increased by 37%. These measures stayed in effect in 2009. In 2010 the maximum rebate amount increased by 47-62% and the net worth ceiling was reduced significantly. The rate of taxable income which is subtracted from the interest expense was increased from 6% to 8% and further to 8.5% in 2014. In addition to the ordinary interest payment relief, a temporary interest cost rebate was in effect in 2010-11; see Section 1.122.

4.6. *Transferability of basic tax credit between spouses*

The basic tax credit was made transferable between spouses in stages; see section 1.121 above. In fiscal year 2001, 90% of the credit became transferable, rising to 95% in 2002 and 100% in 2003.

5. Memorandum items

5.1. *Identification of AW (only eight categories) and valuation of earnings*

The data on average earnings refers to average workers in eight categories according to the NACE rev. 2 classification which corresponds to the ISIC rev.4 system. The categories are C – Manufacturing, D – Electricity, gas, steam and air conditioning supply (from 2008), E – Water supply; sewerage, waste management and remediation activities (from 2008) F – Construction, G – Wholesale and retail trade, repair of motor vehicles, motorcycles, H – Transport, storage, and J – Information and communication K – Financial and insurance activities. Public sector employees are not included. Together, these categories comprise approximately 80% of Iceland's private sector labour force.

The original data are obtained from a monthly survey among Icelandic firms with 10 or more employees.

5.2. *Employer contributions to private pension funds, health and related schemes*

By law, all employees and employers must contribute to pension funds. These funds are private, generally linked to unions and employee associations. The private pension funds are not part of the government-run social security system, to which a payroll tax is paid as described under Section 2.2 above. Compulsory and voluntary payments to such funds are described in Section 4.1 above.

2015 parameter values

Average earnings/yr	Ave_earn	7 440 480	Secretariat estimate
Pension rate for tax allowance	pension_rate	0.04	
Tax credit	Basic_crd	610 824	
	Married_propn	1	
Central income tax	tax_sch	0.2286	3 709 680
		0.253	10 036 847
		0.318	
Special tax	special_rate	0	
threshold	special_thrsh		
Local tax	local_rate	0.1444	
Church tax	church_tax	0	
Social Security Contr.	SSC_fixed	26 864	
	SSC_thrsh	1 637 598	
Employer SSC	SSC_empr	0.0749	
General child allowance:			
child allowance	CA	119 300	
Maximum number of children under 7	max_child_under7	1	
Supplement child allowance:			
Married couple case			
first child	SA_first_m	199 839	
other children	SA_others_m	237 949	
income threshold	SA_tresh_m	4 800 000	
Single parent case			
first child	SA_first_s	332 950	
other children	SA_others_s	341 541	
income threshold	SA_tresh_s	2 400 000	
reduction rate (one child)	SA_redn_1	0.04	
reduction rate (two children)	SA_redn_2	0.06	
reduction rate (tree or more children)	SA_redn_3	0.08	

2015 tax equations

The equations for the Iceland system are mostly on an individual basis. But the tax credit for married couples is relevant only to the calculation for the principal earner and child benefit is calculated only once. This is shown by the Range indicator in the table below.

The functions which are used in the equations (Taper, MIN, Tax etc) are described in the technical note about tax equations. Variable names are defined in the table of parameters above, within the equations table, or are the standard variables "married" and "children". A reference to a variable with the affix "_total" indicates the sum of the relevant variable values for the principal and spouse. And the affixes "_princ" and "_spouse" indicate the value for the principal and spouse, respectively. Equations for a single person are as shown for the principal, with "_spouse" values taken as 0.

	Line in country table and intermediate steps	Variable name	Range	Equation
1.	Earnings	earn		
2.	Allowances:	tax_al	B	earn*pension_rate
3.	Credits in taxable income	taxbl_cr	B	0
4.	CG taxable income	tax_inc	B	earn-tax_al
5.	CG tax before credits	CG_tax_excl	B	tax(tax_inc, tax_sch)
6.	Tax credits :	tax_cr	P	MIN(CG_tax_excl_princ,Basic_crd+MAX(Married*Basic_crd-CG_tax_excl_spouse-(tax_inc_spouse*local_rate),0))
			S	MIN(Married*Basic_crd, CG_tax_excl_spouse)
		special_tax	J	0
7.	CG tax	CG_tax	B	CG_tax_excl-tax_cr+special_tax
8.	State and local taxes	local_tax	P S	MAX(tax_inc_princ*local_rate-MAX(Basic_crd+ Max(Married*Basic_crd-CG_tax_excl_spouse-(tax_inc_spouse*local_rate),0)-CG_tax_excl_princ,0),0) MAX(tax_inc_spouse*local_rate-MAX(Married*Basic_crd-CG_tax_excl_spouse,0),0)
9.	Employees' soc security	SSC	B	SSC_fixed*(earn>SSC_thrsh)
11.	Cash transfers:			
	Total family income	inc_tot	J	earn_total
	Child allowance	cash_trans	J	Positive(MIN(Children,max_child_under7)*CA-Positive(inc_total*(1-pension_rate) -IF(Married,SA_tresh_m,SA_tresh_s))*SA_redn_1) +(Children>0)*(IF(Married, SA_first_m+ Positive(Children-1)*SA_others_m,SA_first_s+ Positive(Children-1)*SA_others_s) - Positive(inc_tot*(1-pension_rate)-IF(Married,SA_tresh_m,SA_tresh_s))*IF(Children=1, SA_redn_1,IF(Children=2,SA_redn_2,SA_redn_3)))
13.	Employer's soc security	SSC_empr	B	earn*SSC_empr_rate

Key to range of equation B calculated separately for both principal earner and spouse P calculated for principal only (value taken as 0 for spouse calculation) J calculated once only on a joint basis.

Ireland

This chapter includes data on the income taxes paid by workers, their social security contributions, the family benefits they receive in the form of cash transfers as well as the social security contributions and payroll taxes paid by their employers. Results reported include the marginal and average tax burden for eight different family types.

Methodological information is available for personal income tax systems, compulsory social security contributions to schemes operated within the government sector, universal cash transfers as well as recent changes in the tax/benefit system. The methodology also includes the parameter values and tax equations underlying the data.

Ireland 2015

The tax/benefit position of single persons

	Wage level (per cent of average wage)	67	100	167	67
	Number of children	none	none	none	2
1.	**Gross wage earnings**	23 348	34 847	58 195	23 348
2.	**Standard tax allowances**	0	0	0	0
3.	**Tax credits or cash transfers included in taxable income**	0	0	0	0
4.	**Central government taxable income (1 - 2 + 3)**	23 348	34 847	58 195	23 348
5.	**Central government income tax liability (exclusive of tax credits)**	4 670	7 179	16 518	4 670
6.	**Tax credits**				
	Basic credit	1 650	1 650	1 650	1 650
	Single, head of family	0	0	0	1 650
	Children				
	Other	1 650	1 650	1 650	1 650
	Total	3 300	3 300	3 300	4 950
7.	**Central government income tax finally paid (5-6)**	2 148	5 463	16 436	779
8.	**State and local taxes**	0	0	0	0
9.	**Employees' compulsory social security contributions**				
	Gross earnings	934	1 394	2 328	934
	Taxable income				
	Total	934	1 394	2 328	934
10.	**Total payments to general government (7 + 8 + 9)**	3 082	6 857	18 764	1 713
11.	**Cash transfers from general government**				
	For head of family	0	0	0	5 802
	For two children	0	0	0	3 240
	Total	0	0	0	9 042
12.	**Take-home pay (1-10+11)**	20 265	27 991	39 431	30 676
13.	**Employer's compulsory social security contributions**	2 510	3 746	6 256	2 510
14.	**Average rates**				
	Income tax	9.2%	15.7%	28.2%	3.3%
	Employees' social security contributions	4.0%	4.0%	4.0%	4.0%
	Total payments less cash transfers	13.2%	19.7%	32.2%	-31.4%
	Total tax wedge including employer's social security contributions	21.6%	27.5%	38.8%	-18.6%
15.	**Marginal rates**				
	Total payments less cash transfers: Principal earner	31.0%	51.0%	51.0%	64.4%
	Total payments less cash transfers: Spouse	n.a.	n.a.	n.a.	n.a.
	Total tax wedge: Principal earner	37.7%	55.8%	55.8%	67.9%
	Total tax wedge: Spouse	n.a.	n.a.	n.a.	n.a.

Ireland 2015

The tax/benefit position of married couples

		Wage level (per cent of average wage)	100-0	100-33	100-67	100-33
		Number of children	2	2	2	none
1.	**Gross wage earnings**		34 847	46 347	58 195	46 347
2.	**Standard tax allowances**		0	0	0	0
3.	**Tax credits or cash transfers included in taxable income**		0	0	0	0
4.	**Central government taxable income (1 - 2 + 3)**		34 847	46 347	58 195	46 347
5.	**Central government income tax liability (exclusive of tax credits)**		6 969	9 269	11 639	9 269
6.	**Tax credits**					
	Basic credit		3 300	3 300	3 300	3 300
	Single, head of family		0	0	0	0
	Children					
	Other		2 460	3 300	3 300	3 300
	Total		5 760	6 600	6 600	6 600
7.	**Central government income tax finally paid (5-6)**		2 793	4 253	7 402	4 253
8.	**State and local taxes**		0	0	0	0
9.	**Employees' compulsory social security contributions**					
	Gross earnings		1 394	1 394	2 328	1 394
	Taxable income					
	Total		1 394	1 394	2 328	1 394
10.	**Total payments to general government (7 + 8 + 9)**		4 187	5 647	9 730	5 647
11.	**Cash transfers from general government**					
	For head of family		1 040	0	0	0
	For two children		3 240	3 240	3 240	0
	Total		4 280	3 240	3 240	0
12.	**Take-home pay (1-10+11)**		34 940	43 940	51 705	40 700
13.	**Employer's compulsory social security contributions**		3 746	4 724	6 256	4 724
14.	**Average rates**					
	Income tax		8.0%	9.2%	12.7%	9.2%
	Employees' social security contributions		4.0%	3.0%	4.0%	3.0%
	Total payments less cash transfers		-0.3%	5.2%	11.2%	12.2%
	Total tax wedge including employer's social security contributions		9.5%	14.0%	19.8%	20.3%
15.	**Marginal rates**					
	Total payments less cash transfers: Principal earner		31.0%	31.0%	31.0%	31.0%
	Total payments less cash transfers: Spouse		21.7%	20.0%	31.0%	20.0%
	Total tax wedge: Principal earner		37.7%	37.7%	37.7%	37.7%
	Total tax wedge: Spouse		27.9%	26.3%	37.7%	26.3%

The national currency is the Euro (EUR). In 2015, EUR 0.90 was equal to USD 1. In that year, the average production worker earned EUR 34 847 (Secretariat estimate).

1. Personal income tax systems

1.1. Central/federal government income taxes

1.1.1. Tax unit

Tax is levied on the combined income of both spouses. Either spouse may, however, opt for separate assessment, in which case the tax payable by both spouses must be the same as would be payable under joint taxation. A further option allows either spouse to opt for assessment as single persons in which case they are treated as separate units. The calculations presented in this Report are based on family taxation.

1.1.2. Tax credits

1.1.2.1. Standard reliefs:

- *Basic reliefs:* The single person's credit is EUR 1 650 per year.
- *Standard marital status reliefs:* The married person's credit is EUR 3 300 per year (i.e. twice the basic credit of EUR 1 650).
- *Employee credit:* With the exception of certain company directors and their spouses and the spouses of partners in partnership cases, all employees, including (subject to certain conditions) children who are full-time employees in the business of their parents, are entitled to an employee credit of EUR 1 650.
- *Single-Parent Family Relief:* The single parent family credit is EUR 1 650.

1.1.2.2. Main non-standard tax reliefs applicable to an APW

- *Interest on qualifying loans:* This relief can no longer be claimed by new applicants but those who had claimed prior to 2012 are still eligible.

	First time mortgage holders	Other mortgage holders
Married couple	• EUR 8 000	• EUR 5 079
Widowed person	• EUR 8 000	• EUR 5 079
Single person	• EUR 4 000	• EUR 2 539

- *Medical Insurance:* Relief at the taxpayer's standard rate of tax is available for taxpayers who make a payment to an authorised insurer under a contract which provides for the payment of medical expenses resulting from sickness of the person, his wife, child or other dependants. This *relief is now granted at source and is paid to the insurance provider.*
- *Mortgage Interest Relief:* Mortgage interest relief is discontinued for any mortgage over 7 years from 1 May 2009.
- *Work-related Expenses:* These are relieved to the extent that they are wholly, exclusively and necessarily incurred in the performance of the duties of an employment.

- *Home Carers Allowance:* This is a tax credit of EUR 810 for families where one spouse works at home to care for children, the aged or incapacitated persons, where the carer spouse's income does not exceed EUR 5 079. A reduced measure of relief is granted for income between EUR 5 080 and EUR 6 700: if the income exceeds EUR 5 080 the tax credit is reduced by one half of the income of the Home Carer that exceeds this limit. This credit and the increased standard rate tax band for two income couples (see tax schedule below) are mutually exclusive but the person may opt for whichever is the more beneficial. If the Home Carer earns income of up to EUR 5 080 in his/her own right for the tax year, the full tax credit may be claimed. For the purposes of this tax credit, income means any taxable income such as income from a part-time job, dividends, etc. but does not include the Carer's Allowance payable by the Department of Social and Family Affairs.

1.1.3. *Tax schedule*

Band of taxable Income (EUR)				Rate (%)
Single/widow(er)	Married couple (one income)	Married couple (two incomes)	One-parent Families	
Up to 33 800	Up to 42 800	Up to the lesser of: 67 600; 42 800 plus the amount of the lowest income	37 800	20
Balance	Balance	Balance	Balance	40

1.1.4. *Low income exemption and marginal relief tax*

Where total income is less than or equal to the income exemption limit that income is exempt from tax.

Exemption limits:

	EUR
Single/widowed	
Under 65	5 210
65 and over	17 000
Married	
Under 65	10 420
65 and over	34 000
Children	
One or two children (each)	575
Subsequent children	830

The marginal relief rate of tax applies where liability to tax at the marginal relief rate is less than that which would be chargeable under the normal tax schedule and where total income is less than twice the relevant exemption limit, otherwise tax is charged under the normal tax schedule.

Marginal relief tax is charged, where applicable, at a rate of 40% on the difference between total income and the relevant exemption limit.

1.1.5. *Universal Social Charge (USC)*

In 2011, the Universal Social Charge (USC) replaced the Income and Health Levies that were introduced in 2009 in the income tax. The USC applies at a low rate on a broad base.

The USC is charged on an individualised basis on gross income at 1.5% on income up to and including EUR 12 012, at 3.5% for income in excess of EUR 12 012 but not greater than EUR 17 576, at 7% for income in excess of EUR 17576 but not greater than EUR 70 044, and at 8% above that level. Those aged over 70 years pay 1.5% on income up to EUR 12 012 and at 3.5% above that level up to and including EUR 60 000. The lower exemption threshold has been increased from EUR 10 036 to EUR 12 012. The USC does not apply to social welfare payments, including contributory and non-contributory social welfare State pensions.

Individuals in possession of full medical card, including a Health Amendment Act card, will only pay USC at a max rate of 3.5% irrespective of the level of their income. However, when an individual has self-employment income in excess of EUR 100 000 for a tax year, the max rate is 6.5% on the amount of the excess. Non-medical card holders are subject to a maximum rate of 11% on such income.

USC rates for individuals aged 70 years and over and individuals who hold FULL medical cards: The 3.5% rate applies to all income over EUR 12 012. There is a surcharge of 3% on individuals who have income from self-employment that exceeds EUR 100 000 in a year, regardless of age. Where such individuals are aged over 70 years or hold a full medical card, a rate of 6.5% applies.

1.2. State and local income taxes

No State or local income taxes exist in Ireland.

2. Compulsory social security contributions to schemes operated within the government sector

2.1. Employees' contributions

Contributions are payable at a rate of 4 per cent of an employee's gross earnings less allowable superannuation contributions. No distinction is made by marital status or sex. Those earning less than EUR 352 per week are exempt. The following is a breakdown of the 2015 rate of contribution together with ceilings where applicable:

Description	Rate	Threshold (EUR)	Ceiling (EUR)
Pension and social insurance	4.00	352 per week	

2.2. Employers' contributions

Like employees' contributions, employers' contributions are payable as a percentage of gross employee earnings less allowable superannuation contributions. The following is a breakdown of the 2015 rate of contribution:

Description	Rate %
Occupational injuries	0.50
Redundancy contribution	0.40
Pension and social insurance	9.85
TOTAL	10.75

The employers' contribution is reduced from 10.75% to 8.5% in respect of employees earning less than EUR 356 per week.

3. Universal cash transfers

3.1. *Transfers related to marital status*

None.

3.2. *Transfers for dependent children*

These are payable to all children under the age of 16 (or under 18 years, if the child is undergoing full-time education by day or is incapacitated and likely to remain so for a prolonged period). These payments do not depend on any insurance or on the means of the claimant. Entitlements to higher rate for the third and subsequent child are being phased out over two years. The amounts payable in 2015 are as follows:

Period	Monthly rate per child	
January 2015 to December 2015	First to second child: EUR 135.00	Subsequent children: EUR 135.00

3.3. *Transfers for low income families*

A non-taxable family income supplement is payable to low income families where either the principal earner and/or the spouse are in full-time employment. Full-time employment is defined as working nineteen hours per week or more. The hours worked by the principal and the spouse can be aggregated for the purposes of this definition. When calculating income for the purposes of the relief superannuation payments, social welfare payments, tax payments, health and employment and training levies are all subtracted to arrive at disposable income.

The level of payment is dependent on the amount of family income and the number of children. The supplement payable is 60% of the difference between the family income and the income limit applicable to the family. A minimum of EUR 20 per week is payable to eligible families. No supplement is payable to families with income in excess of the relevant income limit.

The income limit for a family with two children in 2015 is EUR 602 per week.

One Parent Family Payment: This new non-taxable payment is available for men and women who for a variety of reasons are bringing up a child or children without the support of a partner. The payment which is means tested is payable in full where the persons earnings does not exceed EUR 7 618. Where earnings are between EUR 7 618 and EUR 22 100 a reduced payment is received. The amount of the full payment for 2015 is EUR 6 552 plus EUR 1 550 for each child. Because of the complex means testing system this type of person is excluded from the AW examples.

4. Other main changes in tax/benefit system since 2014

4.1. *One-parent family tax credit*

This was replaced with a new Single Person Child Carer Tax Credit from 1 January 2015. The new credit is of the same value but ONLY available to the principal carer of the child.

5. Memorandum items

5.1. *Employer contributions to private social security arrangements*

Information not available, although such schemes do exist.

2015 parameter values

Average earnings/yr	Ave_earn	34 847	Secretariat estimate
Tax allowances			
Tax Credits	Basic_al_at_standardrate	1 650	
	Married_al_at_standardrate	1 650	
	Empl_al_at_standardrate	1 650	
	Singleparent_at_standardrate	1 650	
	Carers_allow	810	
	Carers_thrsh1	5 080	
	Carers_thrsh2	6 700	
	Carers_taper_rt	0.5	
Exemption amount	Single_ex	5 210	
	Married_ex	5 210	
	Child_ex	575	
	Child_ex_3	830	
Marginal relief limit	Single_MR	10 420	
	Married_MR	10 420	
	Child_MR	1 150	
	Child_MR_3	1 660	
Marginal relief	marg_rel_rate	0.4	
Income tax	Single_sch	0.2	33 800
		0.4	
	Single_sch_child	0.2	37 800
		0.4	
	Married_sch_oneinc	0.2	42 800
		0.4	
	Married_sch_twoinc	0.2	67 600
		0.4	
Universal Social Charge	USC	0.015	12 012
		0.035	17 576
		0.07	70 044
		0.08	
	USC_sch_med_card	0.015	12 012
		0.035	
	USC threshold	12012	
Maximum increase in first band	Band_increase_lim	27 400	
Social security contributions	SSC_thresh	18 304	
Employees	pension_rate	0.04	
	pension_ceil	0	
	Non_cum_Allc	0	
Employers	Empr_rate	0.1075	
	Empr_lower_rate	0.085	
	Empr_thrsh	18 512	
Child benefit	Ch_ben	1 620	
	Ch_ben_3	1 620	
Family income supplement	FIS_pay_limit	31 304	
	FIS_min	1 040	
	FIS_rate	0.6	
Medical card	single_med_card	9 568	
	married_med_card	13 858	
	child_add_med_card	1 976	

2015 tax equations

The equations for the Irish system in 2015 are mostly on a family basis using mainly a tax credit system for the first time. But social security contributions are calculated separately for each spouse. This is shown by the Range indicator in the table below.

The functions which are used in the equations (Taper, MIN, Tax etc) are described in the technical note about tax equations. Variable names are defined in the table of parameters above, within the equations table, or are the standard variables "married" and "children". A reference to a variable with the affix "_total" indicates the sum of the relevant variable values for the principal and spouse. And the affixes "_princ" and "_spouse" indicate the value for the principal and spouse, respectively. Equations for a single person are as shown for the principal, with "_spouse" values taken as 0.

	Line in country table and intermediate steps	Variable name	Range	Equation
1.	Earnings	earn		
2.	Allowances:			(provided at standard rate (tax credit equivalent))
3.	Credits in taxable income	taxbl_cr	J	0
4.	Taxable income	tax_inc	J	earn
	New carers allowance (provided as a tax credit)	career_allow		IF((Married*Children)>0, IF(earn_spouse<=Carers_thrsh1, Carers_allow, IF(earn_spouse>Carers_thrsh2, 0, Positive (Carers_allow-Carers_taper_rt*(earn_spouse-Carers_thrsh1)))), 0)
	Preliminary Tax Liable (including carers allowance)	tax_prel	J	IF(Married=0, IF(Children=0, Tax(tax_inc, Single_sch), Tax(tax_inc, Single_sch_child)), IF(AB7=0, Tax(tax_inc, Married_sch_oneinc)-AG7, Tax(earn_principal+Positive(earn_spouse-Band_increase_lim), Married_sch_oneinc)+Tax(MIN (earn_spouse, Band_increase_lim), Married_sch_oneinc)))
5.	Tax before credits (but including carers allowance)	_tax_excl	J	IF((Married*earn_spouse)>0, MINA(tax_prel, (Tax(tax_inc, Married_sch_oneinc)-career_allow)), tax_prel)
	Universal social charge	USG	J	IF(earn>USC_threshold,IF(med_crd_fac=1,Tax(earn,USC_sch),Tax(earn,USC_sch_med_card)),0)
6.	Tax credits :	basic_cr	J	Basic_al_at_standardrate+(Married*Married_al_at_standardrate)
		single_par_cr		IF(Married=0, IF(Children>0, Singleparent_at_standardrate, 0), 0)
		other_cr		Empl_al_at_standardrate+ (IF(earn_spouse>0, Empl_al_at_standardrate, 0))
		tax_cr		basic_cr+single_par_cr+other_cr
	Exemption amount	exemp_amt	J	Single_ex+Married*Married_ex+Child_ex*MIN(2, Children)+ (Children>2)*(Children-2)*Child_ex_3
	Marginal relief limit	MRL	J	Single_MR+Married*Married_MR+Child_MR*MIN(2, Children)+ (Children>2)*(Children-2)*Child_MR_3
7.	Net tax	CG_tax	J	If(earn_total<=MRL, MIN(marg_rel_rate*positive(earn_total-exem_amt), positive(_tax_excl-tax_cr)), positive(_tax_excl-tax_cr))+USG
8.	State and local taxes	local_tax	J	0
	Employees' soc security			
	weekly allowance	weekly_allce	B	IF(earn=0,0,MINA(Non_cum_Allc,earn))
	Medical card factor	Med_crd_fac	J	(single_med_card+Married*(married_med_card-single_med_card) +child_add_med_card*Children<earn_princ+earn_spouse)
	employees' soc security	SSC	B	IF(earn>SSC_thresh, pension_rate*Positive(earn-weekly_allce), 0)
11.	Cash transfers			
		Child_benefit	J	Children*Ch_ben+(Children>2)*(Children-2)*(Ch_ben_3-Ch_ben)
		FIS	J	(Children>0)*IF((earn-_tax-SSC)<=FIS_pay_limit , MAXA((FIS_pay_limit-(earn-_tax-SSC))*FIS_rate, FIS_min), 0)
	Total cash transfers	cash_trans		Child_benefit+FIS
13.	Employer's soc security	SSC_empr	B	IF(earn<=Empr_thrsh, Empr_lower_rate, Empr_rate)* MIN(earn, Empr_ceil)

Key to range of equation B calculated separately for both principal earner and spouse P calculated for principal only (value taken as 0 for spouse calculation) J calculated once only on a joint basis.

Israel

This chapter includes data on the income taxes paid by workers, their social security contributions, the family benefits they receive in the form of cash transfers as well as the social security contributions and payroll taxes paid by their employers. Results reported include the marginal and average tax burden for eight different family types.

Methodological information is available for personal income tax systems, compulsory social security contributions to schemes operated within the government sector, universal cash transfers as well as recent changes in the tax/benefit system. The methodology also includes the parameter values and tax equations underlying the data.

Israel 2015

The tax/benefit position of single persons

	Wage level (per cent of average wage)		67	100	167	67
	Number of children		none	none	none	2
1.	**Gross wage earnings**		92 432	137 958	230 390	92 432
2.	**Standard tax allowances**					
	Basic allowance		0	0	0	0
	Married or head of family					
	Dependent children					
	Deduction for social security contributions and income taxes					
	Work-related expenses		0	0	0	0
	Other					
		Total	0	0	0	0
3.	**Tax credits or cash transfers included in taxable income**		0	0	0	0
4.	**Central government taxable income (1 - 2 + 3)**		92 432	137 958	230 390	92 432
5.	**Central government income tax liability (exclusive of tax credits)**		10 411	18 882	44 543	10 411
6.	**Tax credits**					
	Basic credit		5 886	5 886	5 886	7 194
	Married or head of family		0	0	0	2 616
	Children		0	0	0	5 232
	EITC		0	0	0	0
	Unused wastable tax credits		0	0	0	4 631
		Total	5 886	5 886	5 886	15 042
7.	**Central government income tax finally paid (5-6)**		4 525	12 996	38 657	0
8.	**State and local taxes**		0	0	0	0
9.	**Employees' compulsory social security contributions**					
	Gross earnings		5 425	10 888	21 980	5 425
	Taxable income					
		Total	5 425	10 888	21 980	5 425
10.	**Total payments to general government (7 + 8 + 9)**		9 950	23 883	60 637	5 425
11.	**Cash transfers from general government**					
	For head of family					
	For two children		0	0	0	6 938
		Total	0	0	0	6 938
12.	**Take-home pay (1-10+11)**		82 482	114 075	169 753	93 945
13.	**Employer's compulsory social security contributions**		4 168	7 468	14 170	4 168
14.	**Average rates**					
	Income tax		4.9%	9.4%	16.8%	0.0%
	Employees' social security contributions		5.9%	7.9%	9.5%	5.9%
	Total payments less cash transfers		10.8%	17.3%	26.3%	-1.6%
	Total tax wedge including employer's social security contributions		14.6%	21.6%	30.6%	2.7%
15.	**Marginal rates**					
	Total payments less cash transfers: Principal earner		26.0%	33.0%	43.0%	12.0%
	Total payments less cash transfers: Spouse		n.a.	n.a.	n.a.	n.a.
	Total tax wedge: Principal earner		31.0%	37.5%	46.9%	17.9%
	Total tax wedge: Spouse		n.a.	n.a.	n.a.	n.a.

Israel 2015

The tax/benefit position of married couples

			Wage level (per cent of average wage)	100-0	100-33	100-67	100-33
			Number of children	2	2	2	none
1.	**Gross wage earnings**			137 958	183 484	230 390	183 484
2.	**Standard tax allowances**						
	Basic allowance			0	0	0	0
	Married or head of family						
	Dependent children						
	Deduction for social security contributions and income taxes						
	Work-related expenses			0	0	0	0
	Other						
			Total	0	0	0	0
3.	**Tax credits or cash transfers included in taxable income**			0	0	0	0
4.	**Central government taxable income (1 - 2 + 3)**			137 958	183 484	230 390	183 484
5.	**Central government income tax liability (exclusive of tax credits)**			18 882	23 434	29 292	23 434
6.	**Tax credits**						
	Basic credit			5 886	13 080	13 080	13 080
	Married or head of family			0	0	0	0
	Children			0	5 232	5 232	0
	EITC			0	0	0	0
	Unused wastable tax credits			0	7 873	2 015	2 641
			Total	5 886	18 312	18 312	13 080
7.	**Central government income tax finally paid (5-6)**			12 996	12 996	12 996	12 996
8.	**State and local taxes**			0	0	0	0
9.	**Employees' compulsory social security contributions**						
	Gross earnings			10 888	12 481	16 313	12 481
	Taxable income						
			Total	10 888	12 481	16 313	12 481
10.	**Total payments to general government (7 + 8 + 9)**			23 883	25 477	29 308	25 477
11.	**Cash transfers from general government**						
	For head of family						
	For two children			3 824	3 824	3 824	0
			Total	3 824	3 824	3 824	0
12.	**Take-home pay (1-10+11)**			117 899	161 831	204 906	158 007
13.	**Employer's compulsory social security contributions**			7 468	9 039	11 636	9 039
14.	**Average rates**						
	Income tax			9.4%	7.1%	5.6%	7.1%
	Employees' social security contributions			7.9%	6.8%	7.1%	6.8%
	Total payments less cash transfers			14.5%	11.8%	11.1%	13.9%
	Total tax wedge including employer's social security contributions			18.9%	15.9%	15.3%	17.9%
15.	**Marginal rates**						
	Total payments less cash transfers: Principal earner			33.0%	33.0%	33.0%	33.0%
	Total payments less cash transfers: Spouse			3.5%	3.5%	12.0%	3.5%
	Total tax wedge: Principal earner			37.5%	37.5%	37.5%	37.5%
	Total tax wedge: Spouse			6.7%	6.7%	17.9%	6.7%

The Israeli currency is the Israeli Shekel (ILS). In 2015, ILS 3.8869 was equal to USD 1. In that year, the average worker in Israel earned ILS 137 958 (Secretariat estimate).

1. Personal income tax system

1.1. Central government income tax

1.1.1. Tax unit

In general, spouses are taxed separately on their earned income, subject to the condition that its sources are independent. The household is taxed jointly if their earned income is deemed to be interdependent. The conditions for interdependence involve situations where one spouse works in a business which the other spouse either owns or has certain levels of capital or management/voting rights.

1.1.2. Tax allowances and credits

1.1.2.1. Standard tax credits

The standard tax credits are given in the form of credit points subtracted from the tax liability. Each point is worth ILS 2 616 in 2015.

- *Basic credit*: Every resident taxpayer is entitled to 2.25 credit points (ILS 5 886 in 2015).
- *Additional credit for women*: Women are entitled to a further half credit point (ILS 1 308 in 2015).
- *Child credit*: Working mothers (and fathers in one parent families) with children aged under 18 are entitled to one additional credit point per child (ILS 2 616 in 2015). In 2012 this credit was increased to 2 credit points per child aged under 5 (ILS 5 232 in 2015). Since 2012, married working fathers with children aged under 2 are also entitled to 2 credit points per child.
- *Single parent credit:* Single parents (male or female) are entitled to one additional credit point (ILS 2 616 in 2015).

1.1.2.2. Non-standard tax credits applicable to income from employment

- Tax credits are awarded for contributions to approved pension schemes, up to a ceiling which varies according to the employee's circumstances.
- Employees living in certain development areas or in conflict zones receive credits as a percentage of their income up to ceiling. In 2015 the credits range from 10 % in the lowest category to 22% in the highest category with ceilings of ILS 160 560 and 241 080 respectively. About 9% of the population lives in these areas.
- New immigrants are entitled to three additional credit points in their first eighteen months in Israel, two additional credit points in the following year, and one credit point in the year after.
- Discharged soldiers receive 2 credit points for three years after the completion of at least 23 months of service or 1 credit point for a shorter service.

- Graduates of academic studies receive 1 credit point for three years after the completion of a B.A. degree (or after the completion of 1 700 study hours that led to a professional certificate) and 0.5 credit point for two years after the completion of a M.A. degree.

1.1.3. *Tax schedule*

The tax schedule for earned income in 2015 is as follows:

Taxable income (ILS)	Tax rate (%)
0-63 240	10
63 240-108 000	14
108 000-167 880	21
167 880-239 760	31
239 760-501 480	34
501 480-810 720	48
Above 810 720	50

1.2. *Regional and local income tax*

There are no regional or local income taxes.

2. Compulsory social security insurance system

Social security contributions are made up of a combination of those for National Insurance and Health Insurance. The tax rates paid by employees and employers are applied in two brackets:

- A reduced rate for income up to a level of 60% of the average wage per employee post (ILS 5 556 per month in 2015).
- A full rate for income exceeding 60% of the average wage per employee post and up to a level of around 5 times the average wage per employee post (ILS 43 240 per month in 2015).

2.1. *Employees' contributions*

The taxable base for social security insurance contributions paid by employees is the total amount of the gross wage or salary including fringe benefits. The assessment period is the calendar month. The effective employees' contribution rates in 2015 are as follows:

Insurance branch	Full rate contribution (%)	Reduced rate contribution (%)
Total for National Insurance branches	7.00	0.40
Health	5.00	3.10
Total contributions	12.00	3.50

2.2. *Employers' contributions*

Social security insurance contributions are also paid by employers on behalf of their employees. These relate to National Insurance only – employers do not pay any contributions for health insurance.

The employers' contribution rates in 2015 are as follows:

Insurance branch	Full rate contribution (%)	Reduced rate contribution (%)
Total for National Insurance branches	7.25	3.45
Health	–	–
Total contributions	7.25	3.45

3. Payroll taxes

The following payroll taxes exist in Israel but neither of them is included in the modelling as they have limited coverage:

- Wage tax on the non-profit institutions: the VAT law imposes a 7.5 per cent on the wage-bill on the non-profit sector including Government,
- Wage tax on the financial institutions: the VAT law also imposes a 18 per cent tax on the wage-bill of the financial institutions.

4. Universal cash transfers

4.1. *Transfers related to marital status*

None.

4.2. *Transfers for dependent children*

A monthly child allowance is paid to the parent (usually the mother) of unmarried children aged up to 18. The amount of the entitlement for each child depends on the date of birth of the child. Between August 2003 and June 2009, all children born after 1 June 2003 received the same benefit as the first child. But, according to the Coalition agreement signed in March 2009, the benefits for the second, third and fourth child (including those born after June 2003) were increased gradually over a period of four years (i.e. from 2009 to 2012). In August 2013 the allowance for all children born after June 2003 were decreased to ILS 140 per month per child.

In December 2015 (retroactively from May 2015) the allowance for all children were increased.

In 2015 the monthly payments per child are shown in the following table. The "average" figure is used in the modelling.

	Children born before 1 June 2003			Children born on or after 1 June 2003		
	Average	Jan-Apr	May-Dec	Average	Jan-Apr	May-Dec
First child	146.67	140	150	146.67	140	150
Second child	172.00	140	188	172.00	140	188
Third child	182.67	172	188	172.00	140	188
Fourth child	336.00	336	336	172.00	140	188
Fifth child and above	354.00	354	354	146.67	140	150

Moreover, the government will open a closed saving account for each child and deposit ILS 50 per child per month, starting with May 2015. The savings will be liquid only at the age of 18. However, the actual deposit for the period May 2015-December 2016 will be only delivered in 36 equal installements in January 2017-December 2019. This element is not included in the Taxing Wages modelling for 2015.

In addition a Study Grant is paid to lone parents with children aged 6 to 14. The grant is paid in one instalment, usually in September at the beginning of the school year. In 2015, the rates of grant per child were ILS 1 557 and ILS 865 respectively for children aged 6-11 and 12-14.

5. Main changes in the tax and benefit systems since 2002

- There has been a policy of gradually reducing the level of personal income taxes since 2003. This policy was expected to continue till 2016 but came to an end in 2012 with the top tax bracket increasing from 45% to 48% although the rate of one middle income tax bracket was further decreased from 23% to 21%. The rates were further increased in 2013. In 2013 a surtax of 2% was imposed on total income above ILS 811 560, effectively increasing the top marginal rate to 50 %. In 2013 the value of some tax brackets weren't fully indexed to the CPI and even suffered a nominal decrease. In 2014 the value of all tax brackets and of the "credit point" weren't indexed to the CPI.

- The full contribution rate for employee social security contributions was increased gradually from 9.7% in 2002 to 12% in 2006. The reduced contribution rate was lowered from 5.76% in 2002 to 3.5% in 2006. The upper threshold for contributions was removed in July 2002 but re-instated one year later. In August 2009, as a temporary measure until December 2011, it was increased to 10 times the average wage per employee post until December 2010 and to 9 times the average wage per employed post until December 2011.
- Prior to July 2005, there was only one contribution rate for employer social security contributions and this was set at 5.93% between July 2002 and June 2005. The upper threshold for contributions was removed in July 2002 but was re-instated one year later. The current system of two tax brackets was introduced in July 2005 with a reduced contribution rate of 5.33% and a full rate of 5.68%. There has been a lowering of rates in each year between 2006 and 2009. In August 2009, as a temporary measure until March 2011, the reduced rate was increased from 3.45% to 3.85%. In April 2011 the regular rate was increased to 5.9%. It was increased again to 6.5% in January 2013, 6.75% in January 2014, 7.25% in January 2015 and will continue to increase to 7.5% in 2016.
- The Employers tax on wage bill of the non-profit sector excluding Government was abolished in 2008.
- In the period between August 2003 and June 2009, all children that were born on or after 1 June 2003 received the same level of benefit payment as the first child. The 2009 Coalition agreement introduced a gradual increase in the benefit payments for the second, third and fourth children in all families (including those where children were born after June 2003) over a period of four years from July 2009 to Apr 2012. In August 2013 the allowance for all children born after June 2003 was decreased to ILS 140 per month per child.

6. Memorandum items

6.1. *Average gross annual wage earnings calculation*

The average wage figures represent the amount earned for a full time post by employees working 35 hours per week or more. Until 2011 the AW data came from a combination of 2 sources - the income and expenditure survey and the labour force survey. Since 2012 the data come exclusively from the income and expenditure survey as the labour force survey has no more data on income. The Central Bureau of Statistics has now computed a new AW series based exclusively on the income and expenditure survey back from 2000.

The 2014 and 2015 data used in the modelling are estimates.

As to the economic classification, until 2012, Israel used a modified version of ISIC 3 where the B-I industries (see Table below) are a very close equivalent of C-K industries in ISIC 3.1. Israel's Central Bureau of Statistics adopted ISIC 4 in 2012 and since 2013 the Average Wage used in the modelling is based on ISIC 4.

A	Agriculture.
B	Manufacturing.
C	Electricity and water supply.
D	Construction (building and civil engineering projects).
E	Wholesale and retail trade and repairs.
F	Accommodation services and restaurants
G	Transport, storage and communication.
H	Banking, insurance and other financial institutions.
I	Business activities.
J	Public administration.
K	Education.
L	Health, welfare and social work services.
M	Community, social, personal and other services.

6.2. *Employer contributions to private pension*

Until 2007 employers were not legally obliged to pay into a pension plan for their employees. Pension rights were guaranteed in collective agreements that covered less than half of the labour force. About one million employees in Israel had no pension arrangement (mainly those earning a relatively low wage, temporary workers and those working for subcontractors).

In 2008, a compulsory employment pension was introduced for employees with a period of employment of at least 6 months. The minimum rate of contributions in 2015 is 17.5 per cent of the employee's salary (up to the level of the average wage of ILS 9 260 per month), one third to be paid by the employee and two thirds by the employer.

6.3. *Earned income tax credit*

A non-wastable earned income tax credit was implemented in 2008 in selected geographical areas of Israel covering 15 % of the population. Entitlement to this credit is established based on earnings in the previous year. The tax credit was extended to all areas of Israel in 2012 (based on the earnings in 2011 and therefore we already included it in the 2011 version of the model). For mothers of children up to the age of 2 and for single parents the full coverage started in 2011 (based on earnings in 2010).

Under the law, workers aged 23 or more who are parents of one or two children aged less than 18 (or workers aged 55 or more even without children), and earn at least ILS 2 100 per month (about 45 per cent of the minimum wage) but not more than ILS 6 330 per month are eligible for a monthly increment of up to ILS 330. The corresponding figure for a family with 3 or more children is ILS 490. Since 2013 (based on earnings in 2012), these sums were increased by 50% for working mothers (and fathers in one-parent family). Families in which both parents work, and their joint income does not exceed ILS 12 180, are entitled to these benefits for each wage-earner. The grant is paid four times a year directly into the account of the eligible persons.

2015 parameter values

Average earnings/yr	Ave_earn	137 958	(Secretariat estimate)
Income tax	Tax_sch	0.10	63 240
		0.14	108 000
		0.21	167 880
		0.31	239 760
		0.34	501 480
		0.48	810 720
		0.50	
Employees SSC	SSC_sch	0.035	66 672
		0.12	518 880
		0	
Employers SSC	SSC_rate2	0.0345	66 672
		0.0725	518 880
		0.0000	
Child benefit	CB_firstchild	1 760	
	CB_secondchild	2 064	
	Studygrant_rate	1 557	
Wastable tax credits			
Basic element	WTC_Basic	5 886	
Lone parent	WTC_lone	2 616	
Parents/per child	WTC_Child	2 616	
Women	WTC_woman	1 308	
Negative Income tax			
Family with 1 or	NIT_sch1	0	25 200
2 children		0.161	43 088
		0	43 800
		0	58 440
		-0.23	75 960
Family with 3 or	NIT_sch2	0	25 200
more children		0.235	43 788
		5.985	43 800
		0	58 440
		-0.235	83 280
	NIT_basic1	1 080	
	NIT_basic2	1 440	
	NIT_min	240	
	NIT_MinIncome	25 200	
	NIT_MaxIncome	146 160	
	Nit_AddIncome	17 520	
	NIT_Bonus	1.50	
Days in tax year	numdays	366	

2015 tax equations

	Line in country table and intermediate steps	Variable name	Range	Equation
1.	Earnings	earn		
2.	Allowances:	Tax_al	B	0
3.	Credits in taxable income	taxbl_cr	B	0
4.	CG taxable income	tax_inc	B	Earn
5.	CG tax before credits	CG_tax_excl	B	Tax(tax_inc, tax_sch)
6.	Tax credits (nonwastable):			
	Principal	tax_cr_princ	B	(earn>0)*(wtc_basic+(IF(married=0)*(children>0),wtc_woman+wtc_lone+(wtc_child*children))
	Spouse	tax_cr_spouse	B	(earn>0)*(wtc_basic+wtc_woman+(wtc_child*children))
	Tax credits (nonwastable)	NIT_princ	B	NIT=+MAX(0, MAX(0,+IF(princ_earnings<NIT_MinIncome,0,IF(Children=0,0,IF (Children<3,NIT_basic1+Tax(princ_earnings ,NIT_sch1),NIT_basic2+Tax(princ_earnings,NIT_sch2)))))+NIT_sch1_rate5*MAX(0,+(princ_earnings + spouse_earnings)-NIT_MaxIncome-MIN(MAX(princ_earnings - NIT_sch1_inc4,0),(NIT_AddIncome))-MIN(MAX(spouse_earnings - NIT_sch1_inc4,0),(NIT_AddIncome))))IF(NIT<NIT_min,NIT=0,NIT)*if((married=0)*(children>0)=1,NIT_Bonus,1)
		NIT_spouse	B	NIT=+MAX(0, MAX(0,+IF(spouse_earnings<NIT_MinIncome,0,IF(Children=0,0,IF(Children<3,NIT_basic1+Tax(spouse_earnings ,NIT_sch1),NIT_basic2+Tax(spouse_earnings,NIT_sch2)))))+NIT_sch1_rate5*MAX(0,+(princ_earnings + spouse_earnings)-NIT_MaxIncome-MIN(MAX(princ_earnings - NIT_sch1_inc4,0),(NIT_AddIncome))-MIN(MAX(spouse_earnings - NIT_sch1_inc4,0),(NIT_AddIncome)))) IF(NIT<NIT_min,NIT=0,NIT)* if((children>0)=1,NIT_Bonus,1)
7.	CG tax	CG_tax	B	Positive(CG_tax_excl-tax_cr)-NIT
8.	State and local taxes	local_tax	B	0
9.	Employees' soc security	SSC	B	Tax(earn, SSC_sch)
11.	Cash transfers	cash_trans	J	IF(children=1,CB_firstchild,IF(Children=2,CB_firstchild+CB_secondchild)+(IF(married=0)*(children>0),Studygrant_rate*children)
13.	Employer's soc security	SSC_empr	B	Tax(earn, SSC_rate2)

Key to range of equation B calculated separately for both principal earner and spouse P calculated for principal only (value taken as 0 for spouse calculation) J calculated once only on a joint basis.

Italy

This chapter includes data on the income taxes paid by workers, their social security contributions, the family benefits they receive in the form of cash transfers as well as the social security contributions and payroll taxes paid by their employers. Results reported include the marginal and average tax burden for eight different family types.

Methodological information is available for personal income tax systems, compulsory social security contributions to schemes operated within the government sector, universal cash transfers as well as recent changes in the tax/benefit system. The methodology also includes the parameter values and tax equations underlying the data.

Italy 2015

The tax/benefit position of single persons

			67	100	167	67
	Wage level (per cent of average wage)		67	100	167	67
	Number of children		none	none	none	2
1.	**Gross wage earnings**		20 576	30 710	51 286	20 576
2.	**Standard tax allowances**					
	Basic allowance					
	Married or head of family					
	Dependent children					
	Deduction for social security contributions and income taxes		1 953	2 914	4 919	1 953
	Work-related expenses					
	Other					
		Total	1 953	2 914	4 919	1 953
3.	**Tax credits or cash transfers included in taxable income**		0	0	0	0
4.	**Central government taxable income (1 - 2 + 3)**		18 623	27 796	46 367	18 623
5.	**Central government income tax liability (exclusive of tax credits)**		4 428	6 905	13 940	4 428
6.	**Tax credits**					
	Basic credit		1 401	987	313	1 401
	Married or head of family		0	0	0	0
	Children		0	0	0	1 578
	Other		960	0	0	960
		Total	2 361	987	313	3 939
7.	**Central government income tax finally paid (5-6)**		2 067	5 918	13 627	489
8.	**State and local taxes**		788	1 176	1 961	788
9.	**Employees' compulsory social security contributions**					
	Gross earnings		1 953	2 914	4 919	1 953
	Taxable income					
		Total	1 953	2 914	4 919	1 953
10.	**Total payments to general government (7 + 8 + 9)**		4 808	10 008	20 507	3 229
11.	**Cash transfers from general government**					
	For head of family					
	For two children		0	0	0	2 619
		Total	0	0	0	2 619
12.	**Take-home pay (1-10+11)**		15 768	20 702	30 779	19 965
13.	**Employer's compulsory social security contributions**		6 601	9 852	16 453	6 601
14.	**Average rates**					
	Income tax		13.9%	23.1%	30.4%	6.2%
	Employees' social security contributions		9.5%	9.5%	9.6%	9.5%
	Total payments less cash transfers		23.4%	32.6%	40.0%	3.0%
	Total tax wedge including employer's social security contributions		42.0%	49.0%	54.6%	26.5%
15.	**Marginal rates**					
	Total payments less cash transfers: Principal earner		41.8%	41.8%	51.5%	43.4%
	Total payments less cash transfers: Spouse		n.a.	n.a.	n.a.	n.a.
	Total tax wedge: Principal earner		56.0%	56.0%	63.3%	57.1%
	Total tax wedge: Spouse		n.a.	n.a.	n.a.	n.a.

Italy 2015

The tax/benefit position of married couples

	Wage level (per cent of average wage)		100-0	100-33	100-67	100-33
	Number of children		2	2	2	none
1.	**Gross wage earnings**		30 710	40 844	51 286	40 844
2.	**Standard tax allowances**					
	Basic allowance					
	Married or head of family					
	Dependent children					
	Deduction for social security contributions and income taxes		2 914	3 876	4 867	3 876
	Work-related expenses					
	Other					
		Total	2 914	3 876	4 867	3 876
3.	**Tax credits or cash transfers included in taxable income**		0	0	0	0
4.	**Central government taxable income (1 - 2 + 3)**		27 796	36 968	46 419	36 968
5.	**Central government income tax liability (exclusive of tax credits)**		6 905	9 015	11 333	9 015
6.	**Tax credits**					
	Basic credit		987	2 814	2 388	2 814
	Married or head of family		690	0	0	0
	Children		1 420	1 420	1 499	0
	Other		0	960	960	960
		Total	3 097	5 194	4 847	3 774
7.	**Central government income tax finally paid (5-6)**		3 808	3 820	6 486	5 240
8.	**State and local taxes**		1 176	1 417	1 964	1 417
9.	**Employees' compulsory social security contributions**					
	Gross earnings		2 914	3 876	4 867	3 876
	Taxable income					
		Total	2 914	3 876	4 867	3 876
10.	**Total payments to general government (7 + 8 + 9)**		7 898	9 113	13 316	10 533
11.	**Cash transfers from general government**					
	For head of family					
	For two children		1 579	926	844	0
		Total	1 579	926	844	0
12.	**Take-home pay (1-10+11)**		24 391	32 657	38 813	30 311
13.	**Employer's compulsory social security contributions**		9 852	13 103	16 453	13 103
14.	**Average rates**					
	Income tax		16.2%	12.8%	16.5%	16.3%
	Employees' social security contributions		9.5%	9.5%	9.5%	9.5%
	Total payments less cash transfers		20.6%	20.0%	24.3%	25.8%
	Total tax wedge including employer's social security contributions		39.9%	39.5%	42.7%	43.8%
15.	**Marginal rates**					
	Total payments less cash transfers: Principal earner		43.4%	43.4%	42.6%	41.8%
	Total payments less cash transfers: Spouse		18.4%	36.8%	42.6%	36.8%
	Total tax wedge: Principal earner		57.1%	57.1%	56.6%	56.0%
	Total tax wedge: Spouse		38.2%	52.1%	56.6%	52.1%

The national currency is the Euro (EUR). In 2015, EUR 0.90 was equal to USD 1. In that year the average worker earned EUR 30 710 (Secretariat estimate).

1. Personal income tax

1.1. *Central government income tax*

1.1.1. *Tax unit*

Spouses are taxed separately.

1.1.2. *Tax allowances and tax credits*

1.1.2.1. Tax allowances

- Social security contributions due by law

1.1.2.2. Tax credits

Italy increased the basic employee tax credit from EUR 1 840 to EUR 1 880 and for 2014 introduced an additional refundable tax credit of EUR 640 for employees with income between EUR 8 146 and EUR 24 000, with a phase-out for income between EUR 24 000 and EUR 26 000. The Government announced that a similar tax credit of EUR 960 would be introduced on a permanent basis as of 2015.

Taxable income (EUR)	Fiscal bonus (EUR)
Up to 8 145	0
From 8 146 to 24 000	960
From 24 001 to 26 000	640*(26 000 - taxable income)/2 000
More than 26 000	0

- Standard tax credits (not refundable)

The PAYE tax credit is defined as a function of net income:

Taxable income (EUR)	PAYE tax credit (EUR)
Up to 8 000	1 880
From 8 001 to 28 000	Maximum tax credit + 902*(28 000 - taxable income)/20 000
From 28 001 to 55 000	Maximum tax credit*(55 000 - taxable income)/27 000
More than 55 000	0

The maximum value for the tax credit depends on the level of taxable income:

Level of taxable income (EUR)	Maximum tax credit (EUR)
From 8 001 to 15 000	978
From 15 001 to 23 000	978
From 23 001 to 24 000	978
From 24 001 to 25 000	978
From 24 001 to 26 000	978
From 26 001 to 27 700	978
From 27 701 to 28 000	978
From 28 001 to 55 000	978

- Tax credits for family dependents (not refundable)

The tax credits for family dependants, which have replaced the former tax allowances, are as follows:

Family tax credit (EUR)*	Amount (EUR)
Spouse	800 decreasing to 0 for net income over 80 000
Children	
Under three years of age	1 220 decreasing to 0 for net income over 95 000
Over three years of age	950 decreasing to 0 for net income over 95 000
Other dependent relatives	750 decreasing to 0 for net income over 80 000

* Tax credits are granted for family dependents earning less than EUR 2 840.51

The spouse tax credit is calculated as a function of net income:

Level of taxable income (EUR)	Amount of tax credit (EUR)
Up to 15 000	800-110*taxable income/15 000
From 15 001 to 29 000	690
From 29 001 to 29 200	700
From 29 201 to 34 700	710
From 34 701 to 35 000	720
From 35 001 to 35 100	710
From 35 101 to 35 200	700
From 35 201 to 40 000	690
From 40 001 to 80 000	690*(80 000-taxable income)/40 000
More than 80 000	0

The child tax credit is calculated as a function of net income:

- for families with only one child: 950*(95 000-taxable income)/95 000;
- for families with more than one child the amount of 95 000 is increased by 15 000 for each child other than the first, for every children (including the first one).

Families with more than 3 children receive an additional tax credit of EUR 200 per child.

A lone parent receives an actual tax credit for the first child equal to the maximum of the spouse tax credit and the child tax credit.

Tax credits for children have to be equally shared between the parents; different shares are no longer allowed.

If the spouse's tax liable net of the PAYE tax credit is less than his/her share (50%) in the child tax credit, the entire child tax credit is provided to the principal earner.

1.1.2.3. Main non-standard tax allowances and tax credits

- Other compulsory contributions;
- Periodical benefits allowed to the spouse fixed by judicial authority;
- Charitable donations to certain religious institutions (up to EUR 1 032.91);
- Medical and assistance expenses incurred by handicapped persons;
- Expenses to restore one's own residence at 50% for 2015 of full expenses up to EUR 96 000, apportioned into 10 annual allowances of the same amount;
- Expenses for energy requalification of buildings at 65% for 2015 of full expenses apportioned into 10 annual allowances of the same amount;
- Expenses for the replacement of covers, windows and shutters and for the installation of solar panels (only for hot water production) at 65% of full expenses (up to EUR 60 000).

For the following expenses, a tax credit of 19% of each incurred expense is allowed:

- Mortgage loan interest (up to EUR 4 000);
- Most medical expenses that exceed EUR 129.11;
- Payments to insurance funds up to EUR 1 291.14;
- Expenses to attend secondary school and university courses; in case such courses are private, the expenses allowed cannot exceed those foreseen for State courses;
- Expenses for nursery school (up to EUR 632 for each child);
- Rents paid by out of town students (up to EUR 2 633);
- Funeral charges up to EUR 1 549.37;
- Expenses for disabled persons;
- Donations to political parties (ranging from EUR 51.65 to EUR 103 291.38);
- Payments to foundations (up to EUR 2 065.83);
- Expenses related to sport activities for children between 5 and 18 years of age (up to EUR 210 per child).

1.1.3. *Tax schedule*

The following tax schedule is applied to taxable income:

Bracket (EUR)	Rate (%)
up to 15 000	23
over 15 000 up to 28 000	27
over 28 000 up to 55 000	38
over 55 000 up to 75 000	41
over 75 000	43

Decree-Law No. 138 of 13 August 2011 introduced the "Contributo di Solidarietà" for the 2011-13, (extended up to 2016), tax periods, that is a 3% "solidarity contribution" on the portion of income higher than EUR 300 000 (the amount paid is deductible from PIT base)".

1.2. *State and local taxes*

These surcharges are due only by taxpayers who pay individual income tax IRPEF (imposta sul reddito delle persone fisiche).

Regional surcharge tax

This surcharge tax has been introduced in 1997. The tax is levied by each region on resident taxpayers' total taxable income at a discretionary rate, which must fall within an established range. As from the year 2000 this range is 0.9%-1.4%.

In December 2011, with the DL 201/2011, the minimum state rate has been increased from 0.9% to 1.23%

The figure given in the 2015 parameter values table under the heading "Regional and local tax" includes the regional surcharge tax paid in the most representative city which is Rome (Lazio); the rate is 3.33% in 2015. The rate is 1.73% for income under EUR 15 000.

Local surcharge tax

This surcharge tax has been introduced in 1999. The tax may be levied by each local government at an initial rate that cannot exceed 0.2%. If the tax is levied, the local government can increase the initial rate, on a yearly basis, up to a maximum of 0.5%. Each yearly increase cannot exceed 0.2%. As from 2012, municipalities can increase the rate up to 0.8. A 0.9 special rate can be introduced by Roma Capitale Local Government.

The figure given in the 2015 parameter values table under the heading "Regional and local tax" includes the local surcharge tax paid in the most representative city which is Rome; the rate is 0.9% in 2015.

Starting from 2011, exemption is provided to taxpayers whose total income consists of retirement income not exceeding EUR 8 000, income from land not exceeding EUR 185.92, and income from primary residence. The ordinary rate is applied if any one of these limits is passed.

The surcharge rates can be adjusted above the fixed roof because of the health care losses

2. Compulsory social security

2.1. Employee contributions

- Rate and ceiling
  - The average rate is 9.49% on earnings up to EUR 46 123;
  - The average rate is 10.49% on earnings over EUR 46 123 and up to EUR 100 324;
  - For earnings exceeding EUR 100 123, the employee pays a fixed amount given by (0.0949 × 46 123) + 0.1049 × (100 324 - 46 123).
- Distinction by marital status or sex
  - None.

2.2. Employer contributions

- Contributions equal 32.08% on earnings up to EUR 100 324. For earnings exceeding EUR 100 324, the employer pays a fixed amount given by 0.3208 × 100324.
- A General Government employer work-related accident insurance exists in Italy. It is compulsory for employers with employees and contract workers in activities involving the use of machinery and in risky activities as defined by the law. The standard premium to be paid is calculated by applying to remuneration the rates linked to the activity in which the employee works. The rates that vary between 0 to about 13% are provided by

a special classification that takes into account the different categories of risk between the various activities. It is not possible to provide a representative or average rate since the contribution rates vary depending on the industrial activities and also other factors of risk. Those contributions are not included in the Report.

3. Universal cash transfers

3.1. *Amount for spouse and for dependent children*

Cash transfers are granted for family income that is:

- composed of at least 70% wage and/or pension income;
- below a given threshold set by law each year.

Family income is the sum of the incomes of all individuals comprising the family.

Cash transfers are determined each year by INPS (Istituto Nazionale di Previdenza Sociale), the public body that collects and manages the social security contributions for dependent workers for the period beginning in July of that year (t) to June in the following year (t+1) and relate to family income earned in the previous year (t-1).

As such, the transfers granted in any given year t are determined by the family income in the previous two years. The following table provides a description of the calculations.

Transfer granted in year t	Relevant amounts as given in INPS tables
January–June	The amount of cash transfers is that given in the INPS table published in July t-1. The transfers are granted with reference to family income earned in year t-2.
July–December	The amount of cash transfers is that given in the INPS table published in July t. The transfers are granted with reference to family income earned in year t-1.

For the purposes of Taxing Wages, the cash transfers that are calculated represent those amounts that would be received by the family based on their incomes for that year even though these amounts would only begin to be paid in July of the following year.

4. Main changes

The Fiscal Bonus, already introduced for 2014, for employees with a taxable income between 8 146 and 26 000 euros, has become permanent. The amount is EUR 960.

5. Memorandum item

5.1. *Identification of an AW*

The data refer to the annual earnings of average workers.

5.2. *Contributions by employers to private pension, health, etc. schemes*

In addition to the mandatory social security contributions employers may pay contributions to private pension schemes (currently about forty pension funds). Employer's contributions are included in the taxable income of the employee.

Employees may also choose to contribute to the pension funds with all or part of the retirement allowance that is otherwise withheld by the employers. In this case the employee can deduct from his taxable income an amount equal to twice the amount of the contribution paid to fund.

Employer's contributions to private health insurance schemes are not included in the taxable income of the employee up to the limit of EUR 3 615.20.

2015 parameter values

Average earnings/yr	Ave_earn	30 710	Secretariat estimate
Tax schedule	tax_sch	0.23	15 000.00
		0.27	28 000.00
		0.38	55 000.00
		0.41	75 000.00
		0.43	999 999 999.99
Sloidarity contribution	sol_tax	0.03	
	sol_inc_limit	300 000	
Tax credits			
Fiscal bonus	thre_min	8 146	
	thre_max	24 000	
	f_bonus	960	
Employment			
	emp_add	0	1 880.00
		8 000	978.00
		15 000	978.00
		23 000	978.00
		24 000	978.00
		25 000	978.00
		26 000	978.00
		27 700	978.00
		28 000	978.00
		55 000	0.00
Spouse	Spouse_cred	0	800.00
		15 000	690.00
		29 000	700.00
		29 200	710.00
		34 700	720.00
		35 000	710.00
		35 100	700.00
		35 200	690.00
		40 000	690.00
		80 000	0
limit	Sp_crd_lim	2 840.51	
Child credit	Child_credit	950	
Additional child credit	add_child	200	
Regional and local tax	reg_rt	0.0423	
	reg_rt_2	0.0263	
Social security contributions	SSC_sch	0.0949	46 123
		0.1049	100 324
		0.00	999 999 999.99
Employer contributions	Empr_sch	0.3208	100 324
		0.00	999 999 999.99
Cash transfers:			
family allowance schedule (t)			
married couple	trans_sch	Table is too long to be included	
single parent	Trans_sch_sp	Table is too long to be included	

2015 tax equations

The equations for the Italian system in 2015 are mostly repeated for each individual of a married couple. But the spouse credit is relevant only to the calculation for the principal earner and any child credit which the spouse is unable to use is transferred to the principal. This is shown by the Range indicator in the table below.

The functions which are used in the equations (Taper, MIN, Tax etc) are described in the technical note about tax equations. Variable names are defined in the table of parameters above, within the equations table, or are the standard variables "married" and "children". A reference to a variable with the affix "_total" indicates the sum of the relevant variable values for the principal and spouse. And the affixes "_princ" and "_spouse" indicate the value for the principal and spouse, respectively. Equations for a single person are as shown for the principal, with "_spouse" values taken as 0.

	Line in country table and intermediate steps	Variable name	Range	Equation
1.	Earnings	earn		
2.	Allowances:	tax_al	B	SSC
		Sol_tax	B	sol_tax*Positive(Gross-sol_inc_limit)
3.	Credits in taxable income	taxbl_cr	B	0
4.	CG taxable income	tax_inc	B	earn-tax_al1-sol_tax
5.	CG tax before credits	CG_tax_excl	B	Tax(tax_inc, tax_sch)
6.	Tax credits :			
	Employment credit	emp_cr_max	P	VLOOKUP(tax_inc, emp_add, 2))
		emp_cr_max_ spouse	S	IF(tax_inc_spouse=0,0,(VLOOKUP(tax_inc_spouse,emp_add,2)))
		emp_cr	P	MIN(CG_tax_excl, IF(tax_inc<=8000,emp_cr_max, IF(tax_inc<=28000,emp_cr_ max+902*(28000-tax_inc)/20000, IF(tax_inc>55000,emp_cr_max,emp_cr_max*(55000-tax_inc)/27000))))+
			S	MIN(CG_tax_excl_spouse, IF(tax_in_spousec<=8000,emp_cr_max_spouse, IF(tax_inc_spouse<=28000,emp_cr_max_spouse+902*(28000-tax_inc_spouse)/ 20000, IF(tax_inc_spouse>55000,emp_cr_max_spouse,emp_cr_max_spouse*(55000-tax_inc_spouse)/27000))))+
	Fiscal bonus	fiscal_b	B	IF(tax_inc<=thre_min,0,IF(tax_inc<=thre_max,f_bonus,IF(tax_inc<=26000,f_bonu s*(26000-tax_inc)/2000)))
	Spouse credit	spouse_cr	P	IF(Married=1, IF(tax_inc_spouse>Sp_crd_lim,0, IF(tax_inc>80000,0, IF(tax_inc <15000,800-110*tax_inc/15000, IF(tax_inc>40000,690*(80000-tax_inc)/ 40000,VLOOKUP(tax_inc,Spouse_cred,2))))),0)
	Child credit	child_cr_princ	P	IF(Children=0,0,IF(Married=1,(800*(95000-tax_inc)/95000+(Children-1)*800*(110000-tax_inc)/110000)*(1-child_crpct_spouse), MAX(800*(95000-tax_inc)/ 95000, IF(tax_inc>80000,0,IF(tax_inc<15000,800-110*tax_inc/15000, IF(tax_inc> 40000,690*(80000-tax_inc)/40000, VLOOKUP(tax_inc,Spouse_cred,2)))))+(Children-1)*800*(110000-tax_inc)/110000))
		child_crfull_spo use	S	IF(Children=0,0,(spouse_cr=0)*Married*(800*(95000-tax_inc_spouse)/ 95000+(Children-1)*800*(110000-tax_inc_spouse)/110000))
		child_crpct_spo use	S	IF(child_crfull_spouse>0,IF((CG_tax_excl_spouse-emp_cr_spouse)/ child_crfull_spouse<0.5,0,0.5),0)
		child_cr_spouse	S	child_crfull_spouse*child_crpct_spouse
	Total	tax_cr	B	MIN(emp_cr+spouse_cr+child_cr, CG_tax_excl)
7.	CG tax	CG_tax	B	Positive(CG_tax_excl-tax_cr)+sol_tax-fiscal_b
8.	State and local taxes	reg_rt	B	IF(CG_tax<=0, 0, IF(tax_inc>15000,tax_inc*reg_rt,tax_inc*reg_rt_2))
9.	Employees' soc security	SSC	B	Tax(earn, SSC_sch)
11.	Cash transfers		J	IF(Children=0,0,12*VLOOKUP(earn_total, IF(Married,trans_sch,trans_sch_sp),1+Children))
13.	Employer's soc security	SSC_empr	B	Tax(earn, Empr_sch)

Key to range of equation B calculated separately for both principal earner and spouse P calculated for principal only (value taken as 0 for spouse calculation) J calculated once only on a joint basis.

Japan

This chapter includes data on the income taxes paid by workers, their social security contributions, the family benefits they receive in the form of cash transfers as well as the social security contributions and payroll taxes paid by their employers. Results reported include the marginal and average tax burden for eight different family types.

Methodological information is available for personal income tax systems, compulsory social security contributions to schemes operated within the government sector, universal cash transfers as well as recent changes in the tax/benefit system. The methodology also includes the parameter values and tax equations underlying the data.

Japan 2015

The tax/benefit position of single persons

		Wage level (per cent of average wage)	67	100	167	67
		Number of children	none	none	none	2
1.	**Gross wage earnings**		3 353 890	5 005 807	8 359 697	3 353 890
2.	**Standard tax allowances:**					
	Basic allowance		380 000	380 000	380 000	380 000
	Married or head of family		0	0	0	0
	Dependent children		0	0	0	0
	Deduction for social security contributions and income taxes		479 472	715 630	1 114 206	479 472
	Work-related expenses		1 186 167	1 541 161	2 035 970	1 186 167
	Other					
		Total	2 045 639	2 636 791	3 530 175	2 045 639
3.	**Tax credits or cash transfers included in taxable income**		0	0	0	0
4.	**Central government taxable income (1 - 2 + 3)**		1 308 251	2 369 015	4 829 521	1 308 251
5.	**Central government income tax liability (exclusive of tax credits)**		66 786	142 329	549 711	66 786
6.	**Tax credits**					
	Basic credit					
	Married or head of family					
	Children					
	Other					
		Total	0	0	0	0
7.	**Central government income tax finally paid (5-6)**		66 786	142 329	549 711	66 786
8.	**State and local taxes**		138 325	244 402	490 452	138 325
9.	**Employees' compulsory social security contributions**					
	Gross earnings		479 472	715 630	1 114 206	479 472
	Taxable income					
		Total	479 472	715 630	1 114 206	479 472
10.	**Total payments to general government (7 + 8 + 9)**		684 583	1 102 361	2 154 369	684 583
11.	**Cash transfers from general government**					
	For head of family					
	For two children		0	0	0	240 000
		Total	0	0	0	240 000
12.	**Take-home pay (1-10+11)**		2 669 307	3 903 446	6 205 328	2 909 307
13.	**Employer's compulsory social security contributions**		504 626	753 174	1 176 903	504 626
14.	**Average rates**					
	Income tax		6.1%	7.7%	12.4%	6.1%
	Employees' social security contributions		14.3%	14.3%	13.3%	14.3%
	Total payments less cash transfers		20.4%	22.0%	25.8%	13.3%
	Total tax wedge including employer's social security contributions		30.8%	32.2%	34.9%	24.6%
15.	**Marginal rates**					
	Total payments less cash transfers: Principal earner		22.7%	27.6%	31.2%	22.7%
	Total payments less cash transfers: Spouse		n.a.	n.a.	n.a.	n.a.
	Total tax wedge: Principal earner		32.8%	37.0%	35.3%	32.8%
	Total tax wedge: Spouse		n.a.	n.a.	n.a.	n.a.

Japan 2015

The tax/benefit position of married couples

			100-0	100-33	100-67	100-33
	Wage level (per cent of average wage)		100-0	100-33	100-67	100-33
	Number of children		2	2	2	none
1.	**Gross wage earnings**		5 005 807	6 657 723	8 359 697	6 657 723
2.	**Standard tax allowances**					
	Basic allowance		380 000	760 000	760 000	760 000
	Married or head of family		380 000	0	0	0
	Dependent children		0	0	0	0
	Deduction for social security contributions and income taxes		715 630	951 788	1 195 102	951 788
	Work-related expenses		1 541 161	2 201 928	2 727 328	2 201 928
	Other					
		Total	3 016 791	3 913 716	4 682 431	3 913 716
3.	**Tax credits or cash transfers included in taxable income**		0	0	0	0
4.	**Central government taxable income (1 - 2 + 3)**		1 989 015	2 744 007	3 677 266	2 744 007
5.	**Central government income tax liability (exclusive of tax credits)**		103 531	161 472	209 115	161 472
6.	**Tax credits**					
	Basic credit					
	Married or head of family					
	Children					
	Other					
		Total	0	0	0	0
7.	**Central government income tax finally paid (5-6)**		103 531	161 472	209 115	161 472
8.	**State and local taxes**		211 402	289 401	382 727	289 401
9.	**Employees' compulsory social security contributions**					
	Gross earnings		715 630	951 788	1 195 102	951 788
	Taxable income					
		Total	715 630	951 788	1 195 102	951 788
10.	**Total payments to general government (7 + 8 + 9)**		1 030 563	1 402 661	1 786 944	1 402 661
11.	**Cash transfers from general government**					
	For head of family					
	For two children		240 000	240 000	240 000	0
		Total	240 000	240 000	240 000	0
12.	**Take-home pay (1-10+11)**		4 215 244	5 495 062	6 812 753	5 255 062
13.	**Employer's compulsory social security contributions**		753 174	1 001 721	1 257 800	1 001 721
14.	**Average rates**					
	Income tax		6.3%	6.8%	7.1%	6.8%
	Employees' social security contributions		14.3%	14.3%	14.3%	14.3%
	Total payments less cash transfers		15.8%	17.5%	18.5%	21.1%
	Total tax wedge including employer's social security contributions		26.8%	28.3%	29.2%	31.4%
15.	**Marginal rates**					
	Total payments less cash transfers: Principal earner		27.6%	27.6%	27.6%	27.6%
	Total payments less cash transfers: Spouse		22.5%	21.2%	22.7%	21.2%
	Total tax wedge: Principal earner		37.0%	37.0%	37.0%	37.0%
	Total tax wedge: Spouse		32.7%	31.5%	32.8%	31.5%

The national currency is the Yen (JPY). In 2015 JPY 121.00 was equal to USD 1. In that year, the average worker is assumed to earn JPY 5 005 807 (Secretariat estimate). In Japan, the central government income tax year is a calendar year and the local government income tax year is from April to March. The calculations in this report are based on the tax rules and rates, which are applicable the 1 April.

1. Personal income tax systems

1.1. Central government income tax

1.1.1. Tax unit

Each individual is taxed separately.

1.1.2. Allowances and tax credits

1.1.2.1. Standard reliefs

- *Basic allowance*: a taxpayer may deduct JPY 380 000 as a basic allowance from his or her income.
- *Allowance for spouse*: allowance equal to JPY 380 000 is given to a resident taxpayer who lives with a spouse whose income does not exceed JPY 380 000.
- *Special allowance for spouse*: the allowance included in the following table is given to a resident taxpayer who lives with a spouse:

Spouse's income	Amount
0-380 000	0
380 001-399 999	380 000
400 000-449 999	360 000
450 000-499 999	310 000
500 000-549 999	260 000
550 000-599 999	210 000
600 000-649 999	160 000
650 000-699 999	110 000
700 000-749 999	60 000
750 000-759 999	30 000
760 000 or more	0

- *Allowance for dependents*: if a resident taxpayer has children and other relatives over 15 years old whose income does not exceed JPY 380 000 and who live with the resident, an allowance of JPY 380 000 is given for each dependent.
- *Special allowance for dependents*: if a resident taxpayer has dependents between 19 and 22 years old whose income does not exceed JPY 380 000 and who live with the resident, an allowance of JPY 630 000 is given for each dependent instead of the allowances for dependents mentioned above.

- *Deduction for social insurance premiums:* the whole amount of social insurance premiums for a resident taxpayer or his/her dependents shall be deducted from his/her income.
- *Employment income deduction:* the following amounts may be deducted from employment income in calculating taxable income:
  - If gross employment income does not exceed JPY 1 800 000, the deduction is 40% of salaries (etc.), but the minimum amount deductible is JPY 650 000.
  - If gross employment income exceeds JPY 1 800 000, but not JPY 3 600 000, the deduction is JPY 180 000 plus 30% of salaries.
  - If gross employment income exceeds JPY 3 600 000, but not JPY 6 600 000, the deduction is JPY 540 000 plus 20% of salaries.
  - If gross employment income exceeds JPY 6 600 000, but not JPY 10 000 000, the deduction is JPY 1 200 000 plus 10% of salaries.
  - If gross employment income exceeds JPY 10 000 000, but not JPY 15 000 000, the deduction is JPY 1 700 000 plus 5% of salaries.
  - If gross employment income exceeds JPY 15 000 000, the deduction will be fixed at JPY 2 450 000.

1.1.2.2. Main non-standard tax reliefs applicable to an AW

- *Credit for housing loans:* A resident taxpayer who constructs, purchases, enlarges or rebuilds a house and finances the cost by means of a housing loan and uses the property as his or her own dwelling is entitled to an income tax credit up to the amount described below for 10 years [or 15 years] after the first use of the house, provided that the floor space is not less than 50m^2 and that at least half of the floor space is used as the owner-occupied dwelling. The base of the tax credit equals the balance of the housing loan debt amount, calculated at the end of each year, consisting of the loan obtained not only from private financial institutions but also from public institutions. This tax credit cannot be claimed by those whose total income is more than JPY 30 million.

The rates of the tax credits correspond to the year in which residence in the house commenced. The rates are as follows:

Residence starts:	From 1 January 2005 to 31 December 2005	From 1 January 2006 to 31 December 2006	From 1 January 2007 to 31 December 2007
Tax credit rate	For the part of remaining housing loan balance at the end of year (R.H.L.B). within JPY 40 million : The R.H.L.B. x 1.0% (for first 8 years) The R.H.L.B. x 0.5% (for last 2 years)	For the part of R.H.L.B. within JPY 30 million : The R.H.L.B. x 1.0% (for first 7 years) The R.H.L.B. x 0.5% (for last 3 years)	For the part of R.H.L.B. within JPY 25 million: The R.H.L.B. x 1.0%[or 0.6%] (for first 6 years [or 10 years]) The R.H.L.B. x 0.5%[or 0.4%] (for last 4 years [or 5 years])
Maximum tax credit amount (for each year)	JPY 400 000 JPY 200 000 (for last 2 years)	JPY 300 000 JPY 150 000 (for last 3 years)	JPY 250 000 [or 150 000] JPY 125 000 [or 100 000] (for last 4 years [or 5 years])
Maximum tax credit amount (for the deductible period in total)	JPY 3.6 million	JPY 2.55 million	JPY 2 million

Residence starts:	From 1 January 2008 to 31 December 2008	From 1 January 2009 to 31 December 2010	From 1 January 2011 to 31 December 2011
Tax credit rate	For the part of R.H.L.B. within JPY 20 million: The R.H.L.B. x 1.0%[or 0.6%] (for first 6 years [or 10 years]) The R.H.L.B. x 0.5%[or 0.4%] (for last 4 years [or 5 years])	For the part of R.H.L.B. within JPY 50 million: The R.H.L.B. x 1.0%	For the part of R.H.L.B. within JPY 40 million: The R.H.L.B. x 1.0%
Maximum tax credit amount (for each year)	JPY 200 000 [or 120 000] JPY 100 000 [or 80 000] (for last 4 years [or 5 years])	JPY 500 000	JPY 400 000
Maximum tax credit amount (for the deductible period in total)	JPY 1.6 million	JPY 5 million	JPY 4 million

Residence starts:	From 1 January 2012 to 31 December 2012	From 1 January 2013 to 31 March 2014	From 1 April 2014 to 31 December 2017
Tax credit rate	For the part of R.H.L.B. within JPY 30 million: The R.H.L.B. x 1.0%	For the part of R.H.L.B. within JPY 20 million: The R.H.L.B. x 1.0%	For the part of R.H.L.B. within JPY 40 million: The R.H.L.B x 1.0% If the rate of tax(consumption tax etc.) included in the amount of cost etc. of housing is other than 8% or 10%; For the part of R.H.L.B. within JPY 20 million: The R.H.L.B x 1.0%
Maximum tax credit amount (for each year)	JPY 300 000	JPY 200 000	JPY 400 000 If the rate of tax(consumption tax etc.) included in the amount of cost etc. of housing is other than 8% or 10%; JPY 200 000
Maximum tax credit amount (for the deductible period in total)	JPY 3 million	JPY 2 million	JPY 4 million If the rate of tax(consumption tax etc.) included in the amount of cost etc. of housing is other than 8% or 10%; JPY 2 million

- *Deduction for life insurance premiums:* If a resident taxpayer pays insurance premiums on life insurance contracts and the recipient of the insurance proceeds is the taxpayer, his/her spouse or other relatives living with him/her, the portion of these insurance premiums which does not exceed the maximum prescribed below, is deductible from ordinary income, retirement income or timber income.
- In addition, if a resident taxpayer pays insurance premiums for a "qualified personal pension plan (insurance type)", and the recipient of the pension payment is the taxpayer or his/her spouse under a specific condition, the portion of such premiums which does not exceed the maximum prescribed below, is deductible from ordinary income, retirement income, or timber income.
- Furthermore, if a resident taxpayer pays insurance premiums on nursing and medical insurance contacts and the taxpayer receipts the nursing and medical proceeds caused by payments for medical expenses, the portion of such premiums which does not exceed the maximum prescribed below, is deductible from ordinary income, retirement income, or timber income.

Annual premium paid (JPY)		Deduction
Over	Not over	
	20 000	Total amount of premiums paid (1)
20 000	40 000	(1) x 1/2 + JPY 10 000
40 000	80 000	(1) x 1/4 + JPY 20 000
80 000	–	JPY 40 000

- For the insurance contracts made on or after 1 January 2012 the maximum deduction is JPY 120 000. A resident taxpayer can claim the deduction up to JPY 40 000 for life insurance premiums, personal pension plan premiums and nursing and medical insurance premiums respectively.
- For the insurance contracts made on or before 31 December 2011, a resident taxpayer can claim the deduction up to JPY 50 000 for life insurance premiums, personal pension plan premiums respectively. Thus, a resident tax payer can claim the deduction up to JPY 100 000 in total. *Deduction for medical expenses:* If a resident taxpayer pays bills for medical or dental care for himself/herself or for his/her spouse or other relatives living with him/her and the amount of such expenses (excluding those recovered by insurance) exceeds the lesser of JPY 100 000 or 5% of the total of his/her ordinary income, retirement income and timber income, the excess amount is deductible from his/her ordinary income, retirement income or timber income. The maximum deduction is JPY 2 million.
- *Deduction for earthquake insurance premiums*: Earthquake insurance premiums up to JPY 50 000 can be deducted from income. Although the income deduction for casualty insurance premiums was basically abolished, the deduction for long-term casualty insurance premiums remains available if contracted before 31 December, 2006. The maximum deduction for long-term casualty insurance premiums is JPY 15 000. If an individual applies for both a deduction for earthquake insurance premiums and a deduction for long-term casualty premiums, the maximum deductible amount is JPY 50 000 in total.

1.1.3. *Tax schedule*

Taxable income (JPY) [1]		Tax rate (%)	Deductible amounts for each bracket (JPY)
Over	Not over	(A)	(B)
	1 950 000	5	–
1 950 000	3 300 000	10	97 500
3 300 000	6 950 000	20	427 500
6 950 000	9 000 000	23	636 000
9 000 000	18 000 000	33	1 536 000
18 000 000	40 000 000	40	2 796 000
40 000 000		45	4 796 000

1. The fraction of taxable income that is less than JPY 1 000 is rounded down.

Tax liability is obtained by multiplying the taxable income by tax rate (A) and deducting the amount (B). For example, income tax due on taxable income of JPY 7 million is:

7 000 000 × 0.23 (A) - 636 000 (B) = JPY 974 000.

In addition, a taxpayer is required to file tax returns and make tax payments for additional 2.1% of the base income taxes from 2013 through 2037 (special income tax for reconstruction) annually together with the regular income tax of respective years.

1.2. State and local income taxes

1.2.1. General description of the system

State and local income taxes in Japan consist of prefectural inhabitant's tax levied by prefectures and municipal inhabitant's tax levied by cities, towns and villages. The prefectural inhabitant's tax is collected together with the municipal inhabitant's tax by cities, towns and villages.

1.2.2. Tax base

Basically, prefectural and municipal inhabitants' taxes (local taxes) consist of two parts; one is proportional taxable income and the other is a fixed per capita amount. The way to compute the taxable income of local taxes is similar to that of the previous year's national income tax. The main difference is the amount of reliefs. For example, the amount of Basic Allowance, Allowance for Spouse, Allowance for Dependants is JPY 330 000, the amount of Special Allowance for dependants is JPY 450 000, etc. Allowance for Dependents is available for dependents 16 years or older excluding the specified dependents. Special Allowance for dependents is available for the specified dependents (between 19 and 22 years old).

1.2.3. Tax rate

- The standard fixed (annual) per-capita amount of Prefectural inhabitants tax is JPY 1 500;
- The standard fixed (annual) per-capita amount of Municipal inhabitants tax is JPY 3 500;
- The standard rate of the local taxes equals a proportional rate of 10% (Prefectural inhabitant's tax: 4%, Municipal inhabitant's tax: 6%).*

Taxable income for local income tax purposes	The tax credit
JPY 2 000 000 or less	5% of the lesser of: • total amount of differences in personal reliefs between those for national income tax purposes and for local income tax purposes; or • taxable income for local income tax purposes
More than JPY 2 000 000	((total amount of differences in personal reliefs between those for national income tax purposes and for local income tax purposes) – (taxable income for local income tax purposes – JPY 2 000 000)) * 5%. The minimum credit is JPY 2 500

Note: Local authorities do not levy the per-capita rate and the proportional rate on a taxpayer whose previous year's income does not exceed a certain amount. For example, in special wards of Tokyo, this threshold is calculated as follows:
per-capita rate: (1 + number of spouse and dependent(s) qualified for the allowance for spouse/dependents) * 350 000 [+ 210 000 in case the taxpayer has a qualified spouse or dependent(s)])
proportional rate: (1 + number of spouse and dependent(s) qualified for the allowance for spouse/dependents) * 350 000 [+ 320 000 in case the taxpayer has a qualified spouse or dependent(s)])

1.2.4. Tax rate selected for this study

Country-wide rates as described above. The local income tax rates chosen for the purpose of this Report represent the standard rate.

* The local tax rate and the central government income tax rate were changed in the FY2006 tax reform. Also a new local income tax credit regime was introduced in order to alleviate the tax burden increase arising from the changes in the tax rates and from the difference between the personal reliefs (Basic Allowance, Allowance for Spouse, Allowance for Dependents, Special Allowance for dependents, etc.) for national income tax purposes and for inhabitant tax purposes.

2. Compulsory social security contribution to schemes operated within the government sector

2.1. Employees' contributions

2.1.1. Pension

8.737% (8.914% as from September 2015) of total remuneration (standard remuneration and bonuses). The insurable ceiling of the monthly amount of pensionable remuneration is JPY 620 000 and the insurable ceiling of the standard amount of bonus is JPY 1 500 000.

2.1.2. Sickness

As from April 2012 about 5.00%, (about 4.75% before March 2012), of total remuneration, (standard remuneration and bonuses), up to the insurable ceiling of JPY 1 210 000, (monthly).

2.1.3. Unemployment

0.5% of total remuneration.

2.1.4-1.5. Work injury and family allowance

None.

2.2. Employers' contributions

2.2.1. Pensions

8.737% (8.914% as from September 2015) of total remuneration. The insurable ceiling of the monthly amount of pensionable remuneration is JPY 620 000 and the insurable ceiling of the standard amount of bonus is JPY 1 500 000.

2.2.2. Sickness

As from April 2012, about 5.00% (about 4.75% before March 2012) of total remuneration up to the insurable ceiling of JPY 1 210 000 (monthly).

2.2.3. Unemployment

0.85% of total remuneration.

2.2.4. Work injury

0.25% to 8.8% of total remuneration, the contribution rate depending on each industry's accident rate over the last three years and other factors. There are twenty-nine rates for fifty-four industrial categories at present.

2.2.5. Family allowance

0.15% of total remuneration.

3. Universal cash transfers

3.1. Transfers related to marital status

Not available.

3.2. Transfers for dependent children

From April 2012 (Income caps are applied beginning from June 2012 payments):

a) For persons earning incomes below the income cap

JPY 15 000 (per month) is paid to parents/guardians for each child who is under 3 years old or for the third or subsequent child from 3 years old until he/she graduates from elementary school.

JPY 10 000 (per month) is paid to parents/guardians for each child who is for the first or second child from 3 years old until he/she graduates from elementary school or who is a junior high school student.

b) For persons earning incomes no less than the income cap

JPY 50 00 (per month) is paid to parents/guardians for each child until he/she graduates from junior high school as the Special Interim Allowances.

The income cap is set at JPY 6 220 000 (the principal's gross earnings net of certain deductions, plus JPY 380 000 per dependent).

4. Main changes in the tax/benefit systems since 1998

As part of the Fiscal Year 1999 tax reform, the highest marginal rate of the personal income tax imposed by the central government was reduced from 50% to 37%. The top rate of the local inhabitants' tax was reduced from 15% to 13%. A proportional tax reduction was granted with respect to the national income tax and the local inhabitants tax. The amount is equal to the lesser of 20% (local inhabitants tax: 15%) of the amount of tax before reduction or JPY 250 000 (local inhabitants tax: JPY 40 000).

As part of the FY 2005 tax reform, the rate of the reduction was reduced from 20% to 10% (local inhabitants tax: from 15% to 7.5%) and the ceiling was reduced from JPY 250 000 to JPY 125 000 (local inhabitants' tax from JPY 40 000 to JPY 20 000) as from 2006 (local inhabitants tax: FY 2006). And as part of the FY 2006 tax reform, the reduction was abolished as from 2007 (local inhabitants tax: FY 2007).

As part of the FY 2006 tax reform, the progressive rate structure of national income tax was reformed into a 6 brackets structure with tax rates ranging from 5% to 40%, and the rate of local inhabitants' tax became proportional at a rate of 10%.

Eligible age for transfers for dependent children was raised from three to six as from 1 June 2001, from six to nine as from 1 April 2004 and from nine to twelve as from 1 April 2006. It has been doubled to JPY 10 000 for the first and second child under the age of three as from 1 April, 2007.

As from 2010, JPY 13 000 per month is paid to parents/guardians regardless of their income for each child until he/she graduates from junior high school.

As from April 2012 (Income caps are applied beginning from June 2012 payments):

a) For persons earning incomes below the income cap

JPY 15 000 (per month) is paid to parents/guardians for each child who is under 3 years old or for the third or subsequent child from 3 years old until he/she graduates from elementary school.

JPY 10 000 (per month) is paid to parents/guardians for each child who is for the first or second child from 3 years old until he/she graduates from elementary school or who is a junior high school student.

b) For persons earning incomes no less than the income cap

JPY 5 000 (per month) is paid to parents/guardians for each child until he/she graduates from junior high school as the Special Interim Allowances.

As part of the FY 2012 tax reform, the upper limit on employment income deduction (JPY 2 450 000) was set for those who earn employment income more than JPY 15 000 000 as from 2013 (local inhabitants tax: FY2014).

5. Memorandum item

5.1. *Average gross annual wage earnings calculation*

The source of calculation is the *Basic Survey on Wage Structure*, published by the Ministry of Health, Labour and Welfare. This survey covers establishments with ten or more regular employees over the whole country, and contains statistical figures for monthly contractual cash earnings in June and annual special cash earnings (such as bonuses) received by various categories of workers. Male and female workers of the manufacturing, mining and quarrying, construction, wholesale and retail trade, accommodation and food service activities, financial and insurance activities, real estate activities sector are the point of departure. Their gross annual earnings have been calculated by multiplying monthly contractual cash earnings by 12 and adding any annual special cash earnings. In the *Basic Survey*, sickness and unemployment compensations are excluded from cash earnings, but average overtime and bonuses are included.

As far as the *Basic Survey* is concerned, it covers the whole country, and no special assumption is made regarding the place of residence of the average worker.

5.2. *Employer contributions to private pension and health schemes*

DB: JPY 3 595 455 million

Employees' Pension Funds (EPFs): JPY 1 296 443 million

DC: JPY 610 641 million

Data of DB and EPFs are the total amount of employers' contribution and employees' one and there is no data of those which indicates only employers' contribution. It is regulated by law that employers' contribution must be higher than employees' one.

2015 parameter values

Average earnings/yr	Ave_earn	5 005 807	Secretariat estimate
Allowances for central tax	basic_al	380 000	
	spouse_al	380 000	
	Spouse_al_sp	0	0
		380 001	380 000
		400 000	360 000
		450 000	310 000
		500 000	260 000
		550 000	210 000
		600 000	160 000
		650 000	110 000
		700 000	60 000
		750 000	30 000
		760 000	0
spouse_al_ceil		380 000	
	child_al	0	
Employment income deduction	emp_inc_min	650 000	
	emp_inc_sch	0.4	1 800 000
		0.3	3 600 000
		0.2	6 600 000
		0.1	10 000 000
		0.05	
	emp_inc_max	2 450 000	
Central gov't tax schedule	tax_sch	0.05	1 950 000
		0.10	3 300 000
		0.20	6 950 000
		0.23	9 000 000
		0.33	18 000 000
		0.40	40 000 000
		0.45	
	surtax	1.021	
Allowances for state/local tax	s_basic_al	330 000	
	s_spouse_al	330 000	
	s_spouse_al_sp	0	0
		380 001	330 000
		450 000	310 000
		500 000	260 000
		550 000	210 000
		600 000	160 000
		650 000	110 000
		700 000	60 000
		750 000	30 000
		760 000	0
	S_spouse_al_ceil	380 000	
	s_child_al	0	
Prefectural tax	pref_per_cap	1 500	
Municipal tax	mun_per_cap	3 500	
	local_sch	0.1	
Social security contributions	SSC_pens	0.08796	
	pens_ceil	7 440 000	
	SSC_sick	0.05	
	sick_ceil	14 520 000	
	SSC_unemp	0.0050	
Employer contribution proportion	SSC_empr_unemp	0.0085	
	SSC_empr_oth	0.0040	
Child transfer	Child_transfer	120 000	
	Child_transfer2	90 000	
	Child_transfer_lim	6 220 000	
	Child_transfer_lim_incr	380 000	

2015 tax equations

The equations for the Japanese system are mostly on an individual basis. But the tax allowances for the spouse and for children are relevant only to the calculation for the principal earner. This is shown by the Range indicator in the table below.

The functions which are used in the equations (Taper, MIN, Tax etc) are described in the technical note about tax equations. Variable names are defined in the table of parameters above, within the equations table, or are the standard variables "married" and "children". A reference to a variable with the affix "_total" indicates the sum of the relevant variable values for the principal and spouse. And the affixes "_princ" and "_spouse" indicate the value for the principal and spouse, respectively. Equations for a single person are as shown for the principal, with "_spouse" values taken as 0.

	Line in country table and intermediate steps	Variable name	Range	Equation
1.	Earnings	earn		
2.	Allowances:			
		tax_al	P	basic_al + Married*(earn_princ - (earn_princ>0)*MIN(emp_inc_max,MAX(emp_inc_min,Tax(earn_princ, emp_inc_sch)))<=spouse_al_ceil)*spouse_al + Married* VLOOKUP(Positive(earn_princ - (earn_princ>0)*MAX(emp_inc_min,Tax(earn_princ, emp_inc_sch))),spouse_al_sp,2,TRUE) + Children*child_al + MAX(emp_inc_min,Tax(earn_princ,emp_inc_sch)) + SSC_princ
			S	MIN(earn_spouse, basic_al + MAX(emp_inc_min, Tax(earn, emp_inc_sch)) + SSC_spouse)
3.	Credits in taxable income	taxbl_cr	B	0
4.	CG taxable income	tax_inc	B	Positive(earn-tax_al)
5.	CG tax before credits	CG_tax_excl	B	Positive(Tax(tax_inc, tax_sch))
6.	Tax credits :	tax_cr	B	0
7.	CG tax	CG_tax	B	CG_tax_excl*surtax
8.	State and local taxes			
	Local taxable income	local_tax_inc	P	Positive(earn_princ- (s_basic_al+Married*((earn_spouse-(earn_spouse>0)*MAX(emp_inc_min,Tax(earn_spouse,emp_inc_sch))<=s_spouse_al_ceil)*s_spouse_al +VLOOKUP(Positive(earn_spouse-(earn_spouse>0)*MAX(emp_inc_min,Tax(earn_spouse,emp_inc_sch))),s_spouse_al_sp,2,TRUE))+Children*s_child_al+ MAX(emp_inc_min,Tax(earn_princ,emp_inc_sch))+SSC_princ))
			S	Positive(earn_spouse- (s_basic_al+(earn_spouse>0)*MAX(emp_inc_min,Tax(earn_spouse,emp_inc_sch))+SSC_spouse))
	Local tax	local_tax	P	(earn_princ-MAX(emp_inc_min,Tax(earn_princ,emp_inc_sch))>350000+ (Married*(earn_princ - (earn_princ>0)*MAX(emp_inc_min,Tax(earn_princ, emp_inc_sch))<=s_spouse_al_ceil)+Children>0)*((Married*(earn_princ - (earn_princ>0)*MAX(emp_inc_min,Tax(earn_princ, emp_inc_sch))<=s_spouse_al_ceil)+ Children)*350000+210000))*(pref_per_cap+mun_per_cap)+(earn_princ-MAX(emp_inc_min,Tax(earn_princ,emp_inc_sch))>350000+(Married*(earn_princ - (earn_princ>0)*MAX(emp_inc_min,Tax(earn_princ, emp_inc_sch))<=s_spouse_al_ceil)+Children>0)*((Married*(earn_princ - (earn_princ>0)*MAX(emp_inc_min, Tax(earn_princ, emp_inc_sch))<=s_spouse_al_ceil)+Children)*350000+ 320000))*Positive(Tax(Positive(earn_spouse-tax_al_spouse),local_sch)- IF(Positive(earn_spouse-tax_al_spouse)>2000000,MAXA(2500,((Positive(earn_spouse-tax_al_spouse)-MAX(emp_inc_min,Tax(earn_princ,emp_inc_sch)))- (Positive(earn_spouse-tax_al_spouse)-2000000))*5%),MINA((Positive(earn_spouse-tax_al_spouse)-MAX(emp_inc_min,Tax(earn_princ,emp_inc_sch))), Positive(earn_spouse-tax_al_spouse))*5%))
			S	(earn_spouse - (earn_spouse>0)*MAX(emp_inc_min,Tax(earn_spouse, emp_inc_sch))>350000)*(pref_per_cap+mun_per_cap+Positive(Tax(local_tax_inc_spouse,local_sch)-IF(local_tax_inc_spouse>2000000,MAXA(2500,((local_tax_inc_spouse-tax_inc_spouse)-(local_tax_inc_spouse-2000000))*5%),MINA((local_tax_inc_spouse-tax_inc_spouse),local_tax_inc_spouse)*5%)))

	Line in country table and intermediate steps	Variable name	Range	Equation
9.	Employees' soc security	SSC	B	SSC_pens*MIN(earn, pens_ceil)+SSC_sick*MIN(earn, sick_ceil)+SSC_unemp*earn
11.	Cash transfers	cash_trans	B	IF(Children>0,IF(Positive(princ_inc - princ_empl_inc)<Child_transfer_lim+(Child_transfer_lim_incr*Children), Child_transfer,Child_transfer2)*Children,0)
13.	Employer's social security	SSC_empr	B	SSC_pens*MIN(earn, pens_ceil)+SSC_sick*MIN(earn, sick_ceil)+(SSC_empr_unemp+SSC_empr_oth)*earn

Key to range of equation B calculated separately for both principal earner and spouse P calculated for principal only (value taken as 0 for spouse calculation).

Korea

This chapter includes data on the income taxes paid by workers, their social security contributions, the family benefits they receive in the form of cash transfers as well as the social security contributions and payroll taxes paid by their employers. Results reported include the marginal and average tax burden for eight different family types.

Methodological information is available for personal income tax systems, compulsory social security contributions to schemes operated within the government sector, universal cash transfers as well as recent changes in the tax/benefit system. The methodology also includes the parameter values and tax equations underlying the data.

Korea 2015

The tax/benefit position of single persons

		Wage level (per cent of average wage)	67	100	167	67
		Number of children	none	none	none	2
1.	**Gross wage earnings**		28 249 025	42 162 723	70 411 748	28 249 025
2.	**Standard tax allowances**					
	Basic allowance					
	Married or head of family					
	Dependent children					
	Deduction for social security contributions and income taxes					
	Work-related expenses					
	Other					
		Total	12 258 560	16 609 244	19 778 634	16 258 560
3.	**Tax credits or cash transfers included in taxable income**		0	0	0	0
4.	**Central government taxable income (1 - 2 + 3)**		15 990 465	25 553 480	50 633 114	11 990 465
5.	**Central government income tax liability (exclusive of tax credits)**		1 318 570	2 753 022	6 931 947	719 428
6.	**Tax credits**					
	Basic credit		850 571	666 698	500 000	825 685
	Married or head of family					
	Children					
	Other					
		Total	850 571	666 698	500 000	825 685
7.	**Central government income tax finally paid (5-6)**		467 999	2 086 324	6 431 947	0
8.	**State and local taxes**		46 800	208 632	643 195	0
9.	**Employees' compulsory social security contributions**					
	Gross earnings		2 368 340	3 534 835	5 008 046	2 368 340
	Taxable income					
		Total	2 368 340	3 534 835	5 008 046	2 368 340
10.	**Total payments to general government (7 + 8 + 9)**		2 883 138	5 829 791	12 083 188	2 368 340
11.	**Cash transfers from general government**					
	For head of family					
	For two children					
		Total	0	0	0	0
12.	**Take-home pay (1-10+11)**		25 365 886	36 332 932	58 328 560	25 880 685
13.	**Employer's compulsory social security contributions**		2 919 196	4 357 008	6 381 075	2 919 196
14.	**Average rates**					
	Income tax		1.8%	5.4%	10.0%	0.0%
	Employees' social security contributions		8.4%	8.4%	7.1%	8.4%
	Total payments less cash transfers		10.2%	13.8%	17.2%	8.4%
	Total tax wedge including employer's social security contributions		18.6%	21.9%	24.0%	17.0%
15.	**Marginal rates**					
	Total payments less cash transfers: Principal earner		17.7%	21.9%	27.9%	8.4%
	Total payments less cash transfers: Spouse		n.a.	n.a.	n.a.	n.a.
	Total tax wedge: Principal earner		25.4%	29.2%	31.9%	17.0%
	Total tax wedge: Spouse		n.a.	n.a.	n.a.	n.a.

Korea 2015

The tax/benefit position of married couples

			100-0	100-33	100-67	100-33
		Wage level (per cent of average wage)	100-0	100-33	100-67	100-33
		Number of children	2	2	2	none
1.	**Gross wage earnings**		42 162 723	56 076 422	70 411 748	56 076 422
2.	**Standard tax allowances**					
	Basic allowance					
	Married or head of family					
	Dependent children					
	Deduction for social security contributions and income taxes					
	Work-related expenses					
	Other					
		Total	21 109 244	29 300 840	32 367 804	26 300 840
3.	**Tax credits or cash transfers included in taxable income**		0	0	0	0
4.	**Central government taxable income (1 - 2 + 3)**		21 053 480	26 775 582	38 043 944	29 775 582
5.	**Central government income tax liability (exclusive of tax credits)**		2 078 022	2 556 348	3 546 592	3 006 348
6.	**Tax credits**					
	Basic credit		966 698	1 236 028	1 780 662	936 028
	Married or head of family					
	Children					
	Other					
		Total	966 698	1 236 028	1 780 662	936 028
7.	**Central government income tax finally paid (5-6)**		1 111 324	1 336 324	1 765 930	2 086 324
8.	**State and local taxes**		111 132	133 632	176 593	208 632
9.	**Employees' compulsory social security contributions**					
	Gross earnings		3 534 835	4 701 331	5 903 175	4 701 331
	Taxable income					
		Total	3 534 835	4 701 331	5 903 175	4 701 331
10.	**Total payments to general government (7 + 8 + 9)**		4 757 291	6 171 287	7 845 698	6 996 287
11.	**Cash transfers from general government**					
	For head of family					
	For two children					
		Total	0	0	0	0
12.	**Take-home pay (1-10+11)**		37 405 432	49 905 135	62 566 050	49 080 135
13.	**Employers' compulsory social security contributions**		4 357 008	5 794 821	7 276 204	5 794 821
14.	**Average rates**					
	Income tax		2.9%	2.6%	2.8%	4.1%
	Employees' social security contributions		8.4%	8.4%	8.4%	8.4%
	Total payments less cash transfers		11.3%	11.0%	11.1%	12.5%
	Total tax wedge including employer's social security contributions		19.6%	19.3%	19.5%	20.7%
15.	**Marginal rates**					
	Total payments less cash transfers: Principal earner		21.9%	21.9%	21.9%	21.9%
	Total payments less cash transfers: Spouse		10.2%	8.4%	14.4%	8.4%
	Total tax wedge: Principal earner		29.2%	29.2%	29.2%	29.2%
	Total tax wedge: Spouse		18.6%	17.0%	22.4%	17.0%

The national currency is the Won (KRW). In 2015, KRW 1 131.31 was equal to USD 1. In this year, the average worker is expected to earn KRW 42 162 723 (Secretariat estimate).

1. Personal income tax system

1.1. Central government income tax system

1.1.1. Tax unit

Each individual is taxed on his/her own income.

Non-taxable wage income includes the:

- national pension, medical insurance, unemployment insurance and work injury insurance that are borne by employer;
- overtime payment to productive workers: up to KRW 2 400 000 of overwork payment of productive workers in manufacturing and mining sectors whose monthly wage is less than KRW 1 500 000 and whose yearly wage is less than KRW 25 000 000.

1.1.2. Allowances and tax credits

1.1.2.1. Standard reliefs

- *Employment income deduction*: the following deduction from gross income is provided to wage and salary income earners:

Salary	Deduction
Up to KRW 5 000 000	70%
KRW 5 000 000 to KRW 15 000 000	KRW 3 500 000 plus 40% of the salary over KRW 5 000 000
KRW 15 000 000 to KRW 45 000 000	KRW 7 500 000plus 15% of the salary over KRW 15 000 000
KRW 45 000 000 to KRW 100 000 000	KRW 12 000 000 plus 5% of the salary over KRW 45 000 000
Over KRW 100 000 000	KRW 14 750 000 plus 2% of the salary over KRW 100 000 000

- *Basic allowance*: a taxpayer can deduct KRW 1 500 000 from his/her income for each person who meets one of following conditions:
  - the taxpayer him/herself;
  - the taxpayer's spouse whose taxable income (gross earnings net of employment income deduction) is less than KRW 1 000 000;
  - the taxpayer's (including the spouse's) dependents (parents, siblings, children) within the same household whose income after accounting for the employment income deduction is less than KRW 1 000 000 and whose age is:
    1. parents: 60 years or older;
    2. brother/sister: 60 years or older or 20 years or younger;
    3. children: 20 years or younger (if both partners in the household earn wage-income, this Report assumes that the principal wage earner will claim the allowance).

- *Additional allowance:* a taxpayer can deduct KRW 1 000 000 (500 000 in the case of [c], KRW 2 000 000 in the case of[b])from his/her gross income when the taxpayer or his/her dependents fall into one of the following categories (for this report, only cases [c] are modelled):
  - a person aged 70 years or older(a)
  - a handicapped person (b)
  - a female wage earner who is the head of a household with dependents (but without spouse) or a female wage earner with spouse when her taxable income is not more than KRW 30 million(c)
  - a single parent with descendants including adoptees*(f)
- *National pension deduction*: employees can deduct 100% of their National Pension contributions
- *Working Tax credit*: wage and salary income earners obtain the following tax credit, :

Calculated tax	Amount of tax credit
Up to KRW 1 300 000	55% of calculated tax
Over KRW 1 300 000	KRW 715 000 plus 30% of the calculated tax over KRW 1 300 000

Total wage and salary income	Ceiling on credit amount
Not more than KRW 33 million	KRW 740 000
Not more than KRW 70 million	The greater of KRW 660 000 and KRW 740 000 - [(total wage and salary income - KRW 33 million) × 0.8%]
Exceeding KRW 70 million	The greater of KRW 500 000 and KRW 660 000 - [(total wage and salary income - KRW 70 million) × 50%]

1.1.2.2. Main non-standard tax reliefs

Wage and salary income earners may deduct from gross income the expenses for the following items during the tax year:

- *Insurance premiums:* the Medical insurance premium and the Unemployment insurance premium can be entirely (100%) deducted from taxable income.
- *Saving/Payment for housing:* 40% of deposits of an account for purchasing a house, which is held by a person who does not own a house, or owns only one house that is smaller than 85 square miles in size and whose price is KRW 300 million or less, 40% of repayments of loans including interest borrowed for the purpose of the lease by a person owning no house may be deducted up to three million won per year.
- *Credit card purchases:* Employees may deduct 15% of their credit card (30% of their debit card, prepaid card or cash receipt) purchases that exceed 25% of their total income up to lesser of KRW 3 000 000 or 20% of their total income. However, for expenditures spent for traditional markets and public transportation, the allowed deduction is equivalent to 30% of the expenditure and the ceiling is raised by an additional KRW 1 000 000 respectively.

1.1.2.3. Child tax credit

- Where a resident with taxable income has dependent children including adoption, he/she gets annual tax credit of KRW 150 000 for having a child, KRW 300 000 for having two

* Overlapping of deductions for (c) and (f) is not allowed. So a taxpayer should select only one.

children and KRW 300 000 plus KRW 300 000 per an excess child over two children in case of having more than three children.

- Resident gets additional tax credit of KRW 150 000 per a child who is under 6 years of age from second child;
- Resident gets tax credit of KRW 300 000 per child for birth and adoption of the year;

1.1.2.4. Credit for Pension insurance premiums

- A resident who paid pension contributions to a pension account may deduct the amount equal to 12% of the premiums paid from his/her global income tax amount, only up to KRW 4 million for pension account as well as KRW 7 million for sum of the pension account and retirement –pension account
- A resident whose labour income is not exceeding KRW 55 million when he has labour income only or whose global income is not exceeding KRW 40 million would deduct 15% of the premium.

1.1.2.5. Special tax credit

Wage and salary income earners may obtain following tax credit during the tax year:

- Insurance premiums (a):12% of the general insurance premium up to KRW 1 000 000 can be deducted from his/her income tax amount.
- Medical expenses (b):15% of the medical expenses exceeding 3% of taxable income can be deducted from his/her income tax amount. The medical expenses for taxpayer's dependents who are eligible for the basic deduction is limited KRW 7 000 000 and the medical expenses for the taxpayer himself, taxpayer's dependents who are aged 65 years or older and handicapped persons is not limited.
- Educational expenses (c):15% of tuition fees for pre-school, elementary, middle school and college (but the graduate school fee deduction is allowed only for the taxpayer himself), either for the taxpayer himself or his/her dependents (including the taxpayer's spouse, children, and siblings), can be deducted from his/her income tax amount. The tuition fee for the taxpayer himself is not limited. For the taxpayer's dependents, the limits of tuition fees are as follows:
  - For pre-school: up to KRW 3 000 000 per child;
  - For elementary, middle and high school: up to KRW 3 000 000 per student;
  - For college/university: up to KRW 9 000 000 per student.
- Charities (d):15% of the amount of donation (in case of the donation exceeding KRW 30 million, 25% of the excess over KRW 30 million) is deducted from income tax amount. The limits of donations are as follows:
  - donations to a government body, donations for national defence, natural disaster, and certain charitable associations: up to gross income;
  - donations to public welfare or religious associations: up to 30% of gross income.
- Standard Credits: Alternatively, a taxpayer may elect to choose an annual standard credit of KRW 70 000 (KRW 130 000 for wage and salary earners and KRW 120 000 for business owners meeting certain requirements), if he or she fails to claim deductions for insurance premium, saving/payment for housing and special tax credit.

1.1.3. Tax schedule

Over (KRW)	Not more than (KRW)	Marginal tax rate (%)
0	12 000 000	6
12 000 000	46 000 000	15
46 000 000	88 000 000	24
88 000 000	150 000 000	35
150 000 000		38

1.2. Local income tax

1.2.1. Tax base

The *local* income tax base is the income tax paid to the central government.

1.2.2. Tax rate

A uniform rate of 10% is applied. However, the local government can adjust the rate between the lower limit of 5% and the upper limit of 15%.

1.2.3. Tax rate (selected for this study)

A country-wide rate of 10% is used in this Report.

2. Compulsory social security contribution to schemes operated within the government sector

2.1. Employees' contribution

2.1.1. National pension

The National pension contribution rate is 4.5% of the standardised average monthly wage income as of 2014.

The scope of the standardised average monthly wage income is from KRW 270 000 to KRW 4 210 000 as of 1 July, 2015

2.1.2. Medical insurance

The Medical insurance premium, which has a rate of 3.2337925% (Health insurance: 3.035%, Long term care insurance: 6.55% of Health insurance premium rate), is levied on average monthly wage income as of 1 January201 5.

The scope of the average monthly wage income is from KRW 280 000 to KRW 78 100 000.

2.1.3. Unemployment insurance

0.65% of gross income.

2.1.4. Industrial accident compensation insurance (premiums)

Compulsory application, premiums paid only by employers.

2.2. Employers' contribution

2.2.1. National pension

The national pension contribution rate is 4.5% of the standardised average monthly wage income as of 2014.

The scope of the standardised average monthly wage income is from KRW 270 000 to KRW 4 210 000 as of 1 July, 2015.

If the average monthly wage income of a person is less than KRW 270 000, the average monthly wage income of the person is regarded as KRW 270 000 and the rate (0.045) is applied. If the average monthly wage income of a person is more than KRW 4 210 000, the average monthly wage income of the person is regarded as KRW 4 210 000 and the rate (0.045) is applied; so the maximum of the national pension contribution per year is KRW 2 273 400 (= KRW 4 210 000 × 0.045 × 12 months).

2.2.2. Medical insurance

The Medical insurance premium, which has a rate of 3.2337925% (Health insurance: 3.035%, Long term care insurance: 6.55% of Health insurance premium rate), is levied on average monthly wage income as of 1 January, 2015.

The scope of the average monthly wage income is from KRW 280 000 to KRW 78 100 000.

2.2.3. Unemployment insurance

- the insurance premium is between 0.9% and 1.5% of total wage;
- the insurance premium selected for this study is 0.9%.

2.2.4. Work injury insurance

- the insurance premium consists of an industry-specific rate which is set by the Ministry of Employment and Labour multiplied by total wage;
- the average rate of all industries (selected for this study) is 1.70%.

3. Universal cash transfers

Child Benefit

Child benefit is paid every month to those who have children aged 5 years or younger: KRW 200 000 for a child aged 12 months or younger, KRW 150 000 for a child aged 1 to 2 years and KRW 100 000 for a child aged 2 to 5 years.

If a child attends a nursery or pre-school, childcare benefit is paid instead every month: KRW 394 000 for a child aged 0, KRW 374 000 for a child aged 1 year, KRW 286 000 for a child aged 2 years and KRW 220 000 for a child aged 3 to 5 years.

The above child benefits are not included in the Taxing Wages calculations that consider children aged between 6 and 11 inclusive.

4. Main changes in tax/benefit system since 2000

2000	Contribution to National Pension are to be deductible from 2001, upper cap of employment income deduction limit (KRW 12 000 000) is abolished from 2001
2001	Personal income tax rates are lowered by 10% (10, 20 ,30, 40% were reduced to 9, 18, 27, 36%, respectively) from 2002
2002	Limits of deduction for education fees are expanded from 2003. For pre-school: from KRW 1 000 000 to KRW 1 500 000. For elementary, middle school and high school: from KRW 1 500 000 to KRW 2 000 000. For college and university: from KRW 3 000 000 to KRW 5 000 000. Limit of deduction for interest of long-term mortgage loan for housing is expanded from KRW 3 000 000 to KRW 6 000 000 from 2003
2003	Employment income deduction and tax credit applicable to low income are increased. The deduction rate for the taxable wage income range of KRW 5 000 000 to KRW 15 000 000 is increased from 45% to 47.5%. The tax credit rate for calculated tax below KRW 500 000 is increased from 45% to 50% and the maximum tax credit is increased from KRW 400 000 to KRW 450 000.
2004	Limits of deduction for education fees are expanded. For pre-school: from KRW 1 500 000 to KRW 2 000 000. For college and university: from KRW 5 000 000 to KRW 7 000 000. Limit of deduction for interest on long-term mortgage loan for housing is expanded from KRW 6 000 000 to KRW 10 000 000. The marginal deduction rate for the taxable wage income range from KRW 5 000 000 to KRW 15 000 000 is increased from 47.5% to 50%. The tax credit rate for tax amounts below KRW 500 000 is increased from 50% to 55% and the maximum permitted tax credit goes up from KRW 450 000 to KRW 500 000.
2005	Personal income tax rates are lowered by 1% point (9, 18, 27, 36% were reduced to 8, 17, 26, 35%, respectively). Lump-sum tax relief are expanded from KRW 600 000 to KRW 1 000 000.
2007	Eligibility for the extra allowance amount has been changed. Previously, an income earner with a small number of dependents (e.g. spouse, child) eligible for basic allowance was eligible for an allowance of up to KRW 1 000 000 depending on the number of dependents. As from 2007, however, an income earner with two or more dependent children eligible for basic allowance is eligible for an allowance equivalent to KRW 500,000 if there are 2 children plus an additional KRW 1 000 000 for every additional child (e.g. 2 children: KRW 500 000; 3 children: KRW 1 500 000; 4 children: KRW 2 500 000, etc.).
2008	Tax schedule has been changed : from KRW 10 000 000, KRW 40 000 000 , KRW 80 000 000 to KRW 12 000 000, KRW 46 000 000, KRW 88 000 000; New items have been added to the additional allowance with respect to lineal descendants who are born or adopted during the concerned taxable year; Credit card purchase deduction has been changed : Employees may deduct 20% (previously 15%) of their credit/debit card purchases that exceed 20% (previously 15%) of their total income; Deduction for donations to public welfare or religious associations has been increased up to 15% of gross income. Previously, the limit was 10% of gross income.
2009	Personal income tax rates have been changed: from 8%, 17%, 26%, 35% to6%, 16%, 25%, and 35%. Employment income deduction has been changed: from 100%, 50%, 15%, and 10% 5% to 80%, 50%, 15%, and 10%. 5%
2010	Personal income tax rates have been changed: from 6%, 16%, 25%, 35% to6%, 15%, 24%, and 35%.
2012	Personal income tax rates have been changed: from6%, 15%, 24%, and 35% to 6%, 15%, 24%, 35% and 38%
2013	• A new additional allowance is added: a single parent with lineal descendants or adopted children who are eligible for basic exemption can deduct KRW 1 000 000. • Insurance premiums, medical expenses, education expenses, loans for house, designated donations, saving deposits for housing subscription, investment in employee stock ownership associations or in associations for investment in start-ups, and credit cards are allowed income deduction with a ceiling at KRW 25 000 000 in total. However, for the amount of designated donations exceeding the ceiling, deduction canbe carried forward for 5 years.
2014	• Tax schedule has been changed : KRW 300 000 000 to KRW 150 000 000 • Personal and special income deductions(e.g. medical expenses, educational expenses) have been shifted toward tax credit • Employment income deduction has been changed : 80% to 70%, 50% to 40%. • The ceiling amount of earned income tax credit has been changed : KRW 500 000 to KRW 740 000(the salary < 33 000 000), KRW 660 000 (the salary < 70 000 000)

5. Memorandum item

5.1. *Identification of the Average Worker (AW)*

Sectors used: industry Sectors B-N with reference to the International Standard Industrial Classification of All Economic Activities, Revision 4 (ISIC Rev. 4)

Geographical coverage: whole country

Type of workers: wage workers (male and female).

5.2. *Method to calculate wages*

Report on Labour Force Survey at Establishments covering data in 2014 by the Ministry of Employment and Labour is used to calculate the annual wages of the AW. The statistics were obtained through a sample survey of 12 000 firms with five or more permanent employees throughout the whole country.

Basic method of calculation used: average monthly wages multiplied by 12.

5.3. *Employer's reserve for employee's retirement payment*

An employer should pay to a retiree the retirement payment which is not less than 30 days' wage and salary per one year of service (about 8.3% of gross income or more). An employer can contribute to the Retirement Payment Reserve Fund established within the company or Retirement Insurance Fund established outside the company to prepare for the retirement payment. Such contribution is treated as business expense under certain constraints. Because contribution to the Retirement Fund is not compulsory, this survey does not include such contribution except the contribution converted to employer's contribution to the national pension plan (see Section 2.2.1).

2015 parameter values

Average earnings/yr	Ave_earn	42 162 723	Secretariat estimate
Tax allowances	basic_al	1 500 000	
spouse	spouse_al	1 500 000	
dependents including children	dep_al	1 500 000	
additional allowance	add_all	500 000	
additional allowance 2	add2_all	1 000 000	
Employment income deduction	empdedsch	0	0.7
		5 000 000	0.4
		15 000 000	0.15
		45 000 000	0.05
		100 000 000	0.02
Earned income special credit threshold	earntaxcred	0.55	
		0.3	1 300 000
credit limit	credlimit	740 000	Ave_earn < 33000000
		660 000	Ave_earn < 70000000
		500 000	Ave_earn > 70000000
Child tax credit	child_cred	150 000	
Lump sum tax credit	lump_cred	130 000	
	lump_thresh	1 428 571	
Tax schedule	tax_sch	0.06	12 000 000
		0.15	46 000 000
		0.24	88 000 000
		0.35	150 000 000
		0.38	
Local tax rate	local_rate	0.1	
Social security contributions	SSC_pens	0.045	
	SSC_pens_max	2 273 400	
	SSC_sick	0.03234	
	SSC_sick_max	30 307 103	
	SSC_unemp	0.0065	
Employer contributions	emp_pens	0.045	
	emp_sick	0.03234	
	emp_unemp	0.009	
	emp_inj	0.0170	

2015 tax equations

The equations for the Korean system are independent between spouses except that the principal earner has tax allowances for the spouse and for any children.

The functions which are used in the equations (Taper, MIN, Tax etc) are described in the technical note about tax equations. Variable names are defined in the table of parameters above, within the equations table, or are the standard variables married and children. A reference to a variable with the affix total indicates the sum of the relevant variable values for the principal and spouse. And the affixes princ and spouse indicate the value for the principal and spouse, respectively. Equations for a single person are as shown for the principal, with spouse values taken as 0.

	Line in country table and intermediate steps	Variable name	Range	Equation
1.	Earnings	earn		
2.	Allowances:			
	employment income	emp_al	B	Empincded(earn, empincdedsch)
	basic	bas_al	B	basic_al
	spouse	sp_al	P	Married*spouse_al*(earn_spouse-emp_al_spouse<=spouse_al)
	dependents	dp_al	P	Children*dep_al
	additional allowances	add_al_princ	P	IF(AND(Married=0,Children>0), add2_all,0)
	additional allowances	add_al_spouse	S	(earn_spouse>0)*add_all
	national pension deduction	np_de	B	Min(earn*SSC_pens, SSC_pens_max)
	Main non-standard tax relief	non-std_al	B	IF(earn*(SSC_sick+SSC_unemp)>lump_thresh,earn*(SSC_sick+SSC_unemp),0)
	Total	tax_al	B	emp_al+bas_al+sp_al+dp_al+add_al+np_al
3.	Credits in taxable income	taxbl_cr	B	0
4.	CG taxable income	tax_inc	B	Positive(earn-tax_al)
5.	CG tax before credits	CG_tax_excl	B	Tax(tax_inc, tax_sch)
6.	Tax credits :	earn_cr	B	MIN(earntaxcred(CG_tax_excl), credlimit(earn))
	earned income	child_cr	P	Children*child_cred
	special tax credit	lump_cr	B	IF(non-std_al=0, lump_cred, 0)
	child tax credit	tax_cr	B	earn_cr+child_cr+lump_cr
	lump-sum tax credit			
	Total			
7.	CG tax	CG_tax	B	CG_tax_excl-tax_cr
8.	State and local taxes	local_tax	B	local_rate*CG_tax
9.	Employees' soc security	SSC	B	MIN(earn*(SSC_pens),SSC_pens_max)+MIN(earn*(SSC_sick),SSC_sick_max)+earn*(SSC_unemp)
11.	Cash transfers	cash_trans	J	
13.	Employer's soc security	SSC_empr	B	MIN(earn*(SSC_pens),SSC_pens_max)+MIN(earn*(emp_sick),SSC_sick_max)+earn*(emp_unemp+emp_inj)

Key to range of equation B calculated separately for both principal earner and spouse P calculated for principal only (value taken as 0 for spouse calculation) S calculated for spouse only J calculated once only on a joint basis.

Luxembourg

This chapter includes data on the income taxes paid by workers, their social security contributions, the family benefits they receive in the form of cash transfers as well as the social security contributions and payroll taxes paid by their employers. Results reported include the marginal and average tax burden for eight different family types.

Methodological information is available for personal income tax systems, compulsory social security contributions to schemes operated within the government sector, universal cash transfers as well as recent changes in the tax/benefit system. The methodology also includes the parameter values and tax equations underlying the data.

Luxembourg 2015

The tax/benefit position of single persons

			67	100	167	67
		Wage level (per cent of average wage)	67	100	167	67
		Number of children	none	none	none	2
1.	**Gross wage earnings**		37 220	55 553	92 773	37 220
2.	**Standard tax allowances**					
	Basic allowance		480	480	480	480
	Married or head of family					
	Dependent children					
	Deduction for social security contributions and income taxes		4 113	6 139	10 251	4 113
	Work-related expenses		540	540	540	540
	Other		0	0	0	0
		Total	5 133	7 159	11 271	5 133
3.	**Tax credits or cash transfers included in taxable income**		0	0	0	0
4.	**Central government rounded taxable income (1 - 2 + 3)**		32 050	48 350	81 500	32 050
5.	**Central government income tax liability (exclusive of tax credits)**		3 981	10 249	24 083	2 218
6.	**Tax credits**					
	Basic credit		300	300	300	300
	Married or head of family					
	Children					
	Other		0	0	0	750
		Total	300	300	300	1 050
7.	**Central government income tax finally paid (5-6)**		3 681	9 949	23 783	1 168
8.	**State and local taxes**		0	0	0	0
9.	**Employees' compulsory social security contributions**					
	Gross earnings		4 739	7 113	11 933	4 739
	Taxable income					
		Total	4 739	7 113	11 933	4 739
10.	**Total payments to general government (7 + 8 + 9)**		8 421	17 062	35 716	5 908
11.	**Cash transfers from general government**					
	For head of family					
	For two children		0	0	0	7 522
		Total	0	0	0	7 522
12.	**Take-home pay (1-10+11)**		28 800	38 490	57 057	38 835
13.	**Employer's compulsory social security contributions**		4 563	6 811	11 374	4 563
14.	**Average rates**					
	Income tax		9.9%	17.9%	25.6%	3.1%
	Employees' social security contributions		12.7%	12.8%	12.9%	12.7%
	Total payments less cash transfers		22.6%	30.7%	38.5%	-4.3%
	Total tax wedge including employer's social security contributions		31.1%	38.3%	45.2%	7.1%
15.	**Marginal rates**					
	Total payments less cash transfers: Principal earner		39.6%	50.1%	50.1%	44.4%
	Total payments less cash transfers: Spouse		n.a.	n.a.	n.a.	n.a.
	Total tax wedge: Principal earner		46.2%	55.5%	55.5%	50.4%
	Total tax wedge: Spouse		n.a.	n.a.	n.a.	n.a.

Luxembourg 2015

The tax/benefit position of married couples

	Wage level (per cent of average wage)	100-0	100-33	100-67	100-33
	Number of children	2	2	2	none
1.	**Gross wage earnings**	55 553	73 885	92 773	73 885
2.	**Standard tax allowances**				
	Basic allowance	480	960	960	960
	Married or head of family				
	Dependent children				
	Deduction for social security contributions and income taxes	6 139	8 164	10 251	8 164
	Work-related expenses	540	1 080	1 080	1 080
	Other	0	4 500	4 500	4 500
	Total	7 159	14 704	16 791	14 704
3.	**Tax credits or cash transfers included in taxable income**	0	0	0	0
4.	**Central government rounded taxable income (1 - 2 + 3)**	48 350	59 150	75 950	59 150
5.	**Central government income tax liability (exclusive of tax credits)**	3 811	6 513	12 003	6 513
6.	**Tax credits**				
	Basic credit	300	600	600	600
	Married or head of family				
	Children				
	Other	0	0	0	0
	Total	300	600	600	600
7.	**Central government income tax finally paid (5-6)**	3 511	5 913	11 403	5 913
8.	**State and local taxes**	0	0	0	0
9.	**Employees' compulsory social security contributions**				
	Gross earnings	7 113	9 407	11 853	9 407
	Taxable income				
	Total	7 113	9 407	11 853	9 407
10.	**Total payments to general government (7 + 8 + 9)**	10 624	15 319	23 255	15 319
11.	**Cash transfers from general government**				
	For head of family				
	For two children	7 522	7 522	7 522	0
	Total	7 522	7 522	7 522	0
12.	**Take-home pay (1-10+11)**	52 451	66 087	77 039	58 566
13.	**Employer's compulsory social security contributions**	6 811	9 058	11 374	9 058
14.	**Average rates**				
	Income tax	6.3%	8.0%	12.3%	8.0%
	Employees' social security contributions	12.8%	12.7%	12.8%	12.7%
	Total payments less cash transfers	5.6%	10.6%	17.0%	20.7%
	Total tax wedge including employer's social security contributions	15.9%	20.3%	26.0%	29.4%
15.	**Marginal rates**				
	Total payments less cash transfers: Principal earner	32.0%	37.7%	47.2%	37.7%
	Total payments less cash transfers: Spouse	25.6%	37.7%	47.2%	37.7%
	Total tax wedge: Principal earner	39.4%	44.5%	53.0%	44.5%
	Total tax wedge: Spouse	33.7%	44.5%	53.0%	44.5%

The national currency is the euro (EUR). In 2015, EUR 0.90 equalled USD 1. The Secretariat has estimated that in that same year the average worker earned EUR 55 553 (Secretariat estimate).

1. Personal income tax system

1.1. *Taxes levied by central government*

1.1.1. *Tax unit*

Spouses and partners are taxed jointly on their income. The income of minor children is included in determining the couple's taxable income. However, any earned income that children may derive from work is excluded from joint taxation.

1.1.2. *Tax reliefs and tax credits*

1.1.2.1. Standard reliefs in the form of deductions from income

- Wage-earners are entitled to a standard minimum deduction of EUR 540 for work-related expenses other than travel, unless their actual deductible expenses are higher. This deduction is doubled for spouses taxed jointly.
- The first 4 distance units (i.e. 4 * 99 = EUR 396 per year) of the lump sum deduction for travel expenses between a taxpayer's home and his working places are abolished. The maximum deduction will be limited to EUR 2 574 per year.
- Like other taxpayers, wage-earners having no special expenses (interest charges, insurance premiums or contributions other than for social security) may take a standard deduction of EUR 480 for special expenses. Actual insurance premiums are deductible up to the limit set by law.
- If both spouses have earned income and are taxed jointly, they qualify for an earned income allowance of EUR 4 500.
- Social security contributions: contributions paid to compulsory health insurance and pension schemes are deductible in full.
- Dependency insurance: the dependency contribution is not deductible for income tax purposes.

1.1.2.2. Standard reliefs in the form of tax credits

- Wage-earners and pensioners receive a refundable tax credit of EUR 300 per annum.
- Single-parents receive a refundable tax credit of EUR 750 per annum.

1.1.2.3. Non-standard allowances deductible from taxable income

- Interest charges are deductible insofar as they are not considered operating expenses or acquisition expenses, and provided they are unrelated economically to the exempt income. However, the deduction of interest charges is capped at EUR 336 per year. This ceiling is increased by EUR 336 for the taxpayer's spouse/partner and for each child.

- Taxpayers may deduct premiums paid to insurers licensed in an EU country in respect of life, death, accident, disability, illness or liability insurance, as well as dues paid to recognised mutual assistance companies. However, deductions are capped at EUR 672 per year.
- Payments to an insurance company or credit institution in respect of an individual retirement scheme are deductible. These payments are capped according to the subscriber's age and must meet certain investment policy constraints. The ceiling varies between EUR 1 500 and EUR 3 200. Each spouse/partner may take out such a contract and qualify for the respective ceilings.
- Contributions to building society savings are deductible up to the limit of EUR 672.
- Interest charges in respect of the rental value of owner-occupied housing are deductible only up to an annual ceiling. During the first five years, the ceiling is EUR 1 500; for the following five years it is EUR 1 125; thereafter it is EUR 750. These ceilings are increased by an equal amount for the taxpayer's spouse/partner, and for each qualifying child.
- As from 1 January 2009, the maximal deduction of premium related to the mortgage life insurance on the taxpayer's principal residence is EUR 6 000. This ceiling is increased by an equal amount for the taxpayer's spouse/partner and by 1 200 for each qualifying child. For taxpayers over the age of 30, the allowable deduction of EUR 6 000 is increased by 8% for each year over 30, with a ceiling of 160%.
- Upon request, taxpayers may be granted exemptions for extraordinary expenses that are unavoidable, and that considerably reduce their ability to pay taxes (*e.g.* uninsured health care costs, support for needy relatives, uninsured funeral costs beyond the taxpayer's means, domestic or childcare expenses, expenses for children outside the taxpayer's household, or expenses for children in a single-parent household).

1.1.3. *Tax schedule reliefs*

Income tax is determined on the basis of the following schedule (amounts in Euros):

0% for the portion of income between 11 265
8% for the portion of income between 11 265 and 13 173
10% for the portion of income between 13 173 and 15 081
12% for the portion of income between 15 081 and 16 989
14% for the portion of income between 16 989 and 18 897
16% for the portion of income between 18 897 and 20 805
18% for the portion of income between 20 805 and 22 713
20% for the portion of income between 22 713 and 24 621
22% for the portion of income between 24 621 and 26 529
24% for the portion of income between 26 529 and 28 437
26% for the portion of income between 28 437 and 30 345
28% for the portion of income between 30 345 and 32 253
30% for the portion of income between 32 253 and 34 161
32% for the portion of income between 34 161 and 36 069
34% for the portion of income between 36 069 and 37 977
36% for the portion of income between 37 977 and 39 885
38% for the portion of income between 39 885 and 41 793
39% for the portion of income between 41 793 and 100 000
40% for the portion exceeding 100 000

The income tax liability of *single* taxpayers is determined by applying the above schedule to taxable income.

The income tax liability of *married* taxpayers and partners corresponds to double the amount obtained if the above schedule is applied to half of their income (class 2).

For widow(er)s, taxpayers with a dependent child allowance and persons over 64 years of age (class 1a), tax is calculated as follows: the schedule is applied to adjusted taxable income reduced by half of the difference between that amount and EUR 45 060, with the marginal tax rate capped at 40%.

Income tax as determined by the applicable schedules is subject to a 7% "solidarity" surtax to finance the employment fund. The rate is 9% for the taxable income exceeding EUR 150 000 (tax classes 1 and 1a), respectively EUR 300 000 (tax class 2).

1.1.4. *Income exemptions*

A taxpayer may claim a deduction for a dependent child under 21 years of age who is not part of the household. This deduction is allowed for expenses actually incurred but may not exceed EUR 3 480.

1.2. *Local (municipal) taxes*

No particular income tax is levied by municipalities, which receive a direct share of the income tax revenue collected by the State. This share is equal to 18% of tax revenue.

2. Compulsory social security contributions to schemes operated within the government sector

	Employer's share (%)	Employee's share (%)	Ceiling on contributions (in euros)
a) Pension and disability insurance	8	8	115 377.84
b) Health insurance	3.05	3.05	115 377.84
c) Dependency insurance		1.4	Monthly allowance 480.26[1]
d) Health in the workplace	0.11		
e) Accident insurance	1.10		

1. (Monthly allowance: EUR 480.26 = 0.25* social minimum salary / 12). The social minimum salary in 2015 is equal to EUR 23 075.52.

No distinction is made according to family status or gender.

As from 1 January 2009 the differences in social security contributions between workers and employees are abolished.

A temporary budget balancing tax, the "impôt d'équilibrage budgétaire temporaire" (IEBT), was introduced for the year 2015. The tax rate of 0.5% will be withheld on all categories of income (professional and replacement income and non-professional income, except on supplements for overtime) for all individuals affiliated to the Luxembourg social security system.

This measure was introduced for the tax years 2015 and 2016.

3. Universal cash transfers

3.1. *For married persons*

None.

3.2. *For dependent children*

Every child raised in the Grand Duchy entitles the person on whom the child is dependent to a monthly family allowance. Family allowances are adjusted regularly for the cost of living. For 2015, the amounts are:

Effective date	As of 1 July 2006
1 eligible child	EUR 185.60
2 eligible children	EUR 440.72
3 eligible children	EUR 802.74

Starting with the fourth eligible child, the allowance is raised by EUR 361.82 per child.

The amounts indicated above are increased by EUR 16.17 for children aged 6 to 11 and by EUR 48.52 for those aged 12 years or older.

Additionally, a child bonus amounting to EUR 76.88 per child per month is paid in cash irrespective of the taxable income of the parents as from 1 January 2009. This amount is paid by the National Family Benefits Administration.

4. Main changes since 2008

4.1. *Partnerships*

The Act of 9 July 2004 introduced the notion of partnerships into tax law. The Act construes the term "partnership" as a relationship between two persons, called "partners", of opposite sex or the same sex, who live together as a couple and declare themselves as such.

As from 1 January 2008, the fiscal treatment of the partnerships is modified. The deduction for extraordinary expenses is replaced by the joint taxation of partners as it already exists for spouses.

4.2. *Introduction of tax credits*

The following changes were made as of 1 January 2009:

- Four tax allowances have been replaced by refundable tax credits. Instead of reducing their taxable income by EUR 600, wage-earners get a tax credit of EUR 300 per annum. A similar tax credit is allowed for pensioners.
- The tax exemption of EUR 1 920 for single-parent households is replaced by a tax credit of EUR 750 per annum.
- A tax credit of EUR 300 per annum is granted to self-employed persons deriving income from trade or business, income from agriculture and forestry or income from self-employment. This tax credit substitutes the allowance for business income and the agricultural allowance.

5. Memorandum item

5.1. *Identification of the average worker*

Average gross hourly wages by industry and by gender are determined on the basis of biannual surveys on industry wages and working hours. These surveys cover gross compensation for regular hours (working hours + leave time) plus overtime pay. Hourly wages include bonuses and allowances such as premiums for output, production or productivity. In contrast, non-periodic compensation (bonuses, profit-sharing) that is not paid systematically in each pay period is not included. Nevertheless, in order to allow for comparisons between countries, gross annual pay is adjusted on the basis of average non-periodic compensation as calculated from triennial surveys of labour costs.

Regarding working hours, the time taken into account is the time effectively offered, including regular working hours, overtime, night shifts and work on Sunday.

2015 parameter values

Average earnings/yr	Ave_earn	55 553	Secretariat estimate
Tax allowances: general	gen_dedn	480	
professional expenses	prof_exp	540	
travel expenses	travel_exp	0	
extra if both spouses earning	extra_dedn	4 500	
Low earner allowance	allow_1		
Low earner allowance (couples)	allow_2		
Class 1a limit	cl_1a_lim	45 060	
Tax schedule	tax_sch	0	11 265
		0.08	13 173
		0.1	15 081
		0.12	16 989
		0.14	18 897
		0.16	20 805
		0.18	22 713
		0.2	24 621
		0.22	26 529
		0.24	28 437
		0.26	30 345
		0.28	32 253
		0.3	34 161
		0.32	36 069
		0.34	37 977
		0.36	39 885
		0.38	41 793
		0.39	100 000
		0.40	
Child credit maximum	ch_cred	0	
Social Minimum Salary	min_salary	23 075.52	
Multiplier for unemployment	unemp_rate_1	1.07	
	Unemp_rate_2	1.09	
	Unemp_lim	150 000	
Social security contributions	SSC_rate	0.1105	
	SSC_ceil	115 377.84	
	infirm	0.014	
	infirm_abatement	0.25	
IEBT	iebt_rate	0.005	
Employer contributions	workhealth	0.0011	
	SSC_empr	0.1105	
	SSC_acc	0.011	
Child benefit (1 child)	CB_1	185.6	
2 children	CB_2	440.72	
extra age 6-11	CB_ex	16.17	
Child bonus	ch_bonus	922.50	
Worker tax credit	worker_credit	300	
Single parent tax credit	cr_monoparent	750	
Class 1a Discount	discount	0.50	
Maximum Marginal Rate	max_rate	0.40	

2015 tax equations

The equations for the Luxembourg system are on a joint basis except for social security contributions.

The functions which are used in the equations (Taper, MIN, Tax etc) are described in the technical note about tax equations. Variable names are defined in the table of parameters above, within the equations table, or are the standard variables "married" and "children". A reference to a variable with the affix "_total" indicates the sum of the relevant variable values for the principal and spouse. And the affixes "_princ" and "_spouse" indicate the value for the principal and spouse, respectively. Equations for a single person are as shown for the principal, with "_spouse" values taken as 0.

	Line in country table and intermediate steps	Variable name	Range	Equation
1.	Earnings	earn		
2.	Allowances:			
	Basic	basic	J	IF(earn_spouse=0, 1, 2)*gen_dedn
	work-related	work_rel	J	IF(earn_spouse=0, 1, 2)*(prof_exp)
	Other	other_al	J	(earn_spouse>0)*extra_dedn
	Total	tax_al	J	min(basic+work_rel+other_al+SSC_ded_total, earn)
3.	Credits in taxable income	taxbl_cr	J	0
	family quotient	quotient	J	1+Married
4.	CG taxable income unadjusted taxable income	tax_inc	J	earn-tax_al
5.	CG tax before credits	tax_excl	J	((Children=0)*IF(Married=0,Tax(tax_inc, tax_sch), quotient*Tax(tax_inc/quotient, tax_sch)) + (Children>0)*IF(Married=0, Taxclass1a(tax_inc, tax_sch, discount, cl_1a_lim, max_rate), quotient*Tax(tax_inc/quotient, tax_sch)))*IF(tax_inc> unemp_lim*(1+Married,unemp_rate_2,unemp_rate_1)
6.	Tax credits :	worker_cr	J	IF(earn_spouse=0,1,2)*worker_credit
		monoparent_cr	J	cr_monoparent*(AND(Married=0,Children>0))
		tax_cr	J	worker_cr+monoparent_cr
7.	CG tax	CG_tax	J	tax_excl-tax_cr
8.	State and local taxes	local_tax	J	0
9.	Employees' soc security	SSC	B	SSC_rate*MIN(earn, SSC_ceil)+infirm*Positive(earn-infirm_abatement*min_salary)+(iebt_rate*earn)
	deductible portion	SSC_ded	B	SSC_rate*MIN(earn, SSC_ceil)
11.	Cash transfers	cash_trans	J	((Children=1)*(CB_1+CB_ex)+ (Children=2)*(CB_2+2*CB_ex))*12+Children*ch_bonus
13.	Employer's soc security	SSC_empr	B	(SSC_empr+workhealth)*MIN(earn, SSC_ceil)+SSC_acc*MIN(earn, SSC_ceil)

Key to range of equation B calculated separately for both principal earner and spouse P calculated for principal only (value taken as 0 for spouse calculation) J calculated once only on a joint basis.

Mexico

This chapter includes data on the income taxes paid by workers, their social security contributions, the family benefits they receive in the form of cash transfers as well as the social security contributions and payroll taxes paid by their employers. Results reported include the marginal and average tax burden for eight different family types.

Methodological information is available for personal income tax systems, compulsory social security contributions to schemes operated within the government sector, universal cash transfers as well as recent changes in the tax/benefit system. The methodology also includes the parameter values and tax equations.

Mexico 2015

The tax/benefit position of single persons

		Wage level (per cent of average wage)	67	100	167	67
		Number of children	none	none	none	2
1.	**Gross wage earnings**		70 969	105 924	176 893	70 969
2.	**Standard tax allowances**					
	Basic allowance		2 342	2 485	2 777	2 342
	Married or head of family					
	Dependent children					
	Deduction for social security contributions and income taxes					
	Work-related expenses					
	Other					
		Total	2 342	2 485	2 777	2 342
3.	**Tax credits or cash transfers included in taxable income**		0	0	0	0
4.	**Central government taxable income (1 - 2 + 3)**		68 628	103 439	174 116	68 628
5.	**Central government income tax liability (exclusive of tax credits)**		4 936	9 478	23 882	4 936
6.	**Tax credits**					
	Basic credit		3 536	0	0	3 536
	Married or head of family					
	Children					
	Other		0	0	0	0
		Total	3 536	0	0	3 536
7.	**Central government income tax finally paid (5-6)**		1 401	9 478	23 882	1 401
8.	**State and local taxes**		0	0	0	0
9.	**Employees' compulsory social security contributions**					
	Gross earnings		887	1 441	2 612	887
	Taxable income					
		Total	887	1 441	2 612	887
10.	**Total payments to general government (7 + 8 + 9)**		2 288	10 919	26 494	2 288
11.	**Cash transfers from general government**					
	For head of family					
	For two children		0	0	0	0
		Total	0	0	0	0
12.	**Take-home pay (1-10+11)**		68 681	95 005	150 400	68 681
13.	**Employers' compulsory social security contributions**		9 833	12 426	17 819	9 833
14.	**Average rates**					
	Income tax		2.0%	8.9%	13.5%	2.0%
	Employees' social security contributions		1.3%	1.4%	1.5%	1.3%
	Total payments less cash transfers		3.2%	10.3%	15.0%	3.2%
	Total tax wedge including employer's social security contributions		15.0%	19.7%	22.8%	15.0%
15.	**Marginal rates**					
	Total payments less cash transfers: Principal earner		12.1%	19.5%	22.9%	12.1%
	Total payments less cash transfers: Spouse		n.a.	n.a.	n.a.	n.a.
	Total tax wedge: Principal earner		17.5%	25.2%	28.4%	17.5%
	Total tax wedge: Spouse		n.a.	n.a.	n.a.	n.a.

Mexico 2015

The tax/benefit position of married couples

		100-0	100-33	100-67	100-33
	Wage level (per cent of average wage)	100-0	100-33	100-67	100-33
	Number of children	2	2	2	none
1.	**Gross wage earnings**	105 924	140 879	176 893	140 879
2.	**Standard tax allowances**				
	Basic allowance	2 485	4 065	4 827	4 065
	Married or head of family				
	Dependent children				
	Deduction for social security contributions and income taxes				
	Work-related expenses				
	Other				
	Total	2 485	4 065	4 827	4 065
3.	**Tax credits or cash transfers included in taxable income**	0	0	0	0
4.	**Central government taxable income (1 - 2 + 3)**	103 439	136 814	172 066	136 814
5.	**Central government income tax liability (exclusive of tax credits)**	9 478	11 347	14 415	11 347
6.	**Tax credits**				
	Basic credit	0	4 879	3 536	4 879
	Married or head of family				
	Children				
	Other	0	0	0	0
	Total	0	4 879	3 536	4 879
7.	**Central government income tax finally paid (5-6)**	9 478	6 468	10 879	6 468
8.	**State and local taxes**	0	0	0	0
9.	**Employees' compulsory social security contributions**				
	Gross earnings	1 441	1 878	2 328	1 878
	Taxable income				
	Total	1 441	1 878	2 328	1 878
10.	**Total payments to general government (7 + 8 + 9)**	10 919	8 346	13 207	8 346
11.	**Cash transfers from general government**				
	For head of family				
	For two children	0	0	0	0
	Total	0	0	0	0
12.	**Take-home pay (1-10+11)**	95 005	132 533	163 686	132 533
13.	**Employers' compulsory social security contributions**	12 426	19 917	22 258	19 917
14.	**Average rates**				
	Income tax	8.9%	4.6%	6.2%	4.6%
	Employees' social security contributions	1.4%	1.3%	1.3%	1.3%
	Total payments less cash transfers	10.3%	5.9%	7.5%	5.9%
	Total tax wedge including employer's social security contributions	19.7%	17.6%	17.8%	17.6%
15.	**Marginal rates**				
	Total payments less cash transfers: Principal earner	19.5%	19.5%	19.5%	19.5%
	Total payments less cash transfers: Spouse	-7.4%	7.4%	12.1%	7.4%
	Total tax wedge: Principal earner	25.2%	25.2%	25.2%	25.2%
	Total tax wedge: Spouse	11.6%	13.0%	17.5%	13.0%

The national currency is the peso (MXN). In 2015, MXN 15.87 was equal to USD 1. In 2015, the estimated earnings of the average worker are MXN 105 924 (Secretariat estimate).

1. Personal income tax

1.1. Central government income tax

1.1.1. Tax unit

Each person is taxed separately.

1.1.2. Tax allowances and tax credits

1.1.2.1. Standard tax reliefs

There are two basic allowances, a yearly holiday bonus and an end-of-year bonus.

- *Holiday Bonus:* Mexico's Labour Law stipulates a minimum holiday bonus of 25% of six days of the worker's wage. The maximum exemption according to Tax Law is equivalent to 15 days of the minimum wage (the minimum wage for the whole country).* Given these two restrictions, the allowance is estimated as the minimum established by the Labour Law, up to the amount that is exempt according to Tax Law.
- *End-of-year bonus:* The minimum end-of-year bonus established in the Labour Law is 15 days of the worker's wage. Tax Law exempts end-of-year-bonuses up to 30 days of the minimum wage (the amount for the whole country). The allowance is estimated as the minimum established by the Labour Law, up to the amount that is exempt according to Tax Law.

1.1.2.2. Main non-standard tax reliefs

Deductions:

- Compulsory school transportation costs.
- Medical expenses (doctor and dental fees and hospital expenses): An unlimited deduction is allowed for the taxpayer's medical expenses. For those made by the taxpayer, on behalf of his or her spouse and straight line relatives, the deduction is allowed only if the person, for whom the taxpayer makes the expense, earns less than the minimum annual wage of his geographical area.
- Complementary contributions of certain retirement accounts are considered eligible as long as they do not exceed 10% of taxable income and MXN 124 702 (five annual minimum wages).

* Until October 2015 there were two minimum wage rates established in Mexico depending upon geographical location (in Zone A the minimum wage is equal to MXN 70.10 on a daily basis and in Zone B it is MXN 66.45. For the purposes of this Report, the calculations are either based on the minimum wage that applies within the Federal District of Mexico City (Zone A) or a representative value for the country as a whole (the average minimum wage is equal to MXN 68.33). The latter is used in the evaluation of the holiday bonus and the end-of-year bonus. In October 2015 minimum wage zone B was homologated to zone A establishing a nationwide minimum wage of MXN 70.1.

- Funeral charges: for the spouse and straight-line relatives up to a minimum annual wage of the taxpayer's geographical area.
- Charitable donations made to institutions such as:
  - Federal, state, and municipal governments.
  - Non-profit organisations involved in the fields of social beneficence, education, culture and research and technology.
- Deposits on special savings accounts, payments of insurance premium of pension plans and for the acquisition of shares of investment societies as long as they do not exceed MXN 152 000.
- Health insurance premiums for individuals, if the beneficiary is the taxpayer, and/or his family.
- Real interest expenditure for the payment of mortgage loans for housing purposes that do not exceed MXN 3 969 905. Real interest expenditure is considered the excess of interest expense over the inflation rate.*
- Deduction of taxpayer's educational expenditures for himself, on behalf of his/her spouse, parents or children, among others, for the following educational levels.

Educational level	Maximum annual deduction (MXN)
Kinder garden	14 200
Primary education	12 900
Secondary education	19 900
Technical profession	17 100
High school	24 500

Since 2014, there is a limitation of the total amount of personal deductions. They cannot be higher than the minimum between 10 % of the taxpayer's gross income or an amount equivalent to 4 annual minimum wages of the of the taxpayer's geographical area (MXN 99 762 in 2015). The limit is not applicable to donations or private educational services.

1.1.2.3. Employment subsidy credit

The employment subsidy credit is assigned through a table and this amount is decreasing in the level of income obtained by each worker. For monthly income higher than MXN 7 382, no employment subsidy credit is given. Employees with an income tax lower than the credit receive in cash the difference along with their salary. The rest of the workers that receive the credit are entitled to a reduction in their tax burden. The employment subsidy credit is paid by the employers who may credit it against their tax liabilities; the credit therefore represents a fiscal cost for the government.

1.1.3. *Tax schedule and other tables*

1.1.3.1. Tax schedule**

Since 2014 three additional brackets were included with a maximum marginal rate for income over MXN 3 million of 35%.

* Since 2010, this exemption is applicable only if in the immediate previous five years the taxpayer has not sold any other house for which he/she obtained this exemption.

** The income tax schedule and the employment subsidy credit table are updated every time the accumulated inflation reaches 10%.

Taxable income (MXN)		Fixed quota (MXN)	Tax on the amount in excess of the lower limit (%)
Lower limit	Upper limit		
0	5 952.84	0	1.92
5 952.85	50 524.92	114.29	6.40
50 524.93	88 793.04	2 966.91	10.88
88 793.05	103 218.00	7 130.48	16.00
103 218.01	123 580.20	9 438.47	17.92
123 580.21	249 243.48	13 087.37	21.36
249 243.49	392 841.96	39 929.05	23.52
392 841.97	750 000	73 703.41	30.00
750 000.01	1 000 000.00	180 850.82	32.00
1 000 000.01	3 000 000.00	260 850.81	34.00
3 000 000.01	And over	940 850.81	35.00

1.1.3.2. Employment subsidy credit table

For taxable income in a certain income range, the employment subsidy credit is given in the third column of the following table:

Lower limit (MXN)	Upper limit (MXN)	Tax credit (MXN)
0.0	21 227.52	4 884.24
21 227.53	31 840.56	4 881.96
31 840.57	41 674.08	4 879.44
41 674.09	42 454.44	4 713.24
42 454.45	53 353.80	4 589.52
53 353.81	56 606.16	4 250.76
56 606.17	64 025.04	3 898.44
64 025.05	74 696.04	3 535.56
74 696.05	85 366.80	3 042.48
85 366.81	88 587.96	2 611.32
88 587.97	And Over	0.00

1.2. *State and local income taxes*

States do not levy taxes on income.

1.3. *Payroll taxes*

Mexico does not have a Federal pay-roll tax. However, most States apply a state pay-roll tax with an average rate of 2.25%. These taxes are not considered in this Report since there are a wide range of practices with respect to the definition of the tax base that does not allow obtaining a reliable estimation.

2. Compulsory social security contributions to schemes operated within the government sector

2.1. *Employees' contributions*

Social security contributions are divided as follows:

For sickness and maternity insurance, 0.625% of the workers monthly wage, plus 0.40% of the amount in excess of three times the minimal legal wage (the amount that applies within the Federal District of Mexico City MWFD). For disability and life insurance, 0.625% of the monthly wage.

In 2015 a ceiling of 25 MWFD applies to the salary that is used to calculate the social security contributions.

2.2. *Employers' contributions*

- For sickness and maternity 20.40% of the MWFD, plus 1.10% of the amount in excess of three times the MWFD, plus 1.75 of the monthly wage.
- For disability and life insurance, 1.75% of worker's monthly wage.
- For social services and nursery, 1% of worker's monthly wage.
- For insurance for work injuries of employees, 2.00% of worker's monthly wage.*

In 2015 a ceiling of 25 MWDF applies to the salary that is used to calculate the social security contributions.

3. Universal cash transfers

3.1. *Transfers related to marital status*

None.

3.2. *Transfers for dependent children*

None.

4. Main changes in the tax/benefit system since 1995

The Social Security Law enacted in July 1997 changed fundamentally the financing of non-government employees' social security, which shifted from a pay-as-you-go scheme to funded individual accounts. The government does not manage these accounts; new private financial institutions were created specifically for this purpose. However, the contractual obligation is between the workers and the government, not with the private administrator of the fund, because legally they are still considered as contributions to social security, independently of who manages the fund. It should be noted that the federal government also contributes to each pension account, and guarantees a minimum pension to every beneficiary of the social security system, again independently of the administration of the fund.

5. Memorandum items

5.1. *Method used to identify an average worker and to calculate his gross earnings*

The income data refer to average workers. It should be noted that in the sample used for this survey, medium and large size firms are over-represented. In Mexico, there are no state or local government income taxes. Information on non-standard tax reliefs is not available.

Figures for 1999 and subsequent years cannot be compared with preliminary figures from previous editions of this publication for two reasons: first, the wage level of the average worker is now based on observed data instead of being estimated; second, social security contributions taken into account no longer include contributions made by employers and employees to privately managed individual accounts. Contributions no longer included in the calculation of social security contributions are specified in the table below.

* The amount of the work injury fee depends on the risk level in which the company is classified. The Mexican Institute of Social Security provided a weighted average rate that considers the economic activities from C to K of the International Standard Classification.

5.2. *Main employees' and employers' contributions to private pension, health, etc. schemes*

	Account	Per cent of workers' monthly wage
Employers' contributions	Retirement	2.00
	Discharge and old age insurance	3.15
	Housing Fund (INFONAVIT)	5.00
Employees' contributions	Discharge and old age insurance	1.125

2015 parameter values

Average earnings/yr	Ave_earn	105 924	Secretariat estimate	
(general min wage per day)	min_wage	68.33		
(general min wage per day for the Federal District of Mexico City)	min_wage_FD	70.10		
Income tax	tax_table	0.00	0	0.0192
		5 952.85	114.29	0.0640
		50 524.93	2 966.91	0.1088
		88 793.05	7 130.48	0.1600
		103 218.01	9 438.47	0.1792
		123 580.21	13 087.37	0.2136
		249 243.49	39 929.05	0.2352
		392 841.97	73 703.41	0.3000
		750 000.01	180 850.82	0.3200
		1 000 000.01	260 850.81	0.3400
		3 000 000.01	940 850.81	0.3500
Tax credit basic	Basic_crd	0.0	4 884.24	
		21 227.53	4 881.96	
		31 840.57	4 879.44	
		41 674.09	4 713.24	
		42 454.45	4 589.52	
		53 353.81	4 250.76	
		56 606.17	3 898.44	
		64 025.05	3 535.56	
		74 696.05	3 042.48	
		85 366.81	2 611.32	
		88 587.97	0.00	
Employees SSC	SSC_rate	0.0125		
	SSC_rate_sur	0.0040		
Employers SSC	SSC_empr	0.0650		
	SSC_empr_min	0.2040		
	SSC_empr_sur	0.0110		

2015 tax equations

The equations for the Mexican system in 2015 are on an individual basis.

The functions which are used in the equations (Taper, MIN, Tax etc) are described in the technical note about tax equations. Variable names are defined in the table of parameters above, within the equations table, or are the standard variables "married" and "children". A reference to a variable with the affix "_total" indicates the sum of the relevant variable values for the principal and spouse. And the affixes "_princ" and "_spouse" indicate the value for the principal and spouse, respectively. Equations for a single person are as shown for the principal, with "_spouse" values taken as 0.

	Line in country table and intermediate steps	Variable name	Range	Equation
1.	Earnings	earn		
2.	Allowances	tax_al	B	MIN(earn, MIN(earn*(6/365)*0.25, min_wage*15)+ MIN(earn*(15/365), min_wage*30))
3.	Credits in taxable income	taxbl_cr	B	0
4.	CG taxable income	tax_inc	B	Positive(earn-tax_al)
5.	CG tax before credits	CG_tax_excl	B	Tax(tax_inc, Tax_sch)
6.	Tax credits	tax_cr	B	VLOOKUP(tax_inc, Basic_crd, 2)
7.	CG tax	CG_tax	B	CG_tax_excl-tax_cr
8.	State and local taxes	local_tax	B	0
9.	Employees' soc security	SSC	B	MIN(earn*ssc_rate, min_wage_FD*25*365*ssc_rate)+MIN(Positive(earn-(3*365*min_wage_FD))*ssc_rate_sur, min_wage_FD*(25-3)*365*ssc_rate_sur)
11.	Cash transfers	cash_trans	B	0
13.	Employer's soc security	SSC_empr	B	MIN(earn*ssc_empr, min_wage_FD*25*365*ssc_empr)+365*min_wage_FD*ssc_empr_min+MIN(Positive(earn-(3*365*min_wage_FD))*ssc_empr_sur, min_wage_FD*(25-3)*365*ssc_empr_sur)
	Memorandum item: Non-wastable tax credit			
	tax expenditure component	taxexp	B	tax_cr-transfer
	cash transfer component	transfer	B	IF(CG_tax<0, -CG_tax, 0)

Key to range of equation B calculated separately for both principal earner and spouse P calculated for principal only (value taken as 0 for spouse calculation).

Taxing Wages 2016

Netherlands

This chapter includes data on the income taxes paid by workers, their social security contributions, the family benefits they receive in the form of cash transfers as well as the social security contributions and payroll taxes paid by their employers. Results reported include the marginal and average tax burden for eight different family types.

Methodological information is available for personal income tax systems, compulsory social security contributions to schemes operated within the government sector, universal cash transfers as well as recent changes in the tax/benefit system. The methodology also includes the parameter values and tax equations.

Netherlands 2015

The tax/benefit position of single persons

	Wage level (per cent of average wage)	67	100	167	67
	Number of children	none	none	none	2
1.	**Gross wage earnings**	32 987	49 235	82 223	32 987
2.	**Standard tax allowances:**				
	Basic allowance				
	Married or head of family				
	Dependent children				
	Deduction for social security contributions and income taxes	0	0	0	0
	Work-related expenses				
	Other				
	Total	0	0	0	0
3.	**Tax credits or cash transfers included in taxable income**	0	0	0	0
4.	**Central government taxable income (1 - 2 + 3)**	31 621	46 726	77 395	31 621
5.	**Central government income tax liability (exclusive of tax credits)**	3 289	9 080	23 941	3 289
6.	**Tax credits :**				
	Basic credit				
	Married or head of family				
	Children				
	Other				
	Total	949	869	562	1 430
7.	**Central government income tax finally paid (5-6)**	2 340	8 210	23 379	1 859
8.	**State and local taxes**	0	0	0	0
9.	**Employees' compulsory social security contributions**				
	Gross earnings	0	0	0	0
	Taxable income (net of credits)	5 701	6 526	7 560	4 079
	Total	5 701	6 526	7 560	4 079
10.	**Total payments to general government (7 + 8 + 9)**	8 041	14 736	30 940	5 938
11.	**Cash transfers from general government**				
	For head of family				
	For two children	0	0	0	5 914
	Total	0	0	0	5 914
12.	**Take-home pay (1-10+11)**	24 946	34 499	51 283	32 964
13.	**Employers' compulsory social security contributions**	3 149	4 830	5 415	3 149
14.	**Average rates**				
	Income tax	7.1%	16.7%	28.4%	5.6%
	Employees' social security contributions	17.3%	13.3%	9.2%	12.4%
	Total payments less cash transfers	24.4%	29.9%	37.6%	0.1%
	Total tax wedge including employer's social security contributions	31.0%	36.2%	41.5%	8.8%
15.	**Marginal rates**				
	Total payments less cash transfers: Principal earner	41.2%	41.2%	52.1%	43.8%
	Total payments less cash transfers: Spouse	n.a.	n.a.	n.a.	n.a.
	Total tax wedge: Principal earner	46.7%	46.7%	52.1%	49.0%
	Total tax wedge: Spouse	n.a.	n.a.	n.a.	n.a.

Netherlands 2015

The tax/benefit position of married couples

	Wage level (per cent of average wage)	100-0	100-33	100-67	100-33
	Number of children	2	2	2	none
1.	**Gross wage earnings**	49 235	65 483	82 223	65 483
2.	**Standard tax allowances:**				
	Basic allowance				
	Married or head of family				
	Dependent children				
	Deduction for social security contributions and income taxes	0	0	0	0
	Work-related expenses				
	Other				
	Total	0	0	0	0
3.	**Tax credits or cash transfers included in taxable income**	0	0	0	0
4.	**Central government taxable income (1 - 2 + 3)**	46 726	62 784	78 347	62 784
5.	**Central government income tax liability (exclusive of tax credits)**	9 080	10 420	12 369	10 420
6.	**Tax credits :**				
	Basic credit				
	Married or head of family				
	Children				
	Other				
	Total	1 138	2 066	2 299	1 728
7.	**Central government income tax finally paid (5-6)**	7 942	8 354	10 069	8 693
8.	**State and local taxes**	0	0	0	0
9.	**Employees' compulsory social security contributions**				
	Gross earnings	0	0	0	0
	Taxable income (net of credits)	5 619	7 009	10 604	8 151
	Total	5 619	7 009	10 604	8 151
10.	**Total payments to general government (7 + 8 + 9)**	13 561	15 363	20 674	16 844
11.	**Cash transfers from general government**				
	For head of family				
	For two children	1 862	1 862	1 862	0
	Total	1 862	1 862	1 862	0
12.	**Take-home pay (1-10+11)**	37 536	51 981	63 411	48 638
13.	**Employers' compulsory social security contributions**	4 830	6 285	7 979	6 285
14.	**Average rates**				
	Income tax	16.1%	12.8%	12.2%	13.3%
	Employees' social security contributions	11.4%	10.7%	12.9%	12.4%
	Total payments less cash transfers	23.8%	20.6%	22.9%	25.7%
	Total tax wedge including employer's social security contributions	30.6%	27.6%	29.7%	32.2%
15.	**Marginal rates**				
	Total payments less cash transfers: Principal earner	41.2%	41.2%	41.2%	41.2%
	Total payments less cash transfers: Spouse	11.1%	11.9%	37.5%	15.6%
	Total tax wedge: Principal earner	46.7%	46.7%	46.7%	46.7%
	Total tax wedge: Spouse	18.4%	18.8%	43.3%	22.2%

The national currency is the Euro (EUR). In 2015, EUR 0.90 was equal to USD 1. In this year, the average worker earned EUR 49 235 (Secretariat estimate).*

1. Personal income tax system (central government)

1.1. *Central government income tax*

There are three categories ("boxes") of taxable income:

- Taxable income from work and owner-occupied housing;
- Taxable income from a substantial interest in a limited liability company;
- Taxable income from savings and investments.

This description is limited to the most relevant aspects of taxable income from the first category, "taxable income from work and owner-occupied housing", because of its relevance for the AW.

1.1.1. *Tax unit*

Husbands and wives are taxed separately on their personal income, which includes income from business, profession and employment, pensions and social security benefits. Certain parts of income may be freely split between husbands and wives, such as the net-income from owner-occupied housing and the income from savings and investments.

1.1.2. *Tax allowances*

1.1.2.1. Standard allowances

Related to wage earnings:

- Employees' social security contributions (see Section 2.1.) are deductible, whereas the health insurance contribution is not deductible and is not a part of the Taxing Wages model (for more information, see the Special Feature on "non-tax compulsory payments" in the 2009 edition of the Taxing Wages Report). In the Taxing Wages model the employers' income dependant health insurance contribution was subject to income tax for the employee. In 2013 the income base for SSC and Income-Tax is harmonised. Standardising or harmonisation of the income tax base for levying SSC and Taxes was introduced in 2013 and was called the Law "WUL" i.e. harmonising the income base for SSC and Taxes (see publication CPB the Netherlands). So the income tax base is since 2013 exclusive the income dependant health care contribution and employees will no longer have to pay taxes over income dependant health care contributions, instead they pay a higher tax rate in the first tax bracket and mainly Work credit is adjusted. The tax rate in the first tax bracket has been increased from 1.95% (in 2012) till 5.85% (in 2013)

* The Dutch labour market is characterized by a substantial share of part-time employees. As explained in the methodological section of this volume, the average wage measure used in the tax burden calculations refer to full-time employees only. If the wages of part-timers were taken into account, the average wage would be substantially lower.

and the Work credit is reduced for employees with a higher income such that the effect of this harmonisation is budgetary neutral.

- In 2014 this system of harmonisation remains and is operational. Only the income tax rate in the first tax bracket became 5.10%. In 2015 the tax rate in the first bracket becomes 8.35%.

1.1.2.2. Non-standard allowances applicable to AW

Related to wage earnings:

- For distances of more than 10 km between home and work, fixed amounts for travel expenses with public transportation are deductible. The maximum deduction for employees who travel by public transport is EUR 1 951 for distances of more than 80 km. If the travel expenses are reimbursed or the employer provides transport, there is no deduction; the reimbursement is untaxed (also for employees who travel by car) if it is below certain specified amounts;
- Employee contributions to private (company provided) pension schemes.

Related to owner-occupied housing:

- Excess of mortgage interest over net imputed rent.

Related to personal circumstances:

- Medical expenses and other exceptional expenses:
  - Fiscal deduction of exceptional health expenses will be reduced to the specific costs as a result of the chronic illness. As specific costs are seen diet costs, special medicine described by a doctor and transportation costs. Visual tools and insurance premiums are not seen as specific costs and are therefore no longer deductible.
  - For a single person: the specific expenses in excess of 1.65% of income are deductible if income exceeds EUR 7 525 and is below EUR 39 975. If income is lower than or equal to EUR 7 525, the non-deductible limit is EUR 127. For a person with a partner: the joint income is used to determine the non-deductible amounts and the non-deductible limit is EUR 254.
  - If income exceeds EUR 39 975 the specific expenses in excess of 1.65% of EUR 39 975 increased with 5.75% of income above EUR 39 975 are deductible.
- Some educational expenses: in direct connection with vocational education. Expenses above the threshold of EUR 500 are deductible. Expenses above EUR 15 000 are not deductible.
- Donations to certain institutions (charity) that serve the public good are deductible if in excess of 1% of the income and in excess of EUR 60. No more than 10% of the income may be deducted in this way.

1.1.3. *Tax schedule*

The tax schedule for income from work and owner-occupied housing is as follows:

Taxable income (EUR)	Tax rate (%)	Social security contributions	
		< 65 years	*> 65 years*
0-19 822	8.35	28.15	10.25
19 822-33 589	13.85	28.15	10.25
33 589-57 585	42	-	-
57 585 and over	52	-	-

The contributions for the general social security schemes are levied on income from work and owner-occupied housing in the first and second income tax bracket. These social security contributions are not deductible for income tax purposes. Individuals of 65 years and older pay 10.25% (for widows and orphans pensions, and exceptional medical expenses). Individuals younger than 65 years and a few month pay 28.15%, (for widows and orphans pensions, exceptional medical expenses, and old age income provision). For further information see Section 2.1.

In 2015 the SSC for specific medical expenses and long term health care is modernised. The rate (For AWBZ) is therefore reduced with 3% points and instead the tax rates in the first two brackets are raised with 3% points. The spendings for long term health care are reduced due to more responsibility for your own living in long term. These Social spendings will be used for other general social purposes and therefore the tax rates in the first two brackets are raised.

1.1.4. *Tax credits*

1.1.4.1. Standard tax credits

The tax credits are deducted partly from the income tax liability and partly from the contributions that are made to the general social security schemes (see Section 1.13). For most families, the share of the credit attributed to tax is related to the ratio of the tax rate to the sum of the tax rate and the social security contributions rate in the first bracket of the tax schedule. In 2015, this ratio was 22.88% (= 8.35% /(8.35% + 28.15%), implying that 22.88% of the (tax) credit is attributed to the personal income tax and the remaining 77.12% to social security contributions. If the individual's total tax credit is higher than the total tax and social security contributions levied on the first tax bracket, the shares of the residual amount of the tax credit that are attributed to the personal income tax and social security contributions are based on the rates of deduction in the second tax bracket in order that the employee can benefit from the full amount of the credit where the level of income allows it. As a result, the ratio of the tax rate to the sum of the tax rate and social security contribution rates is increased to 32.98% for the residual amount in 2015 (i.e. 13.85%/(28.15%+13.85%)).

For example in 2015, the total tax credit of a single parent with 2 children earning 67% of the average wage amounts EUR 6 253. The total tax and social security contributions levied on the first tax bracket equals EUR 7 235.03 (= 19 822*(28.15%+8.35%). The total tax credits in 2015 are capitalized in the first tax bracket (EUR 6 253 < EUR 7235). The residual tax credit equals zero due to tax alterations in tax credits against cash transfer for single parents with children, see paragraph 3.2.

Then the part of the total tax credit that is attributed to personal income tax is EUR 1 430.44 (= 22.88% *EUR 6 253). The remaining EUR 4 822.56 (i.e. EUR 6 253 – EUR 1 430.44) is attributed to the social security contributions.

Division of credits for tax and social security contributions is essential in the OECD publications. In the Netherlands no division is made in the general tax scheme between tax and SSC.

Note that the tax/benefit position tables show the total amount of social security contributions net of the credits that are claimed.

- *General tax credit*: The general tax credit is made dependent on income in 2015. This credit amounts at it maximum EUR 2 203 when no reduction is applicable and taxable income is below or equal to EUR 19 822. For higher income above EUR 19 822 but until maximal EUR 56 935 the reduction of this credit is 2.32% (per euro) in 2015. So the maximum of the general credit reduction is EUR 861 in 2015. The transfer of the general tax credit of the spouse to the principal will diminish with 6.67% per year in the period 2009-2024, such that in 15 year time the general tax credit for a non-working spouse cannot be capitalised against the tax paid by the principal

- This reduction of the transfer of the general tax credit started in 2009. In 2024 the general tax credit can only be capitalised against the tax and premiums paid on own earned income. In 2012 a reduction of the general tax credit for non-working spouses born after 31 December 1962 and before 1 January 1972 is introduced. The reduction will be equal to the reduction of non-working spouses born before 1 January 1963 in year 2015. For Household types in de Taxing Wages model no difference is made between year of birth before 1963 or after 1963, idem before or after 1972. For that reason the additional reduction of the general tax credit is not added to the Taxing Wages model.
- *Work credit:* The Work credit is the sum of 1.810% of taxable income from work with a maximum of EUR 163 and 19.679% of taxable income from work with a franchise of EUR 9 010. The work credit is income dependent and will be reduced by 4% of taxable income above EUR 49 770; the reduction will be maximised till EUR 1 730; so the reduction stops at a taxable income of EUR 100 670. The maximum work credit before it is reduced is EUR 2 220; the maximum reduced work credit is EUR 184.
- *Combination credit:* The combination credit is abolished in 2009.
- *Income dependant combination credit:* The additional combination credit is replaced with the income dependent combination credit. A taxpayer who is either a single parent or the partner with the lowest income, who has children below the age of 12 and has his/her taxable income from work exceeding EUR 4 857, is entitled to an income dependent combination credit of EUR 1 033 plus an extra combination credit of 4% of taxable income above EUR 4 857. The maximum total combination credit is EUR 2 152.
- The child arrangements are modernised and reduced from 10 measurements to 4 measurements. The single parents credits have stopped and instead the cash transfers become more of importance. In the TW model the adjustments mean an extra cash transfer of EUR 3050 per year for single parents with children and a low income.
- *Single parent credit:* A single parent under certain conditions is entitled to the single parent credit of EUR 947. Has stopped in 2015 see explanation above.
- *Additional single parent credit:* A single parent who is entitled to the single parent credit receives an additional credit of 4.3% of his or her income from work, with a maximum of EUR 1 319. Has stopped in 2015, see explanation above.

The amount of the tax credit is limited to the amount of tax and premiums payable (non-refundable tax credit). If, however, a taxpayer with insufficient income to fully exploit his/her tax credit has a partner with a surplus of tax and premiums payable over his/her own tax credit, the tax credit of the former taxpayer is increased by (at most) the surplus tax and premiums payable by his/her fiscal partner. As a consequence, the tax credit of the former taxpayer will exceed tax and premiums payable, resulting in a payout of the residual tax credit to the taxpayer by the tax authority.

1.2. State and local income taxes

None.

2. Compulsory social security contributions to schemes operated within the government sector

2.1. Employees' contributions

Schemes for employees:

- Unemployment: 0% of the gross earnings between EUR 17 888 and EUR 51 976 (this contribution is only for the general unemployment fund); employees do not have to pay an unemployment premium in order to reduce administration costs. Employers pay both an unemployment premium and a premium for invalidity for their employees (see par.2.2).
- For basic health insurance each adult pays an average amount of EUR 1 158 a year to a self-chosen private health insurance company. This premium is a non-tax compulsory payment and is not included in the Taxing Wages calculations but only in the NTCP calculations. Employees might obtain compensation for this nominal contribution, depending on the household's personal situation and taxable income. This is called the health care benefit. This benefit is included in the NTCP calculations as it compensates for the basic health insurance premium of on average EUR 1 158. Also 6.95% of gross earnings net of employees' pension premiums and unemployment social security contributions is paid for health care until a maximum of net earnings of EUR 51 976. Since 2013 employers contribute the Health care Fund directly for the health care of their employees, these costs remain labour costs in the Taxing Wages model. These Health care costs for employers are no longer included in the taxpayer's taxable income.The income dependent health care contribution itself, however, is not modelled (as an employer SSC) in Taxing Wages because it is seen as a Non Tax Compulsory Payment.
- Employees might obtain compensation for the nominal contribution of on average EUR 1 158 for the basic health insurance, depending on the household's personal situation and taxable income. This is called the health care benefit. The care benefit is calculated as follows:

Single parent households: 1408 - 2.395% * 19 463 - 13.40% * (taxable income - 19 463)

Married couples: number of adults * 1408 5.265% *19463 - 13.40% * (taxable income principal and spouse 19 463).

This health care benefit is a non-tax compulsory payment and is not included in the Taxing Wages calculations but only in the "non-tax compulsory payment" calculations (see *www.oecd.org/ctp/taxingwages* for more details on non-tax compulsory payments as well as the Special Feature in the 2009 edition of the Taxing Wages Report).

- Old age pension: The age is adjusted such that elderly will receive Old Age (state) pension at the age of 66 years old in 2018 and at 67 years old in 2021. The Old age premium percentage is 17.9% of taxable income in the first and second tax bracket. This scheme does not apply to individuals aged 65 and two month(and in future aged 66 or 67) or older;
- Widows and orphans pension: 0.60% of taxable income in the first and second tax bracket;
- Exceptional medical expenses and disability: The rate is reduced with 3% point until 9.65 (see paragraph 1.13)% of taxable income in the first and second tax bracket.

2.2. *Employers' contributions*

Schemes for employees:

- Unemployment: 2.07% of gross earnings between EUR 17 888 and EUR 51 976 for the general unemployment fund and a contribution of 2.16% of gross earnings below EUR 51 976 for the industrial insurance associations redundancy payments fund;
- Invalidity: 6.90% of gross earnings below EUR 51 976;
- For medical care employers contribute 6.95% of gross earnings net of employees' pension premiums and unemployment social security contributions until a maximum of gross earnings of EUR 51 976. The premium itself, however, is not modelled (either as an employee or employer SSC) in Taxing Wages. Instead, it is modelled as a NTCP from the employer to a public-man The spending of this fund mainly compensates private insurance companies for their (public) obligation to insure individuals with a high health risk.

3. Universal cash transfers

3.1. *Transfers related to marital status*

None.

3.2. *Transfers for dependent children*

Families with children receive a tax free benefit, depending on the number and age of the children. For a family with two children in the age group of 6 to 12 years, the total benefit amounts to EUR 1 862 a year. Indexation of the child benefits was frozen for three years (period 2009-11).

An additional income dependent child benefit was introduced in 2008. As of 2009, this benefit also depends on the number of children per family. A family can only claim the extra child benefit when it has children under the age of 18 years old for whom it also receives the tax free and income independent child benefit. Indexation of the extra child benefit was frozen until 2011but is used for adjustments and reductions of child arrangements. The maximum value of EUR 1 017 has increased to EUR 1 032 per year for families with one child. The child credit increases to EUR 1 823 a year in 2015 for families with two children. The benefit is reduced at a rate of 6.75% per euro when the family's yearly taxable income exceeds EUR 19 463 and is completely withdrawn for families with two children when the taxable income is at least EUR 46 470.

4. Main changes in the tax/benefit systems since 2000

In 2001, the tax system was changed thoroughly. The tax rates have been lowered; the basic allowance and its supplements have been transformed into tax credits. The deduction for labour costs has also been replaced by a tax credit. Certain other deductions have been reduced or abolished. Extra tax credits for households with children were introduced.

In 2002 and 2003 the tax system was only slightly changed. The additional combination credit was introduced in 2004. The various child credits were integrated and streamlined in 2006.

Public insurance for medical care has been reformed in 2006 A new standard health insurance system was introduced. Until 2005, no public health insurance contributions were levied on income in excess of EUR 33 000. However, taxpayers earning more than EUR 33 000 were obliged to take a private insurance. These private health insurance contributions were not included in the Taxing Wages calculations because they were made to a privately-managed fund (and are therefore not taxes). Since 2006, every individual contributes a nominal contribution to a privately-managed fund (on average EUR 1 064, depending on the competition between insurance companies, a year in 2009) and, in addition for employees, a percentage of gross income (6.9%) net of employees' pension premiums and unemployment social security contributions until a maximum of gross income of EUR 32 369 (in 2009). For this last contribution, the employee receives mandatory compensation of his employer for the same amount. The premium itself, however, is not modelled (either as an employee or employer SSC) in Taxing Wages. Instead it is modelled as a non-tax compulsory payment from the employer to a public-managed health insurance fund. The spending of this fund mainly compensates private insurance companies for their (public) obligation to insure individuals with a high health risk. Taxpayers might obtain compensation for the nominal contribution to the private insurance company of on average EUR 1 064 in 2009, depending on the households personal situation and taxable income. This is called the health care benefit and is part of the NTCP (see Section 2.1).

In 2007, the tax system has not been changed, except for some parameter updates. In 2008, the child credit has been replaced by an extra child benefit.

In 2009 the general tax credit will be reduced for non-working spouses in order to cut down the capitalization of this tax credit in 2024. A non-working spouse can in 2024 capitalise the general tax credit only against his/her own earned income. In 2009 the employment credit is extended for income exceeding EUR 42 509. This credit will be reduced by maximum EUR 24, whereas the employment credit is increased for lower incomes. The income dependant combination credit is introduced in order to promote the labour participation of single parents or partners of married workers. The income-dependent combination credit has been increased considerably. The extra child benefit depends on the total income of the family and the number of children per family. The income-dependent child benefit is higher when more children under the age of 18 years are member of the family. As from 2009 onwards, employees do not have to pay an unemployment premium mainly to reduce administration costs for employers. Employers pay now both an unemployment premium and a premium for invalidity for their employees (see also par. 2.2).

In 2013 the income base for SSC and Income-Tax is harmonised. Standardising or harmonisation of the income tax base for levying SSC and Taxes is introduces in 2013 and is called the Law "WUL" i.e. Harmonising the income base for SSC and Taxes (see publication CPB the Netherlands). So the income tax base is since 2013 exclusive the income dependant health care contribution and employees will no longer have to pay taxes over income dependant health care contributions, instead they pay a higher tax rate in the first tax bracket and mainly Work credit is adjusted. The tax rate in the first tax bracket has been increased from 1.95% to 5.85% and the Work credit is reduced for employees with a higher income such that the effect of this harmonisation is budgetary neutral.

The main adjustment in 2014 is the General tax credit which is made income dependent. Higher income will receive less general credit and the reduction is 2% per euro of income between EURO 56 495 and EURO 19 645 per year. See also par 1.14.1.

In 2015 the child arrangements are reduced from 10 items to 4 items. For that reason Single parent credits have stopped. Cash transfers for parents with children and low income increase. And for single parents with children an extra cash benefit of EUR 3 050 is introduced to compensate the loss of single parent credits.

Not all child arrangements are part of the TW model because these are quite specific arrangements for disabled children and parents with low income with children.

- Long term health care is modernised. The SSC rate for (AWBZ Dutch) reduced with 3% to 9.65% of taxable income. The tax rates in the first two brackets are raised with 3% because Social spending is still used but now for other general social purposes.

5. Memorandum items

5.1. *Identification of the AW and calculation of the AW's gross earnings*

The calculation of the annual gross earnings of an AW is based upon data on gross earnings of full-time workers in industry C-K. These data have been obtained through a yearly sample survey carried out by the Central Bureau of Statistics. Included in the AW annual salary are irregular payments, such as holiday allowances, loyalty payments and bonuses. Payments for working overtime are not included. However, the CBS has stopped carrying out the 'employment and wages' survey in July 2006 due to new legislation. On Inquiry at the Central Bureau of Statistics (CBS) the information from the wage declarations by employers, delivered nowadays at the tax department, will be implemented by the CBS for the new survey about employment and wages. These changes produced a delay in delivery of the information on wages and employment for 2006.

As the AW figure for 2005 and 2006 are not available, the 2004 figure was taken and adjusted for the wage increases in 2005, 2006 and 2007 by the OECD Secretariat based on wage increase estimates from the most recent issue of the *OECD Economic Outlook*. On the base of new information on wages per industry sector, the AW is delivered to EUROSTAT in November 2009 by the CBS for years 2006 and 2007. The standard classification NACE Rev. 1 for industrial sectors C-K is used.

The new classification NACE Revision 2 (sectors B-N) will be applicable as from 2008 onwards. The estimation of the AW for 2008 according to the new classification is applicable at the beginning of May 2010. The AW for 2009 is available since November 2010. For 2008 the average annual gross earnings (full-time NACE REV 2) comes to EUR 43 146, for 2009 EUR 44 412, and EUR 45 215 in 2010. The latest information according to Eurostat is an AW in 2011 of EUR 46 287 (NACE Rev 2)

No new data is found on EU site: *http://epp.eurostat.ec.europa.eu/portal/page/portal/statistics/search_database*.

5.2. *Main employers' contributions to private pension, health and related schemes*

In addition to the obligatory contributions of employees to private insurance companies, all employers pay contributions to a public-managed health fund. More information is included in the Special Feature where the contributions to the public-managed health funds are also presented.

Employers have to pay at least 70% of the gross wage of their sick employees for two years. Many employers have insured themselves privately for the risks of their employees being sick. This insurance for illness of their employees is not compulsory.

2015 parameter values

	Ave_earn	49 235	Secretariat estimate
Social security contributions	SSC_ceil	51 976	
Employees' schemes	Unemp_rate1	0.0	
	Unemp_franchise1	17888	
Medical care	Med_rate	0.0695	
	Med_limit	999 999	
	Med_ceil	51 976	
	Med_adult	1 158	
	Med_child	0	
	Med_compensation1	0.02395	
	Med_compensation2	0.13400	
	Med_compensation3	0.05265	
	Med_compensation4	0.13400	
	Med_key	19 463	
	Med_aldult for care benefit	1 408	
General schemes	Old_rate	0.179	
	Wid_rate	0.006	
	Ex_med_rate	0.0965	
	Gen_Schemes_thrsh	33 589	
	Unemp_empr1	0.0207	
	Unemp_empr2	0.0216	
	Unemp_unempr_franchise1	17 888	
	Unemp_unempr_franchise2	0	
	Inv_empr_rate	0.0690	
	Inv_empr_franchise	0	
	Med_empr	0.0695	
	Med_franchise		
Tax schedule	Tax_sch	0.0835	19 822
	"tax_sch_lowest"	0.1385	33 589
	"tax_thrsh_1"	0.42	57 585
		0.52	
Tax credits	Gen_credit_1	2 203	
	Gen_credit_2	1 342	
	Gen_credit1_thr	19 822	
	Gen_credit2_thr	56 935	
	Gen_credit_per	0,0232	
	Red_gen_credit	1 175	
	Emp_credit1	163	
	Emp_credit2	2 057	
	Emp_credit3	21	
	Emp_credit1_thr	9 010	
	Emp_credit2_thr	19 463	
	Emp_credit3_thr	49 770	
	Emp_credit4_thr	100 670	
	Comb_credit	Nvt	
	Comb_credit_franchise	4 857	
	add_comb_credit	Nvt	
	Income_dependant_comb_comb_credit1	1 033	
	Income_dependant_comb_credit_max	2 152	
	Income_dependant_comb_par_credit_per	0,04	
	Sing_par_credit	it has stopped	
	Ex_sing_par_credit_per	stopped	
	Ex_sing_par_credit_max	stopped	
Family cash transfers	Ch1_trans	931	
	Ch2_trans	1 862	
	Child_ben_1child	1 032	
	Child_ben_2children	1 823	
	Child_ben_redn	0.0675	
	Child_ben_ceil	19 463	
	Extra_cash_single_par	3050	
Payroll tax	Extra_wage_tax	it has stopped in 2015	
	EWT_threshold	idem has stopped	

2015 tax equations

The equations for the tax system in the Netherlands in 2015 are repeated for each individual of a married couple. Tax credits, except a part of the general credit of the spouse, depend also on the tax paid by the principal if the spouse's income is zero or very low, and the cash transfers are calculated only once. The functions which are used in the equations (Taper, MIN, Tax etc) are described in the technical note on the tax equations. Due to the adjustment of the employment credit in 2009, the function Emp_credit(Value) was altered in 2009; no changes were made in 2010 until 2012. Variable names are defined in the table of parameters above, within the equations table, or are the standard variables "married" and "children". A reference to a variable with the affix "_total" indicates the sum of the relevant variable values for the principal and spouse. And the affix "_spouse" indicates the value for the spouse. No affix is used for the principal values. Equations for a single person are as shown for the principal, with "_spouse" values taken as 0.

	Line in country table and intermediate steps	Variable name	Range	Equation
1.	Earnings (gross)	gr_earn		
	Earnings (net)	earn	B	gr_earn
2.	Social security contributions	SSC_al	B	SSC_f(earn,Unemp_rate1,SSC_ceil,Unemp_franchise1)
3.	Credits in taxable income	taxbl_cr	B	MIN(earn-SSC_al, Med_ceil)*Med_rate
4.	CG taxable income	tax_inc	B	earn-SSC_al
5.	CG tax before credits	CG_tax_excl/ tax_liable	B	Tax(tax_inc,Tax_sch)
6.	Tax credits	tax_cr	P	MIN(CG_tax_excl+SSC_taxinc,IF((tax_inc<Gen_credit1_thr),Gen_credit_1,(Gen_credit_1-MIN(Gen_credit_per*(Gen_credit2_thr-Gen_credit1_thr),Gen_credit_per*(tax_inc-Gen_credit1_thr))))+Emp_credit(tax_inc)+IF(AND(Children>0,tax_inc>Comb_credit_franchise),IF(Married=0,income_dependant_comb_credit1+MIN(income_dependant_comb_credit_max-income_dependant_comb_credit1, income_dependant_comb_par_credit_per*(tax_inc - Comb_credit_franchise)),0)
		tax_cr_spouse	S	IF(Married>0,MIN(CG_tax_excl_spouse+SSC_taxinc_spouse+CG_tax_excl+SSC_taxinc-tax_cr,IF(tax_inc_spouse>0,IF((tax_inc_spouse<Gen_credit1_thr),Gen_credit_1,(Gen_credit_1-MIN(Gen_credit_per*(Gen_credit2_thr-Gen_credit1_thr), Gen_credit_per*(tax_inc_spouse-Gen_credit1_thr)))),Red_gen_credit)+Emp_credit(tax_inc_spouse)+IF(AND(Children>0,tax_inc_spouse>Comb_credit_franchise),income_dependant_comb_credit1+MIN(income_dependant_comb_credit_max-income_dependant_comb_credit1,income_dependant_comb_par_credit_per*(tax_inc_spouse - Comb_credit_franchise)),0)),0)
		tax_cr_inc	B	IF(tax_cr>Tax_thrsh_1*SUM(Old_rate+Wid_rate+Ex_med_rate+tax_sch_lowest),(tax_sch_2/SUM(Old_rate+Wid_rate+Ex_med_rate+tax_sch_2))*(tax_cr-(SUM(Old_rate+Wid_rate+Ex_med_rate+tax_sch_lowest)*Tax_thrsh_1))+(tax_sch_lowest/SUM(Old_rate+Wid_rate+Ex_med_rate+tax_sch_lowest))*(Tax_thrsh_1*SUM(Old_rate+Wid_rate+Ex_med_rate+tax_sch_lowest)),tax_sch_lowest/SUM(Old_rate+Wid_rate+Ex_med_rate+tax_sch_lowest)*tax_cr)
7.	CG tax	CG_tax	B	tax_liable-tax_cr_inc
8.	State and local taxes	local_tax	B	0
9.	Employees' soc security' based on earnings	SSC_earn	P	SSC_f(earn,Unemp_rate1,SSC_ceil,Unemp_franchise1)
		SSC_earn_spouse	S	SSC_f(earn_spouse,Unemp_rate1,SSC_ceil,Unemp_franchise1)
	Based on taxable income	SSC_taxinc	B	(Old_rate+Wid_rate+Ex_med_rate)*MINA(tax_inc,Gen_Schemes_thrsh)
	Total employees' soc security	SSC_liable	J	SSC_earn+SSC_taxinc+SSC_earn_spouse+SSC_taxinc_spouse

Line in country table and intermediate steps	Variable name	Range	Equation
	tax_cr_SSC	B	IF(tax_cr>Tax_thrsh_1*SUM(Old_rate+Wid_rate+Ex_med_rate+tax_sch_lowest), ((Old_rate+Wid_rate+Ex_med_rate)/SUM(Old_rate+Wid_rate+Ex_med_rate+tax_sch_2))*(tax_cr-(SUM(Old_rate+Wid_rate+Ex_med_rate+tax_sch_lowest)*Tax_thrsh_1))+((Old_rate+Wid_rate+Ex_med_rate)/SUM(Old_rate+Wid_rate+Ex_med_rate+tax_sch_lowest))*(Tax_thrsh_1*SUM(Old_rate+Wid_rate+Ex_med_rate+tax_sch_lowest)),SUM(Old_rate+Wid_rate+Ex_med_rate)/SUM(Old_rate+Wid_rate+Ex_med_rate+tax_sch_lowest)*tax_cr)
Total	SSC	J	SSC_liable-tax_cr_SSC
10. Total payments	total_payments	J	CG_tax+local_tax+SSC
11. Cash transfers	cash_trans	J	IF(Children=1,Ch1_trans,IF(Children=2,Ch2_trans,0))+ IF(Children=2;1;0)* MAX(0;(Child_ben_2children+IF(Married=0;1;0)*Extra_cash_sing_par-IF((tax)inc+ tax_inc_spouse)>Child_ben_ceil;1;0)* Child_ ben_redn*(tax_inc+tax_inc_spouse – Child_ben_ceil)))

13. Employer's soc security	SSC_empr	B	If Value <= 0 Then
			Emp_credit = 0
			ElseIf Value <= Range("Emp_credit1_thr").Value Then
			Emp_credit = (Value / Range("Emp_credit1_thr").Value) * Range("Emp_credit1").Value
			ElseIf Value <= Range("Emp_credit2_thr").Value Then
			Emp_credit = Range("Emp_credit1").Value + ((Value - Range("Emp_credit1_thr").Value) / (Range("Emp_credit2_thr").Value - Range("Emp_credit1_thr").Value)) * Range("Emp_credit2").Value
			ElseIf Value <= Range("Emp_credit3_thr").Value Then
			Emp_credit = Range("Emp_credit1").Value + Range("Emp_credit2").Value
			ElseIf Value <= Range("Emp_credit4_thr").Value Then
			Emp_credit = Range("Emp_credit1").Value + Range("Emp_credit2").Value - ((Value - Range("Emp_credit3_thr").Value) / (Range("Emp_credit4_thr").Value - Range("Emp_credit3_thr").Value)) * (Range("Emp_credit2").Value - Range("Emp_credit3").Value)
			Else
			Emp_credit = Range("Emp_credit1").Value + Range("Emp_credit3").Value
			End If

Key to range of equations B calculated separately for both principal earner and spouse P calculated for principal only (value taken as 0 for spouse calculation) J calculated once only on a joint basis.

New Zealand (2015-16 income tax year)

This chapter includes data on the income taxes paid by workers, their social security contributions, the family benefits they receive in the form of cash transfers as well as the social security contributions and payroll taxes paid by their employers. Results reported include the marginal and average tax burden for eight different family types.

Methodological information is available for personal income tax systems, compulsory social security contributions to schemes operated within the government sector, universal cash transfers as well as recent changes in the tax/benefit system. The methodology also includes the parameter values and tax equations underlying the data.

New Zealand 2015

The tax/benefit position of single persons

	Wage level (per cent of average wage)		67	100	167	67
	Number of children		none	none	none	2
1.	**Gross wage earnings**		37 594	56 110	93 704	37 594
2.	**Standard tax allowances:**					
	Basic allowance					
	Married or head of family					
	Dependent children					
	Deduction for social security contributions and income taxes					
	Work-related expenses					
	Other					
		Total	0	0	0	0
3.	**Tax credits or cash transfers included in taxable income**		0	0	0	0
4.	**Central government taxable income (1 - 2 + 3)**		37 594	56 110	93 704	37 594
5.	**Central government income tax liability (exclusive of tax credits)**		5 599	9 853	21 842	5 599
6.	**Tax credits :**					
	Basic credit		520	0	0	0
	Married or head of family					
	Children					
	Other					
		Total	520	0	0	0
7.	**Central government income tax finally paid (5-6)**		5 079	9 853	21 842	5 599
8.	**State and local taxes**		0	0	0	0
9.	**Employees' compulsory social security contributions**					
	Gross earnings		0	0	0	0
	Taxable income					
		Total	0	0	0	0
10.	**Total payments to general government (7 + 8 + 9)**		5 079	9 853	21 842	5 599
11.	**Cash transfers from general government**					
	For head of family					
	For two children		0	0	0	11 029
		Total	0	0	0	11 029
12.	**Take-home pay (1-10+11)**		32 515	46 257	71 861	43 024
13.	**Employer's compulsory social security contributions**		0	0	0	0
14.	**Average rates**					
	Income tax		13.5%	17.6%	23.3%	14.9%
	Employees' social security contributions		0.0%	0.0%	0.0%	0.0%
	Total payments less cash transfers		13.5%	17.6%	23.3%	-14.4%
	Total tax wedge including employer's social security contributions		13.5%	17.6%	23.3%	-14.4%
15.	**Marginal rates**					
	Total payments less cash transfers: Principal earner		17.5%	30.0%	33.0%	38.7%
	Total payments less cash transfers: Spouse		n.a.	n.a.	n.a.	n.a.
	Total tax wedge: Principal earner		17.5%	30.0%	33.0%	38.7%
	Total tax wedge: Spouse		n.a.	n.a.	n.a.	n.a.

New Zealand 2015

The tax/benefit position of married couples

		Wage level (per cent of average wage)	100-0	100-33	100-67	100-33
		Number of children	2	2	2	none
1.	**Gross wage earnings**		56 110	74 626	93 704	74 626
2.	**Standard tax allowances:**					
	Basic allowance					
	Married or head of family					
	Dependent children					
	Deduction for social security contributions and income taxes					
	Work-related expenses					
	Other					
		Total	0	0	0	0
3.	**Tax credits or cash transfers included in taxable income**		0	0	0	0
4.	**Central government taxable income (1 - 2 + 3)**		56 110	74 626	93 704	74 626
5.	**Central government income tax liability (exclusive of tax credits)**		9 853	12 113	15 452	12 113
6.	**Tax credits :**					
	Basic credit		0	0	0	0
	Married or head of family					
	Children					
	Other					
		Total	0	0	0	0
7.	**Central government income tax finally paid (5-6)**		9 853	12 113	15 452	12 113
8.	**State and local taxes**		0	0	0	0
9.	**Employees' compulsory social security contributions**					
	Gross earnings					
	Taxable income					
		Total	0	0	0	0
10.	**Total payments to general government (7 + 8 + 9)**		9 853	12 113	15 452	12 113
11.	**Cash transfers from general government**					
	For head of family					
	For two children		7 094	3 159	0	0
		Total	7 094	3 159	0	0
12.	**Take-home pay (1-10+11)**		53 351	65 672	78 252	62 513
13.	**Employer's compulsory social security contributions**		0	0	0	0
14.	**Average rates**					
	Income tax		17.6%	16.2%	16.5%	16.2%
	Employees' social security contributions		0.0%	0.0%	0.0%	0.0%
	Total payments less cash transfers		4.9%	12.0%	16.5%	16.2%
	Total tax wedge including employer's social security contributions		4.9%	12.0%	16.5%	16.2%
15.	**Marginal rates**					
	Total payments less cash transfers: Principal earner		51.2%	51.2%	30.0%	30.0%
	Total payments less cash transfers: Spouse		33.5%	38.7%	17.5%	17.5%
	Total tax wedge: Principal earner		51.2%	51.2%	30.0%	30.0%
	Total tax wedge: Spouse		33.5%	38.7%	17.5%	17.5%

The national currency is the New Zealand dollar (NZD). In 2015, NZD 1.43 was equal to USD 1. In that year the average worker earned NZD 56 110 (Country estimate).

1. Personal income tax system

1.1. *Central/federal government income taxes*

1.1.1. *Tax unit*

Members of the family are taxed separately.

1.1.2. *Tax allowances and tax credits*

None.

1.1.2.1. Standard reliefs

1.1.2.2. Main non-standard tax reliefs applicable to an AW

None.

1.1.3. *Schedule*

- Rates of income tax for individuals:
  - On so much of the income as does not exceed NZD 14 000: 10.5%;
  - On so much of the income as exceeds NZD 14 000 but does not exceed NZD 48 000: 17.5%;
  - On so much of the income as exceeds NZD 48 000 but does not exceed NZD 70 000: 30%;
  - On so much of the income as exceeds NZD 70 000: 33%.

1.2. *State and local income taxes*

New Zealand has no state or local income tax.

2. Compulsory social security contributions to schemes operated within the government sector

New Zealand has no compulsory social security contributions to schemes operated within the Government sector.

It should be noted that there is an accident compensation scheme administered by the Accident Compensation Corporation for residents and temporary visitors to New Zealand. This scheme is funded in part by premiums paid by employees and employers. For employees, the premium represents 1.45% of their gross earnings. For employers and the self-employed, the premiums are based on a percentage of the total payroll and the applicable rate varies depending upon the associated accident risk (the average rate is 1.04%). This scheme is not considered as a compulsory social security contribution for the purposes of the Report.

3. Universal cash transfers

3.1. *Amount for marriage*

None.

3.2. *Amount for children*

The Parental Tax Credit provides NZD 220 per week for the first ten weeks of each child's life. This tax credit abates under the same regime as the Family Tax Credit, although it is unaffected until both the Family Tax Credit and In Work Tax Credit have been abated to zero.

3.3. *Family tax credit*

For an eldest child aged 16-18, the rate of the Family Tax Credit is NZD 5 303 per year, while the rate of NZD 4 822 applies if the eldest child is younger than 16. For subsequent children the rate depends on the age of the child; NZD 4 745 per year for 16-18 year-olds, NZD 3 822 per year for 13-15 year-olds and NZD 3 351 per year for children under 13 years of age. The total credit is abated by 21.25 cents on each dollar earned over NZD 36 350. The abatement is based on the combined income of the parents.

3.4. *In work tax credit*

The In Work Tax Credit is available to families with dependent children who are not receiving an income-tested benefit, veteran's pension, New Zealand Superannuation or student allowance. The level of assistance it provides is NZD 3 120 per family per year, plus an additional NZD 780 per year for fourth and subsequent children. It is only available to couple families working a total of 30 hours or more per week, or to sole parents working 20 hours or more per week. It is also affected by the abatement regime used with the Family Tax Credit, although it is unaffected until the latter has been abated to zero.

3.5. *Minimum family tax credit*

The Minimum Family Tax Credit is a scheme that ensures a guaranteed minimum family net income for all full-time earners with dependent children. The guaranteed minimum after-tax income is NZD 23 036 per year plus the Family Tax Credit and In Work Tax Credit.

3.6. *Independent earner tax credit*

The Independent Earner Tax Credit of NZD 520 is available to individuals with annual net income between NZD 24 000 and NZD 48 000 that do not receive other forms of tax credits or benefits. It is abated by 13 cents on each dollar earned over NZD 44 000.

4. Main changes in tax/benefit systems over 2014/15

The rate and entitlement duration of the Parental Tax Credit changed to those detailed above on 1 April 2014. These changes applied from 1 April 2015.

5. Memorandum items

5.1. *Method used to identify AW and to calculate the AW's gross earnings*

The Annual Earnings figure is derived from the *Quarterly Employment Survey* for those employees in the B-N industry groups. The annual earnings figure for the average worker is the sum of the four quarterly earnings figures, with each quarterly figure calculated by taking the average total weekly earnings and multiplying it by 13 weeks per quarter.

5.2. *Employer's contributions to private pension, health schemes, etc.*

No information available.

2015 parameter values

	Ave_earn	56 110	Country estimate
Income tax schedule	Tax_sch	0.105	14 000
		0.175	48 000
		0.3	70 000
		0.33	
Family tax credit	Fam_sup_eld	4 822	
	Fam_sup_oth	3 351	
	Fam_sup_thrsh	36 350	
	Fam_sup_rate	0.2125	
In-work tax credit	In_work_children123	3 120	
	In_work_children4plus	780	
Minimum Family Tax Credit	Min_inc	23 036	
Independent Earner Tax Credit	IETC	520	
	IETC_thrsh1	24 000	
	IETC_thrsh2	44 000	
	IETC_rate	0.13	

2015 tax equations

The equations for the New Zealand system in 2015 are mostly repeated for each individual of a married couple. But the cash transfer is calculated only once. This is shown by the Range indicator in the table below. The functions which are used in the equations (Taper, MIN, Tax etc) are described in the technical note about tax equations. Variable names are defined in the table of parameters above, within the equations table, or are the standard variables "married" and "children". A reference to a variable with the affix "_total" indicates the sum of the relevant variable values for the principal and spouse. And the affixes "_princ" and "_spouse" indicate the value for the principal and spouse, respectively. Equations for a single person are as shown for the principal, with "_spouse" values taken as 0.

	Line in country table andintermediate steps	Variable name	Range	Equation
1.	Earnings	earn		
2.	Allowances	tax_al	B	0
3.	Credits in taxable income	taxbl_cr	B	0
4.	CG taxable income	tax_inc	B	earn
5.	CG tax before credits	CG_tax_excl	B	Tax(tax_inc, Tax_sch)
6.	Tax credits :			
	Guaranteed minimum income	GMI	J	(Children>0)*Min_inc
	Independent Earner Tax Credit	IETC_rebate	B	=AND(Children=0,earn>IETC_thrsh1)*Taper(IETC,earn,IETC_thrsh2,IETC_rate)
6.	Tax credits:	tax_cr	B	IETC_rebate
7.	CG tax	CG_tax	B	CG_tax_excl-tax_cr
8.	Local tax	local_tax	B	0
9.	Employees' soc security	SSC	B	0
11.	Cash transfers:			
	Family tax credit (unabated)	fam_tax_cr	J	Fam_sup_eld*(Children>0)+ Fam_sup_oth*Positive(Children-1)
	In-work tax credit (unabated)	in_work_tax_cr	J	(Children>0)*(In_work_children123+Positive(Children-3)*In_work_children4plus)
	Tax credits abated	tax_cr_ab	J	Taper(fam_tax_cr+in_work_tax_cr, earn_total, Fam_sup_thrsh1, Fam_sup_rate1)
	Minimum Family tax credit	min_fam_tax_cr	J	Positive(GMI-(earn_total-CG_tax_excl_totall))
	Cash transfers	cash_trans	J	tax_cr_ab + min_fam_tax_cr
13.	Employer's soc security	SSC_empr	B	0

Key to range of equation B calculated separately for both principal earner and spouse P calculated for principal only (value taken as 0 for spouse calculation) J calculated once only on a joint basis.

Norway

This chapter includes data on the income taxes paid by workers, their social security contributions, the family benefits they receive in the form of cash transfers as well as the social security contributions and payroll taxes paid by their employers. Results reported include the marginal and average tax burden for eight different family types.

Methodological information is available for personal income tax systems, compulsory social security contributions to schemes operated within the government sector, universal cash transfers as well as recent changes in the tax/benefit system. The methodology also includes the parameter values and tax equations underlying the data.

Norway 2015

The tax/benefit position of single persons

		Wage level (per cent of average wage)	67	100	167	67
		Number of children	none	none	none	2
1.	**Gross wage earnings**		369 848	552 012	921 861	369 848
2.	**Standard tax allowances**					
	Basic allowance					
	Married or head of family					
	Dependent children					
	Deduction for social security contributions and income taxes					
	Work-related expenses					
	Other					
		Total	139 450	139 450	139 450	188 254
3.	**Tax credits or cash transfers included in taxable income**		0	0	0	0
4.	**Central government taxable (ordinary) income (1 - 2 + 3)**		230 398	412 562	782 411	181 594
5.	**Central government income tax liability (ordinary + personal)**		30 297	54 384	137 393	23 880
6.	**Tax credits (applicable against local tax)**					
	Basic credit					
	Married or head of family					
	Children		0	0	0	0
	Other					
		Total	0	0	0	0
7.	**Central government income tax finally paid (5-6)**		30 297	54 384	137 393	23 880
8.	**State and local taxes (net of tax credits)**		31 910	57 140	108 364	25 151
9.	**Employees' compulsory social security contributions**					
	Gross earnings		30 328	45 265	75 593	30 328
	Taxable income					
		Total	30 328	45 265	75 593	30 328
10.	**Total payments to general government (7 + 8 + 9)**		92 535	156 788	321 349	79 358
11.	**Cash transfers from general government**					
	For head of family					
	For two children		0	0	0	34 920
		Total	0	0	0	34 920
12.	**Take-home pay (1-10+11)**		277 313	395 224	600 511	325 410
13.	**Employer's compulsory social security contributions**		48 080	71 762	119 842	48 080
14.	**Average rates**					
	Income tax		16.8%	20.2%	26.7%	13.3%
	Employees' social security contributions		8.2%	8.2%	8.2%	8.2%
	Total payments less cash transfers		25.0%	28.4%	34.9%	12.0%
	Total tax wedge including employer's social security contributions		33.6%	36.6%	42.4%	22.1%
15.	**Marginal rates**					
	Total payments less cash transfers: Principal earner		35.2%	44.2%	47.2%	35.2%
	Total payments less cash transfers: Spouse		n.a.	n.a.	n.a.	n.a.
	Total tax wedge: Principal earner		42.7%	50.6%	53.3%	42.7%
	Total tax wedge: Spouse		n.a.	n.a.	n.a.	n.a.

Norway 2015

The tax/benefit position of married couples

		Wage level (per cent of average wage)	100-0	100-33	100-67	100-33
		Number of children	2	2	2	none
1.	**Gross wage earnings**		552 012	734 176	921 861	734 176
2.	**Standard tax allowances**					
	Basic allowance					
	Married or head of family					
	Dependent children					
	Deduction for social security contributions and income taxes					
	Work-related expenses					
	Other					
		Total	163 300	268 181	278 900	268 181
3.	**Tax credits or cash transfers included in taxable income**		0	0	0	0
4.	**Central government taxable (ordinary) income (1 - 2 + 3)**		388 712	465 996	642 961	465 996
5.	**Central government income tax liability (ordinary + personal)**		51 247	61 410	84 681	61 410
6.	**Tax credits (applicable against local tax)**					
	Basic credit					
	Married or head of family					
	Children		0	0	0	0
	Other					
		Total	0	0	0	0
7.	**Central government income tax finally paid (5-6)**		51 247	61 410	84 681	61 410
8.	**State and local taxes (net of tax credits)**		53 837	64 540	89 050	64 540
9.	**Employees' compulsory social security contributions**					
	Gross earnings		45 265	60 202	75 593	60 202
	Taxable income					
		Total	45 265	60 202	75 593	60 202
10.	**Total payments to general government (7 + 8 + 9)**		150 349	186 153	249 324	186 153
11.	**Cash transfers from general government**					
	For head of family					
	For two children		23 280	23 280	23 280	0
		Total	23 280	23 280	23 280	0
12.	**Take-home pay (1-10+11)**		424 943	571 304	695 817	548 024
13.	**Employer's compulsory social security contributions**		71 762	95 443	119 842	95 443
14.	**Average rates**					
	Income tax		19.0%	17.2%	18.8%	17.2%
	Employees' social security contributions		8.2%	8.2%	8.2%	8.2%
	Total payments less cash transfers		23.0%	22.2%	24.5%	25.4%
	Total tax wedge including employer's social security contributions		31.9%	31.1%	33.2%	33.9%
15.	**Marginal rates**					
	Total payments less cash transfers: Principal earner		44.2%	44.2%	44.2%	44.2%
	Total payments less cash transfers: Spouse		19.7%	23.6%	35.2%	23.6%
	Total tax wedge: Principal earner		50.6%	50.6%	50.6%	50.6%
	Total tax wedge: Spouse		28.9%	32.4%	42.7%	32.4%

The national currency is the Kroner (NOK). In 2015, NOK 8.06 was equal to 1 USD. In that year the average worker earned NOK 552 012 (Secretariat estimate).

1. Personal income tax system

The personal income tax has two tax bases: *personal income* and *ordinary income*. Personal income is defined as income from labour and pensions. Personal income is a gross income base from which no deductions are made. Ordinary income includes all types of taxable income from labour, pensions, business and capital. Certain costs and expenses, including interest paid on debt, are deductible in the computation of ordinary income.

1.1. Central government income tax

1.1.1. Tax unit

The tax unit is in most cases the individual (tax class 1), but joint taxation (tax class 2) is also possible. Children aged below 17 are generally taxed together with their parents, but they may be taxed individually. All other income earners are taxed on an individual basis (class 1).

1.1.2. Tax allowances applicable to an AW

There are no tax allowances applicable to an AW under the central government income tax (surtax). The tax base is personal income from which no deductions are allowed. As part of the overall tax rate of 27% on ordinary income, 13.15% is considered to be the central government income tax.

1.1.3. Rate schedule (surtax)

Rate (%)	NOK
0	0-550 550
9.0	550 550-885 600
12.0	885 600 and over

1.2. Local government income tax

The overall tax rate on ordinary income is 27%. The local government (municipal and county) income tax is 13.85% points of the overall rate. Tax on ordinary income is levied after taking into account a standard allowance of NOK 50 400 (class 1) and NOK 74 250 (class 2) in 2015. Single parents are eligible to an additional special tax allowance of NOK 48 804. The deductions in the computation of ordinary income are:

1.2.1. Standard reliefs

- Basic allowance: each individual receives a minimum allowance equal to 43% of personal income, with a minimum of NOK 4 000 and a maximum of NOK 89 050. For wage income each individual can choose a separate allowance of NOK 31 800 instead of the basic allowance. Hence, wage earners would opt to choose this separate allowance as long as it exceeds the basic allowance to which they are entitled.

1.2.2. Non-standard reliefs

The main non-standard allowances deductible from ordinary income are:

- Parent allowance: Documented expenses for child care limited to:
  - maximum NOK 25 000 for one child
  - plus NOK 15 000 for each subsequent child.

The allowance applies in general to the spouse who has the highest income. Unused parent allowance may be transferred to the other spouse. The allowance is also applicable to single parents.

- Travel expenses related to work exceeding NOK 16 000;
- Labour union fees up to NOK 3 850;
- Donations to voluntary organisations up to NOK 20 000;
- Contributions to individual pension agreement schemes, maximum NOK 15 000;
- Premiums and contributions to occupational pension schemes in the private and public sector, unlimited;
- Unlimited deduction for interest payments.

The main non-standard tax credits are:

- Home savings scheme (BSU): The BSU scheme aims to encourage young people (under 34 years old) to save for a future home purchase. A wastable *tax credit* of 20% of annual savings up to NOK 25 000 in special accounts is granted. Total savings may not exceed NOK 200 000.

2. Social security contributions

2.1. Contributions to the national insurance scheme

2.1.1. Employees' contributions

Employees' contributions to the National Insurance Scheme generally amount to 8.2% of personal wage income. Employees do not make contributions if their wage income is less than NOK 49 650. Once wage income exceeds this floor, an alternative calculation is made where the contributions equal 25% of the wage income in excess of the floor. The actual contributions made would represent the minimum between the alternative calculation and 8.2% of the total wage income.

Contributions from the self-employed are 11.4% of personal income attributable to labour.

2.1.2. Employers' contributions

Employer's social security contributions are due for all employees in both the private and the public sector. The contribution is geographically differentiated according to the municipality where the work-place is. The standard rates are 14.1%, 10.6%, 7.9%, 6.4%, 5.1% or 0% of gross wages. The highest rate applies to central parts of southern Norway. Lower rates may apply under certain circumstances. The weighted average rate is approximately 13%.

3. Universal cash transfers

3.1. *Transfers related to marital status*

None.

3.2. *Transfers for dependent children (child support)*

The following transfers are available:

NOK 11 640 per child aged 0-18 years.

Single parents receive transfers for one more child than their actual number of children.

4. Main changes in tax/benefit systems since 2002

- Most important changes related to wage taxation in 2015:
  - The threshold in surtax bracket 1 was increased by NOK 5 750.
  - The upper limit of the basic allowance for wage income/social security benefits was increased by NOK 2 100.
  - The lower threshold for the payment of employee's social security contributions was increased from NOK 39 600 to NOK 49 650.
- Most important changes related to wage taxation in 2014:
  - The general tax rate on ordinary income was reduced from 28% to 27%.
  - The employee's social security contributions were increased by 0.4 percentage points.
  - The rate in the basic allowance against wage income was increased to 43%.
  - Tax class 2 for married couples was reduced.
- Most important changes in 2013:
  - The personal allowance for labour income was increased for low income earners (below NOK 213 950) by 2 percentage points from 38% to 40% of their labour income.
  - The taxable value of second homes and commercial property for the purposes of net wealth tax was increased from 40% to 50% of estimated market value.
  - The basic allowance in the net wealth tax was increased from NOK 750 000 to NOK 870 000. Married couples will thus have a total basic allowance of NOK 1 740 000.
  - The current class 2 for sole providers was replaced by a special allowance for ordinary income which provides an equivalent tax benefit.
  - The maximum deduction for labour union fees was increased from NOK 3 750 to NOK 3 850.
- Most important changes in 2012:
  - The personal allowance for labour income was increased for low income earners (below NOK 217 000) by 2 percentage points from 36% to 38% of their labour income.
  - For self-employed the wage allowance was abolished to eliminate residual discrimination between sole proprietorships with employees and limited companies.
  - In the deduction for travel expenses for travels between home and work the deduction rate per kilometre was increased for tax payers travelling between 35 000 km and 50 000 km per year.
  - The maximum deduction for labour union fees was increased by NOK 90 to NOK 3 750.

- In 2011 changes to the tax system was made to provide better incentives for people to work when drawing a pension. The tax limitation rule for early-retirement and old-age pensioners was replaced by a new tax allowance for pension income. The allowance ensures that people who only receive the minimum pension will continue not to pay income tax. The allowance is scaled down against pension income, so that the marginal tax on earned income is reduced to the same level as for wage earners. The marginal tax on capital for low-income pensioners is also reduced to the same level as for other taxpayers. The new tax allowance is determined regardless of the spouse's income and married early-retirement and old-age pensioners will each have their own allowance. In addition, the pension income social security contribution is increased and the special allowance for age is discontinued.
- In 2010 a new formula-based system for determining the tax-assessed value of homes was introduced. The new tax-assessed value will be determined by multiplying the floor space of the dwelling by a square metre price based on the geographical location (neighbourhood, municipality, sparsely populated vs. densely populated area), size, age and type (detached, semi-detached, terraced, flat) of the property. For *primary homes* (owner-occupied), the per square metre rate will be set at 25% of the estimated sale price per square metre, whereas the rate for *second homes*, i.e. any other dwellings in addition to the primary home that are not defined as business or recreational properties, will be set at 40% of the estimated sale price per square metre. The current "safety valve" system is being continued so that taxpayers can appeal and have the tax-assessed value reduced to 30% of the documented fair market value (60% for second homes). In addition, the tax-assessed values of recreational properties are increased by 10%.
- Most important changes in 2009 were the abolition of the 80% rule, which primarily reduced the wealth tax of the richest. The wealth tax on equities for those who fall within the scope of the 80% rule has been more than doubled since 2005.
- The home savings scheme (BSU) was expanded in 2009 by increasing the annual savings amount to NOK 20 000 and the maximum aggregate savings amount to NOK 150 000.
- The rates of the inheritance tax were reduced and the exempted amount was increased in 2009. The instalment scheme for family businesses was expanded through the abolition of the upper limit, and the payment period was increased from 7 to 12 years.

Other changes in the personal tax base in 2009:

- The fishermen's allowance was increased from NOK 115 000 to NOK 150 000.
- The reindeer husbandry allowance was increased to the same level as the agriculture allowance.
- The allowance for labour union fees was increased by NOK 450 to NOK 3 600.
- The rate of the travel allowance was increased from NOK 1.40 per km to NOK 1.50 per km.
- The tax-free net income thresholds under the tax limitation rule were increased such as to ensure that singles and couples who receive the minimum state pension will still not be paying tax following the favourable social security settlement they benefited from in 2008.
- A tax favoured contributions to individual pension agreement schemes was reintroduced as of 2008.
- From 1 January, 2008 the employees' SSC rate for self-employed was increased from 10.7% to 11.0%.

- The upper threshold in the surtax schedule was substantially reduced from 2006 to 2007.
- The surtax rates were reduced in 2005 and 2006, as part of a reform of the dual income tax system. The basic allowance has been substantially increased.
- From 1 January, 2006 the supplementary employer's social security contribution at 12.5% for gross wage income that exceeds 16 times "G" (average "G" is estimated to be NOK 74 721 in 2010) was removed.
- From 1 January, 2006 the class 2 in the surtax was removed.
- From 1 January, 2005 the ceiling in the parent allowance for two and more children was removed, and the maximum allowance was increased with NOK 5 000 for each child after the first. From 2008 the maximum allowance will be increased with NOK 15 000 for each child after the first.
- The additional child support of NOK 7 884 for children aged 1 and 2 years was abolished as of 1 August 2003.
- An allowance of maximum NOK 6 000 for donations to voluntary organisations was introduced as of 1 January, 2003. Previously this allowance was coordinated with the allowance for labour union fees (with a combined maximum allowance). The allowance was increased to NOK 12 000 as of 1 January, 2005.
- As of 1 July, 2002 the employer's social security contribution rates for employees aged 62 years or older were reduced by 4 percentage points, although not below 0%. From 2007 the reduction was abolished.

5. Memorandum items

5.1. *Identification of an AW and calculation of earnings*

The wage series used refers to full time employees in the B-N industry group (ISIC rev.4).

The calculation of annual wage earnings is as follows:

- Weighted average monthly wage plus overtime times 12.

The average monthly wage is agreed payment for a wage earner working a normal agreed working-year. It includes bonus payments and other allowances, but not payments for overtime, sick leave, and an establishment's indirect wage costs. The sum is weighted with the number of persons employed in the different industry groups.

5.2. *Employers' contributions to private health and pension schemes*

No information available.

2015 parameter values

Average earnings/yr	Ave_earn	552 012	Secretariat estimate
Central rate (pers)	Tax1_sch	0	550 550
class 1		0.09	885 600
		0.12	
class 2	Tax2_sch	0	550 550
		0.09	885 600
		0.12	
Central rate (ord)	Cent_rate_ord	0,1315	
Local rate (ord)	Local_rate	0.1385	
Allowances	Class_al_1	50 400	
	Class_al_2	74 250	
	Special_al	48 804	
Basic relief	Basic_min	4 000	
	Basic_max	89 050	
	Basic_rel_rate	0.43	
	Basic_min_wage	31 800	
Soc security contribs	SSC_rate	0.082	
Employer	SSC_empr	0.13	
Trygd. low.lim	SSC_low_lim	49 650	
pct.rate	SSC_low_rate	0.25	
Ref. Income "G"	SSC_G	89 502	
Child cash transfer	Child_sup	11 640	

2015 tax equations

The equations for the system for Norway in 2015 may be calculated on an individual or joint basis for married couples. Social security contributions are calculated on an individual basis. The calculation for Class 2 is chosen for married couples whenever this gives a lower value of tax than the corresponding Class 1 calculations. The functions which are used in the equations (Taper, MIN, Tax etc) are described in the technical note about tax equations. Variable names are defined in the table of parameters above, within the equations table, or are the standard variables "married" and "children". A reference to a variable with the affix "_total" indicates the sum of the relevant variable values for the principal and spouse. And the affixes "_princ" and "_spouse" indicate the value for the principal and spouse, respectively. Equations for a single person are as shown for the principal, with "_spouse" values taken as 0.

	Line in country table and intermediate steps	Variable name	Range	Equation
1.	Earnings	earn		
2.	Allowances:	tax_al	J	IF(class=1, tax1_al_princ+tax1_al_spouse, tax2_al)
	Class 1 tax allowance (ordinary)	tax1_al_princ	P	MIN(MAX(Basic_min_wage, MIN(earn_princ*Basic_rel_rate, Basic_max)) +Class_al_1+IF(AND(Married=0,Children>0),Special_al,o), earn_princ)
	Class 1 tax allowance (ordinary)	tax1_al_spouse	S	MIN(MAX(Basic_min_wage, MIN(earn_spouse*Basic_rel_rate, Basic_max)) +Class_al_1, earn_spouse)
	Class 2 tax allowance (ordinary)	tax2_al	J	MIN(MAX(Basic_min_wage, MIN(earn_princ*Basic_rel_rate, Basic_max)), earn_princ)+MIN(MAX(Basic_min_wage, MIN(earn_spouse* Basic_rel_rate, Basic_max)), earn_spouse)+Class_al_2
3.	Credits in taxable income	taxbl_cr	J	0
4.	CG taxable income (ordinary)			
	Class 1 taxable income	tax1_inc	B	Positive(earn-tax1_al)
	Class 2 taxable income	tax2_inc	J	Positive(earn_total-tax2_al)
5.	CG tax	CG_tax		IF(class=1, CG1_tax, CG2_tax)
	Class 1 tax (personal+ordinary)	CG1_tax	B	Tax(earn, Tax1_sch)+Cent_rate_ord*tax1_inc
	Class 2 tax (personal+ordinary)	CG2_tax	J	Tax(earn_p, Tax2_sch)+ Tax(earn_s, Tax2_sch)+Cent_rate_ord*tax2_inc
6.	Tax credits :	tax_cr	P	0
7.	CG tax	CG_tax	B	CG_tax
8.	State and local taxes	local_tax	J	IF(class=1, local1_tax_total, local2_tax)
	Class 1 local tax	local1_tax	B	(Local_rate*(tax1_inc_princ+tax1_inc_spouse))-tax_cr
	Class 2 local tax	local2_tax	J	(Local_rate*tax2_inc)-tax_cr
	Favourable class	class	J	1+((CG2_tax_excl+local2_tax)<(CG1_tax_excl_total+local1_tax_total))
9.	Employees' soc security	SSC	B	MIN(earn*SSC_rate, Positive(SSC_low_rate*(earn-SSC_low_lim)))
11.	Cash transfers	cash_trans	J	(children>0)*Child_sup
13.	Employer's soc security	SSC_empr	B	earn*SSC_empr

Key to range of equation B calculated separately for both principal earner and spouse P calculated for principal only (value taken as 0 for spouse calculation) J calculated once only on a joint basis.

Poland

This chapter includes data on the income tax paid by workers, their social security contributions, the family benefits they receive in the form of cash transfers as well as the social security contributions and payroll taxes paid by their employers. Results reported include the marginal and average tax burden for eight different family types.

Methodological information is available for personal income tax systems, compulsory social security contributions to schemes operated within the government sector, universal cash transfers as well as recent changes in the tax/benefit system. The methodology also includes the parameter values and tax equations underlying the data.

Poland 2015

The tax/benefit position of single persons

	Wage level (per cent of average wage)	67	100	167	67
	Number of children	none	none	none	2
1.	**Gross wage earnings**	30 499	45 521	76 021	30 499
2.	**Standard tax allowances**				
	Basic allowance				
	Married or head of family				
	Dependent children				
	Deduction for social security contributions and income taxes	3 068	4 579	7 648	3 068
	Work-related expenses	1 335	1 335	1 335	1 335
	Other				
	Total	4 403	5 914	8 983	4 403
3.	**Tax credits or cash transfers included in taxable income**	0	0	0	0
4.	**Central government taxable income (1 - 2 + 3)**	24 983	37 945	64 263	24 983
5.	**Central government income tax liability (exclusive of tax credits)**	3 941	6 274	11 011	3 384
6.	**Tax credits**				
	Basic credit	556	556	556	1 112
	Married or head of family				
	Children	0	0	0	2 224
	Other (health insurance)	2 040	3 044	5 084	2 040
	Total	2 596	3 600	5 640	5 376
7.	**Central government income tax finally paid (5-6)**	1 345	2 674	5 371	- 1 992
8.	**State and local taxes**	0	0	0	0
9.	**Employees' compulsory social security contributions**				
	Gross earnings	3 068	4 579	7 648	3 068
	Taxable income	2 369	3 535	5 904	2 369
	Total	5 437	8 115	13 551	5 437
10.	**Total payments to general government (7 + 8 + 9)**	6 782	10 788	18 922	3 445
11.	**Cash transfers from general government**				
	For head of family				
	For two children	0	0	0	0
	Total	0	0	0	0
12.	**Take-home pay (1-10+11)**	23 718	34 733	57 098	27 054
13.	**Employers' compulsory social security contributions**	5 118	7 638	12 756	5 118
14.	**Average rates**				
	Income tax	4.4%	5.9%	7.1%	-6.5%
	Employees' social security contributions	17.8%	17.8%	17.8%	17.8%
	Total payments less cash transfers	22.2%	23.7%	24.9%	11.3%
	Total tax wedge including employer's social security contributions	33.4%	34.7%	35.7%	24.0%
15.	**Marginal rates**				
	Total payments less cash transfers: Principal earner	26.7%	26.7%	26.7%	26.7%
	Total payments less cash transfers: Spouse	n.a.	n.a.	n.a.	n.a.
	Total tax wedge: Principal earner	37.2%	37.2%	37.2%	37.2%
	Total tax wedge: Spouse	n.a.	n.a.	n.a.	n.a.

Poland 2015

The tax/benefit position of married couples

		Wage level (per cent of average wage)	100-0	100-33	100-67	100-33
		Number of children	2	2	2	none
1.	**Gross wage earnings**		45 521	60 543	76 021	60 543
2.	**Standard tax allowances**					
	Basic allowance					
	Married or head of family					
	Dependent children					
	Deduction for social security contributions and income taxes		4 579	6 091	7 648	6 091
	Work-related expenses		1 335	2 670	2 670	2 670
	Other					
		Total	5 914	8 761	10 318	8 761
3.	**Tax credits or cash transfers included in taxable income**		0	0	0	0
4.	**Central government taxable income (1 - 2 + 3)**		37 945	49 573	62 928	49 573
5.	**Central government income tax liability (exclusive of tax credits)**		5 717	7 810	10 214	7 810
6.	**Tax credits**					
	Basic credit		1 112	1 112	1 112	1 112
	Married or head of family					
	Children		2 224	2 224	2 224	0
	Other (health insurance)		3 044	4 049	5 084	4 049
		Total	6 380	7 385	8 420	5 161
7.	**Central government income tax finally paid (5-6)**		- 663	425	1 794	2 650
8.	**State and local taxes**		0	0	0	0
9.	**Employees' compulsory social security contributions**					
	Gross earnings		4 579	6 091	7 648	6 091
	Taxable income		3 535	4 702	5 904	4 702
		Total	8 115	10 792	13 551	10 792
10.	**Total payments to general government (7 + 8 + 9)**		7 452	11 218	15 346	13 442
11.	**Cash transfers from general government**					
	For head of family					
	For two children		0	0	0	0
		Total	0	0	0	0
12.	**Take-home pay (1-10+11)**		38 070	49 326	60 675	47 102
13.	**Employers' compulsory social security contributions**		7 638	10 159	12 756	10 159
14.	**Average rates**					
	Income tax		-1.5%	0.7%	2.4%	4.4%
	Employees' social security contributions		17.8%	17.8%	17.8%	17.8%
	Total payments less cash transfers		16.4%	18.5%	20.2%	22.2%
	Total tax wedge including employer's social security contributions		28.4%	30.2%	31.7%	33.4%
15.	**Marginal rates**					
	Total payments less cash transfers: Principal earner		26.7%	26.7%	26.7%	26.7%
	Total payments less cash transfers: Spouse		25.1%	26.7%	26.7%	26.7%
	Total tax wedge: Principal earner		37.2%	37.2%	37.2%	37.2%
	Total tax wedge: Spouse		35.8%	37.2%	37.2%	37.2%

The national currency is the Zloty (PLN). In 2015, PLN 3.77 was equal to USD 1. In that year, the average worker earned PLN 45 521 (Secretariat Estimate).

1. Personal income tax system

An individual being a tax resident in Poland is liable to tax on the basis of world-wide income, irrespective of the source and origin of that income. (The term "residency" is understood similarly to Article 4 paragraph 2 point a) of the OECD Model Tax Convention on Income and Capital).

1.1. *Central government income tax*

1.1.1. *Tax unit*

Individuals are taxed on their own income, but couples married during the whole calendar year* can opt to be taxed on their joint income. In the latter case, the "splitting" system applies: the tax bill for a couple is twice the income tax due on half of joint income, provided the joint income does not include capital income taxed at the flat 19 per cent rate. Single individuals with dependent children are also entitled to use the splitting system (their family quotient is two). For the purpose of this report, it is assumed that married couples are taxed on joint income.

1.1.1.1. Tax base

1.1.1.1.1. Gross employment income

For taxation purposes, taxable gross employment income in Poland includes both cash income and the value of benefits in kind. More specifically, gross employment income includes base salary, overtime payments, bonuses, awards, compensation for unused holidays, and costs that are paid in full or in part by the employer on behalf of the employee.

1.1.2. *Tax allowances and tax credits*

1.1.2.1. Standard reliefs

- Basic relief: A non-refundable tax credit of PLN 556.02 per person.
- Marital status relief: None.
- Relief for children: Yes.**

* However, a widowed spouse is entitled to apply the join income taxation.

** It concerns a child of 18 years old or younger or a child up to 25 years old provided they are students or a disabled child irrespective of their age. The actual description in Section 4.

A taxpayer can deduct from the due tax decreased by the amount of health contributions specified in the PIT Act, the amount, which is equal for each month of raising a child:

- PLN -92.67 (annually PLN 1 112.04) for the first child, if the income received by parents (married or single parent, who meets special requirements) doesn't exceed in the tax year the amount of PLN 112 000. For other parent the threshold of income is PLN 56 000;
- PLN -92.67 (annually PLN 1 112.04) for the second child;
- PLN -166.67 (annually PLN 2 000.04) for the third child;
- PLN -225.00 (annually PLN 2 700.00) for the fourth and every next child.
- Since 1st of January 2015 taxpayers whose due tax is lower than the amount of relief for children, may claim for cash refund for amount of relief which has not been utilized. However, such cash refund cannot exceed the amount of deductible social security and health insurance contributions paid by taxpayer (with some exceptions).
- Relief for health insurance contributions: A tax credit is almost equal to health insurance contribution paid to the National Health Fund. The contribution is 9 per cent of the calculation basis whereas the tax credit is 7.75 per cent of this basis.
- Relief for other social security contributions: An allowance is provided for all social insurance contributions paid by the taxpayer.
- Relief for selected work-related expenses: Standard deductions depend on the number of workplaces and on whether place of residence and workplace are within the same town/city or not. The annual amounts in PLN (deductible from income) are:

	One workplace	Two/more workplaces
Workplace in the same town/city as place of residence	1 335.00[1]	2 002.05
Workplace in different town/city as place of residence	1 668.72	2 502.56

Note: If the actual commuting expenses exceed standard deduction, relief can be determined by the actual expenses incurred solely on personal season tickets.

1. For the purpose of the calculations in this publication, it is assumed that the worker has the same town/city as place of residence.

1.1.2.2. Main non-standard tax reliefs applicable to an average worker

Allowances:

- Expenses for the purpose of rehabilitation incurred by a taxpayer who is a disabled person, or a taxpayer, who supports the disabled;
- Equivalent of blood donations, donations made for the purposes of public benefit activity and of religious practice – in the amount of donation, no more than 6 per cent of income;
- Donations made for charity church care – in the amount of the donation;
- Expenses incurred for the use of the Internet – a taxpayer is entitled to deduct the Internet tax allowance within the next two years, providing that during the phase preceded this period he did not deduct Internet for the use of the Internet (up to PLN 760);
- Abolished allowance (since 2007 continued on the acquired right basis) for interests payments on mortgage loans raised no later than in 2006 on acquisition of housing property on the primary market – up to the amount of interests related to the part of loan not exceeding PLN 325 990 for investments finished in 2015.

Tax credits:

- Donation made to public benefit organizations – up to 1 per cent of due tax.*
- Abolished tax credits (continued on the acquired rights basis), i.e. expenses for saving with the aim of buying a house or flat, the amount of social contributions paid on income of an unemployed person hired by a taxpayer in order to take care of their children and/or house.

1.1.3. *Tax schedule*

The tax schedule is as follows:

Tax base (in PLN)		Tax amount
Over	Below	
0	85 528	18 % of the tax base, less a basic tax credit of PLN 556.02
85 528		PLN 14 839.02 + 32 % of surplus over PLN 85 528

A tax-free threshold of PLN 3 091 is applied in the income tax calculations.

1.2. *State and local income tax*

There are no regional or local income taxes.

1.3. *Wealth tax*

There is no wealth tax.

2. Social security contributions

2.1. *Employees' contributions*

Employees pay 13.71 per cent of the gross wage. This contribution includes:

- Pension insurance contribution – 9.76 per cent of the gross wage.** 3.65 percentage points of the pension contribution are treated as non-tax compulsory payments because these payments are either made to the OPF (1.46 per cent) and to personal sub-account in ZUS (2.19 per cent) or only to sub-account in ZUS (3.65 per cent).Disability insurance contribution – 1.5 per cent of the gross wage,
- Sickness/maternity insurance contribution – 2.45 per cent of the gross wage,
- In case of pension and disability insurance, contributions are not paid on the part of the wage that exceeds PLN 118 770.***

* This relief is distinct from an allowance for donations deducted from income.

** Since July 2014 out of total 19.52% of social contributions 7.3% goes to subaccount in ZUS either – if voluntarily stated by insured person – 2.92% goes to account in open ended funds and 4.38% to subaccount in ZUS.

*** The contribution ceiling of pension and disability insurance funds for a given calendar year may not exceed thirty times the amount of the projected average monthly remuneration in the national economy for that year, as set forth in the Budgetary Act.

2.2. Employers' contributions

In respect of income paid under an employment contract with a Polish entity, employers have an obligation to pay social security contributions equal to 20.43 per cent of gross wage. This value consists of:

- 9.76 percentage points are aimed for pension insurance.* 3.65 percentage points of the pension contribution are treated as non-tax compulsory payments because these payments are either made to the OPF (1.46 per cent) and to personal sub-account in ZUS (2.19 per cent) or only to sub-account in ZUS (3.65 per cent).-.
- 6.5 percentage points are aimed for disability insurance,
- 4.17 percentage points are aimed for other insurances i.e. 1.62 percentage points (on average) accident insurance, 2.45 percentage points for Labour Found and 0.1 percentage points for the Guaranteed Employee Benefit Fund.
- In case of pension and disability insurance, contributions are not paid on the part of the wage that exceeds PLN 118 770.

3. Universal cash transfers

3.1. Transfers related to marital status

None.

3.2. Transfers for dependent children

From 1st of November 2012 families where the average monthly income per household member for the previous period is no greater than PLN 539 or PLN 623 when there are one or more disabled children in the household) are entitled to family allowances. From 1st of November 2014 the income criteria will be as high as PLN 574 and PLN 664. Families receive PLN 77 monthly for a child no older than 5 years, PLN 106 monthly for a child of 5 up to 18 years old, and PLN 115 monthly for a child of 18 up to 24 years old. The calculations in this Report are based on the assumption that the children are aged between 5 and 18 years.

Single parents are entitled to a supplement of PLN 170 for each child up to a maximum of PLN 340 for all children (and PLN 250 for a disabled child up to a maximum of PLN 500 for all children).

There are several supplements to family allowances:

- for large families – PLN 80 monthly for the 3rd and next children in the family;
- for education of disabled children – PLN 60 monthly for children not older than 5 years and PLN 80 for children older than 5 years.

4. Main changes in tax/benefit systems since 2012

There were no changes in taxation of wages. Tax schedule, work-related expenses, tax allowances, relieves are the same as in previous years.

There were only changes in Social Security Contribution. Since February 2014, 14.96% of the old-age insurance contribution (2.92 percentage points) are transferred by ZUS to a privately-managed fund (OPF) but since July 2014 this part of contribution will be

* Since July 2014 out of total 19.52% of social contributions 7.3% goes to subaccount in ZUS either – if voluntarily stated by insured person – 2.92% goes to account in open ended funds and 4.38% to subaccount in ZUS.

transferred only if insured persons decides to – otherwise all 7.3 percentage points of the contributions will be passed to subaccount in ZUS.

5. Memorandum items

5.1. *Identification of AW and valuation of earnings*

The Polish Central Statistical Office calculates average monthly wages and salaries for employees on the basis of reports of enterprises. The figures include overtime and bonus payments and also include information for part-time employees converted to full-time equivalents. Male and female workers are included. The information, which includes estimates for different sectors, is published in the monthly *Statistical Bulletin*.

5.2. *Employers' contributions to private pension, health and related schemes*

No information provided.

2015 parameter values

Average earnings/yr	Ave_earn	45 521	(Secretariat Estimate)
Work expenses	work_exp	1 335.00[1]	
Income tax schedule	tax_sch	0	3 091
		0.18	85 528
		0.32	
Tax credits			
Basic credit	basic_cr	556.02	
Health insurance	health_ins	0.09	
	health_ins_credit	0.0775	
Children	Child_cr	1 112.04	
	Child_cr_lim	112 000	
Social security contributions			
Employers	SSC_empr	0.20433	
old-age pension and disability pension insurance	SSC_old	0.097676	
	SSC_old_ZUS	0.061176	
	SSC_old_ZUSII	0.0365	
	SSC_old_OPF	0	
	SSC_dis	0.065	
other insurances	SSC_a	0.0417	
Employees	SSC	0.1371	
old-age pension and disability pension insurance	SSC_old_e	0.0976	
	SSC_old_e_ZUS	0.0611	
	SSC_old_e_ZUSII	0.0365	
	SSC_old_e_OPF	0	
	SSC_dis_e	0.015	
sickness insurance	SSC_s	0.0245	
Contribution ceiling	SSC_c	118770	
Family benefit	fam_ben	1 272	
single parent additional family benefit	fam_ben_Spsup	170	
single parent additional family benefit ceiling	fam_ben_Spsup_lim	340	
income limit	fam_ben_lim	6 468	
income limit for single parent	fam_ben_lim_sp	6 468	

1. Lump-sum annual work expenses for an employee having one workplace and living in the place (town, city) where the workplace is; employees living outside the city (town) where their workplace is may deduct 1668,72 PLN annually.

2015 tax equations

The equations for the Polish system are mostly calculated on a family basis.

The standard functions which are used in the equations (Taper, MIN, Tax etc) are described in the technical note about tax equations. Two additional functions (Tax93 and ftax) have been incorporated to carry out an iterative calculation for central government tax. These allow for the fact that the church tax is calculated as 9 per cent of Central Government tax and is also allowed as a deduction when calculating taxable income. Variable names are defined in the table of parameters above, within the equations table, or are the standard variables "married" and "children". A reference to a variable with the affix "_total" indicates the sum of the relevant variable values for the principal and spouse. And the affixes "_princ" and "_spouse" indicate the value for the principal and spouse, respectively. Equations for a single person are as shown for the principal, with "_spouse" values taken as 0.

	Line in country table and intermediate steps	Variable name	Range	Equation
1.	Earnings	earn		
	Quotient for tax calculation	quotient	J	1+MAX(Married,(Children>0))
2.	Allowances:	tax_al	J	work_exp+MIN(earn_spouse,work_exp)+SSC+SSC_old_e_OPF*MIN(earn, SSC_c)
3.	Credits in taxable income	taxbl_cr	J	0
4.	CG taxable income	tax_inc	J	Positive(earn-tax_al)
5.	CG tax before credits	CG_tax_excl	J	quotient*Tax(tax_inc/quotient,tax_sch)
6.	Tax credits :			
	Basic credit	basic_cr	J	basic_cr*quotient
	Health insurance	health_ins_cr	B	health_ins_credit*(earn-SSC-SSC_old_e_OPF*MIN(earn, SSC_c))
	Child credit	child_cr	J	If(earn_total<Child_cr_lim,children*child_cr,0)
	Total tax credits	tax_cr	J	basic_cr+health_ins_cr+child_cr
7.	CG tax	CG_tax	J	IF(AND(ABS(Positive(CG_tax_excl-basic_cr-health_ins)-child_cr)>SSC+health_ins,Positive(CG_tax_excl-basic_cr-health_ins)-child_cr <0),-(SSC+health_ins), Positive(CG_tax_excl-basic_cr-health_ins)-child_cr)
8.	State and local taxes	local_tax	J	0
9.	Employees' soc security	health_ins	B	(earn-(MIN(earn, SSC_c)*(SSC_old_e+SSC_dis_e)+earn*SSC_s))*health_ins
.		SSC	B	(SSC_old_e_ZUS+SSC_dis_e)*MIN(earn,SSC_c)+SSC_s*earn
11.	Cash transfers	cash_tran	J	((earn_total/(1+Married+Children))<(Married*fam_ben_lim+(1-Married)*fam_ben_lim_sp))*(Children*fam_ben+(1-Married)*(Children>0)*MIN(fam_ben_Spsup*Children;fam_ben_Spsup_lim))
13.	Employer's soc security	SSC_empr	B	(SSC_old_ZUS+SSC_dis)*MIN(earn,SSC_c)+SSC_a*earn

Key to range of equation B calculated separately for both principal earner and spouse, P calculated for principal only (value taken as 0 for spouse calculation), J calculated once only on a joint basis.

Portugal

This chapter includes data on the income taxes paid by workers, their social security contributions, the family benefits they receive in the form of cash transfers as well as the social security contributions and payroll taxes paid by their employers. Results reported include the marginal and average tax burden for eight different family types.

Methodological information is available for personal income tax systems, compulsory social security contributions to schemes operated within the government sector, universal cash transfers as well as recent changes in the tax/benefit system. The methodology also includes the parameter values and tax equations underlying the data.

Portugal 2015

The tax/benefit position of single persons

	Wage level (per cent of average wage)		67	100	167	67
	Number of children		none	none	none	2
1.	**Gross wage earnings**		11 578	17 280	28 857	11 578
2.	**Standard tax allowances**					
	Basic allowance		4 104	4 104	4 104	4 104
	Married or head of family					
	Dependent children					
	Deduction for social security contributions and income taxes					
	Work-related expenses		0	0	0	0
	Other					
		Total	4 104	4 104	4 104	4 104
3.	**Tax credits or cash transfers included in taxable income**		0	0	0	0
4.	**Central government taxable income (1 - 2 + 3)**		7 474	13 176	24 753	7 474
5.	**Central government income tax liability (exclusive of tax credits)**		1 150	2 775	6 479	1 084
6.	**Tax credits**					
	Basic credit		0	0	0	0
	Married or head of family					
	Children		0	0	0	650
	Other					
		Total	0	0	0	650
7.	**Central government income tax finally paid (5-6)**		1 164	2 989	7 098	434
8.	**State and local taxes**		0	0	0	0
9.	**Employees' compulsory social security contributions**					
	Gross earnings		1 274	1 901	3 174	1 274
	Taxable income					
		Total	1 274	1 901	3 174	1 274
10.	**Total payments to general government (7 + 8 + 9)**		2 438	4 890	10 272	1 707
11.	**Cash transfers from general government**					
	For head of family					
	For two children		0	0	0	841
		Total	0	0	0	841
12.	**Take-home pay (1-10+11)**		9 140	12 390	18 585	10 711
13.	**Employer's compulsory social security contributions**		2 750	4 104	6 854	2 750
14.	**Average rates**					
	Income tax		10.1%	17.3%	24.6%	3.7%
	Employees' social security contributions		11.0%	11.0%	11.0%	11.0%
	Total payments less cash transfers		21.1%	28.3%	35.6%	7.5%
	Total tax wedge including employer's social security contributions		36.2%	42.1%	48.0%	25.2%
15.	**Marginal rates**					
	Total payments less cash transfers: Principal earner		43.0%	43.0%	51.5%	25.5%
	Total payments less cash transfers: Spouse		n.a.	n.a.	n.a.	n.a.
	Total tax wedge: Principal earner		53.9%	53.9%	60.8%	39.8%
	Total tax wedge: Spouse		n.a.	n.a.	n.a.	n.a.

Portugal 2015

The tax/benefit position of married couples

		Wage level (per cent of average wage)	100-0	100-33	100-67	100-33
		Number of children	2	2	2	none
1.	**Gross wage earnings**		17 280	22 982	28 857	22 982
2.	**Standard tax allowances**					
	Basic allowance		4 104	8 208	8 208	8 208
	Married or head of family					
	Dependent children					
	Deduction for social security contributions and income taxes					
	Work-related expenses		0	0	0	0
	Other					
		Total	4 104	8 208	8 208	8 208
3.	**Tax credits or cash transfers included in taxable income**		0	0	0	0
4.	**Central government taxable income (1 - 2 + 3)**		13 176	14 774	20 649	14 774
5.	**Central government income tax liability (exclusive of tax credits)**		1 911	2 142	3 337	2 251
6.	**Tax credits**					
	Basic credit		0	0	0	0
	Married or head of family					
	Children		650	650	650	0
	Other					
		Total	650	650	650	0
7.	**Central government income tax finally paid (5-6)**		1 261	1 492	2 687	2 273
8.	**State and local taxes**		0	0	0	0
9.	**Employees' compulsory social security contributions**					
	Gross earnings		1 901	2 528	3 174	2 528
	Taxable income					
		Total	1 901	2 528	3 174	2 528
10.	**Total payments to general government (7 + 8 + 9)**		3 161	4 020	5 861	4 801
11.	**Cash transfers from general government**					
	For head of family					
	For two children		701	637	0	0
		Total	701	637	0	0
12.	**Take-home pay (1-10+11)**		14 819	19 599	22 996	18 181
13.	**Employer's compulsory social security contributions**		4 104	5 458	6 854	5 458
14.	**Average rates**					
	Income tax		7.3%	6.5%	9.3%	9.9%
	Employees' social security contributions		11.0%	11.0%	11.0%	11.0%
	Total payments less cash transfers		14.2%	14.7%	20.3%	20.9%
	Total tax wedge including employer's social security contributions		30.7%	31.1%	35.6%	36.1%
15.	**Marginal rates**					
	Total payments less cash transfers: Principal earner		25.5%	25.5%	39.5%	43.0%
	Total payments less cash transfers: Spouse		16.2%	25.5%	39.5%	43.0%
	Total tax wedge: Principal earner		39.8%	39.8%	51.1%	53.9%
	Total tax wedge: Spouse		32.3%	39.8%	51.1%	53.9%

The national currency is the euro (EUR). In 2015, EUR 0.90 equalled USD 1. The Secretariat has estimated that in that same year the average worker earned EUR 17 280 (Secretariat estimate).

1. Personal income tax system

1.1. *Taxes levied by central government*

1.1.1. *Tax unit*

The standard rule is separate taxation. However, families may opt for joint taxation. Income includes the income of any dependent children. Tax is computed on aggregate net income in the various categories of income, i.e. after the deductions specific to each category and standard and non-standard reliefs.

1.1.2. *Standard and non-standard reliefs and tax credits*

1.1.2.1. Standard reliefs

Standard deduction of 72% of 12 times the Social Benefit Index per taxpayer (the 2010 highest monthly minimum wage until the index reaches this value).* If compulsory contributions to social protection schemes and statutory sub-schemes for health care exceed that limit, the deduction will equal the amount of those contributions.

1.1.2.2. Non-standard reliefs

For income received from 1 January 1999 onwards, the majority of the standard reliefs have been replaced by tax credits (see Section 1.14).

Non-standard reliefs still in effect:

- A deduction is provided for the portion of trade union dues not constituting consideration for benefits in the realm of health care, education, assistance for the elderly, housing, insurance or social security, up to 1% of the taxpayer's gross income, increased by 50%. These dues are not taken into account in the calculations underlying this Report.

1.1.3. *Social security contributions*

Social security contributions are totally deductible if they exceed EUR 4 104.00 per taxpayer, in which case the deduction for the contributions replaces the standard earned income deduction (see Section 1.121).

1.1.4. *Tax credits*

Basic credits

- EUR 325 for each dependent child. This tax credit is increased by EUR 125 for dependent children whose age does not exceed 3 years old.

* The corresponding amount equals EUR 4 104.00 (72% × 12 × EUR 475.00).

- EUR 300 for each ascendant whose income does not exceed the minimum pension benefit. When there is only one ascendant, the tax credit increases by EUR 110.

Other tax credits

- 35% of household general expenses up to a limit of EUR 250, per taxpayer; this limit is increased to 45% and EUR 335, respectively.
- Non-reimbursed health care costs, not covered by Social Security: 15% of health care costs plus interest on loans contracted to meet them, with a limit of EUR 1 000 Expenditures for educating the taxpayer or the taxpayer's dependants: 30% of outlays, up to EUR 800.
- Costs for sanatoria or retirement homes for taxpayers, their ascendants and collaterals up to the third degree whose income does not exceed the national minimum wage: 25% of expenses up to EUR 403.75.
- Costs for the acquisition, construction or improvement of the taxpayers' primary, permanent residence, or for renting out property for a permanent residence: 15% of interest up to EUR 296.00. Rent paid by a tenant, for his permanent residence under an agreement typified by the law, up to EUR 502.00. This credit is applicable to contracts up to 31.12.2011. These limits are also increased by 50% for taxpayers in the first tax rate bracket, by 20% for taxpayers in the second tax rate bracket. This credit is to be phased out until 2016 (interests) and 2018 (rents).
- 20% of alimony payments compulsory under court order or court-approved agreement.
- 30% of education expenditures and 25% of life insurance premiums, up to a limit of 15% of the tax liability, for handicapped taxpayers or dependents.
- 15% of VAT paid for certain services (restaurants, lodging, hairdressers, and auto-repair) up to a limit of EUR 250. This benefit is not included on the limits referred to on the next page.

Tax credits from tax benefits

- Individual Retirement Savings Plans (PPRs): 20% of amounts invested, for unmarried taxpayers or for each spouse, up to:
  - EUR 400 for taxpayers under 35;
  - EUR 350 for taxpayers over 35 and under 50;
  - EUR 300 for taxpayers over 50.
- Social Security Individual Accounts: 20% of amounts invested, for unmarried taxpayers or for each spouse, up to a limit of EUR 350.

Donations granted on the conditions stated in the statutes governing charities (grants to central, regional or local government, special "social solidarity institutions", museums, libraries, schools, institutes, educational or research associations, public administrative bodies, etc.): 25% of donations, limited in certain cases to 15% of the donor's tax liability. However the total of tax credits related to health care costs, education and training, alimony, retirement homes, VAT paid, house expenses and tax benefits cannot exceed the values of the following amounts:

Limits are increased in 5% for each dependent.

1.1.5. *Family status*

Each taxpayer has an equal weight of 1, and every dependent has a weight of 0.3 (0.15 if the household files separate tax returns, as the dependent will be included in both parents'

Taxable income (EUR) (R)	Limit
Up to 7 000	Without limit
Between 7 000 and 80 000	$1000+\left[(2500-1000)*\left(\frac{80000-\textit{liable income}}{80000-7000}\right)\right]$
Over 80 000	EUR 1 000

annual tax returns). It is also introduced a limit to the benefit arising from the introduction of the family coefficient.

- For separate tax returns, EUR 300 for a household with one dependant, EUR 625 for a household with 2 dependants and EUR 1 000 for a household with 3 or more dependants;
- For join tax returns, the values are, respectively, EUR 600, EUR 1 250 and EUR 2 000;
- For single parent households the values are, respectively, EUR 350, EUR 750 and EUR 1 200.

1.1.5.1. Determination of taxable income

To determine taxable income, to which the rates listed in the tax schedule are applied, income is divided by the household coefficient.

1.1.6. *Tax rate schedule (applicable to 2015 income)*

Taxable income (EUR) (R)	Marginal tax rate (%) (T)	Amount to deduct (EUR) (K)
Up to 7 000	14.50	–
Over 7 000 up to 20 000	28.50	980
Over 20 000 up to 40 000	37.00	2 680
Over 40 000 up to 80 000	45.00	5 880
Over 80 000	48.00	8 280

In the case of taxpayers whose income stems primarily from dependent employment (earned income), disposable income after application of the tax rates to taxable income may not be less than 120% of the national minimum wage, EUR 8 500.00 in 2015.

For residents in the Autonomous Regions of the Azores, reduced tax rates are applicable. Tax calculation formula (I = Income tax due):

- Unmarried taxpayers: I = R × T – K – C

  Married taxpayers (with one or two earned incomes/see Section 1.151):

- I ={[(R : HC) × T – K] × HC } – C

  Where:

  R = Taxable income, after deduction of standard and non-standard reliefs (see Sections 1.12 and 1.151)

  T = Tax rate corresponding to the taxable income bracket

  K = Amount to be deducted from each bracket

  C = Tax credits (see Section 1.14)

  HC = Household coefficient.

Surtax:

A surtax was introduced by the 2012 State Budget and is applicable on highest income bracket. The surtax is now 2.5% applicable to taxable income between EUR 80 000 and EUR 250 000 and 5% for taxable income above EUR 250 000. Furthermore, a 3.5% surtax was reintroduced, for taxable income above the annual national minimum wage (EUR 6 790), with a tax credit of 2.5% of the annual minimum wage per dependent (EUR 169.75).

1.1.7. *Special family situations*

1.1.7.1. Handicapped taxpayer/spouse, with a disability rating of 60% or more:

- A tax credit corresponding to 4 times the 2010 minimum wage (EUR 1 900) is granted for each taxpayer or spouse.

1.1.7.2. Handicapped dependent children, with a disability rating of 60% or more:

- A tax credit corresponding to 1.5 times the social benefits index (EUR 712.50) is granted for each dependent child.

1.1.7.3. Handicapped taxpayer/spouse or dependent children, with a disability rating of 90% or more:

- An additional tax credit corresponding to 4 times the 2010 minimum wage (EUR 1 900) is granted for each taxpayer or spouse or dependent child.

1.1.8. *Non liable income*

- Lawfully granted family allowances;
- Living expenses per diem, up to the limits established for national civil servants;
- Meal allowances, up to the amount established for national civil servants, increased by 20% or 60% in the event of a meal allowance in the form of meal vouchers.

2. Compulsory social security contributions to schemes operated within the government sector

Rates and ceilings: social security contributions are levied on gross pay and are not subject to any ceiling.

2.1. *Employee contributions*

As a rule, the rate of employee contributions is 11% of gross pay, with no ceiling.

2.2. *Employer contributions*

The employer's rate of social security contributions is 23.75% of gross pay, with no ceiling.

2.3. *Areas of social protection*

- Health (sickness, disability, work accidents, work-related illness);
- Old age, survival;
- Maternity;
- Family (family allowances);
- Unemployment.

3. Universal cash benefits

3.1. *Benefits for dependent children*

The basic principle is to grant higher monthly social benefits to lower-income households.

There are six different levels of monthly allowances for dependent children, depending on the family's reference income. This reference income is determined by dividing the family's annual gross income, including vacation and Christmas allowances, by the number of dependent children plus one:

- Level 1: Families whose reference income is under 50% of 14 times the reference value (i.e. under EUR 2 934.54);
- Level 2: Families whose reference income is over 50% and under 100 percent of 14 times the reference value(i.e. over EUR 2 934.54 and under EUR 5 869.08);
- Level 3: Families whose reference income is over 100% and under 150% of 14 times the reference value (i.e. over EUR 5 869.08 and under EUR 8 803.62);
- Level 4: Families whose reference income is over 150% (i.e. over EUR 8 803.62).

Each level is also divided according to the age of the dependent child. Benefits are higher during the first 12 months of a child's life.

Monthly social benefits per child are as follows:

	Child under 12 months	Child over 12 months old	Additional benefit per child over 12 months and under 36 months in a family with 2 children	Additional benefit per child over 12 months and under 36 months in a family with 3 or more children
Level 1	140.76	35.19	35.19	70.38
Level 2	116.74	29.19	29.19	58.38
Level 3	92.29	26.54	26.54	53.08
Level 4	0	0	0	0

Monthly social benefits per child in a single-parent family are increased by 20%.

In September, families with dependent school children aged between 6 and 16 years receiving child benefits in level 1 receive an additional amount equal to the regular monthly benefit.

An amount equal to the cash benefits for dependent children under 12 months is attributed for each unborn child after the first month following that of the 13th week of gestation.

3.2. *Benefits for handicapped dependent children*

There is also a special family allowance scheme for handicapped children.

The above cash benefits (in Sections 3.1 and 3.2) are not taxable.

4. Main changes in the tax/benefit system since 2006

- The relief for disabled taxpayers was restructured. Former partial exemptions and allowances were replaced by tax credits.
- Tax credits for higher income households were limited or abolished;
- The fiscal autonomy of local authorities (municipalities) increased. They may set the level of their share in the revenue from personal income tax, up to 5% of their resident taxpayers' tax liability. If this rate is set below 5%, the difference will be credited against the taxpayers' tax liability.
- Tax credits for handicapped taxpayers and dependants were increased.
- Social benefits for dependent children were increased for low income families, single-parent families and families with 2 or more children.

- Introduction of social benefits for unborn children.
- Introduction of a family coefficient in 2015.

5. Memorandum items

5.1. *Method used to identify and compute gross wages of the average worker*

The operative concept of monthly compensation is that of amounts paid to full time staff before deductions for tax and compulsory contributions. It therefore includes wages and basic salaries of staff paid by the hour, by the job, or by tasks; benefits in kind or housing, if they are considered an integral part of compensation; cash subsidies for meals, housing or transport; bonuses for regular night shifts and seniority, as well as incentive pay and rewards for diligence and productivity; family allowances, compensation for overtime and work on holidays. Benefits, subsidies and bonuses are taken into account only if paid regularly at each pay period.

Payments in kind are incorporated into the concept of compensation. The statistics record such advantages in kind at their taxable value.

All managerial and supervisory workers are included in the computations.

Average annual pay is based on the average of monthly earnings for April and October multiplied by an adjustment coefficient representing the share of annual bonuses and allowances (including vacation subsidies and the Christmas allowance), which is provided by the labour cost survey.

The following formula is applied:

Average annual pay = Average monthly pay adjusted by the coefficient × 12.

5.2. *Description of the employer's main contributions to private retirement, health insurance schemes, etc.*

Outside the social security system, employers are required to insure their employees against work-related accidents (with private insurance companies). They may also provide their employees with life insurance, although this is optional.

2015 parameter values

Average earnings/yr	Ave_earn	17 280	Secretariat estimate	
Tax allowances	perc	1		
	max_al	4 104		
Household Coefficient	hc_ad	1		
	hc_ch	0.3		
	ben_limit1	600		
	ben_limit2	1 250		
	ben_limit3	2 000		
	ben_limit_sg_1	350		
	ben_limit_sg_2	750		
	ben_limit_sg_3	1 200		
Tax credits				
Married (basic)	married_cred	0		
Single (basic)	single_cred	0		
Single parent	singlepar_cred	0		
Each child credit	child_cred	325		
Tax schedule	tax_sch	0.145	7 000	
		0.285	20 000	
		0.37	40 000	
		0.45	80 000	
		0.48		
	tax_floor	na		
Surtax	surtax_rate	0.025		
	surtax_rate2	0.05		
	surtax_thrs	250 000		
	add_surtax_rate	0.035		
	add_surtax_cred	0.025		
Social security contributions	SSC_rate	0.11		
ceiling	SSC_empr	0.2375		
Child benefit - Schedule	ch_ben_sch	0	457.47	1st echelon
		2 934.54	350.28	2nd echelon
		5 869.08	318.48	3rd echelon
		8 803.62	0	4th echelon
Extra child benefit for lone parents	ch_ben_lone	0.2		
Minimum Wage	MW	7 070		
Minimum Disposable Income	MinDispY	8 500		

2015 tax equations

The equations for the Portuguese system in 2015 are mostly calculated on a family basis.

The functions which are used in the equations (Taper, MIN, Tax etc) are described in the technical note about tax equations. Variable names are defined in the table of parameters above, within the equations table, or are the standard variables "married" and "children". A reference to a variable with the affix "_total" indicates the sum of the relevant variable values for the principal and spouse. And the affixes "_princ" and "_spouse" indicate the value for the principal and spouse, respectively. Equations for a single person are as shown for the principal, with "_spouse" values taken as 0.

	Line in country table and intermediate steps	Variable name	Range	Equation
1.	Earnings	earn		
	Household coefficient	hd_coef	J	((1+Married)*hc_ad)+(Children*hc_ch)
2.	Allowances:	tax_al	J	MAX((MIN(perc*earn_princ, max_al)+MIN(perc* earn_spouse, max_al)), SSC_princ+SSC_spouse)
3.	Credits in taxable income	taxbl_cr	J	0
4.	CG taxable income	tax_inc	J	earn-tax_al
	Adjusted taxable income	tax_inc_adj		tax_inc/hd_coef
5.	CG tax before credits	CG_tax_excl	J	IF(Married>0,IF(((2*Tax(tax_inc/2,tax_sch))-(hd_coef*Tax(tax_inc_adj,tax_sch)))<=((ben_limit1*(Children=1))+(ben_limit2*(Children=2))+(ben_limit3*(Children>=3))),hd_coef*Tax(tax_inc_adj,tax_sch),2*Tax(tax_inc/2,tax_sch)-((ben_limit1*(Children=1))+(ben_limit2*(Children=2))+(ben_limit3*(Children>=3)))),IF(Children>0,IF((Tax(tax_inc,tax_sch)-(hd_coef*Tax(tax_inc_adj,tax_sch)))<=((ben_limit_sg_1*(Children=1))+(ben_limit_sg_2*(Children=2))+(ben_limit_sg_3*(Children>=3))),hd_coef*Tax(tax_inc_adj,tax_sch),Tax(tax_inc,tax_sch)-((ben_limit_sg_1*(Children=1))+(ben_limit_sg_2*(Children=2))+(ben_limit_sg_3*(Children>=3)))),Tax(tax_inc,tax_sch)))
6.	Tax credits :		J	
	Basic credit	basic_cr	J	IF(Married, 2*married_cred, IF(children, singlepar_cred, single_cred))
	Child credit	child_cr	J	Children*child_cred
	Total	tax_cr	J	basic_cr+child_cr
	Surtax	surtax	J	IF(Married>0,IF(tax_inc/2>surtax_thrs,(surtax_rate*(surtax_thrs-TopIncBracket)+surtax_rate2*((AG/2)-surtax_thrs))*2,surtax_rate*Positive((tax_inc/2)-TopIncBracket)*2)+Positive((add_surtax_rate*Positive((tax_inc/2)-MW)*2)-(add_surtax_cred*MW*Children)),IF(tax_inc>surtax_thrs,(surtax_rate*(surtax_thrs-TopIncBracket)+surtax_rate2*(tax_inc-surtax_thrs)),surtax_rate*Positive(tax_inc-TopIncBracket))+Positive((add_surtax_rate*Positive(tax_inc-MW))-(add_surtax_cred*MW*Children)))
7.	CG tax	CG_tax	J	IF(earn-CG-tax-excl> MinDispY,Positive(CG_tax_excl-tax_cr),0)+surtax
8.	State and local taxes	local_tax	J	0
9.	Employees' soc security	SSC	B	earn*SSC_rt
11.	Cash transfers	cash_trans	J	=IF(Married=0, VLOOKUP(earn/(Children+1),ch_ben_sch,2,1)*Children*(1+ch_ben_lone), VLOOKUP(earn/(Children+1),ch_ben_sch,2,1)*Children)
13.	13. Employer's soc security	SSC_empr	B	earn*SSC_empr

Key to range of equation B calculated separately for both principal earner and spouse P calculated for principal only (value taken as 0 for spouse calculation) J calculated once only on a joint basis.

Taxing Wages 2016

Slovak Republic

This chapter includes data on the income taxes paid by workers, their social security contributions, the family benefits they receive in the form of cash transfers as well as the social security contributions and payroll taxes paid by their employers. Results reported include the marginal and average tax burden for eight different family types.

Methodological information is available for personal income tax systems, compulsory social security contributions to schemes operated within the government sector, universal cash transfers as well as recent changes in the tax/benefit system. The methodology also includes the parameter values and tax equations underlying the data.

Slovak Republic 2015

The tax/benefit position of single persons

		Wage level (per cent of average wage)	67	100	167	67
		Number of children	none	none	none	2
1.	**Gross wage earnings**		7 113	10 616	17 729	7 113
2.	**Standard tax allowances**					
	Basic allowance		3 803	3 803	3 803	3 803
	Married or head of family		0	0	0	0
	Dependent children		0	0	0	0
	Deduction for social security contributions and income taxes		953	1 423	2 376	953
	Work-related expenses					
	Other					
		Total	4 756	5 226	6 179	4 756
3.	**Tax credits or cash transfers included in taxable income**		0	0	0	0
4.	**Central government taxable income (1 - 2 + 3)**		2 357	5 390	11 550	2 357
5.	**Central government income tax liability (exclusive of tax credits)**		448	1 024	2 195	448
6.	**Tax credits**					
	Basic credit		0	0	0	0
	Married or head of family		0	0	0	0
	Children		0	0	0	514
	Other (ETC)		0	0	0	0
		Total	0	0	0	514
7.	**Central government income tax finally paid (5-6)**		448	1 024	2 195	- 66
8.	**State and local taxes**		0	0	0	0
9.	**Employees' compulsory social security contributions**					
	Gross earnings		953	1 423	2 376	953
	Taxable income					
		Total	953	1 423	2 376	953
10.	**Total payments to general government (7 + 8 + 9)**		1 401	2 447	4 570	887
11.	**Cash transfers from general government**					
	For head of family					
	For two children		0	0	0	564
		Total	0	0	0	564
12.	**Take-home pay (1-10+11)**		5 712	8 170	13 159	6 790
13.	**Employers' compulsory social security contributions**		2 219	3 312	5 532	2 219
14.	**Average rates**					
	Income tax		6.3%	9.6%	12.4%	-0.9%
	Employees' social security contributions		13.4%	13.4%	13.4%	13.4%
	Total payments less cash transfers		19.7%	23.0%	25.8%	4.5%
	Total tax wedge including employer's social security contributions		38.8%	41.3%	43.4%	27.2%
15.	**Marginal rates**					
	Total payments less cash transfers: Principal earner		29.9%	29.9%	29.9%	29.9%
	Total payments less cash transfers: Spouse		n.a.	n.a.	n.a.	n.a.
	Total tax wedge: Principal earner		46.5%	46.5%	46.5%	46.5%
	Total tax wedge: Spouse		n.a.	n.a.	n.a.	n.a.

Slovak Republic 2015

The tax/benefit position of married couples

	Wage level (per cent of average wage)	100-0	100-33	100-67	100-33
	Number of children	2	2	2	none
1.	**Gross wage earnings**	10 616	14 120	17 729	14 120
2.	**Standard tax allowances**				
	Basic allowance	3 803	6 977	7 607	6 977
	Married or head of family	3 803	0	0	0
	Dependent children	0	0	0	0
	Deduction for social security contributions and income taxes	1 423	1 752	2 376	1 752
	Work-related expenses				
	Other				
	Total	9 029	8 729	9 982	8 729
3.	**Tax credits or cash transfers included in taxable income**	0	0	0	0
4.	**Central government taxable income (1 - 2 + 3)**	1 587	5 390	7 747	5 390
5.	**Central government income tax liability (exclusive of tax credits)**	302	1 024	1 472	1 024
6.	**Tax credits**				
	Basic credit	0	0	0	0
	Married or head of family	0	0	0	0
	Children	514	514	514	0
	Other (ETC)	0	0	0	0
	Total	514	514	514	0
7.	**Central government income tax finally paid (5-6)**	- 212	510	958	1 024
8.	**State and local taxes**	0	0	0	0
9.	**Employees' compulsory social security contributions**				
	Gross earnings	1 423	1 752	2 376	1 752
	Taxable income				
	Total	1 423	1 752	2 376	1 752
10.	**Total payments to general government (7 + 8 + 9)**	1 210	2 262	3 334	2 776
11.	**Cash transfers from general government**				
	For head of family				
	For two children	564	564	564	0
	Total	564	564	564	0
12.	**Take-home pay (1-10+11)**	9 971	12 422	14 960	11 344
13.	**Employers' compulsory social security contributions**	3 312	4 055	5 532	4 055
14.	**Average rates**				
	Income tax	-2.0%	3.6%	5.4%	7.3%
	Employees' social security contributions	13.4%	12.4%	13.4%	12.4%
	Total payments less cash transfers	6.1%	12.0%	15.6%	19.7%
	Total tax wedge including employer's social security contributions	28.4%	31.7%	35.7%	37.6%
15.	**Marginal rates**				
	Total payments less cash transfers: Principal earner	29.9%	29.9%	29.9%	29.9%
	Total payments less cash transfers: Spouse	30.0%	9.4%	29.9%	9.4%
	Total tax wedge: Principal earner	46.5%	46.5%	46.5%	46.5%
	Total tax wedge: Spouse	42.3%	25.2%	46.5%	25.2%

As from 1.1.2009 Slovakia has joined the Euro zone; the national currency became the Euro (EUR). In 2015, EUR 0.90 was equal to USD 1. In that year, the average worker earned EUR 10 616 (Secretariat estimate).

1. Personal income tax system

1.1. Central government income taxes

1.1.1. Tax unit

The tax unit is the individual.

1.1.2. Tax allowances and tax credits

1.1.2.1. Standard reliefs

- *Basic relief:* An allowance for all taxpayers is set at 19.2 times the minimum living standard (MLS) for a basic adult as of 1 January 2015 (EUR 3 803.33). In 2015, the basic personal allowance for taxpayers with gross earnings net of employee social security contributions in excess of the threshold of EUR 19 809 per year (19 809 = 100 × MLS, which is approximately equal to an employee's monthly gross wage of EUR 1 906) is gradually withdrawn. If gross earnings net of employee social security contributions exceed EUR 19 809, the personal allowance is calculated as 44.2 times the minimum living standard minus 0.25 times gross earnings net of employee social security contributions. The basic personal allowance reaches 0 if the gross earnings net of employee social security contributions amount to EUR 35 022.31 per year (employee's monthly gross wage of approximately EUR 3 370). The value of the basic tax allowance cannot become negative.

The regressive tax allowance is taken into account only once a year (when the tax return is filed or when the annual clearing is performed). Monthly tax prepayments during the year are therefore not affected.

- *Marital status relief:* An additional allowance is given to the principal earner in respect of a spouse living in a common household if the spouse earns no more than EUR 3 803.33. As from 1 January 2007 the value of the spouse allowance depends on the gross earnings net of employee social security contributions of both principal and spouse. As of 2013, to be entitled to spouse allowance one of the following conditions should be met:
  - spouse is taking care of (not necessarily personally) children up to 3 years (or up to 6 years if child is disabled) or
  - spouse is unemployed or
  - spouse is receiving nursing allowance or
  - spouse is disabled.

If the principal's gross earnings net of employee social security contributions in 2015 are lower or equal to EUR 35 022.31 (= 176.8 times MLS) and the spouse's gross earnings net of employee social security contributions are lower than EUR 3 803.33, the spouse allowance is calculated as the difference between 19.2 times MLS and the spouse's gross earnings net of employee social security contributions. If the gross earnings net of employee social security contributions of the spouse exceed EUR 3 803.33, the spouse allowance is 0. If the principal's gross earnings net of employee social security contributions exceed EUR 35 022.31 (= 176.8 times MLS), the spouse allowance is calculated as 63.4 times MLS minus 0.25 times the principal's gross earnings net of employee social security contributions. This amount is reduced by the spouse's gross earnings net of employee social security contributions. The value of the spouse allowance cannot become negative.

The digressive tax allowance is taken into account only once a year (when the tax return is filed or when the annual clearing is performed). Monthly tax prepayments during the year are therefore not affected.

For the purposes of this Report, only families with unemployed spouse are entitled to spouse allowance (spouse income does not influence any equations of spouse allowance as of 2013). Child care up to 3 years does not affect the calculation of tax wedges as according to the Taxing wages methodology any children in the household are assumed to be aged between six and eleven inclusive.

- *Relief for children*: The prior allowance for children has been replaced by a non-wastable tax credit as from January 2004. As from July 2007, the monthly tax credit is automatically indexed by MLS growth as of 1st July when also the new amount of MLS comes into force. Monthly tax credit in 2015 is EUR 21.41 per child for the whole year as MLS did not change during the year. The annual amount will be EUR 256.92. The tax credit for each dependent child is deducted from the tax liability; if the credit exceeds the tax liability, the excess will be paid to the taxpayer. In order to receive this credit, the parent must annually earn at least 6 times the minimum monthly wage, which for 2015 is set at EUR 380.0 (the total annual earnings must therefore be at least EUR 2 280.0). The credit can be taken only by one partner. It can be taken by one partner for part of the tax period (year) and by the other partner for the rest of the tax period (year); this choice will have to hold for all dependent children. (For the purposes of this Report, it is assumed that the credit is claimed by the principal wage earner).
- *Relief for social and health security contributions*: Employee's social security contributions (see Section 2.1.) are deductible for income tax purposes.

1.1.2.2. Main non-standard tax reliefs applicable to an average wage worker

- Supplementary pension insurance, special-purpose savings and life insurances repealed as from January 2011. As of 2014 allowance for supplementary pension insurance has been reintroduced. Supplementary pension contributions are tax-deductible up to the maximum limit of EUR 180 per year.
- As of 2013 voluntary contributions to the privately managed fully funded pillar up to 2% of gross earnings net of employee social security contributions are tax-deductible. Maximum yearly limit for this tax relief is calculated as: 2% × 60 × AW(t-2), where AW(t-2) average wage two years ago. It is legislated that this relief will be automatically abolished as of 2017.

1.1.2.3. Non-wastable tax credit: employee tax credit (ETC/zamestnanecká prémia)

Prior to 2015 low-income workers were eligible for employee tax credit. The employee tax credit was effective since 2009 and depended on employee's earnings and the number of months worked. In order to receive employee tax credit, earnings should be at least 6 times of the minimum wage and 12 times the minimum wage. The credit was than calculated as a 19% of the difference between the basic allowance and the tax base (gross earnings net of employee SSC). Since 2015 the tax base (at the level of the minimum wage, EUR 3 948.96) is higher than the basic allowance (EUR 3 803.33) the tax credit is automatically zero (so effectively anyone can be eligible).

1.1.3. *Tax schedule*

As from 2013 the previous flat tax rate of 19% was replaced by new tax schedule with two tax brackets. The ceiling for the first bracket is set out as 176.8 times MLS (equal to EUR 35 022.31) what secure its automatic indexation. The tax schedule is as follows:

Annual taxable income (EUR)*	Rate (%)
0-35 022.31	19
35 022.31 and over	25

* Employee's social security contributions (see 1.12.) are deductible for income tax purposes.

1.2. *State and local income tax*

No separate state and local income tax exist. As from 2015 the share of distribution of PIT revenue has changed. Out of the total revenue from the personal income tax (PIT) collected by the central government, 68.5% of PIT is transferred into the budget of the municipalities and 29.2% of PIT is transferred into the budget of the self-governing regions. The remaining revenue of the state budget is 2.3% of PIT.

2. Compulsory social security contributions to schemes operated within the government sector

2.1. *Employees' contributions*

Compulsory contributions of 13.4% of gross wages and salaries are paid by all employees into government operated schemes. The total is made up as follows:

Health Insurance		4.0%
Social Insurance		9.4%
of which:		
Sickness	1.4%	
Retirement	4.0%	
Disability	3.0%	
Unemployment	1.0%	

There are maximum assessment bases MSSAB (maximum threshold for contributions to apply) that apply to social security contributions. From 2004 these MSSAB are no longer fixed values but depend upon the average wages (AW). As of 2013 formulae for calculation of all maximum assessment bases has been unified. Monthly MSSAB for social security contributions are calculated as: 5 × AW(t-2), where AW(t-2) is the average wage two years ago. The average wage (AW) is determined by the Statistical Office of the Slovak Republic – for 2013 it was EUR 824 per month.

As of 2015 the health insurance contribution (HIC) allowance has been introduced. The allowance decreases the employee's and employer's assessment base for the health insurance. It amounts to EUR 380 per month (EUR 4 560 annually) and decreases with rising income up to EUR 570 (EUR 6 840 annually) when it reaches zero. With EUR 1 rise in the monthly income the monthly allowance is reduced by EUR 2. The HIC allowance is applicable only on standard employment income (not self-employed income or income based on temporary contracts). However, to determine the amount of allowance all types of incomes are assessed, to target only low income workers.

2.2. Employers' contributions

The total contribution for employers is 35.2% of gross wages and salaries. The contribution comprises the health insurance contribution (10% of gross wages and salaries) and the social insurance contribution (25.2%). The social insurance rate reflects contributions to sickness insurance (1.4%), disability insurance (3%), retirement insurance (14%), the Guaranteed Fund (0.25%), accident insurance (0.8%), for unemployment (1%) and to the Reserve Fund (4.75%). All contributions are rounded down on two decimal places.

Since January 2005, Slovakia has introduced the privately managed fully funded pillar. This means that a given proportion (9 percentage points) of social contributions paid by the employer for retirement insurance flew directly to the private pension funds and not to the Social insurance agency as in previous years. As from September 2012 pension sharing scheme has been changed. Employer's retirement contribution rate to the fully funded pillar has been reduced from 9% to 4% (for more see pension contribution sharing scheme table below). Private pension funds are treated outside of general government; these contributions are therefore not taken into account in the calculations of average and marginal tax rates. For the purposes of this Report, the total contribution rate for employers in 2015 is 31.2%.

As of 2015 the health insurance contribution (HIC) allowance has been introduced (for more see 2.1).

The MSSAB also applies to the employer's SSC. The next table presents the annual values of MSSAB:

	Formula for MSSAB	Value of MSSAB
Health insurance	5.0 × AW (t-2)	49 440.00
Social insurance		
of which		
sickness, retirement, unemployment, disability, Guarantee fund, Reserve fund	5.0 × AW (t-2)	49 440.00
accident		No limit

SSC: Pension – contribution sharing in case of II. Pillar participation

Period	Percentage of gross earnings		
	I Pillar	II Pillar	Total
Previous system (up to September 2012)	9% (5% employer + 4% employee contribution)	9% (employer contribution)	18%
Current system (from September 2012)	14% (10% employer + 4% employee contribution)	4% (employer contribution)	18%

* As from 2017 contribution rate to the II. pillar will automatically increase by 0.25 p.p. per year (i.e. contribution rate to the I. pillar will decrease in the same volume), stopping at 6% in 2024.

3. Universal cash transfers

3.1. *Transfers related to marital status*

None.

3.2. *Transfers for dependent children*

The central government pays an allowance in respect of each dependent child in the amount of EUR 23.52 per month in 2015. In January 2008 an extra allowance for dependent children whose parents are not eligible for the non-wastable child tax credit was introduced. The monthly amount of this allowance is EUR 11.02. For the purpose of the tax wedge calculations this allowance is not relevant, as only non-workers and taxpayers with annual earnings lower than six times the minimum monthly wage (which is the condition for eligibility for the non-wastable child tax credit) are entitled to the extra allowance.

The non-wastable tax credit mentioned in Section 1.121 is part of the social support for families with dependent children. However, it is not considered as a transfer for the purposes of this Report.

3.3. *Transfers related to social status*

To determine the claim to state social benefits (for example the allowance for housing costs), the minimum living standard amounts are relevant as they form the basis of the income test. For 2015, these amounts are:

	MLS monthly (1.1.2015-31.12.2015)
First adult	198.09
Second adult	138.19
Child	90.42

A family is entitled to a social allowance if the total combined net monthly income of the family is less than the calculated MLS for this family. The allowance varies with the family type.

The benefits available to a family in material need (valid since 1st of January 2014) are:

- EUR 61.60 per month for an individual;
- EUR 117.20 per month for an individual with between one and four children;
- EUR 107.10 per month for a couple without children;
- EUR 160.40 per month for a couple with between one and four children;
- EUR 171.20 per month for an individual with more than four children;
- EUR 216.10 per month for a couple with more than four children.
- activation allowance: EUR 63.07 per month – for people who become active either by accepting qualifying employment opportunities or participating in retraining courses.
- housing allowance: EUR 55.80 per month for individual in material need, EUR 89.20 for a household in material need (if household has more than 1 person).
- protection allowance: EUR 63.07 per month for an individual in material need where employment is not possible due to such circumstances as a disability or old age, EUR 34.69 per month for individual on sick leave for at least 30 consecutive days and EUR 13.50 for a pregnant woman from 4th month of the pregnancy and lasts until the

child's age of 1 year (for the purpose of this Report, protection allowance is assumed to be EUR 63.07 for each individual).

- specific allowance: EUR 63.07 per month – entitlement arise for long-term unemployed individuals who move into work for 6 months (does not affect the calculations in this Report).
- dependent child allowance: EUR 17.20 per month for a child who properly fulfils compulsory school attendance.

4. Main changes in tax/benefit systems since 2014

The main change relate to introduction of the health insurance contribution allowance (HIC). Other changes relate to change in PIT revenue distribution between municipalities, self-governing regions and state budget. Since the MLS has not been indexed since 2014 all allowances, credits and brackets related to MLS have not changed as well.

5. Memorandum items

5.1. *Identification of AW and valuation of earnings*

The Ministry of Finance of the Slovak republic estimates the average earnings of the AW based on the data supplied by the Statistical Office of the Slovak republic, Labour Force Survey data (LFS). Earnings data (without self-employees) are based on average wage definition including industries falling under categories B to N inclusive, with reference to International Standard Industrial Classification of All Economic Activities, Revision 4.

2015 parameter values

Average earnings/yr	Ave_earn	10 616	Secretariat estimate
Minimum living standard (MLS) 2015	basic_adult	198.09	
	basic_adult1	138.19	
	basic_child	90.42	
Basic allowance	basic_al_mult	19.2	
	basic_al	3 803.33	
	basic_al_mult1	100	
	basic_al_mult2	44.2	
	basic_al_redn	0.25	
Spouse allowance	spouse_al_limit	3 803.33	
	spouse_al_mult1	176.8	
	spouse_al_mult2	63.4	
	spouse_al_redn	0.25	
Income tax rate	Tax_sch/tax_rate	0.19	35 022.312
		0.25	
Tax credits - nonwastable	tax_cr	256.92	
	min_wage	380	
	minwage_mult	6	
	etc_thresh	3 948.96	
Employee social security contributions	SSC_rate	0.134	
	SSC_sick	0.014	
	SSC_ret	0.04	
	SSC_dis	0.03	
	SSC_unemp	0.01	
	SSC_health	0.04	
Employer social security contributions	SSC_empr	0.304	
	SSC_empsick	0.014	
	SSC_empret	0.1	
	SSC_empdis	0.03	
	SSC_empunemp	0.01	
	SSC_emphealth	0.1	
	SSC_gua	0.0025	
	SSC_acc	0.008	
	SSC_fund	0.0475	
Health Insurance Contribution allowance	HIC_treshold	4 560	
	HIC_rate	2	
Maximum assessment base	MSSAB	49 440	
Cash transfers	transf_1	282.24	
	transf_indiv	739.2	
	transf_indiv_child	1 406.4	
	transf_couple	1 285.2	
	transf_couple_child	1 924.8	
	transf_hous_indiv	669.60	
	transf_hous_couple	1 070.40	
	transf_activ	756.84	
	transf_dep	206.40	

2015 tax equations

	Line in country table and intermediate steps	Variable name	Range	Equation
1.	Earnings	earn		
2.	Allowances:			
	Basic	basic_allce	B	IF(earn-SSC<=basic_al_mult1*basic_adult, basic_al,MAXA(basic_al_mult2*basic_adult-basic_al_redn*(earn-SSC),0))
	Spouse	spouse_allce	P	IF(earn_spouse=0,1,0)*Married*Positive(IF(earn_princ-SSC_princ<=spouse_al_mult1*basic_adult, basic_al_mult*basic_adult,spouse_al_mult2*basic_adult-spouse_al_redn*(earn_princ-SSC_princ)))
	Social security contributions	SSC_al	B	SSC
	Total	tax_al	B	basic_allce+spouse_allce+SSC_al
3.	Credits in taxable income	taxbl_cr	B	0
4.	CG taxable income	tax_inc	B	Positive(earn-tax_al)
5.	CG tax before credits	CG_tax_excl	B	Tax(tax_inc,tax_sch)
6.	Tax credits:			
	Employee tax credit	etc_cr	B	IF(earn>=min_wage*minwage_mult, tax_rate*Positive(basic_al-MAX(etc_thresh, earn-SSC)), 0)
	Children	child_cr	P	(earn>=min_wage*minwage_mult)*Children*tax_cr
	Total	tax_cr	B	etc_cr+child_cr
7.	CG tax	CG_tax	B	CG_tax_excl-tax_cr
8.	State and local taxes	local_tax	B	0
9.	Employees' soc security	SSC	B	MINA(earn,MSSAB)*SSC_rate+MINA(MAX(0;(earn-MAX(0;HIC_treshold-MAX(0;(earn-HIC_treshold)*HIC_rate))));MSSAB)*SSC_health
11.	Cash transfers	cash_trans	J	Children*transf_1+Positive(IF(0,75*((earn-SSC-CG_tax_excl)/12)<(basic_adult+Married*basic_adult1+ Children*basic_child); ((1-Married)* (IF(Children>0;transf_indiv_child;transf_indiv))+ Married*(IF(Children>0;transf_couple_child;transf_couple))+IF((Married+Children)>0;transf_hous_couple;transf_hous_indiv)+(Children*transf_dep)+IF(A7>0;transf_activ;0)+IF(B7>0;transf_activ;0)-0,75*(earn-SSC-CG_tax_excl));0))
13.	Employer's soc security	SSC_empr	B	MINA(earn,MSSAB)*SSC_empr+earn*SSC_accMINA(MAX(0;(earn-MAX(0;HIC_treshold-MAX(0;(earn-HIC_treshold)*HIC_rate))));MSSAB)*SSC_emphealth

Key to range of equation B calculated separately for both principal earner and spouse P calculated for principal only (value taken as 0 for spouse calculation) J calculated once only on a joint basis.

Slovenia

This chapter includes data on the income taxes paid by workers, their social security contributions, the family benefits they receive in the form of cash transfers as well as the social security contributions and payroll taxes paid by their employers. Results reported include the marginal and average tax burden for eight different family types.

Methodological information is available for personal income tax systems, compulsory social security contributions to schemes operated within the government sector, universal cash transfers as well as recent changes in the tax/benefit system. The methodology also includes the parameter values and tax equations underlying the data.

Slovenia 2015

The tax/benefit position of single persons

	Wage level (per cent of average wage)		67	100	167	67
	Number of children		none	none	none	2
1.	**Gross wage earnings**		12 133	18 109	30 242	12 133
2.	**Standard tax allowances**					
	Basic allowance		4 419	3 303	3 303	4 419
	Married or head of family					
	Dependent children					5 086
	Deduction for social security contributions and income taxes		2 681	4 002	6 683	2 681
	Work-related expenses		0	0	0	0
	Other					
		Total	7 100	7 305	9 986	12 186
3.	**Tax credits or cash transfers included in taxable income**		0	0	0	0
4.	**Central government taxable income (1 - 2 + 3)**		5 033	10 804	20 256	0
5.	**Central government income tax liability (exclusive of tax credits)**		805	2 035	4 768	0
6.	**Tax credits**					
	Basic credit					
	Married or head of family					
	Children		0	0	0	0
	Other					
		Total	0	0	0	0
7.	**Central government income tax finally paid (5-6)**		805	2 035	4 768	0
8.	**State and local taxes**		0	0	0	0
9.	**Employees' compulsory social security contributions**					
	Gross earnings		2 681	4 002	6 683	2 681
	Taxable income					
		Total	2 681	4 002	6 683	2 681
10.	**Total payments to general government (7 + 8 + 9)**		3 487	6 037	11 451	2 681
11.	**Cash transfers from general government**					
	For head of family					
	For two children		0	0	0	3 210
		Total	0	0	0	3 210
12.	**Take-home pay (1-10+11)**		8 646	12 072	18 790	12 662
13.	**Employer's wage dependent contributions and taxes**		1 953	2 916	4 869	1 953
	Employer's compulsory social security contributions		1 953	2 916	4 869	1 953
	Payroll taxes		0	0	0	0
14.	**Average rates**					
	Income tax		6.6%	11.2%	15.8%	0.0%
	Employees' social security contributions		22.1%	22.1%	22.1%	22.1%
	Total payments less cash transfers		28.7%	33.3%	37.9%	-4.4%
	Total tax wedge including employer's social security contributions		38.6%	42.6%	46.5%	10.1%
15.	**Marginal rates**					
	Total payments less cash transfers: Principal earner		34.6%	43.1%	54.0%	22.1%
	Total payments less cash transfers: Spouse		n.a.	n.a.	n.a.	n.a.
	Total tax wedge: Principal earner		43.6%	51.0%	60.4%	32.9%
	Total tax wedge: Spouse		n.a.	n.a.	n.a.	n.a.

Slovenia 2015

The tax/benefit position of married couples

			100-0	100-33	100-67	100-33
		Wage level (per cent of average wage)	100-0	100-33	100-67	100-33
		Number of children	2	2	2	none
1.	**Gross wage earnings**		18 109	24 085	30 242	24 085
2.	**Standard tax allowances**					
	Basic allowance		3 303	7 958	7 721	7 958
	Married or head of family					
	Dependent children		5 086	5 086	5 086	
	Other dependent family member		2 437			
	Deduction for social security contributions and income taxes		4 002	5 323	6 683	5 323
	Work-related expenses		0	0	0	0
		Total	14 828	18 367	19 491	13 281
3.	**Tax credits or cash transfers included in taxable income**		0	0	0	0
4.	**Central government taxable income (1 - 2 + 3)**		3 281	5 718	10 751	10 804
5.	**Central government income tax liability (exclusive of tax credits)**		525	915	1 720	2 035
6.	**Tax credits**					
	Basic credit					
	Married or head of family					
	Children		0	0	0	0
	Other					
		Total	0	0	0	0
7.	**Central government income tax finally paid (5-6)**		525	915	1 720	2 035
8.	**State and local taxes**		0	0	0	0
9.	**Employees' compulsory social security contributions**					
	Gross earnings		4 002	5 323	6 683	5 323
	Taxable income					
		Total	4 002	5 323	6 683	5 323
10.	**Total payments to general government (7 + 8 + 9)**		4 527	6 238	8 404	7 357
11.	**Cash transfers from general government**					
	For head of family					
	For two children		2 469	1 509	1 124	0
		Total	2 469	1 509	1 124	0
12.	**Take-home pay (1-10+11)**		16 051	19 357	22 962	16 727
13.	**Employer's wage dependent contributions and taxes**		2 916	3 878	4 869	3 878
	Employer's compulsory social security contributions		2 916	3 878	4 869	3 878
	Payroll taxes		0	0	0	0
14.	**Average rates**					
	Income tax		2.9%	3.8%	5.7%	8.4%
	Employees' social security contributions		22.1%	22.1%	22.1%	22.1%
	Total payments less cash transfers		11.4%	19.6%	24.1%	30.5%
	Total tax wedge including employer's social security contributions		23.7%	30.8%	34.6%	40.2%
15.	**Marginal rates**					
	Total payments less cash transfers: Principal earner		34.6%	34.6%	34.6%	43.1%
	Total payments less cash transfers: Spouse		44.7%	22.1%	34.6%	22.1%
	Total tax wedge: Principal earner		43.6%	43.6%	43.6%	51.0%
	Total tax wedge: Spouse		52.4%	32.9%	43.6%	32.9%

The Slovenian currency is the euro (EUR). In 2015, EUR 0.90 was equal to USD 1. In that year, the average worker in Slovenia earned EUR 18 109 (Secretariat estimate).

1. Personal income tax system

1.1. *Central government income tax*

1.1.1. *Tax unit*

The tax unit is the individual.

1.1.2. *Tax allowances*

1.1.2.1. Standard tax reliefs

- A *general (basic) allowance* of EUR 3 302.70 is deductible from income in 2015. For lower income groups an additional general allowance of EUR 3 217.12 is deductible when taxable income is lower than EUR 10 866.37 and of EUR 1 115.94 when taxable income is between EUR 10 866.37 and EUR 12 570.89.
- *Family allowances* are also deductible from the tax base in the same way as for the general allowance. The allowances for 2015 are as follows:
  - EUR 2 436.92 for the first dependent child;
  - EUR 2 649.24 for the second child;
  - EUR 4 418.54 for the third child;
  - EUR 6 187.85 for the fourth child;
  - EUR 7 957.14 for the fifth child;
  - EUR 1 769.30 for the sixth and all additional maintained children relative to the level of relief for the preceding maintained child;
  - EUR 8 830.00 for a dependent child who requires special care;
  - EUR 2 436.92 for any other dependent family member.
- *Relief for social security contributions*: Employee's compulsory contributions for the social insurance system are deductible for income tax purposes.
- *Tax credits*: None for employees.

1.1.2.2. Non-standard tax reliefs applicable to income from employment

- *Additional voluntary pension insurance premiums*: Premiums paid by a resident to the provider of a pension plan based in Slovenia or in another EU Member State according to a pension plan that is approved and entered into a special register in accordance with the pension legislation are deductible from taxable income. In 2015 such deductions are subject to an annual limit of EUR 2 819.09 or a sum equal to 24 % of the employee's contribution for compulsory pension and disability insurance if that is a lower figure.
- *Reimbursement of expenses associated with work*, such as in-work meals, transport to and from work, in-the-field supplements (per diem when an employee works outside his or

her working place) and compensation for being away from home, are exempt subject to statutory conditions and upper limits.

- *Reimbursement of expenses associated with business travel* such as: per diem allowances, transport costs (including the use of the employee's private vehicle for work purposes), and the costs of overnight accommodation, are exempt subject to statutory conditions and upper limits.
- The cost of purchasing and maintaining uniforms and personal protection work equipment defined in special regulations is exempt from income tax.
- *Compensation for the use of an employee's own tools* and other equipment (except private vehicles) necessary for the performance of work at the work place, is exempt up to a level of 2% of the monthly wage or salary of the employee, subject to an upper limit of 2% of the average gross monthly wage (AGMW).
- Long service bonuses, severance pay upon retirement and payments related to accidents, long term sickness and other unexpected events are exempt subject to statutory conditions and upper limits.
- *Severance pay* on redundancy is exempt subject to an upper limit of ten times the AGMW.
- *Compensation for the use of an employee's own possessions and property when working at home* in accordance with statutory regulations is exempt up to a level of 5% of the monthly wage or salary of the employee, subject to an upper limit of 5% of the AGMW.

1.1.3. *Tax schedule*

The tax schedule for 2015 is as follows:

Taxable income (EUR)	Tax rate (%)
Up to 8 021.34	16
8 021.34-18 960.28	27
18 960.28-70 907.20	41
Above 70 907.20	50

1.2. *Regional and local income tax*

There are no regional or local income taxes.

2. Compulsory social security insurance system

The compulsory social security insurance system consists of four schemes as follows:

- pension and disability insurance;
- health insurance;
- unemployment insurance;
- parental leave insurance.

2.1. *Employees' contributions*

The taxable base for social security insurance contributions paid by employees is the total amount of the gross wage or salary including vacation payments, fringe benefits and remuneration of expenses related to work above a certain threshold. The assessment period is the calendar month. Employees contribute an amount as a percentage of their remuneration as follows:

Scheme name	Rate of contribution (%)
Pension insurance	15.50
Health insurance	6.36
Unemployment insurance	0.14
Parental leave insurance	0.10
Total	22.10

2.2. *Employers' contributions*

Social security insurance contributions are also paid by employers on behalf of their employees. The taxable base and the assessment period are the same as for employees' contributions. The employers' contribution rates are as follows:

Scheme name	Rate of contribution (%)
Pension insurance	8.85
Health insurance	7.09
Unemployment insurance	0.06
Parental leave insurance	0.10
Total	16.10

The only change to these rates since 1996 has been the 0.2% increase in the employers' contribution rates for health insurance in 2002.

3. Payroll tax

None.

4. Universal cash transfers

4.1. *Transfers related to marital status*

None.

4.2. *Transfers for dependent children*

On 1.1.2012 the Exercise of Rights to Public Funds Act (ZUPJS-A) entered into force. Regarding to a new act child allowance is a supplementary benefit for maintenance, care and education of children when the family income per family member does not exceed statutorily defined percentage of the average net wage in the previous year.

The new legislation changes family income which is the basis for the income classes from gross family income to net family income. Income includes taxable income and non-taxable income defined by the Personal Income Tax Act as for instance social benefits. Income is defined as gross income plus social benefits received but excluding the normalized cost and actual cost recognized under the law governing income tax, taxes and mandatory social security contributions levied on such income.

The new legislation also reduces the age of a child's entitlement. The right to a child benefit is held only until the child reaches 18 years. Besides, the child benefit is higher for eligible students included in higher secondary education (aged less than 18 years and with an income per family member below the average net wage).

Applications for the allowance are made on an annual basis and the payments are not taxable.

- The amount of the allowance is calculated for each child separately according to the level of net family income per family member as a percentage of the average net wage and the ranking of the child in the family. Each family is assigned to one of 8 income classes on this basis as follows:

Income class	Net family income per family member as a percentage of the average net wage
1	Up to 18%
2	18%-30%
3	30%-36%
4	36%-42%
5	42%-53%
6	53%-64%
7	64%-82%
8	82%-99%

- The relevant income is the average monthly income per family member in the calendar year prior to the claim (or one year previous if the claim is made in the month of January, February or March).
- Each child is allocated in one of 3 ranking levels (the level of payments increases with the ranking level - the lowest for the first child, higher for the second child and the highest for the third and any subsequent child). When a child lives in a one-parent family, the amount of the allowance is increased by 30%. When a pre-school child does not attend kindergarten, the amount of the allowance is increased by 20%.
- The details for the calculation of the net income per family member was prescribed by the Minister, as follows:

All income and receipts, namely net disposable income (after deduction of the normalized cost and actual cost recognized under the law governing income tax, taxes and mandatory social security contributions levied on such income) are taken into account, except those that are designed to cover the specific needs (such as allowance and attendance allowance, a large family, etc...). Property is also taken into account like immovable property, cars and other vehicles, watercraft, etc. Property is assigned a value and then it is calculated the amount of interest that would be received within one year from the value of assets deposited in a bank account in the form of time deposits.

- On 1.6.2012 the Public Finance Balance Act entered into force. Regarding to the Act the amounts of transfers for a children in fifth and sixth income classes are reduced for 10%. Moreover, transfers for children in the seventh and eighth income classes are abolished. This is a temporary measure, which applies up to the year following the year in which economic growth exceeds 2% of gross domestic product.
- The monthly amounts of transfers for a child **from birth to the end of primary school** in a two-parent family according to the Exercise of Rights to Public Funds Act and Public Finance Balance Act were the following for the year 2015:

In 2015, the maximum annual benefit levels for children in a two-parent family were the following:

- EUR 1 371.72 for the first child;
- EUR 1 508.76 for the second child;
- EUR 1 646.16 for the third or subsequent child.

Net family income per family member as a percentage of the average net wage	1st Child	2nd Child	3rd Child
	Monthly (EUR)	Monthly (EUR)	Monthly (EUR)
00	114.31	125.73	137.18
2 171.52	97.73	108.04	118.28
3 619.20	74.48	83.25	91.98
4 343.04	58.75	67.03	75.47
5 066.88	43.24	50.45	57.63
6 393.92	27.40	34.29	41.14
7 720.96	0	0	0

The amounts decline as the level of income per family member increases. The benefit ceases according to the Public Finance Balance Act to be available for families where the average income per member is higher than 64 % of the average net wage for the year 2015.

5. Main changes in tax/benefit system since 2005

- In 2006 the taxation of income of individuals changed from global tax to a kind of a dual income tax system. Active income (from employment, business, basic agriculture and forestry, rents, royalties and other income) is taxed aggregated at progressive rates and taking into account the allowances and deductions; capital income (interest, dividends and capital gains) is taxed at proportionate rates on a scheduler basis.
- In 2007 the number of income tax brackets was reduced from five to three. At the same time, some non-standard tax reliefs for certain expenses and for interest paid on loans for housing were abolished.
- In 2008 additional general allowances were introduced for people on low incomes.
- The payroll tax was phased out at the start of 2009.
- The Exercise of Rights to Public Funds Act entered into force on 1.1.2012 changes family income which is the basis for the income classes from gross family income to net family income, which also includes social benefits received.
- Regarding to the Public Finance Balance Act which entered into force on 1.6.2012, the amounts of transfers for children in fifth and sixth income classes are reduced for 10%. Transfers for children in the seventh and eighth income classes are abolished.
- In 2013 the second bracket in the PIT schedule was broadened according to the Public Finance Balance Act. For the years 2013 and 2014 also the threshold for the third bracket (with the rate 41%) was increased and a new, top bracket with a rate 50% was introduced.
- For the year 2013 the special relief for students was reduced by 25 % compared to the tax relief in 2012 (the tax relief for 2014 amounts to EUR 2 477.03).
- Concerning rental income deriving renting of immovable and movable property a new scheduler principle of taxation was introduced in the year 2013 with proportional rate of 25%. The standardised costs were reduced from 40% to 10% of the rental income.
- The main and most important substantive change for the year 2014 and beyond eliminates the automatic adjustment of tax credits and net annual tax basis in the scale for assessing personal income tax with the growth in consumer prices.
- For the year 2014 were also introduced another amendments to the personal income tax, that is the abolishment of the tax benefits to certain groups of taxpayers (special relief for daily migrants, relief for the residents over 65 years of age).

- In 2014, the amendments to the Law on Parenthood and Family Incomes increased child benefit for a child who lives in a single-parent family, namely, the individual amount of child benefit increased from 10 to 30 percent.
- The scale of assessment for income tax as a temporary measure that applies to 2013 and 2014, with the addition of a fourth class tax rate of 50% was extended for the year 2015.

6. Memorandum items

6.1. *Average gross annual wage earnings calculation*

In Slovenia the gross earnings figures cover wages and salaries paid to individuals in formal employment including payment for overtime. They also include bonus payments and other payments such as pay for annual leave, paid leave up to seven days, public holidays, absences due to sickness for up to 30 days, job training, and slowdown through no fault of the person in formal employment.

The average gross wage earnings figures of all adult workers covering industry sectors B-N are provided by the Statistical Office of the Republic of Slovenia.

6.2. *Employer contributions to private pension and health schemes*

Some employer contributions are made to private health and pension schemes but there is no relevant information available on the amounts that are paid.

2015 parameter values

Ave_earn	18 109	Secretariat estimate					
Ave_earn_1	17 948						
Ave_net_earnfam	12 064						
Basic_al	0	6 519.82					
	10 866.37	4 418.64					
	12 570.89	3 302.70					
Child_al1	2 436.92						
Child_al2	5 086.16						
Child_al3	9 504.70						
Child_al4	15 692.55						
Child_al5	23 649.69						
Depend_al	2 436.92						
Tax_sch	0.16	8 021.34					
	0.27	18 960.28					
	0.41	70 907.20					
	0.50						
SSC_rate1	0.221						
SSC_rate2	0.161						
		Ist child monthly	2nd child monthly	3rd child monthly	1 child-total annual	2 children-total annual	3 children-total annual
Fam_allow_mc	0	114.31	125.73	137.18	1 371.72	2 880.48	4 526.64
	2 171.52	97.73	108.04	118.28	1 172.76	2 469.24	3 888.60
	3 619.20	74.48	83.25	91.98	893.76	1 892.76	2 996.52
	4 343.04	58.75	67.03	75.47	705.00	1 509.36	2 415.00
	5 066.88	43.24	50.45	57.63	518.88	1 124.28	1 815.84
	6 393.92	27.40	34.29	41.14	328.80	740.28	1 233.96
	7 720.96	0.00	0.00	0.00	0.00	0.00	0.00
Fam_allow_spup	0.3						
		Ist child monthly	2nd child monthly	3rd child monthly	1 child-total annual	2 children-total annual	3 children-total annual
Fam_allow_sp	0	148.60	163.45	178.33	1 783.24	3 744.62	5 884.63
	2 171.52	127.05	140.45	153.76	1 524.59	3 210.01	5 055.18
	3 619.20	96.82	108.23	119.57	1 161.89	2 460.59	3 895.48
	4 343.04	76.38	87.14	98.11	916.50	1 962.17	3 139.50
	5 066.88	56.21	65.59	74.92	674.54	1 461.56	2 360.59
	6 393.92	35.62	44.58	53.48	427.44	962.36	1 604.15
	7 720.96	0.00	0.00	0.00	0.00	0.00	0.00
numdays	365						

2015 tax equations

	Line in country table and intermediate steps	Variable name	Range	Equation
1.	Earnings			
	Current year	earn		
	Net earnings Year-1	net_earn_1		
2.	Allowances:			
	Principal	tax_al_princ	P	VLOOKUP(earn;Basic_al;2)+SSC+IF(children=0,0,IF(children=1,child_al1,IF(children=2,child_al2,child_al3)+IF(Married=0,0,IF(S_earn=0,Depend_al,0))
	Spouse	Tax_al_ spouse	S	MINA(VLOOKUP(earn;Basic_al;2), earn)+SSC
3.	Credits in taxable income	taxbl_cr	B	0
4.	CG taxable income	tax_inc	B	Positive(earn-tax_al)
5.	CG tax before credits	CG_tax_excl	B	Tax(tax_inc, tax_sch)
6.	Tax credits (nonwastable)	Tax_cr	B	0
7.	CG tax	CG_tax	B	CG_tax_excl
8.	State and local taxes	local_tax	B	0
9.	Employees' soc security	SSC	B	earn* SSC_rate1
11.	Cash transfers	cash_trans	J	IF(Children=0,0;VLOOKUP((net_earn_1)/(1+married+children),IF(Married=0;Fam_allow_sp,Fam_allow_mc),IF(Children=1,5,IF(Children=2,6,7))))
13.	Employer's wage dependent contributions and taxes			
	Employer's soc security	SSC_empr	B	earn*SSC_rate2

Key to range of equation B calculated separately for both principal earner and spouse P calculated for principal only (value taken as 0 for spouse calculation) J calculated once only on a joint basis.

Spain

This chapter includes data on the income taxes paid by workers, their social security contributions, the family benefits they receive in the form of cash transfers as well as the social security contributions and payroll taxes paid by their employers. Results reported include the marginal and average tax burden for eight different family types.

Methodological information is available for personal income tax systems, compulsory social security contributions to schemes operated within the government sector, universal cash transfers as well as recent changes in the tax/benefit system. The methodology also includes the parameter values and tax equations underlying the data.

Spain 2015

The tax/benefit position of a single persons

		Wage level (per cent of average wage)	67	100	167	67
		Number of children	none	none	none	2
1.	**Gross wage earnings**		17 594	26 259	43 853	17 594
2.	**Standard tax allowances:**					
	Basic allowance					
	Married or head of family		0	0	0	2 150
	Dependent children					
	Deduction for social security contributions and income taxes		1 117	1 667	2 748	1 117
	Work-related expenses		2 000	2 000	2 000	2 000
	Other					
		Total	3 117	3 667	4 748	5 267
3.	**Tax credits or cash transfers included in taxable income**		0	0	0	0
4.	**Central and state government taxable income (1 - 2 + 3)**		14 477	22 592	39 106	12 327
5.	**Central and state government income tax liability (exclusive of tax credits)**		2 924	5 056	10 476	2 404
6.	**Central and state government tax credits**					
	Basic credit		1 082	1 082	1 082	3 277
	Married or head of family					
	Children					
	Other					
		Total	1 082	1 082	1 082	3 277
7.	**Central government income tax finally paid (5-6)**		899	1 944	4 600	- 1 041
8.	**State and local taxes**		943	2 030	4 793	168
9.	**Employees' compulsory social security contributions**					
	Gross earnings		1 117	1 667	2 748	1 117
	Taxable income					
		Total	1 117	1 667	2 748	1 117
10.	**Total payments to general government (7 + 8 + 9)**		2 959	5 641	12 141	244
11.	**Cash transfers from general government**					
	For head of family					
	For two children		0	0	0	0
		Total	0	0	0	0
12.	**Take-home pay (1-10+11)**		14 635	20 618	31 712	17 350
13.	**Employer's compulsory social security contributions**		5 261	7 852	12 938	5 261
14.	**Average rates**					
	Income tax		10.5%	15.1%	21.4%	-5.0%
	Employees' social security contributions		6.35%	6.35%	6.27%	6.35%
	Total payments less cash transfers		16.8%	21.5%	27.7%	1.4%
	Total tax wedge including employer's social security contributions		36.0%	39.6%	44.2%	24.1%
15.	**Marginal rates**					
	Total payments less cash transfers: Principal earner		29.3%	34.9%	38.0%	24.6%
	Total payments less cash transfers: Spouse		n.a.	n.a.	n.a.	n.a.
	Total tax wedge: Principal earner		45.6%	49.9%	38.0%	42.0%
	Total tax wedge: Spouse		n.a.	n.a.	n.a.	n.a.

Spain 2015

The tax/benefit position of married couples

			100-0	100-33	100-67	100-33
		Wage level (per cent of average wage)	100-0	100-33	100-67	100-33
		Number of children	2	2	2	none
1.	**Gross wage earnings**		26 259	34 925	43 853	34 925
2.	**Standard tax allowances**					
	Basic allowance					
	Married or head of family		3 400	0	0	0
	Dependent children					
	Deduction for social security contributions and income taxes		1 667	2 218	2 785	2 218
	Work-related expenses		2 000	7 700	4 000	7 700
	Other					
		Total	7 067	9 918	6 785	9 918
3.	**Tax credits or cash transfers included in taxable income**		0	0	0	0
4.	**Central and state government taxable income (1 - 2 + 3)**		19 192	25 007	37 069	25 007
5.	**Central and state government income tax liability (exclusive of tax credits)**		4 080	5 527	7 980	5 527
6.	**Central and state government tax credits**					
	Basic credit		2 077	2 050	3 159	1 553
	Married or head of family					
	Children					
	Other					
		Total	2 077	2 050	3 159	1 553
7.	**Central government income tax finally paid (5-6)**		980	1 702	2 358	1 944
8.	**State and local taxes**		1 023	1 775	2 463	2 030
9.	**Employees' compulsory social security contributions**					
	Gross earnings		1 667	2 218	2 785	2 218
	Taxable income					
		Total	1 667	2 218	2 785	2 218
10.	**Total payments to general government (7 + 8 + 9)**		3 670	5 694	7 606	6 192
11.	**Cash transfers from general government**					
	For head of family					
	For two children		0	0	0	0
		Total	0	0	0	0
12.	**Take-home pay (1-10+11)**		22 589	29 231	36 247	28 734
13.	**Employer's compulsory social security contributions**		7 852	10 443	13 112	10 443
14.	**Average rates**					
	Income tax		7.6%	10.0%	11.0%	11.4%
	Employees' social security contributions		6.35%	6.35%	6.35%	6.35%
	Total payments less cash transfers		14.0%	16.3%	17.3%	17.7%
	Total tax wedge including employer's social security contributions		33.8%	35.6%	36.4%	36.7%
15.	**Marginal rates**					
	Total payments less cash transfers: Principal earner		29.3%	34.9%	34.9%	34.9%
	Total payments less cash transfers: Spouse		23.4%	6.3%	29.3%	6.3%
	Total tax wedge: Principal earner		45.6%	49.9%	49.9%	49.9%
	Total tax wedge: Spouse		41.0%	27.9%	45.6%	27.9%

The national currency is the Euro (EUR). In 2015, EUR 0.90 was equal to USD 1. In that year the average worker earned EUR 26 259 (Secretariat estimate).

1. Personal income tax system

1.1. Central government income tax

1.1.1. Tax unit

As a general rule, the tax unit is the individual. Nevertheless, families have the options of being taxed:

- As married couples filing jointly on the combined income of both spouses and dependents.
- As heads of households (only unmarried or separated individuals with dependents).

1.1.2. Tax allowances and tax credits

1.1.2.1. Standard reliefs

- *Basic reliefs*: Married couples filing jointly may claim an allowance of EUR 3 400. This figure amounts to EUR 2 150 for heads of households.
- *Maternity tax credit*: a non-wastable tax credit addressed to working females with children under 3 years of age up to EUR 1 200.
- *Large families(3 or more children) or dependent family members with disabilities tax credits*: this additional non-wastable tax credit (up to EUR 1 200) also may be claimed (within the Taxing Wages framework) by single-parent households with two children .
- *Relief for social security contributions*: All social security payments are fully deductible.
- *Other expenses allowance*: up to EUR 2 000, which may be increased by the same amount in case of accepting a job in a different location implying a change of residence.
- *Employment related* allowance: Net employment income (gross income – employee social security contributions) may be reduced according to the following rules:
  - Taxpayers with net employment income equal or less than EUR 11 250: EUR 3 700.
  - Taxpayers with a net employment income between EUR 11 250.01 and EUR 14 450: EUR 3 700 less the result of multiplying by 1.15625 the difference between net employment income and EUR 11 250.
- *Disabled workers allowance*: an allowance of EUR 3 264 for disabled salary earners. Those with reduced mobility may claim an augmented allowance of EUR 7 242.

As a result of the application of the above rules, net income cannot become negative.

1.1.2.2. Main non-standard reliefs applicable to an AW

- *Contributions to Pension Plans*. Contributions made by each member of the household may reduce taxable income up to the lower of the following amounts:
  - 30% of net income;
  - EUR 8 000.

Moreover, those households whose second earner has net labour income below EUR 8 000 may reduce taxable income up to a maximum of EUR 2 500 on a yearly basis if the principal earner contributes to a Pension Fund for the spouse.

- *Relief for subscriptions paid in respect of membership* of a trade union and business or professional associations (last item is limited to mandatory membership) up to EUR 500.
- *Relief for expenses made for the legal defence* of the taxpayer for labour-related conflicts up to a maximum limit of EUR 300.

Other non-standard reliefs provided as deductions are:

- *Investment in the acquisition and rehabilitation of own-housing*: As a general rule, up to 1 January 2013, taxpayers were allowed to deduct from their tax liability 15% of the investment made during the year, up to a maximum of EUR 9 040.
- Furthermore, disabled taxpayers were also allowed to deduct from their tax liability 20% of the investment expenses incurred in the repairs carried out for housing adaptation to the handicapped personal needs according up to a maximum of EUR 12 080.
- With effect from 1 January 2013, the above tax credit has been abolished. Nevertheless, grandfathering rules apply for those taxpayers who before 1 January 2013 had acquired their main residence; had made some payments for it to be built; had made some payments for restoration/enlargement of their main residence or had made some payments to carry out the adaptation of the main residence of disabled people. However, in the latter two cases the works performed should be completed before 1 January 2017. For these taxpayers, the above tax credit can still be applied in accordance with the rules set up above.
- *Gifts*: 50% of the amounts (below EUR 150) donated to the State (its different levels) public universities and othe qualifying institutions. For larger gifts, 27.5% on the excess, which may be increased to 32.5% when meeting certain conditions and 10% of the amount donated non-qualifying foundations or associations.
- *Investments and expenses in goods of cultural interest:* 15% of the amounts granted to the importation, restoration, exhibition, etc. of certain goods listed in the General Register of Goods of Cultural Interest.

Each of these last two amounts cannot exceed 10% of taxable income.

1.1.2.3. Exempt Income

- The base amount is EUR 5 550 per taxpayer. The same amount is granted for family units filing jointly. Taxpayers aged over 65 years may add EUR 1 250 to the former amount. Those aged over 75 years may claim additionally EUR 1 400.
- Dependent children (under 25 years): EUR 2 400 for the first dependent child; EUR 2 700 for the second one; EUR 4 000 for the third, and EUR 4 500 for any additional child.
- Child care allowance: an additional allowance of EUR 2 800 for each of the above dependent children under 3 years of age.
- In case of disabled workers and additional amount of EUR 3 000 also applies. In case of great disability prior amount reaches EUR 9 000.

Child allowances have to be shared equally between spouses when they file separately.

1.1.3. *Tax schedule*

General rates of tax – resident individuals:

Taxable income (EUR)	Tax at the lower limit (EUR)	Tax rate on taxable income in excess of the lower limit (%)
0-12 450	0	9.50
12 450-20 200	1 182.75	12.00
20 200-34 000	2 112.75	15.00
34 000-60 000	4 182.75	18.50
Over 60 000	8 992.75	22.50

1.2. *State and local income taxes*

Regional rates of tax – resident individuals: (in case that Regional Governments do not exercise its rights to set their own tax rates).

Taxable income (EUR)	Tax at the lower limit (EUR)	Tax rate on taxable income in excess of the lower limit (%)
0-12 450	0	10.00
12 450-20 200	1 245.00	12.50
20 200-34 000	2 213.75	15.50
34 000-60 000	4 352.75	19.50
Over 60 000	9 422.75	23.50

2. Compulsory social security contributions to schemes operated within the government sector

Social Security contributions are assessed on the basis of employees' gross earnings taking into account certain ceilings of gross employment income. In 2015, these ceilings are:

- Lower ceiling: EUR 9 079.20
- Upper Ceiling: EUR 43 272.

These ceilings are based on a full-time job. For part-time workers, ceilings are proportional to the real hours worked (the tax equations used for this Report do not take into account the lower ceiling).

2.1. *Employees' contributions*

- Old age pension/sickness and disability 4.7%
- Unemployment 1.55%
- Professional Training 0.1%

2.2. *Employers' contributions*

- Old age pension/sickness and disability 23.6%
- Unemployment/Work injuries 5.50%
- Wages fund 0.2%
- Professional Training 0.6%

3. Universal cash transfers

3.1. *Transfers related to marital status*

None.

3.2. *Transfers for dependent children*

EUR 291 for 1-child families with annual gross earnings below EUR 11 547.96; the child transfer decreases with income between EUR 11 547.96 and EUR 11 814.71; the value is 0 for gross earnings exceeding EUR 11 814.71. EUR 582 for families with 2 children with annual gross earnings below EUR 13 280.15; the child transfer decreases with income between EUR 13 280.15 and EUR 13 813.65; the value is 0 for gross earnings exceeding EUR 13 813.65.

4. Main changes in tax/benefit systems in 2015

In 2015 the Spanish Government carried out a tax reform. Main PIT measures affecting earned income perceived by PIT taxpayers have been described above. Nevertheless, following SSC concessions also apply:

- Aimed to foster new indefinite hirings, since 2 March 2014 employers hiring new workers under a non-fixed term contract (contracts between 25 February and 31 December 2014) may also apply a flat social security contribution (covering general risks). The flat contribution rate is: EUR 100 monthly contribution for full-time hirings (lower contribution also applies for part-time newcomers). The flat contribution will apply for a 24-month period.
- Furthermore, since 1 March 2015 employers hiring new staff under a non-fixed term contract may claim a partial exemption on their SSC for the first EUR 500 of monthly salaries paid to workers. This SSC concession will apply for a 24-month period

5. Memorandum items

5.1. *Identification of an AW and calculation of earnings*

Refer to the information provided in the Annex of this Report.

2015 parameter values

Average earnings/yr	Ave_earn	26 259	Secretariat estimate	
Work related allowance	wr_rate	1.15625		
	wr_lim_max	14 450		
	wr_lim_min	11 250		
	wr_allow_max	3 700		
Other deductible expenses	oth_ded_exp	2 000		
Personal & family exempt income	Per_fam_exempt_inc	5 550		
Joint taxation allowance	Joint_tax_allow_fam1	3 400		
	Joint_tax_allow_fam2	2 150		
Dependent children	dep_child	2 400		
	dep_child2	2 700		
	dep_child3	4 000		
	dep_child4	4 500		
Single parent tax credit (chld>=2)	SP_tax_credit	1 200		
Tax Schedule	tax_sch_sg	0	0	9.50%
		12 450	1 182.75	12.00%
		20 200	2 112.75	15.00%
		34 000	4 182.75	18.50%
		60 000	8 992.75	22.50%
	tax_sch_sa	0	0	10.00%
		12 450	1 245	12.50%
		20 200	2 213.75	15.50%
		34 000	4 352.75	19.50%
		60 000	9 422.75	23.50%
Social security contributions				
Employee:				
Pension	pension_rate	0.047		
Unemployment	unemp_rate	0.0155		
Other	oth_rate	0.001		
Employer				
Pension	pension_empr	0.236		
Unemployment	unemp_empr	0.055		
Other	oth_empr	0.008		
Ceiling and Floor	min_lim	0	9 079.2	
	top_lim	43 272		
Child benefit	SS_child_benefit	291		
	SS_child_table	1	11 547.96	11 814.71
		2	13 280.15	13 813.65
		3	17 380.39	18 180.64
		4	20 195.53	21 262.53
		5	23 010.67	24 344.42

2015 tax equations

The functions which are used in the equations (Taper, MIN, Tax etc) are described in the technical note about tax equations. Variable names are defined in the table of parameters above, within the equations table, or are the standard variables "married" and "children". A reference to a variable with the affix "_total" indicates the sum of the relevant variable values for the principal and spouse. And the affixes "_princ" and "_sp" indicate the value for the principal and spouse, respectively. Equations for a single person are as shown for the principal, with "_sp" values taken as 0.

	Line in country table and intermediate steps	Variable name	Range	Equation
1.	Earnings	earn	B	for individual taxation: earn=earn_princ, or earn=earn_sp for joint (family) taxation: earn=earn_princ+earn_sp
2.	Allowances:			
	Work related, individual	work_ind	B	IF(earn-SSC<=wr_lim_min,wr_allow_max+oth_ded_exp,IF(earn-SSC<=wr_lim_max,wr_allow_max-wr_rate*((earn-SSC)-(wr_lim_min))+oth_ded_exp,oth_ded_exp))
	Work related, family	work_fam	J	IF(AND(earn_sp=0,married=0,children=0),0,IF(earn_total-SSC_fam<=wr_lim_min, wr_allow_max+oth_ded_exp,IF(earn_total-SSC_fam=wr_lim_max,wr_allow_max-wr_rate*((earn_total-SSC_fam)-(wr_lim_min))+oth_ded_exp,oth_ded_exp)))
	Joint taxation allowance	joint_allow_fam	J	IF(AND(Married=0,Children=0),0,IF(AND(Married=0,Children>0),joint_tax_allow_fam2,joint_tax_allow_fam1))
	Personal and family exempt income, individual	ex_inc_ind	B	per_fam_exempt_inc
	Personal and family exempt income, family	ex_inc_fam	J	IF(AND(Married=0,Children=0),0,per_fam_exempt_inc)
	Children exempt income, individual	child_ex_inc_ind	P	IF(earn_sp=0, (children>0)*(dep_child+(children>1)*dep_child2+(children>2)*dep_child3+(children>3)*(children-3)*dep_child4), (children>0)*(dep_child+(children>1)*dep_child2+(children>2)*dep_child3+(children>3)*(children-3)*dep_child4)/2)
			S	IF(earn_sp=0, 0, (children>0)*(dep_child+(children>1)*dep_child2+(children>2)*dep_child3+(children>3)*(children-3)*dep_child4)/2)
	Children exempt income, family	child_ex_inc_fam	J	(children>0)*(dep_child+(children>1)*dep_child2+(children>2)*dep_child3+(children>3)*(children-3)*dep_child4)
3.	Credits in taxable income	taxbl_cr	B, J	0
4.	CG taxable income	tax_inc	B, J	IF(AND(Married=0, Children=0), tax_inc_princ, MINA(tax_inc_princ+tax_inc_sp, tax_inc_fam))
		tax_inc_ind	B	Positive(earn-(work_ind+SSC))
		tax_inc_fam	J	IF(AND(Married=0, Children), 0, Positive(earn-(work_fam+joint_allow_fam+SSC_princ+SSC_sp)))
5.	CG tax before credits	CG_tax_ind_excl	B	MAXA(0, VLOOKUP(tax_inc_ind, tax_sch_sg, 2)+(tax_inc_ind-VLOOKUP(tax_inc_ind, tax_sch_sg, 1))*VLOOKUP(tax_inc_ind, tax_sch_sg, 3))
		CG_tax_fam_excl	J	MAXA(0, VLOOKUP(tax_inc_fam, tax_sch_sg, 2)+(tax_inc_fam-VLOOKUP(tax_inc_fam, tax_sch_sg, 1))*VLOOKUP(tax_inc_fam, tax_sch_sg, 3))
6.	CG tax credits :	CG_tax_cr_ind	B	MAXA(0,VLOOKUP(ex_inc_ind+child_ex_inc_ind,tax_sch_sg,2)+ ((ex_inc_ind+child_ex_inc_ind)-VLOOKUP(ex_inc_ind+child_ex_inc_ind,tax_sch_sg,1))*VLOOKUP(ex_inc_ind+child_ex_inc_ind,tax_sch_sg,3)+IF(AND(earn>0,married=0,children>=2),MIN(SP_tax_credit,(SSC+SSC_empr)),0)
		CG_tax_cr_fam	J	MAXA(0,VLOOKUP(ex_inc_fam+child_ex_inc_fam,tax_sch_sg,2)+ ((ex_inc_fam+child_ex_inc_fam)-VLOOKUP(ex_inc_fam+child_ex_inc_fam,tax_sch_sg,1))*VLOOKUP(ex_inc_fam+child_ex_inc_fam,tax_sch_sg,3)+ IF(AND(earn_total>0,married=0,children>=2),MIN(SP_tax_credit,(SSC_fam+SSC_empr_fam)),0)
7.	CG tax	CG_tax_ind	B	CG_tax_ind_excl-CG_tax_cr_ind
		CG_tax_fam	J	CG_tax_fam_excl-CG_tax_cr_fam
8.	State and local tax before credits	local_tax_ind_excl	B	MAXA(0, VLOOKUP(tax_inc_ind, tax_sch_sa, 2)+(tax_inc_ind-VLOOKUP(tax_inc_ind, tax_sch_sa, 1))*VLOOKUP(tax_inc_ind, tax_sch_sa, 3))

	Line in country table and intermediate steps	Variable name	Range	Equation
		local_tax_fam_excl	J	MAXA(0, VLOOKUP(tax_inc_fam, tax_sch_sa, 2)+(tax_inc_fam-VLOOKUP(tax_inc_fam, tax_sch_sa, 1))*VLOOKUP(tax_inc_fam, tax_sch_sa, 3))
	local tax credits	local_tax_cr_ind	B	MAXA(0,VLOOKUP(ex_inc_ind+child_ex_inc_ind,tax_sch_sa,2)+ ((ex_inc_ind+child_ex_inc_ind)-VLOOKUP(ex_inc_ind+child_ex_inc_ind,tax_sch_sa,1))*VLOOKUP(ex_inc_ind+child_ex_inc_ind,tax_sch_sa,3))
		local_tax_cr_fam	J	MAXA(0,VLOOKUP(ex_inc_fam+child_ex_inc_fam,tax_sch_sa,2)+ ((ex_inc_fam+child_ex_inc_fam)-VLOOKUP(ex_inc_fam+child_ex_inc_fam,tax_sch_sa,1))*VLOOKUP(ex_inc_fam+child_ex_inc_fam,tax_sch_sa,3))
	State and local tax	local_tax_ind	B	Positive(local_tax_ind_excl-local_tax_cr_ind)
		local_tax_fam	J	Positive(local_tax_fam_excl-local_tax_cr_fam)
9.	Employees' soc security	SSC	B	IF(AND(earn>0, earn<=min_lim), min_lim*(pension_rate+unemp_rate+oth_rate), IF(earn>=top_lim, top_lim*(pension_rate+unemp_rate+oth_rate), earn* (pension_rate+unemp_rate+oth_rate)))
		SSC_fam	J	SSC_princ+SSC_sp
11.	Cash transfers	Child_transf		IF(Children=0,0,IF(earn<=VLOOKUP(Children, SS_child_table,2),SS_child_benefit*Children, IF(earn<=VLOOKUP(Children, SS_child_table, 3), VLOOKUP (Children, SS_child_table, 3)-earn, 0)))
13.	Employer's SSC	SSC_empr		IF(AND(earn>0, earn<=min_lim), min_lim*(pension_empr+unemp_empr+ oth_umpr), IF(earn>=top_lim, top_lim*(pension_empr+unemp_empr+oth_empr), earn*(pension_empr+unemp_empr+oth_empr)))

Key to range of equation B calculated separately for both principal earner and spouse P calculated for principal only S calculated for spouse only J calculated once only on a joint basis.

Sweden

This chapter includes data on the income taxes paid by workers, their social security contributions, the family benefits they receive in the form of cash transfers as well as the social security contributions and payroll taxes paid by their employers. Results reported include the marginal and average tax burden for eight different family types.

Methodological information is available for personal income tax systems, compulsory social security contributions to schemes operated within the government sector, universal cash transfers as well as recent changes in the tax/benefit system. The methodology also includes the parameter values and tax equations underlying the data.

Sweden 2015

The tax/benefit position of single persons

		Wage level (per cent of average wage)	67	100	167	67
		Number of children	none	none	none	2
1.	**Gross wage earnings**		282 314	421 364	703 678	282 314
2.	**Standard tax allowances**					
	Basic allowance		19 900	13 100	13 100	19 900
	Married or head of family					
	Dependent children					
	Deduction for social security contributions and income taxes		0	0	0	0
	Work-related expenses					
	Other					
		Total	19 900	13 100	13 100	19 900
3.	**Tax credits or cash transfers included in taxable income**		0	0	0	0
4.	**Central government taxable income (1 - 2 + 3)**		262 400	408 200	690 500	262 400
5.	**Central government income tax liability (exclusive of tax credits)**		0	0	55 780	0
6.	**Tax credits**					
	Basic credit					
	Married or head of family					
	Children					
	Other		41 361	55 986	59 286	41 361
		Total	41 361	55 986	59 286	41 361
7.	**Central government income tax finally paid (5-6)**		- 41 361	- 55 986	- 3 506	- 41 361
8.	**State and local taxes**		83 941	130 583	220 890	83 941
9.	**Employees' compulsory social security contributions**					
	Gross earnings		19 800	29 500	32 800	19 800
	Taxable income					
		Total	19 800	29 500	32 800	19 800
10.	**Total payments to general government (7 + 8 + 9)**		62 380	104 097	250 184	62 380
11.	**Cash transfers from general government**					
	For head of family					
	For two children		0	0	0	27 000
		Total	0	0	0	27 000
12.	**Take-home pay (1-10+11)**		219 934	317 267	453 494	246 934
13.	**Employer's wage dependent contributions and taxes**					
	Employer's compulsory social security contributions		60 049	89 624	149 672	60 049
	payroll taxes		28 654	42 768	71 423	28 654
		Total	88 703	132 392	221 095	88 703
14.	**Average rates**					
	Income tax		15.1%	17.7%	30.9%	15.1%
	Employees' social security contributions		7.0%	7.0%	4.7%	7.0%
	Total payments less cash transfers		22.1%	24.7%	35.6%	12.5%
	Total tax wedge including employer's social security contributions		40.7%	42.7%	51.0%	33.4%
15.	**Marginal rates**					
	Total payments less cash transfers: Principal earner		28.4%	32.0%	57.0%	28.4%
	Total payments less cash transfers: Spouse		n.a.	n.a.	n.a.	n.a.
	Total tax wedge: Principal earner		45.5%	48.2%	67.3%	45.5%
	Total tax wedge: Spouse		n.a.	n.a.	n.a.	n.a.

Sweden 2015

The tax/benefit position of married couples

	Wage level (per cent of average wage)	100-0	100-33	100-67	100-33
	Number of children	2	2	2	none
1.	**Gross wage earnings**	421 364	560 414	703 678	560 414
2.	**Standard tax allowances:**				
	Basic allowance	13 100	47 400	33 000	47 400
	Married or head of family				
	Dependent children				
	Deduction for social security contributions and income taxes	0	0	0	0
	Work-related expenses				
	Other				
	Total	13 100	47 400	33 000	47 400
3.	**Tax credits or cash transfers included in taxable income**	0	0	0	0
4.	**Central government taxable income (1 - 2 + 3)**	408 200	512 900	670 600	512 900
5.	**Central government income tax liability (exclusive of tax credits)**	0	0	0	0
6.	**Tax credits**				
	Basic credit				
	Married or head of family				
	Children				
	Other	55 986	77 552	97 347	77 552
	Total	55 986	77 552	97 347	77 552
7.	**Central government income tax finally paid (5-6)**	- 55 986	- 77 552	- 97 347	- 77 552
8.	**State and local taxes**	130 583	164 076	214 524	164 076
9.	**Employees' compulsory social security contributions**				
	Gross earnings	29 500	39 200	49 300	39 200
	Taxable income				
	Total	29 500	39 200	49 300	39 200
10.	**Total payments to general government (7 + 8 + 9)**	104 097	125 724	166 477	125 724
11.	**Cash transfers from general government**				
	For head of family				
	For two children	27 000	27 000	27 000	0
	Total	27 000	27 000	27 000	0
12.	**Take-home pay (1-10+11)**	344 267	461 690	564 201	434 690
13.	**Employer's wage dependent contributions and taxes**				
	Employer's compulsory social security contributions	89 624	119 200	149 673	119 200
	payroll taxes	42 768	56 881	71 422	56 881
	Total	132 392	176 081	221 095	176 081
14.	**Average rates**				
	Income tax	17.7%	15.4%	16.7%	15.4%
	Employees' social security contributions	7.0%	7.0%	7.0%	7.0%
	Total payments less cash transfers	18.3%	17.6%	19.8%	22.4%
	Total tax wedge including employer's social security contributions	37.8%	37.3%	39.0%	41.0%
15.	**Marginal rates**				
	Total payments less cash transfers: Principal earner	32.0%	32.0%	32.0%	32.0%
	Total payments less cash transfers: Spouse	15.6%	28.4%	28.4%	28.4%
	Total tax wedge: Principal earner	48.2%	48.2%	48.2%	48.2%
	Total tax wedge: Spouse	35.8%	45.5%	45.5%	45.5%

The national currency is the Swedish Kronor (SEK). In 2015, SEK 8.43 was equal to USD 1. In that year, the average worker earned SEK 421 364 (Secretariat estimate).

1. Personal income tax systems

1.1. Central government income taxes

1.1.1. Tax unit

Spouses are taxed separately.

1.1.2. Tax allowances and tax credits

1.1.2.1. Standard reliefs

- *Basic reliefs*: A basic allowance is given for assessed earned income and varies between SEK 13 100 and SEK 34 300, depending on income. When individuals pay central government income tax, the basic allowance is at its lowest level, which equals SEK 13 100. The basic allowance depends on the assessed earned income and the basic amount, which equals SEK 44 500 in 2015.

Assessed-earned- income (SEK) Relative to Basic Amount (BA)	Share of BA at lower bracket	For exceeding income
-0.99	0.423	
0.99-2.72	0.423	+0.2
2.72-3.11	0.77	
3.11-7.88	0.77	-0.1
7.88-	0.293	

- *Standard marital status reliefs*: None.
- *Relief(s) for children*: None.
- *Work-related expenses*: None.
- *Other*: None.

1.1.2.2. Main non-standard tax reliefs applicable to an AW

- Interest on qualifying loans: Interest payments are offset against capital income. The resulting net capital income is the tax base. A tax credit is given in the case of negative capital income.
- Contributions to pensions, life insurance, superannuation schemes: A deduction of maximum SEK 1 800 can be claimed for premiums paid to private pension arrangements. Medical expenses: None.
- Other allowances are given for:
  - the amount of commuting expenses exceeding SEK 10 000;
  - other types of work-related expenses exceeding SEK 5 000; examples are the costs of tools, work-related phone calls using the taxpayer's private telephone;

- increased living expenses while on business trips, e.g. such as the use of a private car if these costs are not reimbursed by the employer;
- double housing expenses due to *temporary* work at other geographical locations (too far from home for commuting), or if the family for some reason can't move, even if the job is of a *permanent* nature;
- travelling expenses for travelling home if the taxpayer works in another place than his/her place of residence.

1.1.3. *Tax schedule*

Taxable Income (SEK)	Tax (SEK) at lower bracket	For exceeding income, %
0-430 200	0	0
430 200-616 100	0	20
over 616 100	37 180	25

1.1.4. *Tax credits*

A tax credit equal to 100% of the compulsory social security contributions paid by the employee is granted.

For a person aged 65 or less, an annual Earned Income Tax Credit (EITC) worth up to SEK 26 486 at the average local tax rate is granted on labour income. For those older than 65, a higher credit worth up to SEK 30 000 is granted. For a person aged 65 or less the EITC is calculated as follows: EITC = (Special Amount – Basic Allowance) * local tax rate. For those older than 65 a simplified EITC was introduced in 2009 so that it is no longer connected to the local tax rate, the basic allowance or the basic amount. The Basic Allowance is determined in Section 1.121; the local tax rate is discussed in Section 1.2. The Basic Amount (BA) in 2015 is SEK 44 500. The Special Amount is based on the taxpayer's (gross) earned income.

For taxpayers younger than 65, the Special Amount is calculated as follows:

Earned Income (EI)	Special Amount
-0.91 BA	EI
0.91 BA-2.94 BA	0.91 BA + 0.332 * (EI-0.91 BA)
2.94 BA-8.08 BA	1.584 BA + 0.111 * (EI-2.94 BA)
8.08 BA-	2.155 BA

BA = SEK 44 500

For taxpayers older than 65, the EITC is calculated differently:

Earned Income (EI)	EITC
-100 000 SEK	0.2*EI
100 001-300 000 SEK	15 000 SEK + 0.05*EI
300 001 SEK-	30 000 SEK

1.2. *Local government income taxes*

1.2.1. *General description of the systems*

Sweden has both a central government and a local government personal income tax. They are completely coordinated in the assessment process and refer to the same period, i.e. the income year coincides with the calendar year.

1.2.2. Tax base

The tax base is the same as for the central government income tax. The basic allowance for individuals paying local government tax varies between SEK 13 100 and SEK 34 300; it depends on the taxpayer's income. For a taxpayer earning the AW, this basic allowance amounts to SEK 13 100 (based on an AW equal to SEK 407 974 – subject to revision with the AW).

1.2.3. Tax rates

The local government personal income tax is proportional and differs between municipalities. The average rate amounts to 31.99% in 2015, with the maximum and minimum rates being 34.70% and 29.19%, respectively.

2. Compulsory social security contributions to schemes operated within the government sector

2.1. Employees' contributions

A general pension contribution of 7% of personal income is paid by employees and the self-employed when income is equal to or greater than 42.3% of the basic amount underlying the basic allowance (see Section 1.121). The contribution cannot exceed SEK 32 800 since the general pension contributions are not paid for income over SEK 468 900 (= 8.07*58 100). The employees' contribution is offset with a tax credit.

2.2. Employers' contributions

The employers' contributions are calculated as a percentage of the total sum of salaries and benefits in a year. For the self-employed, the base is net business income. The rates for 2015 are listed below.

Program	Employer (%)	Self-employed (%)
Retirement pension	10.21	10.21
Survivor's pension	1.17	1.17
Parental insurance	2.60	2.60
Health insurance	4.35	4.44
Labour market	2.64	0.10
Occupational health	0.30	0.30
General wage tax	10.15	10.15
Total	31.42	28.97

In certain regions, a reduction of 10% of the base, maximum SEK 7 100 per month, is granted (SEK 18 000 per year for self-employed) (it is not included in the calculations underlying this Report). For employees aged under 25 a reduced SSC rate of 25.46% is applied (23.69% for self-employed). For employees who are over 65 years old and born after 1937 only the retirement pension contribution (10.21%) is applicable. For persons born in 1937 or earlier no employers' social security contributions are applied. On premiums for occupational pensions paid by the employer a reduced SSC rate (24.26%) is applied.

For self-employed a general reduction of 7.5% on the SSC is applicable if the income exceeds SEK 40 000 per year. The maximal reduction is SEK 15 000 per year.

3. Universal cash transfers

3.1. *Transfers related to marital status*

None.

3.2. *Transfers for dependent children*

The transfers are tax exempt and independent of the parents' income. The transfers for each child are as follows:

First child	12 600
Second child	14 400
Third child	18 048
Fourth child	24 720
Fifth and subsequent child	27 600

4. Main changes in tax/benefit systems since 1998

A tax credit of SEK 1 320 was introduced for low- and average income earners in 1999. The credit is reduced by 1.2% of taxable income above SEK 135 000. This reduction was abolished in 2003 and was replaced by an increase in the basic allowance.

A tax credit of 25% of the social security contribution paid by employees and the self-employed was introduced in 2000. The tax credit has been gradually increased to 100% in 2006.

In 2004, a special tax credit equal to SEK 200 was provided for the statutory minimum local income tax. The special tax credit was abolished in 2005 as was the statutory minimum state income tax (a lump sum tax) of SEK 200. The central government income tax bracket is indexed with the consumer price index plus 2%. However, in 2004, 2005 and 2006 the central government income tax bracket was restricted to be indexed with the consumer price index plus 1%. In order to reduce the number of people paying the central income tax, there was an additional increase of the tax bracket in 2009.

The child allowance was raised by SEK 1 200 per year in 2000, 2001, 2006 and in 2010 the child allowance for multiple children was raised by SEK 50 for the second child, SEK 100 for the third, SEK 150 for fourth and SEK 200 for the fifth and subsequent children.

Maximum fee for childcare was introduced in 2002.

The basic allowance has been increased in 2001, 2002, 2003, 2005 and 2006.

Regarding the unemployment benefit the higher benefit level of SEK 730 for the first 100 days was removed in 2007 and the maximum unemployment benefit was set to SEK 680 during the entire benefit period of 300 days (or 450 days for persons with children under the age of 18). In August 2015, the maximum unemployment benefit was raised to SEK 910 per day in day 1-100 and to SEK 760 per day in day 101-300 (or day 101-450). The compensation in the sick leave was raised from 75 to 80% in 1998. In 2003 the compensation was lowered to 77.6% and, at the same time, the number of days for which the employer is responsible was increased from 14 to 21 days. In 2005 the compensation in the sick leave and the number of days for which the employer is responsible were set to their before-2003 level.

The lowest level of compensation in the parental leave was raised on 1 July 2006 from SEK 60 to SEK 180 per day. In 2006 also the maximum income compensated for in the parental leave was raised from 7.5*Basic Amount to 10* Basic Amount.

An earned income tax credit was introduced in 2007 with the purpose of making work economically more rewarding relative to unemployment or inactivity. The earned income tax credit was increased in 2008, 2009, 2010 and 2014.

In 2007, the social security contributions for 18-24-year-old employees and self-employed were reduced. In 2009 the reduction were increased and expanded to include all aged under 26. From 1 August 2015 the reduction was reduced by half with the intention to abolish the reduction in 2016. A special wage tax for persons older than 65 was abolished in 2007 for persons born after 1937 and in 2008 for persons born in 1937 or earlier.

An increased basic allowance for persons older than 65 was introduced in 2009 and extended in 2010, 2011, 2013 and 2014.

A general reduction on the SSC for self-employed was introduced in 2010 and increased in 2014.

The deduction for premiums paid to private pension arrangements was lowered in 2015 with the intention to abolish the deduction in 2016 (see section 1.12).

5. Memorandum items

5.1. *Identification of an AW and calculation of earnings*

Basic data for gross earnings are taken from the series *Official Statistics of Sweden*, published by Statistics Sweden. The calculation is based upon total average monthly or hourly earnings, primarily in September of the calendar year. To arrive at the annual earnings, data have been multiplied by the normal amount of hours worked during the year or the stipulated monthly salary has been multiplied by a factor of 12.2. The figures are representative for the country as a whole. The branch classification is NACE Rev. 2 B-N according to the OECD recommendation.

5.2. *Employer contributions to private health, pension, etc. schemes*

There are a handful of widespread private social security schemes. The employers' contributions to these systems for the blue-collar workers in the private sector equalled to 6.3% of wage earnings in 2007. For white-collar workers in the private sector the employers' contributions to private social security schemes was 14% in 2007. These figures are based on the statistics of labour costs in the private sector, published by Statistics Sweden.

2015 parameter values

Average earnings/yr	Ave_earn	421 364	Secretariat estimate
Central income tax			
	tax_rate	0.2	
	tax_rate2	0.05	
	tax_thrsh	430 200	
	tax_thrsh2	616 100	
Basic Allowance			
	gr1	0.99	
	gr2	2.72	
	gr3	3.11	
	gr4	7.88	
	gp1	0.423	
	gp2	0.2	
	gp3	0.1	
	gp4	0.293	
	gp5	0.77	
Local income tax			
	local_rate	0.3199	
	min_taxl	0	
Soc. security amount			
	basic_amt	44 500	
	basic_ant	58 100	
Soc. security contributions			
employee	SSC_rate	0.07	
employer	SSC_empr	0.3142	
ceiling	SSCC	8.07	
Child benefit			
	Child 1	12 600	
	Child 2	14 400	
	CB	13 500	
Tax credits			
	TC1	0	
	TC1gr1	0	
	TC1gp1	0	
	TC2gp1	1	
EITC	er_1	0.91	
	er_2	2.94	
	er_3	8.08	
	ep_1	1.584	
	ep_2	0.332	
	ep_3	0.111	
	ep_4	2.155	
Employer payroll tax	PRT	0.1015	

2015 tax equations

The equations for the Swedish system are mostly repeated for each individual of a married couple. But the cash transfer is calculated only once. This is shown by the Range indicator in the table below.

The functions which are used in the equations (Taper, MIN, Tax etc) are described in the technical note about tax equations. Variable names are defined in the table of parameters above, within the equations table, or are the standard variables "married" and "children". A reference to a variable with the affix "_total" indicates the sum of the relevant variable values for the principal and spouse. And the affixes "_princ" and "_spouse" indicate the value for the principal and spouse, respectively. Equations for a single person are as shown for the principal, with "_spouse" values taken as 0.

1.	Earnings	earn		
		truncearn	B	TRUNC(earn, -2)
2.	Allowances:	basic_al	B	IF(truncearn<=gr_2*basic_amt, MINA(ROUNDUP(MAXA(gp_1*basic_amt, (gp_1+gp_2*(gr_2-gr_1))*basic_amt-gp_2*MAXA(gr_2*basic_amt-truncearn, 0)), -2), truncearn), MINA(ROUNDUP(MAXA(gp_4*basic_amt, gp_5*basic_amt-gp_2*MAXA(gr_2*basic_amt-truncearn, 0)-gp_3*MAXA(truncearn-gr_3*basic_amt, 0)), -2), truncearn))
		ssc_al	B	0
	Total	tax_al	B	basic_al
3.	Credits in taxable income	taxbl_cr	B	0
4.	CG taxable income	tax_inc	B	Positive(earn-basic_al)
5.	CG tax before credits	CG_tax_excl	B	tax_rate*Positive(tax_inc-tax_thrsh)+ tax_rate2* Positive(tax_inc-tax_thrsh2)
6.	Tax credits :	ssc_credit	B	Trunc(SSC, -2)
		localtax_credit	B	0
		eitc	B	=TRUNC(MAX((((TRUNC(IF(earned_income>er_2*basic_amt; IF(earned_income>er_3*basic_amt;ep_4*basic_amt;ep_1*basic_amt+ep_3*(earned_income-er_2*basic_amt));MIN(earned_income;er_1*basic_amt+ep_2*(earned_income-er_1*basic_amt)));0))-basic_allowance)*local_rate);0);0)
		Final_eitc	B	MIN(eitc, CG_tax_excl+ local_tax- ssc_credit)
		tax_cr	B	ssc_credit+localtax_credit+final_eitc
7.	CG tax	CG_tax	B	CG_tax_excl-tax_cr
8.	State and local taxes	local_tax	B	IF(tax_inc>0, TRUNC(local_rate*tax_inc, 0)+min_taxl, 0)
9.	Employees' soc security	SSC	B	(truncearn>=gp_1*basic_amt)*MINA(ROUNDSSC(truncearn*SSC_rate), ROUNDSSC(SSCC*basic_ant*SSC_rate))
11.	Cash transfers	cash_trans	J	Children*CB
13.	Employer's contributions		B	
	Employer's SSC	SSC_empr	B	TRUNC(earn*SSC_empr)-Payroll_empr
	Employer's payroll tax	Payroll_empr	B	TRUNC(earn*PRT)
	Total	Cont_empr	B	SSC_empr+Payroll_empr

Key to range of equation B calculated separately for both principal earner and spouse P calculated for principal only (value taken as 0 for spouse calculation) J calculated once only on a joint basis.

Switzerland

This chapter includes data on the income taxes paid by workers, their social security contributions, the family benefits they receive in the form of cash transfers as well as the social security contributions and payroll taxes paid by their employers. Results reported include the marginal and average tax burden for eight different family types.

Methodological information is available for personal income tax systems, compulsory social security contributions to schemes operated within the government sector, universal cash transfers as well as recent changes in the tax/benefit system. The methodology also includes the parameter values and tax equations underlying the data.

Switzerland 2015

The tax/benefit position of single persons

	Wage level (per cent of average wage)	67	100	167	67
	Number of children	none	none	none	2
1.	**Gross wage earnings**	60 492	90 286	150 778	60 492
2.	**Standard tax allowances**				
	Basic allowance				
	Married or head of family	0	0	0	0
	Dependent children	0	0	0	13 000
	Deduction for social security contributions and income taxes	6 557	10 728	19 048	6 557
	Work-related expenses	2 000	2 539	4 000	2 000
	Other	1 700	1 700	1 700	3 100
	Total	10 257	14 967	24 748	24 657
3.	**Tax credits or cash transfers included in taxable income**	0	0	0	6 000
4.	**Central government taxable income (1 - 2 + 3)**	50 200	75 300	126 000	41 800
5.	**Central government income tax liability (exclusive of tax credits)**	450	1 262	5 083	135
6.	**Tax credits**				
	Basic credit				
	Married or head of family				
	Children	0	0	0	502
	Other				
	Total	0	0	0	502
7.	**Central government income tax finally paid (5-6)**	450	1 262	5 083	0
8.	**State and local taxes**	4 487	8 766	19 189	1 445
9.	**Employees' compulsory social security contributions**				
	Gross earnings	3 781	5 643	9 275	3 781
	Taxable income				
	Total	3 781	5 643	9 275	3 781
10.	**Total payments to general government (7 + 8 + 9)**	8 718	15 672	33 547	5 226
11.	**Cash transfers from general government**				
	For head of family				
	For two children	0	0	0	6 000
	Total	0	0	0	6 000
12.	**Take-home pay (1-10+11)**	51 774	74 614	117 231	61 266
13.	**Employer's compulsory social security contributions**	3 781	5 643	9 275	3 781
14.	**Average rates**				
	Income tax	8.2%	11.1%	16.1%	2.4%
	Employees' social security contributions	6.3%	6.3%	6.2%	6.3%
	Total payments less cash transfers	14.4%	17.4%	22.2%	-1.3%
	Total tax wedge including employer's social security contributions	19.4%	22.2%	26.8%	4.7%
15.	**Marginal rates**				
	Total payments less cash transfers: Principal earner	21.7%	27.6%	32.2%	13.8%
	Total payments less cash transfers: Spouse	n.a.	n.a.	n.a.	n.a.
	Total tax wedge: Principal earner	26.3%	31.8%	35.9%	18.9%
	Total tax wedge: Spouse	n.a.	n.a.	n.a.	n.a.

Switzerland 2015

The tax/benefit position of married couples

		Wage level (per cent of average wage)	100-0	100-33	100-67	100-33
		Number of children	2	2	2	none
1.	**Gross wage earnings**		90 286	120 081	150 778	120 081
2.	**Standard tax allowances**					
	Basic allowance					
	Married or head of family		2 600	15 566	16 000	15 566
	Dependent children		13 000	13 000	13 000	0
	Deduction for social security contributions and income taxes		10 728	14 987	19 284	14 987
	Work-related expenses		2 539	2 539	2 539	2 539
	Other		4 900	4 900	4 900	3 500
		Total	33 767	50 992	55 724	36 592
3.	**Tax credits or cash transfers included in taxable income**		6 000	6 000	6 000	0
4.	**Central government taxable income (1 - 2 + 3)**		62 500	75 000	101 000	83 400
5.	**Central government income tax liability (exclusive of tax credits)**		499	874	2 018	1 207
6.	**Tax credits**					
	Basic credit					
	Married or head of family					
	Children		502	502	502	0
	Other					
		Total	502	502	502	0
7.	**Central government income tax finally paid (5-6)**		0	372	1 516	1 207
8.	**State and local taxes**		4 104	7 019	11 309	9 257
9.	**Employees' compulsory social security contributions**					
	Gross earnings		5 643	7 505	9 424	7 505
	Taxable income					
		Total	5 643	7 505	9 424	7 505
10.	**Total payments to general government (7 + 8 + 9)**		9 747	14 896	22 249	17 969
11.	**Cash transfers from general government**					
	For head of family					
	For two children		6 000	6 000	6 000	0
		Total	6 000	6 000	6 000	0
12.	**Take-home pay (1-10+11)**		86 539	111 185	134 529	102 112
13.	**Employer's compulsory social security contributions**		5 643	7 505	9 424	7 505
14.	**Average rates**					
	Income tax		4.5%	6.2%	8.5%	8.7%
	Employees' social security contributions		6.3%	6.3%	6.3%	6.3%
	Total payments less cash transfers		4.1%	7.4%	10.8%	15.0%
	Total tax wedge including employer's social security contributions		9.8%	12.9%	16.0%	20.0%
15.	**Marginal rates**					
	Total payments less cash transfers: Principal earner		17.2%	21.5%	25.0%	22.3%
	Total payments less cash transfers: Spouse		17.3%	20.6%	25.6%	21.0%
	Total tax wedge: Principal earner		22.1%	26.1%	29.4%	26.9%
	Total tax wedge: Spouse		22.2%	25.3%	30.0%	25.6%

The national currency is the Swiss franc (CHF). In 2015, CHF 0.96 equalled USD 1. The Secretariat has estimated that in that same year the average worker earned CHF 90 286 (Secretariat estimate).

Cantonal and communal income taxes are very substantial in relation to direct federal tax. Here, the canton and commune of Zurich have been selected as an example of the tax system of the 26 cantons. Local income tax is not deductible when calculating federal income tax.

1. Personal income tax systems

1.1. *Income tax collected by the federal government (Confederation)*

1.1.1. *Tax unit*

The income of spouses living together is taxed jointly, regardless of the property regime under which they were married. Income of children living under parental authority is added to the income of their custodian. Children's labour income is taxed separately and in some cases, as in Zurich, is exempt from tax.

1.1.2. *Tax reliefs and tax credits*

1.1.2.1. Standard reliefs for "postnumerando" taxation [i.e. annual taxation on the basis of actual earned income, assessed at the end of the year].

- Basic deduction

There is a basic deduction of CHF 2 600 for married couples for direct federal tax.

- Deduction for children

A CHF 6 500 deduction is allowed for each child under 18 years of age; the deduction is allowed for older children if they are apprentices or still in school.

- Tax credit for children

A CHF 251 deduction from the tax liability is allowed for each child under 18 years, the deduction is allowed for older children if they are apprentices or still in school.

- Deductions for social insurance contributions and other taxes

Premiums for old age and disability insurance (5.15% of gross earned income) and for unemployment insurance (1.1% for income up to CHF 126 000, 0.5% for income over CHF 126 000) are deductible in full. Compulsory contributions of approximately 7.75% to private pension funds are also fully deductible. Health and life insurance premiums are deductible from federal income tax up to CHF 3 500 for married persons and CHF 1 700 for taxpayers who are widow(er)s, divorced or single (such premiums are not considered social contributions). These amounts are increased by CHF 700 for each dependent child.

- Work-related expenses

Taxpayers are allowed a deduction corresponding to 3% of net income (i.e. gross income less contributions for old age and disability insurance, unemployment insurance and work-related provident funds). This deduction may be no less than CHF 2 000 and no more than CHF 4 000.

- Deduction for two-income couples

50% of the smaller income can be deducted, but no less than CHF 8 100 and no more than CHF 13 400.

1.1.2.2. Main non-standard reliefs available to the average worker

- Interest payments on qualifying loans

This is the main non-standard relief available to the average worker. It is allowed for all sorts of loans.

- Medical expenses

Expenses incurred as a result of illness, accidents or disability of the taxpayer or one of its dependants are deductible if the taxpayer bears the expenses personally and they exceed 5% of his or her net income.

1.1.3. *Tax base*

Allowable deductions from gross income	Single taxpayer (CHF)	Married taxpayer, 2 children (CHF)
Work-related expenses[1]	2 000-4 000	2 000-4 000
Personal deduction	–	2 600
Deduction for 2 dependent children	–	13 000 (6 500*2)
Social contributions		
Old age insurance	5.05%	5.05%
Unemployment insurance	1.1%[2]	1.1%[2]
Pension fund	7.75%	7.75%
Maximum deductions for health insurance premiums and loan interest[3]	1 700 plus 700 per child	3 500 plus 700 per child
Deduction for two-income couples[4]		8 100–13 400

1. 3% of net income, minimum CHF 2 000, maximum CHF 4 000.
2. 1.1% of income up to CHF 126 000; 0.5% of income between CHF 126 000 and CHF 315 000.
3. For the purposes of this publication, taxpayers are assumed to always receive the relevant maximum deduction.
4. 50% of smaller income, minimum the lower of CHF 8 100 or adjusted smaller income, maximum CHF 13 400.

In addition, for the married taxpayer with 2 children, there is a tax credit for 2 dependent children amounting to CHF 502, thus reducing the tax liability by CHF 502.

1.1.4. *Tax schedules*

1.1.4.1. Rates for persons living alone

Taxable income (CHF)[5]	Base amount (CHF)	Plus % of excess (CHF)	
Up to 14 500	–	–	–
14 500 to 31 600		0.77	14 500
31 600 to 41 400	131.65	0.88	31 600
41 400 to 55 200	217.90	2.64	41 400
55 200 to 72 500	582.20	2.97	55 200
72 500 to 78 100	1 096.00	5.94	72 500
778 100 to 103 600	1 428.60	6.60	78 100
103 600 to 134 600	3 111.60	8.80	103 600
134 600 to 176 000	5 839.60	11.00	134 600
176 000 to 755 200	10 393.60	13.20	176 000
Over 755 200[6]	–	11.5 of total income	

5. Fractions of less than CHF 100 are disregarded.
6. The calculation model disregards this part of the schedule.

1.1.4.2. Rates for spouses living together and for widowed, separated, divorced taxpayers or unmarried taxpayers living with their own children.

Taxable income (CHF)[7]	Base amount (CHF)	Plus % of the excess (CHF)	
Up to 28 300	–	–	–
28 300 to 50 900		1	28 300
50 900 to 58 400	223	2	50 900
58 400 to 75 300	373	3	58 400
75 300 to 90 300	877	4	75 300
90 300 to 103 400	1 477	5	90 300
103 400 to 114 700	2 127	6	103 400
114 700 to 124 200	2 799	7	114 700
124 200 to 131 700	3 457	8	124 200
131 700 to 137 300	4 057	9	131 700
137 300 to 141 200	4 552	10	137 300
141 200 to 143 100	4 942	11	141 200
143 100 to 145 000	5 151	12	143 100
145 000 to 895 800	5 379	13	145 000
For 895 900	103 028.50		
Over 895 900[8]	–	11.5 of total income	

7. Fractions of less than CHF 100 are disregarded.
8. The calculation model disregards this part of the schedule.

1.2. Taxes levied by decentralised authorities (Canton and commune of Zurich)

1.2.1. General description of the system

The system of cantonal and communal taxation has the same features as that of direct federal tax.

The tax base is comprised of income from all sources.

Once the basic amount of tax is set, cantons, communes and churches levy their taxes by applying a multiple, which may change from year to year. In 2012, for example, the canton applied a multiple of 1.0, the commune of Zurich 1.19 and the reformed church 0.10. The basic amount of tax is therefore multiplied by a total of 2.29. However, following the decision no longer to include church tax in *Revenue Statistics*, it is no longer included in the calculations for *Taxing Wages*. The basic amount of tax is therefore multiplied by a total of 2.19.

1.2.2. *Tax base*

Allowable deductions from gross income	Single taxpayer (CHF)	Married taxpayer, 2 children (CHF)
Work-related expenses[9]	2 000-4 000	2 000-4 000
Personal deduction	–	–
Deduction for 2 dependent children	–	18 000 (9 000*2)
Social contributions		
Old age insurance	5.15%	5.15%
Unemployment insurance	1.1%[10]	1.1%[10]
Pension fund	7.75%	7.75%
Maximum deductions for health insurance premiums and loan interest[11]	2 600 plus 1 300 per child	5 200 plus 1 300 per child
Deduction for two-income couples		5 900

9. 3% of net income, minimum CHF 2 000 CHF, maximum CHF 4 000.
10. 1.1% of income up to CHF 126 000; 0.5% of income between CHF 126 000 and CHF 315 000.
11. For the purposes of this publication, taxpayers are assumed to always receive the relevant maximum deduction.

1.2.3. *Postnumerando tax rates*

Cantonal income tax (Zurich)

a) Basic income tax rates for married, divorced, widowed or single taxpayers living with children:

Taxable income (CHF)[12]	Base amount (CHF)	Plus % of the excess (CHF)	
Up to 13 500	–	0	–
13 500 to 19 600	–	2	13 500
19 160 to 27 300	122	3	19 600
27 300 to 36 700	353	4	27 300
36 700 to 47 400	729	5	36 700
47 400 to 61 300	1 264	6	47 400
61 300 to 92 100	2 098	7	61 300
92 100 to 122 900	4 254	8	92 100
122 900 to 169 300	6 718	9	122 900
169 300 to 224 700	10 984	10	169 300
224 700 to 284 800	16 434	11	224 700
284 800 to 354 100	23 045	12	284 800
Over 354 100	31 361	13	354 100

12. Fractions below CHF 100 are disregarded.

b) Basic income tax rates for other taxpayers (single without children).

Taxable income (CHF)[13]	Base amount (CHF)	Plus % of the excess (CHF)	
Up to 6 700	–	0	–
6 700 to 11 400	–	2	6 700
11 400 to 16 100	94	3	11 400
16 100 to 23 700	235	4	16 100
23 700 to 33 000	539	5	23 700
33 000 to 43 700	1 004	6	33 000
43 700 to 56 100	1 646	7	43 700
56 100 to 73 000	2 514	8	56 100
73 000 to 105 500	3 866	9	73 000
105 500 to 137 700	6 791	10	105 500
137 700 to 188 700	10 011	11	137 700
188 700 to 254 900	15 621	12	188 700
Over 254 900	23 565	13	254 900

13. Fractions below CHF 100 are disregarded.

c) Annual multiple as a percentage of basic tax rates:

Canton of Zurich	100
Commune of Zurich	119
Roman Catholic church tax	10 (for info.)
Reformed Church tax	10 (for info.)

A personal tax of CHF 24 is added.

1.2.4. *Tax rates used for this study*

This study uses the rates of tax levied by the federal, cantonal and communal tax authorities.

2. Compulsory social security contributions to schemes operated within the government sector

2.1. Employee contributions

2.1.1. *Retirement pensions*

5.15% of gross income for old age insurance.

2.1.2. *Health insurance*

–

2.1.3. *Unemployment*

1.1% on the portion of income up to CHF 126 000; 0.5% for income over CHF 126 000.

2.1.4. *Work-related accidents*

–

2.1.5. *Family allowances*

–

2.1.6. Other

–

2.2. Employer contributions

2.2.1. Retirement pensions

5.15 % of gross income for old age insurance.

2.2.2. Health insurance

–

2.2.3. Unemployment

1.1% on the portion of income up to CHF 126 000; 0.5% for income over CHF 126 000.

2.2.4. Work-related accidents

–

2.2.5. Family allowances

The employer pays a benefit for dependent children of an employee. The effective benefits paid depend on the Canton of residence and the respective employer. As of 1 January 2009, a new Swiss-wide minimum amount of CHF 2 400 (for children up to 16 years of age and CHF 3 000 for children in education between 16 and 25 years of age) has been established. In most cases, the benefit paid exceeds this minimum. The average family benefit is estimated to amount to CHF 3 000 per child per year.

This benefit is taxable along with other components of income.

The family allowance contributions are not included in the Taxing Wages results either as they are paid to a privately-managed fund. These contributions therefore qualify as non-tax compulsory payments (see also Section 5.3).

2.2.6. Other

–

3. Universal cash benefits

3.1. Benefits linked to marital status

No such benefits are paid.

3.2. Benefits for dependent children

The employer pays a benefit of, on average, approximately CHF 3 000 per year for each dependent child of an employee. This benefit is taxable along with other components of income. See 2.25.

4. Main changes in the tax/benefit system since 1998

On 1 January 1999, the canton of Zurich switched from biennial praenumerando taxation to annual postnumerando taxation on individual income. As a result, the direct federal tax is based on annual postnumerando taxation as well.

As of 1 January 2008, the basic deduction for married couples and the deduction for two-income couples were introduced. These measures are intended to minimise the marriage penalty and to reduce the high taxation of secondary earners, thereby increasing labour force participation of skilled secondary earners.

As of 1 January 2012, the tax credit for children reduces the tax liability by CHF 251 per child.

5. Memorandum item

5.1. *Identification of the average worker*

The population includes men and women working in industry, arts and crafts. The stated income is for the average of workers in the same sector. The geographical scope is the entire country, whereas the amount of tax is computed in respect of the canton and commune of Zurich.

5.2. *Method of calculation used*

- Unemployment benefits: not included;
- Sick leave payments: not included;
- Paid leave allowances: included;
- Overtime: included;
- Periodic cash bonuses: included;
- Fringe benefits: not included;
- Basic method used for calculation: monthly wages are multiplied by 12;
- Close of the income tax year: 31 December;
- Reference period for computing wages: from 1 January to 31 December of the year in question.

5.3. *Calculation of non-tax compulsory payments*

Switzerland imposes some important non-tax compulsory payments (NTCPs). These NTPCs are not included in the Taxing Wages models except when they qualify as standard personal income tax reliefs. Compulsory payments indicators, which combine the effect of taxes and NTCPs, are calculated by the OECD Secretariat and presented in the OECD Tax Database (See: *www.oecd.org/ctp/taxdatabase*). Switzerland levies the following employee and/ or employer NTCPs:

- Contributions to the second pillar of the pension system (occupational pension funds): Occupational pension funds are mandatory for salaried persons earning at least CHF 21 150 annually. Old age insurance is based on individual savings. The savings assets accumulated by the insured person on his individual savings account over the years serve to finance the old age pension. The constituted capital is converted into an annual old age pension on the basis of a conversion factor. Contribution rates depend on the occupation and the pension fund. An estimated representative rate amounts to 7.75% for employees and 10.27% for employers in 2015.
- Health insurance is compulsory for all persons domiciled in Switzerland. Every family member is insured individually, regardless of age. Health insurance contributions are lump sum contributions per capita depending on age, sex, canton of residence and

insurer. The national average rates for 2015 amount to CHF 4 942 for adults and CHF 1 140 for children per year. Health insurance premiums can be reduced depending on the contributor's income level and his family situation. Each canton has its own definition of the income thresholds and the reduction regime. The health insurance premium and reduction rates of the Canton of Zurich are used in the calculations.

- Family allowance: Employers have to make family allowance contributions. The contribution rates differ among cantons and family contribution funds. A representative rate has to be estimated, for 2015 it amounts to 1.1%.
- Accident insurance: Accident insurance is compulsory for every employee. Employees are automatically insured by their employer, whereas the employers are more or less automatically assigned to a particular insurance company depending on their branch of trade. The risk and associated costs of the respective business activity determines the insurance premiums. A representative rate would have to be estimated.

2015 parameter values

Average earnings/yr	Ave_earn	90 286	Secretariat estimate
Tax allowances	fed_child_al	6 500	
Tax credit	fed_child_cred	251	
Partner Allowance	partner_rate_fed	0.5	
	partner_min_fed	8 100	
	partner_max_fed	13 400	
Basic deduction for married couples	Married_ded_fed	2 600	
Partner income local	partner_local	5 900	
Single parent	sing_par_al	0	
Workrelated	work_exp	0.03	
	work_exp_min	2 000	
	work_exp_max	4 000	
Allowances for local tax	local_basic	0	
	local_child	9 000	
Federal tax	IFD_min_s	-	
Single	IFD_sch_s	0	14 500
		0.0077	31 600
		0.0088	41 400
		0.0264	55 200
		0.0297	72 500
		0.0594	78 100
		0.066	103 600
		0.088	134 600
		0.11	176 000
		0.132	752 200
		0.115	
Married	IFD_min_m	-	
	IFD_sch_m	0	28 300
		0.01	50 900
		0.02	58 400
		0.03	75 300
		0.04	90 300
		0.05	103 400
		0.06	114 700
		0.07	124 200
		0.08	131 700
		0.09	137 300
		0.1	141 200

2015 parameter values

		0.11	143 100
		0.12	145 000
		0.13	895 900
		0.115	
Cantonal tax	Zurich_min	24	
Single	Zurich_sch_s	0	6 700
		0.02	11 400
		0.03	16 100
		0.04	23 700
		0.05	33 000
		0.06	43 700
		0.07	56 100
		0.08	73 000
		0.09	105 500
		0.1	137 700
		0.11	188 700
		0.12	254 900
		0.13	
Married	Zurich_sch_m	0	13 500
		0.02	19 600
		0.03	27 300
		0.04	36 700
		0.05	47 400
		0.06	61 300
		0.07	92 100
		0.08	122 900
		0.09	169 300
		0.1	224 700
		0.11	284 800
		0.12	354 100
		0.13	
Canton and Commune Tax Mutiple	statetax_mult	2.19	
Social security contributions	old_age	0.0515	
Pension	pension_rate	0	
Pillar 2 pension	NTCP_old_age_max	28 080	
	NTCP_pension_ee	0.0775	
Unemployment	unemp_rate	0.011	
	unemp_rate2	0.005	
income ceiling	unemp_ciel	126 000	
Cantonal deductible limit	local_dedn	2 600	
deductible extra for child	local_dedn_c	1 300	
Max other insurance deduction			
single	max_dedn_s	1 700	
married couples	max_dedn_m	3 500	
child	max_dedn_c	700	
Child cash transfer	child_ben	3 000	

2015 tax equations

The equations for the Swiss system in 2015 are mostly calculated on a family basis.

Variable names are defined in the table of parameters above, within the equations table, or are the standard variables "married" and "children". A reference to a variable with the affix "_total" indicates the sum of the relevant variable values for the principal and spouse. And the affixes "_princ" and "_spouse" indicate the value for the principal and spouse, respectively. Equations for a single person are as shown for the principal, with "_spouse" values taken as 0.

	Line in country table and intermediate steps	Variable name	Range	Equation
1.	Earnings	earn		
2.	Allowances:	partner_al	J	IF(earn_spouse-work_al_spouse-SSC_spouse>partner_min_fed,(Married*MAX(partner_min_fed,MIN(partner_max_fed,partner_rate_fed*(earn_spouse-work_al_spouse-SSC_spouse)))),earn_spouse-work_al_spouse-SSC_spouse)+Married*Married_ded_fed
	Children	children_al	J	Children*fed_child_al+ (Children>0)*(Married=0)*sing_par_al
	Soc sec contributions	SSC_al	B	SSC + NTCP_pension_ee*IF(earn_princ>0.75*NTCP_old_age_max,MAX(0.125*NTCP_old_age_max,earn_princ-0.875*NTCP_old_age_max),0)+NTCP_pension_ee*IF(earn_spouse>0.75*NTCP_old_age_max,MAX(0.125*NTCP_old_age_max,earn_spouse-0.875*NTCP_old_age_max),0)
	Work related	work_al	B	IF(earn-SSC>work_exp_min,MAX(work_exp_min,MIN(work_exp_max,work_exp*(earn-SSC))),earn-SSC)
	Other	oth_al	J	IF(Married,IF(Children>0,max_dedn_m+Children*fed_dedn_c,max_dedn_m),IF(Children>0,max_dedn_s+Children*fed_dedn_c,max_dedn_s))
	Total	tax_al	J	partner_al+children_al+SSC_al+work_al+oth_al
3.	Credits in taxable income	taxbl_cr	J	Cash_tran
4.	CG taxable income	tax_inc	J	positive(earn_total-tax_al+taxbl_cr)
5.	CG tax before credits	CG_tax_excl	J	IF(Married+Children=0, Tax(tax_inc, IFD_sch_s)+IFD_min_s*(Tax(tax_inc, IFD_sch_s)>0), Tax(tax_inc, IFD_sch_m)+IFD_min_m*(Tax(tax_inc, IFD_sch_m)>0))
6.	Tax credits :	Children_cred	J	Child_cred*Children
7.	CG tax	CG_tax	J	Positive(CG_tax_excl- Children_cred)
8.	State and local taxes	local_tax_inc	J	MAX(earn_total+taxbl_cr-local_basic*(1+Married)-Children*local_child-work_al_total-SSC_total-(local_dedn*(1+Married)+Children*local_dedn_c)-(earn_spouse>0)*partner_local,0)
		local_tax		IF((Married+Children)>0, Tax(local_tax_inc, Zurich_sch_m)*statetax_mult+(1+Married)*Zurich_min*(Tax(local_tax_inc, Zurich_sch_m)>0), Tax(local_tax_inc, Zurich_sch_s)*statetax_mult+(Tax(local_tax_inc, Zurich_sch_s)>0)*Zurich_min)
9.	Employees' soc security	SSC	B	(old_age)*earn+IF(earn<=unemp_ciel,earn*unemp_rate,unemp_ciel*unemp_rate+(earn-unemp_ciel)*unemp_rate2)
11.	Cash transfers	Cash_tran	J	Children*child_ben
13.	Employer's soc security	SSC_empr	B	SSC

Key to range of equation B calculated separately for both principal earner and spouse P calculated for principal only (value taken as 0 for spouse calculation) J calculated once only on a joint basis.

Turkey

This chapter includes data on the income taxes paid by workers, their social security contributions, the family benefits they receive in the form of cash transfers as well as the social security contributions and payroll taxes paid by their employers. Results reported include the marginal and average tax burden for eight different family types.

Methodological information is available for personal income tax systems, compulsory social security contributions to schemes operated within the government sector, universal cash transfers as well as recent changes in the tax/benefit system. The methodology also includes the parameter values and tax equations underlying the data.

Turkey 2015

The tax/benefit position of single persons

			67	100	167	67
	Wage level (per cent of average wage)		67	100	167	67
	Number of children		none	none	none	2
1.	**Gross wage earnings**		21 472	32 048	53 520	21 472
2.	**Standard tax allowances**					
	Basic allowance		0	0	0	0
	Married or head of family					
	Dependent children					
	Deduction for social security contributions and income taxes		3 221	4 807	8 028	3 221
	Work-related expenses					
	Other					
		Total	3 221	4 807	8 028	3 221
3.	**Tax credits or cash transfers included in taxable income**		0	0	0	0
4.	**Central government taxable income (1 - 2 + 3)**		18 251	27 241	45 492	18 251
5.	**Central government income tax liability (exclusive of tax credits)**		3 050	4 848	9 653	3 050
	Stamp tax		163	243	406	163
		Total	3 213	5 091	10 059	3 213
6.	**Tax credits**					
	Basic credit		1 081	1 081	1 081	1 406
	Married or head of family					
	Children					
	Other					
		Total	1 081	1 081	1 081	1 406
7.	**Central government income tax finally paid (5-6)**		2 132	4 010	8 978	1 807
8.	**State and local taxes**		0	0	0	0
9.	**Employees' compulsory social security contributions**					
	Gross earnings		3 221	4 807	8 028	3 221
	Taxable income					
		Total	3 221	4 807	8 028	3 221
10.	**Total payments to general government (7 + 8 + 9)**		5 353	8 817	17 006	5 028
11.	**Cash transfers from general government**					
	For head of family					
	For two children		0	0	0	0
		Total	0	0	0	0
12.	**Take-home pay (1-10+11)**		16 119	23 231	36 514	16 444
13.	**Employer's compulsory social security contributions**		3 758	5 608	9 366	3 758
14.	**Average rates**					
	Income tax		9.9%	12.5%	16.8%	8.4%
	Employees' social security contributions		15.0%	15.0%	15.0%	15.0%
	Total payments less cash transfers		24.9%	27.5%	31.8%	23.4%
	Total tax wedge including employer's social security contributions		36.1%	38.3%	41.9%	34.8%
15.	**Marginal rates**					
	Total payments less cash transfers: Principal earner		32.8%	32.8%	38.7%	32.8%
	Total payments less cash transfers: Spouse		n.a.	n.a.	n.a.	n.a.
	Total tax wedge: Principal earner		42.8%	42.8%	47.8%	42.8%
	Total tax wedge: Spouse		n.a.	n.a.	n.a.	n.a.

Turkey 2015

The tax/benefit position of married couples

			100-0	100-33	100-67	100-33
	Wage level (per cent of average wage)		100-0	100-33	100-67	100-33
	Number of children		2	2	2	none
1.	**Gross wage earnings**		32 048	42 624	53 520	42 624
2.	**Standard tax allowances**					
	Basic allowance		0	0	0	0
	Married or head of family					
	Dependent children					
	Deduction for social security contributions and income taxes		4 807	6 394	8 028	6 394
	Work-related expenses					
	Other					
		Total	4 807	6 394	8 028	6 394
3.	**Tax credits or cash transfers included in taxable income**		0	0	0	0
4.	**Central government taxable income (1 - 2 + 3)**		27 241	36 230	45 492	36 230
5.	**Central government income tax liability (exclusive of tax credits)**		4 848	6 197	7 898	6 197
	Stamp tax		243	243	243	243
		Total	5 091	6 440	8 142	6 440
6.	**Tax credits**					
	Basic credit		1 622	2 487	2 487	2 163
	Married or head of family					
	Children					
	Other					
		Total	1 622	2 487	2 487	2 163
7.	**Central government income tax finally paid (5-6)**		3 469	4 033	5 818	4 357
8.	**State and local taxes**		0	0	0	0
9.	**Employees' compulsory social security contributions**					
	Gross earnings		4 807	6 394	8 028	6 394
	Taxable income					
		Total	4 807	6 394	8 028	6 394
10.	**Total payments to general government (7 + 8 + 9)**		8 277	10 427	13 846	10 751
11.	**Cash transfers from general government**					
	For head of family					
	For two children		0	0	0	0
		Total	0	0	0	0
12.	**Take-home pay (1-10+11)**		23 771	32 197	39 675	31 873
13.	**Employer's compulsory social security contributions**		5 608	7 459	9 366	7 459
14.	**Average rates**					
	Income tax		10.8%	9.5%	10.9%	10.2%
	Employees' social security contributions		15.0%	15.0%	15.0%	15.0%
	Total payments less cash transfers		25.8%	24.5%	25.9%	25.2%
	Total tax wedge including employer's social security contributions		36.9%	35.7%	36.9%	36.4%
15.	**Marginal rates**					
	Total payments less cash transfers: Principal earner		32.8%	32.8%	32.8%	32.8%
	Total payments less cash transfers: Spouse		18.3%	28.5%	32.8%	28.5%
	Total tax wedge: Principal earner		42.8%	42.8%	42.8%	42.8%
	Total tax wedge: Spouse		30.5%	39.2%	42.8%	39.2%

The national currency unit is the "Türk Lirası" (TL). In 2015, TL 2.72 was equal to USD 1. In that year, the average worker earned TL 32 048 (Country estimate).

1. Personal income tax systems

1.1. *Central government income tax*

1.1.1. *Tax unit*

Spouses are taxed separately on earned income. This rule has been applied since 1 January 1999.

1.1.2. *Tax allowances and tax credits*

1.1.2.1. Standard reliefs:

- *Reliefs for social security contributions:* Employee's social security contributions are deductible from gross earnings. These contributions are 15% of gross income as stated by the Social Insurance Act. The contribution to the unemployment fund is included in this amount and equals 1% of gross income.
- Contributions to public pension funds established by law are deductible.
- *Work-related expenses*: None.
- *Minimum Living Relief*: The calculation of the minimum living allowance is based on the annual gross amount of the minimum wage for employees older than 16 at the beginning of the calendar year in which the income is obtained multiplied by the following rates:
  - 50% for the taxpayer him or herself;
  - 10% for the spouse who neither works nor has an income;
  - 7.5% for each of the first two children;
  - 10% for third child;
  - 5% for each additional child.

This total amount is then multiplied by the rate (15%) which is applied to the first income bracket of PIT Schedule stated in Article 103 of PIT Law, and then minimum living relief is calculated by offsetting 1/12 of the allowance amount against monthly calculated tax due on employment income. Any excess is non-refundable.

1.1.2.2. Main non-standard tax reliefs applicable to an AW

- *Reliefs for disabled*: Article 31 of PIT Law (implemented in 01.01.2004 by the law 4842) regulates tax relief for disabled persons. The employee who lost his/her working capacity with at least 80% is considered to be disabled in the 1st degree; employees are disabled in the 2nd respectively 3rd degree if they lost their working capacity with at least 60% respectively 40%. In these cases, the following amounts are deductible from monthly wages:

  - Disabled in the 1st degree: TL 880
  - Disabled in the 2nd degree: TL 440
  - Disabled in the 3rd degree: TL 200
- Legal deductions for public institutions such as OYAK (Social Aid Institution for Military Officers).
- 50% of the premiums paid by the wage-earner for life insurance policies which belong to himself (or herself), the spouse and dependent children and all of the premiums paid by the wage- earner for personal insurance policies including death, accident, health, illness, disablement, unemployment, maturity, birth, education, etc. provided that the insurance is contracted with a company establishment in or with a main office in Turkey. (The total amount of deductible premiums cannot exceed 15% of the wage that is earned in the current month. The annual amount cannot exceed the annual minimum wage.
- Membership payments made to labour unions.

1.1.3. *Tax schedule*

The tax schedule in 2015 is as follows:

Taxable income (TL)	Tax on lower threshold (TL)	Tax on excess amount above lower threshold (%)
Up to 12 000		15
12 000 up to 29 000	1 800	20
29 000 up to 106 000	5 200	27
Over 106 0000	25 990	35

1.2. *State and local income taxes*

Income tax is levied only by the central government.

1.3. *Stamp tax*

The stamp tax base is gross earnings. The tax rate is 0.759% in 2015.

2. Compulsory social security contributions to schemes operated within the government sector

2.1. *Employees' contributions*

2.1.1. *Pensions (disability, old age and death insurance):*

9%

2.1.2. *Sickness:*

5%

2.1.3. *Unemployment:*

1%

2.2. *Employers' contributions*

2.2.1. *Pensions (disability, old age and death insurance):*

11%

2.2.2. *Sickness:*

7.5%

2.2.3. *Unemployment:*

2%

2.2.4. *Pensions (for short term insurance branches):*

2%

In order to increase employment and reduce regional imbalances in Turkey; various incentives policies have been implemented by state, by laws 4447, 4857, 5084, 5225, 5510, 5746, 6111, 6486 by Council of Minister's Decree of 2012/3305(Unemployment Law No: 4447, Labour Law No: 4857, Investment and Employment Promotion Law No. 5084, Investment Incentives and The Law of Cultural Initiatives Law No: 5225, Social Security General Health Insurance Law No: 5510, Promotion Research and Development Activities Law No: 5746, Law On The Restricting Of Certain Receivables and Amendment To The Law Of Social Insurance and General Health Insurance and Certain Other Laws And Decree Laws No: 6111, Amendment To The Law Of Social Insurance and General Health Insurance and Certain Other Laws No: 6486, Council of Minister's Decree No: 2012/3305 on Government Subsidies for Investments).

One of the various incentives is reduction of premiums. If disability, old age and death insurance premiums paid regularly by employers as stated law 5510 article of 81 (Social Security and General Health Insurance Law), 5% of total 11% premiums are paid by state on behalf of employers. (5% discount applied in employers share). In addition to 5% discount, 6% discount is implemented from 2013 in the working places, which employ ten or more workers, located in 51 provinces, Gökçeada and Bozcaada determined by taking into account the social-development index.

There is no distinction by marital status or sex and the contributions apply to gross earnings. Compulsory social security contributions of employees and their employers are calculated according to the schemes presented above.

For employees whose gross earnings are below the base or above ceiling earnings, which are determined at least twice in a year, these contribution rates are applied to the base or ceiling amounts respectively. In 2015, the base amount is approximately TL 14 850 and the ceiling amount is approximately TL 96 525. Under the Law No. 5510 **(Social Security and General Health Insurance Law),** the base wage for social security contributions is equal to the minimum wage. Because employees cannot be less than the minimum wage, the base wage is not considered in this publication. However, the ceiling earnings are considered for the purposes of this Report.

3. Universal cash transfers

Employees obtain universal cash transfers according to the collective labour agreements that are signed between their employer and the labour union(s). These agreements vary with the bargaining power of the different parties in the different sectors in the economy. This explains why there is no standard amount reflecting these general transfers.

4. Main changes in tax/benefit system since 2004

Personal Income Tax Law (No. 193) which is about income tax, Social Security and General Health Insurance Law (No: 5510) which is about social security contributions and

Unemployment Insurance Law (No: 4447) which is about unemployment insurance fund are the main laws about tax/benefit system.

The main changes have been made to the following laws 5615, 6009, 6327 and 6645 which are as follows:

- According to Act No. 5615, the new application "*Minimum Living Relief*" began to be implemented (see the Section 1.1.2).
- According to Act No. 6009, the taxation of the wages are differentiated than the taxation of the other taxable revenue resources like trading income, income from immovable property or income from investments. By this way, it is ensured that wages (comparative to other income items) are later entered into the 3rd bracket on the income tax schedule.
- According to Act No. 6327, (published in the Official Gazette issue 28338 on 29 June 2012.) there are important amendments in the Private Pension System Regulations. According to this law, any citizen of the Republic of Turkey will have the right for state subsidy for his/her paid contributions to the Private Pension Account. The contribution upper limit to favour this incentive is the annual amount of minimum wage 25% of this amount shall be transferred to the account of the insured party as a state subsidy. The state subsidy shall be earned in proportion to the amount of time within the system.
- According to Act No. 6645, "Minimum Living Relief" rate is changed from 5% to 10% which is used for third child's rate.

5. Memorandum items

5.1. *Identification of an AW*

Weighted mean, by the number of employees, of the monthly average wage* information obtained from "Structure of Earnings Survey, 2010", published by TURKSTAT, according to NACE Rev. 2 classification for B-N sections is calculated** and B-N aggregated data is gained. (The annual average wage data is calculated by multiplying the monthly average wage values by 12.)

The data from 2011-15 is reached by using 2010 = 100 base year "Hourly Earnings Index" and 2010 annual average wage data.

5.2. *Contribution to private pension and health schemes*

Business enterprises (employers) are permitted to make additional contributions for pension savings of their employees. However, these amounts of additional premiums are limited by main tax laws. Such additional pension arrangements, which are optional, are not widely used.

* Monthly wage: Include the sum of monthly basic wages, over time payments, payments for shift work/night work and other regular payments paid to employees in November 2010 by employers.

** The average wage amount from 2010 is calculated as a result of a joint working performed by authorities from TURKSTAT and Ministry of Finance.

2015 parameter values

Average earnings/yr.	Ave_earn	32 048	Country estimate
Income tax	Tax_sch	0.15	12 000
		0.20	29 000
		0.27	106 000
		0.35	
Stamp tax	Stamp_rate	0.00759	
Employees SSC	SSC_rate	0.15	
	SSC_ceil	96 525	
Employers SSC	SSC_empr	0,175	
Minimum living relief	credit_rate	0.15	
	basic_allow	0.5	
	spouse_allow	0.1	
	child_allow	0.075	
	third_child_allow	0.1	
	add_child_allow	0.05	
	min_wage	14 418	

2015 tax equations

The equations for the Turkish system are on an individual basis.

The functions which are used in the equations (Taper, MIN, Tax etc) are described in the technical note about tax equations. Variable names are defined in the table of parameters above, within the equations table, or are the standard variables "married" and "children". A reference to a variable with the affix "_total" indicates the sum of the relevant variable values for the principal and spouse. And the affixes "_princ" and "_spouse" indicate the value for the principal and spouse, respectively. Equations for a single person are as shown for the principal, with "_spouse" values taken as 0.

	Line in country table and intermediate steps	Variable name	Range	Equation
1.	Earnings	earn		
2.	Allowances:	tax_al	B	SSC
3.	Credits in taxable income	taxbl_cr	B	0
4.	CG taxable income	tax_inc	B	Positive(earn-tax_al)
	Stamp tax	stamp_tax	B	earn*stamp_rate
5.	CG tax before credits	CG_tax_excl	B	Tax(tax_inc,tax_sch)
6.	Tax credits :	tax_cr	P	=credit_rate*min_wage*(basic_allow+spouse_allow*(IF(Wife=0;Married;0))+ IF(OR(Children=1;Children=2); Children*child_allow;0)+IF(Children=3;(2*child_ allow) +(Children-2)*third_child_allow;0)+IF(Children>3;(2*child_allow) +(1* third_child_allow)+(1*add_child_allow);0))
			S*	IF(spouse_earn>0,credit_rate*min_wage*basic_allow,0)
7.	CG tax	CG_tax	B	positive(CG_tax_excl-tax_cr)+stamp_tax
8.	State and local taxes	local_tax	B	0
9.	Employees' soc security	SSC	B	Min(earn,SSC_ceil)*SSC_rate
11.	Cash transfers	cash_trans	B	0
13.	Employer's soc security	SSC_empr	B	Min(earn,SSC_ceil)*SSC_empr

Key to range of equation B calculated separately for both principal earner and spouse P calculated for principal only (value taken as 0 for spouse calculation) J calculated once only on a joint basis.

* In the case where the spouse earns 33% of the average wage: Taxing Wages assumption on the working spouse earning 33% of the AW does not comply with the Turkish legislation. 33% of AW in Turkey is below the minimum wage and a person cannot be employed below minimum wage. According to the Turkish legislation, it is assumed that (because he/she doesn't obtain "wage") the spouse should not obtain income in the calculation for this case, and another minimum living allowance is not also calculated for the spouse. Minimum living allowance should be only calculated for the principle earner.

United Kingdom
(2015-16 income tax year)

This chapter includes data on the income taxes paid by workers, their social security contributions, the family benefits they receive in the form of cash transfers as well as the social security contributions and payroll taxes paid by their employers. Results reported include the marginal and average tax burden for eight different family types.

Methodological information is available for personal income tax systems, compulsory social security contributions to schemes operated within the government sector, universal cash transfers as well as recent changes in the tax/benefit system. The methodology also includes the parameter values and tax equations underlying the data.

United Kingdom 2015

The tax/benefit position of single persons

		Wage level (per cent of average wage)	67	100	167	67
		Number of children	none	none	none	2
1.	**Gross wage earnings**		24 131	36 017	60 148	24 131
2.	**Standard tax allowances**					
	Basic allowance		10 600	10 600	10 600	10 600
	Married or head of family					
	Dependent children					
	Deduction for social security contributions and income taxes					
	Work-related expenses					
	Other					
		Total	10 600	10 600	10 600	10 600
3.	**Tax credits or cash transfers included in taxable income**		0	0	0	0
4.	**Central government taxable income (1 - 2 + 3)**		13 531	25 417	49 548	13 531
5.	**Central government income tax liability (exclusive of tax credits)**		2 706	5 083	13 462	2 706
6.	**Tax credits**					
	Basic credit					
	Married or head of family					
	Children		0	0	0	3 634
	Other					
		Total	0	0	0	3 634
7.	**Central government income tax finally paid (5-6)**		2 706	5 083	13 462	- 928
8.	**State and local taxes**		0	0	0	0
9.	**Employees' compulsory social security contributions**					
	Gross earnings		1 929	3 355	4 474	1 929
	Taxable income					
		Total	1 929	3 355	4 474	1 929
10.	**Total payments to general government (7 + 8 + 9)**		4 635	8 438	17 936	1 000
11.	**Cash transfers from general government**					
	For head of family					
	For two children		0	0	0	1 799
		Total	0	0	0	1 799
12.	**Take-home pay (1-10+11)**		19 496	27 578	42 211	24 929
13.	**Employer's compulsory social security contributions**		2 211	3 851	7 181	2 211
14.	**Average rates**					
	Income tax		11.2%	14.1%	22.4%	-3.8%
	Employees' social security contributions		8.0%	9.3%	7.4%	8.0%
	Total payments less cash transfers		19.2%	23.4%	29.8%	-3.3%
	Total tax wedge including employer's social security contributions		26.0%	30.8%	37.3%	5.4%
15.	**Marginal rates**					
	Total payments less cash transfers: Principal earner		32.0%	32.0%	42.0%	73.0%
	Total payments less cash transfers: Spouse		n.a.	n.a.	n.a.	n.a.
	Total tax wedge: Principal earner		40.2%	40.2%	49.0%	76.3%
	Total tax wedge: Spouse		n.a.	n.a.	n.a.	n.a.

United Kingdom 2015

The tax/benefit position of married couples

	Wage level (per cent of average wage)		100-0	100-33	100-67	100-33
	Number of children		2	2	2	none
1.	**Gross wage earnings**		36 017	47 902	60 148	47 902
2.	**Standard tax allowances**					
	Basic allowance		10 600	21 200	21 200	21 200
	Married or head of family					
	Dependent children					
	Deduction for social security contributions and income taxes					
	Work-related expenses					
	Other					
		Total	10 600	21 200	21 200	21 200
3.	**Tax credits or cash transfers included in taxable income**		0	0	0	0
4.	**Central government taxable income (1 - 2 + 3)**		25 417	26 702	38 948	26 702
5.	**Central government income tax liability (exclusive of tax credits)**		5 083	5 340	7 790	5 340
6.	**Tax credits**					
	Basic credit					
	Married or head of family					
	Children		0	0	0	0
	Other					
		Total	0	0	0	0
7.	**Central government income tax finally paid (5-6)**		5 083	5 340	7 790	5 340
8.	**State and local taxes**		0	0	0	0
9.	**Employees' compulsory social security contributions**					
	Gross earnings		3 355	3 814	5 283	3 814
	Taxable income					
		Total	3 355	3 814	5 283	3 814
10.	**Total payments to general government (7 + 8 + 9)**		8 438	9 154	13 073	9 154
11.	**Cash transfers from general government**					
	For head of family					
	For two children		1 799	1 799	1 799	0
		Total	1 799	1 799	1 799	0
12.	**Take-home pay (1-10+11)**		29 377	40 546	48 873	38 748
13.	**Employer's compulsory social security contributions**		3 851	4 372	6 061	4 372
14.	**Average rates**					
	Income tax		14.1%	11.1%	13.0%	11.1%
	Employees' social security contributions		9.3%	8.0%	8.8%	8.0%
	Total payments less cash transfers		18.4%	15.4%	18.7%	19.1%
	Total tax wedge including employer's social security contributions		26.3%	22.4%	26.2%	25.9%
15.	**Marginal rates**					
	Total payments less cash transfers: Principal earner		32.0%	32.0%	32.0%	32.0%
	Total payments less cash transfers: Spouse		6.0%	32.0%	32.0%	32.0%
	Total tax wedge: Principal earner		40.2%	40.2%	40.2%	40.2%
	Total tax wedge: Spouse		10.0%	40.2%	40.2%	40.2%

The national currency is the Pound Sterling (GBP). In 2015, GBP 0.65 was equal to USD 1. In 2015-16, the Average Worker is estimated to earn GBP 36 017 (Secretariat estimate).

1. Personal income tax system

1.1. Central government income taxes

1.1.1. *Tax unit*

The tax unit is the individual, but certain reliefs depend on family circumstances (see Section 1.121).

1.1.2. *Tax allowances and tax credits*

All figures shown are those applying at the start of the tax year in April.

1.1.2.1. Standard reliefs

- Basic reliefs: A personal allowance of GBP 10 600 is granted to each individual with income below GBP 100 000. The personal allowance is then tapered away by GBP 1 for every GBP 2 of income above GBP 100 000.
- Standard marital status reliefs: None.
- Working Tax Credit (WTC): A non-wastable tax credit available to low income families with or without children. It is available for families with children where one person works at least 16 hours a week (though hours must be at least 24 overall for a couple). It is also available for people with a disability who work at least 16 hours a week and for families without children where one person works at least 30 hours a week. The amount depends upon the hours worked, the ages of children, eligible childcare costs, and gross income. A family with a child 16 or under where the claimant (or, where applicable, their partner, or both claimants jointly) works at least 30 hours a week, would get a maximum credit of GBP 4 780 per year (assuming neither the adult(s) nor the child were disabled) before taking into account eligible childcare costs.* This credit is reduced by 41 pence for each GBP 1 of net income above a threshold of GBP 6 420 per year. WTC was introduced on 6th April 2003.
- Relief for social security contributions and other taxes: None.
- Child Tax Credit (CTC): A non-wastable tax credit available to low and middle income families with children. It provides support for children until 1st September following their 16th birthday, and beyond that date to the age of 19 for those who continue in full-time non-advanced education. The amount depends on gross income and the number and age of the children. A family with two children would get a maximum credit

* The amount of credit received is calculated by dividing separately each element of the credit by the number of days in the tax year and rounding up to the nearest penny to give a daily rate. These daily rates are then multiplied by the number of days in the relevant period (for the purposes of this Report, the tax year) and added together.

GBP 6 105 per year, which is reduced by 41 pence for each GBP 1 of gross income above a threshold of GBP 16 105 if the family is not working. A higher threshold applies if the family is working; their CTC is reduced at the same rate once their WTC has been tapered to zero. CTC was introduced on 6th April 2003.

1.1.2.2. Main non-standard tax reliefs applicable to an AW.

- Work-related expenses: Flat rate expenses for tools and special clothing are allowed to certain occupational categories. Since this provision is not applicable to all manufacturing occupations, and hence average workers, and because the rates vary slightly across categories, this relief is considered here as non-standard;
- Contributions to approved superannuation schemes or personal pension schemes are deducted when calculating taxable income. Premiums on approved life assurance policies payable to life assurance companies attract 12.5% tax relief for policies entered into force before 13 March 1984.

1.1.3. *Tax schedule*

In 2015-16 all taxpayers are liable on taxable income other than savings and dividend income at the basic rate of 20% on the first GBP 31 785, 40% over the basic rate limit of GBP 31 785 and 45% over the higher rate limit of GBP 150 000. (Taxable Income is defined as gross income for income tax purposes less allowances and reliefs available at the marginal rate.) Dividend income is charged at 10% up to the basic rate limit of GBP 31 785, 32.5% above GBP 31 785 and 37.5% above GBP 150 000. Savings income is charged at 0% up to the starting rate limit on the first GBP 5 000, at 20% up to GBP 31 785, 40% above GBP 31 785 and 45% above GBP 150 000.

Taxable income (GBP)	Rate %
0-31 785	20
31 785-150 000	40
Over 150 000	45

1.2. *State and local income tax*

There are no regional or local income taxes.

2. Compulsory social security contributions to schemes operated within the government sector

2.1. *Employees' contributions*

National Insurance contributions are payable by employees earning more than GBP 155 in any week. These are 12% of earnings between GBP 155 and GBP 815 and 2% of earnings above GBP 815 for employees not contracted out of the state second pension scheme (additional state pension which supplements the basic retirement pension). For employees who are contracted out, there is a rebate of 1.4% on earnings between GBP 112 and GBP 770. Depending on eligibility, members of the National Insurance scheme qualify for pensions, sickness, industrial injury, unemployment benefits, etc. All employees earning under GBP 155 per week have no National Insurance contribution liability but a notional contribution will be deemed to have been paid in respect of earnings between GBP 112 and GBP 155 to protect benefit entitlement.

2.2. *Employers' contributions*

Employer's contributions are not payable for employees earning less than GBP 156 per week. The rate of employers' contributions for employees not contracted out of the additional (earnings related) scheme is 13.8% of earnings above GBP 156 per week. For employees who are contracted out, there is a rebate of 3.4% on earnings between GBP 112 and GBP 770 per week.

3. Universal cash transfers

3.1. *Transfers related to marital status*

None (widows' benefit is covered by the government pensions scheme noted above).

3.2. *Transfers for dependent children*

A child benefit of GBP 20.70 per week is paid in respect of the first child in the family up to the age of 19 (if the child aged 16-19 is in education or training) with GBP 13.70 per week paid for each subsequent child.

From January 2013, a new tax charge has been introduced for a taxpayer who has income over GBP 50 000 and either they or their partner are in receipt of Child Benefit. For those with income between GBP 50 000 and GBP 60 000, the amount of the charge will be 1% of the Child Benefit for every GBP 100 of income over GBP 50 000. For those with income over GBP 60 000, the amount of the charge will equal the amount of Child Benefit. Where both adults are over the threshold, the liability falls on the adult with the highest adjusted net income (ANI).

4. Memorandum items

4.1. *Identification of AW and valuation of earnings*

A new Annual Survey of Hours and Earnings (ASHE) has been developed to replace the New Earnings Survey (NES) (results of which are published in *Labour Market Trends*) and shows the average weekly earnings of full-time employees in April each year. It covers men and women at adult rates in the United Kingdom (excluding Northern Ireland). The annual figure used for the gross earnings of the AW in the United Kingdom is the annual equivalent of the arithmetic average of the weekly earnings figures for April at the beginning and end of the fiscal year, as published in *Labour Market Trends*.

The earnings figures exclude the earnings of those whose pay was affected by absence (due to sickness etc.). They include overtime, payment by results and shift payments. But they do not include benefits in kind (which could in some circumstances be included in the employee's taxable income in the United Kingdom).

4.2. *Employers' contributions to private pension, health etc. schemes*

In 2008, there were 9.0 million active members of occupational pension schemes with two or more members in the UK, of whom 3.6 million were in the private sector and 5.4 million in the public sector.

2015 parameter values

Average earnings/yr	Ave_earn	36 017	Secretariat Estimate	
Allowances	Basic_al	10 600		
	PA taper start	100 000		
	Married_al	0		
	Married_rate	0		
Income tax	Tax_sch	0.2	31 785	
		0.4	150 000	
		0.45		
Employees SSC				
Primary threshold	SSC_sch	0	8 060	PT
Upper earnings limit		0.12	42 385	UEL
		0.02		
Employers SSC	SSC_rate2	0.138		
	ST	8 112		
Child benefit (first)	CB_first	20.70		
Child benefit (others)	CB_others	13.70		
	CB_1st_thres	50 000.00		
	CB_2nd_thres	60 000.00		
	CB_taper1	0.01		
	CB_taper2	100.00		
NEW TAX CREDITS				
WTC				
Basic element	WTC_Basic	1 960		
Couple/Lone parent	WTC_couple_or_lone	2 010		
30 Hour element	WTC_30hr	810		
CTC				
Family element	CTC_family	545		
Child element	CTC_child	2 780		
Baby element	CTC_baby			
Threshold	NTC_1st_thres	6 420		
	NTC_1st_taper	0.41		
Days in tax year	Numdays	366		

2015 tax equations

The equations for the UK system are mostly on an individual basis. But Child and Working tax credits are calculated on a family basis and child benefit is calculated only once. This is shown by the Range indicator in the table below.

The functions which are used in the equations (Taper, MIN, Tax etc) are described in the technical note about tax equations. Variable names are defined in the table of parameters above, within the equations table, or are the standard variables "married" and "children". A reference to a variable with the affix "_total" indicates the sum of the relevant variable values for the principal and spouse. And the affixes "_princ" and "_spouse" indicate the value for the principal and spouse, respectively. Equations for a single person are as shown for the principal, with "_spouse" values taken as 0.

	Line in country table and intermediate steps	Variable name	Range	Equation
1.	Earnings	Earn		
2.	Allowances:	tax_al	B	Tax_al =IF(earn<PA_taper,Basic_al,IF(earn>(PA_taper+(Basic_al*2)),0,MAX(0,(Basic_al-((earn-PA_taper)/2)))))
2.	PA Start	PA_taper	B	IF(earn<PA_taper,Basic_al,IF(AA7>(PA_taper+(Basic_al*2)),0,MAX(0,(Basic_al-((AA7-PA_taper)/2)))))
3.	Credits in taxable income	taxbl_cr	B	0
4.	CG taxable income	tax_inc	B	Positive(earn-tax_al)
5.	CG tax before credits	CG_tax_excl	B	Tax(tax_inc, tax_sch)
6.	Tax credits (nonwastable)	tax_cr	J	IF(Children>0, (Taper(ROUNDUP(CTC_family/numdays, 2)*numdays+Children*ROUNDUP(CTC_child/numdays, 2)*numdays+ROUNDUP(WTC_Basic/numdays, 2)*numdays+ROUNDUP(WTC_30hr/numdays, 2)*numdays+ROUNDUP(WTC_couple_or_lone/numdays, 2)*numdays, earn_total, NTC_1st_thres, NTC_1st_taper), Taper(ROUNDUP(WTC_Basic/numdays, 2)*numdays+ROUNDUP(WTC_30hr/numdays, 2)*numdays+IF(Married=1, ROUNDUP(WTC_couple_or_lone/numdays, 2)*numdays, 0), earn_total, NTC_1st_thres, NTC_1st_taper))
7.	CG tax	CG_tax	B	CG_tax_excl-tax_cr
8.	State and local taxes	local_tax	B	0
9.	Employees' soc security	SSC	B	Tax(earn, SSC_sch)
11.	Cash transfers	cash_trans	J	=IF(princ_earn>CB_1st_thres,IF(princ_earn>CB_2nd_thres,0,((1-(AA7-CB_1st_thres)/(CB_taper2/CB_taper1)))*(numdays/7*((Children>0)*CB_first+CB_others*Positive(Children-1)))),(numdays/7*((Children>0)*CB_first+CB_others*Positive(Children-1))))
13.	Employer's soc security	SSC_empr	B	(earn>ST)*(earn-ST)*SSC_rate2
	Memorandum item: Non-wastable tax credit			
	tax expenditure component	Taxexp	J	Tax_cr-transfer
	cash transfer component	Transfer	J	IF(CG_tax_excl<0, -CG_tax_excl, 0)

Key to range of equation B calculated separately for both principal earner and spouse P calculated for principal only (value taken as 0 for spouse calculation) J calculated once only on a joint basis.

United States

This chapter includes data on the income taxes paid by workers, their social security contributions, the family benefits they receive in the form of cash transfers as well as the social security contributions and payroll taxes paid by their employers. Results reported include the marginal and average tax burden for eight different family types.

Methodological information is available for personal income tax systems, compulsory social security contributions to schemes operated within the government sector, universal cash transfers as well as recent changes in the tax/benefit system. The methodology also includes the parameter values and tax equations underlying the data.

United States 2015

The tax/benefit position of single persons

		Wage level (per cent of average wage)	67	100	167	67
		Number of children	none	none	none	2
1.	**Gross wage earnings**		34 146	50 964	85 110	34 146
2.	**Standard tax allowances**					
	Basic allowance		10 300	10 300	10 300	13 250
	Married or head of family					
	Dependent children		0	0	0	8 000
	Deduction for social security contributions and income taxes					
	Work-related expenses					
	Other					
		Total	10 300	10 300	10 300	21 250
3.	**Tax credits or cash transfers included in taxable income**		0	0	0	0
4.	**Central government taxable income (1 - 2 + 3)**		23 846	40 664	74 810	12 896
5.	**Central government income tax liability (exclusive of tax credits)**		3 116	5 960	14 496	1 290
6.	**Tax credits**					
	Basic credit		0	0	0	2 171
	Married or head of family					
	Children		0	0	0	2 000
	Other					
		Total	0	0	0	4 171
7.	**Central government income tax finally paid (5-6)**		3 116	5 960	14 496	- 2 881
8.	**State and local taxes**		2 088	3 207	5 478	1 594
9.	**Employees' compulsory social security contributions**					
	Gross earnings		2 612	3 899	6 511	2 612
	Taxable income					
		Total	2 612	3 899	6 511	2 612
10.	**Total payments to general government (7 + 8 + 9)**		7 816	13 065	26 485	1 324
11.	**Cash transfers from general government**					
	For head of family					
	For two children		0	0	0	0
		Total	0	0	0	0
12.	**Take-home pay (1-10+11)**		26 330	37 899	58 625	32 821
13.	**Employer's compulsory social security contributions**		3 207	4 494	7 106	3 207
14.	**Average rates**					
	Income tax		15.2%	18.0%	23.5%	-3.8%
	Employees' social security contributions		7.7%	7.7%	7.7%	7.7%
	Total payments less cash transfers		22.9%	25.6%	31.1%	3.9%
	Total tax wedge including employer's social security contributions		29.5%	31.7%	36.4%	12.1%
15.	**Marginal rates**					
	Total payments less cash transfers: Principal earner		29.3%	39.3%	39.3%	46.6%
	Total payments less cash transfers: Spouse		n.a.	n.a.	n.a.	n.a.
	Total tax wedge: Principal earner		34.3%	43.6%	43.6%	50.4%
	Total tax wedge: Spouse		n.a.	n.a.	n.a.	n.a.

United States 2015

The tax/benefit position of married couples

			100-0	100-33	100-67	100-33
		Wage level (per cent of average wage)	100-0	100-33	100-67	100-33
		Number of children	2	2	2	none
1.	**Gross wage earnings**		50 964	67 782	85 110	67 782
2.	**Standard tax allowances**					
	Basic allowance		20 600	20 600	20 600	20 600
	Married or head of family					
	Dependent children		8 000	8 000	8 000	0
	Deduction for social security contributions and income taxes					
	Work-related expenses					
	Other					
		Total	28 600	28 600	28 600	20 600
3.	**Tax credits or cash transfers included in taxable income**		0	0	0	0
4.	**Central government taxable income (1 - 2 + 3)**		22 364	39 182	56 510	47 182
5.	**Central government income tax liability (exclusive of tax credits)**		2 432	4 955	7 554	6 155
6.	**Tax credits**					
	Basic credit		0	0	0	0
	Married or head of family					
	Children		2 000	2 000	2 000	0
	Other					
		Total	2 000	2 000	2 000	0
7.	**Central government income tax finally paid (5-6)**		432	2 955	5 554	6 155
8.	**State and local taxes**		2 660	3 778	4 931	4 143
9.	**Employees' compulsory social security contributions**					
	Gross earnings		3 899	5 185	6 511	5 185
	Taxable income					
		Total	3 899	5 185	6 511	5 185
10.	**Total payments to general government (7 + 8 + 9)**		6 991	11 918	16 995	15 483
11.	**Cash transfers from general government**					
	For head of family					
	For two children		0	0	0	0
		Total	0	0	0	0
12.	**Take-home pay (1-10+11)**		43 973	55 863	68 114	52 299
13.	**Employer's compulsory social security contributions**		4 494	6 375	7 701	6 375
14.	**Average rates**					
	Income tax		6.1%	9.9%	12.3%	15.2%
	Employees' social security contributions		7.7%	7.7%	7.7%	7.7%
	Total payments less cash transfers		13.7%	17.6%	20.0%	22.8%
	Total tax wedge including employer's social security contributions		20.7%	24.7%	26.6%	29.5%
15.	**Marginal rates**					
	Total payments less cash transfers: Principal earner		29.3%	29.3%	29.3%	29.3%
	Total payments less cash transfers: Spouse		29.3%	29.3%	29.3%	29.3%
	Total tax wedge: Principal earner		34.3%	34.3%	34.3%	34.3%
	Total tax wedge: Spouse		36.4%	34.3%	34.3%	34.3%

The national currency is the dollar (USD). In 2015, the average worker earned USD 50 964 (Secretariat estimate).

1. Personal income tax system

1.1. *Central/federal government income taxes*

1.1.1. *Tax unit*

Families are generally taxed in one of three ways:

- As married couples filing jointly on the combined income of both spouses;
- As married individuals filing separately and reporting actual income of each spouse; or
- As heads of households (only unmarried or separated individuals with dependents).

All others, including dependent children with sufficient income, file as single individuals.

1.1.2. *Tax allowances and tax credits*

1.1.2.1. Standard reliefs

- *Basic reliefs*: In 2015 a married couple filing a joint tax return is entitled to a standard deduction of USD 12 600. The standard deduction is USD 9 250 for heads of households and USD 6 300 for single individuals. This relief is indexed for inflation. More liberal standard deductions are available for taxpayers who are age 65 or older and taxpayers who are blind. Special rules apply to children who have sufficient income to pay tax and are also claimed as dependents by their parents.
- In addition to the standard deduction, in 2015 a USD 4 000 *personal exemption* is given to every taxpayer (including both husband and wife filing a joint return). The personal exemption is indexed annually for inflation. In 2015, there is a phase out for personal exemptions.
- Personal exemption phase out: Personal exemptions are phased out in 50 steps for taxpayers with incomes in excess of certain amounts. All of a taxpayer's exemptions are phased out simultaneously. For each USD 2 500 or fraction thereof by which income exceeds the beginning of the phase out range, personal exemptions are phased down by two percentage points.

Filing status	Beginning of phase out range (USD)
Single	258 250
Joint return	309 900
Head of household	284 050

- *Standard marital status reliefs*: Married couples generally benefit from a more favourable schedule of tax rates for joint returns of spouses (see Section 1.13). There are no other general tax reliefs for marriage.

- *Relief for children*: For each child and other person claimed as a dependent on a taxpayer's return, the taxpayer is entitled to a dependency exemption of USD 4 000 in 2015. Low income workers with dependents are allowed a refundable (non-wastable) earned income credit. For taxpayers with one child, the credit is 34% of up to USD 9 880 of earned income in 2015. The credit phases down when income exceeds USD 18 110 (23 630 for married taxpayers) and phases out when it reaches USD 39 131 (44 651 for married taxpayers). The earned income threshold and the phase-out threshold are indexed for inflation. For taxpayers with two children, the credit is 40% of up to USD 13 870 of earned income in 2015. The credit phases down when income exceeds USD 18 110 (23 630 for married taxpayers) and phases out when it reaches USD 44 454 (49 974 for married taxpayers). For taxpayers with three or more children the credit is 45% of up to USD 13 870 of earned income. The credit phases down when income exceeds USD 18 110 (23 630 for married taxpayers) and phases out when it reaches USD 47 747 (53 267 for married taxpayers).

Since 1998, taxpayers are permitted a tax credit for each qualifying child under the age of 17. In 2015 the maximum credit is USD 1 000. The maximum credit is reduced for taxpayers with income in excess of certain thresholds. The credit is reduced by USD 50 for each USD 1 000 of income in excess of USD 110 000 for married taxpayers (USD 75 000 for single and head of household taxpayers). These threshold amounts are not indexed for inflation. The child credit is refundable (non-wastable) to the extent of 15% of earned income in excess of USD 3 000. A taxpayer with three or more qualifying children may be allowed a supplemental refundable (non-wastable) child credit, subject to certain restrictions. The refundable credit is the excess of the taxpayer's share of social security (including Medicare) taxes over his earned income tax credit for the year not used to offset income tax liability.

- *Relief for low income workers without children*: In 1994 and thereafter, low income workers without children are eligible for the earned income credit. In 2015 low income workers without children are permitted a non-wastable earned income credit of 7.65% of up to USD 6 580 of earned income. The credit phases down when income exceeds USD 8 240 (13 750 for married taxpayers) and phases out when income reaches USD 14 820 (20 330 for married taxpayers). This credit is available for taxpayers at least 25 years old and under 65 years old.
- *Relief for social security and other taxes*. In 2015, the withholding rate for Social Security taxes for employees is 6.2%. The earned income credits described above are sometimes considered an offset to social security contributions made by eligible employees. Furthermore, only a portion of social security benefits are subject to tax.

1.1.2.2. Main non-standard reliefs applicable to an AW

- The basic non-standard relief is the deduction of certain expenses to the extent that, when itemised, they exceed in aggregate the standard deduction. For the purposes of this Report, it is assumed that workers claim the standard deduction. The principal itemised deductions claimed by individuals where the standard deduction is not being claimed are:
- *Medical and dental expenses that exceed* 10% of income (7.5% for taxpayers age 65 and over);
- State and local income taxes, real property taxes, and personal property taxes. Home mortgage interest;

- Investment interest expense up to investment income with an indefinite carry forward of disallowed investment interest expense;
- Contributions to qualified charitable organisations (including religious and educational institutions);
- *Casualty and theft losses* to the extent that each loss exceeds USD 100 and that all such losses combined exceed 10% of income; and
- Miscellaneous expenses such as non-reimbursed employee business expenses (union dues, work shoes, etc.), investment expenses, tax return preparation fees and educational expenses required by employment, to the extent that, in aggregate; they exceed 2% of income.
- In 2012, the most recent year for which such statistics are available, the 45% of taxpayers with income between USD 50 000 and USD 75 000 (the AW range) who itemised their deductions claimed average deductions as follows: medical expenses, USD 7 877; taxes paid, USD 5 445; charitable contributions, USD 2 818; interest expense, USD 7 968.
- *Contributions to pension and life insurance plans.* No relief is provided for employee contributions to employer sponsored pension plans or for life insurance premiums. However, tax relief is provided for certain retirement savings.

1.1.3. *Tax schedule*

Federal income tax rates

Taxable income bracket (USD)[1]			Marginal tax rate (%)
Single individual	Joint return of married couple	Head of household	
0 to 9 225	0 to 18 450	0 to 13 150	10
9 225 to 37 450	18 450 to 74 900	13 150 to 50 200	15
37 450 to 90 750	74 900 to 151 200	50 200 to 129 600	25
90 750 to 189 300	151 200 to 230 450	129 600 to 209 850	28
189 300 to 411 500	230 450 to 411 500	209 850 to 411 500	33
411 500 to 413 200	411 500 to 464 850	411 500 to 439 000	35
413 200 and over	464 850 and over	439 000 and over	39.6

1. The taxable income brackets are indexed for inflation.

In addition starting in 2013, there is a 3.8% tax on certain net investment income of individuals if their income exceeds USD 200 000 (USD 250 000 for joint returns). Net investment income includes interest, dividends, capital gains, rental and royalty income, and income from businesses trading financial instruments.

1.2. *State and local income taxes*

1.2.1. *General description of the system*

The District of Columbia and 41 of the 50 States impose some form of individual income tax. In addition, some local governments (cities and counties) impose an individual income tax, although this is not generally the case. State individual income tax structures are usually related to the federal tax structure by the use of similar definitions of taxable income, with some appropriate adjustments. This linkage is not a legal requirement but a practical convention that functions for the convenience of the taxpayer who must fill out both federal and State income tax returns.

The AW calculations assume that the average worker lives in Detroit, Michigan. The state of Michigan permits a personal exemption of USD 3 950 for the taxpayer, the taxpayer's spouse and each child, and taxes income at the rate of 4.25%. Michigan allows taxpayers who are eligible to claim the federal earned income tax credit to claim a Michigan earned income tax credit. The Michigan earned income tax credit is a refundable (non-wasteable) credit equal to 6% of the federal earned income tax credit.

The city of Detroit permits a personal exemption of USD 600 and taxes income at the rate of 2.4%.

2. Compulsory social security contributions to schemes operated within the government sector

2.1. Employees' contributions

2.1.1. Pensions

In 2015, the rate for employee contributions is 7.65% (6.2% for old age, survivors, and disability insurance, and 1.45% for old age hospital insurance). The 6.2% rate applies to earnings up to USD 118 500. Beginning in 1994, there is no limit on the amount of earnings subject to the 1.45% rate. Beginning in 2013, there is an additional 0.9% tax on employee wages and salaries that exceed USD 200 000 (USD 250 000 for joint returns) as the additional hospital insurance tax on high-income taxpayers. The additional tax on wages and salaries is subject to withholding (but without regard to the earnings of the spouse) when wages from a particular job exceed USD 200 000 per year. These thresholds are not indexed for inflation.

There is no distinction by marital status or sex.

2.1.2. Other

No compulsory employee contributions exist.

2.2. Employers' contributions

2.2.1. Pensions

The rate for employers' contributions is 6.2% on earnings up to USD 118 500 and 1.45% of all earnings (without limit).

2.2.2. Unemployment

Employers are required by the federal government to pay unemployment tax of 6% on earnings up to USD 7 000. Taxes are also paid to various state-sponsored unemployment plans which may generally be credited against the required federal percentage. In 2014 the average unemployment insurance tax rate in Michigan was 5.82% of the first USD 9 500 of wages. The model considers that the Federal government allows employers to take a credit for state unemployment taxes of up to 5.4%, resulting in a net Federal tax of 0.6% on earnings up to USD 7 000.

3. Universal cash transfers

3.1. Transfers related to marital status

None.

3.2. *Transfers for dependent children*

No general cash transfers exist, although low-income mothers qualifying for categorical welfare grants may receive cash transfers.

4. Principal changes since 2011

None.

5. Memorandum items

5.1. *Identification of an AW at the wage calculation*

- The AW is identified from monthly data compiled from establishment questionnaires covering more than 40 million non-agricultural full- and part-time workers. Beginning in March 2006, data on average weekly hours and average hourly earnings cover all employees rather than solely production or non-supervisory workers. To obtain average annual wages, the product of average weekly hours (including overtime) and average hourly earnings (including overtime) is multiplied by 52 and is adjusted to reflect a full-time equivalent worker. The AW wage is estimated to be USD 50 099 for 2014.

5.2. *Employer contributions to private social security arrangements*

Employers commonly contribute to private pension plans, health insurance and life insurance. Data for these contributions are available only on a total workforce basis. It is not possible to state with accuracy the levels applicable to the AW. The following are estimates for 2014 for employees in private industry:

	Pension	Health	Life
Per cent of workers covered	48	58	59
USD per covered employee	n.a.	11 307 (family) 4 806 (single)	n.a.

2015 parameter values

APW earnings	Ave_earn	50 964	Secretariat estimate			
Standard deductions	Married_al	12 600				
	hh_al	9 250				
	single_al	6 300				
Personal exemption	pers_ex	4 000				
Dependency exemption	dep_ex	4 000				
Personal exemption reduction	ex_dedn_rate	0.02				
unit of earnings	ex_dedn_unit	2 500				
threshold single (no children)	ex_thrsh_s	258 250				
threshold single (with children)	ex_thrsh_hh	284 050				
threshold joint	ex_thrsh_m	309 900				
Federal tax schedules	Fed_sch_s	0.1	9 225			
		0.15	37 450			
Single individuals		0.25	90 750			
		0.28	189 300			
		0.33	411 500			
		0.35	413 200			
		0.396				
Married filing jointly	Fed_sch_m	0.1	18 450			
		0.15	74 900			
		0.25	151 200			
		0.28	230 450			
		0.33	411 500			
		0.35	464 850			
		0.396				
Head of household	Fed_sch_h	0.1	13 150			
		0.15	50 200			
		0.25	129 600			
		0.28	209 850			
		0.33	411 500			
		0.35	439 000			
		0.396				
Earned income credit	EIC_sch	rate	income limit	threshold	thresh-married	phase-out
	no children	0.0765	6 580	8 240	13 750	0.0765
	1 child	0.34	9 880	18 110	23 630	0.1598
	2 children	0.4	13 870	18 110	23 630	0.2106
	3 or more children	0.45	13 870	18 110	23 630	0.2106
Child credit	chcrd_max	1 000				
	chcrd_rdn	50				
	chcrd_thrsh_m	110 000				
	chcrd_thrsh_oth	75 000				
	chcrd_ref_perct	0.15				
	chcrd_ref_thresh	3 000				
Detroit	Detroit_ex	600				
	Detroit_rate	0.024				
Michigan	Mich_ex	3 950				
	Mich_ex_child	0				
	Mich_rate	0.0425				
Michigan's earned income tax credit	Mich_EIC_rate	0.06				
credit schedule on city tax	Mich_cr_sch	0				
		0				
		0				
maximum	Mich_cr_max	0				
Pension contributions	pens_rate_er	0.062				
	pens_rate_ee	0.062				

2015 parameter values *(cont.)*

	hosp_rate	0.0145
	add_hosp_rate	0.009
Ceiling for employers and employees	pens_ceil	118 500
	add_hosp_thresh_m	250 000
	add_hosp_thresh_oth	200 000
Unemployment insurance tax	Unemp_rate	0.006
	Unemp_dedn_rate	0.054
	Unemp_max	7 000
Michigan unemploy insur	Mich_unemp_rate	0.0582
	Mich_unemp_max	9 500

2015 tax equations

The equations for the US system in 2015 are mostly calculated on a family basis. There is a special function EIC which is used to calculate the earned income credit. Variable names are defined in the table of parameters above, within the equations table, or are the standard variables "married" and "children". A reference to a variable with the affix "_total" indicates the sum of the relevant variable values for the principal and spouse. And the affixes "_princ" and "_spouse" indicate the value for the principal and spouse, respectively. Equations for a single person are as shown for the principal, with "_spouse" values taken as 0.

	Line in country table and intermediate steps	Variable name	Range	Equation
1.	Earnings	earn		
2.	Allowances:	tax_al	J	IF(Married, Married_al, IF(Children=0, single_al, hh_al)) + +((1+Married)*pers_ex+ Children*dep_ex)-(ROUNDUP(Positive(earn_total-IF(Married,ex_thrsh_m,IF (Children>0,ex_thrsh_hh,ex_thrsh_s)))/ex_dedn_unit,0)*ex_dedn_rate*((1+ Married)*pers_ex+Children*dep_ex))
3.	Credits in taxable income	taxbl_cr	J	0
4.	CG taxable income	tax_inc	J	positive(earn-tax_al+taxbl_cr)
5.	CG tax before credits	CG_tax_excl	J	Tax(tax_inc, IF(Married, Fed_sch_m, IF(Children, Fed_sch_h, Fed_sch_s)))
6.	6. Tax credits :	EIC	J	EIC(Children, earn_total, EIC_sch)
		ch_crd_max	J	Children*Positive((chcrd_max-chcrd_rdn*Positive(TRUNC(earn,-3)-IF(Married>0, chcrd_thrsh_m, chcrd_thrsh_oth))/1000))
		ch_crd_tax	J	IF(ch_crd_tax>0, MIN(ch_crd_max, CG_tax_excl), 0)
		ch_crd_ref		IF(ch_crd_tax<ch_crd_max, MIN(ch_crd_max-ch_crd_tax, MAX(chcrd_ref_perct* (earn-chcrd_ref_thresh), 0)), 0)
		tax_cr	J	EIC+ch_crd_tax+ch_crd_ref
7.	CG tax	CG_tax	J	CG_tax_excl-tax_cr
8.	State and local taxes	local_tax	J	Detroit_rate* Positive(earn_total-Detroit_ex*(1+Married+Children))+ Mich_rate* Positive(earn_total - Mich_ex*(1+Married+Children) - Mich_ex_child*Children) - MIN(Mich_cr_max, Tax(AJ7, Mich_cr_sch)) -Mich_EIC_rate*EIC
9.	Employees' soc security	SSC	B	pens_rate_ee*MIN(earn, pens_ceil)+hosp_rate*earn+add_hosp_rate*Positive (earn-IF(Married,add_hosp_thresh_m,add_hosp_thresh_oth))
11.	Cash transfers	Cash_tran	J	
13.	Employer's soc security	SSC_empr	B	pens_rate_er*MIN(earn, pens_ceil)+hosp_rate*earn+MIN(earn,Unemp_max)* Unemp_rate +MIN(earn,Mich_unemp_max)*Mich_unemp_rate
	Memorandum item: non-wastable tax credits			
	tax expenditure component	taxexp		(rate_rd_crd+EIC)-transfer
	cash transfer component	transfer		IF(CG_tax<0, -CG_tax, 0)

Key to range of equation B calculated separately for both principal earner and spouse P calculated for principal only (value taken as 0 for spouse calculation) J calculated once only on a joint basis.

ANNEX

Methodology and limitations

Methodology

Introduction

The personal circumstances of taxpayers vary greatly. This Report therefore adopts a specific methodology to produce comparative statistics covering taxes, benefits and labour costs across OECD member countries. The framework of the methodology is as follows:

- The Report focuses on eight different family types which vary by household composition and level of earnings.
- Each household contains a full-time adult employee working in one of a broad range of industry sectors of each OECD economy. Some of the households also have a spouse working less than full-time.
- The annual income from employment is assumed to be equal to a given fraction of the average gross wage earnings of these workers.
- Additional assumptions are also made regarding other relevant personal circumstances of these wage earners in order to calculate their tax/benefit position.

The guidelines described in the following paragraphs form the basis for the calculations shown in Chapter 1 and Parts I, II and III. Table A.1 sets out the terminology that is used. Where a country has had to depart from the guidelines, this is noted in the text and/or in the country chapters contained in Part III of the Report. The number of taxpayers with the defined characteristics and the wage level of the average workers differ between OECD economies.

Taxpayer characteristics

The eight household types identified in the Report are set out in Table A.2. Any children in the household are assumed to be aged between six and eleven inclusive.

The family is assumed to have no income source other than from employment and cash benefits.

The range of industries covered

The standard assumption for calculating average wage earnings is based on Sectors B-N of the *International Standard Industrial Classification of All Economic Activities* (ISIC Revision 4, United Nations) [1](see Table A.3). Many countries (for more detailed country information, see Table 0.6) have now adopted this approach

Table A.1. **Terminology**

	General terms
Average worker (AW)	An adult full-time worker in the industry sectors covered whose wage earnings represent the average for workers.
Single persons	Unmarried men and women.
Couple with two children	Married couple with two dependent children between six to eleven years of age inclusive.
Labour costs	The sum of gross wage earnings, employers' social security contributions and payroll taxes.
Net take-home pay	Gross wage earnings less the sum of personal income tax and employee social security contributions plus cash transfers received from general government.
Personal average tax rate (tax burden)	The sum of personal income tax and employee social security contributions expressed as a percentage of gross wage earnings.
Tax wedge	The sum of personal income tax, employee and employer social security contributions plus any payroll tax less cash transfers expressed as a percentage of labour costs.
Elasticity of income after tax	Percentage change in "after-tax" income following an increase in one currency unit of income before tax (defined more precisely as one minus a marginal tax rate divided by one minus a corresponding average tax rate).
	Terms used under the income tax
Tax reliefs	A generic term to cover all the means of giving favourable income tax treatment to potential taxpayers.
Tax allowances	Amounts deducted from gross earnings to arrive at taxable income.
Tax credits	Amounts which a taxpayer may subtract from his tax liability. They are described as payable if they can exceed tax liability (sometimes the terms "refundable" and "non-wastable" are used).
Standard tax reliefs	Reliefs unrelated to the actual expenses incurred by taxpayers and automatically available to all taxpayers who satisfy the eligibility rules specified in the legislation are counted as standard reliefs. These also include deductions for compulsory social security contributions.
Basic relief	Any standard tax relief available irrespective of marital or family status.
Marriage allowance	Additional tax relief given to married couples. (In some countries, this is not distinguished from the basic relief which may be doubled on marriage).
Non-standard tax reliefs	Reliefs wholly determined by reference to actual expenses incurred.
Average rate of income tax	Amount of income tax payable after accounting for any reliefs calculated on the basis of the tax provisions covered in this Report, divided by gross wage earnings.
Schedule rate	The rate which appears in the schedule of the income tax and in the schedule of social security contributions.
	Terms used under cash transfers
Cash transfers	Cash payments made by general government (agencies) paid to families usually in respect of dependent children.

Table A.2. **Characteristics of taxpayers**

Marital status	Children	Principal earner	Secondary earner
Single individual	No children	67% of average earnings	
Single individual	No children	100% of average earnings	
Single individual	No children	167% of average earnings	
Single individual	2 children	67% of average earnings	
Married couple	2 children	100% of average earnings	
Married couple	2 children	100% of average earnings	33% of average earnings
Married couple	2 children	100% of average earnings	67% of average earnings
Married couple	No children	100% of average earnings	33% of average earnings

This approach broadly corresponds to the previous calculation based on sectors C-K incl. defined in the *International Standard Industrial Classification of All Economic Activities* (ISIC Revision 3.1, United Nations) which was adopted in the 2005 edition of *Taxing Wages*. The reasons for moving to a broadened average wage definition were set out in the Special Feature of *Taxing Wages* 2003-04.

Table A.3. International Standard Industrial Classification of All Economic Activities

	Revision 3.1 (ISIC Rev. 3.1)
A	Agriculture, hunting and forestry
B	Fishing
C	Mining and quarrying
D	Manufacturing
E	Electricity, gas and water supply
F	Construction
G	Wholesale and retail trade; repair of motor vehicles, motorcycles and personal and household goods
H	Hotels and restaurants
I	Transport, storage and communications
J	Financial intermediation
K	Real estate, renting and business activities
L	Public administration and defence; compulsory social security
M	Education
N	Health and social work
O	Other community, social and personal service activities
P	Activities of private households as employers and undifferentiated production activities of private households
Q	Extraterritorial organisations and bodies
	Revision 4 (ISIC Rev. 4)
A	Agriculture, forestry and fishing
B	Mining and quarrying
C	Manufacturing
D	Electricity, gas, steam and air conditioning supply
E	Water supply; sewerage, waste management and remediation activities
F	Construction
G	Wholesale and retail trade; repair of motor vehicles and motorcycles
H	Transportation and storage
I	Accommodation and food service activities
J	Information and communication
K	Financial and insurance activities
L	Real estate activities
M	Professional, scientific and technical activities
N	Administrative and support service activities
O	Public administration and defence; compulsory social security
P	Education
Q	Human health and social work activities
R	Arts, entertainment and recreation
S	Other service activities
T	Activities of households as employers; undifferentiated goods- and services-producing activities of households for own use
U	Activities of extraterritorial organizations and bodies

Defining gross wage earnings

This section sets out the assumptions underlying the calculation of the average earnings figures for "the average worker". The gross wage earnings data have been established using statistical data and the methodologies for calculating the earnings data in each country are set out in Table A.4. Further information on the calculation of the earnings figures is provided in the country chapters in Part III. The sources of the statistical data for each country are set out in Table A.5.

The main assumptions are as follows:

- The data relate to the average earnings in the relevant industry sectors for the country as a whole.

Table A.4. **Method used to calculate average earnings**

	Items included and exluded from the earnings base					Types of worker included and excluded in the average wage measure			Basic method of calculation used	Income tax year ends	Period to which the earnings calculation refers
	Sickness[1]	Vacations	Overtime	Recurring cash payments	Fringe Benefits	Supervisory workers	Managerial workers	part-time workers			
Australia	Inc	Inc	Inc	Inc	Exc	Inc	Inc	Exc	Average weekly earnings x 52	30th June	Fiscal year
Austria	Exc	Inc	Inc	Inc	Taxable value Inc	Inc	Inc	Exc	Average annual earnings	31st December	Calendar year
Belgium	Exc	Inc	Inc	Inc	Exc	Inc	Inc	Exc	Monthly earnings in October x 12 (plus recurring bonuses)	31st December	Calendar year
Canada	Exc	Inc	Inc	Inc	Exc	Inc	Inc	Inc[6]	Average weekly hours x average hourly earnings x 52	31st December	Calendar year
Chile	Exc	Inc	Inc	Inc	Exc	Inc	Inc	Inc	Hourly earnings x hours worked	31st December	Calendar year
Czech Republic	Exc	Inc	Inc	Inc	Exc	Inc	Inc	Inc[6]	Average monthly earnings x 12	31st December	Calendar year
Denmark	Exc	Inc	Exc	Inc	Exc	Inc	Inc	Inc[6]	Hourly earnings x hours worked	31st December	Calendar year
Estonia	Inc	Inc	Inc	Inc	Exc	Inc	Inc	Inc	Average earnings	31st December	Calendar year
Finland	Exc	Inc	Inc	Inc	Exc	Inc	Inc[5]	Exc	Hourly wages x usual working time or (monthly earnings x months) + vacation payments+ end of year bonuses	31st December	Calendar year
France	Exc	Inc	Inc	Inc	Exc	Inc	Inc	Exc	Annual earnings	31st December	Calendar year
Germany	Exc	Inc	Inc	Inc	Exc	Inc	Inc	Exc	Annual earnings	31st December	Calendar year
Greece	Exc	Inc	Inc	Inc[2]	Inc	Inc	Inc	Exc	Hourly earnings x hours worked	31st December	Calendar year
Hungary	Exc	Inc	Inc	Inc	Exc	Inc	Inc[5]	Exc	Average monthly earnings x 12	31st December	Calendar year
Iceland	Exc	Inc	Inc	Inc	Exc	Inc	Inc	Exc	Hourly earnings x hours worked x 12	31st December	Calendar year
Ireland	Exc	Inc	Inc	Inc	Exc	Exc	Exc	Inc	Average weekly earnings in each quarter for four quarters/4*52	31st December	Calendar year
Israel	Exc	Inc	Inc	Inc	Exc	Inc	Inc	Exc	Average earnings	31st December	Calendar year
Italy	Exc[3]	Inc	Inc	Inc	Exc[4]	Inc	Inc	Inc[6]	Average monthly earnings x 12	31st December	Calendar year
Japan	Exc	Inc	Inc	Inc	Exc	Inc	Inc	Exc	Monthly earnings in June x 12	31st December	Calendar year
Korea	Exc	Inc	Inc	Inc	Exc	Inc	Inc	Exc	Average monthly earnings x 12	31st December	Calendar year
Luxembourg	Exc	Inc	Inc	Inc	Exc	Inc	Inc	Exc	Aggregate annual earnings divided by annual average number of full-time employees. Any parts of earnings that exceed the upper social contribution limit (7 times the minimum wage) are not recorded.	31st December	Calendar year
Mexico	Exc	Inc	Exc	Inc	Exc	Inc	Inc	Exc	Average monthly earnings x 12	31st December	Calendar year
Netherlands	Exc	Inc	Exc	Inc	Exc	Inc	Inc	Exc	Annual gross earnings	31st December	Calendar year
New Zealand	Exc	Inc	Inc	Inc	Exc	Inc	Inc[5]	Inc[6]	Average weekly earnings in each quarter x 13	31st March	Tax year
Norway	Exc	Exc	Inc	Inc	Exc	Inc	Inc	Inc[6]	Annual wages + estimated overtime	31st December	Calendar year
Poland	Inc	Inc	Inc	Inc	Exc	Inc	Inc	Inc[6]	Average monthly earnings x 12	31st December	Calendar year
Portugal	Exc	Inc	Inc	Inc	Inc	Inc	Inc	Exc	Weighted monthly average x 12	31st December	Calendar year

Table A.4. **Method used to calculate average earnings** *(cont.)*

	Items included and exluded from the earnings base					Types of worker included and excluded in the average wage measure			Basic method of calculation used	Income tax year ends	Period to which the earnings calculation refers
	Sickness[1]	Vacations	Overtime	Recurring cash payments	Fringe Benefits	Supervisory workers	Managerial workers	part-time workers			
Slovak Republic	Exc	Inc	Inc	Inc	Inc	Inc	Inc	Inc	Average monthly earnings x 12	31st December	Calendar year
Slovenia	Inc	Inc	Inc	Inc	Exc	Inc	Inc	Inc	Average monthly earnings * 12	31st December	Calendar year
Spain	Exc	Inc	Inc	Inc	Exc	Inc	Inc	Exc	Weighted monthly average x 12	31st December	Calendar year
Sweden	Exc	Inc	Inc	Inc	Actual value Inc	Inc	Inc	Inc[6]	Average hourly earnings in September x hours worked; and monthly earnings in September * 12	31st December	Calendar year
Switzerland	Exc	Inc	Inc	Inc	Exc	Inc	Inc	Inc[6]	Monthly earnings x 12	31st December	Calendar year
Turkey	Exc	Inc	Inc	Inc	Actual value inc	Exc	Exc	Inc	Average annual earnings	31st December	Calendar year
United Kingdom	Exc	Inc	Inc	Inc	Exc	Inc	Inc	Exc	Average gross annual earnings	5th April	Fiscal year
United States	Exc	Inc	Inc	Inc[2]	Exc	Inc	Inc	Inc[6]	Average weekly earnings x 52	31st December	Calendar year

Note: Exc = Excluded, Inc = Included, '-' = information not available.

1. Usually includes compensation paid by employer whether paid on behalf of the government or as part of a private sickness scheme.
2. Excludes profit sharing bonuses in Greece and the United States plus end of year bonuses in the United States.
3. Sickness payments are only included to the extent that they are paid by the employer. For manual workers, this is only the case during the first three days of sick leave, while payments for the fourth day onwards are made by INPS.
4. Partly: the (small) taxable part of fringe benefits is included.
5. Except for top management (Finland); except if income from profits exceeds 50% of total income (Hungary); except for proprietors (New Zealand).
6. Part-time wages are converted to full-time equivalents before calculating the average wage measure.

Table A.5. **Source of earnings data, 2015**

Country	Type of sample	Source
Australia	Quarterly survey of firms resulting in a representative sample of wage and salary earners in each industry.	Australian Bureau of Statistics "Average Weekly Earnings, Australia" and "Labour Force, Australia".
Austria	Annual Wage Tax Statistics.	"Lohnsteuerstatistik".
Belgium	Data collected or estimated on the basis of an annual establishment survey and social insurance registers of employees.	Statistics Division of the Ministry of Economy (Federal Public Service, Economy, SMEs, Self-employed and Energy). Same source as for Eurostat "Annual gross earnings" data.
Canada	Monthly survey of all firms.	Statistics Canada, "Survey of Employment Payrolls and Hours".
Chile	Monthly sample of businesse with 10+ employees.	National Statistics Institute of Chile (INE).
Czech Republic	Employer survey data.	National Statistical Office.
Denmark	Danish Employers Confederation survey of earnings.	Annual Report Danish Employers Confederation (Dansk Arbejds Giverforening).
Estonia	-	Statistics Estonia/Ministry of Finance.
Finland	(1) Finnish Employers Federation survey of hourly and monthly earnings; (2) Survey for unorganized employers "Structure of Earnings Statistics" published by the Central Statistical Office.	"Wages Statistics" published by the Central Statistical Office.
France	Social insurance registers covering all employers.	INSEE, "Déclarations Annuelles des Données Sociales" (DADS).
Germany	Survey carried out by the Federal Statistical Office.	National Statistical Office.
Greece	Survey carried out by National Statistics Service and Social Security Institutions.	National Statistical Service Labour Statistics. Same source as for Eurostat "Annual gross earnings" data.
Hungary	Monthly surveys among enterprises with at least five employees.	Central Statistical Office.
Iceland	Monthly survey of earnings in the private sector market.	Statistics Iceland.
Ireland	Quarterly surveys of industrial employment, earnings and hours worked.	Central Statistics Office.
Israel	-	Central Bureau of Statistics.
Italy	Quarterly indicators of wages in industry and services (OROS).	National Institute of Statistics.
Japan	Basic survey on wage structure of all establishments with more than 10 employees.	Ministry of Health, Labour and Welfare, Annual Report.
Korea	Labour Force Survey at Establishments.	Ministry of Employment and Labour.
Luxembourg	Monthly aggregated files of Social security services.	National Statistical Office and Social Security Services.
Mexico	Administrative data from the Mexican Social Security Institute (Instituto Mexicano del Seguro Social (IMSS)).	The National Minimum Wage Commission (Comisión Nacional de Salarios Mínimos (CONASAMI)).
Netherlands	Survey "Employment and Wages".	Central Bureau of Statistics, Statline.
New Zealand	The quarterly employment survey is a sample survey of significant business with an employment count of 1 or more.	Statistics New Zealand INFOS.
Norway	Sample of enterprises based on published sector statistics for 3rd quarter – except agriculture, forestry and fishing and private households.	Statistics Norway Wage.
Portugal	April and October survey of earnings carried out by the Ministry of Labour.	Ministry of Labour.
Poland	Estimates for different sectors.	Monthly Statistical Bulletin.
Slovak republic	Quarterly and annual statistical data.	Slovak Statistical Office.
Slovenia	Monthly survey of employees.	Statistical Office of the Republic of Slovenia.
Spain	Quarterly survey of firms.	Instituto Nacional de Estadistica "Encuesta Trimestral de Coste Laboral" (Labour Cost Survey).
Sweden	September survey of Swedish employers.	Statistics Sweden.
Switzerland	Swiss Statistics Office. Personnes actives occupées selon la branche économique.	La vie économique, SECO (Secrétariat d'État à l'économie) table B.8.1, *www.bfs.admin.ch/bfs/portal/fr/index/themen/03/04.html.*
Turkey	Annual Manufacturing Industry Survey.	Turkish Statistical Institute.
United Kingdom	1% sample of PAYE earnings.	Office for National Statistics, Annual Survey of Hours and Earnings (ASHE).
United States	Monthly surveys by Department of Labour on the basis of a questionnaire covering more than 40 million non-agricultural wage and salary-workers.	Employment, Hours, and Earnings from the Current Employment Statistics Survey.

- The calculations are based on the earnings of a full-time adult worker (including both manual and non-manual). They relate to the average earnings of all workers in the industry sectors covered. No account is taken of variation between males and females or due to age or region.
- The worker is assumed to be full-time employed during the entire year without breaks for sickness or unemployment. However, several countries are unable to separate and exclude part-time workers from the earnings figures (see Table A.4). Most of them report full-time equivalent wages in these cases. In four countries (Chile, Ireland, Slovak Republic and Turkey), the wages of part-time workers can be neither excluded nor converted into full-time equivalents because of the ways in which the earnings samples are constructed. As a result, average wages reported for these countries will be lower than an average of full-time workers (for example, an OECD Secretariat analysis of available Eurostat earnings data for selected European countries has shown that including part-time workers reduces average earnings by around 10%). Also, in most of the OECD countries where sickness payments are made by the employer, either on behalf of the government or on behalf of private sickness schemes, these amounts are included in the wage calculations. It is unlikely that this has a marked impact on the results since employers usually make these payments during a short period and the amounts usually correspond very closely to normal hourly wages.
- Two of the household types include a second earner at 33% of average earnings. Such individuals are more likely to be working part-time rather than full-time (as shown in the Special Feature of the 2005 edition). However, the Special Feature also showed that the assumption of all employees working full-time does not significantly affect the tax rates calculated in *Taxing Wages*, except in the case of Belgium for married couples where the spouse is earning 33% of the average wage level. This is because any special provisions made for part-time workers tend to be either of minor importance or not applicable for the household types currently presented in *Taxing Wages*.
- The earnings calculation includes all cash remuneration paid to workers in the industries covered taking into account average amounts of overtime, cash supplements (e.g. Christmas bonuses, thirteenth month) and vacation payments typically paid to workers in the covered industry sectors. However, not all countries are able to include overtime pay, vacation payments and cash bonuses according to the definition.
- The earnings figures include supervisory and/or management employees, though some countries are not able to do this. In such countries, the reported averages are lower than would otherwise be the case (for example, an OECD Secretariat analysis of available Eurostat earnings data for selected European countries has shown that excluding this type of workers can reduce average earnings by 10% to 18%).
- Fringe benefits – which include, for example, provision of food, housing or clothing by the employer either free of charge or at below market-price – are, where possible, excluded from the calculation of average earnings. This could affect comparability of tax wedges – as the reliance on fringe benefits may vary between countries and over time. However, the lack of comparability is limited as fringe benefits rarely account for more than 1-2% of labour costs and are normally more common among high-income employees than in the income ranges covered by *Taxing Wages* (33% to 167% of average earnings). Table A.4 shows that some Member countries are not able to exclude fringe

benefits from the earnings figures reported and used in *Taxing Wages*. The decision to exclude was been taken because:

- these types of benefits are difficult to evaluate in a consistent way (they may be valued at the actual cost to the employer, their value to the employee or their fair market value).
- in most countries, they are of minimal importance for workers at the average wage level.
- the tax calculations would be significantly more complicated if the tax treatment of fringe benefits were to be incorporated.

- Employers' contributions to private pension, family allowance or health and life insurance schemes are excluded from the calculations, though the amounts involved can be significant. In the United States, for example, these contributions can account for more than 5% of the earnings of employees. The country chapters in Part III indicate of the existence of schemes which may be relevant for an average worker.

Calculating average gross wage earnings

Table A.4 indicates the basic calculation method used in each country while more details are, where relevant, provided in the country chapters in Part III. In principle, countries are recommended to calculate annual earnings by referring to the average of hourly earnings in each week, month or quarter, weighted by the hours worked during each period, and multiplied by the average number of hours worked during the year, assuming that the worker is neither unemployed nor sick and including periods of paid vacation. A similar procedure was recommended to calculate overtime earnings. For countries unable to separate out part-time employees from the data, it is recommended that earnings of part-time employees should if possible be converted into their full-time equivalents.

Statistical data on average gross wage earnings in 2015 are generally not available at present. For most countries, estimates of gross wage earnings of average workers in 2015 were therefore derived by the Secretariat on the basis of a uniform approach: year 2014 earnings levels are multiplied by the country-specific annual percentage change of wages for the whole economy reported in the most recently published edition of the *OECD Economic Outlook*.[2] This transparent procedure is intended to avoid any bias in the results. In some countries, there were varying different approaches;

- The final 2015 average gross wage earnings was used for Australia.
- National estimates were used for the Chile, Estonia, New Zealand and Turkey as the *OECD Economic Outlook* does not provide percentages changes in wages for those countries.
- In some countries, average wage earnings were also estimated for prior years – Finland (2014), France (from 2012 to 2014), the Netherlands (from 2012 to 2014), Portugal (2013 and 2014) and Switzerland (2007, 2009, 2011, 2013 and 2014) as no country information on average wage earnings levels was available for these years in these particular countries.

Fifteen OECD member countries have opted to provide national estimates of the level of gross wage earnings of average workers in 2015. These estimates were not used in the Taxing Wages calculations (except for the countries listed above) because of potential inconsistency with the Secretariat estimates derived for other countries. However they are included in Table A.6 to enable comparisons to be made between the estimates obtained by applying the Secretariat formula and those from national sources. In most cases, the two categories are fairly close.

Table A.6. **Estimated gross wage earnings, 2014-15 (in national currency)**

	Average wage 2014	Average wage 2015 (Secret. estimates)	Average wage 2015 (country estimates)	EO98 forecasted rates for 2015[1]
Australia[2]	79 409	79 769	80 774	0.5
Austria	42 814	43 484	43 456	1.6
Belgium	46 451	46 693	46 683	0.5
Canada	49 821	50 877		2.1
Chile[2]	7 019 299		7 556 043	
Czech republic	308 688	317 924	315 660	3.0
Denmark	397 600	405 876	404 359	2.1
Estonia[2]	12 338		12 926	
Finland	43 035	43 536		1.2
France	37 307	37 792		1.3
Germany	45 700	47 042		2.9
Greece	20 450	20 296		-0.8
Hungary	3 054 276	3 172 122	3 167 284	3.9
Iceland	6 960 000	7 440 480		6.9
Ireland	34 178	34 847	32 986	2.0
Israel	134 748	137 958		2.4
Italy	30 400	30 710		1.0
Japan	4 972 455	5 005 807		0.7
Korea	41 428 224	42 162 723	42 037 356	1.8
Luxembourg	54 920	55 553		1.2
Mexico	103 246	105 924	107 672	2.6
Netherlands	49 155	49 235		0.2
New Zealand[2]	54 733		56 110	
Norway	537 195	552 012		2.8
Poland	44 083	45 521		3.3
Portugal	17 411	17 280		-0.8
Slovak republic	10 422	10 616	10 693	1.9
Slovenia	17 948	18 109	17 917	0.9
Spain	26 191	26 259		0.3
Sweden	408 188	421 364	418 801	3.2
Switzerland	89 779	90 286		0.6
Turkey[2]	27 487		32 048	
United Kingdom	35 182	36 017		2.4
United States	50 099	50 964		1.7

1. Increase of compensation per employee in the total economy (*Economic Outlook* No. 98).
2. The country AW estimate is used instead of the OECD Secretariat's AW estimate in the Taxing Wages calculations.

StatLink http://dx.doi.org/10.1787/888933341257

Table A.7 indicates the exchange rates and purchasing power parities of national currencies for 2015 that are used to calculate comparative earnings figures across countries in the report.

Coverage of taxes and benefits

The Report is concerned with personal income tax and employee and employer social security contributions payable on wage earnings. In addition, payroll taxes (see section on *Payroll taxes*) are included in the calculation of the total wedge between labour costs to the employer and the corresponding net take-home pay of the employee.

Table A.7. **Purchasing power parities and exchange rates for 2015**

	Monetary unit	Exchange rates[1]	Purchasing power parities
Australia	AUD	1.33	1.44
Austria	EUR	0.90	0.81
Belgium	EUR	0.90	0.82
Canada	CAD	1.28	1.22
Chile	CLP	654.32	390.74
Czech Republic	CZK	24.59	12.99
Denmark	DKK	6.73	7.51
Estonia	EUR	0.90	0.54
Finland	EUR	0.90	0.92
France	EUR	0.90	0.82
Germany	EUR	0.90	0.78
Greece	EUR	0.90	0.59
Hungary	HUF	279.19	130.50
Iceland	ISK	131.90	145.38
Ireland	EUR	0.90	0.85
Israel	ILS	3.89	4.03
Italy	EUR	0.90	0.74
Japan	JPY	121.00	106.04
Korea	KRW	1131.31	891.65
Luxembourg	EUR	0.90	0.91
Mexico	MXN	15.87	8.23
Netherlands	EUR	0.90	0.81
New Zealand	NZD	1.43	1.42
Norway	NOK	8.06	9.17
Poland	PLN	3.77	1.78
Portugal	EUR	0.90	0.58
Slovak Republic	EUR	0.90	0.49
Slovenia	EUR	0.90	0.59
Spain	EUR	0.90	0.66
Sweden	SEK	8.43	9.03
Switzerland	CHF	0.96	1.29
Turkey	TRL	2.72	1.24
United Kingdom	GBP	0.65	0.70
United States	USD	1.00	1.00

1. Average of 12 months daily rates.

StatLink http://dx.doi.org/10.1787/888933341268

The calculation of the after-tax income includes family benefits paid by general government as cash transfers (see section on *Family cash benefits from general government*). Income tax due on capital income and non-wage labour income, several direct taxes (net wealth tax, corporate income tax) and all indirect taxes are not considered in this Report. However, all central, state and local government income taxes are included in the data.

In this study, compulsory social security contributions paid to general government are treated as tax revenues. Being compulsory payments to general government they clearly resemble taxes. They may, however, differ from taxes in that the receipt of social security benefits depends upon appropriate contributions having been made, although the size of the benefits is not necessarily related to the amount of the contributions. Countries finance compulsory public social security programmes to a varying degree from general tax and non-tax revenue and earmarked contributions, respectively. Better comparability between countries is obtained by treating social security contributions as taxes, but they are listed under a separate heading so that their amounts can be identified in any analysis.

Calculation of personal income taxes

The method by which income tax payments are calculated is described in the country chapters in Part III. First, the tax allowances applicable to a taxpayer with the characteristics and income level related to gross annual wage earnings of an average worker are determined. Next, the schedule of tax rates is applied and the resulting tax liability is reduced by any relevant tax credits. An important issue arising in the calculation of the personal income tax liability involves determining which tax reliefs should be taken into account. Two broad categories of reliefs may be distinguished:

- *Standard tax reliefs*: reliefs which are unrelated to actual expenditures incurred by the taxpayer and are automatically available to all taxpayers who satisfy the eligibility rules specified in the legislation. Standard tax reliefs are usually fixed amounts or fixed percentages of income and are typically the most important set of reliefs in the determination of the income tax paid by workers. These reliefs are taken into account in the calculations – they include:
  - The *basic relief* which is fixed and is available to all taxpayers or all wage earners, irrespective of their marital or family status;
  - The *standard relief* which is available to taxpayers depending on their *marital status*;
  - The *standard child relief* granted to a family with two children between the ages of six to eleven inclusive;
  - The *standard relief* in respect of *work expenses*, which is usually a fixed amount or fixed percentage of (gross) wage earnings; and,
  - Tax reliefs allowed for *social security contributions* and other (sub-central government) *income taxes* are also considered as standard reliefs since they apply to all wage earners and relate to compulsory payments to general government.[3]
- *Non-standard tax reliefs*: These are reliefs which are wholly determined by reference to actual expenses incurred. They are therefore neither fixed amounts nor fixed percentages of income. Examples of non-standard tax reliefs include reliefs for interest on qualifying loans (e.g. for the purchase of a house), private insurance premiums, contributions to private pension schemes, and charitable donations. These are not taken into account in calculating the tax position of employees.

Standard reliefs are separately identified and their impact on average tax rates is calculated in the results tables shown in the Country chapters. The latter include a brief description of the main non-standard reliefs in most cases.

State and local income taxes

Personal income taxes levied by sub-central levels of government – state, provincial, cantonal or local – are included in the scope of this study. State income taxes exist in Canada, Switzerland and the United States. Since 1997, Spain has an income tax for the Autonomous Regions. Local income taxes are imposed in Belgium, Denmark, Finland, Iceland, Italy, Japan, Korea, Norway, Sweden, Switzerland and the United States. In Belgium, Canada (other than Quebec), Denmark, Iceland, Italy, Korea, Norway and Spain they are calculated as a percentage of taxable income or of the tax paid to central government. In Finland, Japan, Sweden and Switzerland, local government provides different tax reliefs from central government. In the United States, the sub-central levels of government operate a separate system of income taxation under which they have discretion over both the tax base and tax rates. Except for Canada, Spain and Switzerland, the rate schedule of these sub-central taxes consists of a single rate.

When tax rates and/or the tax base of sub-central government income taxes vary within a country, it is sometimes assumed that the average worker lives in a typical area and the income taxes (and benefits) applicable in this area are presented. This is the procedure followed in Canada, Italy, Switzerland and the United States where the tax base and tax rates vary very widely throughout the country. Belgium, Denmark, Finland, Iceland and Sweden have preferred to select the average rate of sub-central government income taxes for the country as a whole. The local rates do not vary in practice in Korea and Norway. Japan and Spain have used the widely prevalent standard schedule.

Social security contributions

Compulsory social security contributions paid by employees and employers to general government or to social security funds under the effective control of government are included in the coverage of this Report. In most countries, contributions are levied on gross earnings and earmarked to provide social security benefits. In Finland, Iceland and the Netherlands, some contributions are levied as a function of taxable income (i.e. gross wage earnings after most/all tax reliefs). Australia and New Zealand do not levy social security contributions.

Contributions to social security schemes outside the general government sector are not included in the calculations. However, information on "non-tax compulsory payments" as well as "compulsory payment indicators" is included in the OECD Tax Database, which is accessible at *www.oecd.org/ctp/taxdatabase*.

Payroll taxes

Payroll taxes have a tax base that is either a proportion of the payroll or a fixed amount per employee. In the OECD *Revenue Statistics*, payroll taxes are reported under heading 3000. Fifteen OECD countries report revenue from payroll taxes: Australia, Austria, Canada, Denmark, France, Hungary, Iceland, Ireland, Israel, Korea, Mexico, New Zealand, Poland, Slovenia and Sweden.

Payroll taxes are included in total tax wedges reported in this publication, given that they increase the gap between gross labour costs and net take-home pay in the same way as income tax and social security contributions do. The main difference with the latter is that the payment of payroll taxes does not confer an entitlement to social security benefits. Also, the tax base of payroll taxes may differ from the tax base of employer social security contributions. For example, certain fringe benefits may only be liable to payroll tax. Because this Report presents the standard case, the payroll tax base can be – depending on the relevant legislation – gross wage (excluding fringe benefits and other items of compensation that vary per employee), gross wage plus employer social security contributions, or a fixed amount per employee.

Four of the OECD member countries include payroll taxes in the *Taxing Wages* calculations: Australia, Austria, Hungary and Sweden. The other countries reporting payroll tax revenue in *Revenue Statistics* have not included these taxes in the calculations for the present Report for a variety of reasons.

Family cash benefits from general government

Tax reliefs and family cash transfers universally paid in respect of dependent children between the ages of six to eleven inclusive who are attending school are included in the scope of the study. If tax reliefs or cash transfers vary within this age range, the most generous provisions are adopted, except that the case of twins is explicitly disregarded. The implications of this are illustrated below - suppose the child benefit programme of a country is structured as follows:

Age group	Benefits per child
Children 6-8	100 units
Children 9-10	120 units
Children 11-14	150 units

The most favourable outcome arises in the case of 11-year old twins: 300 units. However, as the case of twins is excluded, the best outcome now becomes 270 units (one child 11 years old, one child 9 or 10 years old). This amount would be included in the country table. Often, the amount in benefits is raised as children grow older. The calculations assume that the children have been born on 1 January so the annual amount received in child benefits may be calculated from the benefit schedule that is in place at the start of the year with any revisions to these amounts during the year being taken into account.

Relevant cash payments are those received from general government. In some cases, the cash benefits include amounts that are paid without consideration to the number of children.

Payable tax credits

Payable (non-wastable) tax credits are tax credits that can exceed tax liability, where the excess, if any, can be paid as a cash transfer to the taxpayer. In principle, these credits can be treated in different ways according to whether they are regarded as tax provisions or cash transfers or a combination of these. A Special Feature in the 2001 edition of *Revenue Statistics* discusses these alternative treatments and the conceptual and practical difficulties that arise in deciding which is the most appropriate approach for the purpose of reporting internationally comparable tax revenue figures.[4]

Based on this review, the Interpretative Guide of the *Revenue Statistics* requires that

- only the portion of a payable tax credit that is claimed to reduce or eliminate a taxpayer's liability (the "tax expenditure" component)[5] should be deducted in the reporting of tax revenues;
- the part of the tax credit that exceeds a taxpayer's tax liability and is paid to him (the "cash transfer" component) should be treated as an expenditure item and not deducted in the reporting of tax revenues.

However, additional information is provided in *Revenue Statistics* on aggregate tax expenditure components and aggregate transfer components of payable tax credits to show the effect of alternative treatments.[6]

In *Taxing Wages,* the situation is different as the full amount of the payable tax credit is taken into account in the income tax calculation.

Strict consistency with the *Revenue Statistics* would require that only the tax expenditure component be offset against derived income tax, with the excess (if any) treated as a cash transfer. However, this approach would diminish rather than strengthen the informational content of the derived results in *Taxing Wages*. In particular, limiting tax credit claims to tax expenditure amounts would yield a zero income tax liability and zero average income tax rate where cash refunds are provided. Where tax credits claims are not constrained in this way, negative income tax liabilities and negative average income tax rates would result where cash transfers are provided. Arguably, these negative amounts more clearly convey the taxpayer's position (which is improved relative to the no-tax situation). Also, not including the cash transfer portion of payable tax credits in the "cash transfers from general government" item of the country tables permits greater transparency of the latter which focuses on 'pure' cash transfers only.

However, in order to improve the informational content of country tables as regards payable tax credits, the memorandum item reporting at the bottom of the relevant country tables shows tax expenditure amounts on one line, with a second line showing cash transfer amounts. Where more than one payable tax credit program applies, the figures represent aggregates covering all the programs. Total program costs in each of the household cases considered can be derived by adding the tax expenditure and cash transfer amounts.

The calculation of marginal tax rates

In all except one case, the marginal tax rates are calculated by considering the impact of a small increase in gross earnings on personal income tax, social security contributions and cash benefits. The exception is the case of a non-working spouse where the move from zero to a small positive income is unrepresentative of income changes and therefore of little interest. So, for this case, the marginal rates for the spouse are calculated by considering the impact of an income increase from zero to 33% of the average wage.

Limitations

General limitations

The simple approach of comparing the tax/benefit position for eight model families avoids many of the conceptual and definitional problems involved in more complex international comparisons of tax burdens and transfer programmes. However, a drawback of this methodology is that the earnings of an average worker will usually occupy a different position in the overall income distribution in different economies, although the earnings relate to workers in similar jobs in various OECD member countries.

Because of the limitations on the taxes and benefits covered in the Report, the data cannot be taken as an indication of the overall impact of the government sector on the welfare of taxpayers and their families. Complete coverage would require studies of the impact of indirect taxes, the treatment of non-wage labour income and other income components under personal income taxes and the effect of other tax allowances and cash benefits. It would also require that consideration be given to the effect on welfare of services provided by the state, either free or below cost, and the incidence of corporate and other direct taxes on earnings and prices. Such a broad coverage is not possible in an international comparison of all OECD countries. The differences between the results shown here and those of a full study of the overall impact on employees of government interventions in the economy would vary from one country to another. They would depend on the relative shares of different kinds of taxes in government revenues and on the scope and nature of government social expenditures.

The Report shows only the formal incidence of taxes on employees and employers. The final, economic incidence of taxes may be quite different, because the tax burden may be shifted from employers onto employees and *vice versa* by market adjustments to gross wages.

The income left at the disposal of a taxpayer may represent different standards of living in various countries because the range of goods and services on which the income is spent and their relative prices differ as between countries. In those countries where the general government sector provides a wide range of goods and services (generous basic old age pension, free health services, public housing, university education, etcetera), the taxpayer may be left with less cash income but may enjoy the same living standards as a taxpayer receiving a higher cash income but living in a country where there are fewer publicly provided goods and services.

As mentioned in Chapter 1 and detailed in the Special Feature of the 2005 edition of *Taxing Wages*, second earners who are earning 33% of the average wage are very likely to be working part-time, although the *Taxing Wages* methodology generally assumes that they are working full-time. However, this only affects the accuracy of the results in *Taxing Wages* for one family type in Belgium (married couple where a second earner is earning 33%of average wages). Therefore, one should be cautious when interpreting the results for this family type for Belgium. In addition, for all countries with hour-based rules, (see the 2005 Special Feature), caution should be used in applying the results in this Report to other household types.

Some specific limitations on the income tax calculation

The exclusion of non-wage income and the limited number of tax reliefs covered mean that the average rates of income tax in the tables in this publication do not necessarily reflect the actual rates confronting taxpayers at these levels of earnings. Actual rates may be lower than the calculated rates because the latter do not take into account non-standard expense-related reliefs. On the other hand, actual rates may be higher than calculated rates because the latter do not take into account tax on non-wage income received by employees.

The decision not to calculate separately average rates of income tax taking into account the effect of non-standard tax reliefs was taken because:

- In many cases, expense-related reliefs are substitutes for direct cash subsidies. To take into account these reliefs while ignoring any corresponding direct subsidies would distort comparisons of take-home pay plus cash transfers;
- The special tax treatment of certain expenses may be linked to special treatment of any income associated with these expenses (e.g. the tax treatment of social security contributions and pension income) which is beyond the scope of this study;
- A few countries were unable to estimate the value of these reliefs and even those countries which could do so could not limit their estimates to taxpayers with the characteristics assumed in the above part on methodology; and,
- Not all countries could calculate separately the reliefs available to different family-types. Where a split is provided between single individuals and families with children, there are large differences in the value of the reliefs typically received by these two categories of households.

Limitations to time-series comparisons

The calculations of the tax burden on labour income in OECD countries reported in the 2004 and previous editions of *Taxing Wages*, are based on an average earnings measure for manual full-time workers in the manufacturing sector (the "average production worker").

Any analysis of the results over time has to take into account the fact that the earnings data do not necessarily relate to the same taxpayer throughout the period. The average earnings are calculated for each year. As such, the results do not reflect the changing earnings and tax position of particular individuals over time but rather to the position of workers earning a wage equal to average earnings in the covered industry sectors in each particular year. This, in turn, may mean that the earnings levels referred to may be at different points in the income distribution over the period covered and changes in tax rates may be influenced by these trends.

There have been changing definitions of the average worker over time. From the 2005 edition, *Taxing Wages* has reported tax calculations under a broadened average worker definition that includes all full-time employees covering industry sectors C-K (reference to ISIC Rev. 3.1). The implications of adopting this new definition for time-series comparisons are discussed in the 2005 edition of Taxing Wages. As of the 2010 edition of the Taxing Wages Report, many countries have started reporting average wage earnings for full-time employees covering industry sectors B-N of the ISIC Rev. 4 industry classification (which broadly corresponds to sectors C-K in ISIC Rev. 3.1).

A Note on the tax equations

Each country chapter contains a section describing in a standard format the equations under-pinning the calculations required to derive the amounts of income tax, social security contributions and cash transfers. These algorithms represent in algebraic form the legal provisions described in the chapter and are consistent with the figures shown in the country and comparative tables. This section describes the conventions used in the definition of the equations and how they could be used by those wishing to implement the equations for their own research.

The earlier sections of the country chapters describe how the tax and other systems work and present the values of the parameters of those systems such as the levels of allowances and credits, and the schedule of tax rates.

In the first part of the equations section is a table showing a brief description of each parameter (such as "Basic tax credit"), the name of the parameter as used in the algebraic equation ("Basic_cred") and the actual value for the relevant year (such as "1098"). Where there is a table of values – for example a schedule of tax rates and the associated thresholds of taxable income – a name is given to the entire table (for example "tax_sch"). These variable names are those used in the equations.

After each table of parameters is the table of equations. The four columns contain information as follows:

- The first two columns give a description and a variable name for the result of the equation on that row of the table. These always include the thirteen main financial value entries in the country tables. Additional rows define any intermediate values which are calculated either to show the detail included in the tables (such as the subdivision of total tax allowances into the different categories) or values which make the calculation clearer.

- The third column shows the range of the calculation in that row. This is necessary to allow for the different way that tax may be calculated for married couples. The options are:
  - B The calculation is carried out separately for both the principal earner and the spouse using their individual levels of earnings. This applies in the case of independent income tax and usually also in respect of social security contributions.
  - P The calculation applies for the principal earner only. An example is where the principal earner can use any of the basic tax allowance of the spouse which cannot be set against the income of the spouse.
  - S The calculation applies for the lower earning spouse only.
  - J The calculation is carried out only once on the basis of joint income. This applies to systems of joint or family taxation and is also usual for the calculation of cash transfers in respect of children.
- The final column contains the equation itself. The equation may refer to the variables in the parameters table and to variables which result from one of the rows of the equations table itself. Use is also made of the two standard variables "Married", which have the value 1 if the family consists of a married couple and 0 in the case of a single individual, and "Children" which denotes the number of children. Sometimes there is a reference to a variable with the affix "_total" which indicates the sum of the relevant variable values for the principal earner and the spouse. Similarly, the affixes "_princ" and "_spouse" indicate the value for the principal earner and spouse, respectively.

In the equations a number of functions are used. Some of these are used in the same way as in a number of widely available "spreadsheet" computer packages. For example, MAX(X,Y) and MIN(X,Y) find the maximum and minimum of the two values, respectively. IF(condition X,Y) chooses the expression X if the condition is true and the expression Y if it is false. Boolean expressions are also used and are taken to have the value 1 if true and 0 if false. As an example, (Children=2*CB_2 is equivalent to IF(Children=2, CB_2,0).

There are also three special functions commonly used which denote calculations often required in tax and social security systems. These are:

- Tax (taxinc, tax_sch): This calculates the result of applying the schedule of tax rates and thresholds in "tax_sch" to the value of taxable income represented by "taxinc". This function may be used in any part of the equations, not just in the income tax calculation. For some countries it is used for social security contributions or even for allowance levels which may be income dependent.
- Positive (X): This gives the result X when this value is positive and zero otherwise. It is therefore equivalent to MAX(0,X).
- Taper (value, income, threshold, rate): This gives the amount represented by "value" if "income" is less than "threshold". Otherwise, it gives "value" reduced by "rate" multiplied by (income- threshold), unless this produces a negative result in which case zero is returned. This provides the calculation which is sometimes required when a tax credit, for example, is available in full provided that total income is below a threshold but is then withdrawn at a given rate for each currency unit in excess of the threshold until it is withdrawn completely.

In some circumstances, there are country specific special functions. These functions involve programming that is designed to simplify the tax calculations. The programming underlying these functions is based on the description of the particular measure given in the relevant country chapter found in Part III. For example, the Earned Income Credit in the United States is calculated using the function called EIC.

Anyone wishing to make their own implementation of the equations will have to write functions corresponding to these special functions or make appropriate modifications to any equations that use them.

Notes

1. Not all national statistical agencies use ISIC Rev.3.1 or ISIC Rev.4 to classify industries. However, the Statistical Classification of Economic Activities in the European Community (NACE), the North American Industry Classification System (NAICS) and the Australian and New Zealand Standard Industrial Classification (ANZSIC) include a classification which is broadly in accordance with industries C-K in ISIC Rev. 3.1 or industries B-N in ISIC Rev. 4.
2. The Wage estimates reported in the *Economic Outlook* are prepared by the Economics Department (ECO) of the OECD. They are consistent with the December 2015 issue of the *Economic Outlook*.
3. In this case, the amount of tax relief is related to actual social security contributions paid by the employee or withheld from his wage – thus in this respect this item deviates from the general definition of standard tax relief under which relief is unrelated to actual expenses incurred.
4. OECD, *Revenue Statistics1965-2000*, p. 28-31.
5. This characterisation must be viewed as informal, as the determination of tax expenditures requires the identification of a benchmark tax system for each country, or preferably, a common international benchmark. In practice it has not been possible to reach agreement on a common international benchmark for such purposes.
6. See Table D in *OECD Revenue Statistics 2015*.

ORGANISATION FOR ECONOMIC CO-OPERATION AND DEVELOPMENT

The OECD is a unique forum where governments work together to address the economic, social and environmental challenges of globalisation. The OECD is also at the forefront of efforts to understand and to help governments respond to new developments and concerns, such as corporate governance, the information economy and the challenges of an ageing population. The Organisation provides a setting where governments can compare policy experiences, seek answers to common problems, identify good practice and work to co-ordinate domestic and international policies.

The OECD member countries are: Australia, Austria, Belgium, Canada, Chile, the Czech Republic, Denmark, Estonia, Finland, France, Germany, Greece, Hungary, Iceland, Ireland, Israel, Italy, Japan, Korea, Luxembourg, Mexico, the Netherlands, New Zealand, Norway, Poland, Portugal, the Slovak Republic, Slovenia, Spain, Sweden, Switzerland, Turkey, the United Kingdom and the United States. The European Commission takes part in the work of the OECD.

OECD Publishing disseminates widely the results of the Organisation's statistics gathering and research on economic, social and environmental issues, as well as the conventions, guidelines and standards agreed by its members.

OECD PUBLISHING, 2, rue André-Pascal, 75775 PARIS CEDEX 16
(23 2016 11 1 P) ISBN 978-92-64-25187-8 – 2016

www.ingramcontent.com/pod-product-compliance
Lightning Source LLC
LaVergne TN
LVHW080114011026
849160LV00013B/1101